Test Pilot

Test Pilot

An Extraordinary Career Testing Civil Aircraft

Chris Taylor

AIR WORLD

First published in Great Britain in 2022 by
Pen & Sword Air World
An imprint of
Pen & Sword Books Ltd
Yorkshire – Philadelphia

ISBN 978 1 39908 534 2

Typeset by Mac Style
Printed and bound in the UK by CPI Group (UK) Ltd,
Croydon, CR0 4YY.

Pen & Sword Books Limited incorporates the imprints of Atlas,
Archaeology, Aviation, Discovery, Family History, Fiction, History,
Maritime, Military, Military Classics, Politics, Select, Transport,
True Crime, Air World, Frontline Publishing, Leo Cooper, Remember
When, Seaforth Publishing, The Praetorian Press, Wharncliffe
Local History, Wharncliffe Transport, Wharncliffe True Crime
and White Owl.

For a complete list of Pen & Sword titles please contact

PEN & SWORD BOOKS LIMITED
47 Church Street, Barnsley, South Yorkshire, S70 2AS, England
E-mail: enquiries@pen-and-sword.co.uk
Website: www.pen-and-sword.co.uk

Or

PEN AND SWORD BOOKS
1950 Lawrence Rd, Havertown, PA 19083, USA
E-mail: Uspen-and-sword@casematepublishers.com
Website: www.penandswordbooks.com

Contents

Introduction

Holy Moses!
I was doing over 30 mph …
I was in a helicopter …
I was on the ground …
I was going sideways …
I couldn't steer and sparks were flying everywhere …
I could do nothing but 'Keep calm and hang on' …

I was testing the emergency landing characteristics of a Polish helicopter in Arizona, USA on a very warm day at an airfield that was a mile above sea level. As I slid sideways with the metal skids kicking up an almighty cascade of sparks from the tarmac runway you might conclude that I was mad, bad or stupid; for me this was just another typical working day in my life as a test pilot.

A couple of years ago I reached one of those milestone birthdays – you know, one with a zero. This was significant in a number of ways. Once pilots turn 60 they can no longer fly passengers around on their own. For me this brought an end to a very enjoyable aspect of my aviation career, that of police and air ambulance helicopter pilot. More importantly, I had just become a grandpa and I'd already bought the trainset and dusted off my Scalextric. Even more importantly, I had reached the age at which my father had suffered a catastrophic stroke leaving him unable to speak.

My dad was a prolific storyteller. He had a gift. He would always have us in hysterics as he narrated his various escapades from childhood or wartime experiences in the RAF. Sunday lunchtimes, my brother and I would ask again and again for our favourites and, despite us all growing older, it never crossed my mind that we might suddenly be denied access to all those stories, all his wisdom and all his so valuable advice.

My stories aren't as good or as funny as my dad's, but I suddenly started to consider how little my grandchildren would know of my life should I suffer a similar fate.

My dad, Edward Taylor of Burnley, Lancashire was born on Trafalgar Day (21 October) in 1921. In 1940, as an 18-year-old clerk, he joined the RAF, mainly in the hope that the uniform would help him pull the girls; not that he needed any help in that department if his collection of sepia photos of glamorous sirens was anything to go by. He'd wanted to fly but the RAF was desperate for medically fit clerks to join the squadrons as they expected them to be deployed overseas. After basic training my dad joined 222 Squadron operating Spitfires (Vbs) and in 1943 he was transferred to 65 Squadron flying Mustangs (IIIs then IVs). He spent lots of time in Scotland and the south of England but then found himself in France shortly after D-Day as 65 Squadron flew ground-attack missions from dirt strips just behind the front line. Some of his funnier and scarier stories were generated in this period, including driving a jeepload of pilots into Brussels to get hammered, only on the way home to notice blokes in grey uniforms standing on street corners. The Germans (who clearly hadn't seen the memo my dad thought he had read about the city's liberation) were so stupefied, to see a bunch of drunks being driven at such speed, that they had no time to unsling their rifles. With their heads down and Dad driving for his life they made their escape. Throughout the war his mates were all pilots and, as the squadron clerk, he had the unenviable task of drafting the letters home following sorties when they failed to return. As a consequence our holidays to France and Germany included tours of numerous cemeteries as we identified the gravestones of his former comrades.

My quick tempered dad almost certainly suffered from what we would now describe as PTSD. He spent several weeks in an RAF hospital at one stage and had a nervous breakdown just before his planned wedding years after the war.

I certainly owe my dad my love of flying and, amongst other things, my 'terrier like' stubbornness and commitment to always completing what I promise to do. Beach holidays were taken in Anglesey, just along from RAF Valley. Shiny Lightning jet fighters, bright yellow (then red) Gnat trainers and Whirlwind search and rescue helicopters would all overfly us while building our sandcastles. Kites made way for Keil Kraft balsa-wood elastic-band-powered aircraft and hard-earned pocket money was spent every Saturday morning at the local newsagent who sold Airfix bagged models of Spitfires and Hurricanes which could be built in a day and hung from bedroom ceilings without delay. Dad loved it that I wanted to be a pilot – and I did, from as long ago as I can remember. I dreamt of flying Sopwith Camels and Spitfires and read all of W.E. Johns' books about my all-time hero, James Bigglesworth, aka Biggles. There was nothing he couldn't fly or do with an aeroplane. However, in my teens I became more aware of the activities of the Fleet Air Arm and at the age of 16 spent two weeks drinking at the expense of the taxpayer in the wardroom bar at Royal Naval Air Station Culdrose where every day the Royal Navy flew me in a different aircraft. Not content with that sales pitch, they awarded me a Flying Scholarship, as a member of my school Combined Cadet Force (CCF), which allowed me to be awarded a Private Pilot's Licence (PPL) before I could drive.

Despite his stroke Dad continued to encourage me and must have been the proudest and drunkest 60-something bloke at my 'Wings Day'.

I went on to fly the Westland Wasp and then Lynx helicopter and as such was known affectionately as a 'Pronger' or more fully 'Third Pronger' based on the idea that a fork has three prongs with one prong being those that flew to hunt out submarines, the second to support and transport the Royal Marines and thirdly – well, us – those that flew off smallish ships that carried a single helicopter with a single crew. As a Lynx pilot I became an instructor and continued to teach and fly at numerous air displays before running the Lynx training simulator complex at RNAS Portland.

However, in 1976, shortly after gaining my PPL, Thames Television aired a documentary about attending the Empire Test Pilots' School (ETPS) to become a test pilot. Although barely able to fly a simple Cessna training aeroplane at the time, this TV programme sowed the seed and I knew then that I wanted to test aircraft for a living. So much so that it skewed my thinking regarding degree courses and I opted for Electrical Engineering in the hope that it would prepare me for a life in flight test; if only I had realised how hard the maths was going to be. Ironically the BBC made a very similar programme which aired at the end of 1986 when I was converting from the Wasp to the Lynx helicopter. The latter programme had the opposite effect as I watched students, who were later to become colleagues and friends, struggle with the workload … especially the maths.

As a Wasp/Lynx flight commander I was the only pilot on board the ship and aviation adviser to the captain and warfare team. It was a huge responsibility but very rewarding, and when disembarked I was able to be my own boss and run my flight with fun firmly on the agenda. I equally enjoyed my time instructing immensely but I'm obviously wired to seek out new challenges; that or more likely I have a short attention span. So now having become bored of 'just flying the Lynx' I started to get itchy feet and came very close to joining the RAF to fly jets. As you will read later, I had to rethink that opportunity but that only rekindled my slow-burning aspiration to become a test pilot. At the time competition for the single RN place on the course was fierce and the assessment incorporated two interviews, a technical written exam and, wait for it – a dreaded maths paper.

Fortunately I was able to blag my way to pole position and joined 32 Rotary Wing Test Pilot Course/ Class of 1994 at ETPS, Boscombe Down. Two years of flying a wide variety of aircraft for research and development led me back to the school as an instructor. As a flight test instructor I spent four more years in uniform followed by three years as a civilian designing, developing and delivering flight test training to both aeroplane and helicopter crews. Ten years at Boscombe Down paved the way for ten years working in a very small, but highly competent, Flight Test Department of the UK Civil Aviation Authority (CAA) based at Gatwick. It was in this job, and a subsequent period of being self-employed, that I have been able to fly a wide variety of aircraft, meet a vast array of people and hopefully have generated enough anecdotes to fill a book, but you had better be the judge of that.

This book is predominantly written for my children and grandchildren. It is for them to read about some of the things I have got up to, and scrapes I have got out of. Hopefully when I'm 'six foot under' or stricken speechless, some of the stuff their cranky old dad/grandpa talks about will make more sense.

And to some extent this book is inspired by Emily Maitlis, the journalist and presenter of Newsnight. I read her book 'Airhead' a while back and loved the style of it. It wasn't a chronological account of her life to date but a string of chapters based on characters she'd interviewed. The chapters were effectively her version of 'escapades' and that is what I hope to present here.

I am currently testing an aeroplane for a company and the CEO recently remarked that without me being available there would be no one suitably experienced or qualified to undertake the task. When I left the CAA I was able to organise a meeting with the then Minister for Aviation in the Houses of Parliament. My main aim in meeting was to discuss the flight test capabilities that the UK then had, but was rapidly losing. It is hard to imagine how a youngster learning to fly today could come close to acquiring the experience, expertise and qualifications I've been fortunate enough to gain over more than four decades. The tagline for my company, Dovetail Aviation, is 'Making Flying Safer' and I hope that is what I have achieved during my operational flying, instructing a whole generation of Lynx pilots, flying for a number of research and development projects, teaching others how to do flight test and finally, ensuring every aircraft or situation I've been involved with has resulted in the world being a less dangerous place.

Invariably when pilots gather, much ale is consumed, and witty and often educational, 'dits' flow freely. In the Fleet Air Arm we would be invited to 'pull up a bollard' or 'swing the lamp' and each 'salty tale' of heroism would inspire the gathering to 'black cat' the previous story by telling one funnier or scarier or, as the session went on, ruder.

This book seeks to present a collection of tales where I hope truth (or too much technical detail) hasn't been allowed to ruin a good story. Hopefully there is enough content to entertain, educate, enlighten and perhaps challenge us to appreciate when abilities and experience are used to make the lives of others safer. See what you think – then in a future volume I can always add the 'back-story' of my military test pilot escapades and time as a Fleet Air Arm pilot that there isn't room for here.

NB: Skip to Chapter 18 to read more about the first few words of this introduction.

Flight Test Engineers

Just before you properly dive in to the book, I would feel guilty if I didn't explain one particular topic: the role of the Flight Test Engineer (FTE). You will see mention of Ray and Jeff and Nick, David and John in some of the text that lies ahead. As CAA and/or EASA FTEs these guys were teamed up with me from time to time – although they would I say I was teamed up with them. The FTE is a very clever sort of person who has degrees and the like. They tend to be good at analysing the complex data gathered on some flight test sorties and they will, more often than not, do most of the planning on complex flight test programmes, producing reams of paperwork including flight test plans and the final reports. When flight testing, if there were enough seats in the aircraft, they would invariably fly with me, leading me through the sortie plan and writing down all my observations and the various numbers I would gather. In particular, when working together, we would support each other and discuss everything, often over supper and a few glasses of wine at the end of exhausting days. Much of the work I've had to do has had to be done without their support and invariably the work on smaller aircraft has prevented them being able to fly with me. But when we were able to work together they formed an equal and invaluable part of the flight test team – and they had to trust my shabby flying to get us home again safely. I salute them.

Chapter 1

Boeing Stearman

'**** me!'

A grammar school education, followed by over twenty years in the Royal Navy, had equipped me with a very full, and varied, vocabulary. Despite my need, as a parent, to set a good example to my children, and their children, there are times when this particular phrase is 'just the ticket'. I say this, despite being previously challenged, by my then 6-year-old son, to chastise some rather large rugby players, who were practising their game and using such expletives within earshot of us both many years ago. Despite them all being six inches taller and many stone heavier than me they were so flabbergasted to be accosted in such a manner that they were instantly very apologetic and, as far as my son was concerned, I acquired super-hero status.

Something had just appeared in my field of view, like as in all unfolding disasters I've experienced to date, in very slow motion. And slow was the last thing I would have expected as I was diving an old Second World War training biplane near vertically at the ground in order to go as fast as this aircraft, and the laws of physics, would possibly allow. With lots of 'shake, rattle and roll', and a gale-force wind buffeting my helmet-clad head, something grabbed my attention and I ducked, despite already being scrunched as low in the cockpit as I could get. My expletive accompanied an upward glance. An object about three feet in length was tumbling towards me. As it passed inches over my head my steely pilot like vision (!) finally recognised the object … it was a leg. A man's leg. In fact it was one of the legs that milliseconds earlier had belonged to, and still been attached to, my passenger, Fred. Perhaps even odder was that Fred was strapped to a frame on the upper wing of my biplane. If all of that wasn't odd enough, Fred's day job was standing in a window at a department store.

Anyway, this was typical of 'another working day in the life of' a test pilot. I'd become quite fond of the Boeing Stearman PT-17 aeroplane which had been used in the USA to teach army and navy pilots to fly in the Second World War. I'd test flown a number of UK registered examples since I joined the CAA with my first example being G-OBEE based at Old Buckenham where actor Martin Shaw based his own Stearman. In the UK we had designed the de Havilland DH-82a Tiger Moth in the 1930s to fulfil the same role, but the Stearman was a different beast. Bigger and heavier they create an impressive sight, often still painted in their US Navy bright yellow and blue or green colours. Although relatively easy to fly they have a number of challenges. They are fitted with large radial engines which are sometimes difficult to start and in the main gutless. The aircraft usually needs some kind of bump on the runway to launch it airborne and then only gives the appearance of climbing as the earth gently curves away from it. It would take an age to get to a safe height to do any of the required testing and this would be rapidly lost as I would invariably have to wingover (see glossary) into a near vertical dive in order to accelerate to the aircraft's maximum permissible speed of 186 mph. Imagine going down the motorway in a Ford Transit Luton van with a top box fitted. Yep, what prevents you from getting above around 50 mph is 'aerodynamic drag' and the Stearman had it in spades.

I have really quite enjoyed flying Stearmans over the years, mainly because they have a better windscreen than the Tiger Moth and are easier to land than most tail draggers, but their large wheels incorporate a very elderly inefficient brake system. Pressing the brake pedals with your feet you are faced with two possible outcomes. Option 1: Next to nothing happens and the aircraft slows to a halt when it jolly well feels like it. Option 2: One or both of the wheels will snatch or lock up and then inertia or momentum, or something like that, will try to tip the aircraft on its nose. Since that's where the rotating propeller is to be found, that would lead to an embarrassing arrival and costly outcome. Thankfully, to date, my rigorous testing prior to take-off tended to head off this misfortune but it was a 'monster waiting in the wings' for the unwary.

Later in the same year I'd flown G-OBEE and, with two further Stearman flight tests under my belt, I had the good (or bad) fortune to find myself at Stacumny House, Celbridge, just west of Dublin, the home of Cathal Ryan, airline pilot and son of Tony Ryan, perhaps best known to most of us as the founder and owner of Ryanair. I confess to being somewhat bowled over by the venue for this particular check flight. It's not often that Georgian mansions have formed the backdrop to airfields I've operated from. Anyway, Cathal owned a G-registered Stearman, G-THEA, which needed an air test.

I was met by a charming airline captain who tended to fly this aircraft frequently and we commenced briefing for the flight. I was on foreign soil and set about making sure that I didn't embarrass myself. This was not helped by discovering that the owner's private strip was located within an army training range (Baldonnel Military Operating Area).

'Begorrah – no bother', was the response to my expressed concern. 'We fly out of here all the time.'

'*How?*'

'We just get airborne and call them on the radio and they're fine about it all.'

I wish I had a beer for every time I've been advised, 'Trust me, all will be OK', only for it to prove a folly.

As with so many days like this, time was against me as my flight home from Dublin International was already restocking the galley bar and the weather, which had started as barely acceptable, was deteriorating before our eyes.

G-THEA on the concrete 'pan' adjacent to the grass strip.

This aircraft presented as a good example of Option 2 when it came to brakes and the taxi out to the runway was in itself a challenging evolution. But getting them fixed prior to my flight was no longer viable if I was to fly at all that afternoon. The good news was that it had a Lycoming engine fitted, which was more powerful than the Continental engine normally used, but it still required all the available grass strip to struggle airborne. I should point out that this flight, like so many, had my poor body coursing with adrenalin from the 'get go' with my pulse racing and my usual sense of foreboding. I was facing dodgy brakes, a short strip which was only just long enough, and the prospect of crappy weather – par for the course.

Immediately I was airborne my expectations were indeed confirmed as the borderline weather really had become very borderline indeed. The aircraft had no clearance or suitable instruments to allow me to climb up into the low cloud and rain so I was committed to trying to stay below the worst of it 'in sight of the surface'. These days, aircraft are fitted with an array of 'gizmos' to help navigate and, in any case, I now have an aviation version of Google Maps on my iPad (Runway HD). I do not leave home if it's not in my flying kit bag as I would, quite literally, be lost without it. Back then, in an open cockpit 1930s' biplane with next to no instruments, not only was I concerned about keeping the aircraft the 'right way up' but, I was also immediately concerned about becoming lost; or as we pilots like to claim, 'unsure of position'. In my pre-flight planning (time limited as always) I had noticed something to prompt optimism.

When the weather is good, and we can see where we are going, we fly by a set of rules creatively called Visual Flight Rules (VFR). If the visibility or cloud prevent such flight we then fly by … wait for it – Instrument Flight Rules (IFR). On this day the IFR stood for something else entirely but equally helpful: 'I Follow Railways'. The main Dublin to Tipperary railway ran just to the south of the landing site, thank goodness. So, whatever happened, I was determined not to lose sight of this railway track.

Meanwhile another, but frequently occurring, challenge had presented itself. In order to talk to the other pilot, aircraft usually have intercom systems so that we can talk and hear over the ever-present wind noise, in this case, created by a 120 mph gale. As often happens, a system that works fine on the ground at low speed and low engine power/noise, suddenly very annoyingly becomes next to useless when full throttle is applied and the aircraft is accelerated to flying speed. Shouting at my co-pilot I asked him politely(?) to kindly talk to the Irish Army so that we wouldn't be shot down or more likely incarcerated after our flight for flying through their live firing exercise. I now discovered that the same crap intercom that almost prevented us talking also had a fault that prevented him using the radio ... great.

I was now, as has often been the case, working my absolute socks off, using every ounce of my ability, experience, guile and cunning, barrelling along in an open-cockpit aeroplane, in worsening weather, rain, low cloud and poor visibility, in an active army range, trying to establish communications on a radio set that would have been better replaced by two tin cans and a piece of string. And guess what? My finely honed Royal Navy officer accent turned out to be entirely unintelligible to the Irish sáirsint (sergeant) who was trying to get some sense out of me despite the 120 mph wind noise accompanying every well accentuated syllable. So, I adopted the classic mantle of the 'Englishman abroad' and in my most pompous fashion broadcast my intentions very loudly, at least hoping that in the subsequent legal battle, I could not be accused of trying to route through an army training area unannounced.

Finally, the weather beat me. A tight 180-degree turn not to lose sight of my saviour, the railway line, and we 'grobbled' back to the estate, from whence we had only recently departed, to squeeze the aircraft gracefully back onto the short strip, trying to remember the dodgy brakes and thus ensure I didn't tip Ryanair's smallest passenger-carrying aircraft on its back after successfully surviving our short flight to Tipperary!

With my commercial return flight almost closing at Dublin International I completed a comprehensive brief to the chap I'd flown with who was still rather dumbstruck by the proceedings. (Later in the week, in much nicer weather, he kindly completed aspects of the flight that the shoddy weather had prevented.)

My first glass of vino on the flight back to Heathrow had me snoozing seconds after take off.

Phew! ... I had survived another.

But I did then wait for many weeks wondering if I was to receive a summons in the mail to attend an Irish Army court to explain myself – after fifteen years I'm hoping they've forgiven me.

Three years later I'd been briefed by a colleague in the CAA about the intention to modify a Stearman to fit a 'Wing-Walking' rig which was designed to allow fare-paying passengers to 'wing walk', or rather not walk, on the upper wing of this biplane. The UK Civil Aviation Authority (CAA) took more than a passing interest in such matters and in this case I was despatched to assess whether the rig and concept could achieve a safe civil certification. What do you think? Other similar rigs were already in existence and similar aircraft registered in America had been seen on the UK air display circuit for many years with very glamorous girls dressed in lycra performing all manner of 'Green Goddess' workout moves. In this case the punter was to be a fare-paying passenger and, unlike the wing walkers who climbed into position after take-off, these poor souls would be strapped into position immediately after passport control.

My principal role was to assess the modification's 'airworthiness', namely whether the aircraft's performance or handling qualities had been degraded in anyway. Minimising risk is at the heart of flight test preparation and so, despite there being numerous live volunteers, I had elected to insist my first passenger for my testing wouldn't mind some of the more extreme tests I needed to do. Fred had found himself in pole position.

Returning to land after a successful first flight.

Final briefing with Fred installed.

The testing was conducted at the delightful grass airfield of Oaksey Park and commenced with me discussing the modification with the engineering organisation that had fitted it and the aircraft's owner, Mike. I then flew with just the rig fitted to effectively get some baseline data for the aircraft itself.

All had gone well, so following a pee and cup of tea, Fred was finally installed for the actual testing.

The weather was pleasant enough and suitable for what I needed to do, so with Fred waving to the crowd (!) I taxied carefully to the end of the grass strip, turned into wind and then using all the available power accelerated as fast as I was able.

I raised the tail as quickly as I could to get into the flying attitude and be better able to see out of the front. The mainwheels eventually lost contact with the ground and without further ado I set about measuring the rate of climb with the extra drag I was now carrying, so I could compare it with the data I'd gathered from my first sortie. Needless to say, it climbed less well.

The handling of the aircraft was still absolutely fine, so the final aspect of the testing was to fly to the aircraft's maximum speed to again see what effect a wing-walker might have and determine whether a reduced speed

Fred waving to the crowd – Well, he would have done if he could.

limit might be appropriate. Having gained as much height as I could, and having done all my checks, I chose an open area and commenced a steepening dive to try and overcome the now considerable aerodynamic drag of biplane and dummy.

Taxiing back to the hangar with my legless passenger.

'**** me!'

And that's where this chapter started.

Fred had lost his leg.

I confess, as aviation incidents go, this was certainly a first. But thankfully it wasn't the most upsetting, once I'd checked to make sure that the leg hadn't taken a damaging kick at my rudder on departure. I returned for a normal landing, with enough flight test data 'in the can' to call it a wrap.

Phew! ... I had survived another.

I was content to approve the airworthiness aspects of the rig and handed it over to the CAA operations team who then had to work out whether or not it was safe to be used by *real* people.

Chapter 2

Spinning

GeDUNK!

What? Right in front of me where the spinning blur of the propeller disc was supposed to be was a very stationary set of three blades. The engine, and propeller attached to it, had stopped. It went from rotating very fast to not rotating at all in an instant – and I mean blink of an eye – in a heartbeat – instant. The rapid change of state from turning to stopped was accompanied by – well … *GeDUNK!*

I was 5,000 feet above Shropshire without an engine …

'Bugger!'

Nearly all conventional aeroplanes need airflow over the wings to generate the lift required to fly. This is why, when you go on your holidays, your Boeing or Airbus aeroplane has to dash along a long stretch of tarmac to gain flying speed. Once airborne, if the aeroplane is allowed to become too slow, the airflow reduces to the point where the aeroplane won't fly properly anymore. Aviators call this the 'stall', and if you're interested I've added some notes at the back of the book to try and explain this more fully (Appendix 1). Stalling an aeroplane can be daunting for some pilots but is a 'bread-and-butter' requirement for test pilots. The speed at which the stall occurs becomes a vital piece of information which determines how fast the aircraft needs to fly and, when considering the landing, it dictates a minimum approach speed. This effectively is the speed your airliner has to fly down to the runway carrying you and all your duty-free. The faster it lands, the longer the runway needs to be in order to have room to stop. If a stall occurs in flight the aircraft can be recovered to 'normal flight' simply by lowering the nose to allow it to accelerate to flying speed again. Problems occur when the aircraft is already too close to the ground to achieve this acceleration in the height available. This brings me on to the next topic. When the aircraft stalls, if it is not recovered, or enters with some yaw or side-slip, then it may enter what we call a 'spin'. Entering a spin accidentally is *always* bad.

Now the aerodynamics and physics of an aeroplane in a spin can easily generate whole books on the subject. Just like with helicopter aerodynamics, this is a subject where experts do not always agree. And it's definitely the case that the designer of an aeroplane will not be 100 per cent sure of the spinning characteristics until the aircraft has actually been flown and spun and data gathered. Can this be dangerous? Yes. Aircraft during test programmes often do not behave 'as advertised' and numerous airframes have tumbled into the ground during such test programmes. Not always, but most of the time, the plucky test pilot will have abandoned the aircraft to float gracefully to earth on a parachute.

Entering a spin accidentally, when not in a test programme, has led to numerous fatalities over the years. (In fact, it's fair to say that most aeroplanes that hit the ground accidentally, without power failure, do it because they've flown too slowly without sufficient height to recover.) The spin, if it occurs, leads to the aircraft spinning around an axis that may or may not run through the middle of the aircraft. The aircraft will also be yawing at a high rate and usually pitching both nose up and nose down in a regular or irregular oscillation. In addition, it will be plummeting earthwards at a great rate of knots. (Pilot speak for 'falling like a brick'.) For the aircraft occupants it is extremely disorientating and stressful. The pilot may well find that they are being pushed by the centrifugal or centripetal forces away from the flying controls. It is difficult to know whether the aircraft is the right side up and the spinning literally slows down most pilots' brains making clear thinking more difficult. The pilot has just 'signed on' to the worst funfair ride on the planet. You can see that if this was to happen to a pilot who wasn't well trained or experienced, and there wasn't sufficient height, the aircraft could hit the ground while still spinning. Sadly that is the outcome more often than we would like.

Anyway, in 'my day job' I am often the poor hapless soul who has to test an aircraft's spin characteristics and, more importantly, ensure it can be recovered using a fairly simple and ideally 'standard spin recovery technique'. Once I've demonstrated an aeroplane can be recovered using an 'optimum technique' I then have to investigate all the incorrect techniques a stressed and disorientated pilot might use. I know, bonkers! And you wonder why my hair is grey?

I tested a microlight aeroplane shortly after setting up Dovetail Aviation Ltd. I have included an explanation of what Microlight aeroplanes are in

Appendix 2. The aircraft I was invited to test was an upgraded version of an aircraft that had been flying safely for years, the Savannah XLS; it had a new design of wing. I did all the right things in terms of research. I then chose to fly out of Old Sarum in Salisbury, Wiltshire so I had all the resources of the MoD Boscombe Down test centre air traffic at my disposal to keep an eye on me. I even alerted my mates at the Wiltshire Air Ambulance as to where I was operating so they could come and get me if I had to take to my parachute.

And then off I set with my test programme, testing the aircraft's performance and handling qualities (how easy or difficult it was to fly) and obviously I tested flying the aircraft slower and slower, as described above, to experience the stall. As always, I tested 'every which way' of stalling the aircraft: with full power, and some power, and no power, and different configurations etc. And as suspected, the aircraft was very benign in slow speed flight and didn't stop flying until it was doing around 30 mph. So that's pretty good; means you can land in a built-up area without breaking the speed limit!

So off to do some spin testing. The word you will often hear used in flight test circles is 'incremental'. The concept is religiously taught by the various test pilot schools and ignored at your peril. The idea is that each

Savannah XLS at Old Sarum during the flight test programme.

test is just very slightly more challenging for the aircraft than the previous one and if the previous test was safe and easy to fly then the next point will still be OK. Eventually the test pilot will start to encounter more and more difficult or challenging characteristics and, when no longer comfortable to proceed further, that usually defines an 'end point'. However, whilst pilots have been fully versed in the incremental approach, aircraft haven't.

With the Savannah, its stalling was very benign and the spins all began as expected with recovery being very easy to do and the aircraft behaving in a very gentlemanly fashion and doing exactly what was expected. So much so that having achieved the certification requirement of a one-turn spin in all configurations and centres of gravity, I elected to fly one last test point – a two-turn spin.

Mistake.

I've lost count of the number of mistakes made in my aviation career to date. Most have been at worst embarrassing, rather than life threatening, but not so today. As I applied the controls in exactly the same way as previously to recover the aircraft, the aircraft decided to 'spool up' to the same rate of rotation as my spin-dryer – very fast; the nose of the aircraft dropped to the vertical and I began staring at a rotating version of the outskirts of Salisbury where my blurring view indicated things on the ground were getting bigger very quickly. As is always the case, things in my head dropped into the, by now, familiar 'slow-motion movie view' and I observed, somewhat remotely, that I had the controls applied correctly.

'I had done everything right', to quote Viper from the Top Gun movie.

But still I went round and round very quickly. There is a school of thought that suggests that, in these situations, it's better to put the controls back to where you started, and then try again. That is one view, but that also means the height you've already lost has added nothing to escaping your demise and you are now about to commence the same evolution again even closer to the ground. I adopted my pre-briefed and rehearsed response which was to be patient. Anyone who has ever met me will confirm that this is not how I'm wired. I can't sit stationary in a traffic jam when racing an extra fifty miles down 'RAC Rally quality' narrow, muddy farm tracks might keep me moving forward. But I did pause … and I waited … and I waited … and I waited … and called on the Almighty to alert my Guardian Angel.

As suddenly as it all started … it stopped.

All I had to do now was recover my lightweight aeroplane from the vertical dive it was now in before it accelerated to a speed that would rip the wings off – easy peasy.

Phew! … Survived another.

And, having lived to tell the tale, I was able to discuss my results with the British Microlight Aircraft Association (BMAA) and I drafted some strong words of warning which would be contained within the aircraft's flight manual to warn other pilots of the unpleasant nature of the spin, should they be unfortunate enough to encounter one.

Thankfully the high rotational aspects of the spin had not fazed me, largely due to another spinning evaluation I had done previously. The certification requirement for this class of (microlight) aeroplanes effectively prevented them from being spun deliberately, but it did contain a slightly folksy comment that manufacturers who wanted their aircraft to be capable of deliberate spinning should 'contact the CAA'.

And so it was that the UK-based importer of the German-built Ikarus aeroplane contacted me. He was a nice chap, and he had a point; that's what the certification code said, although probably only because the person writing the original draft wasn't sure about the topic. And so it was that I found myself staring at the Shropshire countryside going round and round while the cows got bigger.

C42 Ikarus Microlight G-FIFT used for the spin testing.

The first major upset to my relatively fragile morale occurred on the very first test sortie. I was right at the beginning of the test programme exploring the 'easy' test points. Firstly – the aircraft went round very, very fast, a full turn within two or three seconds. Experts on the topic will use phrases like inertia, momentum and A, B and C axes. Suffice to say that, if you were designing a spinning top to go round as fast as possible, the Ikarus designers had nailed it. As I commenced my recovery, expecting to remain spinning for some time, I again was caught out. The first action, usually, is to apply rudder in order to try and reduce or stop the yaw; generally this is then followed by other control inputs. So I confirmed the direction of the spin, ensured the throttle was closed and smoothly and progressively applied opposite rudder …

GeDANG!

Holy Moses! My eyes watered. We went from rotating very fast to not rotating at all – in an instant. And I mean in a blink of an eye – in a heartbeat – instant. The rapid change of state from spinning to stopped was accompanied by, well …

GeDANG!

An explosively loud sound caused when a well-engineered aircraft was suddenly forced to do something it didn't want to, perhaps like jumping your Mini Cooper over a hump-back bridge? (Hasn't everyone?) Just not what the designers originally expected.

Now, this was again very unusual. I had, by then, done a lot of spinning in a lot of different aeroplanes and none had behaved like this. Despite my very best intentions, was this flimsy aluminium-and-fabric-tent-like aircraft being abused too much?

'Time out.'

Discretion being the better part of valour, I headed in a very gentle descent to where I'd just departed. On the ground I explained what I'd seen and heard, to be met with faces that didn't inspire immediate confidence. This scene was to be repeated in a 'Groundhog Day' fashion time and time again in my flight-test career. The crucial question for me concerned the structural integrity of this slack handful of aluminium poles. Were they going to break and send my Ikarus hurtling into the sun…? And guess what – no one knew. Worrying really …

Turns out (and I learn new stuff with every flight/sortie/project) that when you put stressful loads on aluminium (unlike more modern composite materials) it bends in a linear fashion. That means that, as you increase the load, the metal bends progressively. Some other materials hardly bend at all, then break = very bad in an aeroplane. So after much conflab, emails and telephone calls to various experts, it turned out that by putting video cameras on the top of the aeroplane and repeating the manoeuvres already flown (and therefore known to be safe – bit like walking through a minefield and stepping in your mate's footprints) we could see the wings and tail bend and thus someone, a good deal cleverer than me, could work out whether we were close to breaking anything. It turns out this Ikarus was built like the proverbial 'brick shithouse' and my abuse to date had not come close to snapping off crucial components, like wings. Or the tail assembly.

I now felt very confident that the aircraft would recover 'easily', and we could offer the pilot a very simple technique to recover the aeroplane – or so we thought; but no.

Having completed testing at a mid-range centre of gravity I embarked on the typically more exciting aft centre of gravity test points. With the

Video camera mounted on the test aircraft facing aft to film the tail. It was also mounted to point at the wing tips for other tests.

centre of gravity moved rearwards, our benign spinning-top took on horns. It laughed at my naïve attempts to recover as previously.

Not only did it need full rudder to be applied but the joystick needed to be moved forward also. This stick moved the elevator at the back of the plane in an effort to push the nose down so I could gain some airspeed. As with the Savannah this had the initial consequence of speeding up the spinning.

I know – it was already going around as fast as I thought possible.

But just before my eyeballs burst out of their sockets the aircraft recovered into a conventional dive …

Phew! … survived another.

So far so good and onto the next test point. This involved all the 'abuse' cases including applying aileron during the stall.

So, here we go – entering the spin,

I closed the throttle … I slowed, … I stalled, … I yawed and …

GeDUNK!

What? Right in front of me, where the spinning blur of the propeller disc was supposed to be, was a very stationary set of three blades. The engine, and propeller attached to it, had stopped.

'Oh, bugger!'

It went from rotating very fast to not rotating at all, in an instant. And I mean in a blink of an eye – in a heartbeat – instant. The rapid change of state from spinning to stopped was accompanied by, well …

GeDUNK!

So 5,000 feet over Shropshire I was in a glider – again. In fairness, I have lost count of the number of times I've managed to start with a powered aircraft and ended up in a glider. On balance, most of the times deliberately but that still leaves countless unexpected similar occurrences. This aircraft was fitted with an engine made by Rotax; as I came to understand they really don't want to go round. Other engines such as Lycomings or Continentals or Gipsy Majors fitted to other single-engine aircraft do, in the main, want to go around and, as long as they remain connected to their propellers (which act as a giant windmill), they will tend to turn, forced to by airflow. Thus temporary problems such as lack of fuel or spark to the spark plugs can usually be resolved in 'slow time'. Not so the Rotax; it spits in the face of such conventional manners – and – well – when they stop they really stop! And so did this one. There was a time in my aviation career where such an occurrence would have been a drama and I would have been quite upset. However, with each such crisis I was adopting a slightly less ruffled response. By the time I was flying the Ikarus I was able to react relatively calmly; enough to recover the aircraft from the spin I'd entered and start gliding for home. Then, having decided that I wasn't going to die just yet, set about trying to restart the engine which, in fairness to Mr Rotax, was achieved with the minimum of fuss.

The test programme went on to investigate this issue – and time and time again …

GeDUNK!

The airflow around the prop was critical and when the aircraft was already spinning rapidly any airflow from an unexpected direction caused Ronnie Rotax to hand in his cards in disgust.

I'd survived another, without having to pester my Guardian Angel too much. We had encountered an aircraft that frankly seemed to enjoy spinning – happy as Larry they would say – and by varying the centre of gravity different characteristics could be demonstrated to trainee pilots. All of which would make their lives safer in the long run but we had an aircraft engine that just loved to say no.

In military certification certain unhelpful characteristics can be mitigated against by choosing only the most gifted pilots (just ask any Harrier pilot – that's if he hasn't already told you). More comprehensive training and frequent refresher training can be required, but in civil certification (give or take), it's either safe or it isn't. And with the best will in the world it was hard to see how a single-engine aeroplane could routinely accept the engine quitting. So – the CAA had been contacted – and the CAA said,

'Sorry, but *not today* …'

Postscript

Since drafting this chapter I've just completed a further comprehensive flight-test programme on the latest version of the aircraft, the C42C, which has, amongst other things, a different wing. I have to say the aircraft was a delight to fly and after scores and scores of one turn spins I can report that the engine did not stop on me once, almost certainly because after just a single turn, the aircraft had not yet had a chance to reach its very high rotational speed that I'd encountered all those years ago.

C42C test aircraft on completion of testing this latest version at Little Snoring.

Chapter 3

Learning to Fly Autogyros

Just when I thought all was going quite well (always a big mistake in my aviation experience) there was a now familiar string of audio cues …

Cough, Cough – *splutter* – *splutter* – SILENCE!

I was probably about eleven years old when I first saw the James Bond movie 'You Only Live Twice'. Back in those days we would have waited until it appeared on our small black-and-white TV at Christmas. The movie had Sean Connery dashing around Japan doing his usual stuff but in one part of the movie he needs to do an aerial reconnaissance of an old volcano. Q the 'gadget man' turns up with some wooden crates and proceeds to unpack, what I now know to be, an autogyro. Needless to say, Bond's aircraft came with rockets and missiles amongst other things and when attacked by a whole bunch of baddies in Bell 47 helicopters, with mounted machine guns, he is able to fight them all off. That scene sowed the seed, as I guess it did for many aspiring gyro pilots about my age. Ironically, if I google 'Chris Taylor Test Pilot' I find more entries about my test flying of autogyros than anything else. But I'm getting ahead of myself …

I started working for the UK CAA in January 2004 and was walked around the various desks in the first couple of days. On one wall was a large piece of graph paper that measured about one metre high. Along the bottom of the graph was a zigzag line in numerous colours. It was just what I would have expected if I had given my 3-year-old grandson a bunch of coloured pencils! Right at the top, all on its own, was a single red zigzag line. Needless to say I let my curiosity get the better of me and it turned out it was a graph showing the number of fatal aircraft accidents per flying hour split out by type. Thus at the bottom were aeroplanes, gliders, helicopters, jet aircraft, balloons etc. … and right up the top, with an accident rate ten times higher than all the others, was the autogyro line.

I soon discovered that, prior to my joining the CAA, no one within the organisation had thought it sensible to be flown in one, let alone commence test flying them.

I had been recruited to test fly aeroplanes with another team looking after helicopters. Because some people thought gyros and helicopters were 'kind of the same' this team looked after autogyros. In fact they really aren't the same.

I was the wide-eyed innocent and eager to please my new masters and, as you have already guessed, I hadn't been there a full year before my boss tapped me on the shoulder,

'Go and learn how to fly autogyros', he commanded.

A bit unfair, since the rest of the office thought this was potentially a one-way mission and had avoided it successfully for years. But the James Bond movie had already got to me and, like all pilots who stupidly choose to become test pilots, I like variety and I like new challenges. I'm not sure I had fully realised at that point just how perilous aspects of this particular avenue were to become. But more of that in some later chapters ...

For now, the challenge was to familiarise myself with as much info as I could and find the right place to go and learn how to fly them. Now, so far in this book, I've avoided mentioning too many names – I don't want to be sued for defamatory remarks. But the gyro world at the time, and still to some extent, was more about people than machinery. In the UK it was a very small pond with a handful of fish who all the know-how. My colleague and Rotary Wing (RW) Flight Test Engineer (FTE), Ray had largely been conducting the CAA's flight test input to the issues generated by the type for a few years, although he had relied on third party information provided by those who actually flew them. He pointed me towards a very nice chap who earned a living refitting repaired tyres to tractors. Yes – I know. Turns out Dave was one of the country's most experienced gyro pilots; he was approved by the CAA to give instruction and was one of only two examiners. So, by all accounts, he was at the top of this particular food chain, which is, in my limited experience, always the best place to be.

Now another thing I've learnt about flight testing over the last couple of decades is that people with open cockpit aircraft always want to fly in the summer; not unreasonable? But that means people like me who need to test open cockpit aircraft or learn how to fly them end up doing it in the winter.

Dave and Ray standing by our training aircraft, the Magni M16.

And so it was that Ray and I found ourselves in February 2006 rocking up to Melbourne, a disused former Second World War bomber base east of York, used for drag racing and also, it turns out, autogyro training.

Dave met us on arrival but couldn't offer us a well needed coffee as the water in his briefing room, aka rusting caravan, was still frozen. And that set the tone for the next three days where I proceeded to cover the whole autogyro training syllabus, mainly, if I'm honest, driven by a deeply-rooted Royal Navy Fleet Air Arm ethos of getting home for the weekend – come hell or high water.

Dave was slighter in stature than his gravitas implied; despite being from Yorkshire I was actually able to understand every word he said. (I covered a few shifts for the police helicopter units based at Wakefield and Sheffield. Despite hailing from the North of England myself, albeit the other side of the Pennines, not only would I struggle with internal communications but crew members from different parts of Yorkshire needed me to act as interpreter.)

Dave had been flying gyros for decades, following tuition initially from his dad, and built up a good understanding of how to fly them without killing himself – always a good 'skill set' in any aircraft community.

So, some of you will at this point be interested in knowing how gyros fly; the rest of you can skip on a page or so to avoid excessive technical jargon which might induce uncontrolled slumber ...

However, don't let anyone tell you they know how gyros fly, because frankly, no one does. OK, they will tell you what to do to operate one for sure, but try picking up a book that achieves the same as a myriad of text books on aeroplane aerodynamics – they don't exist. Maybe I should write one if I ever finish this?

When I started my Googling and background research I was able to learn all about a chap called Juan de la Cierva y Codorníu, First Count of la Cierva. Now as a helicopter test pilot I had heard a good deal about him already. A wealthy Spaniard born in 1895, he graduated as a civil engineer (what does this tell you already about autogyros?) and started designing an aircraft using a windmill arrangement instead of a wing. Quite rightly (hurrah!) he moved to the UK in 1925 which was, back in the day, when we Brits still loved eccentrics and whacky technical projects. His aircraft had a few very minor, almost inconsequential really, technical snags which caused them to roll over and destroy themselves on take off. His balsa wood models, however, had worked and eventually he realised that the fan blades (rotor blades) on top of the aircraft needed to bend like those of his models. In fact, he eventually fitted hinges to the roots of the blades which allowed them to flap around and find their own way in life – this stopped them forcing the whole aircraft to tip over and was the key to the success of the gyro and, subsequently, helicopter rotor systems. Cierva managed to survive his involvement at the beginning of the Spanish Civil War, assisting Franco return to Spanish Morocco, but sadly was killed in 1936. Ironically he wasn't killed in an autogyro accident but in an aeroplane taking off from Croydon when his hapless pilot flew into a house – those were the days.

Cierva's research led a number of others to 'pick up the baton' and design the helicopter. It's fair to say that all the money and effort then went into building practical helicopters. Ironically the next nation to use autogyros in earnest was Germany and most of the technical papers I could find on gyro aerodynamics came from the Third Reich of the 1930s. They went on to use them during the war, most bizarrely in their U-boats. At sea you can only see as far as the horizon and, due to the curvature of the earth, you can see farther the higher above the water line you are. Remember all those pirate movies with some hapless soul being sent up the crow's nest at the top of the mast with a telescope, all waiting for the 'Land Ho' shout?

A submarine has a relatively short fin or conning tower, so lookout was difficult until the Germans hit upon the idea of using 'aerial reconnaissance'. However, with no flight deck available they couldn't carry an aeroplane but worked out they could put a gyro onboard and, given that these machines are only a few metal tubes and a seat, they could easily collapse them and stow them inside the sub when not in use. To get airborne the sub would motor flat out into wind to create as much airflow over the deck as possible and the gyro would lift off the deck without the need for an engine. It was tethered to the boat with a winch wire that contained the very latest in communication technology, a phone line. As the gyro reached the end of the winch wire the pilot now had an impressive view of tens of miles rather than the handful previously. Pre-radar and other such devices, this was essential for spotting the enemy.

What do you think happened if the pilot spotted a large Royal Navy cruiser coming towards him? Surely he would alert the rest of the crew to their imminent peril so they could cut the winch wire and crash dive?

'Hey Hans, can you see any Royal Navy cruisers?'

'Nein.'

'Bist di Sicher – are you sure?'

'Ja.'

''But what's that black smoke on the horizon?'

'Nothing at all – can you winch me down now please? – It's my lunch break …'

In fact, it was probably we Brits who then built the most promising autogyro. The Cierva designs were taken up by the Fairey Aviation Company who had spent the war years developing and building most of the UK-built aircraft for the Royal Navy's Fleet Air Arm; so, therefore, a company I have a great deal of respect for. Although some of their designs were dreadful, they did at least build the Swordfish which was perhaps even more iconic than the Spitfire to those of us with salt water running in our veins.

Anyway, Fairey took over Cierva's designs, building a number of experimental aircraft in the late 1940s and 1950s, which led to the innovative Fairey Rotordyne – Google it. It was another great British invention that, sadly, didn't quite make it as a commercial success. This was an aircraft that could hover like a helicopter but, in forward flight, it flew like an autogyro …

Which brings me back to explaining how these aircraft fly. So to start with, they have to be propelled forward by either a propeller or jet engine, or more than one. Early aircraft looked like the biplanes of the day with the upper wing replaced by rotors. The individual rotor blades are similar to sycamore seeds. If you ever watch these fall from the tree, nature has designed them as perfect rotating blades. As they fall earthward the airflow spins them around and in doing so creates lift that slows down their descent. If you get a couple of such blades and allow them to spin in the airflow above an aircraft the same thing happens. The spinning blades create lift. If you spin them fast enough they create as much lift as an aeroplane wing, for example. So start with an aeroplane fuselage and an engine then swap the wing for rotors and you have a gyro. In order to steer it through the sky you fit it with an aeroplane rudder which you might as well mount on a fin which will help it fly more like a dart; that is, straight-ish. So we have propulsion that pushes or pulls us forward, lift, and a rudder to steer, but how do we control the rest of the flight path? Well, imagine the rotors spinning create a disc like a dinner plate. If we tilt the rotors so that the dinner plate tilts left or right or farther back the lift axis will also tilt. This will cause the aircraft strapped beneath it to pitch or roll etc.

Tilting the disc is achieved by the pilot moving a simple stick usually hinged on the cockpit floor such that, moving the stick left rolls the aircraft left, pulling it back pitches the aircraft nose up – just like an aeroplane. Uncanny. And also similar to a helicopter, as it happens.

So, armed with my research and with Dave strapped into the rear cockpit off we set in his Italian kit-built aircraft and, notwithstanding the open cockpit and sub-zero airflow, it actually was a lot of fun. Turns out that having flown both helicopters and aeroplanes, with a bit of imagination, I could apply the applicable technique when it mattered – but initially it wasn't always intuitive. What I really did enjoy though was the fantastic field of view with no wing to get in the way. And the aircraft was relatively lightweight so quite 'chuckable', that is manoeuvrable, and it was possible to repeatedly land exactly where I wanted to, even without using the engine.

Setting up for a landing – Note how the rotor disc is tilted back.

In a helicopter the rotors go round at a constant speed but the pilot can change the lift by increasing the angle of the rotor blades. In a gyro this angle is fixed and, like a toy helicopter, varying the rotor speed increases or decreases lift like a piston-engine aircraft propeller. It's also very important to keep the air flowing through the gyro's rotors at all times, otherwise they tend to stop.

A good example of inappropriate technique leading to a one way ticket to 'Cock-up Central' was the 'engine failure shortly after take-off' emergency. If it happens to you in an aeroplane you have to react quickly and push the joystick forward briskly to try and maintain sufficient airspeed to enter a glide and prevent a stall and possibly a spin. But in a helicopter if you push the stick forward briskly after a power loss your rotors will slow down and you will have insufficient lift or control to prevent the crash. So helicopter pilots will instinctively pull the stick back to flare the aircraft following engine failure which keeps the rotors spinning and reduces rate of descent.

So in a gyro the helicopter pilot part of me expected that I would need to do a 'helicopter thing' if the engine stopped in my gyro …

Just airborne from the grass strip. Note the tall power cables to be avoided.

'Noooooooooooo!**!'

As I attempted this on my first simulated 'donk stop' the calm David became quite excited and promptly reversed my instinctive control inputs while he added full power to save us both from embarrassment.

Turns out in a gyro you have to keep your 'flying speed' because without airspeed you can't land at all – you crash. So you have to be an aeroplane pilot in this situation but, like in a helicopter, pushing the stick forward does cause the blades to slow down, so now you are pointing at the ground, going down rapidly with reducing rotor speed. At least if you have airspeed you can, at the critical moment, smoothly pull the stick back which causes the aircraft to level out, and the blades to speed up, and just for a moment, whilst still going forward, the lift from the spinning rotors will plonk you gently on your chosen bit of God's earth, sufficiently gently for you and your aircraft to live to fly another day.

There have been a number of accidents caused by aeroplane pilots flying helicopters and helicopter pilots flying aeroplanes in such circumstances. When I was learning to fly helicopters in the Royal Navy we students were banned from any form of aeroplane flying until we completed the course. Later on in life I finished learning how to fly a Robinson R22 helicopter with a very experienced R22 instructor. There was nothing he couldn't do or cope with in the R22 – he was the UK expert. He was sadly killed a couple of years later when apparently his aeroplane pilot student briskly pushed the stick forward when he shouldn't have done.

The other large area of 'gotchas' was on the ground. Yes, in a gyro you can easily kill yourself, or certainly damage your pride and joy, without ever getting airborne. So much time in learning to 'fly' a gyro is actually spent motoring around an airfield firmly on the ground.

Why so?

Well – how long have we got? But rotors are designed to operate at a certain rotational speed or speed range. Once that speed has been achieved the blades are held rigidly in place by centrifugal or centripetal force, the force that allows you to swing your baby around like Superman as long as you don't get too dizzy first. Oh dear, was I a bad parent? Doesn't everyone want to teach their kids how to fly like the 'man of steel'?

Now, when the blades aren't turning they tend to droop down under their own weight and can easily come into contact with bits of the aircraft they aren't meant to. Additionally, when they are turning slowly they are prone to wander up and down of their own volition, subject to the slightest change in wind etc. All of that is also a challenge for a helicopter pilot, but at least you are able to spin the rotors up to their flying speed whilst the aircraft remains stationary on the ground; not so in a gyro. As you are now fully aware, the rotors on a gyro are not powered but allowed to spin in the breeze unfettered by such punitive measures.

This means that a primary way to get the whole thing spinning is to drive your aircraft along a runway at increasing speed with the airflow spinning the rotors up as you go. That sounds easy enough but if you try to do this too quickly you get too much lift on one side of the rotor disc and the aircraft will roll over, resulting in bruised ego, scratched paintwork, bent blades etc. If you attempt this in a more leisurely and, apparently, safe fashion you will run out of runway before you can take-off and make a nice gyro shaped hole in the hedge at the end of the airfield.

So lots of training and practice is essential to master 'blade handling'. However, many gyro manufacturers have anticipated this challenge. So they have worked out a method of taking a drive from the engine to the rotors so that, before take off, the rotors can be spun up to a sensible

With Ray having survived our gyro training.

speed. This invariably isn't quite enough to fly with but it does circumvent a number of the problems described above.

So with all of this new-found knowledge I set off back home to Salisbury on Friday morning, mission accomplished despite some very red cheeks from frostbite. Now the CAA had an Autogyro Test Pilot.

Shortly thereafter I was at an aviation trade show and mingling like a true pro on the autogyro stand. Bear in mind, this community is a very small pond and word of my successful training had bounced around, probably before I'd completed the five-hour drive home from Yorkshire. When I mentioned to a gyro pilot on the stand that I was now proficient in flying gyros he laughed his head off. He was a grumpy sod and this was the only time I ever saw him laugh.

He said, 'You might know how to fly a two seater, but you know nothing (Jon Snow?) about single seaters. Flying a single seater versus a two seater is like the difference between driving a Ferrari instead of a bus.'

I'm not sure if this chap has ever driven a bus or a Ferrari but I have, and they are really quite different.

So, not to be blown off course, I contacted another living legend in the community – Tony. Tony had also been flying gyros for decades without killing himself and had found a niche as the world's (well the gyro world as I knew it) leading instructor on single-seaters. Now arguably, whilst flying single-seat gyros might not be sane, instructing on them isn't such a bad idea as you do it safely from the comfort of your car as you drive up and down the runway chasing your student with a megaphone or hand-held radio. Quite safe in comparison.

And so it was that Tony invited me to attend Henstridge airfield (ex-Fleet Air Arm Second World War airfield in Somerset) one Saturday morning. I was given no choice but to arrive at the café for breakfast at 8 am. I'm trying to think of the horror movie, where you walk in to the haunted house, which is already full of scores of the 'undead' eating their most recent victims – well that's what this felt like. The café was all steamed up from a tea urn set to permanent boil and, in the resulting mist, I was met by scores of gyro pilots and enthusiasts, munching huge plates of bacon, sausage and eggs, who had driven miles across the UK to take part in what I thought was a day of training, mostly for them. How mistaken was I? As later I started to get to grips with my single-seat gyro it became apparent that the crowd from the café were not flying at all. In fact, they had arrived with their deck chairs and packed lunches as the word had got out that the CAA's newest test pilot was about to make a complete fool himself in a 'Ferrari of the skies' and this would evidently provide the best lightweight entertainment since those chaps in shorts watched the A bombs exploding on Bikini Atoll.

And so I was introduced to a machine (if that was a fair description) – comprising two bits of angle iron welded together with a seat mounted where they joined. A further bit of angle iron ran up behind the seat to which a pair of rotor blades was attached. Behind that was a lawnmower engine with a propeller affixed so as to blow air over the rudder.

The machine had no brakes, no stabiliser, no pre-rotator, no fuselage or windscreen. This really was minimalist aviation I thought. But, undeterred, I listened as Tony (who liked a bottle of whisky from his customers as part of his remuneration to dull the pain of watching people like me learn) explained how I was to learn. I was to motor up and down the runway with him in his trusty Golf (car not buggy) running alongside. We would start with the art of 'spooling

The single seat training gyro.

up' the rotors followed by doing 'wheel balancing'. Now I don't mean adding lead weights to the front wheels of your car, as we did 'back in the day' in an attempt to stop the vibration tearing the steering wheel out of your hands above 50 mph. No, this was a different definition altogether. Mainly, it comprised of getting the gyro to the point where it almost wanted to fly but then only raising the nose wheel off the ground. Harder than it sounds, as the aircraft is not on all three wheels or flying but instead has become a whacky balancing challenge around the pivot of the rear wheels, requiring a surprising amount of deft wiggling of the stick to keep everything in the right place. This all went on for quite a while before my need for a pee and cuppa, in that order, allowed a debrief and brief for the next challenge which was to be 'Bunny Hops'. I'd spent quite some time in Yorkshire practising this in the two seater, but now I had the challenge of getting the rotors whizzing fast enough for me to hop a few inches off the runway before closing the throttle and allowing the aircraft to gracefully alight. With practice I could keep the rotors spinning fast enough to achieve a series of these take offs and landings before running out of tarmac – hurray. Time for another pee.

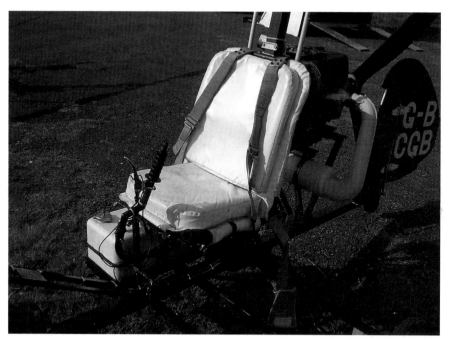

The cockpit. Note the fuel tank under the seat.

Mid-afternoon, realising the punters in the deckchairs needed some real entertainment before they headed home, I asked if I could finally 'slip the surly bonds of earth', which in this case meant getting more than three feet above the runway.

Now over the years I have repeatedly seen the self-same expression on another pilot's face – one of slight bemusement if not disbelief. And I tend not to have learnt my lesson and didn't take the hint on this cold winter afternoon ...

Tony agreed and I asked, as always,

'Is the aircraft still OK? No defects?'

'All OK.'

'And is there enough fuel for my sortie?'

'Loads', came the reply.

So off I set, excited about the prospect of being able to experience this Ferrari thoroughbred of the skies finally being let off the leash.

And so, waving to the spectators in a cheerful fashion, I observed they all waved cheerfully back. Although I think, with hindsight, they were flapping their arms in genuine concern for my welfare.

Just airborne in the single-seater.

All went entirely as planned for the first half of the runway. Smoothly opening the throttle, I gathered speed, with the wind-milling blades starting to spin faster and faster. With no gauge to tell me how fast the blades were turning, I had to rely on my 'considerable experience' gained in the 'forenoon' and, when I judged it was sufficient, let the lawnmower engine have its head and, with a mighty lack of roar, I gently ascended to my previously customary cruise height of three to four feet, accelerating to the 'one speed fits all' of around 45 mph. It was at this best rate of climb speed that I expected to climb away from the air cushion squeezed between the ground and the rotors. By now I was committed to go flying – the large stretch of tarmac I had started with in front of me had ebbed away quite quickly whilst I was concentrating on other things and the now the customary hedge at the end of the runway was filling my view – mmmmmmmmmmm!

A number of choices flooded my numbing brain:

In an aeroplane, I would now be in a very embarrassing predicament, as pulling back on the stick to try and clear the hedge at such a low speed would have had me stall and crash for sure.

In a helicopter this would have been less of a drama as I would have had enough power to climb over the obstacle or I could have flared to stop in good time.

In the gyro I was left with only one realistic option. I continued to fly as fast as I could pointing at the hedge and, just as all appeared lost, eased back on the stick smartly and promptly climbed to clear the hedge. Hurray – but not so quick, young Quixote! One thing I already knew about gyros was if you went slower than a certain crucial speed no amount of power would keep you aloft – and I had just traded speed for height and had slowed below this critical speed …

Eeeek!

In an aeroplane I would now be toast, but in a gyro I was still in full control and now had something else in the bank to trade – height. So, promptly I pushed forward on the stick, entering a dive towards the ground as the airspeed indicator trickled back to the magic 45. Phew! Survived, for now – I'm still flying, albeit now skimming the surface of the field at two feet or less. That expression I'd seen on Tony's face a few minutes earlier I now recognised on the faces of the numerous cows I was hurtling towards about to turn into T-bones and sirloin. Thankfully my newly mastered skill of hopping obstacles was entirely 'fit for purpose' and I scurried across the field leaping cow after cow with gay abandon. I hadn't had so much fun in years. With each cow I gained a little more height so that I was able to turn back to the airfield – ever conscious of my non-fare-paying audience's customer satisfaction. Imagine the cheers as I roared back into view over the hedge which many thought had claimed one of its first victims since 1945. When I say imagine, that's what I had to do, as I couldn't hear them, and was far too busy trying to keep this thing climbing than to worry about the punters. A slight variation in speed found the 'sweet spot' as I rocketed skywards at about 100 feet a minute. Eventually I was high enough to run my planned test programme; to really get to grips with the stability and control characteristics of my new mount. I flew at different speeds, flew turns with different angles of bank, flew slowly to the point where I could descend vertically then dived to accelerate to the fastest anyone had ever flown this Meccano set. Just when I thought all was going quite well (always a big mistake in my aviation experience) there was a now familiar string of audio cues …

Cough, Cough – *splutter* – *splutter* – SILENCE …

Now, this wasn't my first engine failure by any means. In the military I'd ditched my helicopter during training and lost an engine on the Basset twin on my first ever flight flying it. I'd also had the single jet engine on a Hawk flame out on me at 44,000 feet on a Friday afternoon – top tip: never have a problem over Devon on a Friday afternoon in the summer holidays. As I commenced my glide into St Mawgan in Cornwall, all I could concentrate on were the gridlocked roads that would now lie between me and home. It was this, my first 'Mayday' call, that taught me one of the best lessons in test flying to date. If it starts to go 'pear shaped' the first thing you do is point to where you've parked your car. Sadly my car wasn't in Cornwall.

This recently adopted rule stood me in good stead in this gyro. I pointed the nose down to where I'd parked, gathered airspeed and rotor speed and took a moment to congratulate myself on still being alive. Stand down my guardian angel.

With my nerves intact and with lots of speed and rotor rpm I was able to gracefully touch down in front of most of the punters still putting down their flasks of tea. I even managed to maintain enough speed on touch down so that I could roll/coast gracefully off the runway along the taxiway to within a few feet of the essential rusty briefing caravan, my car and perhaps just as important – the bottle of scotch I'd arrived with a few hours earlier.

And the crowd went wild! If there had been ticker tape, they'd have thrown it.

'And so Tony', I asked, 'what's just occurred?'

'Dunno? Ah – there's no fuel in it.'

'So what part of "Yes there's loads of fuel in it" was misleading then?'

'Well', says Tony, 'No one expected you to be able to learn to fly a single seat gyro at all – let alone in a morning. And I thought there was a real risk of you f**king up and crashing, so I lent you this heap which hasn't flown for years. If you crashed it I wouldn't have been too worried. And when you said you wanted to go and do some flight testing I didn't think you'd fly for that long. Why do you think all the spectators are here if not to watch the CAA Test Pilot plough a new furrow on the airfield somewhere?'

Well, how I laughed. What do you think? Still, I had experienced my new favourite sport of 'Cow Hopping' which was much more fun than 'Bunny Hopping' and I'd been able to convince a very sceptical gyro community (most of whom were there that day) that I could fly one of the worst of types and still return it without a scratch – even without any petrol. And, most importantly,

I'd survived another … Phew!

Chapter 4

PZL

'Standby – Three, Two, One, *Now.*'

Before the word 'now' had been fully spoken I was completely out of control, tumbling sidewards through the sky in a helicopter with the warning klaxon blaring in my ears louder than a rock concert.

As you will know by now, my flight test expertise started out in helicopters. As an experienced Royal Navy Wasp and Lynx pilot I fought off all the opposition to be selected for the single RN place on the 1994 ETPS Test Pilot Course. By the time I had become a civil certification test pilot working for the CAA I had spent two years completing some very 'whacky' testing for the Defence Research Agency (DRA) based at RAE Bedford and Farnborough. I then returned to ETPS where I taught rotary wing flight test for seven whole years. In fairness, it turns out, I'd learned next to 'bugger all' during my year as a student, but boy did I have to learn fast when I suddenly had to teach it to others, who all seemed younger, smarter and, if I'm honest, better looking than me. So, I sharpened up and, after ten years at Boscombe Down, thought I could hold my own against the best rotary wing (RW) test pilots (TP) in the world. However, as I was to discover, I was about to start a whole new, and ever so full, chapter of learning, or in other words I still knew 'bugger all'!

I joined the UK CAA to test fly aeroplanes as the department already had a full time RW TP and two RW Flight Test engineers (FTEs).

So, whilst tempted to intrude on the RW turf, I stuck to the aeroplane side of the house until invited otherwise. Well, it turns out I didn't have long to wait. At my interview I had actually asked to do some RW flying in addition to the aeroplane stuff. At the time, the Chief Test Pilot had dollar signs flashing in his eyes, and I was immediately rechristened 'Buy One, Get One Free!' unbeknownst to me for quite a while.

Over a few beers at some social event or other I must have mentioned that as Principal Tutor at ETPS I'd been out to Lublin in Poland to fly a very challenging little helicopter known by the catchy name of SW-4 (dull or what?). Twelve months or so later the European Aviation Safety Agency (EASA) had been formally approached by the helicopter's manufacturer Państwowe Zakłady Lotnicze, which stands for State Aviation Works, thankfully known the world over as PZL. Anyway, PZL had applied to EASA to have their new helicopter certified so it could operate in Europe (although it was already approved by the Polish authority for the Polish military).

Somehow my name came up (funny that) and, before I could spell PZL, I found I had been nominated as the TP for the CAA Certification team working under contract for EASA. I was teamed up with Ray who was later to become my gyro mate and our colleague, Nigel, who was the CAA's then current RW TP and my senior. Now, the immediate good news was that I finally had a cast-iron case for the CAA to provide me with the protective helmet I would almost certainly need to wear. Apparently, flying around for over a year, in all manner of open cockpit biplanes, had not been reason enough so far. So for the sake of a shiny new blue helmet I sold my soul to the 'dark side' and the day came for us

Prototype PZL SW-4 during our initial flight test programme at Swidnik.

to travel to Lublin, which involved a BA flight from London Heathrow to Warsaw on a Sunday. I had been looking forward to getting back into helicopter flight test after my 'sabbatical' and I was determined to make a good impression on the new team I was working with. So, I'd set off from home early and, as I pulled up on the M3 behind some crawling traffic, I was not fazed at all. Ray and Nigel had not even left Gatwick and I had ages before my flight was due to leave. However, this afternoon was about to become one of the most stressful for ages. Initially, I just chilled; I listened to Radio 2 but without any traffic info. It was a Sunday and surely this now stationary jam would clear in good time? But the clock kept on ticking until I was starting to make more frequent phone calls to Ray and Nigel telling them I was going nowhere fast. I had to get there *today*.

Miss my flight and I'd miss the first day at PZL. I really felt I couldn't be late for my very first RW gig. Desperate times required desperate measures and, following a rare flash of inspiration, I managed to get hold of the phone number of the duty manager of Fleet Motorway Services. I was only a couple of hundred yards past the slip road to the service area. The phone rang and rang as my heart sank but then, a very, very, very nice lady answered. I explained, with extremely stressed tones, my dire situation and, although she was based on the south-bound side of the motorway, she took pity on me and agreed to have one of her team let me out of the north side service area using a rear delivery gate. Phew! (If you read this chapter one day, please call me so I can send you a nice bottle of wine.)

Was I chuffed or what?

Now, I wish you had been there to see this. Moses would have been proud. I was log-jammed in the outside lane with bumper to bumper juggernauts on the two inner lanes. So, out of my car I jumped to personally canvas a dozen 'hairy truckers' with my plight. By getting three or four to back up a few inches each and another few to pull forward a few inches I managed to make a corridor about seven feet wide. I three-point-turned my car until it was at right angles to the traffic and quickly slid between the trucks onto the hard shoulder. I had about forty minutes before the flight closed. It was going to be tight …

Now on the hard shoulder I reversed to the entrance, as briskly as one of the cops in 'The Sweeney' would have managed. I then zipped around to the filling station to meet, just like a CIA agent, the pre-briefed colleague who covertly entered the code for the back gate and let me out.

Now it really was 'RAC Rally' time as I found myself pre sat-nav in the rabbit warren of lanes and tracks north of the M3. Thankfully, no tractors, and I made it to the junction beyond the accident in record time. With thirty minutes or so remaining, I floored the accelerator of my abused company car and entered the completely empty motorway. I took a calculated risk that on a Sunday all the local traffic police would be busy sorting out the carnage now thankfully behind me, and I selected a three-digit speed that I felt might just work without getting me immediately imprisoned for life. As I drove I devised a 'cunning plan' to save as much further time as possible. I now used my 'hands free' to set up a taxi to meet me at the CAA's Heathrow office, where I planned to abandon the car, and alerted my mate, Ray, that all was nearly, but not quite yet, lost.

I threw £20 at the taxi driver telling him to keep the change if he could get me to the terminal within five minutes. He didn't quite select the same three-digit speed but clearly £20 was a lot of money for him back then. I bailed out as the taxi slowed and threw myself through the terminal building's sliding doors to be met by Ray and the most charming of BA ladies.

Superhero style she exclaimed, 'Follow me and don't stop for anything!'

And with a flick of her cloak we were off.

Have you seen the movie 'Love Actually' when the young lad leaps the security barriers? We didn't have to. Our superhero used her special powers, or a magic pass, or something, because doors opened, people moved and we threw ourselves on to the Airbus as they closed the cabin door behind me with a thud. I strapped in with sweat pouring. It took four large glasses of Chardonnay before my pulse rate slowed to a level humans can normally cope with for more than a few seconds.

And we were off. Surely the worst part of my trip was behind me? What do you think?

The only realistic way to get to Lublin from Warsaw is along a straightish main road, the S17, which runs south-east on the north bank of the Vistula river. It was what we Brits would call 'single carriageway'. Turns out that doesn't translate at all well within the Polish highway code. Overtaking would routinely take place as if on a dual-carriageway with the overtaking cars forcing themselves down the middle of the road. Avoiding a 'head to head' with overtaking cars relied on the slower vehicles realising that pile ups were imminent, and kindly pulling over as much as they could into the dusty gritty verge. For we three Brit passengers the only saving grace was that our driver seemed to have done this before and the BA staff on the plane seemed to have taken a shine to us sufficiently to ensure we were suitably inebriated to soften the impact of any emergency stop.

We got to the rather dilapidated, although previously splendid, hotel only to discover that the coming Friday was a bank holiday and almost certainly we wouldn't be able to fly that day. Bank holidays on a Friday: who'd have thought it? So we rolled up to the PZL factory complex on the Monday morning with no time to spare.

Now, I had been there eighteen months earlier, unlike my colleagues, and the first impression is interesting. The 'gate guardian' at the front roundabout entrance to the factory was a licence-built Mil helicopter. Although the company built aeroplanes up to 1939, post war, and under Communist management, it had been turned into a major helicopter producer and made all of these helicopters for the Soviets and other aligned countries around the world. The factory buildings could have come from a Hollywood set for a gulag or similar.

Now, if you're my age, you will probably have heard of the Solidarity movement headed by Lech Wałęsa and others who led strikes in the Lenin shipyards in 1980. Well, what I hadn't realised was that the strikes started here. Yes, at this very factory in Swidnik, Lublin. We were walking on cherished ground indeed. By 1989 Communism had collapsed and the Solidarity Union was legalised. So it was about this time in the 1980s when the forward thinkers at PZL set about covertly designing a 'western-type' light helicopter. It was designed in secret, without the knowledge of Soviet supervision, so it could be an army trainer or observation aircraft but mainly it was designed from the outset with a view to selling it to Western Europe and on to the rest of the world.

So, on Monday morning, my little team of Brits was introduced to the PZL flight-test team: Head of Flight Test, Zbigniew, who had studied helicopter aerodynamics in Russia, and had a devilish sense of humour, their Test Pilot, Leszek (who was literally built like a 'brick shit house') and their certification point of contact, Jerzy. To say these guys were friendly would be an understatement. Whilst we met and briefed in

Soviet-era squalor, their good humour and keenness to learn from us was infectious. Perhaps it was partially my background as an instructor and tutor at ETPS but we found that our relationship with PZL was instantly proactive and 'hands-on'.

This was just as well, as this was a helicopter that had arrived 'ugly'. We joke in the flight test world that it is always our job to tell a mother their 'baby is ugly'. No mum thinks her newborn is ugly, although as a parent and grandpa I'm aware it often takes quite a while for babies to stop looking 'squished'. Manufacturers of aircraft always behave in a maternal and protective manner to their offspring; in addition to honesty and integrity, much tact and diplomacy, accompanied by robustness and a thick skin, is a requirement in flight test.

And so we embarked upon our test programme. Nigel, my boss and mentor, took one of the flights so that we could both compare notes

The flight test team – Author, Zbigniew, Ray, Nigel, Leszek and our engineer.

on some of the difficult issues, and that was a really helpful way to do this. Ultimately we had to decide what aspects of the aircraft were OK, were not OK, or were downright dangerous (=unacceptable). Where do I start to tell you about the next four days? Well perhaps I should tell you that our final night was on the Thursday with a plan, as always, to head home on Friday come 'hell or high water'. We typed up our report from midnight that evening, having been plied with more ice-cold glasses of Polish vodka than any of us could count earlier in the evening, perhaps so that it might soften our words. Or perhaps more likely that we, fellow flight-test aviators, had stared death in the face several times very recently and survived to tell the tale. And that's an excuse for a 'lorra vodka'!

The helicopter itself had little to commend it … but I note that in my formal debrief note I said it was strongly built (which it was), had a good view out (field of view) and, really clutching at straws, had comfortable seats with a good range of adjustment. It's a bit like saying you had a good car because there was ample room for the spare tyre.

First up, you had to fly it from the 'wrong seat'. In recent years (since the 60s?) helicopter pilots usually sit in the right-hand seat. This allows

Thursday night – about to start drinking Vodka.

The test aircraft's instrument panel optimised for the pilot to be on the left. Note the additional instrumentation for flight test data gathering.

them to fly with the most important control, the 'cyclic stick' in their right hand (between their knees) and the left hand can adjust power using the 'collective lever' but the left hand can also, temporarily, be moved around the cockpit to operate engine controls or switches etc. By being required to fly from the left-hand seat lots of controls that would normally be 'conventionally operated' now needed a lot of hand swapping and crossed arms. Not ideal, but not an illegal (unacceptable) proposition.

As soon as I set off to fly the aircraft all manner of problems were instantly obvious. Firstly, they had been designing this aircraft for decades and the best engine they could get their hands on at the time was a very gutless version of the Allison (now Rolls Royce) turbine as fitted to the very first version of the popular Bell 206 JetRanger helicopter, amongst others. The snag was that this engine would run hot and would be about to overheat (overtemp) well before it was delivering the amount of power the gearbox and transmission of the aircraft was designed to take. This had a hugely negative impact when trying to hover when heavy, or climb on a warm day, or go faster than about 120 mph. Still, just like it's legal to drive around in a Nissan Micra and hold everyone up behind you when going up even modest hills, so it is with under-powered helicopters. The safest aircraft are those that can't get airborne at all.

Next, it was just really difficult to fly. We flight test folks have developed a whole language and set of jargon to be able to explain this more fully. In the 'longitudinal axis' we want the aircraft to be stable, which means we want it to fly in a given attitude or at a given speed; flying this helicopter was like trying to balance a pencil on its point. It wanted to fly at any other speed apart from the chosen one (known as Negative Longitudinal Static Stability). When manoeuvring, we want an aircraft to require a larger control input to do larger manoeuvres. Thus to get close to breaking something we need a very heavy force on the controls. But not so this aircraft. As soon as you had set it off in one direction you were immediately applying the opposite control input just to stop it running away with you (Manoeuvre Unstable). Additionally the aircraft had a very small fin and didn't want to fly in a straight line (Neutral Directional Stability). The aircraft had very short rotor blades which didn't have much mass/weight. This gave us lots of problems. The rotors are designed to go around at a given speed and the pilot needs to ensure they do. This is assisted by a governor system for normal flight but this wasn't very good and the slightest change in aircraft attitude or power requirement would tend to accelerate or decelerate the rotors very quickly.

A required series of test points is to 'chop the power' from the engine to simulate engine failures. This is very high risk testing and requires very good teamwork, and planning, and briefing. The idea, as always, is to approach the final requirement in an incremental fashion. In this case I, as the handling pilot, couldn't operate the roof-mounted engine throttle while keeping my hands on the controls. So, just as per years of training at ETPS, I briefed how Leszek would assist me. The first test point was without any delay and went as follows:

Me, 'Standby for a throttle-chop on my count of three –

Place your hand on the throttle lever …

Are you ready?'

Leszek, 'Ready.'

Me, 'Standby … Three, Two, One, *Now*.'

As Leszek smoothly closed the throttle I lowered the collective lever, thus removing the pitch or angle on the blades, reducing their drag and turning them into autogyro blades so that the blades would continue to spin at the correct speed, letting me continue to fly.

We continued this technique, working through our test card. Once we had tested successfully at low speed, we increased the aircraft speed in stages, until the last batch of test points, which were undertaken as fast as the helicopter could be flown (Vne). So this also involved immediately slowing down, briskly, to the optimum gliding speed. The rotor system was connected to a very loud klaxon that 'went off' whenever the blades were spinning either too fast, or too slowly.

'So here we go Leszek – final test point – High Speed – are you ready?'
'Ready.'
'Standby … Three, Two, One, *Now.*'
BAAAAAAAAAAAAAAAAAAAAAAAAAAAAAAAARRRPP
BAAAAAAAAAAAAAAAAAAAAAAAAAAARRRPP
BAAAAAAAAAAAAAAAAAAAARRRPP
BAAAAAAAAAAAAAAARRRPP
BAAAAAAAAAAAARRRPP
BAAAAAAAARRRPP
BAAAARRRPP
'Kin Hell!'

I had, for what felt like an eternity, not been in control of my own life or the flight path of this machine. I still have it on tape, on my Dictaphone, a long series of painfully loud klaxon tones finally punctuated by a breathless expletive, followed by the calm ETPS tutor voice which returned in time to ask my Polish colleague,

'So Leszek – did you close the throttle in the same way as all the other times?'

'No – of course not – You were doing so very well I closed it really quick this time!'

So much for the tried and tested incremental approach. He had chopped the throttle so aggressively that, in the blink of an eye, the aircraft had turned sidewards (due to the lack of torque reaction) through about ninety degrees and the rotor rpm had decayed rapidly to the point where it could become unrecoverable very soon. I had to get the aircraft going straight by applying full left yaw pedal with my feet, slam the collective lever to the bottom stop to recover my rotor rpm and apply aft cyclic to flare the aircraft to assist in recovering rotor rpm and slow down! Which wasn't at all easy to do, but in fairness, 'goes with the territory'.

As I tried to slow down, the rotor rpm went up and up, and as I tried to prevent a catastrophic overspeed by then raising the collective lever the rpm plummeted down again. Each low or high speed condition was announced without constraint by the ear piercing klaxon.

'What the hell is going on? This is bloody difficult and we're all going to dieeeeeee!'

After a second or two, which felt like a lifetime, the grey putty in my skull started to sift through the different cues it was receiving. Something very 'Twilight Zone' was going on, and I suspected I was being duped by some of the visual indications. In a helicopter you can actually hear the gearbox whining behind you – like those old Morris Minors that were forced to travel up and down motorways at 70 mph with only four forward gears and a puny A series 1098cc engine.

And the audio cues of the gearbox were what had finally allowed me to bring my mount to heel. With the rotor rpm under control, the speed reduced to a sensible 80 mph or so it was time to breathe again ….

Phew! … Survived another.

Time to head home very carefully for a debrief, followed, as quickly as possible, by large amounts of alcohol. As always, my first suspect in this

Setting off in the prototype SW-4.

kind of tumble was my own gash (rubbish) flying abilities. But I'd become quite good at flying the Gazelle at ETPS which was easier to fly but had some similarities.

'So, dear Polish people, can we meet with your design team and discuss the gauge that tells the pilot how fast the rotors are turning please?'

Needless to say, Ray and I went back to our hotel somewhat perturbed by recent events and spent a good deal of time trawling through everything that we'd done and said to learn valuable lessons to apply in the future, not least rebriefing Leszek on the importance of using a consistent strategy for control operation. A night of troubled sleep followed.

First thing the following day we reconvened at PZL who had been as good as gold. The room was packed with boffins pouring over schematic diagrams of the indicating system. Always crucial to try and pick up key words in such meetings; very hard to do if you can't speak fluent technical Polish, but, thankfully, some terms were not translated, including 'computational delay'. Now I've been around this business long enough to really not like 'computational' or 'delay', but the two together – *aaaaargh!*

It's imperative for information about rotor speed to be accurate and real time, i.e. true. The pilot has to control it, by manipulating all the controls at once, and needs to know what is going on, especially on a helicopter where the rotors wanted to change their speed in a heartbeat. Turns out this gauge had a delay due to 'computational issues' of around four seconds. So this was like a 'Dr Who timey whimey thing'. What I was seeing on the gauge was already four seconds old. A bit like us seeing stars in the sky; some of those stars are now burnt out and dead but we are still seeing the light that originally emanated from them years ago. This gauge would be OK if the rotor speed wasn't varying quickly, and was probably OK therefore for normal flight where the governor was trying to control things, but when we were tumbling sidewards through the sky due to the over enthusiastic 'Polish throttle chop' then it had really not helped. Guess what? This was one item that they were going to have to change. And, amazingly, before the end of the day (try that in the rest of Europe) they'd fitted what they thought was a poorer gauge and was, for sure, less Gucci, but had next to no delay. Hurray, a good result.

Next on the 'scary meter' was to fly some 'Engine-off-landings'. Aircraft with only one engine have to be able to land safely should that engine fail in flight. When a helicopter engine fails the pilot has to remove pitch from the blades, by lowering the collective lever, which turns the helicopter into an autogyro. This state of flight is called 'auto-rotation' because the rotor blades turn round all by themselves, assuming that is there is enough airflow to spin them like a windmill on its side. Aeroplanes have it easier. If the engine stops they convert into gliders, and as long as the pilot pushes the nose down a small amount the airspeed will be retained and all will be well.

In a helicopter entering an auto-rotative state is slightly more challenging. As soon as the engine stops lots of things happen all at once, as you will have read above. The pilot has to get the collective to its bottom stop rapidly and then use it and the other controls to control the rotor rpm – normally within a narrow or small range of speeds. Too fast, and the centrifugal/centripetal forces may rip the blades off = very bad. Too slow and the increasing drag on the blades will get to a point where the airflow is insufficient to turn them and they stop = also very bad.

So the designer works out an acceptable range which the test pilot then goes out to confirm. Yep, another high risk aspect of helicopter testing.

This helicopter could just (and only just) meet a required one-second delay from engine failure to the pilot reacting without the blades slowing down too much and stopping.

When it comes to landing a gliding helicopter, quite a degree of skill, training and practice are required, even if everything is working in your favour. It transpired that this was not to be easy in Swidnik.

Firstly it was June, and it was warm, and there was no wind. Ideal for flight-test purposes but not so good for learning and practising the required technique. And PZL had come up with a rather extreme technique for landing the SW-4 which was 'all or nothing'. So off I went, with my new best mate Leszek (isn't it amazing how surviving near-death experiences with someone makes you mates?).

I did what I have often done in such situations. I'm flying with a guy who has flown hundreds of engine-off-landings in this helicopter. So I invited him to show me one using the company technique, which he proceeded to do …

Now that was scary!

'So that was an engine-off?' I thought. 'I can't do this.'

Although I did a quick practice in a similar helicopter, courtesy of a mate who was working as an instructor (QHI) for the military at RAF

Shawbury a few days earlier, I was still feeling rusty and this looked very difficult. So while I'm thinking about it I get him to show me two more. Not that it showed me anything new; it was just allowing me to build up my 'bottle'. And I confess I was very anxious. Screwing up on my first RW job for the CAA and under contract to EASA was unthinkable. The shame would haunt me forever. But after three such demonstrated landings I had only two choices: crack on with the plan or head back to the hotel for a stiff vodka. The latter was the more tempting option, but my sense of duty or 'can-do' got the better of me and I heard myself saying –

'I have control.'

I have to say that a few years earlier I might have found the testing I was about to commence far too daunting. Even though I'd been flying engine-off landings in Gazelle and Wasp helicopters for years, the step-change for me was when I managed to crash a Scout helicopter doing an engine-off landing during my first year at ETPS. If I write a book about my time at Boscombe it will no doubt feature. When I say crash, it was more of a heavy landing with the aircraft subsequently being repaired and still flying for many years in civilian hands. However, I didn't sleep afterwards for many days and it was one of the most traumatic events in my aviation career to date. The morning after the accident I was called into the Chief Test Pilot's office – like being summoned to see the headmaster.

My interview with the RAF group captain was scheduled to last an hour, but on entering his office I said:

'I'm terribly sorry sir, but I messed up! Error of judgement – no-one else to blame – all my fault.'

It turns out this was more of a Fleet Air Arm pilot type of comment than RAF and I'd been expected to 'do a Donald Trump' and deny everything. So my planned one-hour interrogation was replaced by a five-minute confession and I was allowed to get on. I was also lucky in that my immediate boss was also Fleet Air Arm and rather than 'bollock me rigid' threw me into a waiting Gazelle helicopter and took me back to Netheravon where the accident had happened. He then proceeded to give me more 'throttle chops' than I'd had pink gins. By the end of an hour I knew I could survive pretty much any helicopter engine failure that came my way (thanks, Chris).

That experience, followed by teaching a whole bunch of student test pilots from all over the world how to do them, meant I'd become relatively competent.

Thank Goodness – as right now I really needed to be good at them.

I staggered into an untidy hover (which was the best anyone could manage). Then I proceeded to transition into forward flight climbing to 1,000 feet over the airfield and lining myself up with the grass runway we had been using so far. With the engine throttle being in the roof, once it was closed there was no Plan B, I became a glider and down we went.

Firstly, this aircraft went down very fast indeed. It had all the gliding characteristics of a brick with some lead weights added for good measure, so the instant the throttle was closed the ground seemed to rush up at me.

Secondly, because, as mentioned earlier, the aircraft didn't want to fly at a chosen speed, then this crucial aspect was very difficult to do. And the company technique offered no flex (flexibility). It had to be flown at 110 km/h, or 60 KIAS (70 mph), exactly (a 4 KIAS error was the maximum allowed) so with frequent high gain inputs into the cyclic stick that's what I flew at.

Then the rotor rpm had to be controlled to exactly 105 per cent. A 3 per cent rise would damage the rotors and gearbox. A 3 per cent decrease would result in a heavy landing or, as most readers of this book would call it, a crash. So not only were my inputs to the cyclic 'high gain' but so were my inputs to the collective. I couldn't afford not to nail the optimum rotor rpm for my first attempt.

Then – yes, it gets better – no judgement by the pilot was allowed as to what to do next. Instead a radio altimeter (Rad-Alt) fitted to the aircraft aimed to measure the aircraft's height above ground. When the number on this gauge got to 65 feet above the ground the next thing happened …

Now bear in mind this wind-milling brick was descending at around 2,000 feet per minute. If your maths is any good you can work out how long it will now take me to travel 65 feet if I don't do anything … Well let me put you out of your misery … It's less than two seconds.

So at 65 feet it was essential that I, without delay or procrastination, hoiked the cyclic stick back aggressively and pitched the helicopter to point skywards. In fact the runway had to be viewed through the piece of Perspex next to my feet.

But wait, it's not over yet. Hitting the ground with the back end of the helicopter really is fatal, as it would smash the tail rotor and we'd become a tumbling car wreck like in an old Hitchcock movie.

Having flared the aircraft, and controlled the rotor speed to exactly 105 (no mean feat), I then had to aggressively push forward the cyclic to try and level the helicopter. Meanwhile the helicopter had to be prevented from hitting the ground too hard which might tear the skids off. To do this required me to raise the collective lever at exactly the right moment. The collective was the lever that had to be lowered when the engine stopped (with me so far?). Well now it had to be pulled up, which put the pitch back on the blades which, just for a moment, created lift, but also drag. The lift was good as it briefly allowed the descent of the helicopter to be arrested. The drag was bad, as it caused the blades to stop rotating rather quickly. An ideal helicopter for this kind of thing has big rotors that are very heavy and can store lots of kinetic energy/momentum. (The American Vietnam era Huey is perhaps one of the better examples of this. Even with the engine switched off in a Huey you can actually come into the hover – pause – do a spot turn and then land, all with the stored energy in the blades. Well, if the Huey is at one end of the scale, the SW-4 is at the other.) There was no spare energy in the rotors on this aircraft and in fact, the company technique required me, immediately on levelling, to pull the lever up to the top stop and then accept whatever happened next. Its redeeming feature was, being built like the 'proverbial', the skids were able to absorb some pretty hideous punishment; thank goodness.

'Bang! Rattle, rattle!' I had landed.

Not content with surviving my first attempt, I then went through my test card looking at the challenges faced by being at the wrong speed (bad), having the wrong rotor rpm (bad), commencing the flare too low (very bad), commencing the flare too high (bad).

After more of these landings than I could count and with my fillings now loose in my teeth we taxied back to the safety of the flat piece of tarmac loosely described as 'the dispersal'.

Phew! … survived another.

Surely this sortie was the highest risk of them all?

There was one final aspect to assess, which we expected to be challenging. Very small helicopters like the Robinson R22 can be flown, like an autogyro, with the pilot being able to move the flying controls unaided. The rotors act like a massive gyro and don't like to change their axis of rotation; that, and the aerodynamic feedback, creates large forces. So most helicopters are supplied with a system a bit like a car's servo brakes or power steering. A pump pushes hydraulic fluid around a maze of pipes such that when the pilot moves a control the input is 'boosted' by this hydraulic fluid under pressure. If you want a laugh, and you have a heavy car with power steering and servo brakes, try rolling it down a hill with the engine stopped and the gears in neutral. It can be quite a shock to find steering is difficult and stopping near impossible.

Now, very big helicopters cannot be flown at all without hydraulic boost and, therefore, will have two independent systems in case one springs a leak. Small helicopters are hoping to avoid the extra weight and cost and complexity required by dual systems. So they fit just one, known as a simplex system.

So what happens when it fails I hear you ask, if you haven't lost interest in all things technical at this point?

Well, the deal is that the helicopter has to be capable of being flown without hydraulics if you only fit one system. My new best mate, Leszek (we had now survived even more numerous near-death experiences and were drinking and singing buddies now), remember, he's the guy built like the 'brick shithouse'? Well he had flown about 200 hours of the helicopter flight test programme before they'd even designed the hydraulic system. So it must be easy right? Or at least do-able?

So off we went to test this feature, in an incremental fashion. This commenced with flying at the optimum speed to reduce all the aforementioned forces, about 60 KIAS (70 mph). Then, as I braced myself, Leszek selected the system off.

'Blige!'

I was running out of expletives.

The helicopter, which was already difficult to fly, now became incredibly difficult to fly, even at the easiest speed of 60–62 KIAS. The control forces were very heavy indeed. As I rolled the aircraft to commence a gentle turn, I realised that I could no longer roll the aircraft back to level flight without using both my hands on the stick. At higher airspeed the forces ramped up and, more worryingly, as I slowed towards a hover, they ramped up even further. Back I flew to the airfield only a few minutes away and attempted to land. It is fair to say that helicopter pilots tend to get used to the very light forces of a boosted system, and I certainly was not the sort of chap to go and lift weights or do pull ups in the gym, and landing this helicopter without hydraulics on a 30-degrees C day at Swidnik was right on the limit of what I could do.

In order to give the aircraft another chance, I then went off to investigate the accumulator. So, bearing in mind that when the system failed the aircraft might be flying very fast or very slowly, both of which would make getting to the magic 60 KIAS very difficult, the designer decided to put a 'helpful' device in the system. Imagine a big spring that continues to push the hydraulic fluid for a while after the pump fails. This device is designed to keep pressure to the flying controls for a period after a warning light illuminates. This allows the pilot to rapidly land or at least adjust his speed, attitude etc.

So for this test, rather than deliberately selecting the system off when I was fully prepared, I flew along at the cruise speed and pulled a circuit breaker which failed the pump and waited to see what happened – well, initially, nothing, which was good. Maybe this system was so well designed I could conduct an emergency landing without breaking my wrists? So I started my gentle descent when … *whap*.

The cyclic was almost wrenched from my grip and my shoulder immediately felt like somebody had shot me and we were now rolling past 30 degrees of bank. I already knew that the forces required to roll level would soon be too much – both hands on the stick, and a surprising amount of adrenalin coursing through my system, saved the day and we made yet another untidy running landing on the same grass runway. By the time we'd climbed out I realised I was going to need a good deal of anti-inflammatories for my shoulder but first I needed to kiss the ground.

But that was the last landing of this first week's assessment.

Phew! … survived another.

Off to some Lublin restaurant for lots of vodka and even more toasts as we bonded further with the team responsible for the helicopter that had tried so hard to kill me over a four-day period.

Our debrief writing commenced at midnight and after eight hours of tortured typing we found ourselves in front of the PZL management team.

'I'm sorry – but your baby is ugly', I opened.

Using a hand held force gauge to measure stick forces with Ray taking notes.

Well, actually I didn't, but the faces staring back at me heard exactly that. Now, other companies might well have reacted differently. Perhaps it was the bonding over pizzas covered in tinned peas, ice-cold vodka and some dubious Polish folk songs that helped? Or more likely it was our natural keenness to assist this embryonic company 'get it right'. We talked for ages, giving out all our best 'top tips' for redesign and improvements, and finished by inviting ourselves back for a return visit as soon as they'd made some changes. And, in fairness, we'd become quite fond of Lublin, apart from the Majdanek concentration camp which was a harrowing place to visit. Lublin itself, in the summer, was almost Parisian, with lots of university students and open air cafés on the streets etc.

Coming back again would be a treat if only we could make the drive up the M3 and from Warsaw to Lublin as safe as flying the SW-4.

Chapter 5

Jets

'Drat!'

Undercarriage that wouldn't go up had now decided not to come down and I had run out of airfield opening time and I was running out of ideas.

Having just read all about helicopters in a previous chapter, then your head may well be exploding with technical jargon or your eyelids may have shut already? There's no doubt that helicopters are complicated and that's good news for we test pilots. The next Boeing or Airbus off the drawing board will almost certainly fly exactly as predicted. Regulators are now letting manufacturers do some of their certification testing in the simulator. They are so confident that there will be few surprises. But not so helicopters, which never fly quite as hoped and usually go through all manner of modifications to make them fly in an acceptable fashion.

Now, I think getting your heads around jets is relatively easy. They are aeroplanes, so conventional wings, fuselage, tail plane etc. And they don't even have to worry about propellers, thus no prop wash which creates a lot of asymmetric effects. No, you just stick a jet turbine in the middle of the fuselage, chuck in some jet fuel and air and next thing you know the generated thrust is accelerating you along the runway to flying speed and the 'wide blue yonder'. And that's the other nice thing about jets. They can fly high enough to get above the worst of the weather, cloud, rain etc. And they often have the help of someone on the ground chatting to them on the radio to help them find their way around. So, all in all, a much more pleasant way to aviate rather than grubbing around close to the ground in a helicopter.

Now, I must confess, 'hand on heart', that although I set off to 'sign up' with the sole intention of flying the Wasp helicopter off small ships, I was contemplating this career just as the Sea Harrier was coming into service. My first real look at the Fleet Air Arm had included an auspicious visit to RNAS Culdrose which had included the most exciting displays from the soon-to-be-retired Phantoms and Buccaneer jets from HMS *Ark Royal*. At the Birmingham Royal Navy recruiting office my head had been turned by the particularly good looking and flirtatious second officer WRNS. When dithering over which form to sign and how long to commit myself for, she had fluttered her eye lashes and seductively commented that surely only 'career officers' who commit to serve for at least sixteen years would be allowed to fly the Sea Harrier. And with that, and the desperate need to fund myself through my remaining years at university, I signed up to apply for a university cadetship; which meant learning how to be a ship's navigating/operations officer initially. By the time I commenced flying training, ironically at the start of the Falklands conflict, the Sea Harrier FRS 1 was proving to be a commendable and capable fighter and ground attack aircraft in the hands of Sharkey Ward, Tim Gedge and others. (Read Sharkey's book, 'Sea Harrier over the Falklands', but don't bother with his second book ...)

So it was, halfway through learning to fly the Scottish Aviation Bulldog up in Yorkshire, that I asked Bill, my instructor, if he thought I'd make a good Sea Harrier pilot. Instead of looking up or commenting, he started feverishly scribbling with his chinagraph pencil on his white plastic kneeboard. I had hoped he was making a note of my request for fast jet evaluation ...

Instead I glanced down to notice he had scribbled:

Ha Ha Ha Ha

Ha Ha Ha Ha

Ha Ha Ha Ha

A bit cruel, I thought, as I pulled up gracefully into my not-quite-symmetrical loop. Bill, sadly, was killed years later, teaching someone to fly a Jetstream at Prestwick when the student kicked in the wrong rudder pedal following a simulated engine failure, and rolled them both into the ground.

In fact there were no requirements for any trainee Harrier pilots at the time I went through my course. There had been an initial cadre of ex-Phantom and Buccaneer crew and, along with some RAF exchange pilots, there were no vacancies then for the likes of me. I did consider applying later but by then I was married with children on the way and the concept of months away at a time on a CVS (Through Deck Cruiser) had less appeal than if I'd been single.

Bulldog G-BZDP tested at RAF Colerne in 2004.

A couple of years later, after I'd done everything I could with a Lynx helicopter without getting arrested, I again got itchy feet and applied to, and was accepted by, the RAF as an aspiring jet pilot. They were short of experienced instructors and by then I had considerable instructional experience. So I was off to fly the Jet Provost, then the Tucano which I would fly for a year or two before moving on to the Hawk as an instructor. The intent then would be to convert to an operational type etc. I came within two weeks of swapping my dark-blue uniform for a light-blue one and setting off to Cranwell to learn how to march and salute in a funny fashion, but it was not to be. My wife was very seriously ill at the time and we had two small children to look after. I asked my wife's consultant whether I could sensibly join the RAF which meant moving around the UK quite a lot for the next few years …

I got the medic's equivalent of:

Ha Ha Ha Ha
Ha Ha Ha Ha
Ha Ha Ha Ha

Probably daft to ask really. (Many years later I joined the RAF Reserve in order to fly air cadets around and despite lots of hair-raising times as a fishhead it was the RAF that gave me my only medal.)

Instead of joining the RAF, I requested the RN give me the ideal job to be able to cope with my unfortunate domestic circumstances; that was running the Lynx Simulator complex (three different training devices for

Flying a Grob Tutor as an RAF Reserve pilot.

the various marks of RN Lynx). As the boss, I could manage my diary to suit my domestic crisis, keep flying lots of instructional sorties and, from this book's point of view, I had the chance to study for the very onerous selection for ETPS. Just a single place on the course for the RN, but lots of candidates; you get the gist.

Anyway, moving on to the real content of this chapter, at ETPS we got to fly jets. Not as many as I had hoped, but I flew the Tucano and Hawk and the BAC 1-11 airliner. And I loved it. (Thank you, Gordon and Dave.) Even better, I had chosen to apply for the RN TP job on Experimental Flying Squadron. This was the squadron that flew very quirky, often highly modified, aircraft belonging to the Defence Research Agency (DRA), based initially at RAE Bedford and Farnborough, but by the time I started the aircraft were based at Boscombe Down. Now this squadron was just a complete blast for someone like me. We had Hunters, Jaguars, Canberras, BAC1-11, Andovers and HS748 and Wessex, Lynx and Sea King Helicopters and the best part was – only a handful of TPs. So, we all had to fly everything. In fairness, in the aeroplanes I would be the co-pilot. In the helicopters I would sign for everything, whilst my fast-jet mates, like Trevor or Tim, would have to make like rotary-wing pilots whilst I would supervise and gather the required data. So now I got to fly the Hunter and Jaguar and big airliners. Additionally, I had a former helicopter mate, Roger; I don't know how he wangled it, but he had ended up on RN Fixed Wing Standards at RNAS Yeovilton. He basically had two personal Hawk trainers and would often take part in exercises where we would beat up warships off Portland or Plymouth. Since I was 'current fast jet' and had all the right gear, I was able to call him up whenever I had a spare day and invite myself along for some ship bashing. Now that really was a lot of fun; skimming the waves flat out in the hope that we could 'attack' the fleet before being detected. Later on, when I returned to ETPS as a tutor, I begged sorties from the other tutors to see what other jets were like. So, I was able to fly the Alpha Jet and the Harrier, and Jaguar, Tucano and Hawk some more and was formally qualified on the BAC1-11 to be a 'First Officer' or co-pilot, mainly as we used this aircraft to fly ourselves around the world for various technical visits etc. and when we helicopter guys travelled it meant we only needed one of the proper BAC 1-11 pilots to join us.

I joined the CAA as the 'Light Aircraft Test Pilot'. Whilst this included microlight aeroplanes it also included looking after all the historic aeroplanes as well. So I was responsible for all the Spitfires and Mustangs etc. and all the ex-military jets which included Vampires, various marks of Jet Provost (JP), Strikemasters, Hunters, and Gnats amongst others. I had to oversee the 'flight testing' or 'check flying' of these aircraft for annual airworthiness tests and for a few other specific topics. Since I was a self-confessed amateur when it came to flying these aircraft I'd always try and find a 'grown-up' to fly with me, often a highly experienced pilot who was looking to check fly such aircraft on our behalf. The vetting, approval and training process would involve me flying a genuine check flight and discussing all the required techniques and safety considerations etc. Generally, this meant the guy in the 'other seat' had more fast jet time than I'd ever have. A bit like with gyros, the pool of such people was relatively small; generally ex RAF/RN blokes who had flown similar types within the military during their younger years.

Jet Provost Mk4 G-PROV at North Weald prior to flight test.

Brian was the 'go to guy' for all things Jet Provost or Strikemaster. Like me, he was a 'rote' (rotary-wing pilot) but I think had spent some time as an instructor on the JP. He certainly converted a good number of private owners on to their aircraft. 'Back in the day' you could buy an ex-military jet like this for less money than it cost to fly it for a year. Every time we flew together we would find ourselves gliding jets with dead engines while inverted. I know; what a claim to fame. I can't quite remember what specific part of the schedule required this, but we had to fly inverted and check engine oil pressure, fuel pressure etc. Sometimes the engine stopped or had to be shut down. We also did 'slam checks' which basically means, at high altitude where the air is thin, you slam the throttle from idle to full power as quickly as you can (give or take a second or two or three). Quite often these old engines would not like that at all and complain. We would know they were complaining because they would make a lot of noise (surging) and develop no power. (Just like the grumpy coal trucks that Thomas the Tank Engine had to haul from time to time.) A surging engine had to be shut down. This seemed to happen every time I flew with Brian and we became adept at me pointing the aircraft towards a suitable piece of tarmac whilst he tried to relight the engine, and I have to say it was a successful team as we flew them all back to where we'd parked our cars.

Needless to say, none of these JPs/Strikemasters would have their permits to fly renewed until the various identified defects had been fixed.

Strikemaster at North Weald prior to flight test.

I'd flown the Hunter T.7 at Boscombe so was not too fazed when invited along to Exeter to fly a T.8B version; in fact, I was rather looking forward to being in a type I'd flown previously. There is not much to beat opening the throttle and powering up a Rolls Royce Avon to max chat at a runway threshold. The biggest challenge with this particular Hunter was seeing out. The already relatively small windscreen had suffered over the years from trapped moisture and general wear and tear. A new windscreen would need to be fitted to allow future flights to be conducted safely. Thankfully, lots of flying of Tiger Moths and Stearmans had allowed me to pick up peripheral cues instinctively. Once airborne and high enough to not worry about bumping into anyone else the trip was completed without event. It was an interesting version as it had been used to train Buccaneer pilots for which there were no two-seat trainers, so the instrument panel was laid out like that of the Buccaneer, and what a whacky panel that was. It had a strip indicator for airspeed, for example, well before the big aeroplane manufacturers of today adopted similar ideas.

My trip in a Gnat came at the end of a lot of pestering by the UK civvie Gnat community. It transpires that when the Red Arrows flew them, they had a special dispensation from the RAF to disable an electrical circuit that restricted the rate of roll. So, if it's good enough for the Red Arrows it must be good enough for all the relatively well-heeled private owners of such aircraft, who mostly had a good deal less relevant flying

Hunter T.8 at Exeter prior to flight test.

experience. (Apparently the Red Arrows' jets rolled at 420 degrees per second rather than 210 degrees when limited.) So I needed to investigate and work out whether this request was sensible or reasonable. I flew the air test out of Bournemouth with a different Brian. At the time this Brian, who had been chief pilot for the Royal Navy's 'Fleet Requirements & Air Direction Unit', based at RNAS Yeoviliton, had amassed over 8,000 flying hours on Hunters alone making him then (and probably still) the world's most experienced Hunter pilot. I had flown with him previously and had huge confidence in his ability and relevant experience. So, I was surprised that, during briefing and the subsequent taxi out to the long runway at Bournemouth, he was very concerned about the amount of wind blowing across, rather than along, the runway, and so was I. Even as I taxied at pedestrian pace one of the aircraft's wings kept wanting to lift despite all my efforts to counter it. At the threshold we were within one knot of the crosswind limit for the aircraft and set off down the runway with the joystick applied fully against the stop, with one wing high for a while before flying speed was gained and at last the ailerons became effective and hauled the high wing level again.

Once airborne I was expecting my life to get easier – it didn't. I couldn't keep the wings level. We were 'rocking and rolling' as we barrelled along at increasing airspeed and it took what seemed like an eternity for me to recalibrate my eyes, to brain, to hand, to joystick, to ailerons (which were the moving control surfaces on each wing which allow the aircraft to be rolled). This was an aircraft that really, really loved to roll very fast indeed. The amount of lateral joystick input required to initiate a turn was a gnat's whisker (see what I did there?). Anyway, we hurtled around the sky and safely completed the check flight and set up for the return to Bournemouth. Could I land in this limiting crosswind? The fuselage on the Gnat is so small there is hardly any room to stow the undercarriage wheels when they are retracted. So, they had to make the wheels very slim and fit them with skinny bicycle tyres (well almost). So, the tyres are very prone to damage, especially when landing in a crosswind. During training operations, they quite often would have to change the wheels over during the lunch break before the aircraft was used for further training in the afternoon. Now that must have been a real Achilles heel for a trainer. Anyway, no margin for cock-up as I slowed to 180 KIAS (Knots Indicated Airspeed) to set up for the approach.

In a crosswind, lining up in good time, I have found, is essential for me to work out how to compensate for the drift by cross controlling and applying sufficient aileron to fly along the extended centre line of the runway. Bleeding the speed back progressively I monitored the amount of applied aileron to ensure I didn't run out and crossing the 'piano keys' at

Folland Gnat being pulled out of the hangar at Bournemouth prior to flight test.

140 KIAS I smoothly closed the throttle, applying gentle back pressure on the stick to adopt a marginally nose-high attitude which allowed the aircraft to very gently descend until the right-hand tyre made contact with the tarmac.

Squeeeeeeeeck.

Tyre and wheel now spinning I eased the left wheel and nose wheel onto the ground simultaneously, braking gently to wash off my excess speed before running out of runway.

Phew! … survived another; and frankly no need to increase the roll rate for civilian registered aircraft. It was rolling fast enough to make your eyes pop out of their sockets as it was.

Working at the CAA there was never a dull moment and always lots of issues to resolve, like, for example, the use of ejection seats. Many of you will already be aware that these fast jet aircraft tend to be fitted with an escape system generically referred to as an 'ejection seat' or 'bang-seat'. If the pilot has a problem and needs to abandon the aircraft he only has to pull on a conveniently located black and yellow handle to find himself propelled upwards out of the aircraft on rockets. Within seconds the ejectee will be floating down to earth on a parachute in order to live to tell the tale. The Martin Baker company make the majority of such seats which have been getting more capable with each successive jet they are fitted to. Pilots who have used their seats are entitled to a free tie and usually a few beers whenever the company has a marketing presence at trade fairs. I'm very glad to say that, as yet, I don't have such a tie but I do have a Goldfish Club one – awarded for surviving a ditching in my Wasp helicopter.

Anyway, these seats are life savers, and fitted to these high-performance aircraft for good reason but they are expensive to maintain and need cartridges to fire them which are only given a short life and are difficult to obtain in sensible quantities. So many years ago, the civvie Jet Provost/Strikemaster lobby had made a case to the CAA in order for them to be able to fly with the ejection seats made inert – i.e. not work. The argument was that the JP was a relatively benign, easy to fly aircraft, and could easily be glided into a field or similar in the event of an engine failure, just like the thousands of single piston-engine aircraft out there. My predecessor had agreed that if an aircraft could make a forced landing approach, without a working engine, at 100 KIAS/120 mph or less, then there would be no need for us to insist on the operator or owner retaining live ejection seats. Now in fairness, that's still bloody fast. Imagine hitting a brick wall in your Nissan Micra at 120 mph. I used to fly air ambulance helicopters and went to many a road traffic accident. Nissan Micra versus brick wall was a 'no contest' event. However, this magic number of 100 was now the precedent. So, as with any such precedent, someone else comes along and wants to do something similar, and so it was I found myself testing a couple of de Havilland Vampires; a T.11 then a similar Mk 55. First up was the T.11 at North Weald, where I had tended to fly the JPs and Strikemasters from. I flew with the aircraft owner, Mark, who had relatively little time on the aircraft but was happy to help me start it up. Often, it's the starting that thwarts the TP. Off we went on a relatively uneventful flight, which was good because I was doing a serious investigation of all aspects of the aircraft's handling qualities, particularly slow speed flight. Now there were a couple of things noteworthy about this type. Firstly, it was mostly made of wood. Wood? Yep. In the Second World War we had some aircraft built almost entirely of wood with the Mosquito being perhaps the most successful and well-known example; this allowed furniture makers to turn their hands to making high performance aircraft. The Vampire (first flown in 1943 as the Spider Crab) entered operational service not that long after the end of the war and at that time using wood on a fast jet aircraft didn't seem barking mad. In fact, these aircraft were flown for some years without ejection seats at all. But the crumple zone in front of the pilot was a few planks of balsa and an instrument panel with a bit of aluminium sheeting thrown in for good measure. How fast would you like to be going when you hit the brick wall?

The second quirk involved the airspeed indicating system. In your car your speedo is effectively driven directly from the road wheels (used to be by a Teleflex cable directly into the back of the instrument – dodgy second-hand car salesmen would disconnect the cable and wind your mileage down using an electric drill. I always am wary of apparently low mileage cars that have had to have their mats or carpets renewed).

Well, in an aircraft that system clearly wouldn't work so, in simple terms, the speed of the passing air has to be measured. On the Tiger Moth this used to be done by a bendy piece of metal that would be pushed further over as you went faster and then like on a sundial it would point at

Vampire T.11 at North Weald prior to flight test.

numbers telling the pilot how fast he was going. Later on, things became more sophisticated and it was realised that if you put a tube in the airflow, as the wind whistled down the tube, due to some law or other, the pressure in the tube would rise. If we compared this with the pressure of air that wasn't being forced down this tube we could work out the difference and use this to tell us our airspeed. Clever, eh?

So almost all aeroplanes have one or more of these tubes, called pitot tubes, named after Henri Pitot, the French physicist who worked all this out. They are mounted where they get clean air undisturbed by the mass of aircraft bashing its way through the sky. So, inevitably, they are mounted on the nose of the aircraft or under a wing clear of the fuselage. So where do you think the pitot tube is mounted on a Vampire?

No, sorry, not there … no, not there either … no, sorry, wrong again …

It is mounted at the rear of the aircraft on top of the left hand fin. Yes, I know. And look at the enclosed photo of the Mk 11 I flew. The fins are really, really small.

OK, so what do you think happens when you fly slowly? Well first you end up with the nose pointing higher and higher to try and get more lift from the wings and, if you've already read about my stalling escapades you know this will happen soon. But with the Vampire, before you stalled you suddenly lost all indicated airspeed as the tiny pitot tube on the tiny fin was suddenly deprived of the vital airstream it needed to be in. So, this was news to me and the owner who it appeared had never flown quite so slowly before – that he'd noticed anyway. But I was well prepared with my monochrome Garmin GPS Pilot III device which read out my groundspeed, which with some deft in-air calculations I was able to use to accurately determine our actual stall speed and the like.

But let's not finish up just yet. If this was going to be safe to fly without live seats, I had to have a safe method of gliding this aircraft to a safe landing using the fitted airspeed indicator – and I had to be able to land slower than 100 KIAS and guess when the airspeed indicator stopped working – you are way ahead of me … 100 KIAS it was, almost exactly. However, after a few extra minutes flying I'd come up with a forced landing profile with different speeds for each part of the 'pattern', such that the pilot could come over the 'hedge' decelerating to the point where airspeed gave way to 'visually assessed groundspeed' – and Bob's your uncle – a consistently safe landing could be made. Having practised this 'well high'. I now needed to ensure it could be practised to a runway, so back to an airfield for some glide circuits. Now, another Achilles heel; this aircraft was fitted with a very elderly and simple jet engine called a Goblin. It was designed in 1941, following on directly from the jet engine designed by Frank Whittle, so this was a very early generation, unsophisticated, jet engine. Not only that, but the one in the jet I was flying was probably not much younger than the aircraft which was built in 1954. Let me confidently inform you – jet engines do not, like fine wine, improve with age. They are far more likely to become the vinegar equivalent. Old jet engines take a long time to go from idle power and end up at full power. (If you have hung on so far with this chapter you will have read how testing this feature in JPs and Strikemasters would often lead to the engine needing to be shut down.) The conventional 'work-around' for this characteristic is to fly the latter stages of the approach with the engine already providing a moderately high power. The engine is able to 'spool up' from a high power setting to full power relatively quickly. So, the 'normal' approach for such aircraft is to fly a long shallow approach using a lot of drag from deployed flaps and undercarriage. For me to fly simulated glide approaches I had to have the engine set to idle in the full knowledge that it would not be able to provide me full power quickly if I needed it.

So, guess what? Instead of rushing back to the relatively small North Weald airfield with short runways I called up Cambridge which has a very long runway and would hopefully be more forgiving. Good decision, as my historic jet was able to float majestically just above the tarmac as I was able to coach the Goblin slowly back to life each time.

Phew! … survived another.

Back home for tea and medals and with some caveats about forced landings and keeping in practice etc. I was able to recommend that this aircraft could be safely flown without live seats.

Ten months later I was driving home from Hereford, where I'd been testing some helicopters used by the SAS. I was passing Gloucester when my mobile rang and I took a hands free call from a nice lady at the CAA called Jane:

'Are you by any chance somewhere near Gloucester right now?'

'How do you know?'

'Well – I saw you were due to leave Hereford at lunch time and must be heading home etc.'

'OK, so?'

'Well, since you will be passing close to Kemble, would you mind dropping in to test fly another Vampire? It's a Mk 55 rather than a T.11 and we need to confirm the aircraft can fly at the same speeds.'

Now, one of the many problems in my rather eclectic flight test 'job' is that I bounce around all manner of aircraft types and communities and I need to be able to insert the right SD card into my ageing brain beforehand in order to get my sh*t together. I often used to refer to it as 'heading to the Batcave'! Batman on his way to different missions would always go via the Batcave to pick up the kit he needed, just as Thunderbird 2 always had to insert the pod with the correct gear prior to leaving Tracy Island. I was still in helicopter mode and, of more immediate importance, all my flying kit and equipment in the boot of my car was 'helicopter stuff' not 'fast-jet stuff.' However, I did tend to travel with most of what I needed, to do most things, most of the time. Twenty minutes later I found myself pulling off the main road to wind my way across to Kemble airfield, formally RAF Kemble and home of the Red Arrows, now known as Cotswold Airport.

There I met up with Jon, whom I had flown with before. He had not had any military flying experience but had found himself flying a number of old aircraft owned by Aviation Heritage Ltd (Air Atlantique). A number of challenges lay ahead. The airfield shut at 6 pm and it was now 4 pm. We had to spend a fair amount of time sorting out what flying kit we possessed between us, which we did by tipping everything onto the office floor and then picking up what we each needed. As we did, we formed a 'cunning plan', aware that we also needed to blow the cobwebs off the aircraft which hadn't flown for some months. Anyway, with a good amount of 'can-do' and pooling our flying kit we got enough stuff to go flying, albeit without oxygen masks which prevented us flying too high. As the clock struck five, we walked to the jet, but aircraft just know when you're running late. We had quite a faff starting the Goblin. Once that fired up there were no complicated systems to delay us and we roared off down the long westerly runway at Kemble – safely airborne – wheels selected up – wait for the green lights (that indicate they are safely down) to turn to red as they start to move – then wait for the lights to go out as the wheels lock home in the nose and wings – or in this case ... not.

Blast! How annoying and worrying. We couldn't complete the testing if the wheels weren't fully up. So I tried again and this time the lights went out. Phew! Full power, heading north-west we rattled up to 10,000 feet in next to no time. Now into the brief test plan but my rushed preparation, through no fault of my own, reared its ugly head again. My trusty GPS gizmo was essential for recording stall speeds etc., given the problems with this aircraft's pitot tube. Just when we needed the gizmo its batteries went:

Ha Ha Ha Ha
Ha Ha Ha Ha
Ha Ha Ha Ha

And promptly died on me ...

Not as prepared as usual but still quite well prepared I immediately fished out a new set of batteries from my flying suit pocket and handed the whole lot to Jon as I continued to gather data.

'Oh bugger!'

Not me this time ... Jon.

'What's happened?' He couldn't answer. My previous words had been, 'careful you don't drop the batteries ...'

And now two of them were rolling around the cockpit floor. Who knows where these loose items were going to end up ... would they drop below the floor and jam the flying controls?

'Oh, Pooh!'

One of the major pains of these jets are the seats themselves. Normally you have to strap into a parachute harness and then the very tight harness of the seat itself and you become a stuffed turkey, unable to move hardly at all. So, retrieving two runaway AA batteries content to be liberated from their packaging was a challenge. If I'd been a proper fast-jet pilot, a god of the sky, I would now tell you that I promptly rolled the aircraft inverted, let the batteries fall upwards to the canopy roof where Jon could reach them easily without unstrapping. But I'm not a SkyGod and I'd had numerous bad experiences previously on such aircraft of engines stopping when inverted so instead I slowed down and steadied the aircraft, wings level, to prevent the batteries rolling away from where they'd been dropped. Jon quickly loosened his harness and ...

Phew! ... batteries retrieved and fitted. Test data successfully gathered. Now 5.54 pm.

I pushed the stick forward and left, rolling into a descending wingover with full power applied, accelerating to 'max chat' to join the Kemble circuit in a truly professional and spirited fast-jet fashion. As I pulled around the first bend, with power now at idle, I deftly slowed to the undercarriage limit speed, paused for good measure, then selected the gear DOWN. I waited ever so patiently for the three green lights I'd seen earlier which would indicate I had wheels to land on as I turned onto my final approach at 5.59 pm ...

'Drat!'

Despite a couple of attempts, undercarriage that initially wouldn't go UP had now decided not to come DOWN, and we had run out of airfield opening time ....

Kemble tower told me that they had a Chipmunk aeroplane joining to land just behind me, I think in the hope I'd get out of the way. But, instead, I promptly conducted an immaculate pair of air-display wingovers to position behind the joining Chipmunk, a type I had flown extensively. Rudely using the tower radio frequency as our private chat line, I promptly initiated the 'Chipmunk and Vampire Air Display Duo' and with him flying as quickly as possible and me flying as slowly as I could, we transited the length of the runway in, if I say it myself, a very neat formation with the very friendly Chipmunk pilot passing commentary on the position of my wheels. With my new best mate having passed an optimistic report I bade him farewell and let him land ahead of me and get well away from the runway.

Here I was again, about to determine whether the wheels that appeared down really were. I'd been there before and I've been there since. It's at times like this when someone might wonder what I was feeling? 'Very worried' would be about right. I've already explained that the crashworthiness of the aircraft and its high landing speed was not going to do either of us any good if one of the main undercarriage legs wasn't locked down.

My most perfect Vampire approach was followed by my slowest, and smoothest, touch down … *Squeak – Squeak –* (mainwheels on) *– Squeak* (nosewheel) ….

Phew! … Survived another.

And the crowd went wild again. In fact, it was a major anti-climax – the punters who had all gathered to watch all went home empty-handed with no photos to email to the Daily Mail. Meanwhile, I was already working out where the nearest pub was in order to calm my nerves. Immediately thereafter I intended to call Jane to ensure she never bounced me again with such a short notice request at the end of a busy day. Just another day in the life of …

Chapter 6

Northern Ireland

Sadly, in many respects, I didn't get chance to fly the RN's Wessex 5 helicopters operationally, despite ending up as the project pilot for all marks of Wessex at Boscombe Down. I loved flying the Wessex for a whole bunch of reasons, particularly the very high seating position, the fantastic sliding window/door which allowed you an almost cabriolet flying experience, the spare power when both engines were online, and it had very sprightly handling even when heavy. Lots of my contemporaries were flying the Wessex during 'The Troubles' in Northern Ireland and as a result had usually flown there; but not me.

My first visit came in 2005 when I was invited to fly an Alexander Schleicher K14 self-launching motor glider (SLMG) at the Ulster Gliding Club, based at a grass airfield at Bellarena, north-east of Londonderry. It was not easy to find by car but, thankfully, compared to one of my later operating sites, quite easy to find from the air, being right by the east coast of Lough Foyle, which is the estuary of River Foyle, which flows through Londonderry. The western shore coast of the lough is within Ireland, so overshooting my landing site was not going to be a good move. It turns out that at Lisahally, at the entrance to the lough, was where, at the end of the Second World War, the German U-boat fleet assembled before they were, mostly, taken out to sea to be scuttled.

Well, back to my mission. This was the first of three such aircraft imported into the UK and so the CAA had asked me to conduct a familiarisation as part of their airworthiness oversight; so off I was despatched. The owner met me at the airfield, despite living miles away south of Dublin, and we set about investigating his aircraft which needed my blessing before its Certificate of Airworthiness (just like a car MOT certificate) could be renewed.

Now, yet again, I was about to tick off a number of firsts. Thankfully, as a student at ETPS, I'd been given a familiarisation flight in a glider from Netheravon with a very nice chap, Gerry whom I've subsequently

ASK 14 Motor Glider prior to flight test.

had the pleasure to fly with every couple of years or so. He also took my wife flying on a pleasant summer's evening – a rare treat. At the time, I was just glad to be flying something without having to write a report on it. But here I was, now at Bellarena about to fly my first single-seat motor glider, from a strange airfield, where people spoke with an accent that made broad Yorkshire sound positively tame in comparison. My 'wide-eyed innocence' must have been evident and, in order to help preserve their beloved aircraft for longer than my flight alone, the gliding club decided to take me gliding again first. I'd barely caught my breath since arriving but I was now strapping into the front seat of a Glazer Dirks DG505 high performance glider built in Slovenia. The purpose was, allegedly, to give me a familiarisation of the area so I wouldn't get lost. I suspected I was being assessed by the owner of the ASK 14 to see if I could be trusted with his 'pride and joy'. I wish I had a pint for every time I have had to prove I can fly; mind you, my liver would have packed up long ago.

The DG505 was a lot of fun in fact; excellent field of view and, carried aloft by a tug plane, I was able to get up to around 3,000 feet before being 'cast off'. All I had to do now was demonstrate I could land a glider, again. I'm no expert but, since flying single-engine aircraft means you may become a glider pilot at any minute, I have always tried to keep 'my hand in' at flying to a landing site without an engine. A glider frankly doesn't really want to stop flying; its glide angle is so shallow that you feel you can carry on flying forever (and that's what gliding competitions and records are all about). But my fun had to come to an end and, by pulling on a lever, airbrakes/spoilers could be deployed, which caused the glider to descend much more steeply. With an engine you have a glide angle, which can be made shallower by the use of power; in a glider you have a glide angle that can be made steeper. Either way, the pilot can adjust his angle of approach, as I was able to do, to land on the pre-determined spot.

Phew! …

The glider rumbled to a halt as intact as I'd found it and I climbed out. The crowd didn't quite go wild but I was given leave to head to the loo for a quick 'nervous pee' before being allowed into the ASK. Now this quirky beast had a small engine in the nose powering a two-bladed propeller, which came very, very close to the ground. So, the take-off had to be flown very carefully, without tipping the aircraft too far over onto its nose; otherwise I'd have been digging divots out of their nice grass airfield and no doubt been forced to repair them for the rest of the week. I managed the take-off with the aid of wingwalkers who initially held my wings in the level attitude. With only a single main wheel I couldn't keep the wing tips off the ground until I had some airspeed. But once airspeed was acquired suddenly I was in control, and flying, and off yet again, for another adventure.

Although the climb performance was poor, I eventually struggled above 3,000 feet and flew my usual sequence of test points. All appeared to be well, apart from the fuel cock which was labelled in such a way as to point to OFF when it was ON and ON when it was OFF (not at all helpful if I'm honest) and its main electrical on/off switch was a similar-looking knob, very much like a fuel cock. Anyway, time to head home. Because the prop was so close to the ground it was normal practice to land with the engine stopped with the stationary blades horizontal. So, before commencing my descent I had to shut down a perfectly serviceable engine.

At ETPS I used to teach students how to do engine-off landings in helicopters and also how to restart an engine in flight. So, I had logged literally hundreds of inflight engine shutdowns in a Gazelle, but I had always managed to restart it before I actually landed. Equally, I had already landed numerous aircraft following engine failure. But this was the first time I'd deliberately stopped an engine in flight with no intention of restarting it before I landed.

Anyway, it grabbed my attention for sure. And to be honest, even though I've now completed many similar inflight shutdowns, when it all goes quiet there is a definite sense of imminent foreboding, like buying your first house when you don't know how you're going to ever afford the mortgage repayments.

So now the challenge was not to get too far from where I needed to land. As a helicopter pilot I'm used to very steep glide angles so for me landing a glider can be frustrating due to the fact that they come down so slowly. It can be a real temptation to fly a very wide circuit and then end up too far away in the last few hundred feet. Well not me, not today. The airbrakes worked ever so well and by putting them in a mid-position I could adjust my glide angle both up and down. I adopted my usual forced-landing circuit with a wide base leg curved approach. By then I could see the anxious expressions on the gathered 'goofers'. Nicely into wind as I came over the hedge, airbrakes deployed, a gentle flare and the single main wheel hit the landing spot exactly as planned. And now the crowd did go wild! Given their earlier apprehension I guess they would have been pleased if I'd landed anywhere other than Ireland.

Phew! … survived another.

After documenting the safety issues regarding the fuel cock and electrical switch I was treated to a brisk scenic drive to a posh golf club for a slap up meal with, maybe just a couple of glasses of robust red wine, before heading home to complete my travels …

Now, I mentioned the need for an airborne famil (familiarisation) in light of challenges I was to encounter on a subsequent check flight. If you've flown in Northern Ireland you'll know what I mean; if you haven't, have a look at the place via Google Maps satellite photos. The whole place is a patchwork quilt of thousands of very small fields that all look the same. So, it's now March 2006 and a Pilatus PC-6/B2-H4 Turbo Porter aircraft needed a flight test. It was to be flown from an 'airfield' (if you could really describe this place as such) called Movenis. You will not find it on many maps and certainly you will not find it on aviation maps. It was owned by a parachute training school and is found about ten miles south of Coleraine, if that helps? Basically, it's in the middle of nowhere.

Anyway, as usual, I did my research and had hatched a cunning plan that had me landing in Belfast early afternoon, sorting the rental car, driving to Movenis, checking out the aircraft, doing all the paperwork and then after a good night's rest and suitable reading of the aircraft's flight manual etc., I would do the check flight the following morning and be on the ground in time for a well-earned pub lunch before finally heading back to the mainland for tea and medals at the end of the day. It was a good plan, that I had used both before and since, but what is that expression from the Prussian General Helmuth von Moltke? 'No plan survives first contact with the enemy' – and so it was to be …

I had found the right place, found the aircraft, found the engineer responsible for maintaining the aircraft and started going through the paperwork thoroughly, as I had a couple of hours before my first glass of ale at the local tavern that evening. All was going well until the 'head honcho' at the place asked when I was about to go flying.

'About 9 am tomorrow', I replied with the confidence borne out of my well-honed preparations.

The 'head honcho' gave me one of those looks that had started to become familiar – 'What planet am I coming from?' kind of look.

'By 9 am I expect the aircraft to be over the English Channel heading back to the French parachute centre where it needs to be. It has to be off at dawn.'

'What?'

How did this happen? Does nobody read my emails? No, it turns out, and that has been the case far too often.

'Oh, Bugger!' – what to do?

When was sunset today? Too bloody soon I discovered; but there was nothing for it but to at least show willing. I had not flown a PC-6 before. They are an extremely ugly aircraft and, to be honest, are not at all easy to fly in certain respects. I was to take with me a French chap who was expecting to fly the aircraft back to France the following morning; he turned out not to be a great deal of help.

Anyway, minutes later I was gingerly advancing the power lever and trying to keep the thing straight with a good deal of applied rudder as we 'slipped the surly bonds', about thirty minutes before sunset, hoping to fit everything in before it went 'proper dark'. So off we went with me glancing down at some of the scenery as we climbed north-east towards

PC-6 immediately before flight test. The very narrow tarmac strip can be seen immediately behind the aircraft.

the Glens of Antrim. To be honest it was a beautiful sight to see these hills already bathed in a pinkish light. Such moments are priceless and should be savoured and enjoyed but, in reality, I was more concerned by the reddening sky than I was delighted by its beauty. One thing I've learned repeatedly in my aviation career is, that no amount of enthusiasm or preparation can slow the relentless descent of the sun. So performance climb done, tick; stalling done, tick; systems checked, tick. And so it was, that I now pointed south-west, adding power and dropping the nose to gain maximum speed as a final test point and the now very urgent need to return this beast from whence it came before nightfall.

Mmmmm.

Well, if all those small identical fields were unhelpful on the way outbound, then they were extremely unhelpful now as I looked into the red orb of the setting sun. Back then, I had nothing in the way of GPS nav aids to get me home. I looked hopefully to my French buddy, who raised his arms with a Gallic nonchalance and a franglaised, '*Je suis perdu,*' which even a 'rocket scientist' would conclude meant he didn't know where the airfield was either.

Thankfully, I had noted some scenic markers as we departed and, as the sun sank over the horizon, I identified Movenis. Now, getting airborne from a short strip is one thing, but landing again is quite another. This strip was really short, just over four hundred metres if that means anything to you? About three soccer pitches end to end, which sounds like a lot if you're running after a ball (as I always seemed to be at school) but trust me it's not. My predicament was not helped by the fact that a limiting crosswind was blowing from the south and the strip was in a valley with steeply rising ground at either end. If that wasn't enough, the tarmac 'runway' was less than one metre wider that the width of the aircraft's undercarriage.

Not for the faint-hearted, I concluded, and I set up to have a go at making a dummy approach to get the measure of the field. Yep, it was going to be tight! I trimmed the aircraft out as I reduced power, added flap and was pretty happy that I could have a go at landing next time around. I added power and:

'Bugger!' my eyes watered.

As I added power, the nose on this beast (look at the photo – this thing really had a nose on it) reared up like the pigheaded horse I ended up riding one day when trying to impress a girl at university. I had to add power to get the thing climbing, so as not to fly into the rising ground, but, gosh, did I need to work hard at controlling the aircraft. Initially both my hands were required before I'd retrimmed the aircraft to remove the massive force. Now in fairness to Pilatus, they had festooned the aircraft's flight manual with bold warnings about such characteristics, and advised of the potentially high stick forces, and suggested not trimming the aircraft on the approach but, if you didn't trim the forces with low power for the descent then trying to land on a short strip over a high hedge became almost impossible, especially with my puny helicopter pilot arms. Anyway, undaunted, I flew my circuit to have another approach. This time I planned to do a 'touch and go'; that is put the wheels on the ground, but, rather than jam the brakes on and try and stop in the very short distance, I would add power and fly off again – which is what I did, successfully – hurray!

Now all this fun was gratifying but I was now facing the prospect of failing light and reckoned I had only a few minutes of useable daylight left as the 'runway' was completely unlit. So, round I went again – perfect approach – speed spot on – over the hedge – 'gosh this strip is narrow' – both wheels firmly on – stick full back to get the tail down – and reverse thrust. Yep this aircraft could go backwards; and with a very powerful engine now pushing instead of pulling I was slowing very quickly, but also turning. The engine's massive torque reaction wanted to turn me off the tarmac, as did the strong crosswind which really wasn't helpful. So, applying full rudder and braking the outboard wheel as hard as I dare, I came to a stop in about two hundred metres, still within my one metre allowable error before I came off the tarmac and in so doing impressed the smiling Frenchman who was realising that his departure to France in the morning might be possible after all. Especially as my flight test had confirmed the aircraft was all OK.

Phew! ... survived another without embarrassment.

Off to the pub.

Now, the PC 6 was in fact my third visit to Northern Ireland but I wanted to link my next two tests together as they were flown at the same airfield – Newtownards.

Now, Newtownards is not a place of happy memories for me, I must say. Built in 1934, it served for a while as one of the main ways of getting from Great Britain to Northern Ireland being sited within nine miles of Belfast. During the Second World War it operated Lysanders and numerous target towing aircraft before being returned to civil use and becoming the home of the Ulster Flying Club. For me it is a bleak place.

My first visit was to fly an Aerochute for noise gathering purposes among other things.

Aerochute ready for test at Newtownards.

What the heck is an Aerochute, I hear you ask? Well, that was exactly my reaction when being asked to test fly one. Imagine a shopping trolley, with a lawnmower engine on the back, hung beneath a square parachute and you will have an idea. The one I was asked to fly was a two-seater so I could fly with a rep from the Aerochute company which was based in Australia. My guess was that the testing in Oz was done in warmer weather than this brutal morning at 'Ards' which was about zero degrees at the surface. Firstly, the challenge was to try and get off the ground. I looked to the Aussie who was trying to pitch this device into the UK as a sensible way of flying, especially for SAS types who could whizz around and fly low level into enemy territory. Have you seen the Bond movie 'The World is not Enough' with Pierce Brosnan when he is on skis being chased by blokes with machine guns on these kind of things?

Anyway, the trick was apparently to lay out the parachute behind the cart (putting the chute behind the cart?) then gently open up the throttle in the hope that the airflow generated would 'fill the canopy' – like trying to get one of those really annoying kids' kites airborne as a dad. Never works first time, in my experience. And so it was: we got colder and colder, with a bit of flimsy parachute material making us all look stupid,

The Aerochute ready for start up with the parachute laid out.

until all of a sudden the air 'hit the spot' and without further delay full throttle was applied. The shopping trolley shot forward on its plastic wheels – my fillings fell out of my teeth yet again and we hurtled across a corrugated frozen wasteland of my favourite UK airfield …

All of a sudden, we were airborne. To fly it, if that was the correct expression, I had to reach up above my head so that each hand could pull down on a cord which somehow bent the canopy of the 'chute' to cause some roll and thus yaw. There was no way to control yaw independently of roll or vice versa. Now these two characteristics often work hand in hand but there are times, like when trying to position very accurately over a microphone to measure noise, where being able to achieve one without the other would have really helped. The alternative was to run in for over a mile in order to have a fighting chance of getting into the right area. Holding my hands over my head created a two-inch gap between my trusty Swordfish pilot leather gauntlets (issued by the Fleet Air Arm to any self-respecting pilot even in the 1980s) and my warm synthetic Ozee suit, designed to keep the sub-zero breeze out. After twenty minutes of this my morale was also sub-zero and even pretending to chase Sophie Marceau (fit Bond girl from the aforementioned movie) around snowy mountainsides was failing to maintain my positive attitude.

Just in time, before becoming suicidal, noise data captured – Phew! … And now to the landing …

This thing was a bugger to fly. There was no way to land with any kind of crosswind because you were just blown sideways; so landing on one of the tarmac runways, which would have been kinder on the trolley's plastic wheels, was not going to work – so into wind – point at a flat bit of grass – power back – and down we go – 'flare like a rascal' with ice blocks for hands and …

BAMMMMMMMMMM!

We had returned to earth. Despite the previously frozen ground my nose-wheel now ploughed a deepening furrow covering me in lumps of icy mud.

Great. Barely able to move I crawled out of the shopping trolley and kissed the ground. I couldn't speak as my face was numb, so I staggered off, like a Yeti, to the nearest warm building where medicinal hot coffee could be administered.

Phew! … survived, just.

I should have learnt my lesson but, years later, when working for myself as Dovetail Aviation, I found myself being invited back. Based on my first experience there alone I should have declined, or based on the hassle of getting there and back home, or based on what I was being asked to fly; all would have been sensible reasons to say no.

Elsewhere in this book, you will have read about autogyros where I make mention of the Fairey Rotodyne which flew in forward flight with the main rotors acting as an autogyro. In slow speed flight or in the hover the blades had to be powered to go around and the aircraft used the novel feature of tip jets – a jet engine blasted air along the rotor blades such that it could then escape at the tips and so pushed each of the blades around.

The demise of the Fairey Rotodyne was partially because the method of spinning the blades was very, very noisy and really not a popular way to arrive into a city centre such as London or Paris.

Anyway, someone had got hold of my name from somewhere; I'd like to think it was down to my worldwide reputation as a test pilot, and that I'd already flown an extensive variety of aircraft, rather than because I had sucker stamped on my forehead.

I was approached by a team with expertise from Shorts of Belfast (Bombardier). They had bought an unfinished project from the USA and were now trying to get it moving; would I be interested? Two immediate drawbacks: it was based at my not so favourite airfield, Newtownards, and they wanted me to test it on a weekend. We compromised on a Friday and Saturday in July 2018; at least I wouldn't be quite as cold.

I arrived in Belfast courtesy of Aer Lingus and was whizzed off to the airfield to see the aircraft. It was based on a Rotorway Exec kit helicopter but with an auxiliary power unit (APU) gas turbine, mounted not far behind the pilot, powering an air compressor which forced air through the blades to then emanate from the tips, thus pushing them around. The pilot had some control over the APU which then varied the jet efflux and speed of the rotors via a twist grip on the collective lever.

The yaw control came as a result of the APU efflux being directed over a rudder at the rear of the aircraft. Heath Robinson (First World War cartoonist famous for drawing whacky inventions) would have been proud.

Through the afternoon I adopted my usual pattern for such events; lots of nattering to the gathered experts and lots of 'war stories' shared before

RDL Genesis helicopter awaiting flight test at Newtownards.

trying to ascertain how to fly the thing and how likely it was that it would kill me! I was assured it had flown successfully in the US and I was even shown grainy video footage of a flight. Well, if some American Johnny could fly it so could I. My logic had an element of sense but was, as often, flawed. Many years ago, I landed my RAE Bedford Wessex helicopter on the back of a very small Type 23 frigate flight deck, in a rather rough sea, with only inches to spare between my rotors and the hangar. The bulk of my research had centred on the fact that an RN colleague had already managed it, albeit in flat calm conditions. If he could do it, surely it couldn't be that difficult, could it? Needless to say it turned out to be rather marginal and I had to take the unusual step of asking one of the boffins to hang out of the cabin door to make sure my tailwheel was definitely over the deck before I touched down.

Back to Newtownards; I formed a plan. My first sortie would simply be a ground run to see if I could start and stop it and control this sod of an APU engine which it transpired was like trying to get a 'Game of Thrones' dragon to spit flame just where and when you wanted.

And it was f***ing loud!

There was absolutely no sound proofing between my head and the APU.

Years previously, I had badly deafened myself by testing a single-seat autogyro without a proper helmet. I am mostly deaf in my right ear now and have tinnitus which if you haven't yet got it – please avoid loud noises. I'm left with a lot of white noise hissing in my head most of the time.

So I had jammed ear plugs underneath my bulky and normally effective active noise reduction (ANR) headset. On lighting up the APU my head exploded with the cacophony behind me, but I had come a long way, so I practised controlling rotor rpm and then shut it all down with a view to the next stage which was to get it airborne, at least in a low hover.

Wow – what an experience. I had arrogantly expected to have no major problem getting the thing to hover.

Yes, I'd expected it to be difficult …

Yes, unstable and …

Yes, have lots of vibration …

But what I got was far worse than expected. As I pulled the collective lever up, pitch was added to the blades to create lift and I compensated for the increased drag by pouring more fuel into the APU to spit out more compressed air and the aircraft started to get 'light on the skids'. That is, it was still on the ground but with some of the weight being supported by the blades.

Well, as I achieved this interim state, the cyclic stick between my knees started thrashing itself from side to side, full-scale travel, with me hanging on for grim death. Now some helicopters do have a characteristic whereby they are OK in the hover and OK on the ground but really, really hate being halfway between the two. I hoped this was the case with my Genesis Aerotech Ltd mount, so I pulled the lever some more and added more power until one skid lifted off the ground by around a centimetre; not that much you might think, but Hell's bells was that scary enough! I yet again found myself in an aircraft where I was mostly out of control. Never a good experience. One centimetre was enough for this sortie thank you very much. I promptly plonked it firmly back on the ground winding the APU down to save my knackered hearing as much as I could.

'So guys – what's going on here?'

I hadn't seen this problem in the video footage from the US, although as I re-watched it on my phone, I realised the footage was of it flying, not actually getting airborne. Anyway, I went for a pee and a cuppa as was customary at such stages of a flight test campaign and the assorted experts phoned their mates in the States to find out what 'was occurring'.

I returned from the café with my ears still ringing to find the engineer cramming the rotor head and all moving parts with axle grease. Turns out there were no proper bearings in the moving parts and the experimental flying done to date had only been achieved by thoroughly greasing everything each flight.

So surely this would fix the issue?

What do you think?

Yep indeed, I now became the most efficient grease spreader that Newtownards had ever witnessed, managing to spray everything within a four hundred metre radius with very sticky black grease.

Did it make it easier to fly?

No.

Was I brave enough to lift the skid more than one centimetre off the deck?

Absolutely not.

Was any of this improving my hearing?

**** no!

Time to call it a day. I 'pulled the plug' and turned it all off.

By now it was late in the day, and nearly dark again. What is it about flying in Northern Ireland? So after a depressing debrief we adjourned to our hotel. Well, I call it a hotel only because the other possible descriptions aren't polite. A wedding reception was in full swing and no food was to be had, so off to a local curry house, for the *worst* curry in the world.

'What kind of meat is this?'

'Dunno.'

'Why is it so red?'

'Food Dye.'

'Why?'

'To make it look more appealing.'

'What?'

The fun did not stop as returning to the 'hotel' I found the wedding party had reached the stage of the 'dad dancing contest' in the room above mine. *Aaaaargh* – deaf but not deaf enough it appeared.

A new day dawned and, despite a rumbly tummy, I didn't feel quite as ill as expected – survived another dodgy curry.

Phew! …

If the dodgy curry had not been enough to ruin my morale entirely, I now faced the challenge of my return flight home; an Aer Lingus flight booked through BA. I will never do that again.

My flight was the only flight that day that refused to land in Belfast because it was rather windy. It was windy, sure, but all the other BA flights and Flybe flights landed and departed successfully. My plane was based in Dublin and my guess was the pilot was homesick because that's where the aircraft diverted. Aer Lingus were not interested in a very cross Brit trying to get back to LHR. After a hugely frustrating Saturday in the Belfast City Airport Costa spending my Aer Lingus £5 voucher wisely I caught a coach down to Dublin and just managed to catch the last flight back to London.

Phew! … survived another.

Now all I needed to do was get home despite the M3 having been closed for the night to do roadworks. Who would be daft enough to be trying to use the M3 to get home after 10 pm on a Saturday night anyway … *aaaaaarrrgghhh!*

I haven't been back across the water since.

Chapter 7

Sikorsky S92
Search and Rescue (SAR)

I'm pulling 20 per cent more power than normally allowed. I'm yawing and pitching and I'm rolling. I'm less than 30 feet above the ground and still going down rapidly in a multimillion dollar experimental helicopter …

I don't think I could write down such a collection of short stories without including Sikorsky. My main aim with this book is to make my grandchildren chuckle years from now when they are staring at the pages in disbelief as they get just a glimpse of how I used to earn a living, back in the day. And, as I vomit words on to paper, I would not include my visits to Sikorsky amongst my funniest anecdotes. But the company was a big chunk of my time, energy and stress as a civil certification test pilot … So, here goes …

Firstly, you should know who Igor I. Sikorsky was …

Igor was a Russian pilot who, at the age of 24, was already designing bombers for use in the First World War. He fled from Russia in 1917, arriving in the USA (via a brief time in France) in 1919, setting up a manufacturing company in Stratford, Connecticut, designing and building float/sea planes for Pan Am. By 1939 he had designed the Vought Sikorsky VS300, seen as perhaps the first practical helicopter. By the end of the Second World War, he had designed and built the S-51 which Westland Helicopters of Yeovil were to build for the Royal Navy (RN) as the Dragonfly. In fact, the RN went on to use many of the Sikorsky designs in subsequent years including the Whirlwind (S-55), Wessex (S-58) and Sea King (SH-3/S-61), all of which I've been fortunate enough to fly. The particular Sea King I used to fly extensively, for the Defence Research Agency (DRA) at Boscombe Down, was one of only four Sikorsky SH-3s shipped to the UK. It was assembled as a kit and formed the basis for the design of the incredibly well-respected

Westland Sea King family. It even had the word 'Sikorsky' still written on the pilot's yaw pedals.

Later, as a tutor at ETPS, I was looking after a team of our students who had to assess the Sikorsky CH-53G(D) Sea Stallion helicopter. As a consequence, I was able to conduct my own evaluation. And what an awesome helicopter it was: a huge amount of fun to fly with lots of power and good handling qualities. First flying in 1964, the type flew some impressive missions in the Vietnam War and the latest versions are still being built today, nearly sixty years later.

Anyway, I think the above opening words are probably enough of an intro to explain that I had a 'soft spot' for Igor and his amazing legacy. As a tutor at ETPS we went on technical visits each year and in the late 1990s I found myself at Sikorsky's other plant, West Palm Beach (WPB), Florida, where much of their aircraft development and testing took place. During that ETPS visit we were chuffed to be shown around the brand new S-92 helicopter by the project test pilot, Ron. Although I confess to struggling to take in much of what we saw, largely due to an excessive amount of Bourbon consumed the night before. I'm not sure the 'chain sucking' of extra-strong mints disguised my shabby state. It turns out, Ron and I were to fly together frequently.

My mentor and senior, Nigel, had left the CAA when he was offered more money than he could count from Agusta in Italy. Not only lots of dosh, but he got to live near a big lake, drive a speedboat, drive a flash sports car and, unlike me, managed to completely sidestep having to test fly autogyros for the CAA – what can I say?

So with his departure I had become, in addition to all my aeroplane tasks, the de facto Chief Helicopter Test Pilot for the CAA.

Having taken up the baton from Nigel I promptly learnt that I had become the European Aviation Safety Agency (EASA) project pilot for all types of Sikorsky helicopters. Well, knock me over sideways with a feather duster. I was about to go and fly the very latest aircraft from Igor which was to include the popular S-92A and later the S-76D. But I'm getting ahead of myself; first our visit to WPB in November 2006.

So, I now realise I'm going to have to write some rather dull paragraphs. What do you mean, they're all dull?

I need to explain different types of flight testing and, then later, there is going to be some technical helicopter stuff – 'bear with'!

The S92A SAR flight test team. Ray is wearing a borrowed orange flight suit and standing next to him is Ron who is the tall guy on the right.

I had been 'handed the baton' and Sikorsky had completed the development of a new version of their very large bus-like S-92 aircraft. These are the sort of aircraft that make themselves useful flying oil workers out from the Shetlands and are 'mini airliners' that can land on oil rig platforms. This latest version had been specifically designed for the UK requirement for numerous long-range search-and-rescue (SAR) helicopters which were about to replace the military Sea Kings (talk about keeping it in the family ...). So, we were looking forward to seeing what Igor's team had come up with. The only slight fly in the ointment was that this all absolutely had to be signed off by Christmas in order to deliver aircraft on time and the American certification agency – the Federal Aviation Authority (FAA), bless their cotton socks, hadn't yet had time to complete their certification visits. But this was Sikorsky after all. What could possibly be wrong with their product that we Brits could have a problem with? So, another cunning plan was hatched; that we would 'validate' the FAA's findings first. Yes, you heard me correctly the first time. We would validate what they were about to discover before they did.

Oooohhh.

(Later in this book I talk about doing a validation job on an aeroplane, a Columbia 400.)

Off I jet to WPB to meet up with my colleague Ray. We pitched up at the Sikorsky facility bright and breezy on Monday morning, raring to go. There we met Ron, who thankfully didn't remember me from our ETPS visit, which is just as well given my shabby state and Bourbon breath. Ron gave us the two-dollar tour of the plant and aircraft and started to present the findings of what they had done during their flight-test programme. We organised our first two-hour flight for that afternoon. This was my first flight in an S-92 and Ron beamed at me throughout, like a parent at his son's graduation. This really was his baby. He had been testing it since its first flight six years previously. And in fairness, there is a lot of good about the S-92, but if anyone tells you they've found the perfect

With Ray during the flight test programme at West Palm Beach.

helicopter, drum them out of your gathering, as there really is no such thing.

And so it was, I started making note of what I liked and what I didn't and, along with Ray, starting dropping them into the various categories we used to describe and define such issues. Most manufacturers, apart from companies like PZL, didn't really want to know our top tips for improvement. They just wanted to know if we had identified any 'Unacceptable' issues that were 'show-stoppers' until fixed.

The Monday's flight went well, albeit it was as much about me becoming comfortable with the cockpit and controls as anything else. Tuesday morning dawned with us already en route to the plant. We had a lot to get through within our test plan and we were about to get very interested in the aircraft's flight control system (FCS) and its ability to assist the SAR pilot fish poor drowning souls out of the water. I was going to say this is a thankless task, but actually it's not. Lots of military and civilian SAR crews have won bravery and 'well done' awards for pulling people to safety from sinking ships or cliff tops. But this is not an easy task. In order to do SAR safely over the water at night, pretty much everyone would agree that the helicopter should be equipped with systems that make the job as easy as possible for the pilot. The flight control system (FCS) effectively acts like an airliner autopilot and can fly the aircraft around without any input to speak of from the pilot. And even when the pilot does want to add some personal control inputs the FCS uses computers to drive actuators that will move the controls for the pilot to achieve a smooth ride, or a stable hover etc.

The FCS of the S92 had been approved already but its use for SAR required some modifications and we particularly had to investigate where it would spend a lot of time, in the hover.

So, after lunch, we briefed what we needed to do. We again were met by some of those very concerned faces you see from time to time. It's the sort of face that, if worn by a used car salesman, would prompt you to walk out of the showroom, very briskly.

We wanted to discuss with Ron and his colleagues faults or failures with the FCS. If a manufacturer can determine, by design, that it will not fail more than one time in a billion occurrences (1×10^{-9}) then, effectively, it's nearly 100 per cent reliable. For most of you who don't grasp maths (who does?) let's just say that if you only have a 10^{-9} chance of something happening you can assume that it will never happen – well, just like the Euromillions jackpot, it will never happen to **you** anyway. But it turns out that the design team couldn't quite demonstrate this near 100 per cent reliability with their fancy calculations. So, the next option was to ensure that the pilot could cope with whatever malfunction the FCS created. Check out the chapter on the PZL SW4; for that aircraft with one engine and only a single hydraulic system, we had to assume either would fail and had to ensure a pilot could deal with the problem without too much difficulty.

With flight control systems the principal concern is that the computer will send duff signals to the actuators (which are the hydraulic rams that use the hydraulic system to push a rod connected to the flying controls to boost the pilot's inputs) and that they will run-away. Yep, just like a runaway train or an errant schoolboy worried about his exam results, the actuator will run 'full-travel' pushing the relevant flying control with it. In order for this not to immediately destroy the aircraft, the authority of the actuator is limited; typically it is only allowed to move 10–20 per cent of the total control travel possible, which in a helicopter is still more than enough.

With me so far? So we asked which had been the worst runaways that Ron had encountered – and we were given a couple of examples – but the following was determined to be worst case:

This was a 'multiple axis runaway' where the following all happened at once:

Cyclic stick Aft – which pitched the nose up.

Cyclic stick Left – which rolled the aircraft left.

Yaw pedal Left – which yawed the aircraft left.

Collective lever Down – which dumped the pitch off the rotor blades giving reduced lift and a descent.

What was not going to make my life easier as I contemplated this sortie was that, in order to be deemed acceptable, just as with the PZL SW-4, the pilot must be allowed at least a one-second reaction time before any intervention. We were flying a fully-instrumented aircraft that was recording all my inputs and aircraft reaction. There could be no cheating by reacting 'early'. This, I surmised, was going to be one of the more scary flights of my career to date, and I was not to be disappointed.

Just for extra fun, the aircraft had to be flown at its maximum weight of over 12,000 kg, or 12 tonnes. That was one bloody heavy helicopter; it can take twenty-two passengers in its normal configuration. In the flight test world we are allowed to overload aircraft to ensure that, even as we use fuel, we stay heavy enough for our findings to be valid, which is what we did.

So, having made the briefing as long as I could to delay the inevitable, I strapped in wearing my brown underwear, and cautiously, with a sense of imminent doom, lifted into the hover in the correct place over the runway. We were being filmed and all of the aircraft parameters were being relayed to a telemetry facility. So, one wrong move on my part and everyone would know about it instantly. I started with a very high hover of 100 feet to give me plenty of room. Sikorsky wanted to be able to operate this aircraft down to 30 feet over the sea at night.

You might wonder why I didn't go even higher? When it comes to hovering an aircraft, the pilot is predominantly relying on what they can see out of the window. The closer to the ground, then the easier it is to get a sense of if the aircraft is moving up or down or sliding sideways/backwards etc. So 200 feet would have been much more difficult than 100 feet.

The inputs into the FCS were made by another special box and we carried a Sikorsky flight test engineer (FTE) who sat alongside my buddy, Ray, in the back to assist. On throwing a switch all the actuators in the various control runs would run full travel.

'OK – so here we go.'

'Call On Condition', says Ray.

'On Condition', says I, having established a stable hover with all the engine and gearbox parameters nicely in limits although we were pulling a lot of power just to hover this 12+ tonne beastie.

'Standby then – Input on 3–2–1–Now', says Ray.

'One thousand and one', I say in my head.

'*Now*', says I, when I commence recovery …

This has been a very long second indeed. By the time I get to the second 'one' in my count, we are dropping brick-like towards an accident, with the aircraft nose having already pitched up around 20 degrees, and we are rolling left and turning left also. Frankly, we are well up 'pooh creek' and no mistake.

On calling 'Now' I have had to do lots of things simultaneously. It's hitting the ground that will kill us or, at the very least, write-off millions of dollars' worth of experimental helicopter and my left hand's preservation instinct, almost certainly, reacts first and commences a brisk pull up of the collective lever to add power. In an ideal world, I'd like to just pull this lever up to the top stop but that would destroy the gearbox and damage the engines (= very, very costly). Instead, I have to read a power gauge on the dashboard which gives me a normal limit of 100 per cent (torque). At 100 per cent we are still going down and I pull to a further transient limit, which I am allowed to use for a few seconds, 120 per cent. As I'm doing this, my eyes are feeding signals to my brain, and thankfully, without me being aware of consciously thinking about it, I am correcting the aircraft to a level attitude by inputting right pedal with my right foot, and right and forward cyclic with my right hand. Most of my attention is outside the cockpit, to try and maintain my visual cues, but I am equally having to monitor the torque gauge and radio altimeter (Rad-Alt) which tells me I'm still going down.

'Yikes!'

The beast started to shake and rattle, and groan and moan, and the huge rotor blades with increased pitch on them, slapped the air out of the way as they all did their best to claw some lift out of the warm and humid sky around me and after what felt like a very, very, very, very long time, we stopped going down and inch by inch clawed our way back up to where we had started from. Phew! …

I talked to telemetry on the radio. We had not broken anything but we had lost more than 50 feet during the test point. In order to ensure that my techniques had been good and using the lessons learnt from the last few minutes I agreed to repeat the test point. This time my left hand knew it had to apply 120 per cent torque promptly and my brain knew roughly where in the cockpit my left hand had to be put to get us there.

'OK – here we go again –'

'Call On Condition.'

'On Condition.'

'Standby then – Input on 3–2–1 *Now*.'

'One thousand and one.'

Brrrrrrggrrrrbbrrgghhrr!

120 per cent applied – the panels and rivets and spars and bolts of the S-92 all complained with their own contribution to the audio soundtrack, but we had arrested the descent and noted a 50 feet height loss.

Now, in flight test, there is a concept, which pretty much equates to the idea of flogging a dead horse. Sikorsky thought they would be able to hover at night at just 30 feet and be able to cope with any FCS failure. I'd clearly demonstrated that you needed 50 feet to recover. So game over and no cigar.

'Let's call it a day', says I, and we did.

It was already late in the day and after this kind of high adrenalin aviation we were all knackered. The debrief kind of went along the lines of, from Sikorsky, 'I'm sorry but you didn't get the right result.'

I responded by mumbling something to convey that I thought that we, kind of, had done and that we'd reached an 'end point', so no point in doing anymore. 'But', says Sikorsky – 'you have to do better; because we want to clear the aircraft down to 30 feet!'

So I did what I always do in such situations; I called it a day and headed back to the hotel to:

- Discuss the sortie more fully with my mate Ray.
- Contemplate my own poor flying skills. Trying to evaluate whether a better pilot could do a better job.
- But most importantly, quaff some Californian Cabernet in sufficient quantities to be able to sleep soundly, and during the quaffing mull over our next steps.

Dawn arrived far too quickly (can't hold back the sun) and off we drove in our rental car apprehensively, to more fully debrief and rebrief. Ray and I had decided we would be happy to continue with our test programme, given that we had nailed the required technique etc. Now, you might be wondering what our new best mate Ron was doing during these high workload sorties? Well, I can tell you his outward demeanour was far more relaxed than how he must have really been feeling. Although he had 'signed for the aircraft', given the rapidity of my required responses, there was little he could have done to save the aircraft if I'd 'cocked up' at any stage.

And so off we went for more of the same.

We started at 100 feet as before, and pretty much got the same, albeit slightly better, result. I was now becoming more accustomed to the sights and sounds of this particular form of sadism. I should point out at this stage that, as a tutor at ETPS, I had taught my students how to do this testing in our elderly Sea King, so I should have been well in my comfort zone, but at Boscombe we had built in a bit of a safety margin. We would fly the aircraft quite light and for most of the test points would do away with the one second delay required for civil certification.

Well 100 feet gave way to 95 feet, which led to 90 feet, which led to 85, then 80, then 75, then 70, then 65, then 60, etc.

By the time we got to 60 feet you would have thought we would have been almost hitting the ground wouldn't you? But no, we weren't. What we discovered was that we were tending to use half the available height to recover. So, our 50-feet loss at 100 feet became only 30 feet at 60 feet. And so it was as we continued in this incremental fashion until we reached our final test points at 30 feet. Low and behold we lost only 15 feet. I know, who would have thought it?

So, why might this have been the case? It seems to defy the laws of physics. Another Dr Who phenomenon? Well, for my money, I think a couple of things were occurring. Firstly, there is a thing called ground effect or, sometimes called the ground cushion. All the air coming down through the helicopter's rotors is giving us the lift, as an equal and opposite reaction. Air goes down, we go up. If we now impede the flow of the air downwards by, let's say putting planet earth in the way, then we become more like a hovercraft and the up reaction becomes more effective. The closer to the ground we get then the more effective or noticeable is this particular quirk of helicopters. Now I did say helicopters were complicated already didn't I?

Also the visual cues, to allow the pilot to fly the recovery, were all getting slightly better closer to the ground.

And finally, never ever forget the pucker factor in aviation, i.e. that feeling you get in your backside when you think you're going to die! That, and a bunch of adrenalin, and it's probable that I was nailing the technique required slightly better as we descended.

We repeated the point a couple of times to be sure of our results, and then home for tea and medals, or Bug Juice (see glossary) and burgers in the works canteen.

We lunched with Ron. Ron had a lovely southern drawl and was quietly spoken for such a big man. After we were seated, and my face was filled with fries, he leant across the table.

'You know – we were very worried about today's sortie.'

'Que?'

'We were very worried that you might not be able to fly these test points. We have had some pilots here who are so out of practice, or just so dreadful, that we wouldn't let them continue with their test cards.'

'Wait – so you're saying the Brits did good?'

'Yes indeed – y'all Brits did good.'

Phew! … I'd proved I could fly once more.

But this visit wasn't over, and we were not yet safely in the BA lounge at Miami drinking Napa Valley Chardonnay by the bucketful. During the sorties flown we had spent a good deal of time assessing the instrument panel and its displays to determine whether they would be fit for purpose for the search and rescue mission.

And there was one particular aspect of the displays that I really did not like.

As I mentioned above, the aircraft was fitted with a rad-alt. Normally height is measured a bit like speed (see an earlier chapter about pitot tubes). Essentially an altimeter instrument measures air pressure. As air pressure gets less with increasing height, such a pressure gauge, pointing at a suitable scale, can tell you how high the aircraft is. But this is not very accurate, especially when you need to know how high you are within a foot or two. So, enter the radio altimeter onto the scene. A radio wave bounces from aircraft to ground/sea and then back to the aircraft. A computer then works out how long this took and works out the distance and thus height. Good 'rad-alts' can certainly tell the pilot the aircraft's height to the nearest foot. However, there is next to no help (information) on any aspect of rad-alt performance or displays in the relevant certification codes; it's down to the certification agency to determine if such equipment is fit for purpose and, in my very humble opinion, in this case, it was not.

Ron and the flight test guys knew exactly what we thought of the aircraft in real time as we discussed everything with them during, and after, each flight and on our final evening we wrote up our customary Debrief Note with all our findings. Unlike when we visited PZL in

Poland, we thankfully were not plied with vodka and were able to gather our thoughts over supper back at the hotel. Ray and I always ensured we were totally in agreement during such visits before presenting our findings but, in fairness, my dislike for this matter was largely borne out of my own personal experience.

As you have read my first operational type was the Wasp HAS Mk 1 helicopter which was followed by the Lynx HAS.2 and then HAS.3. All these aircraft were required to be flown at very low level over the sea at night continually. We flew the Wasp everywhere at just fifty feet above the sea. Ironically when I flew the Lynx, with two engines rather than just one, we flew at a hundred feet. As a Lynx instructor I then had to teach ab-initio students all about flying low level over the sea at night. So after about three thousand flying hours of doing all of this I reckon I'd built up a sufficient amount of relevant experience to have some 'street cred' on this topic. And I was convinced that an accurate rad-alt, and an easy to read/use gauge, was absolutely essential if a pilot was to avoid accidently flying into the sea. Certainly monitoring my rad-alt continuously had saved my bacon more often than I could count.

In this case the rad-alt 'gauge' was not where it should have been, on the pilot's Primary Flight Display (PFD) – a TV screen with all the flying instruments displayed – but on an adjacent display mixed in with all the navigation info; not the right place for it at all. So, Ray and I had written up this item as 'unacceptable'. That means it was a 'showstopper' for the certification of this aircraft.

On our final morning we entered a briefing room expecting to debrief the company flight test team. Instead, we found a room crammed with most of the company senior management and as many TPs as they could find. Don't forget, you only need two TPs to get three opinions. (Many years later I was to encounter a very similar situation. I was working as a contractor helping the Norwegian government acquire some brand-new SAR helicopters. The tender had been won by Leonardos with a version of the Merlin or EH101 helicopter. For some reason the cockpit used successfully by the Royal Navy was not to be supplied but a generic export version of the cockpit based on the AgustaWestland 189 helicopter. I think the idea was for AgustaWestland helicopters to all end up with very similar cockpit designs to make certification easier, but again the design of the PFD was 'wanting' and the rad-alt display was very poor indeed. I complained and found myself in a very large room full of lots of TPs and senior management. Deja vu or what?)

Meanwhile, back in Florida in November 2006, Ray manfully explained each aspect of our concerns within the Debrief Note which cited the 'Rad-Alt' display as being unacceptable.

At this point I knew the conversation was about to get heated. Firstly, it was explained, by an already red-faced executive, that the first aircraft had to be shipped before the end of the year (six weeks away) as this was a contractual obligation. Come hell or high water, the first aircraft needed to be shipped and, because the change we were asking for demanded a change to the computer-driven displays, this would mean an update to the software which would take six months to be designed and certified.

This was often the case. Flight test always occurs right at the end of a design/build programme and the milestones or deadlines never seem to get shifted following delays earlier in the process. So, the flight-test programme is always crimped, which is why we were here representing EASA before the FAA had conducted their own assessment. That aspect was now about to become embarrassing as the assumption that allowed us to evaluate it first, had now stumbled because we had found something I was about to die in a ditch over, maybe literally if the glowering faces were to be an indicator.

I looked to my fellow TPs for support …

Now the TP has an unenviable position. A core tenet of our profession is honesty – 'the truth will out'. But we have to pay the mortgage, put food on the table and buy our kids new clogs from time to time, when the old ones wear out. So it is inevitable that loyalty to the hand that feeds you may colour opinion.

Notwithstanding this, I reached out to another TP in the room. In fairness, Ron did not have a navy background and flinched at spending too long over the nearby lake, so this discussion about 'low level over the sea at night' was somewhat outside of his experience. I turned to an ex-United States Navy Seahawk pilot. Like me he had lots of time flying low level over the water at night and, like me, had been a tutor at his country's test pilot school, in his case at Patuxent River, Maryland. He also had a doctorate in Human Factors – Man Machine Interface no less. I gambled that honesty would prevail.

What I got from said fellow TP was perhaps the longest ever sentence I'd ever heard anyone use. A proper politician would be proud. Trump struggles with just a handful of words as we know.

But what did he say? Well, he did his best to agree with everyone at the same time and because, by the time he drew breath, we couldn't remember how he'd started the sentence, we all sat around in silence trying to remember a key phrase that each of us could use to support our argument.

Time to leap in quick …

'So how about we let the aircraft fly around for the next six months but limit its use to daytime only and in good weather?' I found myself saying.

I was new to this game but I had discovered that we, as representatives of EASA, had quite a good deal of clout in such situations.

Well, time for Ray and me to take a well-earned coffee break and leave the grown-ups to chat, which we did.

About to test the production aircraft at Coatesville. Note our brand new matching CAA/EASA navy blue flight suits.

By the time we had returned, the idea of producing a safer aircraft had started to find favour and it turns out the requirement to ship a flyable aircraft was rather vague about whether it needed to fly at night. In truth we were aware that the most it was likely to be needed for, in the short term, would be some PR photos and crew training.

Phew! … the day was saved. We had survived another.

However, the more difficult challenge lay ahead. Since we were meant to be validating the FAA certification, we now had to encourage the FAA to also find the rad-alt unacceptable. Like all these situations, the FAA were now in a corner of their own making and irrespective of what they might have thought of the display had they seen it first it was now very hard for them to dismiss our unacceptable verdict.

Phew! … The FAA also found the display unacceptable.

One of the ironies with these kinds of issues and outcomes is that we will never know how many aircrew lives we might have saved, but if it was only one it had been worth the fight.

In March we returned to the USA to complete our evaluation on a fully completed aircraft at Sikorsky's Keystone facility in Coatesville, Pennsylvania. Here we flew a representative aircraft (the third built) over some rougher water off the east coast and managed some night flying to be sure everything in a production aircraft was as expected, which, thankfully, it was.

Another job in the bag – but not my last visit to West Palm Beach or Coatesville by any means …

Chapter 8

RAF 2000 Autogyro

So, it's September 2006. I've learned how to fly autogyros, both two-seaters and single-seaters and, along with my mate, Ray, I've test flown the new factory-built autogyro, the MT-03. This was the first 'factory built' gyro in the UK to be certified against the relatively new certification code called British Civil Airworthiness Requirements (BCAR) Section T, or just 'Section T' for brevity. This had been, in itself, a steep learning curve, thankfully with a very successful outcome. The newly-certified aircraft was quickly bought up by fledgling training schools and was probably the training aircraft of choice for a time. However, for now, I want to chat about the RAF 2000. This aircraft type had been responsible for a number of fatal accidents in recent years and was a large part of the reason why my boss wanted me to learn to fly them. Before I arrived on the scene the UK CAA had already promised the UK Aircraft Accident Investigation Branch (AAIB) that we would investigate the aircraft further.

So, again I chatted to my mate Ray, and we concluded that there was only one person to go to for this; again he was the chap sitting on top of this particular dung heap and he was, like Dave, a senior examiner. He taught people how to fly the type and he, even more importantly, owned one that he was willing to use to teach me.

So off we went to a dairy farm near Faversham, as you do, to meet up with Marc. I'm not quite sure what he did apart from flying gyros, but he had owned a heck of a lot of cows and sold milk in plastic packets! Later on, I believe he made cheese. 'Blessed are the Cheesemakers' – to quote from the Python movie, 'Life of Brian'!

We met up in what I recollect was yet another caravan on the farm, but in fairness it might have been a portacabin so I was moving up in the world. Marc was a tall, rather imposing chap but with a friendly demeanour and warm, if very firm, handshake. With some trepidation, I opened the conversation and we chewed the fat a bit as I tried to establish my credentials which, when it came to flying the RAF 2000, were, on

Marc's RAF2000 autogyro parked ready for flight. Note the very steep gradient of the runway behind the aircraft.

the face of it, pretty thin. We talked about the RAF 2000 in general and then moved on to discuss his aircraft in particular. Now, it's important to realise that, up until now, the only gyros you could get your hands on to fly in the UK were kitbuilt or home-built designs. These aircraft tended to be like the aircraft I'd learned to fly already and had open cockpits or no cockpit at all. The attraction of the RAF 2000 was that it was a side-by-side two-seater in a fully enclosed cabin – with a *heater*. So a much better bet for all year flying in the UK than the other options.

Marc's own aircraft looked absolutely magnificent – resplendent in a custom-car style of electric metallic blue. Inside, the customary utilitarian instrument panel was replaced by a splendid walnut dashboard that wouldn't have looked out of place in a 1930s Jaguar. In my job I always try to find something nice to say about everything I test. And that was it, because the RAF 2000 was, without any shadow of a doubt, one of the more unpleasant aircraft that I've had the pleasure to fly; and I have a long list to compare it with. But I'm getting ahead of myself …

The first part of my visit was to learn from Marc how to fly this aircraft as safely as it could be flown. So, I inserted my 'student chip' into the grey matter and switched to 'receive' as Marc imparted words of knowledge, wisdom and experience to me in a relaxed and accomplished style. What

The walnut instrument panel fitted to Marc's aircraft.

he thought this muppet from the CAA was going to achieve, in just the two days I'd set aside, I don't know, but I flew five sorties including a flight down to Lydd airfield to use a proper tarmac runway as opposed to the 1-in-3 steep sloping field at the farm that Marc used.

Although there was quite a crosswind blowing at Marc's farm strip, I was able to just about manage take-offs and landings which required maintaining a lot of power to keep blowing prop wash over the rudder.

On the second day the engine stopped.

Was it scary? My recollection is that Marc suddenly became more animated but I was able to ignore him and concentrate on the task in hand. I pushed the stick forward to maintain speed, assessed the wind direction and chose the best place to land that I could get to, and I was able to make a textbook forced landing directly across the runway. Marc was both impressed and relieved that his 'ab initio student' had landed his dead-engined aircraft without even scratching the custom paint job.

Phew! ... survived another.

So, I had, indeed, learnt how to fly it. Then, as often is the case, weather or some such curtailed further flying and the following week I was in Poland flying the SW-4, so a few days went by before Ray and I could return with a cunning test plan. And that's what we did.

I set about to do a full range of tests as I had done recently on the MT-03 factory-built aircraft. I knew this was an 'ugly baby' for sure and I knew that I was about to become the most unpopular man within the RAF 2000 community overnight but these things *kept on killing people*, so something had to be done.

Now, how much technical detail can you stand? 'None', I hear you cry in pain. So, here's the minimum … which you may skip if the bar's already open.

Firstly, the difficulty of flying the aircraft varied greatly with speed. Up to about 50 mph it wasn't easy to fly but it wasn't absolutely dreadful either. But above 50 mph the aircraft, of its own volition, wanted to enter a sinusoidal oscillation in pitch – what? Well imagine a roller-coaster where you go down, then up and then down, like a series of rolling hills. Then imagine that each hill gets bigger than the last one and each valley gets steeper – and then … wait for it … imagine those hills get closer and closer together. And this all happens with increasing magnitude the faster you go. Aeroplanes suffer from an oscillation like this which is called a phugoid, but the period of this oscillation, or the time between hills, can be over a minute. For this aircraft it was a few seconds, which was worse than any of the many helicopters I've flown in this regard. Faster than 70 mph, this oscillation became divergent (got worse and worse) and the pilot had to work harder and harder on keeping the aircraft level with little time or capacity to do anything else like navigate or concentrate on joining a busy airfield for example. Not clever.

There's more? Yep.

I had investigated the aircraft's directional stability. Aircraft should, in the main, have some. That is, they should fly like the darts being thrown by those chaps with the big tummies who like their beer. They should want to fly straight. Another way to think of this is like the weathercock you would get on a barn roof. You want the cock (so to speak) to be moved, by the attached vane, to point into the prevailing breeze.

That's why, pretty much every type of aircraft I can think of has some kind of weathervane down the back, usually known as the fin or fins. And then, again usually, a rudder would be bolted onto the fin so as to move in the airflow and allow the aircraft to be steered. Helicopters tend to have

The aircraft fitted with wool tufts to investigate the reason for the directional instability.

the fin but then mount a tail rotor there which kind of works like a rudder in forward flight.

Well, the RAF 2000 did not want to fly in a straight line and, even worse, instead of pointing into the prevailing breeze, it tended to want to point away from it. This could be overcome by frantically moving the rudder whichever way was required with your feet, but to do this added further 'workload' to the task of flying in a straight line.

Why was this happening, we queried? So, we did what all flight-test professionals do and resorted to lots of pieces, or tufts, of wool, which we taped all over the aircraft (see above photo). When I next flew, we filmed these tufts dancing in the airflow which confirmed exactly what we had guessed; that the cockpit or nose of the aircraft was forming an almost perfect wing shape stood on its end! It was creating lift just like an aeroplane wing. If we turned slightly in flight we created an angle of attack, which created lift, which continued to push the cockpit further away from flying straight (see Appendix 1). We had an aircraft that was directionally unstable. And there was lots of other bad stuff I noted like the difficulty of trimming etc. but for now the above will suffice. I went on to test the aircraft with the doors removed – and guess what?

Flying the RAF 2000 with the doors removed.

Are you ahead of me at this point?

Well the directional stability improved. What? Yep, taking the doors off created a turbulent flow around the aircraft that destroyed the tendency of the cockpit to act like a wing and, although not great, we had an aircraft that was technically compliant with the certification regulations.

So, what next? I'm guessing, by now, you've already worked it out; back to our accommodation for a pint of ale or three, and chance for Ray and I to discuss our thoughts for our Debrief Note. As always, this was a good cards on the table session. As Ray hadn't flown the aircraft he was able to ask me difficult questions and play Devil's Advocate. (We were both churchwardens at the time.)

The following morning, as per usual, we faced the stressful meeting to discuss our findings. At least, as about to be condemned men, we had found time for a hearty breakfast, possibly to delay the next part of the day as much as we could. It's funny – you would think flight test was all technical: computers, engines, gearboxes etc. Frankly, that's the easy part. The real job is all about people and invariably having to win over hearts and minds. In this case, we were not about to face the might of the Sikorsky boardroom but a dairy farmer sitting in a portacabin whose mainstay in life was teaching people to fly his RAF 2000 which we were just about to slag off, and I really, really hated being the bearer of bad news! If just once I could test the perfect aircraft …

A possible option, based on our findings, would have been to 'ground' the fleet of such aircraft. That would clearly have been a 'safe' option. But there would have been a whole host of owners who had spent lots of money on an aircraft that would become worthless overnight – lots of pain.

No, the pragmatic approach, as always, was called for. So, we started addressing each of the issues in turn. Lots of quirky aspects could be accepted given that the cadre of pilots flying these was very few. Marc had trained or flown with most of them, and ironically, they were all competent pilots. You couldn't fly this aircraft unless you were. Something about the Darwin theory of evolution springs to mind …

The worst aspect was the divergent roller-coaster ride that occurred with increasing speed. We were content that, at slower speeds, used when preparing to land etc., the aircraft flew well enough. The main problem was at the higher cruise speeds. So, we started discussing a reduced speed limit. In the USA these aircraft were allowed to fly at 120 mph and up until now, 100 mph in the UK.

We debated where the aircraft's handling went from benign to difficult and, I will not bore you with all the ins and outs but, we ended up with 70 mph as an absolute maximum speed with an expectation that most people would then fly slightly slower.

Next, we turned our attention to the directional instability which was in clear contravention of our certification requirements. We discussed possible solutions which all centred around increasing the fin area at the back of the aircraft and, ideally, having additional fins that were not masked by the relatively large bulk of the cockpit. This kind of 'fix' was going to take a while to sort out but we had already identified that the aircraft was just about compliant with the requirements if we removed the doors. This was a job of only a few seconds as the doors were designed to be removed easily for flying in warmer climates. We wish! … So, if we allowed the aircraft to be flown without the doors fitted, at no faster than 70 mph, we were getting somewhere. Again, this was a pragmatic solution. It kept these aircraft flying until the fix could be sorted but you can imagine how popular I was, with the winter coming up, forcing pilots to fly exposed to the elements. But all the other types of gyros at that time had open cockpits anyway.

So, we said our goodbyes to Marc with the hope that he realised we were doing our best for the community whilst also trying to keep fellow gyro pilots safer.

Ray and I continued to do our best for the poor RAF 2000 and we had been communicating with the manufacturer out in Canada. They had made some changes to their company demonstrator aircraft and told us, in black and white, that their modified aircraft could be flown hands off at 120 mph. Now, this statement, if true, represented a major change to our findings and I was keen to investigate further. So, I pestered until we received an invitation. The next snag was funding … we became victims of our own pragmatic solution. If the aircraft could be flown around, safely enough, slowly without its doors fitted, why spend money on sending me out to the far side of Canada? A good point, which was loudly and repeatedly made. But I persevered in making my case. A few days later I was in Connecticut, visiting Sikorsky for a series of meetings about a new helicopter (S76D) I would be testing in the future, and I received a phone call from my boss,

'How quickly can you be at the local airport?'

'Why?'

'Turns out the AAIB have some funds to enable you to get to Canada and they want you there now.'

This was pre-smartphones, but some frantic phoning around had me in a car being whisked to the airport and on a flight to Toronto. I needed to get to Medicine Hat. Where? Medicine Hat. Google it (started out because the railway went through it). I had never heard of it and hadn't got a clue how to get there but someone was working on that for me and had lined up an onward flight to Calgary. Where? Calgary – known for cattle drives. In the foothills of the Rockies.

My flight was running late and landed at Toronto with a tight connection. Who knew you could build airports with terminal buildings so large? In the UK we are always cramming as much as we can onto a postage stamp of ground. Out there it was the other way around. So where is gate number 125 when I'm now at gate 7? A hell of a long way away it turned out! My casual international traveller image was about to be dashed when I started counting – 8, 9, 10, 11, 12 …

Minutes ebbed away and I realised I was about to miss the last flight out of the place and that was going to be a real drama as I was due to be testing the gyro at dawn the following morning so I could get home again for the weekend. Hurray. And how on earth could I explain a failure to get there when I'd been pushing so hard for so long to justify the trip and the AAIB had struggled to find the funding. I confess, I saw my impending 'Bollocking' flash before me in stark technicolour.

Now, I'm not athletic but, when it comes to running for buses, trains and planes or chasing after my grandson scooting downhill on his two-wheeler, I seem to have developed a different set of legs and those I now employed. How I ran; my poor carry-on wheely-bag wheels were red hot before I sighted my destination gate. No passengers in sight, all already safely onboard reading their in-flight mag, I threw myself forward like a sprinter to scrape through the gate as they pulled the 'closed' rope across. Just like on my earlier trip to Poland, the cabin staff were closing the door as I stepped on board; not at all the suave international traveller, more the sweaty red faced blob too breathless to say my own seat number. But just so incredibly relieved to have made the last flight I sank into my plastic seat, fastened my seat belt and minutes later we were safely airborne for an internal flight that lasted forever before being the last aircraft to land at Calgary. I was the last to make it to the Avis desk and was thrown the keys to their last car that I still can't remember anything about. They gave me a 'map of the world' on a sheet of A4 and off I set heading east, as fast as I dare drive, as it was getting really late. But I can tell you this for free: when the following day, in daylight, I saw all the hazards on the road, such as cattle and train crossings etc., it's probably just as well I couldn't see anything much in the dark.

I have no idea when I got to my motel, but I was checking out, what felt like, moments later, still dark pre-dawn, to meet my host at the local airfield. Now this guy was the company instructor and development test pilot. He had logged about 2,000 flying hours, and all of them in RAF 2000s. Given what I now knew of the aircraft, that made him either an extremely competent pilot, or a very lucky one. But, and this is always a challenge in my game, he knew little else. So when I was trying to explain the issues we'd already identified he had no other benchmark to compare his beloved RAF 2000 with. Anyway, I did the usual, told some war stories, established a rapport (I hope), chatted about him and the aircraft, and then we set off, to hopefully experience an aircraft with all the issues sorted …

And what do you think? Issues sorted, Hurrah?

Well … no. I confess I almost cried. I had so hoped that this version would fly well.

There was some good news.

Firstly, it was an absolutely cracking morning to go flying! The air was beautifully still; not a breath of wind, the air icy cold from the night before, with the cloudless sky still tinged red from a 'Wild West' kind of dawn. I always have to pinch myself when I get to go flying in such moments.

Secondly, the aircraft was being investigated by a company for use as a drone and they had put lots of instrumentation into it to record what all the controls did and how the aircraft responded. So at last I would have the formal proof of how this aircraft flew.

We flew out over a large expanse of nothingness with me applying all my usual tests:

Directional Stability = Pants. Phugoid = still just as bad.

Returning to the airfield, at a punchy 120 mph I was able to gather lots of data which illustrated the aircraft's issues without any further doubt. Landing as smoothly as I could to impress my host I then explained what

Canadian RAF2000 prior to flight testing.

I thought of it. Yep, this remains an ugly baby. That's a hard discussion to have with a bloke that's flown nothing else and relies on the manufacturer as his main source of income. And so before he became too morose I beat a hasty retreat to my rental, to dash back to Calgary, to zip to Toronto, and finally I made it onto my flight to LHR where I could order a large Chardonnay or three and allow my adrenalin to be restored to more normal levels as I reflected on another flight in another potential deathtrap and nearly missed commercial flights of the last twenty-four hours.

Phew! …

But the Gyro world is a small world and someone within it was working on a better solution than the Canadians …

So many, many, many moons ago, a bloke called Ronnie went out with the girl my brother subsequently married. Ronnie was a car mechanic by trade and, despite what you might think would be awkward, he ended up being the go-to fixer of all my brother's cars, including the ex-company car I used to drive. Many years ago I was introduced to Ronnie, who at the time owned a nice, but elderly Jodell D120 aircraft which he flew from a steeply sloping farm strip on the moors somewhere up north, and I was kindly given a go. This was long before my TP days and, to be honest my landing wasn't my best. I half expected the wheels to come up through the wings, but obviously this mostly wooden aeroplane had been well assembled.

Anyway, it turns out Ronnie had become bored with aeroplanes and had learned how to fly gyros, buying himself an RAF 2000 along the way. Being a practical fella, he had done his own investigation of other modifications made to the aircraft and, with plagiarism being all fair in love and aviation, decided to copy and improve upon a replacement tail unit for the aircraft, which he did, and guess what? Yep, suddenly my name was in the frame to test it bolted to another RAF 2000 up in Yorkshire. Not ideal, but it did provide the opportunity to fly with Dave again and we flew a couple of trips together before I went off on my own to do the formal testing.

Ronnie's mod had noticeably improved the way the aircraft flew. It was now directionally stable and the roller-coaster effects were less pronounced and the aircraft could be flown safely a bit faster than before. Well done Ronnie. My flight testing and Ronnie's tail had thankfully produced a safer aircraft.

Flying the RAF 2000 with Ronnie's tail fitted.

Phew! ... Good Result. Break out the fizzy wine.

But the aircraft was not yet done with trying to kill me. Eighteen months later I found myself strapping in to another RAF 2000 at Blackbushe airfield near the M3. We had tested a prototype tail previously and now a production version was available and so I was to test it fitted to two further aircraft. I tested the first aircraft at Little Rissington, an old RAF base in the Cotswolds where my parents had taken me on holidays to watch shiny Jet Provosts of the Central Flying School doing their thing. All went well and I was now due to fly an aircraft that had a reputation for being a bit of a dog. This was my last flight test of the year before I started Christmas leave. In my experience, for some reason, the last flight before a leave period, or even flights late on a Friday afternoon, are more troublesome. I have encountered all sorts of difficulties on such flights with the ramifications often impacting on weekends or days off. Anyway, it was December, it was cold and dank and the cloud was low enough to make my required test flying only just legal. But with lots of folks waiting on my, hopefully, positive, report it was churlish not to do the best I could. I am risk averse; you will have gathered this already. So I commenced my testing with all my test points conducted flying along the in-use runway; therefore an easy decision on where to land should bad things happen.

The first sortie went okay but for some reason this was a dog. And even with the Ronnie tail it didn't fly well. Although in fairness, it would have been an awful lot worse without it. The second sortie involved assessing the aircraft's characteristics following sudden engine failures, known in the trade as 'throttle chops'. I was no fool (or so I thought) and aimed to conduct these at the landing end of the runway just in case.

You are way ahead of me here aren't you?

'Standby' – I say to myself, 'cos I'm on my own … '3–2–1–*now.*'

Throttle smartly closed – stick pushed forward to adopt a glide attitude and maintain my precious airspeed … 'Rather quiet isn't it?'

Yep – this was an engine that didn't like simulation – it liked the real thing.

Great. I was not that surprised, nor that concerned. By now, I was used to engines stopping and generally to quote me, 'If you're going to have an engine failure in a single-engine aircraft then have it in a gyro.'

So I let my Guardian Angel sleep in, and I maintained my glide until the optimum moment then gradually flared the aircraft by smoothly moving the stick aft. The wind was blowing at 10 knots from my left at right angles to the runway. No drama, I think; I just need to ensure I keep the airspeed up in order to have enough airflow over the rudder so that I can keep it straight and, if I say so myself, I was doing an ace job. Nicely on the runway centreline ten inches above the tarmac, speed nicely washing off, rate of descent now all but zero. And the crowd went wild (in my head) as I creamed it onto the ground with the two mainwheels making perfect and gentle contact with Mother Earth.

Phew! … Survived another, I think …

But, what's that expression? – 'It ain't over until the fat lady sings?'

My version, developed over a few years of flight testing, is along the lines of 'it ain't over until I'm on the ground quaffing my first glass of vino!'

And so it was …

My drama wasn't over. It was just beginning.

I was on my own, so that there was minimal weight in the cockpit which meant there was next to no weight over the nose-wheel.

The nose-wheel was connected to the rudder and provided the steering on the ground but couldn't if the nose-wheel wasn't actually on the ground.

The brakes were on the mainwheels and were operated by a foot lever which required the pilot's feet to be removed from the rudder bar to operate. So you could try and steer, or try and slow down, but couldn't do both at the same time.

And so my fun began; on the ground doing 30 mph, which suddenly felt very fast for a change, I was balanced on the rear wheels keeping straight with rudder but now the wind from the left started to take charge and I began to yaw/turn rapidly left, which as a consequence, lifted the left wheel off the ground. So, I'm suddenly piloting a monocycle with a mind of its own.

I was desperate to slam on the brakes but my feet were at this point interested in their own salvation and were pedalling the rudder as fast as they could in an attempt to counter the wind. They succeeded – but too much already – as I rolled the aircraft onto the other mainwheel.

RAF 2000 tested at Blackbushe. Note the tendency for the nose-wheel to end up off the ground.

'Well, keeps the tyre wear even,' I think.

This lurch is worse than the first and there is a danger the rather large rotor blades will make contact with something solid.

'Come on Taylor. More effort required here; get a grip!'

I now had managed to gather quite an audience including the now very bemused and concerned owner.

Anyway, I should have taken tap dancing lessons as a kid, as it appeared I have an aptitude for it. Full rudder, hammer the brake, full rudder, hammer the brake, full stick, keep the rotors level, more rudder, more brake, more dancing ... and, finally, it all stopped. And was very quiet.

Phew! ... I had survived a potentially very embarrassing outcome which would have ruined my Christmas.

My mate, Jeff, has some lovely video of me becoming the lead test pilot in the latest craze of trying not to crash in a 30-mph shopping trolley. Time to beat a hasty retreat and commence my Christmas activities with the application of a large tumbler of white port to calm my nerves as soon as I got home.

Some years later when self-employed I was again invited to fly an RAF2000 in order to clear a modified design for a permit issue. Guess what? The engine stopped – there was a crosswind blowing across the in use runway – what do you think I did?

Yep, a smart wiggling of the controls and I landed directly across the runway – nice and safely into wind – I'm a slow learner but I get there in the end ...

Chapter 9

Achtung Spitfire

We nosed over into the dive to accelerate this Spitfire to the fastest it had flown since it left the Castle Bromwich factory in 1945 and as we flew faster and faster I became more and more concerned we were about to, literally, rip the wings off.

Well, let's be honest. I had always wanted to fly a Spitfire ever since I first started reading war comics as a kid; followed by lots of books from W.E. Johns about Biggles who seemed to fly anything and everything but especially Sopwith Camels and Spitfires. I confess, as a serving RN helicopter pilot I had surmised the chances of my ever having the chance to fly in this iconic aircraft were very slim – well, zero, frankly.

The Fleet Air Arm did own and operate some historic aircraft which serving pilots were sometimes lucky enough to fly but, with a line of Sea

Spitfire TR.9 G-ILDA at Kemble prior to testing.

Harrier pilots well ahead of me in the queue, that was never going to happen. Not helped by my base throughout my operational flying days being Portland, which had a large helipad but did not have a runway long enough for fixed-wing aircraft. However, as you will now have gathered, ten years at Boscombe Down flying all sorts of aeroplanes led the way to my joining the Civil Aviation Authority as their fixed wing aeroplane test pilot for 'light aeroplanes'. This included all the historic types on the UK register. I've already written about the jets but also included on my 'slop chit' were all the warbirds you can think of. I was responsible for answering all manner of difficult questions about these aircraft to my non-flying colleagues. So, I needed to get up to speed as soon as I could.

So easy-peasy you might think? I would be up to my eyes in Merlin-powered aeroplanes before you could blink, but it was not that straightforward. Firstly, it's fair to say that these aircraft generally are worth a heck of a lot of money. In fact, one chap I had dealings with described his P-51D Mustang as his pension plan. He was seeing it accumulate in value and expected it to be a hugely rewarding investment. Sadly, the aircraft collided with another warbird during an air display and was destroyed, with the pilot managing a very fortunate abandonment in a parachute just in the nick of time.

So, I understood that such aircraft were prized assets and, as this book should have made plain, I did not have the arrogance to assume I could leap into a cockpit and fly anything better than a pilot with more relevant experience. Although, as the years have gone by, I have come to believe this false modesty is a flawed view. I set about doing my best to become as well-informed and expert as I could be. We had next to no money in the CAA available for training, but I managed to prise a few quid from the clenched fist of my boss and off I went to Duxford. Duxford has an illustrious history. Built in 1918, it served as an RAF aerodrome until 1961, seeing the first operational Spitfires in 1939 and hosting Douglas Bader for a period. In the second half of the Second World War it hosted numerous American squadrons from the Eighth Air Force and even had a Concorde land there in the 1970s before, sadly, the M11 motorway was built which clipped off one end of the main runway. But, despite that, the airfield has become home to the Imperial War Museum collection of aircraft and the American Air Museum. Additionally, a number of aircraft companies have decided to base their operations there, so it has become a real hub for the restoration, repair and operation of Second World War aircraft, especially the single-engine fighters.

Anyway, off I went and spent my hard-won cash on a training flight, learning how to fly the Harvard. I had already flown the Harvard at Boscombe Down where it was still being used as a photographic chase aircraft for trials. It had two seats in tandem and a big rear cockpit with windows that could be slid wide open to allow good photos to be taken. So, I was happy in the cockpit and filled an enjoyable hour ensuring I could fly the type safely again. The Harvard was a wartime trainer that effectively bridged the gap between lightweight Tiger Moths and the more heavy-metal operational aircraft. Over my years at the CAA I test-flew a good number of various variants of Harvards or T-6 Texans as they were known in the US. In the main it was a relatively straightforward aircraft to operate and fly, but with a significant vice. When you were in the landing configuration (with undercarriage and flap deployed) and flew slowly enough, it would stall with minimal warning. Almost without fail the right wing would drop viciously. Not clever if you were in a right-hand circuit turning at low level onto the final approach. A number of Harvards were lost during the war in training accidents, especially when teaching night flying, when poor visual cues could lead to an unobserved loss of airspeed.

One of the many Harvards flight tested for permit renewal purposes.

Having cracked the Harvard, I continued to grow my warbird experience as best I could and went to visit most of the companies rebuilding such aircraft. I also did my best to spend some of our constrained training budget on a training flight in a two-seat Spitfire but for some reason the aircraft were never available when I was?! So, as with the jets, I restricted my testing to two-seaters where I could fly with the owner or another nominated pilot so that there could be no reasonable objection.

My first such flight was, I can honestly say, amongst my least enjoyable flying experiences to date. At the time these aircraft were issued with Annual Permits that allowed them to fly as UK registered aircraft. As part of the permit renewal a check flight was required to demonstrate that the aircraft still performed and handled as it should do. So, the aircraft would be climbed at full power for five minutes, the speed at which it stalled would be checked and how it handled would be assessed as well as all the various systems such as flaps and undercarriage functioned. It was, I believe, not an overly onerous test and on simple aircraft could be completed in around forty-five minutes without undue haste. I would, as the CAA agent, conduct a number of these MOT test fights, but we would delegate the vast majority to trusted, experienced pilots who we would brief and approve in order for them to be added to our database of bona fide check pilots.

I was in the office on one occasion and I was shown the completed proforma from a recent P-51D check flight. All looked absolutely fine.

'So what's the problem?' I asked.

I was then shown the completed proforma from the previous year's check flight. Apart from the date, it was exactly the same. In fact, I think even the handwritten text was the same. Now call me suspicious if you like, but no aircraft flies an identical five-minute climb every single time. Something was very fishy indeed. I will not bore you with the details but, suffice to say, following a conversation or two, I found myself standing on the grass runway at Compton Abbas awaiting the arrival of this particular P-51D. Surely I was looking forward to this sortie? I was about to fly in an iconic warbird, albeit in the rear passenger seat. I would be lying if I didn't confess to being rather excited when the silver aircraft hove into view and, with the Merlin engine at idle and gear and flap down, it skimmed over the hedge at the easterly end of the airfield and gracefully touched town in a three-point attitude. Despite my distrust of the said

P51D Mustang at Compton Abbas prior to flight test.

pilot we chatted over a coffee and I re-briefed the importance of these check flights. Minutes later the Merlin engine coughed into a noisy existence and we rumbled across the rough chalky surface of the grass runway before gaining flying speed and turning south-east towards the Isle of Wight in order to conduct an academic climb followed by some stalling. Surely this must have been fun? Flying in a genuine Second World War fighter?

How could this not be a pleasant day out? I was doing what loads of folks would have paid good money to do, surely? Well, not really. I was trying to gather data to help determine whether this aircraft was safe to fly and thus have its permit renewed. I was also trying to stop the guy in the front flying me into bits of airspace he wasn't allowed into. For some reason he was making no effort to navigate, perhaps because he was finally having to fly the aircraft as required for the check flight. Where I was positioned was incredibly noisy, the intercom was very poor and my cheap nasty headset was frankly not fit for purpose. Also, I hate being a passenger in an aircraft I have no control over just as I hate riding on the backs of motorbikes. (I only did it once, with a fellow university student, at night, doing 70 mph around the inner ring road in Birmingham through underpass after underpass. I've never been back on a motorbike since.) I'm very happy sitting there letting the other pilot fly so as long as I can intervene if I have to. (Believe me, I have lost count of the number of times as an instructor, examiner and test pilot where I have had to intervene to save our bacon.) It was another flight where I was glad to kiss the ground as soon as I'd extricated myself from my cramped and uncomfortable seat. Still, it was worth it to gain firsthand experience of that type and it had helped to grow my overall knowledge of such aircraft.

For a Fleet Air Arm pilot there are a number of iconic aircraft; certainly, the Fairey Swordfish that flew with open cockpits for many hours over the Atlantic and the Med attacking with its single torpedo such ships as the *Bismarck*. However the post-war Sea Fury was the FAA aircraft of choice. Designed just too late for service in the Second World War it is probably fair to say it marked the pinnacle of single-piston-engine fighter development. In the Korean War the FAA took full part with the Sea Fury being its main fighter – and it shot down a jet. Albeit a rather crude MiG 15, but a jet nonetheless.

So, it was with a real sense of excitement that I 'rocked up' to an airfield not far from the M25 ring where I had been asked to formally test fly a rebuilt Sea Fury T.20.

Sea Fury at North Weald ready to taxi for flight test.

Unfolding the wings after start.

The shakedown flying to date had been done by Chris, a Sea Harrier pilot and a graduate TP of ETPS, and I was confident reading his reports and hearing his debrief that the aircraft had been well put together. I flew from the rear seat but had a good field of view and thoroughly enjoyed unfolding the wings (required for ship-based operations).

Taxiing was straightforward and, despite the huge amount of power on tap, it was easy to keep straight on take-off and we leapt airborne to find a clear bit of suitable airspace. I found the aircraft delightful to fly. It was much like flying the smaller and well-known de Havilland Chipmunk. The controls were all nicely harmonised, the performance was great, and it was mildly stable. The power control was ahead of its time by effectively producing a go-faster lever. The lever managed throttle and pitch on the propeller blades to give the aircraft the optimum combination. The aircraft's only vice seemed to be to flick rather aggressively when getting too slow in manoeuvres. I flew a couple of barrel rolls and with little warning found myself rapidly flicking through 180 degrees.

Back home for tea and medals and a bollocking. Although I answered the phone from the local air traffic control (ATC) agency I had not been made aware that one of our black boxes that transmits a code to the ground wasn't working and we'd had to fly in airspace where we should have had one. Thankfully, I hadn't signed for the aircraft, so promptly passed the phone over to Chris who became somewhat flushed as he appropriately ate humble pie. Chris went on to display the aircraft for a number of summer seasons for the Royal Navy and was boss of the RN's Historic Flight for a while, so his bollocking on this particular day had not held him back any.

So often, as I've already said, the challenges in my job are people rather than machinery. A good example was the North American Yale. The Yale with fixed undercarriage was effectively the predecessor to the Harvard. A batch ordered by the French was diverted to Britain after France fell in 1940 and they were used extensively as wartime trainers in Canada. Again, given that this was the only one of its type in the UK (a two-seater), it was the responsibility of the CAA to ensure the type was safe to be flown. So, the company where the aircraft was rebuilt was duly contacted, the matter discussed and an agreement reached that the CAA would complete the formal flight testing of the aircraft, i.e. I would. It came as a surprise some days later to receive, in the office at Gatwick, completed flight-test paperwork for the aircraft. However, the requirement for the CAA to conduct the testing had been made crystal clear and agreed. So yet again I found myself not receiving the warmest of welcomes to test fly an aircraft. I was looked after by another ex-military

Sea Fury ready to taxi.

helicopter pilot who had flown the aircraft just once. He was happy to sit in the rear seat and help me by scribbling down all the gathered numbers and data, and off we went, on a pleasant January day. All went well up until I got to the part where I tested slow speed flight and allowed the aircraft to stall. As previously mentioned, I was comfortable testing the Harvard and was ready for a Harvard-like response … but that was not what I got at all. Basically, as I slowed down nothing much happened, although the controls became a little sloppy and then – *Whap!* The joystick literally jumped to the right almost out of my hand, with a subsequent instant drop of the right wing through over 90 degrees. Now that was exciting. The stalling was investigated further with similarly very exciting and potentially dangerous characteristics being evident with and without flap, with and without power. So back to base to talk about the ugly baby. On the way I invited the pilot in the rear to stall the aircraft also so that there would be no doubt that this was an aircraft rather than a pilot issue; and he found the same.

On the ground I reviewed the paperwork already submitted. No mention of this alarming characteristic. On phoning the pilot who had submitted this paperwork I queried his findings. And guess what? When pressed,

Yale Aircraft prior to flight test.

he admitted he'd had similar issues. For some reason a slight mismatch in recollection and paperwork methinks? His eventual confession cited his concern that, if he had included the correct data, the CAA might have declined to issue the aircraft with a permit to fly. However, there was no problem with me accepting this aircraft on to a UK permit. It was not a public transport airliner certified in modern times. It was a historic aircraft, with characteristics deemed acceptable in 1935. What I had to do was ensure its modern-day operators were aware of the issue and flew accordingly. Some bold words in the aircraft's manual made sure of that and everyone was happy, and no one died.

Phew! … Good result.

Another challenging conundrum along similar lines was generated from my involvement with the Morane Saulnier MS 733 Alcycon. This was a side-by-side trainer built in the 1950s for the French navy. After less than a decade in military service it had found its way into civilian flying clubs in France and then was eventually bought and brought to the UK. The aircraft was restored and tested from Spanhoe, originally a USAAF wartime base, operating C-47s, until it closed in 1946. Now Spanhoe was not my favourite venue by any means. Located in the black hole north of Corby and east of Leicester it was, frankly, a painful drive to get there. Then there was the issue of runways. The east-west runway comprised a narrow 600-metre part of tatty concrete wartime taxiway with the first 90 metres of the total available distance being rather soggy soft grass. The alternative runway was all grass but also quite soft and only 500 metres long; both runways were approached over tall bushes. In addition, it was always a struggle to get much help from anybody based there; I always felt like I was on my own.

My first take off was undertaken at a modest weight, deliberately not the maximum weight by any means. I taxied the aircraft so that the tail was almost touching the hedge at one end of the field, applying power against the brakes to get the thing spooled up as much as I could. Then, with the aircraft starting to shudder a little and the wheels slipping on the wet grass, I let the brakes go. All of a sudden very little happened, that is apart from the aircraft wanting to skip sideways. It certainly didn't want to accelerate down the runway. Eventually I started gathering speed as grass turned to concrete and the far end hedge grew ever larger. As soon as I dared, I pulled the stick back transiently to force the aircraft to hop

Morane Saulnier MS 733 Alcycon at Spanhoe prior to flight test.

just a few inches into the air, but stayed 'hugging' the ground in ground effect, which helps produce lift. I could then raise the undercarriage which reduced the drag, enough to allow this brick shithouse to accelerate to climbing speed as the end of the runway approached. Oh what fun I mused, as I cleared the far-end hedge.

The landings were OK but it dropped like a brick as soon as power was removed or airspeed reduced, not easy to fly into a short strip. When I complained to the maintenance organisation about the poor performance, they told me to let the engine rev faster. I'd used the book figure of a maximum of 2,530 rpm, but they advocated 2,700 rpm. But based on what? Apparently, it turns out, based on some folklore anecdotal myth that the French revved the engines faster for take-off. Well maybe they did? Or maybe they didn't? But they were not allowed to. The engine speed limits were pretty clearly laid down.

So yet again I was the bearer of bad news. No you can't over-rev the engine to get airborne out of a 700-metre strip. You need to fly from a longer runway. The following year I returned to Spanhoe where the owner swore that he hadn't exceeded the engine limits, although to not do so required an incredibly finely judged take-off technique, particularly at maximum weight and with no wind. During this flight I again had to test the aircraft at its maximum speed. Although I needed a steep dive

MS733 Cockpit. Note the placard that states the maximum engine rpm of 2530 rpm but the red line on the rpm gauge is placed at 2700 rpm.

angle, and had to reduce the propeller rpm to prevent an overspeed, the aircraft seemed to behave itself.

120 … 130 … 140 … 150 … 160 … 170 … 180 … 185 … 187 … 189 … 190 … *Bang!*

Just as I reached max chat, with barely a rattle previously – Bang! My canopy, without warning, jumped off its rails. The rails allowed the heavy canopy to be moved fore and aft to allow entry and egress. Not the biggest drama in my aviation career I initially surmised and I promptly turned for home as I was desperately in need of a pee, as usual. I carried out another of my expert touch-downs, taxiing promptly to where I could exit for the nearest urinal without delay. Parking brake applied, engine fuel cut-off operated, mags off … and simultaneously the canopy opening handle reached for. I had expected a few rapid turns to open a sufficient gap for me to hurl myself out onto the wing. But … no. This aeroplane was about to have the last laugh following my recent criticisms and, despite my desperate demeanour, it just refused to let me out. The heavy canopy, having jumped its rails, was far too heavy for me to move. 'Bugger!'

Stuck in an aeroplane on a deserted airfield with a bursting bladder. It was at times like this that I reflected on the glamorous lifestyle of a modern-day test pilot. I'm pretty sure Chuck Yeager would not have suffered the same fate. Thankfully I had a policy of never getting airborne without my mobile phone and was able to call for help. It took six blokes to lift the canopy back onto the opening mechanism ... Within seconds of this being achieved, I was leaping out and sprinting to the nearest hedgerow ...

Phew! ... the relief ...

I confess, I never did solve the engine rpm issue. I did as much research as I could and found no substantive data that allowed over-revving the engine, even for take off. So, ultimately, I had to follow in the footsteps of my fellow fishhead, Nelson. Knowing that the owner was likely to over-rev the engine, if required, to avoid impacting the hedge, I could only tell him not to and leave him to face any costly engine repairs that might come his way ...

The Nord 1101 was another sorry saga. A 1950s French-built aircraft based on the Messerschmitt Bf 108 which had been built in occupied France in the latter half of the war. This particular example had been crashed, rebuilt and then unsatisfactorily test flown by someone who should have known better and, quite rightly, I was despatched by the CAA to conduct a proper test flight. Now, funny old thing, I pestered and pestered to gain access to the aircraft and finally was invited to fly it at the very end of the day on a Friday afternoon in February. The cynic in me speculated that this was a cunning ploy in the hope that the prospect of driving home in Friday rush hour would deter me, but it took more than that I'm afraid.

Flying late in the day in the winter is less than ideal and this was a very tatty aircraft. I was teamed up with the pilot who hadn't completed the previous testing properly and was able to re-brief him on the error of his ways. Although the aircraft had lots of minor snags which should have been documented and fixed it flew better than it looked and I was able to recommend permit issue once all the defects had been rectified. But I decided I had no great desire to fly any more Nords unless I really had to.

One of the nicest warbirds I was asked to test was the Fieseler Fi.156 Storch. Built in Germany in 1942 but operated in France for many years after the war, the aircraft was owned by Peter who, if memory serves,

Nord prior to flight test late on a Friday afternoon.

made a fair amount of money in the hairdressing business, which he proceeded to spend buying up an interesting collection of historic aircraft, many of German origin. Airworthiness oversight of this aircraft was to be transferred from the CAA to the Light Aircraft Association and, somewhere along the way, it was agreed I would do a formal flight test on the aircraft as part of that process. So, I rocked up to Old Warden where the aircraft was hangared and maintained (and flown from time to time alongside Shuttleworth collection aircraft). The Shuttleworth Collection Chief Pilot and a graduate test pilot from the USAF school at Edwards agreed to ride in the passenger seat in the back (despite there being no flying controls there) and point me in the right direction both in terms of 'knobs, levers and switches' and the local airfield procedures. Now this was more like it, a very nicely presented aircraft with a nearly new appearance in a smart Luftwaffe colour scheme.

Although the aircraft had a very, very poor rate of climb, it flew so slowly that the angle of climb was acceptable. The aircraft was the helicopter of its day and had extremely good low-speed flying characteristics, being able to fly more slowly than most of the current crop of microlight aircraft gracing our skies right now. The stall when it happened was very gentle with no drama and all this led to being able to approach the landing site at around 40 mph. The other really great feature was the long front undercarriage legs with long stroking oleos to damp the bumps on touch-down. I remarked upon the topic, having done one of my best landings

Fieseler Storch at Old Warden prior to flight test.

ever, stating that it was virtually impossible to know quite when you had landed. My back seater for the day told me that one of his colleagues, landing at the end of a display, thought he was about to make a hash of the landing and decided to apply full power and overshoot for a further attempt. In fact, he'd already landed but just didn't know it. Now, if only I could have done my basic Private Pilot's Licence (PPL) training on such an aircraft instead of the Cessnas which I always seemed able to bounce; well with an instructor onboard anyway. The Storch was a really interesting aircraft to test fly and I could now totally believe all the historical anecdotes about Hitler being picked up from the centre of Berlin in such an aircraft. Flown by an experienced pilot into any kind of wind it could be landed on a postage stamp for sure.

But back to the title of the chapter, I had been nobbled by one of the CAA airworthiness guys who wanted me to get involved with this particular warbird project. A Spitfire Mk 9 was being rebuilt as a two-seater with dual controls, not by one of the established companies, but by another team who had refurbished Chipmunks and a Harvard. This was their most complex project to date. So, I contacted the company in my usual friendly manner and asked to conduct one of the planned flight-test sorties with any other pilot they wanted to join me. Well, I have to say my request was again not greeted warmly. Over the next few months, some of the emails originating from this organisation that arrived late in

Storch cockpit.

the evening, and their reluctance to engage with the regulator, frankly gave me countless sleepless nights. But the day came when we had finally agreed I would participate in a single test flight flying from the rear cockpit.

Spitfire TR9 prior to my initial flight test. Note the Dutch colour scheme.

I had already flown previously with their nominated project pilot who, whilst not being a test pilot, was a familiar sight on the UK display circuit and had some previous experience of flying Spitfires. As usual, we chewed the fat as I tried to discover how the flight-test programme had gone so far, what they'd achieved, issues identified etc., but, frankly, I didn't

TR9 Rear cockpit.

learn much. So, after spending some time acquainting myself with all the knobs, levers, dials and controls in my seat and breathing in the aroma of oil and metal and leather evocative of another age, off we set.

So, after all those childhood years of growing up, reading my war comics and building my Airfix kits at the weekends, I was finally fulfilling

Front cockpit.

a genuine aspiration; I was flying a Vickers Supermarine Spitfire Mk 9, just as numerous war heroes and aces who had gone before me. Again, you would have thought this would have been an enjoyable trip, but sadly not. That said, I did have a 'pinch myself', moment when, on a beautifully crisp blue skied December morning, I found myself flying past the Stonehenge stones seen just ahead of my iconic elliptical wing tip. There really isn't a nicer wing, from an aesthetical and to some extent aerodynamic perspective, and placed adjacent to the ancient stones of Stonehenge seemed to capture thousands of years of history in a moment.

The aircraft had been ballasted with 20 kg of lead mounted on the tail so I could test the aircraft with its centre of gravity (CG) at the rear permissible limit. In practice, wartime Spitfires had a more forward CG, especially with lots of ammo to feed their machine guns and cannon, but the agreed test plan required testing at both the full-forward and full-aft limits. The project pilot had flown the forward CG flight solo and apparently checked the accuracy of the airspeed indicator by flying in formation with a Harvard at up to 180 mph. What was the aircraft like to fly? Well, at this loading it was in certain configurations unstable, this included the climb configuration and the approach configuration. It was also laterally unstable on the approach which meant that flying 'cross–controlled' to be able to see past the large nose would be difficult. In practice, wartime pilots of the Spitfire and other aircraft with limited forward view like the Corsair would fly to touchdown in a progressive curved approach, only levelling the wings over the hedge or back of the carrier for my Fleet Air Arm brethren.

Flying the aircraft slowly was very benign and when it stalled it gave good warning and didn't, like the Harvard, drop a wing or some such. So far so good. I was rattling through my test points with most in the bag. The final test was to dive the aircraft to its maximum operational speed plus an extra 11 per cent (to give a safety margin in service) in a similar fashion to the MS 733 as described above. I needed to ensure that all the controls worked normally, that we didn't have any excessive vibration or loose panels and that structurally the aircraft was sound. So, having climbed high enough to allow plenty of room for a shallow dive, I went through my usual routine of doing HASEL checks. These are used by both aeroplane and helicopter pilots prior to doing certain exercises such as stalling, spinning or auto-rotations. I've used them or abused them for my day job modified to suit the task. So in this case:

H   Height: am I starting high enough to achieve the speed before hitting the ground?

A   Airframe: am I sure the flaps and wheels are up and the canopy locked shut etc.

S   Security: am I and my fellow pilot secure in our straps? Are we free of any loose articles?

E   Engine: is the propeller set to the best rpm. Will the engine give enough power? Might it suffer from getting too cold or too hot?

L   Location: am I clear of airfields, built-up areas, controlled airspace and danger areas

L   Lookout: have a good look out below the aircraft to ensure it's clear.

With checks done I could no longer find any excuse for putting off the inevitable, so I applied full power and, with my usual amount of mild trepidation, gently nosed over to accelerate to a target speed of 443 mph. As you've read already, I've had bad things happen previously doing this. In addition to lifting canopies, I've had windscreens bend inwards, had air vents pop open and inspection panels torn off ... So here I go again ...

150 ... 160 ... 170 ... 180 ... 190 ... 200 ...

Phew! ... so far so good – wind noise noticeable but not intrusive, ailerons starting to float up a little, OK, no excessive vibration, OK, ... 210 ... 220 ... 230 ... 240 ... 250 ... 260 ... 270 ... 280 ...

Now one of the joys (or lack thereof) of being a helicopter test pilot is that, for some reason, you develop a canny knack of picking up negative waves (to quote Oddball from 'Kelly's Heroes'). Maybe it's because we are held aloft by hundreds of moving parts, anyone of which might kill us if it breaks? Or maybe it's because we become used to sensing a minimal change in noise or vibration? Or maybe it's because the slightest change in wind direction can easily embarrass us on landing? I don't know; but quite soon after I had passed 200 mph I found the hairs on the back of my neck rising. We were using the airspeed indication from the front cockpit as the master, as allegedly it was the more accurate one and the pilot in the front was urging me to fly faster and faster so we could get the job done and go home.

At an indicated speed of less than 300 mph I took in the wind noise, the vibration, the angle of the ailerons on each wing, the rattle of the canopy, the forward stick force and, despite protestations from the front-seat occupant urging me to dive faster, my personal alarm bells started to ring – very loudly. I decided that discretion was the better part of valour and my feeling of uneasiness needed to be resolved. So, I gently eased back on the joystick, while closing the throttle to return the aircraft to a level attitude and more sensible speed to fly gently home.

Phew! What now?

As is so often the case, on landing I was met by engineers bemused by my unwillingness to fly their beautiful machine as required and I found myself having to justify my reluctance to exceed 300 mph. Back then we didn't have iPads with GPS driven moving maps or the like, but I did have a simple monochrome device which I had referred to during the dive which supported my general feeling of concern. It appeared to be showing a higher speed than expected for the given indicated airspeed. After much debate the engineers gave in and set about using a test kit on both the airspeed indicators (ASIs). For some time, evidence was

In the front cockpit of the TR9 about to conduct an engine ground run.

presented to me that both ASIs were fine, particularly the one in the front. So as usual the CAA TP was in the dog house. But I persevered and pestered, and we retested and eventually a pinprick hole was discovered in the very fine brass pipework behind my instrument. As I've already explained previously, airspeed is determined by measuring the air pressure coming from a pitot tube, so any leak in the system drops the pressure and indicates a correspondingly lower speed.

Phew! … I was right to be concerned after all.

In fairness this leak was unlikely to have affected the lower airspeed readings at lower pressure. But here was a very good example of where my involvement in such a flight-test programme possibly saved the loss of an aircraft and perhaps both pilots as, almost certainly, had I not been onboard, the aircraft would have been flown vastly in excess of its structural limit. Only this week I've read a book by a Second World War pilot called Bob Spurdle who ripped the wings off his Spitfire when diving after a Messerschmitt 109 which apparently was acceptable behaviour back then! And that's when he was flying a brand new aircraft, not one that was over sixty years old.

Chilling out after completing a successful flight test at Kemble.

Needless to say, I wasn't thanked for saving the day. The aircraft was tested some more, and a permit eventually awarded. Sometime later, I invited myself along to fly the aircraft again for its permit renewal check flight. Now with a new owner and a more friendly maintenance organisation I was warmly welcomed, and this time did get the chance to enjoy both flying the aircraft and discussing its weak stability with the organisation's pilots. The aircraft is now flying regular joy rides at an airfield I operate out of regularly and it is without doubt a safer operation following my fleeting involvement.

The aircraft are easy, it's the people that are difficult – or have I said that already?

Chapter 10

Frank Carson

Weeeeeaaarrrgh … Weeeeearrrgh … Whoooooop … Whoooop … Weeeeaaargh

Okay, so how would you write down the sound of a police siren? Not a nice, friendly Brit one, which tends to just go 'Neeee Naaaah' or, back in the days of my youth, was a ringing bell on the front bumper. I remember when, as a young dad, I was flying at night with a younger pilot yet to enjoy the delights of fatherhood. On looking down to see a car meandering around the lanes with a blue flashing light on its roof I remarked without thinking,

'Oh look – a Nee Nah car.'

He laughed out loud and would have fallen off his chair if he hadn't been securely strapped into it.

'A *what?*'

'You know, a Nee Nah car – a police car. Just wait until *you* have kids!'

Anyway, don't think Brit police car – think 'Blues Brothers' movie – think large American county sheriff law enforcement vehicle. And, just like for Elwood and Jake, this one was chasing me.

Now this was not the first time I've been chased by a police car I have to admit. When learning to fly helicopters in Cornwall after a legal amount (just) of beer my mate and I elected to head out to the local hot spot of Truro. On a long straight bit of road, another car came right up behind us. Flushed with the bravado of youth and a couple of beers I was not about to let the honour of my Blackpool-built three-litre TVR Sports car be usurped. So, I punched the accelerator and left the 'pretender to the throne' behind – but only briefly. Within seconds he was right behind me again, so I repeated what I thought was an entirely reasonable manoeuvre in the circumstances, but I now was greeted, not just with dazzling headlights in my rear-view mirrors, but some blue flashing ones thrown in for good measure.

Bugger!

I pulled over and got out of the car to be greeted by two large chaps, donning their white-topped caps as they climbed out of an unmarked Ford Granada – which ironically was equipped with exactly the same engine and gearbox as my nippy glass-fibre two-seater. You could cut the sarcasm with a knife, not helped by my well-pissed passenger trying to engage in witty banter (not witty enough if you ask me).

I ate humble pie (I'm very used to the taste by now) and answered all the questions correctly with an apologetic tone. The fact that they had decided to race me and goaded me into exceeding the 60-mph limit was not an issue I felt I could engage with, but they knew they'd provoked me, and they'd had a lot of fun racing a navy pilot on a quiet Friday evening. So, with a sharp verbal reprimand behind us, we were on our way to the fleshpots of Truro – there aren't any, by the way.

But no, the car of my story was not a nice, friendly Brit car. More like the car that pulled me over in Florida many years earlier. My mate and I were serving on an RN ship, HMS *Londonderry*; a ship I could write a whole book about in itself. Well, we were in Florida for over a week and had earned enough leave, we reckoned, to drive to New Orleans for Mardi Gras; eleven hours one way and thirteen hours the other, because you changed time zones en route. My mate and I shared the driving. He was asleep – I was bored – and the required 55 mph far too soporific, so the needle on the speedo had been creeping up steadily. I noted with mild passing interest a Highway Patrol car on the opposite carriageway, going the other way. Used to the more conventional Brit expectation of a 'traffic car' needing to follow from behind for a while to clock your speed I gave it little attention until out of the corner of my eye I saw clouds of 'dust, shit and derision' flying skyward and I saw, with some amazement and wonder, this same police car now emerging from the hundred-metre-wide central reservation onto my carriageway. Within seconds it had caught up with me and glued itself to my rear bumper as I now nailed the rental car's speedo to exactly 54 mph. But too late. And, without much fuss, the two large blokes in Stetson cowboy hats, clearly visible in my rear-view mirror, pointed their fingers at the hard shoulder. *Blast!*

As I pulled over, trying to anticipate what the Florida version of police sarcasm might sound like, my half-asleep, and still reclined mate, decided to clarify our partnership agreement by muttering:

'By the way; we both pay our own fines, OK?'

'Great, mate – thanks.'

I confess the bloke walking towards me was an impressive sight …

'So y'all got any good reason why y'all exceeding the speed limit?' says the seven-foot bloke in the huge hat with the massive revolver strapped to his belt.

I assumed he had no formal evidence because of his 'cowboy approach' to catching up with me, so I bluffed.

'I'm terribly sorry, officer'. I said in my best toffee-nosed Brit accent. 'The sun was in my eyes (true) and I was having difficulty seeing the speedo (not quite so true) but I thought I was doing fifty-five' (not really true at all).

'Weeeeell, Y'all radar here in y'all interstate highway patrol car says y'all was doin' seventy-five –'

'No, I can't possibly believe that! Surely not? So what are my options?' I asked.

I thought this was an innocent enough question, not being from around these parts. When I got back to Florida and mentioned this to a girl that I was seeing, her response was, 'What? Y'all asked an interstate highway patrol trooper what your options were? Golly Gee – I must tell all my friends!'

And that was about it. The patrolman wrote out a scrap of paper from his book and handed me my first and only citation. Sadly, this was a citation for speeding rather than for anything heroic and I was given six months to pay. Needless to say I wrote a grovelling letter to the county judge when I was safely back in the UK and could probably have got away with not paying it, but I had no enthusiasm to have a criminal record hanging over my head the next time I had to get through Homeland Security at some US airport or other. An EASA colleague of mine, Nick, was always being stopped by US immigration every time we tried to enter because he'd once left the country without handing in his customs slip. He wasn't allowed back in until his leaving had been recorded properly!

So, where was I? Yes, I was again being chased by a large American sedan with blue and red flashing lights everywhere and this ridiculously loud siren was blaring whoop, whoop noises. What was perhaps unusual this time was that I wasn't in my car but in a helicopter.

I had just touched down by performing a running landing as this helicopter had wheels and I was testing out this particular aspect. I had rolled onto the taxiway at around 30 mph when this patrol car pulled out of the bushes and gave chase. My American co-pilot, who had more war stories than hot dinners from his Vietnam days, remarked laconically,

'Whatever you do, don't stop.'

Now, that was a challenge as we needed to pick up some ground crew and ballast which was sited alongside the taxiway a few metres further along.

For this next bit you have to imagine a scene from all those movies where people (often escaped convicts or prisoners of war) are running by a train in order to board it – invariably throwing themselves into the final open truck, with the last bloke running like the clappers with his hand outstretched in the hope his mate will catch it and pull him aboard. And that's exactly what occurred. Our ground crew clearly also had no enthusiasm to spend a night or two in county jail and had clutched in fairly quickly to our demise and their only means of escape. We slowed to around 10 mph and, as we passed each one of them, they threw their kit in the back and then, like catching the train, they, one by one, threw themselves into the helicopter. As the last bloke leapt for the open doorway I briskly pulled up the collective lever to apply maximum power and I hauled this now very heavy old bird into the sky and across the State line to freedom.

What the heck? What was going on here, you might be wondering?

Well let's go back to the beginning of the story which centres around one Frank Carson. Now, many of you will remember the Northern Irish comedian Frank Carson whose catchphrases included 'It's a cracker' and 'It's the way I tell 'em'. I bet many of you are now wishing he wrote this book? Well, he didn't, and it wasn't him. Rather another chap by the same name who got involved in helicopters as far back as 1958 when he started using a Bell 47 helicopter for fire-fighting and other aerial tasks and set up Carson Helicopters based at Perkasie, Pennsylvania. By the 1970s the company had moved on and was using the much larger Sikorsky helicopters, eventually the S-61. The S-61 had a lot in common with the UK's Westland Sea King which was derived from the SH-3 helicopter. These were the aircraft famous for picking up the Apollo astronauts on their return to earth and 'splashdown'. Frank Carson was an entrepreneur and had started to develop the S-61 to make it more efficient at the load lifting and fire-fighting roles, both of which involved lifting very heavy weights. One of his initiatives was to buy up old S-61s and strip all the paint off them. He found that would lighten the aircraft by 1000 lbs. He then sawed out large sections of the fuselage to shorten the aircraft which again saved weight. Not content with this, he had been chatting to a mate from NASA (National Aeronautics and Space Administration) who had developed a rotor-blade profile that Frank thought might work well with the S-61. That, and the increasing use of composite materials led to his design of composite tail rotor and main rotor blades – now known throughout the community as the 'Carson Blade'. Indeed, shortly after our involvement with the project, the UK MoD bought a good number of these blades to be fitted to the Royal Navy Sea Kings operating in Afghanistan where the hot temperatures and high altitudes had meant the classic metal blades were not performing well enough.

As for us, Ray and I were tasked by EASA to conduct a validation of the already certified Carson Blades. All we were asked to do was make sure the composite blades worked 'no worse than' the metal ones, i.e., Carson was not at that time trying to claim the new rotors provided any performance benefit for civil use, but separately they had increased the

Commencing testing of the Carson Blade S61 out of Perkasie.

maximum weight the S-61 could fly at when carrying a load hanging under the aircraft (underslung load) and so we needed to assess this also.

So, off we flew to Philadelphia and, via rental car, arrived at Perkasie, which is in the middle of nowhere, and certainly didn't boast its own airfield at the factory – more that we flew out of what felt like an unused car park. First up was to test the shortened S-61 at its new capability to lift a stupidly heavy weight of 11,000 lbs. The easiest way to do this testing was to use the training area the company had and lift one of their calibrated weights. Being game to try anything once, we briefed the sortie along with the company pilot who had been lent to us as co-pilot and, frankly, he was the chap who was going to tell us where we were in the local area. At the brief Ray and I emphasised the need to be as heavy as possible and therefore we were going to fill all the fuel tanks to the brim, as was our usual practice in flight test when trying to get the aircraft as heavy as possible.

'Oh no we won't', says my co-pilot, Boyd, in a southern drawl all of his own.

'Why not?'

About to lift the load in the shortened S61.

'Well …', he continues to explain, 'if we crash with the underfloor tank full of fuel the impact of the crash will force all the fuel into the back of the aircraft – it will catch fire and we will all die in the massive fire ball long before we can run away.'

Now that got my full attention.

'Two thirds full will be just fine!' we agree.

Weirdly the best way to fly for this task was sitting in the 'wrong front seat'. Normally, modern helicopters are flown from the right seat but see my earlier comments about the PZL SW-4. To do this load-lifting task the pilot had to half-turn in his seat to look sideways out of a massive bubble window – think goldfish bowl. Holding the collective (power) lever in the left hand made it impossible to swivel clockwise and look out of the right window. You had to swivel left. Try it sitting at your kitchen table with your left hand gripping the rear leg of the chair – see what I mean? So off we went, with me in the left seat 'firing up' this clapped-out ancient helicopter which had had more owners than Henry had wives and probably had received as much abuse as any one of them. I have to say that I have been fortunate enough to do a number of difficult aviation tasks over the years. Don't believe any pilot who boosts his own ego by telling you he/she is better than other pilots because they can do 'x'. The RAF has suffered over the years from a so-called streaming process where would-be fast-jet pilots get 'canned' and end up flying C-130s or helicopters because they must be easier to fly. Absolutely not true. It's not just the learning to fly one type or another but what you then go on to do with it.

I was about to lift the heaviest load I had ever lifted in a helicopter, which weighed more than the helicopter did. That in itself was hard enough, but the strop, or wire, from which the load was to be connected, was about 100-feet long. In summary, it was bloody difficult. Just getting the helicopter to hover directly over the load itself was hard. I had to look in about four places at once. I had to stick my head into the bubble so I could look vertically down at the load itself. At the same time I had to scan the surrounding area for hazards and be able to pick up any horizontal or lateral drift or movement of the helicopter. I also had to look out the front and side of the helicopter to pick up the horizon to ensure the hover attitude of the aircraft was correct and, given that we were testing the maximum permissible load, I had to be constantly scanning

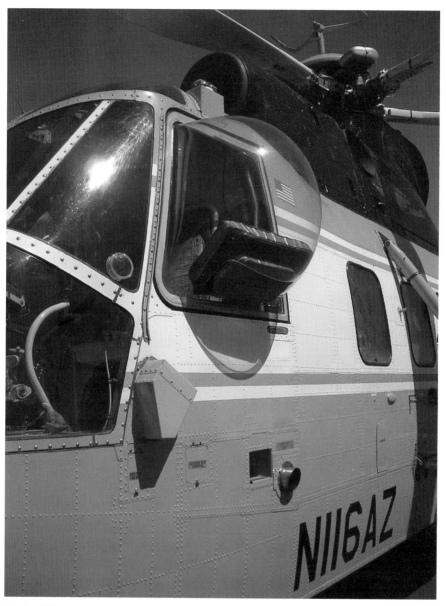

S61 Bubble window on the left hand side.

the engine and gearbox instruments to make sure I wasn't about to 'break' the helicopter. But I managed to lift the load and, in order to do so, pulled every ounce of power the aircraft had to offer. With all the gauges red lining and the tired airframe protesting the inconvenience, I gently nursed the machine into forward flight and, with the load now airborne,

Picking up the calibrated 11,000lbs load.

flew around, aiming to try and dump the load back in the car park where I'd found it. I should have chosen a bigger car park. I'd done a fair amount of load lifting in the navy in my Wasp and Lynx. Frankly, I thought I was quite good at it and used to collect the ship's supply of fresh eggs in a crate that was suspended under my helicopter – which I would then bet I could plonk onto the flight deck without breaking one … and I would win a fair amount of beer money from my various supply officers who were foolish enough to take my bet. I was only once caught out when the load I was tasked to pick up was, it turned out, twice as heavy as advertised and the gearbox on my poor little Wasp didn't approve, but that's another story.

But, back to Perkasie; this was really hard. To give you an idea, four Nissan Micra cars weigh less than the load I was lifting – yes, *four*. That amount of inertia is really difficult to control under a helicopter. I was also desperately missing my crewman. In my Wasp I would always have an experienced aircrewman in the back of the aircraft telling me exactly what the underslung load was doing and, to be honest, what I needed to do to sort it out. But not today. There was just me, and a knackered old S-61, and a bubble window. Coming into the hover the aircraft decided to tell me in no uncertain terms how unhappy she was. The aircraft started to really vibrate – I mean a lot – the sort where you can't speak without using vibrato. Anyway, I could not allow my four Nissan cars to swing. Even a small swing on the end of a 100-foot wire means a lot of movement and I didn't want to ruin the reputation of EASA and the CAA overnight by killing a few folks on the ground just because, when they got out of bed that morning, they weren't expecting to get hit by four flying Micras all at the same time. A few beads of nervous perspiration containing last night's beer dripped into my eyes which I ignored to smoothly lower my load, so to speak, onto the spot where I'd found it.

And the crowd went wild.

Phew! … survived another.

And with the weight of the aircraft halved, a sporty return to the helipad and we had survived to tell the tale. So, that was day one. Off to the hotel for some Californian Cabernet before we pitched up on day two to commence our, hopefully, easier assessment of the new blades.

We had asked to fly the 'N' version of the aircraft. This was the version used in Europe and extensively on the North Sea for ferrying oil workers out to the oil rigs. Unbeknownst to us, when we asked to fly this version,

Returning the load to where it had come from.

was the fact that in the US this was a rare beast. Our flight-test aircraft turned out to be a very old and knackered 'R' version with the sponsons containing the undercarriage bolted on to convert it to an 'N' just before we got there. It's fair to say, I think, that even to this day after flying helicopters for nearly forty years this was the worst helicopter I've had the displeasure to fly. Nothing on it worked properly. The autopilot, which helps make it easier for the pilot, was constantly dropping out and on one of my more gentle landings a panel the size of a typical garage door just fell off the side of the helicopter … much to consternation of the scattering ground crew! Decades of corrosion had beaten the best that Sikorsky could produce. Anyway we briefed to fly the heap including only two-thirds gas in the bottom tank (we learn). But then, at the brief, we were clobbered with another bit of info …

George W. Bush, aka POTUS, aka President of the United States, was visiting Limerick. Not the quaint Irish city in this case; rather the local nuclear power plant which, disturbingly for me, as a lapsed member of Greenpeace, was just a few miles away. He was flying in to somewhere nearby, so the area was going to be a no-fly zone for the day. Thinking outside the box, good ol' Boyd suggested we travel north-east to New Jersey and work out of a quaint little general aviation airfield there. Which is what we did. And very successful the very long day was, with us gathering lots of data for our various test points. A good deal of our testing had involved flying our noisy helicopter quite low over the surrounding suburbs of this rural airfield and guess what? Someone called 911.

And, so it came to pass – thankfully, towards the end of our final sortie – that the local law enforcement turned up to arrest us all for dangerous low-level flying and creating a disturbance. Not something I wanted on my CV and any delay trying to explain what we were up to would have blown our three-day-test programme to pot.

So, on hearing the siren and seeing the flashing lights, I was glad that my conspirator in crime, Good ol' Boyd, suggested we become fugitives. Which we successfully did and landed at Perkasie not wearing handcuffs. The nice thing about the States is that each state is a mini-country. Once we had crossed the state line the nice chaps who had been chasing us had no jurisdiction and we had committed no crime where we landed.

Phew! … escaped another embarrassing moment.

Pulling power to get the heck airborne. Note the yellow sponsons.

But, needless to say, we did phone the NJ PD and explain, and I ate humble pie again – (not as good as the local apple pie) – and said we'd never ever do it again, which I was 101 per cent sure would be the case, since I had no intention whatsoever of returning to that particular airfield in a clapped out S-61N.

The next challenge was catching our flight home. Unbeknownst to we Brits, the Americans have a number of long weekend holidays, a bit like our August Bank Holiday. We might have heard of Labour Day, but who's heard of Memorial Day? Something to do with the way the Confederacy honoured its war dead, which was adopted by Union soldiers and then became a national day of remembrance and celebration. Like all such days, it's now just another 'day off' and marks the start of summer in the US, so is a fiercely enjoyed few days, usually in good weather. Our testing completed as usual on the Thursday evening, the plan, as it invariably was, was to write up our thoughts overnight and present them to the company on the Friday morning before catching our flight home. Our S-61 mechanics, with whom we had shared our near criminal experience, were now honorary Brits and were very concerned about us travelling the interstate on the Friday of Memorial Weekend – each would 'Blackcat'

The Carson flight test team with Ray on my right and Boyd on my left and the ground crew and fellow conspirators.

the other with tales of multi-lane pile ups and gridlock across the country. Needless to say, we went into the debrief with our primary scan, including our wrist watches.

Good ol' Frank was there; and he was a powerful character. We started explaining our issues. These were technical and complex but, in terms of performance, the aircraft did not climb as it should have done, a worrying finding when the new rotor blades were supposed to improve performance and I knew from RN TP colleagues that they were pinning their hopes on these blades saving the day for our RN Sea King fleet operating in the hot and high climates of Afghanistan.

More surprisingly was the negative effect these blades had on handling qualities, given that they were meant to be a one-for-one swap.

Now – this could get technical and boring in a hurry, so skip the next half page if your eyelids are already heavy …

The lift caused by helicopter rotor blades going through the air causes them to flap up; that is they want to fly up. The result of that is that the 'dinner plate' created above the helicopter when the blades are turning has a tendency to want to tilt away from the prevailing airflow. In forward flight this means that increasing airflow from ahead (such as when you fly faster) causes the dinner plate to tilt back and this has to be controlled and minimised by the pilot pushing the stick forward. With our test helicopter, when we had some weight down the back to give us an aft centre of gravity, I found that I eventually reached a situation where, to go faster, my cyclic stick (same as joystick) had to be moved so far forward as to physically hit the dashboard and prevent further forward movement. This was a first for me in an aircraft … to be pushing the stick fully forward to push the nose down and go faster and then find, uncontrollably, the nose of the aircraft pitching up. Yep, here I was again; in a ten-ton helicopter out of control. Thankfully, as the nose of the aircraft came up, the airspeed reduced and the need for full forward stick reduced and I was back in control again. Phew!

The same characteristic also featured with increase in the lateral airflow. The dinner plate would tilt away. So, flying along, a gust from the right caused us to roll to the left and we'd then turn a bit and then we'd have airflow from the other side and roll away and turn some more and this would continue, getting more and more pronounced. To those in the know, this was divergent Dutch Roll. The phenomenon was so called based on the antics of a drunken Dutchman wandering back to his barge after too many lagers – apparently. And who said this was a boring subject?

Anyway, these new blades made this feature of the aircraft bad.

So, here we were on the Friday of Memorial Day weekend looking at our watches as we tried to explain to Frank, who was more interested in green backs than the 'Greek flute music' required to explain helicopter aerodynamics, that his baby was ugly.

When will we ever learn that this does not go down well, especially with the company CEO who was pretty much still responsible for every decision in the company? What really confused him was that the characteristic we had discovered actually made the static stability greater, but that same static stability was like putting a stronger spring on something. It bounced things back very aggressively and in this case created the Dutch Roll.

'Now Listen You ...' Frank opens, *'Are you daring to tell me that my blades make the helicopter less stable?'*

'No, Frank,' I say with my most diplomatic overtones. 'I'm telling you the blades make your aircraft more stable (true).'

But in my head, I'm adding ... 'which is driving an unstable divergent dynamic oscillation', but I keep that to myself.

Standing by the test aircraft in my ex-ETPS flying suit.

My watch has already passed the 'must absolutely leave by now' time and I am starting to get anxious … and then, as if in answer to an unvoiced prayer, Frank's mobile phone rings and as he blusters and protests it becomes apparent that he's forgotten he'd promised to pick up the grandkids. As a grandfather myself now, I realise he was answerable to a higher authority than his own company at this point and he was deeply in the pooh with someone. As his car left the parking lot with a squeal of rubber, we were already strapping into ours, having changed out of our flying kit during our heated debrief. Given our now flagrant disregard for local law enforcement, we proceeded to break a number of speed limits on the way to the local international airport – sipping a cold Chardonnay on the BA flight home with barely minutes to spare.

Phew! … survived another.

But the saga was not complete, and we were invited back by Frank to have another go. But instead of Perkasie, he directed us to Arizona for better weather. This time the 'heap of shit' we'd been asked to fly previously had been replaced by N15456; an airframe of slightly less tired appearance and, it turns out, the last S-61 ever made, a quantum leap better than its sister. Although this was another occasion where we had to drive to work in the dark, to be lifting into the hover as the first pink of the dawn's twilight appeared, was another 'to-die-for' moment. That first hour of the Arizona dawn provided absolutely perfect conditions for helicopter performance testing. This time around, as we pulled power on our heavily-ballasted aircraft, we discovered that, at last, we were meeting the scheduled hover weights or climb performance. So suddenly things were as advertised. Although the dinner-plate effect as above was still in evidence, the autopilot of this aircraft actually worked and was capable of suppressing this nasty characteristic. Therefore, we could effectively deal with the problem by insisting on a speed limit to be applied only if the autopilot failed.

Hurrah! Another good result.

We approved the blades for use and, with a speed limit imposed in case of autopilot failure, we agreed that the Dutch Roll was acceptable and the blades were safe to be used. We later learned that the Royal Navy Sea Kings seemed to perform better in theatre with their new blades which, in fairness, only came into their own in the very thin air caused by high altitudes and high temperatures.

Chapter 11

The Lord

My phone rang.

I answered – and instinctively jumped to attention.

In fairness, after twenty-two years in the Royal Navy and time spent in the Officers' Training Corps, the Army cadets and the Royal Air Force Reserves, I'd become very able to recognise the voice of a senior officer in an instant. Not quite sure what it was; I'd have mates that one minute talked like me, then got promoted and suddenly effected a deep and booming voice that somehow said, *'Listen to me – I'm important.'*

I had been badly caught out during an exercise on my ship when we were in the exercise areas off Portland and we had embarked a whole bunch of navy specialists who were putting us through our paces as we pretended to be at war. It was a Thursday and this exercise was always known therefore, at the time, as 'The Thursday War' (Clever we fishheads, eh?). Anyway, I was looking after my 'part of ship' with my flight/team at the 'back end' on the flight deck. We were all wearing our cumbersome carbon chemical suits, gas masks and bulky rubber overboots. To the uninitiated we were a hilarious sight if I'm honest.

Again, the phone rang.

The phones on our Leander-class frigate were initiated by winding a handle to generate some 'wiggly amps' which would be enough to ring a rather pathetic bell and then we had to shout into the mouthpiece to try and get our voices to carry down some ancient copper wires – the classic and original sound-powered telephone.

I answered, and was greeted with a garbled, muffled muttering which was barely discernible but said something about the emergency steering. So, let me explain. If a warship lost power to the various hydraulic rams that moved an extremely heavy rudder left or right to steer the ship, then the ship couldn't be steered. (This is what did for the German battleship, Bismarck, on the evening of a very blustery miserable 26 May 1941 when Jock Moffat, flying an 818 Naval Air Squadron Swordfish, managed to get his torpedo to hit the ship's stern and jam her rudder. Thereafter, the stricken battleship was locked into a constant left hand turn and it was only a matter of time before the RN warships finished her off. The weather was so bad and the sea so rough that when the aircraft from the mission returned to Ark Royal in the dark many crashed on landing. Another typical day in the life of a Fleet Air Arm pilot.)

But we 'men of oak' on our 'Pusser's Grey Steamer' were not about to let this same fate befall us and in such an eventuality, a team of blokes would rig a makeshift mechanism with some hefty oak beams and numerous block-and-tackle ropes and pulleys. With enough manpower and time, the rudder could usually be forced to move, despite itself, and small course corrections made. This was like one of the classic leadership tasks taught at Britannia Royal Naval College (BRNC) Dartmouth and the like and required a lot of sweat and tears and shouting and swearing. So my immediate response was lacking motivation and I replied with the regrettable expression, 'Do you know who you are talking to? This is the Flight Commander.'

I shouted these words with such authority that, despite my gas mask and the 1940s vintage technology, my words arrived on the bridge of the ship with apparent clarity. The reply was similar in that it started with the same words, but concluded with,

'Do you know who you are talking to? This is the Captain – rig the emergency steering.'

This again was a jump-to-attention moment. If you can't relate to the military, imagine your response, when like me, the headmaster turns to you in the middle of school assembly and shouts directly at you with similar authority, 'Boy – you are talking in assembly – see me in my study.'

Either way, you get the idea. I had been called by someone who just had that kind of authoritative manner.

'Are you the CAA's Light Aeroplane Test Pilot?'

'Yes (sir?) that's me …'

'Well then – you'll be testing my aeroplane', he commands.

And so it came to pass. I had been introduced to the Lord – or Robin, as I was invited to call him later after we'd shared a near-death experience together. Anyway, the initial conversation included a kind invitation to his 'house' for lunch to discuss his aeroplane project and the way ahead. A few days later I found myself in a scene from Netflix's The Crown as I drove, in some awe, up the long tree-lined driveway of Cornbury Park, a large stately home near Oxford, which has hosted the Wilderness music festival for a number of years. Seated in a most splendid dining room, surrounded by suited knights, lunch was a delightful piece of fried fish. I confess, in order to calm my nerves you understand, I had hoped this would have been washed down with a bucket of Pinot Grigio, but fizzy water had to suffice. Clearly, this was going to be a 'working afternoon'.

Following lunch we retired to the stable block which had been converted into a massive workshop big enough to hold an aeroplane. In pride of place was a very nice Glassair III kit plane, built by the lord himself. No expense had been spared in terms of time and quality of components, and that was pleasing since I was being invited to do the first-ever flight and all the test flying of the aircraft, on a type, which having flown previously, I already knew to be extremely difficult to fly, due to its inherent instability.

In fact, the first one I had to fly was out in Germany and I took the owner along with me. He was an airline pilot with Lufthansa, and I thought that if I had any difficulties with navigation or flying this particular machine

The Lord's Glassair III G-USSI prior to flight test.

he'd be able to help. As soon as the wheels came off the runway I realised this was an aircraft that was unstable, twitchy and prone to pilot-induced oscillation (PIO). In other words, I knew immediately this was going to be a challenging task. In fact, like so often in my day job, having managed to get safely airborne my immediate concern was whether or not I'd be able to land safely again. Not a good start, but I decided to worry about that later and got on with climbing to assess the climb performance and check the speeds at which the aircraft stalled. I'd been busy doing this for a few minutes, rattling out numbers for my German mate to write down when I realised his skin colour now resembled the camouflage pattern of a Messerschmitt 109 – namely green.

'Are you OK?' I queried. *'Uuuugggggghhhhh!'* was his only reply.

He frankly looked like he was about to throw up all over the cockpit (including me) or maybe just … die.

So I had to check the maximum speed of the aircraft anyway, which I now used to good effect in a near full-power dive back to the old wartime airfield I'd just departed from. Now I knew what it was like to fly a Typhoon in 1945.

But this aeroplane was one 'son of a B'. Very unstable indeed, and as I slowed down to start my approach, I wondered whether my arrival might be more V2 than 109. Thankfully, as I lowered the wheels and flaps, the aircraft became slightly more controllable and I smoothly skimmed the hedge and, avoiding a bumpy touch-down, floated onto the ground, opening the passenger door as soon as I could with a hope that a blast of fresh air would forestall the inevitable vomit stream for a few seconds, which thankfully worked. As soon as I was stationary, I literally pushed this bloke out of the door and allowed him to 'hooey' all over the surrounding tarmac; tarmac which he embraced like his life depended on it. He subsequently blamed something he ate but, for an airline pilot, I was surprised his career had lasted so long.

So back to the delightful Lord's aeroplane that I was being tasked to fly: the next question was, where was I going to fly it from? So, without further ado, my host invited me aboard a souped-up golf buggy and off we roared in a cloud of two-stroke exhaust fumes to explore the estate, well at least the other side of the rather massive stately home. After bouncing around we just stopped in the middle of a deer park.

'So – what do you think?'

'About the deer?'

'No – about the strip? The runway?'

'What runway?'

'The one we're parked on.'

Well – we had stopped on a gently sloping area with numerous small trees and scores of grazing deer. A delightful scene for a David Attenborough documentary but with none of the trappings normally associated with airfields. Although, in fairness, when I looked along the direction being pointed out there was a wider gap between the small trees and for about 300–400 metres in a south westerly direction was a smoother strip of grass. Immediately behind me was the whacking great building I'd just had lunch in. So, flying over that would be required if I wasn't to emulate James Bond by flying through buildings. As I looked further along the strip there was a definite dip, which we couldn't see into, and then another part of the strip running into a wood of very tall trees.

'So I guess the smooth grass continues down into the dip and on into those trees?' I asked hopefully.

'No – in the dip is a stream with a stone wall on either side of it.'

'So, what am I supposed to do about that?'

'Well, Chris, the idea is you would try to get airborne in the first 300 metres or so, but if that wasn't working you'd have to leap the aeroplane over the wall, the stream, the other wall and land it over there before you hit the trees.'

Sometimes in my job decisions are hard and I take a while to weigh up all the pros and cons, and as you know already, I do hate to upset people, but this was a no-brainer. Leap into a high-performance unstable type with rather fragile undercarriage for its very first flight from a runway that, even on a good day, wasn't long enough and try not to scratch the paintwork …

'I'm sorry', I stated, 'But absolutely no!'

'So what will I have to do?'

'Take it to Oxford Kidlington? It is just down the road and has a massive tarmac runway which will be ideal.'

So despite the free lunch (and there is no such thing in my experience) I had to disappoint him.

Now, one of the challenges in flight test is that if your advice is followed it's hard to prove you were right in the first place. Does that make sense? I mean, I tell the Lord that I can't fly from his less than 400-metre strip because, if I have any problems, I'd crash and burn and die. But obviously by moving to a larger safer airfield sod's law usually means I don't have the problem that would prove my point. Well not so in this case.

On only my second flight I launched airborne with the Lord at my side to commence the formal testing of his aircraft. I flew initially at high power settings and all seemed to be going well but when I needed to reduce the power, to test the slow-speed flying, the engine suddenly went from a Ferrari noise to that of an East European tractor; in other words it sounded like a bag of nails that would cease working at any moment. So my now well-established drill kicked in and I immediately turned to where I'd parked my car – Kidlington. By re-applying full power cautiously the engine recovered its composure and off we set at 200 mph. Time to talk to the nice people in the air traffic control tower. I explained my situation and made it crystal clear there was every likelihood that my engine was about to fail on me. They were very chilled about it; too relaxed by far if you ask me. But I positioned in the overhead of the airfield at 3,000 feet up and, having worked out the duty runway and wind direction and where all the other aircraft were, I gingerly retarded the throttle in the hope of still being able to make a powered, and thus controlled, approach. But my pessimism was, as is often the case, borne out in reality and, with a mighty shudder, rattle and shake, I found myself staring at a wind-milling propeller 'Ho Hum.' Back to being a glider pilot.

Thankfully, on this Glassair the undercarriage at least was behaving, and I lowered all three wheels and praised the Lord (!) for the three green lights indicating the wheels were locked down. Putting my adrenalin to good use I made, dare I say it myself, an absolutely perfect dead-stick landing onto the northerly runway and coasted to a stop. Inside my head – the crowd went wild again. But that was quickly interrupted by ATC coming onto the radio with an expression that in any context is in my top three most annoying, 'You can't park there!'

Now given that I had spent ages on the radio telling them about my ill-fated engine before I commenced my approach, they shouldn't have been too surprised by this potential outcome – but they were. Clearly other people who have engine failures near Oxford have the good grace to crash into a field instead.

G-USSI in the middle of the runway at Oxford, Kidlington about to be towed.

But I explained, and they closed the airfield for forty-five minutes while the slowest aircraft tug on the planet made its way to us from the other side of the airfield. At least it wasn't raining – and, more importantly, I was able to say 'I told you so' to my now best mate, Robin.

It took five months to get the required replacement engine parts delivered and fitted but I'm glad to say I was then able to test this very nicely built aircraft without further incident.

Phew! … survived.

But this isn't the end of the story. For some reason, Robin decided that building one such aircraft wasn't enough and he embarked on building another aircraft to a similar high standard, a Vans RV-8.

Now this machine was a very different beast to the Glassair, which had delicate retractable undercarriage and long take-off run. The RV-8 was designed with grass strips in mind and had a rugged fixed tail-dragger undercarriage and a good power-to-weight ratio for good short-field performance, so I thought there was a much better chance I could fly this off the Cornbury strip, but only if the wind conditions were ideal. My biggest concern for the very first flight was the landing. (I could operate the aircraft much lighter for the first flight and thus give myself good take off performance.) So did I want to fly my first approach between the chimneys of Cornbury Park stately home, thus having to land halfway down an already short strip which sloped down to a stream and two stone walls? Guess.

I elected to make my first approach for my first landing over the open area in the trees which meant landing in a north-easterly direction towards the stately home. If the brakes failed, or I got the touch-down point

Vans RV-8 prior to commencing the flight test programme.

About to conduct the first flight in the RV-8 pointing towards the stately home. Note the stone wall that ran behind the aircraft and along the end of the short strip.

wrong, I'd be back in the baronial dining room but probably not being offered fried fish this time. To mitigate the risk, I needed a headwind for my landing. North-easterly winds in the UK are far rarer than south-westerly ones. This kind of decision plays havoc with your diary which is no fun as, now being self-employed, lost days equal lost income. But, with a bit of faffing, I was able to wait for the right conditions and thankfully the take off and landing were accomplished with aplomb, which is just as well as Robin was videoing them.

Subsequently, I chose to fly with a south-westerly wind which allowed me to take off safely at the maximum permissible weight of the aeroplane, I then accepted a steep approach path, skimming the house roof tiles and side-slipping slightly to drop, more like a helicopter than aeroplane, back into my now familiar landing site.

So again the crowd went wild.

Or rather Robin did as I'd successfully completed all the required testing of his new aircraft, and was able to recommend permit issue, without closing Oxford Kidlington for nearly an hour.

Phew! … such a relief all round.

With the RV-8 outside the stable block on successful completion of the testing.

Chapter 12

Escapades

'Mayday, Mayday, Mayday – I'm on fire and abandoning the aircraft!'

Perhaps I should explain what I mean by a Mayday call? The expression was coined by one Frederick Stanley Mockford in 1923. At the time he was working at Croydon airport as a radio operator. He was searching for an easy to use expression that said 'help me'. Ideally, he wanted a word that couldn't easily be mistaken for anything else. Well ahead of his time, and given that nearly all the flights from Croydon were to France and back, he hit upon the idea of using the French for 'Help Me' and anglicising it; so 'm'aidez' was corrupted into the word 'Mayday'. These days an emergency radio call is initiated by using the words in succession three times, hence 'Mayday, Mayday, Mayday', followed by the nature of the emergency and the pilot's intentions. If the emergency isn't immediately life threatening, or potentially catastrophic, a corruption of the French word for 'breakdown' is used, so the French word 'panne' is replaced within an expression 'Pan-Pan', repeated three times. I'm not sure when the expression went from 'Pan' to 'Pan-Pan'. I certainly had to declare a 'Pan call' early in my Fleet Air Arm training when the engine on my Wasp helicopter started to fail. As a very inexperienced trainee pilot I thought I put out a pretty professional call only to be greeted by the response from my ship,

'Roger, confirm this is for exercise?' which was indicative of the fact that we practised emergencies all the time and didn't have real ones that often. I confess I wasn't expecting this reply and all I could think of to say in response was … 'No – it's a real one!'

However, my current situation was rather unusual, and I thought that perhaps there was a different call I might have used to get the required response – but then and now I can't for the life of me think of one.

You see, I wasn't actually flying. I had started up this single-seat deregulated microlight aeroplane just minutes earlier and was now taxiing with the relaxed confidence of a test pilot well equipped and prepared for the testing he was about to do – always a mistake, I've found, to ever have that confidence in my job. As I taxied over the bumpy grass there was suddenly a very strong smell of burning. Initially I wasn't too alarmed. I thought I was much better placed than when, a few years previously, I'd had a similar experience in a Royal Navy Lynx. On that occasion I was a Qualified Helicopter Instructor (QHI) at RNAS Portland (702 NAS) and the weather was dire, so there was no student flying going on. Being young, keen and not particularly risk averse back then, I decided to take a Lynx up on my own to gather two hours of 'actual instrument flying'; always useful training and experience, but I was aware that getting home again in such marginal conditions might be a challenge. What I hadn't considered particularly was all the possible 'What ifs' which go hand in hand with my current day job. I was thankfully already heading for home when – yep, strong smell of burning. Without much delay the burning was accompanied by black smoke emanating from behind the dashboard or instrument panel. My first response was to reach for the hand-held fire extinguisher. Actually, that isn't true – that was my second response. My first was to chastise myself with a bunch of unrepeatable expletives for being in cloud in the first place, when I didn't have to be, in a now burning aircraft. The fire extinguisher was conveniently located behind the co-pilot's seat and, despite all my best efforts of stretching like a Pilates instructor, I couldn't reach it. It had never crossed my mind to practise grabbing it previously and, in fairness, we flew two-up most of the time. So, I abandoned that vain hope, to observe that, one by one, various instruments in front of me were failing as no doubt the wiring which led to them was burning and short-circuiting. Oh, Bugger!

So I cracked out the 'Pan call' in exemplary fashion, which quite rightly always gets the instant attention of air traffic control who immediately realised that I needed to get my homesick pigeon on the ground very rapidly indeed.

'Roger, your Pan call acknowledged. Stand by for vectors for a PAR to Runway 22.'

Calm as you like, I thought, and right on the money – just what the doctor ordered. All I had to do now was hope that the important instruments or radio didn't pack up soon and I could follow the directions from the air traffic controllers on the ground who would steer me onto the runway centre line for Runway 22 and then give me instructions to descend using their precision approach radar (PAR). And the really good news was that, because I'd declared an emergency, they would talk me right down to the ground. Oh the joys of flying a helicopter in bad weather. Having told me to turn right a couple of times they advised,

'Do not acknowledge further calls unless requested.'

That meant things were going okay and, shortly thereafter, I was asked to commence my descent. So, with my left hand I lowered the collective lever and eased the cyclic a tad forward to maintain my speed at 100 KIAS. I'd already put my landing lamp on but the chances of anyone seeing it were non-existent.

'The cloud base is estimated at fifty feet with a visibility of 500 metres.'

This update from ATC was not good as, normally, I would have to overshoot if I couldn't see the runway at 150 feet. I pressed on down, but gingerly started washing off my forward speed. I could not afford the luxury of going around with smoke still emanating from behind the dashboard. I passed 150 feet at 60 KIAS reducing to 40 KIAS, which was about as slow as you could legally fly on instruments.

Then, all of a sudden, when my levels of concern were at least six out of ten, the runway lights appeared out of the murk, just a few feet away along with the numerous blue flashing lights on the numerous waiting fire trucks. Thankfully, I would have to disappoint the pumped-up fire crews, as by then my electrical fire had finally run out of wiring to burn through.

Phew! … survived another.

But back to my current situation. Based on this experience of my Lynx episode, the smell of burning wasn't too alarming in itself, nor were the black smoke and acrid fumes. But then, all of a sudden, real live flames started appearing from behind the instruments. Now this was a first; I really was on 'proper fire'! And I really needed to get out quickly, and I really needed a brave chap with a fire extinguisher to put out the fire before it caught hold and destroyed this beautiful little aeroplane. Fortuitously, I was right in front of the ageing wartime control tower at Old Sarum when I radioed for help. But a bit like with my Wasp Pan call I was greeted with a reply to my Mayday from the chap in the tower. Not being Navy he said,

'You what?'

'I'm on *fire* – real flames! I need the fire truck.'

As the words passed my lips I was already wriggling out of my harness and parachute and out of the door that I'd already flung open, to run, like an Olympic sprinter, the 50 metres or so I reckoned I could cover without embarrassment. Which I did, only to turn to see the red fire truck now manned by the bloke from the tower about to squirt fire retardant foam at the rate of a hundred litres a second at my stricken bird. Put mildly, being hit by a torrent of high-pressure foam would have killed this particularly small and delicate aircraft for all time. So now I ran the 50 metres in the other direction, desperately throwing my body between aircraft and fire truck, wildly flapping my arms in the hope of communicating, 'Please don't destroy this little aircraft with your mighty foam spray nozzle.'

The message got through, but now I was left, singlehandedly, trying to extinguish the flames with my, thankfully, gloved hands (I still have the gloves to prove it) but without success. I shifted tactics and I managed to negotiate the use of a carbon-dioxide extinguisher from the fire truck which I grabbed, pulled the pin, squeezed the trigger and pointed the nozzle at the source of the flames. With a wooooooshhh and torrent of misty gas, as quickly as the fire had started it was extinguished and I'd saved the day again.

Phew! … fire out.

But what was I doing here in the first place? And why was I testing this little aeroplane? … I hear you ask.

I guess this saga all started when I learned that there was an aircraft importer/manufacturer based just a few miles from my home. Reality Aircraft was then based in Amesbury, near Boscombe Down, and run by a very nice chap called Terry. Working for the CAA at the time I had a remit to oversee aspects of such organisations and it was daft not to oversee one close to home. So I'd spent a day with Terry many years previously. He was creating the kits for home-built aeroplanes in a couple of industrial units.

A few years later I had been talking with the British Microlight Aircraft Association (BMAA). The UK CAA delegated responsibility for aeroplanes weighing less than 472 kg to them and I was overdue to audit their flight-test procedures. In an effort to be helpful and achieve the aim in a slightly less tedious manner than usual, I suggested they simply treat me as one of their test pilots for a specific project. I would use all their paperwork, preparation, risk assessments etc., and get some flying done which needed to be done anyway. Imagine my delight when it turned out the BMAA were short of pilots near my home and they allocated me to the Reality Aircraft Escapade project, the latest version of the very aircraft that I'd been shown by Terry in Amesbury years earlier.

Great stuff. So, I undertook two flights totalling five hours and managed to bash through the BMAA's requirements in good order without any excitement. Excitement is a bad thing in my job. This had included some deliberate engine shut-downs to correctly quantify the aircraft's stall speed; turns out this was a good deal more zealous than other BMAA pilots' take on the same requirement. But the engine re-started each time so all was well.

I returned the following year to fly the same aircraft again which, I have to say, was a pleasant aircraft to fly despite not having enough directional stability; that is that characteristic of the dart which, once thrown, flies straight, due to its tail feathers. Well, this aircraft really needed bigger tail feathers but that would have compromised one of the neat tricks of this aircraft. Both wings, with the removal of just two bolts, could be folded back like on a Fairey Swordfish. This meant the aircraft took up no room in a hangar and could be towed behind a car easily and took only minutes to re-rig and go flying – genius.

I had enjoyed my day or two flying the Escapade. I had also enjoyed my time in Terry's office drinking coffee and chewing the fat with him and a handful of his mates who seemed to come and go and treat the company as a social club. It was during one of these social chats that I was invited to fly another aeroplane; this one was called the Kid – son of the Escapade. It seemed to me to be a scaled-down and single-seat version of the aircraft I'd just tested – and it kinda was.

Interestingly the UK CAA had taken the decision to de-regulate such aeroplanes, as long as they weighed less than 115 kg, which isn't a lot. As the CAA test pilot for microlights, I felt I should have a better understanding of this genre. Were they really safe to be flown without any kind of annual airworthiness check or flight test? Ironically, by the very fact that they were now de-regulated they didn't need a formal flight test by the CAA at all. So, to cut a long story short, given that I had no alternative access to these aircraft, I thought I should seize the day, which justified a flight out of professional curiosity. Terry kindly dragged the aircraft out on to the historic and very pleasant grass airfield at Old Sarum. Fuel topped up, seconds later I was off on my own wondering at what stage of the flight the go-kart Wankel engine would seize up on me. But this little pretender to the throne actually flew okay and, given the rather nice sunny day I'd chosen, proved a pleasant way to spend half an hour or so. I survived the flight and thought my time with the aircraft was over, but Terry convinced me to stay for more coffee and some of my favourite chocolate digestives – there is no such thing as a free chocolate digestive! While sipping and munching, he explained that he hadn't been able to find a suitable test pilot to formally test fly the aircraft, which he needed to do for the BMAA and, subsequently, sales into mainland Europe. It was not the remit of the CAA to undertake such a task but I saw no conflict of interest with me helping out in my spare time and discussed it with and gained the support of the CAA's Chief Test Pilot.

This meant my availability was poor, but living only five minutes from the airfield, it meant as soon as I had a spare minute on a nice-weather day, I could ring up Terry and by the time I got to his office the kettle

The Kid aircraft during the flight test programme at Old Sarum.

was on and the aircraft was outside and ready to fly. Due to poor weather and other snags the testing of this and some associated aircraft lasted over eighteen months, so I had become a regular, if infrequent, visitor to Reality Aircraft.

My first major snag with the aircraft gave me one of the most disturbing emergencies I've had to deal with.

The sun was shining. The sky was, well, sky blue. There were a few white fluffy clouds about, and you could see for miles. All was well with the world and I was flying along in my bright yellow single-seater, minding my own business without much of a care in the world, gathering my flight-test data, as you do, when, all of a sudden, the aircraft started literally shaking itself to death. In particular, the joystick was trying to thrash around the cockpit. Hell's bloody bells!

My heart leapt into my mouth.

This was not an experience I'd had before and I now had to make some extremely difficult decisions very, very quickly indeed.

Some years earlier, a microlight, visiting ETPS at Boscombe Down to give students familiarisation flights, had experienced serious vibration and had immediately landed in a field; it turned out that three of the four bolts holding the engine onto the aircraft had sheared. Had the fourth bolt let go, the loss of the engine would have caused such a massive shift in the centre of gravity of the aircraft that the whole thing would have become uncontrollable and would have crashed, killing both pilots.

So, based on the little that I knew, this ETPS event formed the basis of my working hypothesis. Was this happening to my little Wankel engine? Instinctively, I quickly throttled back with a view to stopping the engine promptly. But throttling back did not change the level or frequency of vibration at all. Bugger! But, curious? I thought, in perhaps my last few seconds on planet Earth. So, hypothesis number one – wrong.

If in doubt, slow down. I had already automatically done this anyway and, as the airspeed reduced, so did the vibration.

'Mmmmmmmmm – maybe all is not lost?'

I slowed to 45 mph, at which point the vibration had calmed down to just 'worrying' rather than 'catastrophically upsetting'. Having adopted my, now, usual policy of always pointing to where I'd parked my car at the first sign of trouble, I was at the geographical location where I would normally call the airfield to let them know I was rejoining. So, I could continue? Or I could land in a field? Decisions, decisions, decisions.

Given that it wasn't engine-related and given that the vibration seemed no longer bad enough to rip my wings off (this was a sturdily-built wee beastie), I elected to fly in a pedestrian manner back to the field while alerting them to my emergency in the customary fashion (see earlier). I landed, taxied back to the office and clambered out.

Phew! … survived another.

What catastrophic damage to the wing or tail might be responsible for the last ten minutes of 'brown adrenalin'? But no, nothing seen. Terry came across with whoever was chewing the fat with him at the time and we searched and investigated, and eventually found the cause of what had felt like the imminent end of my world event. A certain bicycle brake cable had snapped.

'What – just a bike brake cable?'

'Yep'.

So, technical explanation inbound. At the back of the aeroplane is the elevator control surface. This is attached directly to the joystick which, when moved fore and aft, moves the elevator up or down; this directs the airflow over the back of the aircraft and has the effect of being able to push the back end of the aircraft up or down which pitches the attitude of the aircraft so that I can climb or dive or stay straight and level.

As the aircraft's speed changes the elevator has to be moved slightly to keep the aircraft from climbing or descending which means the pilot is usually left having to apply a constant force to the stick, making flying more difficult and tiring. So, many decades ago, shortly after such aeroplanes were invented, someone came across an idea that would allow the pilot to reduce the control stick forces to zero. This was known as 'trimming the aircraft' and was achieved by the addition of a 'trim tab' on the back edge of the elevator. If this trim tab was moved up it tended to push the elevator down and vice versa. In this particular aircraft, weight was absolutely critical. The empty weight had to be kept below 115 kg. So, the trim tab was operated by a simple push-pull bicycle brake cable. And because it was operating at a rather acute angle the inner cable eventually got tired of being pushed around this way and that and promptly snapped. This meant the very small trim tab could flap around freely in the breeze, with the consequence that the elevator was then driven up and down at quite a ferocious pace. The aeroplane did what it was told by the elevator; trying to climb – dive – climb – dive – climb – dive in very rapid succession, which is why I had initially decided I had seconds left to live. All brought about by a £5 item from the Halfords bike shop. Great.

You might wonder why I continued to test fly such an aircraft but there were some really rewarding times and, obviously, there were the copious quantities of coffee and chocolate digestives. Additionally, there were lots of chances to sit and chat aviation and do our level best, as a team, to produce the best aircraft we could. My favourite example was early in the programme when I had started the formal testing of the Kid's stability and control and, like its big brother, it lacked directional stability. It was almost as happy flying sideways as it was flying in a straight line. I landed and complained bitterly about this aspect and was told to go away for lunch and come back in two hours.

I should point out, two hours, in flight-test terms, is the blink of an eye. Modifications to aircraft generally take months or even years. The re-design has to go via a design office, be costed, new risk assessments and test plans have to be approved, the regulator needs to be informed and so on.

After lunch I rocked up to find a cheery bunch of individuals, a bit like those you might find at a surprise party being thrown in your honour. I was invited to have another look at the test aircraft.

The Kid fitted with MDF dorsal fin and rudder extension.

It wasn't subtle. And, frankly, I think it had a lot to do with the aircraft owner who, prior to retirement, ran a kitchen-fitting business. I say that because, now, fastened to the rear of the aircraft with jubilee clips and sticky tape, were two large pieces of MDF, very similar to kitchen worktops!

I was, I confess, both impressed and amazed.

Is it OK to just completely modify the design of an aircraft over the lunch break?

What will the 'grown-ups' say?

But who are the grown-ups here?

Terry was company CEO and chief dishwasher. I was de-facto Head of Flight Test and Chief Test Pilot. Kitchen-fitter, Jim, had taken on the role of chief designer and this aircraft was deregulated. Blige!

Test flying in the 1920s and 1930s must have been like this: rapid prototyping of new ideas – tried out in minutes rather than months – how really refreshing.

And guess what? Yep, the mods worked. The extra dorsal fin area and taller rudder both worked to make the aircraft much more dart-like. Much better than the Escapade two-seater for sure. Further testing allowed us to work out how much of this extra fin area was required and it transpired a taller rudder on its own would be good enough, which was good news indeed as it meant no formal re-design of the fuselage. All we had to do was build a taller rudder that could still be attached to the same attachment points, just as previously.

So, the test programme continued – and although I was only getting to fly the aircraft once or twice a month I was actually quite enjoying it. I was, on each landing, trying to perfect my technique. An aircraft such as this needs to fly from short strips in farmers' fields and the like, and I was perfecting my short-field landings with each successive landing.

One day I came into the approach with a real determination to land on a sixpence. Everything was just right; light wind down the strip, me flying over the hedge at the aircraft's slowest possible speed and then progressively flaring the aircraft to land in the three-point attitude (that is with all three wheels contacting the ground simultaneously). In fact, on this occasion, probably the tail wheel actually touched first. The mainwheels plonked on to the ground with me expecting a nice gentle run on for a short but measureable landing distance. But what happened

The Kid with the extended rudder to improve directional stability.

instead was a skid of about 2 or 3 metres with the tail now lifted back into the flying attitude before I finally came to an ungraceful halt.

'What the hell?'

I tried to taxi off the runway but the wee beastie would have none of it and, yet again, I had closed an airfield by finding myself stuck in the middle of the only useable runway.

On climbing out, the cause of my problem this time was readily apparent. Each main wheel was individually braked by disc brakes. One of the discs now resembled a bent shelf bracket rather than the nice flat disc it had started life as. And this well-bent disc clearly could not turn more than once through the brake pads before jamming which is exactly what had happened. This could have been very, very embarrassing. The aircraft could easily have stood on its nose, writing off the prop and engine and severely denting my pride/ego/reputation as all those watching would have assumed I'd messed up.

Light enough for a few blokes to bodily lift the aircraft, it was easily returned to whence it came, and the dodgy disc diagnosed. Major trauma, thinks me, months of delay, wheel and brake re-design etc. Instead, I was sent to get some lunch and come back in two hours – sound familiar?

I returned to find the aircraft sitting outside the office as if nothing had happened. It turns out the discs fitted to the wheel brakes were identical to those fitted to some high-spec mountain bikes which the posh bike shop in town kept in stock. Great – two new discs, pads and some much tighter bolts holding them in place, and I was good to carry on with the programme.

With most of the required flying done, my attention turned to investigating the spin characteristics of the aeroplane and ensuring it could always be recovered should it get into such a disorientating situation accidentally. As always, with such spin-test programmes, there is always a significant risk that the aircraft might actually not be recoverable during a test point and will continue to spin itself into the ground; not a good outcome for someone hoping to make use of their hard-earned pension fund.

So, an exit strategy had to be devised. Fans of Star Trek would know that pilots were often rescued from their blazing shuttle craft by 'emergency beam out'. If only Scotty, Spock and James T. could have helped with my spinning programmes, I'd have been very happy. Instead, the best option was to wear a parachute, always very uncomfortable, especially in a small aircraft such as the Kid, which was very definitely not designed to accept a parachute-wearing pilot. Getting into the aircraft was one problem, but the far bigger one was how to egress from an uncontrollable spinning aircraft hurtling earthwards with seconds available to get the heck out of it.

The doors on the Kid were quite flimsy, but hinged at the leading edge. So, in order to get them open in flight I would have to push against the prevailing airflow, and probably the airflow would win. So, a better method was discussed whereby I could literally pull the pins out of the door hinges and then pushing against the door would allow the airflow to (probably) rip the door off, allowing me to throw myself out of the opening. Terry, forever the innovator, came up with another metal cable attached to the two hinge-pins, which was fed through the fuselage and could then be pulled by my left hand. The cable was covered in a length of plastic hose to protect it and allow it to move freely.

So, the day came for me to go spinning; always a very tense series of sorties. I had already alerted the ATC unit at Boscombe Down as to what I was up to, since I'd be talking to them and I'd called my mates at Wiltshire Air Ambulance so that, if I did have to jump out, they'd know roughly where to look and what colour of parachute to look for.

Briefed and prepared as best I could be, I started the Wankel and, following a quick check of the brakes with shiny new discs securely bolted in place (!), I taxied forward and turned to travel down to the far end of the runway. I'd barely been moving a few metres when I started to smell the burning. I wasn't particularly worried – I was still on the ground after all – how bad could it be? It never crossed my mind that, within seconds, I would be using the words,

'Mayday, Mayday, Mayday'!

I'm not sure how many Mayday calls have been initiated on the ground within minutes of setting off – not many would be my guess.

Still, with the help of Dave in the tower and a borrowed CO_2 extinguisher, the flames were quickly extinguished, but my gloves were ruined, covered in molten and blackened plastic hose.

Phew! … survived another.

It turns out that when Terry shut my door, with me inside to prevent me having a last-minute change of mind, he tucked the pull/ jettison cable behind the instrument panel. Unfortunately, there was just enough metal not covered in plastic hose to touch the back of the battery master ON/OFF switch. Once the engine was running, I was pumping electrical current through this wire as fast as the 14V charge could muster. It got hot, therefore. The plastic hose reached its ignition temperature or kindling point and, well, you've read the outcome earlier in this chapter.

So we pulled the aircraft back to where I'd started from and amazingly there was no real damage done. A new switch, a quick re-design of the jettison cable and 'Bob's your Uncle' I was off again to complete my sortie. I can't imagine how long the paperwork for a similar incident in a commercial aeroplane would have taken. Let alone fixing it and re-designing a jettison mechanism?

So, all too quickly, the test programme for the Kid was completed and with the report written I thought that would be the end of my time chewing the fat with Terry and team. Then another task came my way to help get the Escapade through German certification.

I was busily testing an Escapade owned by another of Terry's mates to sort this out when his battle with lung cancer took a downward turn and, sadly, Terry died a few months later. Ironically, I now act as Chief Test Pilot for the company that bought Reality Aircraft's designs. Sadly, they aren't based locally but their welcome is equally warm and I have no complaints in being invited to continue flying Escapades.

The first Stearman I had the privilege to flight test in 2005. G-OBEE tested out of Old Buckenham.

Boeing Stearman G-THEA ready for its flight test at Stacumny House.

Just airborne from Oaksey Park in the Boeing Stearman with the Wing Walk Rig fitted.

Landing after the Flight Test with Fred having lost a leg!

Savannah XLS at Old Sarum prior to my spin testing.

The pre-production PZL SW-4 at Lublin just about to get airborne during my flight test programme.

Vampire T.11 at North Weald prior to flight test Note the placement of the pitot tube on the left hand tail fin.

Pilatus PC-6 in the late afternoon prior to test flying past sunset.

Ray and me with the Sikorsky S92 SAR at Coatesville, USA. Initial testing had been completed in Florida.

Testing the RAF 2000 autogyro without the doors fitted which improved the directional stability. Note the electric blue colour scheme.

Sea Fury at North Weald about to taxi for flight test. After the Swordfish the most iconic Fleet Air Arm aeroplane.

Unfolding the wings on the Sea Fury.

Fiesler Storch at Old Warden prior to flight test. The aircraft had very good low speed handling qualities but a poor rate of climb.

Two seat Spitfire TR9 prior to flight test. Notice it is partially painted already in Dutch Airforce Colours. Subsequently it was repainted in RAF colours.

Starting the RYAN ST3KR at Breighton, Yorkshire prior to flight test.

After the Fiesler Storch, the Ryan has the most forgiving undercarriage of any aeroplane I've flown. This example was built in 1942 and was used as a trainer in WW2 for the US military.

Getting airborne in the S61N at Perkasie, Pennsylvania – Notice the yellow sponsons added on specifically for our flight testing.

The Escapade microlight aeroplane prior to my flight testing at Old Sarum, Wiltshire parked in front of the office where I consumed much coffee and chocolate digestives.

The Whirlwind Helicopter prior to my flight test. Note that there are no RAF roundels or other military insignia visible as it was owned and operated in Ireland.

Wasp helicopter prior to my flight test at Thruxton. This is the very helicopter I flew for my Final Handling Test in when I completed my Wasp conversion course back in 1983.

The REGA A109SP helicopter I tested out of Interlaken, Switzerland. Note the large device on the left hand side which mounts a Camera turret on a sliding mount so it can be raised or lowered. The aircraft is used extensively since this mod was approved – searching for survivors lost in the Alps.

Stampe Aeroplane that I tested with brakes that didn't work and nearly came off the side of the runway into a car park.

Stampe Aeroplane modified with enclosed canopies. Another aircraft with an engine prone to stopping.

Me setting off in the Optica for a flight test out of Thruxton.

Tiger Moth at Goodwood – the first I'd had to test to assess its spin recovery characteristics.

Tiger Moth at Chilbolton. Notice the very narrow strip alongside a tall hedge.

Tiger Moth at Henlow that nearly met its match!

The PZL flight test gang at Flagstaff, Arizona just before I tried to get airborne with insufficient power.

Me flying the PZL SW-4 at Lublin for the initial avoid curve testing.

Me starting up a Cavalon autogyro at night.

Me flying an NPAS Police EC135 helicopter – visiting a Welsh Police Station open day.

Me landing the Wiltshire Air Ambulance at a major road traffic accident on the A350 by the A303 intersection.

Chapter 13

Bugs and Yanks

'So Ed, what's your understanding of the certification requirement for this aeroplane's stalling characteristics?'

Ed and I were walking through downtown Bend, a relatively small town in Oregon, 250 miles south-east of Seattle, named after the fact that it was on the bend in the Deschutes river, no doubt a very important aspect of the main navigation feature through the State a hundred and twenty years previously when settlers had first arrived.

Ed was a Federal Aviation Administration (FAA) test pilot, based in Seattle, who had started his life as a US Marine Corps Skyhawk pilot before training at the US Navy Test Pilot School (USNTPS Patuxent River, or Pax River as it was known in TP circles) where he went on to teach fixed-wing flight test for several years. He'd been an FAA TP for seven years and I'd worked for the UK Civil Aviation Authority for less than two. What I'm trying to say is: I was feeling very much like a first-day-at-school rookie in the presence of this guy's experience and résumé.

We were between bars. This was my strategy for the evening – to drink a lot? Nothing new there. Not quite. I'd encountered a problem testing an aeroplane that he had previously tested. He had reported all was okay and I had found it to be horrendously bad. 'Oh dear.' Clearly a different opinion.

Now, I've already mentioned, if you want three different opinions you only need to ask two different test pilots. We are, by training and definition, people who generally feel pretty passionate about our day job and do our level best to nail an opinion about an aircraft that stands scrutiny, but we often do have to argue the case for our view, especially if we are representing the two opposite sides of whichever fence we are meeting over. I began my gentle inquisition by trying to establish whether our interpretation of the written certification requirements was the same.

'Well', says Ed, 'I think the requirement is the same in Europe as in the US.'

'What exactly?' I ask.

By now we have had a couple of jars of typically weak and tasteless American fizzy beer but I'm feeling emboldened.

Ed goes on to explain (you can always tell an ex-test pilot school instructor – but you can't tell them anything). Anyway, his explanation coincided with my own interpretation pretty much exactly.

We have now been to a number of bars and head for a curry, or maybe it was a Mexican? Anyway, chance to drink some more alongside some spicy food so I continue with my interrogation.

'So, when you test-flew the aeroplane, did you find any problems? Did it meet the requirements we're chatting about?'

'Yes absolutely', he states.

Which I was afraid he was going to say. This was going to be very problematic when we would be in a more formal meeting with the company that had designed the offending aircraft. I was going to have to tell an ex-USMC Skyhawk test pilot that his opinion of this aeroplane was – ouch – *wrong*.

Let me rewind a little and try to explain another dry but relevant topic. An aircraft that's new or newly modified has to be approved initially in its home country. This was all decided in a series of meetings held in Chicago during and after the Second World War. Once the home nation had approved, or certified, the design, other countries would then evaluate the aircraft to see if they also believed it was safe to fly in their country. Former nations of the British Empire and Commonwealth accepted the UK CAA's approval without further evaluation; equally many countries would accept the certification process of the USA. In the UK we would accept much of what the FAA had done but, since there were differences in our certification requirements, we would conduct a 'Validation', which meant a scaled-down test programme. When the European Aviation Safety Agency (EASA) came into being they took on the same process. In this case I had been sent to Bend (not round the Bend) with a UK flight test engineer, Nick, under contract to EASA. We were there to test and validate a locally designed and built pair of quite 'punchy' aeroplanes. These had been built by a company called Columbia, who had started life building home-built kit aeroplanes but had recently moved into the big leagues and were producing a four-seat aeroplane with a massively powerful piston engine that could take the aircraft to 25,000 feet, or 5 miles up. Which is very high for a light piston-engine aeroplane. They had experienced a troublesome flight-test programme as they were trying to match the claims of their main competitor. We can go higher, faster, further – that kind of thing. During the company flight testing the pilot lost control of a prototype when testing the recovery from a spin and he had to abandon the aircraft and parachute to safety – *great*. The morning after our pub crawl dawned. As usual, since we were on the west coast, Nick and I had been awake from about 3 am anyway. And after the usual rubbish American buffet breakfast, we headed off to the company for this dreaded meeting.

We were hosted by the company chief test pilot (CTP). She was German and had spent a fair amount of time flying gliders and testing home-built aeroplanes. I even have one of her books in my loft but confess I've never completed reading it.

This meeting was going to be difficult. The way these things work is the company does its own flight testing, then the National Authority does whatever testing it thinks necessary and then certifies the aircraft if it flies okay. So now, on behalf of EASA, I was about to explain that the aircraft doesn't fly okay. The baby is, yet again, *ugly*. But now the FAA will also need to defend its opinion so that, instead of my views being opposed by the company CTP, initially I'm up against ex USMC Skyhawk TP, Ed. In fairness I have already accepted an experience and 'credibility gradient'. And not in my favour.

And so we started with Nick and I presenting our results and explaining why we believe there were unacceptable issues that needed addressing. We look to the company CTP who had flown alongside me in my testing but, whenever I needed confirmation of my results, I was greeted with a Germanic shrug – oh dear. This wasn't going well …

But let me rewind further …

Firstly, let me point out this was my first overseas validation test campaign on behalf of EASA in an aeroplane rather than a helicopter. And at this stage my street cred as a fixed-wing text pilot was in its ascendency. Nick and I had hoped this would be a straightforward validation exercise, given that the FAA had already approved the aircraft. So, what could we possibly find that they hadn't?

We started as usual with a tour of the factory and a brief on the aeroplane and the testing issues encountered by the company, including the spinning accident. We were assured this had been properly sorted and

Columbia 400 test aircraft at Bend.

went off to commence our usual combination of performance testing and assessment of the aircraft's handling qualities. The first couple of trips went okay and we were hoping to get through to Friday morning nicely on time to get our flight home from Seattle that evening, but life is never that easy. And then we got to stalling.

I've talked about stalling elsewhere in the book, but aircraft such as this should be able to be slowed right down and give the pilot plenty of warning when they are flying too slowly. If the pilot continues to slow down, the aircraft will stall (stop flying) but the pilot should be able to maintain the aircraft's wings level, or at least within 15 degrees of level. As I commenced slowing down I was under the watchful eye of the CTP. She had already bollocked me repeatedly for not flying the aircraft quite like her. She didn't quite seem to appreciate that I was here to find any problems with the aircraft, rather than to overcome them with (hopefully) my slightly better than average ability? She had not had the good fortune to attend a test pilot school and I think, for the entire time of our flying together, she didn't quite get what I was trying to discover and document.

Anyway, put it like this, as I slowed she snorted with Bavarian contempt, clearly aware that I would be unable to cope with what was to come next.

I did my usual checks:

Height = sufficient;
Airframe = flaps up;
Security = straps tight, no loose articles;
Engine = prop rpm set fully fine, all temperatures and pressures OK;
Location = over a crackingly beautiful part of the Wild West;
Lookout = nothing seen apart from the sun set high in an azure sky
and not a cloud in sight.

All checks done, I smoothly closed the throttle and commenced a leisurely deceleration at the required one knot every second. All was going well, using a technique I had already had to use countless times before despite my relative inexperience and then … *Whack!*

With no notice, the aircraft stalled and despite my instinctive reactions it promptly rolled itself *upside down.*

Well, perhaps I exaggerate just a teeny bit? But it rolled 110 degrees. Bear in mind that 15 degrees was the allowed limit and 90 degrees is a right angle; that would be the wings not level but pointing at the ground. So by 110 degrees I'm looking up over my head at the ground which by any definition is pretty much upside down.

So with my female companion glaring and tutting at me at the same time for my inept flying, I recovered the aeroplane to level flight, followed by a quick 'team chat'.

'What happened then?'

'I suggest you repeat the test point cautiously', offers Nick.

So I set up to repeat the test point, ensuring I climbed back to a sensible height to be able to cope with whatever this troublesome child threw at me next.

And guess what? Yep, same again, almost exactly. In fact, we knew this was a very contentious finding and, so as to be absolutely confident with our results, we repeated the test point several times, and always got the same outcome.

My new most ardent critic was not impressed and sulked as I flew us (untidily no doubt, in her opinion) back to the airfield. So we debriefed and chatted and were advised that we were flying a prototype and, clearly, the production variant was absolutely fine. So, the following morning, in the still early morning dew-laden air, we rocked up to Bend Airfield where the company pilot had already prepped the shiny brand-new production aircraft. Off we flew, quickly flying high enough to find proper daylight long before the poor earthbound souls below. It was another 'to die for' morning with a stillness that was at contrast to our intentions.

HASEL checks done; again with plenty of height in hand, just in case. Throttle closed, trimmed at just over 100 KIAS, 99, 98, 97 ... 80, 79, 78, 77, 76, 75, 74, 73 ... 72 ... 71 ... *Whack!*

Yep, it was even worse than the prototype. No amount of 'conventional use of the flying controls' could prevent this aircraft rolling onto its back. At least it was consistent. My poor FTE Nick started to complain about spending more time upside down than the right way up. So we flew home for my last landing of that session, which thankfully was perfect, much to my prime critic's annoyance as I think she was hoping to find another excuse to berate me.

So, what now?

Well this was an aircraft already certified and approved by the FAA and we had discovered, without trying that hard, a major 'non-compliance' with the certification requirements. We had found another ugly baby.

The FAA experts responsible for this particular aeroplane were based in Seattle, so agreed to pop down to see us the following morning, and we suggested we meet up for a drink or three that evening so I could employ the haze of alcohol to avoid my embarrassment at clearly not knowing what I was doing. I was evidently not doing this right (as no doubt my Bavarian winger would testify) because I had obtained quite different results from the FAA TP, Ed.

Much beer and much spicy food later, I think I had established that Ed thought the rules read the same way as me, and that the aircraft should stay within 15 degrees of level rather than 110 degrees but he clearly couldn't recollect seeing such bad characteristics when he flew it ... mmmmmmmmmmmmmmmmm.

So another day dawned when, thankfully, none of us had any plans to do any further flying and, after a good deal of black coffee and of course, donuts, we commenced our formal meeting. Nick and I were on one side of the table with Ed and his colleague and the company personnel, including their CTP, on the other. The politics were such that the FAA were now defending the aircraft and their reputation, and they were doing a robust job.

'But', says I, 'the company CTP has witnessed our tests, haven't you?'

'Ja.'

'And you saw that the aircraft rolled on its back?'

'Ja.'

'And you saw that I flew the test technique correctly?'

'Ja', she admitted, somewhat begrudgingly.

So what is going on? Nick and I decided to step out for a well-timed 'comfort break' to give the other side of the table a chance to regroup.

We returned in time to see the company pilot waving a document around thicker than your average Yellow Pages phone directory. She was pointing to a sentence buried deep within the document where she had summarised her own stall test results – and guess what? You're ahead of me …

Yep, she had also had very similar results from her final phase of testing. What? Yep, she'd seen this characteristic herself, and had documented it in her final report which she had submitted to Ed and his team, but had she discussed it with them? Or drawn attention to the non-compliance? Well no, she hadn't. Oh dear.

However, this still didn't explain why my USMC Skyhawk TP drinking buddy hadn't experienced the same phenomenon. So, we got into the detail over more coffee and donuts and finally – 'Eureka!'

It transpired that the aircraft Ed flew for all his testing was a prototype without wheel spats. Wheel spats go over the wheels to make them look pretty and, perhaps, allow the aircraft to fly slightly faster. My aeroplane came with spats fitted to each wheel but his didn't. So, we had been flying quite different aeroplanes.

Phew! … we were both right. Integrity intact.

Ed's aeroplane had stalled okay, but mine hadn't. Three big wheel spats added to the machine, especially on the nose wheel, had clearly made a big difference to the airflow around the wings and thus we had a different result. Hurrah! FAA credibility wasn't quite as eroded as it might have been. However, they proceeded to give the company a bollocking for not drawing their attention to this issue before now.

Phew! … survived another and a very good result all round.

Even better, our BA flight to LHR was delayed, so Nick and I had even longer in the BA business lounge to sample the local Oregon wines which, it turns out, are rather good.

A few months later we were back in Bend, flying with the same company pilot again, following the company's own flight-test programme to sort out the issue. They had flown scores of sorties trying to get to the bottom of the problem and fix it. Now here is one of my favourite questions I used to ask the TP students at ETPS when I went back each year to lecture them on civil flight testing …

'The company found repeatedly that the stall characteristics of the aircraft were better (more benign) in the afternoon than when they had flown in the morning. Why?'

I've had some great answers to that question, even including speculation that the skinny chief test pilot would eat like a horse every lunchtime and thus dramatically change the weight of the aeroplane.

Do you want to know the answer?

Bugs.

Bugs?

Yep, Bugs.

Turns out that in the cold air of the morning the local bugs and flies hadn't yet stirred but in the warmth of the afternoon sun they would be out in abundance. The lucky ones would enjoy a scenic flight and be home in time for tea; the less lucky were impacted by the leading edge of the test aeroplane's wing at over 100 mph – *splat*. Ouch!

By the time the aircraft was flying the stall test points in the afternoon the leading edge of the wing was splattered with unlucky and, now dead, bugs. And the bugs changed the airflow over the wing, and the plane now stalled okay; well, at least better.

So, guess what? They decided to stick a whole bunch of 'bugs' on the leading edge of the wing as a permanent feature. In fairness, they looked more like triangular pieces of chocolate from a Toblerone bar by the time we went testing, but they did indeed work.

Three flights later and we were very happily convinced that the problem was fixed and we could head home rejoicing, waving a, not so sad, Auf Wiedersehen, pet.

Phew! … job done … an unsafe aeroplane now safe to fly.

The triangular bugs affixed to the wing's leading edge.

The following year I was back out to Oregon, but this time flying from Hilsboro, about a hundred and forty miles south-west of Seattle, near the city of Portland. I was with my RW FTE, Jeff, and we were visiting to assess a new system. The system had been developed originally by a US Navy F-18 Hornet fast-jet pilot. He'd tried to use the technology of the fast-jet world (fast) and apply it to helicopters (slow). I think you can guess how this evaluation was going to go.

We flew the system in a Baron twin-engine aeroplane and also in a Bell JetRanger B206. I was a fairly experienced pilot of both such types of aircraft, but we were there to assess the usefulness of the system which had, you've guessed it, already been certified by the FAA. In the Baron we were predominantly dashing along at 150–200 mph. In the JetRanger we weren't!

The system was based on what's called a head-up display (HUD). Thirteen years ago, when we were testing the equipment, that concept was entirely limited to aircraft but right now there are a number of domestic cars where the speedometer reading is projected onto the windscreen so a driver can know how fast they're driving without taking their eyes off the road. In a jet the HUD not just indicates speed but also additional information including the aircraft's attitude (pitch and roll – not how grumpy it was).

The JetRanger was an aircraft flown predominantly by day in good weather and really didn't need this additional device, but it could be legally, and frequently was, flown at night. If the pilot cannot see a natural horizon (the roughly horizontal demarcation between blue sky/clouds and the green ground or grey sea) then it is very possible that the pilot will not know when they are flying level and ultimately could end up with such a large bank angle as to lose control = 'crash, burn, die'.

So, to fly at night, an aircraft has an 'artificial horizon' or 'attitude indicator' which mimics the external view and allows the aircraft to be kept level. Well, this new novel system replaced this relatively simple device with a computer-driven glass screen that tried to do everything including make the half-time tea. The display changed frequently with probably five different pictures depending on what it thought the pilot was trying to do. It determined much of this optimising by use of a speed switch. Rather than using the airspeed, the device used groundspeed derived from tracking satellites (GPS).

Anyway, off we went to evaluate it. I didn't like it during my day flight, but since you didn't legally need it to fly by day, I couldn't claim it was entirely unacceptable. By night it was a different saga altogether. Early on in the sortie I flew a very simple manoeuvre that would be absolutely essential if, for any reason, the single engine lost power. That is, I would slow down, lowering the collective lever to reduce the drag on the rotor blades and then, as they continued to turn, I would be in autorotation or a glide. I then turned through 180 degrees into wind so that I could land in a field or similar. I was flying at around 60 mph and the wind was about 20 mph. So, one minute my ground speed was 80 mph and then, having completed my turn into wind, it was down 40 mph. My airspeed had not changed but this clever (?) system now assumed I was slowing down to land and must now want information about hovering rather than info on which way was up. In fact, during this simple manoeuvre the display format changed three times.

I try not to use the word, but, yes, it was a nightmare.

So, back to the office to tell the F-18 pilot his system sucked (another ugly baby). But, of course, he cited the fact that it was already approved in the US by the FAA. So, when we should have been in the hotel bar quaffing our first glass of Pinot Gris (excellent local wine) we were contacting the FAA's helicopter test pilot, Anne, who had approved of, and signed off, this system.

I have never met the lady face to face, but at this time she had worked for the FAA a good deal longer than I had worked for the CAA and EASA, so I prepared to meet my match and have it explained to me where I was going wrong.

So, we had a conference call, and I introduced myself. We talked about people we might know – did she know Ed? Not so much apparently as he only did aeroplanes and she only did helicopters …

Then we got to crunch time.

'So, Anne, talk me through what you thought of the system.'

She described something similar to the device we'd been looking at, so thankfully no repeat of the wheel spats debacle.

'But, what did you think about the system at night?'

'At night?'

'Yep, what did you think about it when you flew at night?'

'At night?'

'Yes, when it was dark – at night.'

'Night – when it was dark?'

'Yes, like the Flight Manual says you can and when lots of people operate the aircraft – at night?'

Now I can't quite remember where she was speaking from, but my guess is it was Texas where she was based and I could now hear the tumbleweed blowing around in the background as it went quiet for a very long time.

And then in a way that only sounds funny when said with a strong Texan drawl,

'Y'all flew a JetRanger at night?'

'Yes, we did. That's kinda what we do when we evaluate something. We do a comprehensive flight-test programme which meant flying in bright sunlight, overcast conditions and at night.'

'Well … we don't and I didn't!' she stated.

But by now it was evident, like at Bend, that we had, on behalf of EASA, found some unacceptable aspects of the system which were not going to pass muster without being fixed.

So we wrapped up the conversation and dived into our rental just in time to catch last orders at the bar.

Phew! … Survived another; a useful visit and the world now a safer place.

We weren't quite so lucky when I found myself out in Boise, Idaho, flying another JetRanger at night. I was working with Ray, who had travelled from Germany and discovered on the Sunday that German trains don't run on time after they've driven over someone! So he was a day late catching up with me.

We were there on behalf of EASA to assess a Bell JetRanger B206 that could be flown (according to the FAA) using Night Vision Goggles (NVG).

NVG have been used by military operators since the Vietnam War. A tube powered by a battery is able to use very low light levels and, by some technical wizardry, project the outside world view onto a monochrome green screen, a bit like watching a black-and-white TV with your green-tinted sunglasses on. In fact, these days David Attenborough's film crew use the same technology extensively to film animals (without disturbing them) doing their thing at night (bonking?). So if you've watched any wildlife documentaries recently you'll know what I mean. Anyway, this evaluation was all about flying at night. But before we set off we did our level best to ensure there would be somewhere to eat (Idaho potatoes obviously) and some source of vino to quaff once we'd finished. Frankly we were lied to, in more ways than one.

The most important fib was that the restaurants and bars would be open after 11 pm. In Idaho late-night eating was just not the done thing.

Another challenge was the concept of flying a single-engine helicopter at night using these vision aids which was like looking through two toilet rolls taped together, i.e. you couldn't see much. At that stage in the UK we had only ever approved twin-engine helicopters to use NVG so that we hadn't had to assess whether a safe engine-off landing could be performed. So, having voiced our concerns, we found ourselves minutes later skimming the roof tops of Boise with the company pilot frequently rolling the throttle closed to give us chance to fly numerous 'forced landings' into various downtown car parks. Scary, but do-able. We also found, funny old thing, problems with the cockpit design. On the first night it was difficult to complete our evaluation as the Rad-Alt, which

Wearing NVG ready to flight test the B206 at night.

tells you how high you are above the ground, wasn't working properly. The toilet tubes with the monochrome scene projected into our eyes gave us some visual information but provided no useful clues to determining our height accurately above the ground, particularly when we were very close to it and therefore about to crash, burn, die.

So we had knocked off the flying and gone searching for an open bar whilst the Fedex overnight courier service was tasked, at great expense, to fetch us a replacement part for the following day. In fairness we did find an open bar that night but it was definitely not the sort of bar that two middle-class elderly Brits (who were frankly a bit shy of cross dressing and paying for sexual favours) should have entered if they had wanted to keep their reputations intact. But Hurrah! The hotel had an emergency stash of cold tins of beer and, once we'd woken up the only on-call member of staff to let us in, we felt no further embarrassment whilst we kept him up providing us with beer and crisps/chips.

The following evening, we determined to finish earlier so as to improve our diet over and above fried potato products and fizzy beer. So, as soon as it was dark (dark? Night?) we set off to try out the new rad-alt, but guess what?

The new rad-alt did exactly what the old rad-alt had done. Which meant it turned itself OFF just when we needed it most.

'Who approved this?' we asked.

You will not be surprised by the reply!

So another festeringly 'ugly and unsafe baby'; a shame because the company that hosted us were great fun to work with and the guy we flew with was one of those ex-US Army helicopter pilots who was born riding in the back of a Huey and had more night-flying hours using NVG than all of the UK RAF helicopter pilots put together. Another good job, issues found and documented and no approval given.

Sometime later we were back in Florida, Jeff and I, to evaluate the Sikorsky S-92A helicopter again.

We'd been invited by Sikorsky back to West Palm Beach again (tough life, I know) to evaluate some flight profiles, known throughout the industry as Cat A. So short explanation follows – honest.

If you get on an aeroplane with more than one engine and you pay to travel from A to B then the aircraft manufacturer has to provide you with a reasonable chance of not dying on the trip. So, if an engine fails on an airliner you can be 100 per cent confident that the other engine or engines will be able to land you somewhere safe. The tricky bit is when you are taking off and sometimes you need all the engines to be working properly to get you fast enough to fly. In this case the runway has to be long enough for your aircraft to be able to stop before the end if your remaining engines aren't up to the job – see what I mean?

Now a helicopter has to give fare-paying passengers the same deal. If it has two engines (as pretty much all the public transport aircraft do) then at any stage if one engine should fail the aircraft should be able to abort the take-off and land or fly onto a suitable landing site. Needless to say, everything to do with helicopters is far more complicated than it is with aeroplanes. Which is a good thing for me as there will always, always, always, be work for helicopter test pilots. We arrived at Sikorsky's flight-test facility to be greeted by our 'mate' Ron who briefed us on the already FAA-approved profiles that we were to evaluate on behalf of EASA. Surely this trip would be successful and without drama? Ron leapt in the co-pilot's seat and, with much more familiarity than a few years ago, I flashed up both engines and we taxied out to the airfield, where a simulated helicopter landing pad had been marked out, and I invited

Ron to show me these profiles he single-handedly (please note) had developed. Then I had a go. The S-92A hovered with the nose pitched up about 10–12 degrees. So, I set myself up flying towards the helipad exactly as required by the draft flight manual supplement. As I slowed down from forward flight to get into the hover, I had to pitch the nose up further and further and this profile required me to flare the aircraft to about 30 degrees nose up. All of this required good co-ordination between right hand on the cyclic, my feet on the yaw pedals to keep straight and my left hand on the collective as the lever had initially to be lowered to stop the aircraft climbing accidentally and then, as it slowed down, the collective had to be raised briskly to add power to keep the aircraft from hitting the ground. It was extremely difficult to see out of the aircraft at the best of times but pitched 30-degrees nose up I could see bugger all but my flying boots.

We had to evaluate an additional profile by day and, more critically, at night. The profile required us to descend vertically over a hundred feet … oh great. Hitting the ground accidentally was a real possibility. Or if I tried to stop the rate of descent too soon, I would run out of power, the rotor speed would decay and we would literally fall out of the sky. No pressure then.

The first problem was seeing where on earth, literally, I was needing to land! The cockpit of an S-92A is like an airliner and seeing vertically down impossible. But I did my best and when I thought I was in the right place Ron throttled one engine and I lowered the collective lever to preserve my precious rotor rpm, which resulted in us going down – very fast indeed. And then, at the very last minute, when it appeared all was lost, I had to pull up the collective to use all the energy stored in the spinning rotors. I needed to arrest the rate of descent just before our wheels touched down. And I couldn't see the helipad from the helicopter. I couldn't see the ground, so I didn't know when to pull the lever up to avoid the crash, burn, die we all hoped we would avoid. Thankfully, years of having done this sort of testing came good and by monitoring the rad-alt constantly with a squeak, squeak, squeak all three tyres impacted onto the concrete gently enough not to be ripped off their hubs.

Phew! … Survived another hairy flight. Back to the office for a longish debrief methinks.

Before I go on, I should point out that Ron is an extremely friendly guy and good fun to fly with. We had a lot of laughs in the cockpit but I wouldn't let my daughter buy a car from him if you know what I mean?

'So, Ron, which FAA test pilot signed off on this? Which FAA TP apparently can see through the metal airframe?'

'Well, I did.'

'Yes, Ron, we know you designed, developed, evaluated, documented and published these profiles for Sikorsky *but* who was the independent evaluator from the FAA?'

'Well, I was.'

'Noooo, you don't understand', says I, 'who flew these profiles apart from you on behalf of the FAA?'

'Just me.'

So, here's the thing. In the US, the FAA has finite resources (in fairness as do EASA and the UK CAA). One of the ways they get around this problem is a system of 'Designated Engineering Representatives' (DERs). These DERs include test pilots who can sign off certification documentation on behalf of the FAA. That is what Ron had done here, quite properly and legally, but it was just not sensible. Because a lot of this kind of flying is very subjective. Working out whether something is easy or difficult or too difficult can depend on ability, experience and relevant background. Ron had flown most of the test flights on the S-92A over a fifteen-year period and could probably have flown it with his eyes closed sitting backwards in the seat. So, guess what? He had found the profile he had designed to be easy for him to fly.

'But you can't see where you're going, Ron.'

Anyway, he's a nice guy, and I try to be, so we set aside the first option of throwing all our teddy bears out of the cot and, just in time to catch last orders, rewrote all the profiles in a manner which I thought would actually work. The following day/night we re-flew the amended profiles. And on completion Ron remarked, 'Well I'll be. Y'all have made everything a lot easier to fly – even limeys will be able to do it now.'

Phew! … Good result and a safer set of Cat A profiles in the bag.

Working with the Americans was never dull which is probably what they said back in 1944. To some extent we are indeed two nations divided by a common language. Back at the same location the following year I was about to commence testing the brand-new Sikorsky S-76D helicopter and we arrived at the same time as the FAA flight-test team. Our first briefing was held together and their senior TP (they'd brought two!) kept going on about 'cross-eyed viewing'. For me, and my mate Ray, it made the whole brief really hard to comprehend. Who were these cross-eyed pilots? Why were they so important to the FAA? What were they going to do?

The S-76D was the latest development of an aircraft that had been around for decades. It was often flown like a mini-airliner with two pilots but was certified to only need one pilot. The S-76D had all sorts of gizmos in the cockpit which comprised of two TV screens in front of each pilot station which displayed different information. If the aircraft was flying with only one pilot he would only have two screens to view, unless he looked at the screens in front of the empty pilot seat.

It turns out that the FAA team weren't saying 'cross-eyed' at all, but actually saying 'cross-side' which for them meant to look across at the other side of the instrument panel. Well, why didn't you say so? At last we were on the same page and we shared their concerns this time around and so, in the end, we all agreed the aircraft should be flown with two pilots.

Phew! Entente cordiale restored. God bless America!

Chapter 14

Historic Rotors

'Airspeed, Airspeed', I yelled, followed shortly, thereafter, by the classic instructional mantra, 'I have control. *Let go*. I have control.'

I have to say that I am very, very glad that I became an instructor before becoming a test pilot. I confess my motives were two-fold. I was a Royal Navy Lynx pilot at the time and wanted to spend more time flying whereas the RN wanted me to captain a minesweeper which would have meant no flying for a while. Also, my first child, Samuel, was inbound, and I really did not want to be away for six months at a time as my wee boy was growing up. So I pushed the Royal Navy Appointer hard. He was the guy who allocated my jobs every two years or so. Thankfully for me, the Lynx world was short of competent pilots willing to instruct, given it had more than its fair share of career officers who really did want to captain their own ships. So with my wife eight months pregnant, I was despatched to RAF Shawbury in Shropshire in order to learn how to instruct, initially in a Gazelle helicopter. My son announced his impending arrival in the early hours of a Friday morning, and I was able to dash down to Dorchester Hospital in time to be with my wife when he was born later that day. As he'd timed his arrival perfectly at the weekend, I had two full days at home before having to dash back to Shropshire on Sunday night. Being an instructor now finally gave me some 'shore time' and I was thus around for my daughter's birth two years later. As you will have read earlier, I followed my tour on the Lynx instructional squadron (702 NAS) by being appointed to run the Lynx simulator and instruct on all three of the Lynx squadrons at RNAS Portland. Towards the end of my five years instructing, I was discussing my end-of-tour confidential report with the four-ring captain who had previously been in charge of managing aircrew careers. I had already been selected to attend ETPS in just a few weeks' time and had also just had an assessment as an 'Exceptional Instructor'.

Frankly, I was feeling pretty chuffed with myself. The captain read out my report which included mention of the above and then added,

'Taylor has elected to specialise in aviation.'

An innocent enough comment which was 100 per cent true.

'So, what do you think of that?'

'Sounds fine, Sir. Thank you.'

'Do you know what I'm saying?'

'Well, you're reporting on my career aspirations accurately, thank you, Sir.'

'No, Chris, what I'm saying is: don't promote this officer because he is not interested in being the captain of a ship; he just wants to go flying.'

'Well, that's the case, Sir. Thank you.'

Only a year or so later I was up in London trying to sort out a major hiccup in my embryonic RN flight-test career and these words had indeed conspired to prevent further promotion. But that's a story for another book, maybe.

The crucial thing was I had the opportunity, by instructing for over five years, to apparently become an 'exceptional instructor', according to the experts at the Central Flying School (CFS), which also meant I'd had to become a reasonable helicopter pilot in the process being able to save the day on numerous flights as various students tried to kill me.

Only three years later I was back at ETPS as a rotary wing tutor; now teaching flight test to students from all over the world. They also tried to kill me. Frequently!

But on this particular day I was back in Northern Ireland, my favourite place as you will already have read in a previous chapter. I was flying out of Enniskillen (St Angelo) airfield on the shores of Lough Erne and, if the weather had not been so poor, I'm sure the scenery would have been outstanding. I was there to conduct a check flight on the last of the UK's ex-military Westland Whirlwind helicopters. Ironically, the Whirlwind was the first helicopter I flew in when visiting the Royal Naval Air Station Culdrose as a sixteen-year-old interested in becoming a Wasp pilot. The pilot of said Whirlwind took great pleasure in entering an autorotation/ glide with no notice. I was convinced I was about to die. My whole life flashed in front of me, which didn't take long as a very naive schoolboy, but then the engine was re-applied and I lived to tell the tale, several times over, in the bar later that evening.

About to test fly the Whirlwind HAR Mk 10 at Enniskillen Airfield.

This particular aircraft was an ex-RAF HAR Mk 10, powered by a Gnome gas-turbine engine, and was owned by a chap who lived in Ireland but it was kept on the UK register as an ex-military machine. If you look at the enclosed photo you will see it is in RAF Search and Rescue colours, but without any military roundels. This was apparently to ensure the IRA didn't think it had been recalled to service for military duties and thus shoot it down.

As on many occasions in my flying career I was teamed up with a 'living legend'. This guy had joined the RAF as a pilot before I was born, was an aeroplane instructor before becoming a Whirlwind pilot and helicopter instructor for many years. He had over twelve thousand flying hours and was the only examiner still flying the Whirlwind. So he was, as far as I was concerned, within the cockpit, God. He would forget more about the Whirlwind each year than I'd ever learn about it in my lifetime.

I was overdue to test this helicopter as it hadn't been seen by the CAA for a while, nor had I flown with this pilot before who was conducting airworthiness check flights on our behalf.

My guess is he was around seventy years old when we flew together but appeared sharp enough as we set about starting the engine and lifting into the hover. We shared the flying as I was keen to see how well the

The Whirlwind's rather tatty instrument panel.

Whirlwind flew. He was flying the aircraft for the test point that required us to reach the maximum allowed speed on the aircraft (Vne). Invariably, in such types, you need to both apply full power and then dive the aircraft to accelerate it, trying to overcome the drag of the airframe, which is what we'd done. Due to the lowish cloud, we didn't have much room to achieve the required speed before 'tent pegging' this unique aircraft into the muddy Ulster fields below. We rattled and shook as this hero of so many rescues protested at being asked to do such an ungentlemanly thing. As the airspeed indicator reached the limiting speed I had to confess I had fully expected us to slow down quite promptly as the cows were now starting to get quite big in the window.

But we didn't slow down.

After a further slow-motion second,

I called, very urgently,

'Airspeed, airspeed!'

I thought this would be enough to grab the attention of my super experienced colleague in order for him to stop the rotor blades being ripped off their hubs. But it wasn't. Thankfully, my instructor head turned up in the nick of time and, without further thought, I had automatically taken control from my 'student' and voiced the pre-briefed executive command, 'I have control.'

And, since he didn't immediately release control, promptly followed by, 'Let go. I have control.'

I smoothly lowered the collective to reduce the rotor blade pitch and simultaneously gently eased the cyclic stick back to level the aircraft and reduce speed to something more sensible. Once achieved, I breathed a sigh of relief and I asked,

'What happened there?'

'Dunno.'

'Are you alright?'

'Think so.'

'What were you looking at?'

'Dunno.'

Now, this can happen to any of us. I call it the 'brain fart'; when we do something unexplainable for no apparent reason. A mate of mine in my squadron at Boscombe Down dropped a bomb off his Jaguar jet during a trial. Thankfully it was an inert instrumented store, and although expensive, didn't make too much of a hole in the ground.

Another mate dropped a missile off his Lynx helicopter in a similar fashion – why?

Dunno.

It's not fully appreciated, I think, that we humans make cock-ups all the time. In aviation we try to minimise them with various strategies, such as using checklists or having two pilots on airliners to check each other constantly. I tend to assume I'm going to cock up constantly and just try to make sure my mistakes are small enough not to threaten life or aircraft.

One of my big concerns with flying helicopters is that they rely on lots of moving parts, many of which would kill you quite happily were they to finally wear out on your flight. The Whirlwind was built two years before I was born and was no longer a spring chicken, but we all survived, and I learned the same lesson I'd previously learned many score times. Never trust the other chap. Even if he's a living God and 'legend in his own lunchtime'.

Phew! … pride dented but no damage done.

Arguably I'd been flying historic helicopters from as soon as I gained my Royal Navy Wings; I went straight on to fly the Wasp which, by then, had already been around for twenty-four years. At the time, I had arrived at the conclusion that I was a rubbish helicopter pilot because I found the Wasp bloody difficult to fly. Guess what? As I discovered many years later as a test pilot, the Wasp *is* bloody difficult to fly, let alone land it on the pitching, rolling and heaving flight deck at the backend of a frigate on a dark and stormy night.

Ironically, my first helicopter permit renewal check flight undertaken for the UK CAA was flown on Wasp HAS 1 XT420 at Thruxton. This, it turns out, was the very helicopter I had flown twenty-two years earlier when Chris, 829 NAS Senior Pilot, gave me my Final Handling Test (FHT) out of RNAS Yeovilton. He gave me a very hard time, if memory serves. Chris had been flying a Lynx HAS 2 in the Falklands conflict when a couple of Argentinian Dagger jets decided to shoot him down. His nifty flying and a few popped rivets had saved his bacon. He went on to command HMS *Ocean* in the Second Gulf War and retire as an admiral.

Wasp HAS1 XT420 awaiting flight test at Thruxton.

Test flying Wasp G-RIMM at North Weald. This aircraft is now owned by John as discussed in Chapter 15.

I confess that the opportunity to test fly this aircraft, of which I had such fond memories, was quite a treat, although I did find it a good deal harder to climb into than when I was just 25 years old. I was quickly reminded that it really was not an easy helicopter to fly, and I found the 'older me' being quite in awe of the 'younger me' who had operated this machine in all weathers by day and by night for over three years without major incident.

Over my ten years at the CAA I tested nearly all of the still airworthy Wasps and many of the Scouts (the Army version of the Wasp) and even one of the early Saunders-Roe prototypes. Sadly, I didn't get chance to re-fly Scout XP849 which had the misfortune to be owned by ETPS when I took it up for a training flight on a less than ideal day with a blustery wind. To cut a long story short, as described earlier in this book, I crashed it.

I was practising landing with the engine turned off, was caught out by the wind conditions, and landed more heavily than this elderly aircraft was willing to put up with. Given that this airframe was earmarked for retirement a few weeks later, the damage was never repaired until it was sold off at auction and fixed and operated for a few years by a civilian

Test flying Wasp G-RIMM.

private owner before being sold on to New Zealand in 2010. It would have been nice to fly an aircraft again that I had accidently 'killed-off' years earlier.

One of the good things about working for the UK CAA was that, in both my helicopter and aeroplane licences, I had the words 'Licensed to fly all types of aircraft when flown for flight test purposes in the course of his duties as a CAA Test Pilot'.

This was an essential qualification to allow the job to be undertaken. Normally, to get the appropriate type rating, to allow the piloting of a particular type, a formal course of training has to be undertaken, usually including some theory, examinations and a flight with an examiner. Sometimes aircraft were so new, or so old, no such courses or even instructors or examiners existed. In such circumstances, I would be rolled out to get the said aircraft airborne and tested so that it could be awarded a permit so that subsequently permit training could take place to allow it to be flown. All rather complicated and not what would have happened when Lord Brabazon of Tara was issued with the UK's first Pilot's Licence in 1910. But things never get any easier. Anyway, that's how I came to get involved with G-UHIH, which led to my last flight of 2005, getting this venerable warbird (now UK registered) airborne from UK soil for the first time. It was bought by a chap called Phil who had made a good deal of money as a deep-sea diver and then a supplier of diving equipment to the North Sea oil industry. Phil, I think, had seen too many Vietnam War movies as a kid and his hobby now was to buy and then operate some genuine veterans of that war, in the UK for the airshow public. So, a few phone calls and emails later, the day came when I was to flight test this aircraft to recommend, hopefully, permit issue. Thankfully, I had flown a Huey previously, a couple of military ones when working at ETPS, and I also took along another TP, Geoff, an ex-RAF TP who had flown the type far more extensively than I had. With my CAA mate Ray riding shotgun, we flashed up the beast and committed aviation out of Redhill on quite a misty 22 December day.

The biggest challenge was trying to document the climb performance. The Huey has a relatively light empty weight. Even with three of us on board, and as much ballast as we could find, it was difficult to get heavy enough to get close to the aircraft's maximum allowable weight. The Huey has a ride like no other. Its two rotors are massive and literally

Huey G-UHIH awaiting flight test at Redhill. Note the misty weather.

seem to bash the air out of the way as they rotate. If you slide down the simple window in the pilot's door you can feel the swirling air thumping your helmet every time the blades go around. After a gentle taxi about two feet above the muddy grass, and once lined up, I was able to smoothly raise the collective while nudging the cyclic forward to gather flying speed. Within seconds I was departing the circuit at 1,000 feet or so and heading eastbound along the main railway line past Godstone towards Tonbridge. Up to 100 KIAS and the steady *thump, thump, thump* of the rotors threatened to shake my fillings loose. Documenting the climb performance over five minutes was challenging; it is so good on a Huey that at modest weights you can easily climb several thousand feet. So, a descent to skim the blades of grass in an empty field, then a rapid application of pitch to target the maximum allowable torque, with the stopwatch running. The cloud and murk brought our very rapid ascent to an end and, turning for home, the height was used to accelerate to max chat – 120 KIAS. Gosh, you wouldn't want to fly a Huey this fast for long. Testing complete, we thundered noisily back into the circuit at Redhill to give an early Christmas present to Phil as everything was okay.

The Huey flight test team with Ray and Geoff in the middle.

Next time you watch, 'Apocalypse Now' or 'Miss Saigon' just see how many blokes with guns and ammo they can cram into the back, and don't forget the film crew that must be in there somewhere. Talking about Vietnam War films at this stage, I must recommend my favourite helicopter book of all time – 'Chickenhawk' by Rob Mason. By the end of the first few chapters, you know so much about the Huey that you could probably take one into a war zone yourself. I learned quite a few top tips from the book that I applied on a number of occasions when I was flying my very heavy and power-limited Wasp.

I went back to Redhill after Christmas to finish off some testing for them as they had no pilot with a type rating able to do it for some time and then re-flew the aircraft some years later out of its 'home' near Blackpool with Phil along for the ride, just to make sure it was still flying as it should – which thankfully it did.

A couple of years later I got a call about the other Huey in the UK, G-HUEY. Now I confess, as a bit of an anorak, I was keen to help get this aircraft flying again after it had been on the ground and not flown for some years.

Huey G-UHIH instrument panel.

The story of G-HUEY started, I suppose, when one young flight lieutenant attended No. 13 Rotary Wing Test Pilot Course at ETPS in 1975. After a successful tour at Boscombe Down, Rob had ended up as the 'Air Liaison Officer' for No. 5 Infantry Brigade (Yep, not sure what they did either) which found itself fighting in the Falklands conflict in 1982. The troops managed to capture an intact Argentinian Huey helicopter and the Army being the Army, and being very short of support helicopters, said to this RAF TP,

'Hey Rob, you're a test pilot – Come and fly this.'

And he did, very successfully and helpfully. I do wonder what the conversation might have been like had he still been embedded in the 'light blue' rather than the 'khaki'? My experience of the RAF in recent years convinces me that no one would have been able to underwrite the airworthiness of the aircraft, and hence the risk, and as a result they would probably have just torched it.

Anyway, Rob became very fond of his new pet and brought it home with him. He even blagged a further tour of the Falklands so he could

Huey G-HUEY awaiting flight test at North Weald.

roam the islands stripping spare parts off the numerous abandoned and wrecked aircraft left down there. Eventually, after a lot of volunteer help from some RAF engineers, he managed to get it civilian registered and issued with a permit to fly. The aircraft flew at numerous air displays in the 1990s, raising money for the RAF Benevolent Fund, initially in its smart white Argentinian livery and then in some rather 'gopping' multi-coloured scheme. Thankfully when I went to test fly it the colour scheme of a US Army variant had been applied, and, despite shabby weather, we managed to complete the check flight satisfactorily. Basically it still shook your dental fillings out above 100 KIAS. Goodness knows what back and joint problems high-time Huey pilots suffer from.

Phil was not content with just one Vietnam War veteran in his garden shed; he wanted three. His third was to be a Bell Cobra AH-1 attack helicopter. Sadly, for him the US State Department thought he was about to invade France with it post-Brexit and wouldn't let it leave US soil, but he had better luck with his Hughes OH-6. The OH-6 was used in Vietnam as a scout helicopter. I wasn't quite sure what that was until I read another book on the topic, 'Snake Pilot' by Randy R. Zahn. He

Huey G-HUEY instrument panel – a more authentic layout than G-UHIH.

was a Cobra attack helicopter pilot but describes how they were teamed up with the OH-6, which would be flown just above the trees by maniacs waiting to be shot at by the Viet Cong. The Cobras would be flying much higher, but when they saw their mate being shot at would unleash hell in the form of scores of seventeen-pound rockets – 'Take that!'

The OH-6 was a very unstable helicopter with odd control functionality that meant the cyclic control stick worked about 30-degrees offset to other helicopters and the aircraft had negative lateral stability, so rolled into, rather than away from, the prevailing breeze or gusts, making for a very uncomfortable ride. But, as a result, it was very manoeuvrable and loved by its pilots who always put fun first. If you've seen the 1983 movie 'Blue Thunder' you'll know what I mean. In the movie the local state Air Department are trying out a new helicopter which is actually a Gazelle with some fake panels bolted on. The bad guy flies an OH-6 and the whole premise of the movie is that this bad guy ace can fly a loop in his OH-6 and the Gazelle can't. It's a rather cheesy movie but a 'must see' for helicopter fans. The other 'must see' movie to watch to see the OH-6 in action is 'Black Hawk Down'. The OH-6 was used by 160th

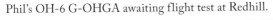

Phil's OH-6 G-OHGA awaiting flight test at Redhill.

Special Operations Aviation Regiment, which provided transport and air support to the US Special Forces. In the movie you see them being used extensively to protect numerous US troops who became trapped in Mogadishu following a botched raid. Good book and good movie.

Anyway, Phil bought his OH-6, which was a genuine war veteran, and which had been shot down when performing the scout role as above. Then it was shipped back to the USA for repair but the major headache for him was that, for a while, it had been lent to the Drugs Enforcement Administration (DEA) under a US government arrangement to help fight the 'war on drugs'. With funding and help from the federal government, the helicopter received numerous upgrades/updates belonging to the more modern civilian version of the aircraft. By the time it arrived in the UK it was neither one thing nor the other, which gave the CAA numerous headaches. One of them was for the guys from licensing. The Hughes 500 was a proper civilian type which meant there were proper training courses and already approved examiners etc. So, could it be that this warbird was really a Hughes 500? If it really was an OH-6, then there was no proper training course and the required pilots would be granted an exemption to fly the aircraft without such expensive and onerous training.

Yours truly was tasked with 'forming a view' and making a formal recommendation. Again, we found ourselves at Redhill on a murky day,

The OH-6 flight test team with Andrew in the middle and Jeff wearing a tie.

The OH-6 instrument panel when tested.

hosted by Andrew, an ex-Army Air Corps pilot with lots of hours flying the Hughes 500. Flying the check flight was the easy bit. I'd already flown the OH-6 before at the US Navy Test Pilot School (USNTPS) and, thankfully, Phil's war veteran was deemed acceptable for permit issue. The next challenge was to sit around a table with a few chocolate biscuits and mugs of coffee to thrash out what we were going to designate it.

I originally thought that calling it a Hughes 500 would make the operators' life easier, but it turns out the opposite was true and they were keen for it to be designated an OH-6. And lo, it came to pass.

Not all the historic helicopters I was required to test were military or ex-military machines. I found myself at Gloucester Airport on one occasion needing to test-fly a Brantly B2B. The aircraft was owned by the editor of Helicopter International. Although he was no longer licensed to fly the type, I took him along with me. I was curious to fly this as the rotor blades were hinged halfway along their length. Whacky. I had thought this was to ensure a softer, more comfortable ride but this couldn't have been further from the truth. And this poor wee machine had lots of snags.

The Brantly B2B awaiting flight test at Gloucester.

Firstly, as soon as I lifted into the hover, the engine began to overheat. I had only seconds to get the thing moving into forward flight in order to get some cooling air to the engine. As soon as I accelerated into forward flight, the vibration levels grew to being unacceptable very quickly and when I went to check whether I could enter autorotation, to be able to glide following an engine failure, I discovered that you couldn't. The rotor blades had been rigged with too much pitch on them, giving excessive drag. So had the overheating engine quit, the blades may well

The Brantly B2B instrument panel.

have slowed down so much that I would literally have fallen from the sky. Time for a swift exit methinks and I plonked the aircraft ungracefully back on the ground from whence it came.

Phew! … survived another.

This was an aircraft that wasn't going to fly again without some serious remedial work doing to it. At the time of writing this, I note the aircraft is still owned by the same owner but no longer flyable.

Now, let's be honest, which bloke, or even girl, doesn't want to be 'James Bond, if just for the day' (check out the song by 'Scouting for Girls'). The movie 'You Only Live Twice' had Sean Connery flying a yellow autogyro over some volcanic island, firing off rockets and machine guns at baddies in helicopters. I was invited by the inventor and owner, Ken, to test fly one of the pair of identical aircraft.

Ken had been at the forefront of UK autogyro design, but his design of controls was at odds with all the others. So, like a good test pilot, I spent a bit of time working out that the throttle actually did something else and the brakes weren't where they normally are. Having finally worked out where all the flying bits and pieces were, I donned my helmet in the hope of looking more like Sean Connery, eased the throttle open and started to taxi. Until meeting me, Ken had been reluctant to let anyone from the CAA test fly his aircraft, so my intended flight had attracted a crowd of

Being greeted by Ken following a successful test flight.

other CAA folks and gyro people. So I had a large and savvy audience and as I set off I promptly lost control of the thing. What? Yep, I couldn't taxi it along the ground in a straight line.

Why? I hear you cry. Surely a bloke that can fly all these different types of aircraft can taxi a simple gyro?

Well, most aircraft have pedals attached to the rudder or tail rotor. Pushing the left pedal = turn left, pushing the right pedal = turn right. The only exception to this fundamentally sound principle is weight-shift microlight aeroplanes. They don't have rudders and turn by the pilot moving his weight within the fuselage beneath the fabric wing. No rudders means no rudder pedals, but to steer it on the ground the pilot puts his feet on the axle-bar of the nose-wheel which works like an old soapbox buggy; and pushing the left pedal moves the wheel clockwise when viewed from above and a right turn ensues – so now left pedal = turn right (See Appendix 2 – Microlights).

But I was in an autogyro, with a rudder which was required to turn the aircraft in flight. Yes, there was a rudder bar, and, yes, the rudder worked conventionally such that left pedal = turn left.

However, Ken had decided that the ground steering should be the opposite way around and rigged it like a soap cart. So there were two control bars for me to operate: one that steered the aircraft that worked the 'wrong way' and one that worked the rudder the 'correct way'. Imagine how you would cope if you got into a rental car and suddenly found you had to move the steering wheel in the opposite direction to the usual one until you got onto the motorway and then everything returned to normal. You'd probably crash before you'd left the car park. That's what I was faced with. Lurching from side to side as I slalomed along the taxi-way forcing my brain to reverse itself despite 8,000 flying hours of expectation.

I made it to the runway in an increasingly straighter path, but how was I to manage the take-off? I had to keep the aircraft straight as I accelerated on the ground using left = right and then, before getting airborne, had to move my feet onto a completely different control where left = left!

The saving grace was that once I had applied full throttle and was moving forward, the rudder became effective enough to override the nose-wheel steering and just before 'slipping the surly bonds of earth', I was able to get back to my usual way of turning left and right. Phew! Now airborne and finally in charge I was able to put Ken's aircraft through its

The Hiller 12E ready for flight test.

paces in full view of the appreciative audience who, only a few minutes earlier, had already written me off as a complete muppet.

And again, the crowd went wild.

So James Bond survived and found himself testing another movie icon. Remember the 1964 movie 'Goldfinger'? Featuring the very alluring Pussy Galore, played by Honor Blackman in a very fetching figure-hugging flying suit? Which bloke of my generation couldn't?

And here I was being invited to test fly the very Hiller 12E helicopter she had 'flown' (with a little help from a friend) in said movie. Now there is an anecdotal question asked of test pilots:

'When test pilots walk around an aircraft they haven't flown before – Why do they walk around it twice?'

'The first time is to work out what on earth it is and the second time is to find the door.'

Well, this helicopter beat me. I walked around it three or four times and couldn't find any way of opening the door whatsoever. I had to eat humble pie and fetch the engineer who had worked on it and he revealed a very sneaky catch that couldn't be seen or felt by the uninitiated. Once I'd gained entry, frankly flying it was a piece of cake, and I spent most of the flight wishing Pussy Galore or one of her glamorous female instructor pilots was alongside me rather than my CAA FTE mate Jeff.

Never mind – always another day to be James Bond.

Hiller 12E instrument panel.

Chapter 15

Italia

Frankly, who wouldn't like flying in Italy? Some fantastic scenery, better weather and good food and wine. What's not to like?

My bond with Italy as a test pilot started way back in 1994. Towards the end of the Test Pilot Course at ETPS there is one big final exercise; in my day it was called the 'Preview Exercise'. We students were sent around the world and asked to fly an aircraft for ten flying hours and then write a whopping great report which was then presented to a full audience of technical experts and staff who liked to outdo each other by asking the most difficult question of the day. We students all wanted to get something new and exciting to fly but I was allocated an elderly search and rescue aircraft, the Agusta Bell 212. This was basically a Huey helicopter with two engines instead of one and made under licence in Italy. What made this aircraft more of a technical challenge was the comprehensive autopilot that flew the aircraft around in all weathers to help the pilots find and rescue survivors from the sea or mountains. Obviously as a Royal Navy Wasp pilot I had no interest in flying any more minutes over the sea than I had to, so spent the bulk of my testing flying around the local mountains. Now that really was a lot of fun. Additionally, we were based at the test centre, Practica de Mara, near Rome, so a weekend in Rome was enjoyed to the full. While working at ETPS, as a member of staff, a few of us went out to Viterbo in the mountains north of Rome to test fly the Italian Army's Mangusta attack helicopter. Again, more scenic mountain flying, although with hindsight we were far too professional and spent much of our flying dicing with death in the dark using night vision goggles – not at all scenic. But at least we visited in the winter which meant night flying started and finished early enough for us to get to the local pizzeria and get some epic fresh pizza, cooked in an open wood burning oven, washed down by buckets of Chianti.

So, as I started this phase of my career as a civilian test pilot, I already had fond memories of the country, people and wine!

I'd been at the CAA a handful of years before, out of the blue, I was tasked with conducting the check flight on a Robinson R22. The R22 is an unforgiving helicopter and the test profile therefore quite challenging. Fortunately, I'd spent a few weeks in the USA when I was first thinking of leaving the RN. I'd taught myself how to fly the R22 (long story) and had added it to my UK licence when I got home. I'd then spent a number of weekends instructing on the type before the training school went bust owing me lots of money. But the flying experience was invaluable. For some bizarre reason the aircraft in question was still on the UK (G) register but owned by some chap in Rome. Bonkers!

The deal with such tasks was that the CAA funded the travel, but the applicant funded the local subsistence costs. This was a really stupid arrangement, from my perspective, as we always were put up in cheap, crappy hotels – funny that …

Before leaping on the first BA flight out of LHR I had the very good sense to remind myself how to fly the thing by spending some of the miserly training budget on forty-five minutes flying a similar aircraft with a mate at Thruxton. I then blatted off to l'Hotel de la Gare, or the Italian equivalent. The one star venue was right behind the very noisy main train station (Stazione Termini) in Rome and I spent most of the evening trying to reduce the local insect population to a tolerable level.

In the morning my host, Dr Luca, arrived late in a somewhat battered Mini Cooper – 'Italian Job' or what? Michael Caine would have been chuffed. Sadly, this bloke couldn't drive anything like as well as the heroes of the heist movie, but what he did do was send text messages on his phone while weaving through traffic at speed as he tried to make up some lost time. By the time we got to our destination I was a gibbering wreck.

Prior to leaving the UK I had emailed clear instructions as to what I would need to operate. This included local area aviation maps, and a comprehensive brief on local procedures and ATC by someone competent.

If you look at the attached photo we arrived at a field (Corcolle Microlight strip) with plastic-sheeted structures looking like a scene from a third world disaster movie. No airfield, no infrastructure, no maps, no one to talk to about the local airspace; a complete shambles.

Luca, it turned out, was an eye surgeon. He was clearly paid by the hour or per operation as his text messages were mostly to patients and the hospital, trying to jam as many 'jobs' as he could into the afternoon

The R22 awaiting flight test at Corcolle. Note the plastic sheet hangars.

– great. He wasn't an experienced pilot and hadn't really got a 'Scooby' about flying legally. I was flying a UK registered aircraft on my EASA licence in Italy. Lots of people would be after my 'guts for garters' if I 'cocked up' today! Luca tried to convince me we were located east of Rome's controlled airspace but as we were talking fast jets kept flying low overhead.

'What are they?'

'Tornados.' (I knew that!)

'Where are they going?'

'They're landing at the military airfield just over there.'

'Great.'

One thing you have to do as a test pilot in this game is to be pragmatic. – The right course of action was to tell Luca to stick his check flight and ask him to drive me back to the hotel for an early supper with much pasta. But then I'd have had to come back another day and how much of a pain would that be?

So, I elected to do what I could. With no map this relied on not getting lost, which meant staying near enough to see the field at all times and trying to talk to Rome ATC in the hope that I could convince them that I wasn't about to bump into any of the numerous inbound commercial flights or some fast jet driven by an Italian intent on getting back in time for their lunch with a large glass of Vino Rosso on the side.

I wanted to take Luca with me so he could share my pain but that would have made the aircraft too heavy as it was already full to the brim with fuel. So off I set, very glad of my short refresher the previous week.

As soon as I was airborne, I tuned into Rome International ATC.

'Hello Rome – This is helicopter G-OCDS – hello?'

Sssssscchhhhh crackle wizz pop scchhhh.

Now my Italian's not great, but neither was this helicopter radio. Climbing higher to get a better signal could have me climbing into controlled airspace and getting into a world of trouble but I had to check the climb performance of the aircraft, 'Bugger!'

I elected to start my climb as I flew just a few inches over the grass strip, calculating that the Microlights from the strip would have some local clearance to fly locally in any regard. So, pretending to be a microlight I climbed for only two minutes before testing the glide/autororotation back down to the airfield. 'High level' stuff done, I completed the other testing by hurtling around the strip in a manic fashion that would have impressed the crowd had one gathered. Thankfully, one hadn't.

Time to get out of Italy quick, just in case. More texting with some crazy driving followed and I was thrown out of Luca's Mini as we barely slowed at the station so he could dash to the hospital in time to conduct eye surgery on some hapless patients who were paying for the privilege.

Phew! ... Survived another.

Only months later, now in January, I was heading back to Italy but Milan this time.

I had been flying autogyros for some time and conducting the certification testing of the main factory-built types. RotorSport was producing aircraft in Germany and Magni were building gyros in Milan, Italy. The CEO of Magni wanted me to test fly their new side-by-side enclosed two-seater, the M24. So off I went, and the really good news was that I was able to catch up with Nigel, who had been the CAA's helicopter test pilot before me, and my RN TP mate, Martin. Both were flying for Agusta which was part of the same company as Westlands of Yeovil. So much merriment was had over spaghetti and vino before the following morning when I had the obligatory marketing spiel and factory tour from Magni before heading off to test their new machine.

The M24 tested wearing my freebee Magni jacket. Note the muddy airfield and low cloud.

It was January. Their test centre was up in the hills away from Milan, and the weather was dire. Cold and very wet with a cloud base only 300 ft above the ground. I was anxious that we wouldn't be allowed to fly but, ironically in Italy, gyro pilots are supposed to fly below 300 feet rather than above 500 feet as we do in the UK. But it was not a pleasant day. Wellies and umbrellas were suddenly a crucial element of our flying clothing. I flew with another Luca. He was the younger of the sons of Signor Vittorio Magni – the company founder and boss. Apart from the fact that I could barely see where I was going, the two of us had quite a fun day out. Luca was a very friendly guy with a great sense of humour, which was just as well. A few months later he tried to demonstrate to me that we could survive an engine failure from a test point that was beyond my capability and, as it turned out, his! How we laughed. Thankfully the undercarriage coped quite well with our real rather than simulated crash landing.

Phew! ... Survived another.

When I started up my own business as Dovetail Aviation Ltd (after being made redundant from the CAA) I had no idea what to expect and

The Magni M24 following flight test with Luca in the flying suit accompanied by his glamorous support crew.

what projects would take me where, but as I write this chapter, I have had another three trips to Italy in recent years and, frankly, they all count amongst my to-die-for flying experiences.

I was working as the Chief Test Pilot for Bond (now Babcocks) Helicopters at Gloucester Airport Staverton. All of the English and Welsh police air support had been taken over by an organisation called National Police Aviation Service (NPAS). At the time I was flying EC135 and MD902 helicopters for them as a police helicopter pilot. NPAS decided that they would acquire some aeroplanes to replace some of their helicopters and put out an invitation to tender for different companies to bid to supply the aircraft. The specification was fairly tight and written around a specific aeroplane type they liked the look of, built in Naples. Bond decided to bid for the work, but also identified another similar aircraft also built near Naples, so hatched a plan to visit the country and, since one of the types was unknown in the UK, asked me to formally evaluate it.

So off again, passport in hand, to find myself in another cheap hotel in the industrial outskirts of said city. The morning dawned with us arriving at the Oma Sud factory in Capua, home of the SkyCar Aeroplane. This was an unusual aeroplane in that, although it had conventional piston engines, they operated pusher propellers at the rear of the wings rather than tractor props on the front of the wings as usual.

Anyway, we were met warmly by our host, the company CEO, and the predictable marketing spiel gave way to the inevitable factory tour.

About to flight test the SkyCar.

I confess I was anticipating the arrival of the company test pilot at any time. Invariably companies like their TP to 'ride shotgun' on such an evaluation. It means they can demo or point out all the good bits and aim to gloss over the bad bits. It also means they can be the insured party, look after all the paperwork, local area knowledge and navigation etc.

But as lunchtime arrived and as there was no sign of such an individual, I asked the CEO ...

'Will your test pilot be joining us soon?'

'No – he won't.'

'I thought he would be flying with me?' I ask politely

'No – he only works for us part-time and today he's flying for an airline, but you can go flying now. Here are the keys!'

Now that was, I have to confess, quite a surprise. Most CEOs wouldn't trust some random Brit turning up to take away their prized prototype and demonstrator, let alone throw them the keys without so much as a safety brief or risk assessment.

'Whoa – hold your horses', thinks I.

And I proceeded to ask for all the relevant paperwork as I started to discuss this with my mates from Bond, one of whom has a UK PPL. He proved an excellent sounding board, as I tried to work out what I could and what I couldn't do – legally.

A few years earlier I would have been faced by flying an Italian aircraft in Italy on a British licence – and the answer would have been to seek approval from the Italian CAA equivalent (ENAC). But now I had an EASA European Licence (albeit issued by the UK CAA). So yes, I could now fly a European registered aircraft in Europe.

We started looking at the other docs and I found an interesting comment about experimental propellers. Turns out the aircraft was certified for use with two bladed propellers and was in the middle of a flight test programme with experimental three bladed props!

So, this was another thing altogether. Could I now fly an uncertified aircraft as part of its flight test programme for an Italian company? Well, only a year or two earlier after much debate and consideration, EASA had introduced Test Pilot ratings and I now had Class 1 Test Pilot ratings for aeroplanes and helicopters (unusual to have both). So, I could conduct flight test in an Italian aeroplane, but I needed to be on the books of Oma Sud to ensure I was covered by their flight test procedures and insurance.

I really thought this would be the showstopper. Had the CEO not heard of this maverick Brit TP that had suffered more engine failures than most would consider sensible. The reverse was true; he promptly 'hired me' on the spot. Well, that sorted out most of the legalities for today but I had to confess the commute from the UK to Capua to fly for the company in the future would be rather onerous – so sadly, tongue in cheek, I had to decline his kind invitation later that day!

But the 'fun and games' were not yet over. On doing my detailed walk around and finding out how to get in (see earlier chapter) I found there was insufficient fuel in the aircraft for my testing. Normally not a big deal; just get the bowser and fill the tanks. But apparently the company didn't have one. So, next thing I know, I'm having to sort out fuel at Naples International.

Next to no time later I'm airborne with my PPL colleague acting as my co-pilot as we follow the main road through the suburbs of Naples, trying to integrate with various Boeing and Airbus aircraft as we 'white stick' our approach; just to get fuel. Thirty minutes or so later, full to the

The SkyCar at Naples awaiting fuel.

gunwales with fuel, we were 'wheels up' heading north again to put the SkyCar through its paces.

I have to say, the scenery north of Naples was spectacular. We flew up towards the Volcano of Roccamonfina which is now part of a national park, Roccamonfina-Foce Garigliano Regional Park; a rather unfortunate turn of phrase, but epic to fly around. My usual concerns regarding engine failure however took the edge off as I'd already worked out that full of fuel, we wouldn't be able to stay airborne should either of the engines fail. Great.

Anyway, scenic tour complete, stability and control and performance assessed; time to 'beat up the tower'. Actually, there wasn't a tower, but I lined up on the grass airfield, applied full power and timed my dive to cross the hedge at about five feet. It was impossible not to imagine myself 'in the flying boots' of an Italian Breda Ba.25 pilot who had been based there during the Second World War, being trained no doubt to subsequently duel with my Fleet Air Arm brethren over the Med near Malta. A pair of sporty wingovers, followed by a double engine throttle chop and glide landing onto the runway just in front of the company offices …

Inside my head the crowd went wild. An impressive beat up, conducted safely and a pleasant way to conclude a very busy and stressful day.

Back to the hotel for copious amounts of lasagne and Taurasi (the local vino rosso).

However, the story of finding an aircraft for NPAS did not finish there. Sadly, for Bond, the tender to source the required aircraft was won by an Austrian company who did work on both aeroplanes and helicopters. I ended up doing some helicopter test flying for them on a Swiss A109 mountain rescue helicopter they had modified. Again, epic scenery, flying from a former Hawker Hunter fighter base at Interlaken, in the foothills of the Alps – awesome. My final flight of the testing was conducted in the evening dusk, flying above purple-tinged cloud and mountain tops at 18,000 feet needing an oxygen mask to breath, always novel in a helicopter.

This company sourced a fleet of aeroplanes from VulcanAir, the other company in Naples. The aircraft were then modified with all the kit they needed for the police role, including special Infra-Red camera, extra radios etc.

The next chapter of this saga commenced when I responded to a tender from NPAS and became their Chief Test Pilot. So, after a couple of helicopter tasks I was despatched to Austria to test fly the lead P68R. I already knew my way around, having visited the company previously, and was met by my mate who took me out to the steak house just across from the cheapo airport hotel. Great steak, great wine, a charming waitress and a 1940s fug of cigarette smoke. We chatted through the aircraft which were pretty much finished and ready for delivery.

So early the next morning I'm safely airborne, at the aircraft's maximum possible weight, enjoying the local scenery – well I was until I turned off one of the engines as I flew up a valley with a gently rising floor. Despite pre-flight planning leading to expectations to the contrary, at my heavy weight, I was barely able to maintain level flight. Time to do a brisk 180 degree turn and find some lower ground quickly. Thankfully,

About to flight test the P68R at Airborne Technologies, Austria.

I was able to nurse the aircraft gently onto a reciprocal heading without further drama, but this was not a good result. Back to the airfield which in the First World War had built the very successful Albatross fighter and, in the 1930s, the Bf109. We managed to get the shutdown engine going again and landed normally to then 'chew the fat' regarding the poor performance. Needless to say, the discussions and emails bounced around for some time before it was concluded I should head back to Naples again. This time to the VulcanAir factory to test fly one of their NPAS aircraft fitted with a different propeller that they had just built. This time I would fly with the VulcanAir Chief Test Pilot, which suited me just fine. Not least because I needed to have the results from my flight witnessed and agreed by a company representative.

We needed really still air, the sort you only get at dawn. So, having briefed the night before, I was at the company premises just as the first ruddy glimmer of light was emanating from the east. We pulled the aircraft out of the hangar, filled it with fuel, and then had a bizarre faff, the sort that seems more typical of Italy than elsewhere. The company hangar was separated from Naples International by a road and two fences. We had to lower the fence on our side, then the airfield had to lower their own fence, but, before they could do that, we needed their local security, and the local police, and their version of Homeland Security. First one car with blue flashing lights would appear and then disappear to be replaced by one from a different agency. This pantomime of coming and going eventually resolved itself and, with more police cars than on the 'Blues Brothers' chase, we finally towed the aircraft across the road to the airfield and got on with the easy bit of flying around with one engine shut down at the maximum weight of the aeroplane.

I confess that I had been so busy doing my TP thing, and trying to get us safely underway, I was caught by surprise when I looked beyond the nose of the aircraft to see the Island of Capri. What a truly beautiful sight – nestling in an incredibly azure flat calm sea against a pinkish dawn sky. This view alone was 'to die for'; and being the 'saddo' that I am, I was really chuffed with the conditions which were quite simply perfect for performance testing – not a breath of wind or any turbulence whatsoever. Whatever the climb performance of this aircraft actually was we were going to 'nail it' for sure this morning. I managed to get the company CTP to fly some test points and with the Austrian company CEO as

Dragging the test VulcanAir P68R across the road to the airport.

witness and 'note scribbler' in the back, there would be no doubt about the fidelity of the data when we got back on the ground.

In fairness, when we did get back to the office, there was a lot of heated discussion because, yet again, I was telling a company that it's 'baby was ugly!' In particular, I was telling them that the performance data in their flight manual was far too optimistic. Eventually they agreed with me and produced an amended flight manual with more realistic information, (albeit still slightly optimistic) which now allows the aircraft to be operated safely if flown at appropriate weights.

Phew! ... Another good outcome. I was able to head home the following day having earned my pay and made the world a safer place.

However, Italy was certainly not done with me yet and the phone rang again one day. The chap on the other end of the line turned out to be a really nice guy who, I confess, I ended up feeling very disappointed for. The story is a long one, but in summary, John had, as a boy, been mad keen to join the Fleet Air Arm to fly helicopters, the Wasp in particular. So already he had my attention.

He rang me to explain he suffered from a condition that meant he had a slightly weak right hand and arm and he wanted to be able to swap the conventional helicopter controls around so that the main cyclic control stick could be operated with his left hand. Now, that might not sound like much of an issue but, believe me, it really is! To completely change the way a helicopter is flown would take a mammoth amount of time and money from a major helicopter manufacturer: not something that could be justified for, or afforded by, an individual by any means. But John had already been out to Italy where they had different regulations from the UK. This had allowed companies to build 'microlight helicopters' that were able to fly under a certain weight, 450 kg. The aircraft in this microlight category were effectively deregulated, so manufacturers had much greater flexibility in what they were able to do.

For two years, John had been talking to a company called CH7 Sport Helicopters. Over the years they had developed a number of aircraft in the microlight category, including one of particular interest, the CH77 Ranabot which was a side-by-side two-seater. The aircraft was powered by a version of the Rotax engine found in autogyros and microlights but had been 'souped up' to give it a few more horsepower. The company was run and managed by three brothers, and they had convinced John that the aircraft would be easy for him to fly and that they could easily modify the controls to allow him to effectively swap hands compared to conventional helicopters. After lots of chatting on the phone I suggested he hire me to take an initial look at the helicopter and carry out a 'Qualeval'; that is conduct a qualitative evaluation of the aircraft so that I could assess its performance and handling qualities and determine if it was a worthy investment of further cash. John had already paid a deposit on a new aircraft that was due to be built soon.

The good news for me was that the company was based near Turin in north-west Italy. Turin was the venue for the 1969 movie 'The Italian Job'. A red, a white and a blue Mini Cooper were used to transport stolen gold bullion out of a gridlocked city by driving though shopping arcades, sewers and, most iconically, across the weir, which was the full span of the main River Po, which passes through the centre of town. So as an owner, over the years, of three Minis, including both a red and a blue Mini Cooper I was rather chuffed to have a few minutes to myself to snap lots of photos of various emotive venues. But the day job eventually beckoned. The usual pattern for such a day started immediately after breakfast, being driven to the factory, getting the usual marketing spiel, followed by a factory tour. In fairness, the engineering was impressive. I'd never seen such small helicopter components before, all beautifully made. I was then driven through the cloud-topped hills to the test airfield in order to fly with one of the three brothers, Igi, who was an instructor on such helicopters but had received no test pilot training (often the case for

The CH77 Ranabot being flown by John.

companies building smaller aircraft). I was hopeful, for John's sake, that this really would be a delightful little aircraft to fly, but I was suspiciously pessimistic, not least because, when the engine stops on such a helicopter, you have to be able to autorotate down to the ground and use the stored momentum in the rotor blades to land safely. But nothing on this aircraft was heavy – quite the reverse. Everything was incredibly light, including the crucial rotor blades.

My first flight that afternoon really was enough to form a view. This was a very 'ugly baby' indeed. The vital rotor rpm had to be controlled manually with a twist grip throttle that was too stiff to move smoothly. In the hover the aircraft was very difficult to control and couldn't cope with any wind from behind. In forward flight it suffered from the issues I'd had with the RAF 2000 autogyro and had a roller-coaster oscillation that just kept getting worse and when turning the aircraft wanted to tighten the turn of its own accord.

Finally, I came to try some engine-off landings; empty satellite airfield located, some smooth flat grass identified and wind direction checked. HASEL checks completed, speed on the numbers, all lined up, throttle closed, and I banged the collective to the 'bottom stop' in less than a second to retain my precious rotor rpm. Then 100 feet … not yet … 80 feet … hold on … 60 feet … wait for it … 50 feet … 40 feet … 30 feet … ooooooooooohhhhhhh … 20 feet … now! An aggressive flare to end up about three feet off the ground trying to wash some of the speed off, and then rapidly levelling at a foot above the ground as the rotor rpm was already decaying, with the collective now raised to the top stop and bang, we'd arrived. Wow! What an exciting ride. Was I able to do a couple? Yes. Was I using every ounce of my considerable experience in having done hundreds and taught even more? Yes, you betcha. It was an 'all or nothing' technique that required the aircraft to be flown onto the ground with minimal chance to slow down. Get it even slightly wrong and you would prang the machine big time. Not an ideal aircraft for a low time PPL with a weakness in one hand …

This was now one very tricky situation. Igi, of course, thought the helicopter was wonderful, but just like the Canadian RAF 2000 pilot, I talked about previously in this book, he had flown nothing else to speak of; so, it was all he knew. He couldn't compare it with the hundred or so helicopters I've flown to realise this was probably at the most difficult and dangerous end of the spectrum.

Now I had to break the news to John. Best to get alcohol involved methinks! So, with little comment expressed I suggested we beat a hasty retreat to our mountaintop hotel overlooking one of the most beautiful valleys I've ever seen from a hotel balcony. Throwing our bags in our rooms we sat in the late afternoon sun with large glasses of Asti Spumante in hand and I went through my thoughts and recollections. I was very keen that John should make his own decision and that we didn't dismiss the aircraft out of hand. I suggested I fly the aircraft again the following morning when there would be less wind in the hope that in less turbulence it would be easier to fly. Frankly it wasn't. I further investigated all the critical areas of poor handling and headed back to the airfield. Again, I said little to Igi but suggested we have a lunch break so I could chat further to John, which we did over plates of pasta in Asti. I outlined all the issues with the aircraft in a quiet corner of the café and suggested he conduct his own evaluation rather than letting Igi demonstrate things. It was a good ploy. John arrived back after his flight both shaken *and* stirred. He realised that, despite the goodwill of the three brothers, this was not an easy aircraft for anyone to fly, and certainly was not for him. We adjourned to the hotel where the chef cooked a single special meal for all the guests. The food and wine really were special, although tainted with some sadness as we effectively had to draw a line under over two years' worth of hope and aspiration.

The good outcome from this story was that sometime later John phoned me to tell me he had bought his own Wasp HAS1 XT435 G-RIMM. Welcome to the club of Wasp pilots, John. The Wasp at least has a good trim system, so the forces required to fly it normally are acceptable. Every cloud does have a silver lining it appears.

Phew! ... Good result.

My most recent adventure in Italy featured some of the most memorable flying of my aviation career to date. I was contacted by an Italian design organisation. They had already produced a flight test plan and had it approved by EASA. They now just needed a Class 1 EASA helicopter

The CH 77 – having survived my flight test programme.

test pilot to fly the aircraft and gather the data. They didn't even want me to write the final report at the end of it all, which was rather unusual. However, it was another paid task, so I wasn't about to complain. So, I hopped on an aeroplane and found myself in a rental car north bound from Turin Airport (again!). I confess I hadn't really taken on board where I was going. I had been manically busy and not being involved in preparing any of the paperwork for the testing I was just planning to turn up. The main road I was on started a gentle ascent into the hills as I glanced down at the satnav. Then the hills got steeper and the road more windy, and then the road stopped. Or rather it went into a tunnel. Without realising where I was going I'd found myself at Entreves, Courmayeur, which is as far north as you can drive in Italy before you enter the tunnel under Mont Blanc to end up in France. It was dark when I arrived and not yet skiing season, so my hotel (highest in Italy) seemed to have only half a dozen guests including me and the two Italian guys paying me to be there. Time for a beer and chance to discuss the plan for the morning. Oh, what a dreadful test plan! I have no idea how EASA had approved it. (I have found that when dealing with EASA, it all depends on the individual assigned to the task).

One cold beer led to another and then a brisk walk down the hill to the only restaurant open in the area for steak, chips and Chianti. Then, as was often sadly the case, back to the laptop to pound the keys and turn this 'pig's ear' of a plan into something that would work.

Dawn was spectacular, looking down over the mist-shrouded valley, but more impressive was the near vertical mountain we were nestled hard up against. Off we went to the very scary small helipad where our host operated a couple of AS350B3 Squirrel helicopters. The pilot I was to fly with was a nice guy but had arrived in his position as chief pilot in what was, for me, an unusual fashion. He was a skier, and over the years had become quite good at it. I think he won competitions or something. Then he got into mountain rescue, all on his home turf, Mont Blanc. After doing that for a few years he decided he could rescue people better if he had a helicopter. So he learned how to fly one and, with some financial help, set up a helicopter base at Entreves. So … interesting. He knew a hell of a lot about Mont Blanc; he knew all the places he was likely to fly to very well and I saw him in action later and he was very efficient doing what he wanted to do. But really, he knew 'bugger all' about aviation! He was a 'mountain rescue guide' who happened to drive a helicopter rather than a helicopter pilot who happened to end up rescuing people. So, he had none of the normal thought processes of a guy who was a pilot first. He had no consideration of aviation emergencies, so he never gave any thought to where he was going to land when the engine failed, mainly because there really was absolutely nowhere to land safely following a 'donk stop'. Believe me, I spend 90 per cent of my attention, when flying a single-engine aircraft, working out where I'm going to land should the engine quit. The ground was either sloping steeply or had something built on it. There was no spare flat ground.

So, off we set; very windy equals lots of turbulence, equals *very* scary. So that was day one! Difficult to get any meaningful data, apart from reminding myself how much red wine is required to calm my nerves after a stressful day. The reason we were there was to test a new rear-view mirror bolted onto the helicopter. This was to allow the single pilot to be able to see an underslung load carried on a hook beneath the helicopter. This aircraft was frequently used as an airborne truck carrying stuff to remote locations in the mountains for various reasons.

About to test fly the AS350B3 at Entreves. Note Mont Blanc in the background.

The following day the weather was better, and I flew a sortie and gathered data. I was debriefing my Italian mates when I heard another helicopter starting up. Clearly it wasn't my helicopter as the modification of the new mirror invalidated the normal airworthiness paperwork and insurance. Right now, it could only be flown by a test pilot for the purposes of flight test. But a few minutes later when I stepped out for some air, I realised someone had stolen my helicopter.

'Now that's embarrassing,' I think! 'How will I explain that?'

Then I saw it crazily descending the side of the mountain to hover briefly over the helipad before a large generator was hooked underneath and, without any real care for wind direction or flight path, it lurched airborne again with its heavy load swinging in the breeze.

Minutes later it was back and my co-pilot, the ski guide, clambered out. I was a guest in his country, in his company and in his helicopter but he had just done something he *wasn't allowed to do*. My efforts to point it out, in typical diplomatic fashion, were greeted with an Italian shrug. What would Nelson have done?

The test flying was both scary and spectacular in equal measure. My final flight had to be on my own for 'weight and balance' reasons and I have to confess I ensured my test plan for the flight included some scenic touring of the local castles and other monuments before I had to climb to 14,000 feet, nearly three miles up. That was *weird*. Probably one of the weirdest things for a helicopter pilot is to be one minute looking a long way down and wondering where I would land if bad things happened, but also skimming inches from the mountainside while looking up at the summit set against an amazingly clear deep blue sky. Very disorientating, very impressive, very memorable.

Sadly that concluded my scenic tour of Italy but,

Phew! ... I had survived another.

Chapter 16

Two in One Day

In 2016 I was invited by the Society of Experimental Test Pilots (SETP) to become a Fellow of the Society. It's hard to describe how chuffed I was to learn this news. I was particularly 'blown away' to be given the news by Tom who was also a graduate of ETPS (Top student in 1975) and had been a Fellow of SETP (and President) for a number of years. His CV is amazing, having test flown for the US Navy, he ended up as a captain before moving on to become chief test pilot for Lockheed – where he worked at the 'Skunk Works' test flying all the super-secret amazing jets that Lockheed were working on covertly. If you get time Google him …

My wife and I had come to know Tom, and his delightful wife Norma, over numerous European symposia of the SETP held in various European countries. They are frankly just the nicest people you will meet – and Tom's modesty, given his incredible career, is particularly impressive. Had I heard the news from anyone else I would have suspected they had got the wrong 'Chris Taylor'! (In fact, when my wife and I went to California to receive the award, there were two Chris Taylors on the attendance list. The other guy was a US Air Force fast-jet pilot. Surely, he was more likely to have received this accolade than me?)

Before I knew too much about the award ceremony itself (a part of the annual conference held in Disney World, Anaheim, USA), I was asked to draft a few words that could be read out by the Society's President before he handed me my ribbon-wrapped certificate. I had no idea that the other new Fellows and I were to be paraded in alphabetical order and, being a 'T', I would be last. I also didn't know that in front of me would be three astronauts – yes, *astronauts*, for Heaven's sake! – And even more fast-jet pilots and a Vietnam War veteran attack helicopter guy … and then 'yours truly' bringing up the rear. I was incredibly glad I'd kept my 'bio' short and humorous and it concluded with the sentence:

'Chris has flown 400 different types, logged 8,000 flying hours; had 2 Maydays, 1 Ditching, 19 engine failures leading to 10 forced landings including **2 on the same day.**'

Thankfully this made the seven hundred fellow TPs in the room laugh. Loudly. Trying to follow astronauts and a whole bunch of fighter pilots any other way and I would have been calling on the floor of the hotel ballroom to open up and swallow me whole. In fact, riding the 'elevator' (lift) back to our room we were surrounded by kids wearing Mickey Mouse ears (following their fun days out on the Disney rides). It made the whole experience quite comic, if not surreal.

The certificate hangs in pride of place in my study but I still have to pinch myself every time I read the CVs/bios of other TPs becoming Fellows; part of me still thinks there is another Chris Taylor somewhere wondering why he hasn't received his certificate yet!

Since I used the expression 'two on the same day' I really ought to spend a few minutes chatting about some more of the 'donk stops' I've suffered to date …

Receiving my SETP Fellowship in Anaheim.

In my first year as the CAA's Light Aeroplane Test Pilot, I test flew over a hundred different types of aeroplane and none of them more than once. It was what we would describe as 'a steep learning curve'. I was flying most days, often on my own but also supporting our flight test engineers who also had their own work load of tests to conduct but would need TP support. David and I found ourselves teamed up together from time to time, invariably testing twin-engine aircraft, often King Airs or Islanders or similar used for commercial air transport. On only our third flight together we found ourselves testing a very tired Piper PA-34 Seneca out of Stapleford Airfield, near where the M25 and M11 cross, adjacent and beneath Heathrow's controlled airspace. This aircraft was used mainly for training and had recently been fitted with two new engines. Great, at last a battered piston twin that might actually perform as intended. Most of these elderly aircraft really struggled to climb as they should do. The way we would test all such twins would be to deliberately shut down one engine and then climb using the other engine alone. In the jargon this is known as flying 'one engine inoperative' or OEI. In the aircraft's flight manual would be tables or graphs telling the pilot how well or how badly an aircraft was supposed to perform following an engine failure. This was essential information for a pilot planning how many people or how much fuel he could carry and still be able to fly should one of the engines stop. Sadly, many of these elderly aircraft couldn't manage to meet their 'book figures' which is why, back then, the CAA, spent a good deal of time trying to identify such aircraft and ensure they were put right.

Anyway, we hoped this aircraft would fly okay, unlike the very similar aircraft David and I had flown the previous day which we had to 'ground'. That is, tell the operator not to use it until the performance problems were resolved. The biggest embarrassment on that occasion was walking past the queue of people about to get on the aeroplane we had just tested in the expectation of flying to the Channel Islands in it … 'Not today I'm afraid'!

Anyway, off we set from Stapleford. Due to its location close to the London airports (which meant lots of airspace above us that we couldn't fly in) we had to fly north-east for about ten minutes before we could commence our performance testing. Now the next bit is technical, but you know the drill; skip on a few lines if you need to for the sake of maintaining your sanity.

Seneca G-TEST at Stapleford prior to flight test.

Some twin-engine aeroplanes have engines set up such that each engine and prop turns in opposite directions. This means that the torque and prop-wash effects for each power-plant tend to cancel out the effect of the other engine. This is known as having 'handed engines'. Other aircraft have to make do with two engines that turn the same way. When they fail one of the engines turns in a 'helpful' way and the other doesn't. If the 'helpful engine' were to fail, the rate of climb would be less and the handling more difficult. So, the 'helpful engine' becomes known as the 'critical engine'. During our testing, therefore, we would normally shut down the 'critical engine' as that would give us the worst case to assess.

The Seneca we were flying on this occasion had 'handed engines', so no 'critical engine'. So, we had to test the performance of each engine in turn. Time to 'flip the coin', metaphorically at least. I, to this day, have no idea why I shut down the left-hand engine first; probably because it was on my side. To do that, I throttled the engine back to a very low power setting to allow the engine to gently cool down. After a couple of minutes, I operated the 'fuel cut-off lever' which starved the engine of fuel and I 'feathered' the propeller which meant that the propeller blades were turned 'end on' to the airflow so that they wouldn't slow the aircraft down too much. I then settled down to flying the aircraft at the optimum speed to climb (best rate of climb speed Vy) and asked David to start the stopwatch. Every thirty seconds he recorded the height we had reached. This we did for five minutes, which later allowed us to plot a graph and work out our rate of climb for comparison with the charts in the book. After five minutes I levelled the aircraft and started up the left-hand engine. Again, in order to be kind to the engine, I left the engine at idle power initially so it could gently warm up before we needed to add power. I was still heading away from where I'd parked my car as the airspace gave us more room to fly the further away from London we were. After another couple of minutes, when I was beginning to think about opening the throttle on the left engine, I was suddenly aware that the said engine started to sound quite rattly. Odd. I started to try and achieve more power, but nothing was working as it should. I had one lever that controlled the engine speed but advancing this fully didn't give me the effect I'd expected. Opening the throttle to achieve more power only worked partially.

This was my first year at the CAA and by this stage I'd only tested half a dozen or so piston twins, so clearly this situation was down to my own 'cock-up' for sure. The question now was to work out what it was. David and I set about trying to work through various options …

'Was there enough fuel? Yes.'

'Was it selected correctly to feed the left engine? Yes.'

'Was the booster pump selected on?' – 'it is now … any change? No.'

'Could it be magnetos?'

There are two sets of spark plugs on an aeroplane engine – so I tried each set in turn …

'Anything?'

'No.'

'It must have iced up then when it was shut down for five minutes'.

'Applying hot air to the engine.'

'Any improvement? – No.'

By now I had turned to point towards where I'd parked my car, but we couldn't fly into Heathrow's airspace. So, I was scanning my map more frequently than Vasco da Gama (fifteenth-century Portuguese explorer). I had begun to run out of ideas and was beginning to suspect I was in for an almighty embarrassment and subsequent 'bollocking' for being inept. The principal concern now shifted to a worry that the engine might seize before we had feathered the propeller. This would have created so much additional drag that we would not have been able to stay aloft on the remaining engine. Time for a new strategy – there was now nothing for it but to shut down the engine again. This I did, and promptly turned my attention to the emergency I now had. The nearest airfield (Southend) involved a longish transit over water. Given that I had no clue as to what had gone wrong, I had to assume that the right-hand engine might suffer the same fate at any minute. So, I ruled out that idea and set off back to where I'd parked my car, giving Heathrow a 'Pan call' (you will have read about Pan calls earlier). They were helpful as I did not want to descend any sooner than I had to. Should the other engine quit I'd be in a really crap glider currently with the wheels up. I'd need all the time and height I could get to find a suitable field, plan a forced landing pattern, maybe get the gear down? Possibly on the emergency system? It was not going to be an easy few seconds.

Eventually Stapleford hove into view and, given my paranoia about losing the second engine, I joined overhead as high as I was allowed and then throttled the good engine to idle and flew, thankfully, a textbook glide approach with the wheels coming down when asked.

Stapleford has a section of tarmac runway and then a further part of the runway which on this day was rather soft, muddy grass. This was another lesson about to be learnt the hard way.

I elected to land 'well in' on the runway as I didn't want to hit the trees on the approach, a reasonable concern I thought. The result was that I landed halfway down the tarmac bit and then rolled to a stop on the grass part. I was already expecting to get a good deal of grief from the operator of the aircraft and his engineers as I was fully expecting to be berated for 'finger trouble' and my inability to restart a piston engine properly, but now my embarrassment was about to be compounded. On the tarmac I could have applied a small amount of power on my right-hand engine and, as I rolled forward, could have steered the aircraft back to the club house using my nose-wheel which I could steer with my feet. Sadly, on this soggy, muddy terrain that I was now sinking into, I needed a lot of power from the right-hand engine to get moving which caused me to start turning to the left. The nose-wheel at this point took umbrage and started to skid sideways and, with everyone watching this incompetent muppet of a test pilot who couldn't restart an engine in flight, I was going round and round in circles. Oh dear.

I had yet again 'blacked' a runway and eventually had to be towed off with a tractor ... How embarrassing – the 'Tow of Shame'. Engineers had gathered and I was greeted with some very dirty looks which continued until the dodgy engine had its covers removed. I expected nothing bad to be evident but thankfully it was instantly obvious some part of its inner workings had been trying to escape, visible by a large domed lump on the casing, literally like a tongue in cheek! So, my initial concerns promptly ebbed away, and the grumpy aircraft owner began to cheer up when I pointed out his new engine was still under warranty. For him, in fairness, it had been 'kinda' helpful of the CAA to discover this problem rather than one of his students. So smiles all round and another knackering drive home around the M25.

Phew! ... Survived another.

It was later in the evening after the usual de-stressing bottle of Australian Shiraz that I began to mentally debrief myself on the adventure. I had shut down the left engine 'on a whim'. On restarting, even at idle power, it had only run for another couple of minutes. At full power this might have only been seconds. So, what if I'd flipped the coin the other way? I'd have shut-down the right-hand engine when still quite low (3,000 feet) due to the London airspace and almost instantly the left hand engine would have suffered its demonstrated unwillingness to keep turning. I'd have been in a gliding brick, with no wheels, and probably insufficient height or time to restart the 'good engine'. I didn't get any sleep that night considering all the 'what ifs' and thanked my 'Guardian Angel' for prompting the result of my 'coin flip'. For all subsequent such shutdowns I always had a plan of exactly where I was going to land and how exactly I was going to restart the other engine, with the help of anyone with me, if required.

I was to encounter a similar situation years later when flying a PA-30 Twin Comanche. That was an aircraft that had been rebuilt following a crash landing and left outside and not flown for over eight years. I was the muppet foolish enough to test fly it out of a very challenging short grass field. I flew the aircraft to a better airfield before I filled it with fuel and ballast to get to the heaviest possible weight and then went off, and as above shut down the left engine. I tried to climb for five minutes but barely stayed level. And then when I came to start the engine – it wouldn't. By this time thankfully I'd gained considerably more experience of dealing with such dramas. Slowly but surely over a period that seemed like an eternity, I coaxed the dead engine back into life. All I had to do then was land back on the very short strip where my car was parked.

Phew! One crappy PA-30 returned to where I'd found it with a long list of defects that had to be fixed before it could be flown again.

It has always annoyed me when I've been put in harm's way by the shoddiness of others. Flight test is dangerous enough as it is. I needed to test fly a Stampe biplane. The Stampe is in some ways similar to the Tiger Moth. It is a tail-dragger bi-plane, originally with a French Renault engine but often re-engined with a Tiger Moth de Havilland Gipsy Major engine. This particular example was owned by a chap who really didn't want to fly in an open cockpit biplane. Instead of buying a more suitable aircraft he elected to take his aeroplane to an engineering organisation west of London to fit canopies over the open cockpits. Because this was a major change to the aeroplane the CAA insisted, quite rightly, on conducting a check flight to see how much the bulky cockpit covers had affected performance and handling qualities. Enter yours truly.

Around the M25 again and I found myself receiving a less than friendly reception.

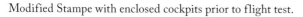
Modified Stampe with enclosed cockpits prior to flight test.

'What did the CAA need to flight test this aircraft for?' They had already flown it and it was all fine …

I did my best to explain that all the paperwork was now in place that required my flight. Easier to let me do it rather than argue about it. So, with a grumpy pilot from the company filling the front passenger seat, off we went heading north-west to again clear Heathrow's airspace. At least the brakes worked on this Stampe, unlike the first Stampe I'd test flown from a very short grass strip at Maypole in Kent.

I was in my first year with the CAA and by then I had only flown a single flight in a Tiger Moth and had never flown a Stampe. So, I elected to sit in the front seat and trust myself to the allegedly experienced Moth and Stampe pilot I was programmed to fly with. As we taxied out to the strip it was evident that the wheel brakes weren't working. These days that might have been enough for me to 'call it a day', but back then I was young, keen to be helpful and the other pilot stated that there was absolutely no need for brakes on this type of aircraft which he instructed on at a nearby field. So off we flew with me doing all the test flying but when it came to the landing this guy was clearly going to be able to land the aircraft safely – wasn't he?

So – 'You have control,' I said instructing him to land the aeroplane for us.

We did land – very fast. To one side of the runway was a car park with scores of families with young children out to watch the aeroplanes – and bizarrely – we were heading straight for them.

'What are you doing?'

'The brakes don't work.'

'I know.'

I had no idea what part of this guy's brain had ceased to work … another 'brain fart'.

'I have control.'

I slammed the throttle forward to give me full power and kicked the rudder hard over with my left foot whilst instinctively applying full left joystick to try and keep level. We didn't. We tipped onto one wheel. But we were no longer pointing at a lot of very white faces and running children. Just before we ran out of runway, I eased the 'just flyable' aircraft off the ground, barely clearing the far end trees. With, now some considerable trepidation, and a bag of useless spuds in the rear seat, I circuited back for another go at a landing – which was clearly going to be difficult given that this 'expert' had just fluffed it and I was positioned in the front seat which was harder to see out of. With the joys of considerable adrenalin coursing through my system I was able to land it smoothly and stay on the runway centre line. A much less spectacular arrival. On the ground this bloke could give no explanation for why he had 'frozen' particularly when he already knew the brakes didn't work. After that experience I didn't fly such aircraft from the passenger seat again.

But back to my original story of the enclosed Stampe now somewhere near Aylesbury. The first test point was a climb for five minutes at the 'best rate of climb speed'. So, having adjusted to the correct speed, I applied full power and started my stopwatch. I started noting the heights every thirty seconds but after a minute or so,

'Splutter, splutter', and the engine promptly stopped.

'Oh, Bugger!'

Close the throttle, stick forward to peg the best glide speed, trim and choose a field …

The bloke in front had no advice to offer so, into the now familiar drill of planning my approach to my chosen field and checking for obvious cause of failure – and there wasn't any. The next part of the drill is to turn the fuel off and then the electrics to the engine but just before I did so there was a splutter and a cough and the propeller that was still spinning seemed to spin a little faster. Could it be that my 'Guardian Angel' has been to an aero engines class recently? Sure enough, the engine continued to pick up such that, as we approached about five hundred feet or so above the ground, I was able to advance the throttle and gingerly add power and stop going down.

'Hurrah!'

I had no idea what had caused the problem and was already pointing to where I'd parked my car. I needed to gain some height and, in fairness, I knew that the likely finding by the engineers when I got back would be 'no fault found'. So I coaxed the aircraft higher, very gently, until I'd reached a safe enough height to try another full power climb …

You guessed it – a minute or so later the engine quit again. Déjà vu or what? Again, it spluttered back to life at around five hundred feet. No more attempts at diagnosis. Time to try and get home without having to walk. At the lowest possible power setting I climbed very, very, gently back to the airfield picking fields to land in every few hundred yards. I managed to join overhead the airfield and do a glide landing and, with the engine still running, taxied back to the hangar. As I suspected, I was greeted by the usual unbelieving faces. I set about explaining the issue. A ground run was completed, apparently successfully, as I got warm again drinking coffee ... and 'no fault found'. What a surprise! I insisted on a recount. And politely suggested the aircraft was put onto chocks so the engine could be run at full throttle ...

At full throttle after a little over a minute the engine spluttered and died – well there's a thing.

To cut a long story short the fuel tank in the wing over the pilot's head fed fuel to the engine below via a beefy rubber pipe. Turns out the pipe was mostly blocked. So, at low power, the engine got enough petrol and when full throttle was applied there was still plenty of fuel in the pipe. Just enough to take-off it would seem. But after a couple of minutes all the fuel in the pipe had been used and the engine stopped.

I was annoyed. This company had claimed that the aircraft had already been adequately tested. Clearly not well enough. In fairness the aircraft owner was very grateful for my discovery as, had I not done my testing, he would have been the first to discover the problem a few weeks later. After a few months and some rectification work I was able to complete my testing and sign the aircraft off as acceptable but still a bonkers concept!

Phew! ... Survived another.

Perhaps my 'most gentlemanly' engine failure in recent years occurred when testing an ETPS helicopter at Boscombe Down; on my 'home turf', so to speak, having spent ten years conducting flight test there, followed by a further dozen flying air cadets around. The UK military over the last three decades has used some fairly entrepreneurial methods of procuring aircraft. In particular, it has obtained 'off-the-shelf' civilian certified aircraft and then put them on the military register. One of the major financial advantages of this methodology was that they could be maintained as civilian aircraft and retained a resale value which reduced their in-service running costs. This method had been used to acquire numerous training and operational helicopters and aeroplanes. ETPS had been using such aircraft since I introduced the concept when I was working there as the Principal Tutor for Rotary Wing flying. I managed to organise the lease of a second-hand civil Squirrel helicopter, which

The ETPS A109E Helicopter prior to my initial testing to approve the addition of the orange boom used for gather accurate pressure data.

was put on the military register and given a very nice shiny new paint job for us to use as a fourth type. This paved the way for two shiny Augusta 109E helicopters to be bought. The Ministry of Defence had placed a contract with the CAA for us to test fly all of these civilian types which were known as 'Civil Owned, Military Registered' (COMR) or Military Registered, Civil Owned Aircraft (MRCOA). So along with one or another of my FTEs I spent a good deal of time dashing around numerous military airfields to conduct regular testing on a wide variety of thankfully well maintained and carefully operated (perhaps with one exception) aircraft. A flight test on one of the ETPS A109s meant I could have a leisurely breakfast for once, since I still lived near to Boscombe Down. I was teamed up with Jeff and ETPS programmed Kev to fly with me; he had been one of my tutors many years earlier when I first attended ETPS as a student. With an experienced crew, newish aircraft and perfect weather I was looking forward to an hour or so of low drama pottering around the Wiltshire countryside – mistake. Early on in the sortie we needed to test the one engine inoperative (OEI) climb performance. Just like on the twin-engine aeroplanes this was accomplished by shutting down one engine and climbing on the other for up to five minutes. In a turbine helicopter the same effect can be achieved by running one engine at idle power as it then runs too slowly to add any power to the gearbox. So in this case I'd identified the left hand engine operating knob and selected it to 'Flight Idle'. The engines were computer controlled and promptly I was left with only the right-hand engine driving. Five minutes later and OEI climb data gathered it was time to return to conventional twin-engined flight. I selected the correct knob and returned it to its normal position – and exactly the 'square root of nothing' happened. This was a new one for both Kevin and myself. I instinctively turned towards where I'd parked my car while Kev worked through our approved check list to try and determine what we might have done wrong. Surely this computer-controlled engine would return to normal if only we had operated it correctly? But sadly not. Without further ado I pushed out the 'Pan call' and lined up on the north-easterly runway of my 'home airfield'. The A109E is fitted with wheels and therefore is allowed to land with forward airspeed. In a helicopter you use a lot of power to hover but a lot less as you fly faster (up to about 60–70 KIAS). So, by choosing to keep my airspeed at 30 KIAS or so, I knew I would have all the power I needed

Edgley Optica at Thruxton prior to initial flight testing.

with just one engine. Being the considerate chap I am, and with memories of the Glassair forced landing at Oxford, Kidlington still relatively fresh, in the final stages of my approach I asked if I could land on a suitable taxiway and with years of practising and teaching such a manoeuvre I was able to conduct a drama-free landing on the spot of my choice.

Phew! … If all my emergencies could be so stress free.

Self-induced engine failures are potentially more embarrassing. Not that long ago I was invited to fly a 'sales demo' in an aircraft I've had quite a history with – the Edgley Optica. Designed many years ago by John Edgley effectively as a replacement for the helicopter in surveillance roles, I had become involved as an EASA test pilot when an elderly example had been bought back by John and returned to flying condition to pave the way for further development and investment. I had subsequently used the aircraft for a number of years on the trot when delivering a short course in flight test under the auspices of the Light Aircraft Association (LAA) at Turweston. On the day in question, I was teamed up with a Chinese investor and pilot and I was asked to put the aircraft through its paces. I elected to show my 'punter' the excellent glide qualities of the aircraft and, somewhere near Andover, explained my intentions and promptly snapped the throttle shut. My patter continued without missing a beat as I instantly recognised a real engine failure. I promptly added this into the narration … 'As you will now see – we have stopped the engine and are now gliding quite successfully.'

With one eye out of the cockpit now searching for a large flat field I am trying also to locate the various required switches which on the Optica are up in the roof. So, throttle reset – and after some deft hand swapping – starter motor engaged and, thankfully as my patter continued unabated, I restarted the engine, added power and soared skyward again. And my punter had remained blissfully ignorant throughout.

Phew! … Got away with that one.

Not many months later I found myself teaching a French test pilot how to fly and subsequently how to test fly autogyros. This had been for a task for which EASA had agreed to use my services but then some paperwork muddle meant that became too difficult. Instead, the plan was hatched where I would use my Autogyro Instructor qualification to deliver a week's training to three other EASA colleagues, a Frenchman, an Italian and a Spaniard. Sounds like one of those jokes about three men going into a bar.

Anyway, I had taught the Frenchman quite a bit when I felt it was time to demonstrate an engine failure after take-off. So, as we crossed the hedge of the airfield boundary I snapped the throttle closed – and quite rightly the Frenchman instantly pushed the stick forward to maintain airspeed – which he did with such gusto that all the fuel flew to the top of the fuel tank starving the engine which instantly stopped.

'I have control,' I called – setting up to land amongst the sheep in front of us.

But 'It's not over until the fat lady sings', and I quickly swapped hands, turned the starter/ignition key fully OFF, which I knew I needed to do from having done a fair amount of flight testing on this type, and then just as quickly turned it fully clockwise to energise the starter which kicked the Rotax engine back into life and, with full throttle applied in an instant, we flew between a couple of sheep – and I mean between – before returning to the heavens followed shortly thereafter by the bar.

Phew! … The Frenchman, Italian and Spaniard went wild.

Which brings me neatly back to the title of the chapter. For a number of years, I'd had to test single seat autogyros for the CAA. Each of these aircraft was different and some were very difficult to fly. I had learned to fly single seat gyros at Henstridge but sometime after that the airfield had

Cricket Autogyro G-CFCH at Little Rissington prior to flight test.

asked the 'gyro nuts' to leave and they had found a new home at Little Rissington. I'd been there a few times and in order to make efficient use of my time I was presented with three single seat autogyros for test, all in one day.

A short brief later and the first aircraft was successfully flown and returned to the hangar from whence it came. I was then presented with G-CFCH – a similar but different machine. I taxied this out towards the end of the long and wide runway at this former military base. As I reached the end there were two conventional aeroplanes, checking their engines and so on, but with nothing really to check on a simple aircraft like mine, I waved cheerfully and moved to the front of the queue. I had no working radio so couldn't chat to anyone, but the pilots of the aeroplanes waved back and let me go ahead. With hindsight this was a mistake.

The runway ahead came into view and I lined up. The runway was built on the top of a hill and had a very distinct slope up to a summit about a third of the way along before starting to slope down again. I added power, the spinning rotors accelerated, and full throttle was then applied with the aircraft leaping airborne. All went well until I reached about a hundred feet or so at which point the engine promptly spluttered and died.

'Bugger!'

No radio, so no Pan Call. In fact, there was minimal time to think and I reacted instinctively – lowering the nose, maintaining speed and then carrying out a textbook power-off landing on the remaining runway ahead. I braked to a stop and breathed a sigh of relief.

Phew! … Survived another.

Then suddenly another penny dropped! I was now stuck in the middle of the runway where, any second, two conventional aeroplanes were about to come barrelling along and, since I was 'over the hill' in more ways than one, they wouldn't know I was there. I had no idea how I or my gyro would fare when run over by a ton of aeroplane, so time for a very swift exit. I jumped out of my harness and pushed this shopping trolley of an aircraft for all I was worth to the side of the runway – to wave again seconds later at the passing aeroplane pilots looking at me in bemusement.

The owner of the first gyro tested had thankfully realised my plight and came walking across the airfield to help me push the now dead gyro back to its home, which thankfully was all downhill.

Merlin Autogyro prior to my third flight test of the day.

A pee and a quick cup of tea to steady the nerves and on to gyro number three. Same brief as last time, so waving at the aeroplane pilots at the end of the runway and shortly thereafter accelerating towards the hump. I might have made it to a hundred and fifty feet or so this time before ... 'Gedunk!'

This engine did not splutter or cough its intentions politely. Without warning it simply seized solid. What do you think? Land on the runway in front of me in line with decades of training? No.

Instead, a flick of stick and rudder turned me 90 degrees left as I dropped the nose to maintain speed and stowed my biro in my pocket, as I'd been writing notes when the engine seized. Now I could also swap hands as I'd been writing with my right (flying hand) hand. I glided steeply towards where my car was parked until the last possible minute before a further 90 degree turn into wind and an aggressive flare to land on the taxiway.

Phew! ... Good result.

At least I was not about to be driven over by some unsuspecting aeroplane pilot and I had shortened the distance to push yet another infernal death trap by a shed load.

And again (in my head) the crowd went wild.

Many pilots survive a whole flying career without experiencing a single engine problem. I'd like to think that I've swayed the statistics in their favour by clocking up more than my fair share. I have mates who have had engine failures and been extremely lucky to survive relatively unscathed. In my case I have for many, many years always had a gloomy disposition and have not only expected the worst to happen to me but have, where possible, planned for it, often by conducting testing over suitable airfields, or in twins, ensuring I'm high enough for the remaining engine to take me to somewhere I can land. Sadly this isn't always possible – and for those situations I'm glad my Guardian Angel is becoming quite technically adept.

Chapter 17

Tiger Moths

Whatever I did I couldn't get away from this huge gang mower that any minute now was going to turn my aeroplane into matchwood.

Whichever way you look at it, I've flown a lot of Tiger Moth aeroplanes over the last seventeen years. For many people sitting outside with a pint of local foaming ale in hand there isn't a prettier sight than a brightly-coloured Tiger Moth pottering overhead with its characteristic Gipsy Major engine emitting the same note as it has done for the last ninety years. Yes, the Tiger Moth first flew in 1931 and the ones still flying are pretty much the same, following a few minor improvements during the 1930s. The aircraft was rapidly purchased by friendly air forces prior to the Second World War and was responsible for training most Allied wartime pilots. A modification of direct relevance from 1941 was to fit anti-spin strakes to the rear fuselage. This followed an RAF accident when a Tiger Moth failed to recover from a spin, although some blame the lightweight bomb-racks it was fitted with at the time.

These anti-spin strakes became the 'normal specification' but I discovered that many owners, when rebuilding pre-1941 vintage aircraft, wanted to fly them without strakes so that they would more accurately resemble their original appearance. The UK CAA had been reluctant to allow such aircraft to fly without strakes but had compromised on a policy which required the CAA to test each example to assess their spin recovery characteristics. So once or twice a year, usually in the winter, I'd get a call inviting me to go spinning in yet another Tiger Moth. I also did a number of 'first flights' following extensive restorations and, sadly, I have flown a number of sorties on behalf of the Air Accidents Investigation Branch to try to help investigate why such a relatively benign aircraft might have caused a fatal accident.

I have always found the Tiger Moth pleasant to fly despite usually having to fly these aircraft in the winter, invariably in sub-zero temperatures at the heights required to safely conduct spin recovery testing. My first such test

Warming the engine of a recently renovated Tiger Moth at Henstridge.

was of G-ANNI, a delightful example resplendent in silver and red with a white and red chequerboard on the wings. I flew from Goodwood on a cold spring morning. It was the first of many spin recovery assessments I flew, and I confess I was somewhat apprehensive. I had yet to spin a Tiger Moth and wasn't quite sure what to expect. Given that I was flying off the south coast of England I decided to wear a lifejacket in addition to my 'Michelin Man' warm clothing and parachute. I needed the help of two chaps just to get in! I was aiming to capture as much data as I could, despite the challenges of flying in an open cockpit, which made writing notes particularly difficult.

So, for this flight I bought myself a new Dictaphone and taped the microphone onto the boom of my helmet microphone. Excellent, strapped in like a Christmas turkey, climbing ever so slowly to 8,000 feet; more spins than I could count, with ailerons applied into and out of the spin to ensure that I couldn't get into a spin from which I couldn't recover. All the time I was gabbling away with all this valuable information into my Dictaphone and then home for tea and medals. But it's never over until it's over. As I attempted my first landing a strong gust of crosswind tried to tip me over at the critical moment. Full aileron had little effect and only full power and a willingness to go around for another go saved the day. It turns out some Tiger Moth ailerons are more efficient than others. Now I know. Still at least I had all my valuable spin data but, on investigation, it quickly became apparent that my spit and saliva had frozen onto the mike and after the first few minutes the audio track became more and more muffled and then stopped. I never made the same mistake again and after I'd done a few of these, I could pretty much remember both the test plan and the subsequent results with next to no notes – as long as I wrote up everything the same evening as I'd flown.

The cold, exposed cockpits were a constant challenge and, as the years went by, I gave up on the authentic Biggles look of leather jacket etc. and wore my Ozee microlight suit and modern Alpha helmet for pretty much all of this flying. One particularly icy early March morning I was tasked with testing G-AOJJ out of White Waltham. The aircraft

Tiger Moth at White Waltham prior to flight testing on a very cold day.

required spinning again and, due to the restricted airspace locally, I had to transit to the west of Reading before I could legally get to the safe height I needed. My concerns were doubled when the elderly owner insisted on coming with me. I tried to talk him out of it but he was very insistent and it was his aeroplane. So, I ensured he was safely strapped into the front cockpit and with some additional engineering support to swing the prop for me (these aircraft don't have starter motors) I was able to start up, and taxi and commence a leisurely climb west bound.

It was bloody cold. It was around zero at the surface and at least twelve degrees below freezing as I reached my planned height. My passenger had started out being reasonably chatty but became less lucid with time and I realised after I'd completed my minimum number of spins he'd stopped talking to me altogether.

'Hello.'

'Hello in the front.'

'Can you hear me?'

'Are you okay?'

'Are you okay?'

No answer... 'Hells Bells! – had he died?'

It was certainly cold enough to get hypothermic very quickly. Time for a swift exit and to get this chap on the ground. Now I faced another conundrum. If I flew as fast as possible, in order to get home as soon as I could, the increase in airflow would increase the wind chill and might make matters worse. If I pottered back as slowly as I could then it would be a greater delay before I could get my passenger into somewhere warm. Another dilemma with life-threatening consequences that I hadn't faced previously. In the end I decided on a compromise and I flew back at a sensible 80 mph or so, but joined the airfield with alacrity and taxied at high speed to get back to the clubhouse expeditiously, wondering whether I would be charged with manslaughter or murder. As soon as we stopped, I realised just how cold my face had become. Meanwhile, my passenger resembled a block of ice, poor soul. Apparently, he'd really enjoyed the flight but by the time we'd reached test altitude had lost the gift of speech. Thankfully only temporarily.

Phew! ... We had both survived another.

For me the real hassle of the Tiger Moth was never flying it, but it was driving it around on the ground. Firstly, it is very difficult to see where you are going; you have to look out of the side of the aircraft and then aggressively slalom to clear the ground in front of you. On landing you have to fly a curved approach or 'crab' sideways so that you can see the runway and as soon as you kick it straight before touch down, you are again relying on looking out of the sides of the aircraft.

Additionally, the aircraft has no brakes at all ... Yes – no brakes. So, on the ground you have to be very careful not to travel too fast. However, if you keep the engine revs too low then the spark plugs oil up and you will lose engine power. Finally, steering on the ground is incredibly challenging. Instead of a tailwheel at the back end of the aircraft, there is a metal skid. On grass airfields, if the ground is soft enough, but not too soft, then the skid digs into the ground and, being connected to the rudder pedals, allows very large radius turns to be conducted as long as the joystick is held fully back. If the airfield is tarmac, then this skid cannot dig into anything and provides no steering or braking help whatsoever, which is one of the reasons grass airfields tend to be the preferred operating homes of such aircraft.

Early on at my time at the CAA I had to test a beautifully rebuilt Moth at Chilbolton. As usual I had assistance to swing the prop and get me started but, thereafter, I was on my own. I managed to get to the grass strip, but I needed to transit to the far end of it and then turn around to start my take-off run. The strip was narrow with a hedge along one side and a very soft ploughed field on the other. At the end of the strip, I manoeuvred as close to the hedge as I could, slowed down as much as possible and then promptly applied full right pedal to cant the rudder and swivel the tail skid, adding a burst of power to blow some propwash over the rudder to help me turn. However, the additional power now started to accelerate me towards the ploughed field, and it was becoming clear I wasn't going to make it. With no brakes I had only two choices. One option was for experienced Moth pilots only, which was to push the joystick fully forward and, with full rudder applied, open the throttle fully. This was a very successful technique if done right. The propwash over the elevator would lift the tail into the air and the propwash over the rudder would turn the tail very smartly in the required direction. The downside was that the additional power accelerated the aircraft forward even more, and, if not done quite right, the nose of the aircraft could tip forward enough for the propeller to strike the ground leading to a destroyed prop and damaged engine – very expensive.

'Quick – decide – *Quick* ...'

So do you think this risk-averse test pilot applied full power?

No. I'm afraid I 'wimped out' and quickly turned off both magnetos so that I came to a halt still on the strip and not stuck in the ploughed field. So not the best possible outcome but certainly not the worst, and with my trusty mobile phone to hand I could eat humble pie and call for reinforcements to help me turn the final 45 degrees and get me restarted. Frankly the flight itself was 'easy peasy' after the hassle of getting to the correct end of the runway pointing in the right direction.

Phew! ... Embarrassed but no damage done.

The ultimate Tiger Moth embarrassment came when I was tasked to fly the club aircraft from RAF Henlow. It is, still to this day, a useable airfield and retains its wartime charm of being completely grass. There are marked-out runways but most of the site is grassed and flat enough to operate from. On the day in question the wind was in excess of 20 knots, excessive for a Tiger Moth, particularly if it's not directly along the runway. Given the nature of the site I thought I'd be able to find at least one suitable runway when I came back to land and, for my take-off, I had

About to flight test a Tiger Moth at Henstridge.

two kind chaps who each held a wing tip in order to help me steer. The aircraft only ever wanted to point into wind so trying to taxi at right angles to the wind direction was tricky. Anyway, the flight was absolutely fine. I returned, chose a runway and, if I say so myself, conducted a very nice landing some way from the clubhouse. All I needed to do now was taxi back. It was then that I realised my troubles were only just beginning, because the large tractor-towed gang-mower rig which I'd spotted earlier was now bearing down on me at a fair rate of knots. My guess was that the tractor driver didn't expect anyone to be daft enough to be flying on such a windy day and wasn't paying attention. As I added power to try and get out of its way the aircraft promptly turned into wind and towards it. Adding power just made it worse as I simply hurtled towards impending doom all the more quickly. Ninety-degree turns were impossible as the aircraft was being forced by the wind in a certain direction. With all nearly lost I tried another trick I'd had to use once before and that was to start my turn in completely the wrong direction.

Madness!

By getting the aircraft swinging I found I could get the aircraft to turn through 270 degrees and thus end up briefly pointing where I needed to go. I have to say it was a close-run thing as the tractor driver constantly changed direction and kept on closing the gap. Finally, the same two blokes who had helped me get airborne ran to greet me and each grabbed a wing tip.

Phew! … I was under control again and had survived perhaps the most unusual 'mid-ground collision' possible.

Chapter 18

What to Avoid

If you have read the first few words of the book you may be wanting to know more about that particular event?

I was testing the 'Avoid Curve' – or 'Height-Velocity curve' of the PZL SW-4. For the non-helicopter pilots, suffice to say HV testing has a similar 'high risk' categorisation as spin recovery testing does for aeroplanes. In fact, it's far worse. Spin recovery usually requires the pilot simply to place the controls against their end stops and wait to see what happens. Testing the engine-off characteristics of a single-engine helicopter requires a good deal of flying ability and currency, in addition to bravery. Two years after the events at Swidnik narrated in Chapter 4, we were invited back to have another look at the helicopter. Thankfully, the company had made good progress on improving some of the things we had criticised and, most importantly, had improved the recommended engine-off landing profile to something slightly more do-able.

Two further years were to go by before we were invited back for our third visit. This time we were being asked to validate the Avoid Curve. The Avoid Curve or the 'Height Velocity Diagram' indicates combinations of height and airspeed which prevent a safe engine-off landing being accomplished. The curve is derived by analysis and then by flight testing. The testing will provide a series of test points along the curve where safe landings can only just be achieved. Flying lower/slower in the shaded region is likely to lead to a crash should the engine fail.

I was teamed up with Leszek again. It turned out that PZL had not properly tested their avoid curve. They had not actually done any real landings. For a whole bunch of reasons that wasn't good enough. Once the engine has been 'chopped' the rotor rpm decays and the rate of descent increases enormously. Even when you recover the rpm your rate of descent may be too high to safely land. So, after lengthy discussions, we elected to fly a fairly comprehensive pair of sorties allowing me the chance to build up to each test point in an incremental fashion, or so I

The SW-4 Height Velocity (Avoid Curve) as presented initially. Note the units used of metres and Km/h rather than feet and KIAS.

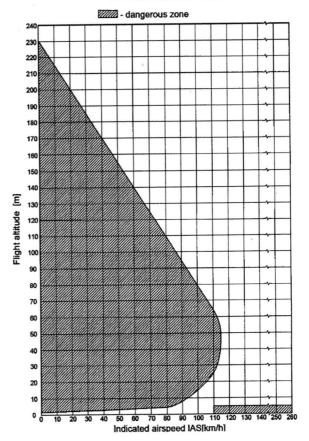

DANGEROUS ALTITUDE AND SPEED ZONES AFTER ENGINE FAILURE

hoped. I started with a couple of 'training engine-off landings' so I could get my 'hand in' and then set up for the first test point. I again made the mistake of asking the company TP to demonstrate the first one which was a high hover.

We positioned at 850 feet which was about 100 feet above the declared limit. (If the engine fails in a high hover the pilot has to expeditiously convert height to speed, such that a conventional glide can be established, followed by a normal variable flare engine-off landing. Without forward airspeed the rate of descent is far too high and cannot be sufficiently arrested to prevent a very serious/fatal crash landing.) The idea was that he would count down as we had done together previously, I would then close the throttle (in the roof) and he would then wait a second before responding.

'So Leszek are you stable and on condition?'
'Yes, on condition; in a stable hover at 850 feet.'
'Standby then for a throttle chop on my count of three.'
'Ready?'
'Ready.'
'Three two one; *Now.*'

I then counted 'one thousand and one' which was the required one second civil certification delay or simulated reaction time, at which point I expected Leszek to demo the perfect entry into autorotation we needed … but nothing happened.

I was, yet again, so glad of my time as an instructor at ETPS when I used to teach this subject. By the time I had silently counted to 'one thousand and two' the grim reaper had already unsheathed his scythe ready for our now imminent demise.

Without thinking, my right hand had flashed from the throttle in the roof to the cyclic control stick and, with the rotor rpm decaying below the published minima, I abruptly pushed the stick forward as I slammed the collective lever fully down with my left hand. We started falling but the fuselage attitude remained level while the rotors, although slowing, were being forced to change their path.

Bang, bang, bang, bang, bang …

The blades almost instantly hit the 'droop stops' – the bits of metal that stopped the blades hanging down too low when they weren't spinning at flying speed. I knew from my previous testing that these droop stops were pretty robust and unlikely to fail … and at that stage I had no other choices apart from dying.

After a painfully long time, the fuselage slowly started to pitch nose down in sympathy with the rotor blades and the banging stopped … Phew! I was now 30 degrees nose down, with no indicated air speed and the vital rotor rpm somewhere near my ankles!

I'm not sure I had time to utter an expletive or even tell Leszek I had taken control but by now he had already released the controls in the hope I could recover the situation. Eventually the airspeed began to build but so did the rate of descent which was really high. At least I knew that if I managed to judge things correctly I could flare very aggressively which would recover my vital rotor rpm and hopefully decrease the rate of descent sufficiently.

100 feet … 90 feet … 80 feet … now … cyclic briskly moved aft … progressive flare commenced … please God let my rotor rpm recover … rotor speed back in limits … Phew! … 60 feet … flare like a bandit … can't see where I'm going … level rapidly by pushing the cyclic forward … collective now snatched to the top stop … and land at over 30 mph …

Bloody Hell!

And that was just the first test point.

Thereafter I flew all the test points myself 'off the bat' which was much better for my stress levels, and we survived the day. What it really brought home to me was how naïve I had been as a young navy Wasp pilot flying around in the dark at 50 feet. I had always assumed my quick wits and 'above average' ability (we all thought we were above average) would allow me to cope with my Rolls Royce Nimbus quitting at almost any stage. How wrong I was. Even allowing just a one second reaction time a lot of height, speed and rotor rpm loss occurs … Blige!

In order for such a helicopter to be certified it has to be tested in all possible conditions with high altitude and high temperatures being particularly challenging for performance, including the dreaded avoid curve.

Two years later, in the middle of August, I had been invited to test the same helicopter again during some very hot days in Arizona. Testing had to start when it was almost too dark to see. After dawn, the temperature rose 1°C every 20 minutes and with each degree rise in temperature the helicopter could lift 20 kg less. Fortuitously, it burnt about the same weight in fuel so we could rattle through limiting performance test points.

We were flying at Prescott which is 5,000 feet above sea level with temperatures getting into the 30s by lunchtime which effectively meant the air was as thin as it would have been at 7,000 feet.

Because the avoid curve is more critical with the 'thin air' found at high altitude and high temperature, we now had to redo the already marginal avoid curve testing. Leszek had left PZL and I was teamed up with his replacement whose grasp of English was more of a challenge. So, without requesting a demo, I set myself up at Prescott for the first high-hover test point. I dropped the lever after exactly one second's delay and managed to get the nose pitching down with no droop stop pounding. Given that the air was much thinner, I knew I would have to use more speed to land with. In Poland, as we would have done in the UK, we had tested on to smooth level grass which also tends to be slightly more forgiving. In the States we were locked into 'doing it their way' which meant landing on the tarmac runways. To that end we fitted additional thin metal plates to the bottom of the skids to protect them.

So here we go …

Descending at 2,000 feet/minute …

100 feet …

Gentle aft cyclic input to flare …

60, 55, 50, 45, 40, 35 KIAS and around 20 feet …

Time to do the hard bit …

Forward cyclic … aircraft levelled … 10 feet … 8 feet … 5 feet …

Collective raised …

Bang … we landed doing about 35 mph … cool … I'm an ace I think … and as I do so we start to yaw to the left. Instinctively I apply full right pedal which has bugger all effect!

The air is thin and the tail rotor, which is effectively connected to the slowing main rotors, is also slowing down rapidly and has reached the point where it no longer can do anything useful.

What to do next?

Well, nothing. I had applied full pedal. I had lowered the collective fully to put as much weight as possible on the skids to slow me down swiftly and I had no engine to use … I was out of control and along for the ride.

I have some great video which makes it all look rather tame … it did not appear to be from where I was sitting. Thankfully, the metal plates on the skids allowed us to slide sideways just as easily as in a straight line. Weird, but thankfully no tendency to tip over which would have been very bad. Phew!

For the rest of the test points, I fed in more right pedal as I touched down, to ensure I prevented any possible yaw and all went well. In fact, the Arizona detachment was successful, apart from the fact that the helicopter's engine was barely powerful enough to cope with the thin air and really struggled. It transpired that the company had almost certainly been allowing the engine to run a lot hotter than permitted before our arrival. Testing at Prescott, given the serious abuse this helicopter had received of late, I spent every minute of every flight expecting the engine to quit on me. For my final day of testing, I needed to fly the aircraft to Flagstaff which is 7,000 feet above sea level. With the warm air this would give the helicopter the challenges of flying at nearly 10,000 feet. My Polish co-pilot was now very much outside his 'comfort zone' and we routed across some very hostile territory, with me trying to ensure that every minute or so I identified where I was going to land when the engine stopped ... *not* a relaxing flight. Having completed our testing, the temperature at the airfield was rising and I had to do some serious mental arithmetic to calculate the maximum weight that the helicopter could get airborne with. This allowed me to work out how much fuel I could carry which I had to ensure was sufficient to get us back to Prescott. I crunched the numbers and decided I would have enough fuel, but with no margin for error. The bowser took a while, and I needed a pee. By the time I clambered into the sweltering cockpit the outside air temperature had risen some more.

Yikes!

No time to waste ... with the rotors spinning and checks done I smoothly raised the collective with both eyes fixed on the engine temperature gauge ... I pulled to the red line ... and ...

Nothing happened.

'Oh Bugger!'

The temperature had risen, and we now had less power available than we needed to get airborne. The more I delayed the worse the situation would get. We had no weight we could offload and burning off fuel couldn't be achieved fast enough to match the rising temperature and we needed it all to get back.

'Double Bugger!'

Time for some rapid lateral thinking. As I've already explained, helicopters need less power to fly if they are moving forward. Helicopters with wheels often do a running take-off and trundle along the ground until they are doing 30–40 mph before pulling power. But my SW-4 had skids and I was parked on a dispersal not the runway.

'Hello Flagstaff Tower this is the SW-4 Helicopter on the dispersal – I need to do a running take-off.'

'Say again.'

'I need to run along your tarmac dispersal and taxiway prior to getting airborne and departing for Prescott.'

'OK SW-4 – good luck with that.'

I had remembered we still had the 'shoes' fitted to the skids to prevent damage if they scraped along tarmac … with ATC vaguely happy, I pulled again to the red line and eased the cyclic stick forward as much as I dared. This caused the thrust to start to tug us forward and, after an agonising second or two, we suddenly overcame the friction and started to slide forward.

Phew!

Sparks flew from the skids as I added more collective to squeeze every ounce of power from the engine and, nudging the cyclic further forward, we started to accelerate … Now a walking pace … Now a fast walk … Now a jog … Now a run … and at last the airspeed indicator started to flicker into life. I quickly changed radio frequency to avoid the potential bollocking I felt sure would be coming my way and, as we reached around 40 mph, I let the aircraft stagger ever so slowly off the ground. By the time I'd achieved 65 KIAS, still within two inches of the ground, I finally could rotate slightly and allow the aircraft to fly away!

Phew! … Survived another.

The next phase of the campaign was to test the aircraft in colder climes. Originally, the testing was scheduled for winter in Yakutsk which, in addition to being on the Risk game board, is, in winter, the coldest place on the planet.

In the end PZL chose to go to Alaska instead and I was raring to go with all my extreme cold-weather clothing already packed. However, after all our extensive preparation, we were contacted to be told that the PZL test aircraft had crashed. The crew were OK but not so the helicopter. That put an end to my association with this particular aircraft which is now owned by Leonardos and is being developed for use as a pilotless drone.

Good Luck with that.

Chapter 19

Finale – Embarrassing Moments

And that's when the hotel manager found me sitting in his chair completely naked apart from the 'flasher mac' I'd stolen earlier!

I confess I have read a number of books by pilots over the years who have tried to impress the reader with their amazing flying abilities and prowess at being the world's best at this or that.

If you've read this book as far as this final chapter, I would hope that you haven't formed a similar opinion about this author, but just in case you have, here are a collection of 'cock-ups', issues and embarrassments that have formed part of my 'day job' for the last seventeen years or so. I'd like to think I survived them due to an element of diligence and good humour in equal measure but I'm also aware that my 'Guardian Angel' hasn't had an easy ride.

I was tasked with conducting a test programme on a Beech Baron (twin-engine piston powered aeroplane). At the time London City Airport

Beech Baron Aeroplane at Gamston prior to commencing our steep approach trial into London City.

not only had relatively short runways but also, due to the surrounding skyscrapers, aircraft had to make an unusually steep approach in order to land. A steep approach in a large aeroplane designed to use minimal fuel can be a problem as they tend to glide quite well and don't want to go down. The unconventional approaches required by this airport resulted in the CAA having to assess each type requiring such a clearance to operate.

Anyway, lots of emails later, Nick (FTE) and I arrived at Gamston Airfield and stood in the car park at the bottom of the ATC control tower waiting to meet the pilot who would be arriving with the required aircraft. After thirty minutes I phoned said pilot to enquire where he was. He was in the car park at the bottom of the tower. But we were at different airfields. When I scrolled through the recent emails, it was obvious we had been at cross purposes for weeks. Happily, the flying

Flying the circuit at London docklands.

Flying the approach into London City.

time from where he was located was minimal and an hour or so later than planned we were able to route down to London for some rare scenic flying over the docklands. After we had confirmed all was safe with the proposed approach profiles we thankfully were able to route back to Gamston – where we had parked our cars.

I was, I confess, more annoyed by the cock-up regarding our planned meeting venue than other people might have been. Professional credibility in flight test is hard won and easily lost. Thankfully, in this case, everything was well planned and, once underway, smoothly executed, so we managed to keep our professional reputation intact – just.

Phew! … Another successful outcome.

The CAA had a system of continued airworthiness testing in place which ensured most aircraft were tested, to ensure they were safe to fly, at least every three years.

I was very proud to oversee a good deal of this activity. A major part of my task was briefing other pilots to act on our behalf. I would give a formal PowerPoint brief and then we would conduct a genuine check flight together. I was asked by a very nice guy if I could brief him at Bidford Airfield and conduct a check flight on a Gardan Horizon aeroplane. Sure thing. Unfortunately, the weather when I arrived was dreadful – heavy rain and low cloud. After several cups of coffee and completing as much of the briefing as I could, it was clearly evident the weather was not going to improve, so I departed and returned again another day … and again it rained all day. On my third visit I was really getting quite keen not to have to drive to Bidford ever again and the weather had brightened but I was concerned about the state of the grass airfield. My very keen 'applicant' had been forced to take another day off work and was, therefore, keen not to squander another day of 'holiday'. He proceeded to convince me that the runway was suitably firm despite resembling a scene from the Somme circa 1916. I elected to taxi along the full length of the runway, in order to try and assess its suitability, and then turned around at the far end. There is nothing more useless than runway behind you. I applied full power and immediately knew this wasn't going to be good … 10 … 15 … 20 KIAS. Halfway down the runway with full power applied we were achieving no more speed than a bloke on a push bike. I use a rule of thumb for my take-offs. I want to achieve 70 per cent of my flying speed by the time I am halfway along the runway. 70 per cent is sometimes simplified to 2/3 or 3/4 depending on my level of pessimism on the day. Today I was definitely not going to get airborne by the end of the runway so, sadly, it was time to abort. As I closed the throttle, we slowed rapidly as the full weight of the aeroplane was taken again by the wheels, and when I tried to turn off the runway it became evident that – we were stuck up to our axles in mud.

'Bugger!'

Another first! After berating my 'applicant' for his optimism we clambered out and, fortuitously, spotted a couple of farmers in a neighbouring field. Much arm flapping later we had attracted their attention. Thankfully, they took pity on us and offered to tow us in their little all-terrain buggy. Ironically it was much quicker than the proper tug I'd had to wait so long for at Oxford, Kidlington.

I never did fly that Gardan Horizon as the next time we met up I found myself testing another quirky aeroplane, the Morane Saulnier MS894A – now that's a catchy name. But at least on our fourth attempt the weather was OK and the runway dry enough.

The Gardan Horizon stuck in the mud at Bidford. Note the friendly chaps with the buggy who were about to tow us out.

Phew! … Job completed … at last.

Bad weather and soft ground have always been a challenge when operating out of numerous grass strips and farmers' fields over the years. In my first week of joining the CAA I travelled around with my colleague Paul, who was the previous holder of my post. I've enclosed a photo of him helping prep the aircraft for flight test on a very wet day on a particularly soggy strip near Salisbury.

I should have learned my lesson then and quit whilst I was ahead. The first time I visited Wing Farm (near Warminster) to test fly a Grob motor glider I was faced with a similar problem, as the guy I was due to brief ran the co-located engineering facility and, despite soft ground, was very happy that the strip was suitable. Having learned my lesson about trying to get airborne from muddy airfields I invited him to have a go first at a very light weight – which he did and was successful. So, with more confidence following this demo, we ballasted to maximum weight and set off to fly the formal check flight. The ground was soft and I would have aborted my take-off had I not witnessed the art of the possible. Although

My colleague and fellow test pilot Paul assisting me get ready to flight test a Fuji at a strip near Salisbury. Note the poor weather.

it took some degree of faith in my decision as we passed the halfway mark only just meeting my take-off airspeed criteria. This was another example of a poor performer.

My five-minute climb was well below scheduled figures which was a 'fail' but the engineer I was with thought he knew better and offered me a particularly interesting challenge … 'This is a motor glider. I bet I can stop the engine and, as a glider, climb better than you did.'

Grob motor glider prior to flight testing at Wing Farm.

Well, this was early days for me doing this kind of thing … and he was very convincing. So with a suitable wager in place, I offered him the controls and he promptly stopped the engine. Another deliberate engine failure. What *fun*. He then did his level best using every glider pilot trick in the book to ride a thermal on the edge of various clouds and we descended. And then again over certain fields … and we descended … and descended. This was about to become a real forced landing in a serviceable aeroplane – too embarrassing by far. Low enough to see the legs of the cows, I insisted we restart the engine.

'Now!'

Phew! It started first time, or I'd have had some explaining to do. Instead, the engineer needed to sort out the aircraft's performance before it could be flown again.

Weather was the major factor in trying to test another quirky aeroplane at Gamston, a Diamond Super Dimona, another motor glider. This aircraft had been bought by Edinburgh University and had two large pods, one under each wing, so that various sensors could be fitted for doing survey work. I'd tried to test fly this aircraft a couple of times already and when I finally went flying the weather was, frankly, still not that great and was already deteriorating from the west. My preparation was as brisk as I could make it and I figured I could fly eastward ahead of the poor weather to get my testing done and then scurry home again before it got too bad. This I managed to achieve, as hoped up until the point of needing to return. This was before I had a moving map driven by GPS and I was relying on my basic navigation skills of comparing compass heading with my map. As the rain arrived and the cloud and visibility lowered, I was really struggling. I was on my own, so no local mate to help, and it was getting really difficult to work out where I was, where I had been and where I was going. Eventually after some IFR flight, ('I follow roads') reminiscent of numerous operational sorties, the runway threshold eventually appeared through the rain and gathering gloom and I threw the aircraft onto the tarmac with huge relief as the last of the visibility disappeared into the dusk. It was then that the main cause for my confusion became blatantly evident. The magnetic compass was reading about 60 degrees off the runway centre line. 'Bugger!' That would explain it.

Grob Dimona prior to flight test at Gamston. Note the big underwing pods and low cloud.

It is normal practice when about to go flying in cloud, to check the compass functionality and accuracy before getting airborne. Although not expecting to fly in cloud, how had I not noticed this during take off? Well to be honest I don't know, but my guess is that I was rushing to get things done in a new aeroplane, at a strange airfield, and I just hadn't noticed. Guess what? Every time I line up on a runway now, I religiously check the compass even when I have no intention of flying in cloud. How could it have been so wrong? Most magnetic compasses are set up by the engineers to within a 1-degree error. So, what on earth had occurred?

It turned out that the engineers were struggling to work out how to ballast the aircraft to its maximum weight. After a few failed ideas they had decided to fill the underwing pods with steel bars. No wonder my poor magnetic compass was confused especially when most of the aircraft was made out of a composite material and not metal. The poor compass needle had been well and truly 'spoofed.' On discovering this, I was relieved that at least I had a partial excuse for my cock-up.

Phew! I had survived another thanks, in no small part, to experiencing many bad weather flights in my trusty Wasp.

My flight in the Rotorway Exec kit-built helicopter had much in keeping with some of the incidents in previous chapters and taught me a similar lesson again. That is the one about not trusting the bloke in the other seat. I had been asked to brief this guy so he could carry out CAA check flights. I had never flown a Rotorway before and given that this was early on in my time at the CAA I assumed that a bloke with over 700 hours on type would be better placed to fly it than me. Wrong.

The helicopter had very limited performance which meant we needed nearly all of the power available just to get it to hover a few inches above the ground. The farm we were operating from was surrounded by hedges, telephone wires and other hazards intent on ruining our day. However, with such a limited amount of power and no way to do a running take-off, the only way to get airborne was to fly what's known as a 'cushion creep'. That is, we hovered very, very close to the ground and then had to gently accelerate into forward flight, to the speed we needed, to have enough power margin to climb. This technique requires a flat smooth area for a whole bunch of reasons. So imagine my surprise when the muppet I was

Rotorway Exec prior to flight test.

with, without warning or discussion, suddenly set off across a ploughed field – at right angles to all the ruts.

'Noooooooooo'

I really thought we were going to hit one of the ruts in the ground at any minute which would have had us tipping over and dying. So that wasn't a good start. Once safely airborne and at a suitable cruise height, passing close to Stansted International, we were asked to change radio frequency, a common enough requirement and simple to do but as this muppet leaned forward to reach the radio he suddenly, again with no warning, completely lost control of the aircraft. My guess is we were milliseconds rather than seconds away from tumbling out of the sky when, without any deliberate bidding from my ageing grey matter, I noted I had taken control.

'I have control,' I heard spout from my mouth.

'Are you Okay?'

'Yeah.'

'You nearly killed us.'

'Yeah – sorry about that.'

'Okay, how about I do the flying for the rest of the flight?'

In fairness, the Rotorway Exec is not the easiest of helicopters to operate. It suffers from static and dynamic instability which is another way of saying – 'bloody difficult to fly'!

The tail rotor, which is an absolutely vital component to allow safe flight, is rotated thanks to six – yes, six – large rubber bands, connected in series such that if any of the six were to fail the tail rotor would stop going round and then the helicopter would go round instead. The flight manual offered this kind of advice:

'You will know when one or more of the rubber drive belts start to slip, as you will be applying full yaw pedal and not getting a satisfactory response.'

Yaw pedal, which changed the pitch on the tail rotor blades to apply clockwise or anti-clockwise thrust, needed to be applied fully (in opposite directions) for both high power and low power conditions – nothing to spare – no margin – great. In fact, when turning the helicopter in autorotation it could only be turned to the right as there was no control authority remaining in order to get it to turn left. Not ideal when the pilot sits in the left seat in this helicopter. At least I was able to make our return to where I'd parked my car a good deal more relaxed than our departure, but I was very glad to be safely on the ground at the end of it all.

Needless to say, the debrief of this particular flight took longer than the flight itself. A pilot, with more experience on type than most Rotorway pilots put together, would have killed himself had I not been there and been able to sort things out without hesitation.

Phew! … I had survived another and formed a very comprehensive opinion of a very challenging helicopter and this particular pilot.

'Making Flying Safer!'

Landing 'tail-draggers' can be more challenging than aeroplanes fitted with the more conventional tricycle undercarriage including a nose-wheel, particularly on tarmac rather than grass runways. Flying a Dauphin at Kemble, a very large ex-military airfield, I was faced with a known problem before I got airborne. The brakes on this aircraft were operated by a lever under the dashboard or instrument panel which was meant to apply braking equally to both main wheels. In fact, it worked much better on one side than the other. With this deficiency noted, I was still able to taxi safely to the runway and take-off without further ado. With the flight test successfully completed, I turned my attention to the landing, still aware of my asymmetric brakes. My touchdown was gracefully flown, with all three wheels making contact simultaneously. I needed to slow down fairly quickly to make the turn-off I needed, and I gently applied the brake lever, fully expecting the aircraft to yaw/turn towards the stronger brake. I was ready for this and was applying rudder to compensate but, without warning, the tail wheel, instead of running straight as it was supposed to, suddenly started to swivel, like on a badly-behaved Tesco shopping trolley. The folks on the ATC tower must have laughed their socks off as I did a left, right, left, right, left…mini slalom before eventually taming the thing and pulling off the runway breathing a sigh of relief.

'Are you alright?' they asked politely.

'I am now', I replied, before promptly completing the paperwork requiring the tail wheel and brakes to be fixed without delay.

The moral of this tale, and the lesson learned, was to be wary of accepting minor snags which of themselves can be safely accommodated. Such snags can really compound difficulties should additional problems present themselves.

Dauphin at Kemble prior to flight test.

Phew! At least in this case the additional snag only caused me mild embarrassment ...

On leaving the CAA I was appointed by an autogyro company as their Test Pilot, amongst other things. This range of gyros was constantly being improved and their capabilities extended. And so, 'it came to pass' that the company sought approval to operate the aircraft at night. This involved a number of challenges. Firstly, being confident that the aircraft was stable and easy enough to fly without good external visual references. Secondly, the cockpit internal lighting had to be suitable. Instruments had to be appropriately lit so that they could be easily read, but dim enough to allow the outside view to be seen clearly without dazzle or unwanted reflections on the canopy. Finally, the external lights had to perform two functions. They needed to provide legally compliant navigation lights so that other aircraft could see the gyro and work out which way it was pointing i.e. a red light fitted to the left side, a green to the right and a white light visible to the rear and they needed to be able to provide sufficient illumination to taxi and take off and land.

Night flying would, in practice, be conducted to an airfield using suitably lit runways, which would provide lighting at regular intervals so that the perspective of the runway could be judged to make a suitable approach.

Cavalon Autogyro prior to night flight testing.

Initial testing was flown at Halfpenny Green, Wolverhampton where the runway lights were good, and we could ask for them to be turned off when required. I thought it was important that the aircraft should have sufficient external illumination in order to make a safe power-off landing should the engine fail somewhere other than at an airfield. This meant the landing lamps had to illuminate the ground satisfactorily at sufficient height for the pilot to judge the final flare manoeuvre – easier said than done. Having tried it at Halfpenny Green we realised we needed more light and therefore had to improve the landing lamps. We initiated a trial to test two different sorts and chose to use Thruxton where there was less ambient/cultural lighting. It was a very dark night with no moon and no visible stars and we were testing the worse of the two lamps. I circuited around to run into the airfield from the east, aiming to be in line with the main tarmac runway. Once over the airfield I closed the throttle sharply, put the 'rubbish landing lamp' on and religiously flew at 70 mph which would be enough speed to allow me lots of 'flare effect'. The wait as I descended was unbearable and then, suddenly, out of the gloom the ground appeared.

'Wait … wait … wait … *now.*'

Judging my moment, I commenced a progressive flare of the aircraft and touched down with next to no forward motion.

Phew! … Safely on the ground, and rather pleased at my gentle landing – but where on earth am I?

I'd been flying out of Thruxton for many years, and still do. I had expected to be on the runway, but it didn't look at all right in the dark. A rough surface with lots of weeds and grass etc. Eventually, the penny dropped. Thruxton had been an old wartime field, operating American P-47 Thunderbolts amongst other things. The once very wide runway had been utilised by resurfacing just half the width. So, to the right of the actual runway was the old overgrown wartime concrete which is where I'd happened to alight. It looked the same in the dark. But at least I had proved I could use even the 'rubbish landing lamp' if required. I went off and flew another dozen or so landings using the better lamp and made the proper runway every time. Although I count this as an embarrassing moment, the ATC tower couldn't see me at all that night so this is the first time this escapade has become public.

Also, at Thruxton I had a requirement to test fly a Harvard, which apparently had completed a successful restoration. I had agreed to let another pilot do the first flight on this particular aircraft, but I had asked to 'ride shotgun' in the rear cockpit. The said pilot had flown check flights on behalf of the CAA previously and I wanted to see whether he was up to the job. After briefing we 'manned up' and I clambered into the rear cockpit and he into the front. Without further ado he rushed to get the engine started and without discussion was calling ATC for permission to taxi. Meanwhile, the aircraft's intercom system wasn't working properly. With hindsight (which is a wonderful thing) I should have insisted we terminate the sortie and get the comms fixed. However, I wasn't the aircraft captain and was just along to observe and, before I had chance to intervene, the bloke in the front seat was heading for the runway.

As soon as we were airborne, I realised the long metal exhaust that runs down the right-hand side of both cockpits was clearly rigged wrongly as I was starting to breathe all manner of noxious fumes. My front seat pilot was paying no attention to the wellbeing of his 'passenger' and rushing to climb clear of the circuit.

'I'm being gassed!

We need to land now.

Harvard with a poor exhaust system prior to flight test at Thruxton.

I'm dying!'

No response from the 'professional' in the front, and in a Harvard the two occupants sit a fair way apart. I couldn't just tap him on the shoulder to get his attention. 'What to do before I die?'

Such circumstances require lateral thinking and, pulling my large map of the South of England out of my leg pocket I unfolded it and rolled it into a tube resembling a Luke Skywalker lightsaber. Fuelled by adrenalin and a strong survival instinct, I swiftly used my weapon to apply a pair of energetic pokes to the back of this chap's head – now I had his full attention. He definitely realised I really wasn't happy, and, still not quite understanding the situation, he thankfully elected to return to the airfield. On eventually climbing out of the aircraft I was asked by one of the engineers if I'd enjoyed my flight …

'No I bloody didn't.

It nearly killed me.

Fix the bloody exhaust!'

I had barely survived another and wondered whether any other 'passenger' would have had the wherewithal to attack the aircraft captain's head with a homemade lightsaber?

A similar issue occurred when again 'riding shotgun' in a Harvard, this time out of Duxford, again for me to check that the front-seat pilot was up to the task. Full power applied, airborne, wheels up, speed gently building as we turned to clear the circuit and

Whoooooosh.

Without any warning a 100 mph blast of air from the floor of the aircraft hit me full in the face. It was so powerful that it immediately blew out the side window of my canopy.

'Bloody Hell!'

At least this time my intercom worked and over the gale force wind I was able to shout to the pilot in the front seat to fly slowly and land as soon as possible. It turned out that a panel on the underside of the aircraft had dropped down and formed an almost perfect air scoop funnelling in 100 mph air between my feet. Not expected or pleasant but thankfully not as traumatic for me as it might have been for anyone else. And it turns out it was fixable before we ran out of daylight.

Phew! ... Mission accomplished.

Harvard following the initial flight test with engineers working to fix the lower fuselage panel.

Trislander awaiting flight test.

At least in all of these examples I completed the day with safety issues identified and, invariably, solutions in place to fix them.

Early in my time at the CAA one of the FTEs, John, asked me to accompany him to Jersey to conduct the check flight on a Trislander, a three engine version of the ubiquitous Islander. The aircraft had apparently been check flown previously and passed its test with flying colours. Hopefully an easy day trip and we'd be back to the mainland in time for tea?

Once we'd safely arrived at the engineering organisation, we, as usual, reviewed the documents previously completed, including the check flight schedule, and set about planning our own flight. As always, we asked for ballast to be able to operate the aircraft as close to its maximum weight as possible and were then told the organisation didn't have any.

'But you did last week when this other pilot flew it', I said as I pointed to the completed schedule.

'*What ballast?*' was the retort.

'The ballast needed to get the aircraft to this heavy weight.'

'*Nope – no ballast fitted when it flew the check flight with the other pilot.*'

The completed schedule for this aircraft appeared to demonstrate that the aeroplane met the required climb rate, but it now appeared 'phantom ballast' might have been fitted to indicate the aircraft was heavier than it really was thus allowing them to obscure the poor performance. It appeared we had identified yet another 'scallywag' conducting check flights on our behalf. So, we really weren't impressed and insisted ballast be found and made available so that we could test the aircraft properly the following day. We adjourned to a seafront hotel and found a delightful pub selling excellent ale within walking distance. We enjoyed a beer or three, in order to numb the pain of our disappointment, before heading back to the hotel to try and get a good night's sleep before facing this dodgy aeroplane again in the morning.

In the middle of the night the beer had exceeded the rather puny 'pain and volume' tolerance of my bladder and I half awoke in the pitch dark of a strange room with an urgent need to pee. With no nearby table lamp, I thought I'd head urgently through into the en suite bathroom where I'd hopefully feel a light switch on the wall. I stepped into the bathroom, still fumbling for a switch and the door swung closed behind me. Eventually, I found the light – turned it on – to find I was now standing in the corridor not wearing a stitch of clothing. Here was I, as an aviation regulator, in the process of giving a local airline a very hard time and was standing outside my locked bedroom door with no key, no wallet, no specs, no phone and no clothes.

'Bugger!'

I pattered quietly down to the reception area. That there wasn't a young female receptionist on duty was a mixed blessing. I had hoped to make contact with the hotel staff only to find it was one of those cheap seaside hotels where everyone goes home at 11pm.

'Double Bugger!'

The only bonus was a long abandoned, grubby mac left hanging on one of the cloakroom hooks.

'Better to look like a "flasher" than be discovered stark bollock naked?'

A difficult decision for sure. 1 had to get back to my room, not least so I'd get some sleep and be fit to fly in the morning.

The reception desk phone had some saved numbers on some speed dial buttons. It was 2 am. Without my specs I couldn't see what the buttons were labelled, so took a decision, created by my desperation, and I started phoning each of them in turn. I must have awoken numerous innocent members of staff before, eventually, I reached the hotel manager. Once he'd stopped laughing (!) he returned with a spare room key to find me sitting in his chair completely naked apart from the grubby flasher mac.

Clearly this was a story that couldn't be kept quiet and one that John always narrates whenever we see each other! Thankfully he's living in Cologne these days, so I don't have to hear it again too often!

Meanwhile, after our flight the following day, we decided the Trislander only just met the required performance. However, I was very keen not to be arrested for indecent behaviour so, discretion being the better part of valour, we accepted the Trislander's performance and leapt on the next available aeroplane heading to the mainland.

Phew! … I seem to have got away with it for now.

Conclusion

If you've read this far – well done! Or maybe you've got bored after the first chapter and skipped to the end like I often do. I usually do that and then can't be bothered reading the bits I've missed. This is probably an odd book to read. It is best read with a pint of foaming ale or large glass of wine in hand, ideally in the sun somewhere. I will almost certainly be criticised for too much technical content, or dumbing it down too much – or most likely both.

I've tried to capture a sense of just a small aspect of the most recent seventeen years of my life. In so doing, I also hope you have learnt something about flying some of the whacky aircraft I've had to fly and obtained a glimpse into the hazardous occupation of being a test pilot. Perhaps being more aware of the rigorous testing aircraft are required to undertake will give you more peace of mind the next time you go flying or see a recreational aircraft potter overhead.

Test flying has been the defining chunk of my professional life but has been squeezed by being an aeroplane and helicopter instructor, a police and air ambulance pilot, a father, husband, grandfather and member of my local church. I am the first to confess that it is unlikely that I will have got the balance right.

One of the challenges for we test pilots is that we crave so much. We crave variety; we want to fly everything ever built or likely to be, although I have heard a few fast jet pilots claim they wouldn't be seen dead flying a helicopter. The keen ones usually find them rather tricky but fun to fly.

We want to excel at everything we do; we want to be good at it! Perhaps most of all, we want to make a difference. We want our involvement in a project to produce a better aircraft and we want to identify any unsafe aspects that may lead to problems or accidents in the future.

These cravings can never be satisfied. To be really good at flying something takes time. Taking time to fly one aircraft prevents us having time to fly all the others. Most operational pilots are lucky these days if they get to fly two or even three types: many fly only one. Equally, airline pilots will often fly one type for decades, maybe again flying only two or three types over their careers. Many test pilots can test fly aircraft for years without finding any serious safety issues. (In fact, that is what we should expect from well-designed aircraft being produced in recent years.)

Unquestionably, I have had a career which has contained more variety than a dozen other TPs might have achieved collectively. And I've had the good fortune to fly extensively as a police and air ambulance pilot – both jobs I have also enjoyed thoroughly. Even the job satisfaction of test flying pales, compared with the experience of getting a paramedic to the side of a severely injured child and in equally rapid measure, zipping them to the nearest suitable Trauma Unit where seconds count, despite the invariably marginal weather and fading light.

I don't know of any other pilot who has managed to fly quite such a wide variety of types in recent years. I also do not know of another pilot who is qualified to conduct Class 1 flight testing of both aeroplanes and helicopters and instruct both aeroplane and helicopter flight test, in addition to being a regular flying instructor and examiner. If there is someone I haven't come across I'd bet my last Euro that they hadn't tested autogyros and microlights and gliders and parachutes also.

So, I count my blessings. Would I have liked to be an F35 test pilot? – you bet. Would I have liked to have flown more historic aeroplanes? – of course. But would I have liked to have spent more time with my children when they were growing up? – absolutely! The grass always tends to be greener on the other side of the fence for most TPs. The other TP always seems to be involved with more interesting projects, or gets to fly more, or gets paid more, or gets treated better. That's the nature of the beast; we are a hard group of people to please.

One of the many downsides of the job is the pervasive aura of gloom and pessimism that intrudes not just my working moments but every corner of my life. I know that 'shit happens', and I know that shit happens to me and I know that shit can happen to me when it's most difficult to deal with. I spend a good number of my waking minutes considering the worst possibility in every situation I might find myself in and working out how I might be best able to respond. If an engine fails at this moment what will I do? How will I land safely? Etc.

It's easy for this 'negative vibe' to read across to trains that never run on time, roads that are always gridlocked, weather that's crap when we have outdoor parties planned and so on.

This negative vibe makes me difficult to live with; of that I have no doubt. My glass is always half empty – I see the dark cloud behind every silver lining – rainbows mean it's raining. I am open and honest and trustworthy and pride myself on my integrity, but I doubt anything and everything I am told or read. I am the ultimate doubting Thomas;

'Unless I see the marks in His hands …'

'Unless I fly it myself how can I be sure it flies okay?'

I have no idea how much damage my day job has done to my body over the years. As a medic once explained – our bodies, when under the stress of flying, are constantly coursing with adrenalin. To get that around our bloodstream at short notice, our blood pressure oscillates constantly. I've lived for days on a diet of bacon sarnies and chocolate bars. Steadying the nerves every evening after numerous cock-ups or near-death experiences requires copious amounts of alcohol that our livers were never designed to deal with. My hair is grey, my hearing shot and my medical certificate insists I carry a spare pair of specs. My knees ache and will eventually need replacing and my back muscles are prone to protest at the least convenient times.

Apparently when pilots retire they typically only survive three or four years – goodness knows what the stats are for test pilots.

This book was predominantly written for my children and grandchildren; to fill in the blanks as to what I was doing when I wasn't fixing broken plastic dinosaurs or emptying out wellies after playing in the puddles in our park. For anyone else dedicated enough to have read it, I would hope it has provided an entertaining few hours which has, perhaps, shone a light on the type of experimental and continued airworthiness testing I've been privileged to have undertaken in the last couple of decades, mostly conducted with little support or a safety net in place. Whatever alternative philosophies you might hear, aircraft of all shapes and sizes must continue to be flight tested by appropriately trained and experienced test pilots. The comedy and terrors of my personal flight test escapades, I strongly believe, have contributed to 'Making Flying Safer'. Perhaps you can form your own view as you finish off that large glass of Californian Chardonnay my ramblings have encouraged you to pour!

Appendix I

Why Aeroplanes Fly – And What is a 'Stall'?

If you're reading this appendix it means you've found a part of the book you don't understand and want me to explain it better. Some readers will know all about stalling, others might think they do, and then there are people, like me, who are aware it's a difficult subject to totally understand, yet it is one of the most fundamental issues for aeroplane designers and pilots.

If we want to go flying, we have relatively few proven ways of doing it. One would be to use a rocket. This technology was around about a thousand years ago. Fireworks and then rockets used as weapons of war have been around in China that long. If the rocket is big and powerful enough it can put men into space as we know. The second method would be to use some form of lighter-than-air gas such as hot air or hydrogen or helium. Enclose this gas in a balloon and it will want to rise taking

On this picture you can see the end of the wing and can identify what we would describe as an 'aerofoil shape'. So let's look at a diagram or two (all following diagrams credited to the New Zealand Civil Aviation Authority website).

anything fastened to it aloft. So hot air balloons found favour. Again the Chinese have been using 'lanterns' propelled aloft by hot air for around eighteen hundred years, with them being used to carry people for the last two hundred years or so. Finally, people like the Wright brothers and others came up with the idea of using a wing which, in forward flight, can generate lift. The same principle is also used in helicopters and autogyros. In this case the lift is generated from rotor blades, which can be considered as wings that are spun around to create the necessary airflow over them.

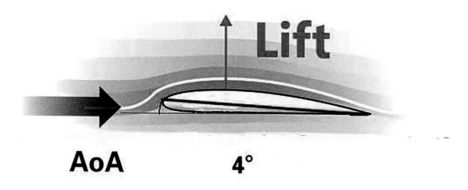

If we consider the above very simplified picture, we can see that as the aeroplane flies from right to left it is met by an airflow. Some of this flow of air has to travel over the top of the wing and some underneath it. The air travelling over the top of the wing has to travel further and in order to catch up with its mates that travel under the wing, it has to speed up. The splitting of the airflow into a faster flow and a slower flow effectively creates lift as the slower molecules try harder to push the wing out of their way. The angle between the initial airflow and the effective centre of the aerofoil as shown in the red line will be at an angle – known as angle of attack, or AoA in the diagram.

Lift is created by an AoA and airspeed. If we increase the AoA and maintain airspeed we get more lift. Conversely if we want to provide the same lift at a reduced airspeed we can achieve this by increasing the AoA.

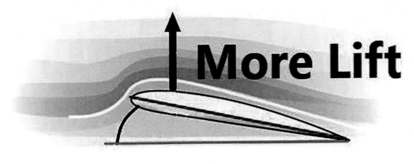

8°

An aeroplane at a given weight will need a matching amount of lift. If it slows down from its cruise speed and wants to remain in level flight the pilot will have to pull back on the joystick, to pitch the aircraft more nose up to increase the AoA. So far, so good. So, no problem then – we can keep flying more and more slowly and increase the AoA to keep the lift constant? This is true, right up until the point where it isn't.

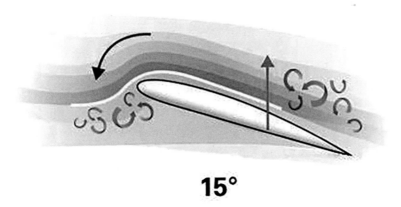

15°

If we look at the above diagram the pilot has increased the 'nose up' attitude of the aircraft and the AoA has reached 15 degrees. The airflow is now struggling to flow smoothly over the top of the wing, and this will only get worse if the AoA is increased further. With all the turbulent air the lift is markedly reduced; also of note is that the lift is generated further back along the wing which has the effect of now trying to tip the aeroplane 'nose down'.

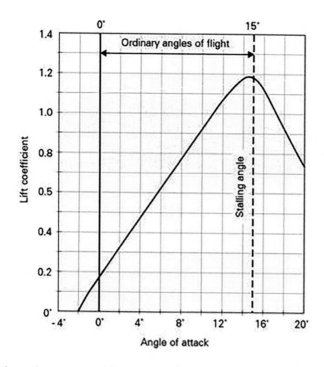

If we plotted a graph of 'lift' versus 'angle of attack' for a typical light aeroplane it might look like this graph. You can see that with increasing angles of attack the lift increases up to a 'Stalling Angle' and then the lift rapidly decreases.

In a given set of circumstances then, the stalling angle will equate to an airspeed. So my job as a test pilot is to determine the exact speed at which the aircraft stalls, in a given set of circumstances; the most important and commonly required 'set of circumstances' is 'The Idle-Power, Wings Level Stall'. That is, I've throttled back to idle power and I am not in a turn – I am wings level. And, in order not to corrupt the exact speed of the stall by pitching the aircraft, I've slowed down to the stall very slowly and carefully – typically at one knot or one mph every second.

A number of other issues merit a mention:

Power and Propeller Wash

If power is applied the aircraft wants to accelerate. To maintain speed, we would pitch the nose up and eventually we would have the aircraft flying 'nose high'. The applied thrust now has a component assisting lift.

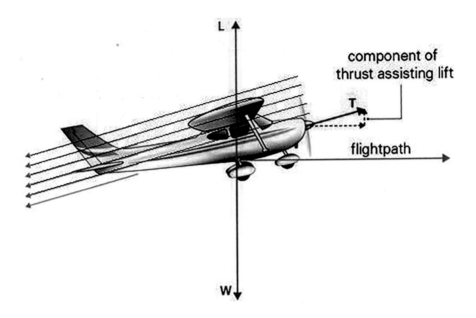

In extreme cases such as the Harrier, or similar very powerful jet aircraft, the thrust can be equal to or exceed the weight of the aircraft allowing it to climb vertically. Of more relevance, to most of the stories within this book, is propeller wash. As high power is applied, and more thrust generated by the propeller, a large additional amount of airflow is created which flows over parts of the wing and tail. This additional airflow provides additional lift so would result in a slower stall speed. Because this can be 'a variable', it's important for the test pilot to document the idle-power stall speed.

Weight

The heavier the aircraft, the faster it has to fly to generate the required amount of lift; or a greater angle of attack will be required. The heavier the aircraft, the higher the stall speed. Since the stall speed dictates the slowest the aircraft can fly, and thus land with, then knowing the stall speed for every possible aircraft weight is important.

Turning Flight

When the aircraft is turning, with angle of bank applied, then the lift vector no longer directly opposes the weight – so more lift is required in the turn, which again means a greater angle of attack. So the more angle of bank, the higher the stall speed.

Centre of Gravity

If the weight is acting at the front of the aeroplane, then it will pitch nose down unless we apply a downward force at the tail. This downward force is in addition to the downward force created by weight. So, aircraft with a forward C of G are effectively heavier and have a consequently higher stall speed than aircraft with aft C of G. Thus, for test purposes, I have to ensure my stall speed data is gathered with a forward C of G which is the 'worst case'.

Wing Drop and Use of Aileron

The lift and airflow along the span of a wing can vary depending on the design of the wing and other factors.

Red = Stalled

Ideally, we want the stall to commence in the middle of the aircraft. This is good for two reasons. Firstly, the turbulent air created will impact on the tail of the aircraft and cause the aircraft, and possibly the controls, to shake. This is known as 'buffet' and is an excellent cue to the pilot of what is happening. Secondly the wing tips are still providing lift and the ailerons which control roll will work normally. As a test pilot this is what I'm hoping to find.

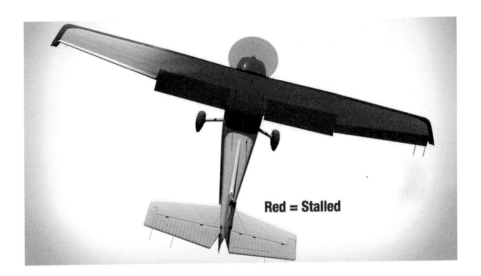

Red = Stalled

If we had a situation where the outer part of one wing, the wing tip, was to stall before the rest of the wing had stalled then the sudden loss of lift at the wing tip would cause that part of the wing to drop, causing the whole aircraft to roll. The modern certification requirements effectively require the designer to prevent this phenomenon or at least minimise it. The Austers in the photographs were known to have a particular problem with this when their flaps were applied. The flaps would lower the stall speed near the fuselage but not at the wings tips which dropped quite briskly as the stall was approached.

Spinning

If the aircraft at the stall drops a wing then the aircraft will start to roll, in this case to the right. Additionally, the aircraft will also start to yaw to the right and due to the usual loss of lift the nose will pitch down.

Ailerons which would normally be used to control roll are now either ineffective or if used will make matters worse. Recovery usually involves trying to stop the yaw with rudder and then pitch the aircraft nose down to accelerate to a speed where the wing is returned to being unstalled. If recovery isn't achieved the aircraft will enter a spin and continue to rotate/yaw in a partially stalled condition. All sorts of factors can complicate this such as the amount of power applied when the spin starts, the amount of aileron applied and in which direction, whether flap and/or undercarriage is lowered and so on. So investigating an aircraft's spin characteristics and subsequent recovery will be time consuming and hazardous.

Appendix II

Microlights

Forgive this Appendix but I feel obliged to explain a bit about microlights.

Until embarking on the path to being a test pilot, I confess, I had only limited exposure to the class of aircraft known as 'Microlights'. During the Falklands War, when I had thought the RN couldn't possibly do without me, they'd sent me on a course in the Brecon Mountains learning how to be a hang-glider pilot. I know. Goodness knows how much longer the conflict would have taken if I'd been invited to take part. Learning how to 'hang-glide' was a hoot and involved consuming copious amounts of ale of an evening, and the 'morning-after' throwing myself off Welsh hills to float, usually a few feet above the ground, until my 'Wright brothers' experience' would be halted by a barbed wire fence or similar. If these prangs were not embarrassing enough, we practised some of our 'handling' of the enlarged kite type apparatus while suspended from the roof of a vehicle shed at Sennybridge Barracks surrounded by Guardsmen and Gurkhas who, just a few days later, would be yomping across the boggy peatland of the Falkland Islands under fire. I confess to being mortified, to this day, as I remember the upturned, incredulous faces of the Gurkhas in particular.

Later I was invited to fly with an ex-university mate in a machine resembling a hang-glider with an engine on the back which, I would later learn, was described as a 'weight shift microlight'. My mate had me whizzing around an old wartime airfield inches off the ground. And, I confess, I rather enjoyed it.

These 'weightshift' machines are flown using quite a different control strategy to conventional aeroplanes. You are effectively 'hanging' beneath a fabric 'wing' using what's known as an 'A-frame' (because it looks a bit like a capital A). To go up, you push the 'bar' on this control frame away from you and the whole wing tilts nose up compared to you. In a conventional aeroplane pushing the stick forward has you pointing earthwards. So, the controls work in exactly the opposite sense to each other. In fairness, as long as you make a mental switch in your 'grey matter' it's not too hard to 'get your head around it'; particularly if you remember you are directly controlling the angle of the wing in respect to any airflow.

However, controlling these things on the ground is quite a different matter. Originally aeroplanes had no assistance with ground handling. They could only be steered on the ground by using airflow over the rudder mounted at the very rear of the aircraft, just as in flight. With single-engine aircraft more airflow over the rudder can be generated by spinning the engine faster (opening the throttle) and a large dose of air known as propwash is generated by the propeller which fortunately tends to flow over the rudder and again give more steerability. However, such aircraft are not easy to steer on the ground. In the First World War Biggles and his mates would operate from very large fields where they could always take-off and land directly into wind. Later on brakes were added to the mainwheels that could be used independently; thus pressing the left wheel brake alone would slow the left wheel and the aircraft would, hopefully, pivot to the left. Eventually, some aircraft had nose-wheels that could be connected to the rudder such that applying left rudder would turn the nose-wheel to the left and the aircraft would, again, deftly turn left. With me so far? In summary: nearly all aircraft including helicopters and most autogyros are steered to the left by pushing with your left foot on the left pedal – simple? BUT not so the weight shift microlight. To steer one of these you have to remember back to your childhood when your dad, mum or other tech savvy relative might have built you a soapbox cart or buggy. In recent years I haven't seen many of these around. Maybe kids today just get some electrically powered thing from China?

My buggy, as a kid, was a plank of wood which was transformed into a vehicle by a redundant set of pram wheels. The front wheels were attached to either end of a piece of timber which was fastened to the plank by a bolt in the middle, so it could pivot. If I pushed forward with my left foot, the whole bar would pivot, with the front left wheel moving forward and the right wheel moving back in an arc. Such a 'control input' would make the cart turn right. As a kid this seemed natural, but at that time I hadn't clocked up thousands of hours flying aircraft where 'left means left'. The weightshift microlight often has no brakes and a very simple nose-wheel with a bar connected directly to it such that it mimics my soapbox. This for me has been the hardest part of flying these aircraft, particularly on take-off when I haven't yet reminded myself to reverse my brain. I have snaked across a number of grass fields only saved by virtue of the fact that the nose-wheel tends to be off the ground quicker than I can work out which foot to use next. In the air, your feet are no longer required as you push and pull the A frame 'this way and that' to manoeuvre around; frankly all quite tiring for my puny under developed helicopter pilot arms.

It wasn't until I joined the CAA that I was able to get some formal training in such aircraft, but in fairness the vast majority of my 'microlight' flying time has been spent in, what most of us would consider, conventional aeroplanes, albeit restricted to a punitive 450 kg maximum all up weight. (If the aircraft is equipped with a parachute, sometimes known as a Ballistic Recovery System, (BRS) then they are allowed to fly at up to 472.5 kg. NB: Since this book was completed the rules have changed again to allow aircraft up to 600 kg to be described as microlights.) These aircraft are all designed to exploit a series of regulations written initially around the powered hang-glider concept. Modern materials and innovative designs have allowed aircraft to be built that weigh around 250 kg. This has allowed two 80 kg blokes to carry a few litres of fuel and get airborne. Given that the costs of running these machines are relatively low, burning around 12–15 litres of petrol to fly for an hour = 38 miles per gallon. However, designing such lightweight conventional aircraft has required some compromises which means they generally are not designed to do whacky aerobatics, fly upside down or similar and are limited to non-aerobatic flight. However, even when not throwing the aircraft around the sky like a Red Arrows Hawk jet, there is always a risk that the pilot may lose control. Hence in the UK such aircraft need to be flight tested to ensure they can be recovered from a single turn spin within one further turn.

Appendix III

Types Flown to Date

Rotorcraft

Autogyros

ArrowCopter AC20
Bensen B8 Rotax 503
Bensen B8MR
Bensen Cricket Mk4
Calidus
Cavalon
Cavalon Pro
Campbell Cricket Replica
Montgomerie Bensen B8MR
   Merlin

Magni VPM M16
Magni VPM14
Magni M16C
Magni M24 Orion
MT-03
MTO Sport
MTO Sport 2017
RAF 2000
VPM M16 (Modified)
Wallis WA 116

Helicopters

Atlas Oryx
Augusta 109A II
Augusta 109P
Augusta A109B
Augusta A109E
Augusta A109 Grand
Augusta A109S
Augusta 129 Mangusta
Augusta Westland AB139
Augusta Westland AW169
BK117
Eurocopter Alouette III
Eurocopter AS 322L2
Eurocopter AS350B1 and BA
Eurocopter AS350B2
Eurocopter AS350B3

Eurocopter AS350BB
Eurocopter AS355F1
Eurocopter AS355F2
Eurocopter AS355N
Eurocopter AS355NP
Eurocopter EC120
Eurocopter EC135T1
Eurocopter EC135P1
Eurocopter EC135P2
Eurocopter EC135 T2
Eurocopter EC135 T2+
Eurocopter EC135 P2+
Eurocopter EC145
Eurocopter EC155
Eurocopter EC225
Eurocopter AS322 Tiger

Eurocopter AS365N
Eurocopter AS365N2
Eurocopter AS365N3
Augusta Bell 212
Augusta Bell 412
Bell AH1W Cobra
Bell OH58C
Bell 47 G2
Bell 47 G5
Bell 204
Bell 205
Bell 205 VSS NRC
Bell 206
Bell 206L
Bell 206L3
Bell 206L4
Bell 212
Bell 412
Bell 407
Bell 430
Bell UH1 Huey
Boeing MD Apache AH64D
Boeing Chinook 2A
Bolkow 105
Brantly B2B
EH101 PP8
Enstrom F28A
Enstrom 480
Hiller 12E Stretched
Hughes OH-6
Hughes/Schweizer 269/300
Hughes/Schweizer 500
HUGHES/MD500E
Kaman SH-2 Seasprite
MD520N
MD902
PZL Sokol SW3

PZL W3AS
PZL SW4
Reaction Drive Rotorcraft RDL
Robinson R22
Robinson R22B
Robinson R44
Robinson R44 Raven II
Robinson R66
Rotorway Exec 162F
Schweizer S269
Schweizer S333
Sikorsky Sea Hawk SH60B
Sikorsky Black Hawk UH60
Sikorsky CH53-G
Sikorsky S61N
Sikorsky S61 Short
Sikorsky S-76A
Sikorsky S-76B
Sikorsky S76C+
Sikorsky S76C++
Sikorsky S76D
Sikorsky S-92A
Sikorsky S-92 SAR
Saunders Roe
Westland Gazelle AH1
Westland Gazelle HT2
Westland Gazelle HT3
Westland Lynx AH1
Westland Lynx AH5
Westland Lynx AH7
Westland Lynx AH9
Westland Lynx HAS2
Westland Lynx HAS3
Westland Lynx HMA8
Westland Puma
Westland Sea King HAS1
Westland Sea King HAS2

Westland Sea King 3
Westland Sea King 3A
Westland Sea King 4
Westland Sea King 4X
Westland Sea King 5
Westland Sea King 6

Westland Scout Mk1
Westland Wasp HAS1
Westland Wessex HC.2
Westland Wessex HU.5
W'land Whirlwind HC.10

Fixed Wing

Alpha Jet
BAe Hawk T1
BAe Jaguar
BAe Jet Provost 4
BAe Jet Provost 5
BAe Strikemaster
BAe Harrier T4
BAC 1-11
BAC Andover
DH Comet Mk4
DH Vampire T11
DH Vampire Mk55
Folland Gnat
Hawker Hunter T7
Hawker Hunter T8
Lockheed P-3 Orion
Jetstream TMk1
HS 748
Shorts Tucano T1
VFW-614
Aero AT-3
Aerochute
Aerprakt A22-L Foxbat
Airtourer
Alpha 160
Alpha R200 R2160
Alpi 300
Alpi Pioneer 400

American Champion 8KCAB
    Super Decathlon
Ask21 Glider
AT-6D Harvard
AT-6G Harvard
Aviat Husky
Aviat Husky – floats
Avions Pierre Robin R1180
Bantam
Beagle E3 Auster 11
Beagle Auster AOP9
Beagle Basset 1
Beagle Basset 2
Beagle Pup 150
Beagle Pup Mk 2
Beech 180 Sundowner
Beech Bonanza
Beech 58PA Baron
Beechcraft Duchess 76
Beech C90
Beech 90B
Beech B90GTI
Beech C90 GTI
Beech 99
Beech B200 King Air
Beech BE200
Beech B200GT
Beech BE300 B350 Super King Air

Beech B300C

Beech Avenger

Beech Shadow

Bellanca 7ECA Citabria

Bellanca 8GCBC Citabria

Breezer M400

Blackshape Prime

BN Islander 2A

BN Islander 2B

BN Islander 2T-4S

BN Islander 2T

BN Trislander

BN Defender

Boeing Stearman PT17
    Continental 220

Boeing Stearman PT17 Lycoming

CAP10B

CAP10C

CAP232

Cessna Bird-Dog

Cessna 120

Cessna 140

Cessna 150

Cessna 150J

Cessna 150M

Cessna 150 Aerobat

Cessna 150TD Tail Dragger

Cessna 152

Cessna 152TD

Cessna 170

Cessna 170B

Cessna 172

Cessna 172N

Cessna 172 – Diesel

Cessna 172 RG

Cessna 172S

Cessna 180

Cessna 182Q

Cessna 182R

Cessna 182T

Cessna 206

Cessna 206H Amphib

Cessna 208 Caravan

Cessna 406

Cessna CJ 525 Citation

Champion 8KCAM Super
    Decathlon

Christen Eagle

Cirrus SR20

Cirrus SR22

Columbia 350

Columbia 400

Consolidated Vultee Stinson
    108-3

Cornwell Eurofox 912

Currie Wot 2 seater

Czech Sport Cruiser

Diamond DA-40TDI

Diamond DA-42

Diamond DA-42M

Diamond HK36 Super Dimona

Dornier Do27

Douglas DC-3

DH Beaver

DH Otter

DH Twin Otter DH-6

DH Chipmunk T10

DHC-1 Chipmunk (Lycoming)
    Super Chipmunk

DH Tiger Moth DH82A

DH 87B Hornet Moth

DR200/120 Robin

DR221

DR253

DR340 (CEA) Major
DR400/160 Robin
DR400/180
DR1050 Ambassadeur
DR1050-M1 Jodell
Pierre Robin R1180T
EuroFox Nosewheel
EuroFox Tailwheel 560kg
Europa
Eurostar
Eurostar SL
Evektor Sportstar
Falco F8L
Flight Design CTLS
Fuji FA200-180
FW Steiglitz
FLS Optica OA7 Series 301
Gardan Horizon
Glassair RG
Glassair III
Glassair Turbine G-ICBM
Glazer Dirks DG505
Grob 109B
Grob 115
Gippsland GA8 AirVan
Grumman GA-5
Harvard2
Harvard 4
Harvard 4M
Harper Falco F8L
HP Jetstream Mk 1 NFLC
Ikarus C42
Ikarus C42C
Jabiru UL-D
Jabiru SP-470
Jodell D120
Lambert M108

Les 82a
Luscombe Silvaire 8A
Maule MX-7 -160
Maule MX-7 -180
Miles Messenger
Mooney M20B
Morane saulnier MS 894A
NAC2-180 Freelance
Nanchang CJ6A
Nord 1101
North American Rockwell OV-
    10B Bronco
North American Yale
OA7 Optica
Oma Sud Skycar
Partenavia Oscar 200
Partenavia P68B
Pegasus Weight shift
Percival P56 Provost T1 (Piston
    Provost)
Percival Proctor 5
Pilatus PC-6 Turboporter
Pilatus PC-12
Piper PA18-95 Cub
Piper PA18-135 Cub
Piper PA18-150 Cub
Piper PA22-108
Piper PA22-135 Tripacer
Piper PA22-160
Piper PA-23-160 Apache
Piper PA24-260
Piper PA25-235 Pawnee
Piper PA28-140 Cherokee
Piper PA28-161 Warrior
Piper PA28-161 Diesel
Piper PA28-181 Warrior
Piper PA28-125

Piper PA28-200R

Piper PA28-235

Piper PA28-RT201T Arrow

Piper PA28-Diesel

Piper PA30 Twin Commanche

Piper PA31-112

Piper PA31-2T

Piper PA31-310

Piper PA32R-301 Saratoga

Piper PA34-200

Piper PA34-220T

Piper PA42-720 Cheyenne II

Piper PA44

Piper PA46-310P Malibu

Piper PA46-350P

Piper L18C Cub

Piper L21B Cub

Piper L21B Modified Cub

Piper J3C-65 Cub

Piper Sport Cruiser

Pipistrel Virus SW

Pipistrel Virus 115

Pipistrel Virus 121

Pitts S2A

Pitts S2B

Pitts S2C

PZL 104 Wilga 35A

Reality Escapade

Reality Escapade Kid

Remos GX

Ryan ST3

Robin ATL L

Rushmeyer R90-230RG

Savannah

Savannah XLS

Sea Fury T20

Socata TB10

Socata TBM700

Siai Marchetti SF260

Scottish Avn Bulldog T1

SA Bulldog 100/101

SA Bulldog 120/125

Scottish Avn Jetstream Mark 1

Scottish Aviation Jetstream 31

Shadow CD

Sherwood Ranger

Sky Ranger

Slingsby T67C Firefly

Slingsby T67C-260

Sportcruiser

Sprint 160

Stampe SV4C

Supermarine Spitfire TR9

Tecnam Sierra

Texan Harvard

Thruster TST1

Thurston Teal

TLAC Scout

TSW 2 Currie Wot

Vans RV-6A

Vans RV-7

Vans RV-8

Vans RV9a

Vans RV10

Vans RV-14

Victa Airtourer

VulcanairP68R

Waco YMF

Yak-3

Yak-11

Yak-52

Yeoman Light A/c Dynamic

Zlin 50

Glossary

Aileron	The control surface at the trailing edge of each wing – operated by moving the joystick laterally. Moving it left causes the left aileron to tilt up and the right aileron to tilt down which causes the aircraft to roll left.
Airbrake	Imagine a plank of wood that pops out of the wing or fuselage of an aircraft to increase drag – which slows an aircraft and increases its rate of descent.
ASI	Air Speed Indicator. Uses pressure measured by the pitot tube which is compared with static pressure around the aircraft – the difference is displayed, usually, by a needle on a gauge and indicates in KIAS or MPH or sometimes Kilometres per hour etc.
ATC	Air Traffic Control. Sometimes conducted from a control tower by looking out of the windows but also often using sophisticated radars and radios.
Autogyro	An aircraft using free-spinning rotors to provide the lift required for flight.
BA	British Airways.
BCAR	British Civil Airworthiness Requirements. These are the certification requirements produced by the UK and were deemed a World Class Standard. Since the UK became more integrated with mainland Europe these standards for larger aircraft were replaced by codes based on those emanating from America – exceptions being Section S for microlight aeroplanes and Section T for autogyros.
Black Cat	Navy expression. Based on the concept of 'my cat is bigger than your cat'. So to Black Cat is to tell a taller tale than the previous one – or funnier or more scary etc.
Blades	Shorthand for rotor blades.
Black – or Blacked	The UK military Met service has abbreviations for the visibility and cloud base and gives them colours. Blue is the best and means Blue Sky...then white, green, yellow, Amber which is dreadful and Red which is thick fog. If the runway is unuseable for another reason the colour code is deemed to be 'Black'. To 'Black the runway' means to block it or crash on it.

BMAA	British Microlight Association. Delegated authority from the UK CAA to look after the airworthiness of microlight aeroplanes.
BRNC	Britannia Royal Naval College (Dartmouth).
CAA	Civil Aviation Authority.
Can-do	Usually used in the phrase 'can-do attitude' associated with military or ex-military personnel who are keen to get the job done despite external pressures or regulations.
Chop	As in 'chop the power' or conduct a 'throttle chop' means to rapidly or instantly fail an engine or throttle it back to idle.
Civil Aviation Authority	The UK aviation Regulator based in London and Gatwick. Responsibilities include the airworthiness of UK registered aircraft although most of the aircraft on the UK register from 2003–2020 were the responsibility of EASA.
CIA	American Central Intelligence Agency.
Civvie	What military people call civilians – the rest of us!
Clutch in	To 'cotton on' To 'get it'
Cock	Used a good deal by aviators! Within this book it refers to an ON/OFF lever – e.g. the fuel cock turns the fuel on or off.
Collective lever	This lever usually operated by a helicopter pilot's left hand changes the pitch on the rotor blades – collectively – that is at the same time. More pitch creates more thrust or lift allowing the aircraft to go up. Lowering the lever fully removes most of the pitch from the blades allowing them to autorotate in a glide.
Condition (On Condition)	'On condition' means the aircraft is flying at a given height, speed, power etc. ready for the next test point.
Control (As in Stability and Control)	In order to fly an aircraft, a pilot has to be able to control it. The flying controls in the cockpit, should allow the pilot to manoeuvre the aircraft as required. Certification requirements include specific tests to ensure required rates can be generated by control inputs.
Convergent	An oscillation that is well damped, will have a decreasing amplitude with each cycle and, is known as convergent.
CTP	Chief Test Pilot.
Cyclic	This is the stick, usually mounted between a helicopter pilot's knees, that controls the pitch on the rotor blades in a cyclical fashion. That means that, pushing the stick forward causes the rotor blades to increase their pitch as they pass over the rear of the helicopter, which causes the rotor disc to be tilted forward, thus angling the rotor thrust or lift forward. This has the consequence of pitching the nose of the helicopter down and allowing the aircraft to accelerate in forward flight. It is the equivalent of the aeroplane's joystick.

CVS	C = Carrier V = Fixed wing S = Short Take-off vertical Landing
Dead Stick	Meaning stationary propeller or stopped engine – as in 'dead stick landing'.
DER	Designated Engineering Representative – used in the USA when the FAA delegates airworthiness acceptance to industry experts.
Directional Stability	Sometimes known as weather cocking – the tendency of an aircraft to point into the prevailing airflow. Aircraft are expected to have positive directional stability.
Disc	Created when helicopter rotor blades spin round. Externally, when spinning, individual blades cannot be seen but the blur of rotating blades form a disc, which can be seen to tilt as if a dinner plate. Tilting the disc changes the main vector of the provided lift.
Dit	Navy slang – short story, anecdote, often humorous.
Divergent	An oscillation that grows in amplitude is known as divergent as opposed to convergent.
Donk	Navy expression, meaning engine or powerplant. Derived from the use of 'donkey engine' which was originally a small steam driven engine often used in winches and cranes.
Donk Stop	Engine failure.
DRA	Defence Research Agency. Flew research and development aircraft from RAE Bedford and RAE Farnborough until 1994, before aircraft transferred to Boscombe Down and Bedford was closed – ultimately taken over by QinetiQ in 2001.
Dutch Roll	Named after Dutch bargees who apparently used to stagger home rather drunk after several lagers in the local tavern. An oscillatory motion of both roll and yaw which, if divergent, means each cycle gets bigger – very unpleasant.
Dynamic Stability	Often the consequence of an aircraft's static stability. Usually referring to an oscillatory response and will be damped/convergent or undamped/divergent. The period and amplitude of oscillations determines whether any dynamic instability is acceptable.
EASA	European Aviation Safety Agency. Formed in 2002 and provided the European Union's aviation regulation function from 2003 – which included the UK until the end of 2020.
Elevator	The control surface at the rear of the aircraft's tail. It is connected to the joystick which, when pushed forwards, tilts the elevator down, causing the aircraft to pitch nose down.
ENAC	Italian CAA

ETPS	Empire Test Pilots' School. Formed in 1943 to teach military and industry pilots how to flight test aircraft. Based at Boscombe Down since 1968.
FAA	Federal Aviation Authority – America's aviation regulator.
FCS	Flight Control System – a computer within an aircraft that helps the pilot fly it.
Fishhead	Slang for someone in the RN. Pongo = Army, Crab = RAF. Other definitions are to be found in the Urban Dictionary much to my horror!
Flame Out	Literally – to put out the flame on a jet engine – 'Flamed out' means the jet engine stopped!
Flaps	Surfaces that can be lowered on the trailing edge of the wing to create more lift and reduce the stalling speed. Normally used for landing.
Flash Up	To get a jet engine started.
Fleet Air Arm	After the First World war the newly formed RAF was to provide aircraft to support the Royal Navy. The outdated aircraft they allocated to this task formed the Fleet Air Arm. By the 1930s pilots were required to hold commissions in both the Royal Navy and Royal Air Force. In 1939 the RAF returned the FAA to Royal Navy control and at the time of writing it has remained independent operating numerous helicopters and fixed wing aircraft including the F35 Lightning.
Forenoon	Navy speak for the morning – it's actually the 'watch' from 0800–1200.
FTE	Flight Test Engineers – the clever people who often team up with test pilots for flight test programmes.
FW	Fixed Wing. Fixed wing aircraft = aeroplane.
G	G is the term relating to acceleration due to gravity. 1G is the normal acceleration we all feel due to gravity. 2G would be twice that acceleration – at 2G our bodies would appear to weigh twice as much as at 1G. 2G could easily be experienced by an aircraft, in a steep turn, for example. Aerobatic aeroplanes typically will pull to around 6G for certain display manoeuvres and military fast jets as much as 9G temporarily.
Gash	Navy expression for rubbish or trash. To 'be gash' is to be rubbish at something.
Goofers	RN speak for a bunch of spectators gathered on a ship to watch aircraft landing.
Gopping	Not very nice, grotty.
Gotcha	A test pilot expression for an aircraft's characteristic that's potentially going to catch you out and lead to an accident. An aircraft may have a number of 'gotchas'.

Grobble, Grobbled	To grobble is to fly low and slow below cloud and murk, trying to stay in contact with the ground and navigate as best one can –often using a series of line features.
Gyro	Short for Autogyro or gyrocopter – an aircraft using free-spinning rotors to provide the lift required for flight.
Handling Qualities	This expression is used to describe what an aircraft feels like to fly. An aircraft with good handling qualities is likely to be stable and easy to fly with easy to use controls.
HAR	Helicopter air/sea rescue.
HAS	Helicopter anti-submarine.
Inceptor	Posh word for flying controls.
IFR	Instrument Flight Rules – used by pilots when they have an instrument rating and a suitably equipped aircraft. Used when the weather is too bad to fly visually (IMC) or when flying in certain types of airspace or sometimes by choice for safety reasons. Jokingly used for 'I Follow Railways or Roads or Rivers' when a pilot may follow a line feature particularly in poor weather to assist with navigation.
IMC	Instrument Meteorological Conditions. Weather with visibility and/or cloud base worse than VMC
KIAS	Knots Indicated Air Speed. This is the speed on the airspeed indicator on the aircraft's instrument panel and the instrument which is used to tell the pilot how fast he is going. For a whole bunch of reasons this indicated airspeed may not be true – but it is the speed the pilot flies to.
Knots	A speed terminology – originally derived from nautical use, when a rope with knots in it would be trailed behind the ship and the rate the knots passed through a sailor's hands would indicate speed. It equates to nautical miles per hour. A nautical mile is bigger than a statute (regular) mile so 100 knots = 115 MPH for example.
LAA	Light Aircraft Association – has delegated authority from UK CAA to look after the airworthiness of home-built aircraft, gyros and some historic types.
Lateral Stability	Sometimes known as dihedral stability. It is the tendency of an aircraft to roll away from sideslip. Aeroplanes are expected to be stable laterally.
LHR	London Heathrow Airport (to be found on baggage labels)
Lift	The term associated with the characteristic that keeps an aircraft in the air and opposes the downward effects of weight. Can be created by a wing or a spinning rotor or other methods.

Longitudinal static stability	This is the tendency for aircraft to stay at a trimmed attitude, angle of attack – effectively airspeed. Aircraft are expected to have positive longitudinal stability – that is they should tend to remain at a trimmed airspeed. If they possess very strong stability the control stick and displacement required to change speed will be large – if stability is weak only small stick forces/displacements are required to change speed.
Manoeuvre Stability	Also known as 'Stick Force per G'. When a pilot pulls back on the stick the aircraft will pitch nose up and the aircraft will experience increasing 'G'. Ideally the G should build in a linear fashion with more force required to achieve more G. The force required to rip the wings off should be high enough for the pilot not to do this by accident! Some aircraft, helicopters amongst them, have a tendency to be manoeuvre unstable and can be pitching with increasing G while the pilot is having to push the stick forward to control it – this instability is not a good characteristic.
Mayday	Urgency radio call – something serious.
Microlight Aeroplane	In the UK, a Microlight has a maximum all up weight of just 450 Kg or 472.5 Kg if fitted with a Ballistic recovery parachute. This weight limit has changed to 600 Kg in 2021. The stall speed must be 35 knots or less or 45 knots at 600 Kg
NAS	Naval Air Squadron.
NASA	National Aeronautics and Space Administration.
NJ PD	New Jersey Police Department.
NPAS	National Police Aviation Service – in charge of all English & Welsh Police aircraft.
NVG/NVD	Night Vision Goggles/Devices.
Ozz	Australia.
Ozzie	Australian.
Pan Call	Emergency less severe than Mayday.
PAR	Precision Approach Radar. Allows ATC to talk an aircraft down to the runway very accurately. Used by the military but not available at civilian airfields.
Part of Ship	A ship's company is normally split into divisions. Each division is responsible for the maintenance and husbandry of a certain area of either the upper decks or lower decks. The Wasp or Lynx flight would look after the hangar and flight deck which was their 'Part of Ship'. Also means something you are responsible for – or if you are claiming it's nothing to do with you – 'That's not my part of ship'.

PFL	Practice Forced landing – usually achieved by throttling the engine back to idle power – or in a helicopter lowering the collective to enter into autorotation.
Phugoid	An oscillatory flightpath where, without pilot intervention, the aircraft climbs, levels dives, levels and climbs again. If the phugoid is divergent the various oscillations get bigger with each cycle. The motion can be likened to being on a roller coaster but can be almost unnoticeable on a large transport aircraft.
Pronger	Or Third Pronger – Fleet Air Arm Helicopter pilots of the third prong (flying Wasp, Lynx, Wildcat). The first prong includes anti-submarine warfare ASW. Pilots flying ASW are known as Pingers (flying Wessex 3, Sea King HAS 1/2/5/7, Merlin). The second prong includes Commando/Support Helicopters. Pilots flying SH are known as Junglies (flying Wessex 1/5, Sea King Mk4, Merlin Mk4).
Prop	Propeller – mounted on an engine and, by rotating, creates thrust.
PTSD	Post Traumatic Stress Disorder – often suffered by those exposed to mortal danger and combat.
Pull up a Bollard	Navy expression – Invitation to listen to tall tales and humorous stories.
Pusser	Navy expression meaning supply officer or anything issued by the navy – a pusser's steamer being a Royal Navy warship etc.
QHI	Qualified Helicopter Instructor.
RAC	Royal Automobile Club.
Rad-Alt Radio Altimeter	Rad-Alt uses radio waves fired from under the aircraft to bounce back from the ground/sea surface which gives a very accurate height above the said surface. Essential for aircraft operating low level over the sea, for example.
RAF	Royal Air Force – Formed on April Fool's Day 1918 by merging the Royal Flying Corps (RFC) and Royal Naval Air Service (RNAS). The Royal Navy recovered its independent Fleet Air Arm in 1939 and has retained its own independent aviation capability ever since.
Reg	Register, as in G Reg = on the UK register.
Ride Shotgun	As in the days of the Wild West, when the driver of stagecoaches would take a mate with a shotgun to help protect him and the coach from robbery – effectively meaning, act as assistant or co-pilot.
RN	Royal Navy.
RNAS	Royal Naval Air Station.
Rote	Shorthand for, rotary wing pilot.

Rotors	Or rotor blades. Helicopters or Gyros have 2 or more rotor blades, which spin to provide lift.
RPM	Revolutions per minute – relating to engine or propeller or rotor speed.
Rudder	The vertical control surface, mounted onto the tail, controlled by rudder pedals, which allows the pilot to yaw(turn) the aircraft.
RW	Rotary wing – a RW aircraft would normally be thought of as a helicopter but would include autogyros.
Salty	Navy expression – due to the salt in sea water, salt would pervade much of a ship's external and internal fixtures and fittings and sailors' clothing. To be salty was to be a more experienced sailor – or a salty tale would be one based on naval adventures. An Old Salt is an experienced mariner.
SAR	Search and Rescue (Helicopter).
SAS	Special Air Service Regiment – Army Special Forces based at Hereford operating helicopters from their own helipad at Stirling Lines.
Slipping the surly bonds (of earth)	Means 'getting airborne' from the poem 'High Flight' by John Gillespie Magee.
Slop Chit	Basically a document issued by stores – something on your slop chit has been issued to you and you are responsible for it.
SME	Subject Matter Expert.
Spear In	To be like a javelin or spear and hit the ground so fast that you dig into it. To spear in = crash.
Spin	An aeroplane enters a spin when it slows down sufficiently for one wing to stall. As one wing stalls, it will drop and, if the aircraft is also allowed to yaw or turn, it will enter a descending fall, where it is gyrating around a spin axis. Spinning is an incredibly complex topic and is expanded upon in the Appendices. Generally, spinning is a bad thing and often leads to aircraft fatalities if the pilot cannot recover before hitting the ground.
Spoiler	Used to spoil airflow thus changing the amount of lift – usually reducing it.
Spool Up	An expression derived from cotton weaving. The spool would have to be spun faster to engage with the machinery. To 'spool up' means to be spun faster – often used in respect of jet engines where the turbines are spun up.
Sqn	Squadron – the Fleet Air Arm also uses the expression NAS = Naval Air Squadron.

Stability	This is a crucial factor for the assessment of an aircraft's handling qualities. If something has positive stability it wants to return to its original state even when displaced – imagine a marble or ball bearing at the bottom of a curved soup bowl. If you move the ball up the sides of the bowl it will, when released, roll back to the bottom of the bowl where it started from. If it stayed where you had moved it to, this would represent neutral stability and instability would be, to displace the ball for it to roll up and out of the bowl of its own accord.
Stall	An aircraft 'stalls' when it is no longer flying fast enough to remain airborne. The stall speed is a very important performance test point, as from it a redefined a number of other speeds, including the landing speeds, which in turn dictate the length of runway required. Some requirements, such as the definition of a Microlight, require the manufacturer to demonstrate the aircraft stalls below a certain speed. (See Appendix 1 for a fuller explanation of the stall).
Stick	The main control used to fly an autogyro- connected to the main rotor to directly pivot the rotor disc to control pitch and roll of the aircraft.
Stick Force per G	See Manoeuvre Stability
Swing the lamp	Navy expression. At sea ships' lamps would be hung from ceilings or deck heads and would swing as the ship rolled. Tall tales would often be told to the accompaniment of swinging lamps – swing the lamp therefore is an expression used to invite you into a session of storytelling.
Temp	Temperature. To 'over temp' means to exceed an engine temperature limit.
Tent Pegging	Diving your aircraft into the ground = crash.
Trim	Trimming the aircraft to a given condition removes the control forces being held by the pilot. Aircraft can be trimmed longitudinally using an elevator trim or pitch trim.
TP	Test Pilot.
USAAF	United States Army Air Forces (WW2). The United States Air Force, USAF was created in 1947
US	United States of America.
USMC	US Marine Corps.
USNTPS	US Navy Test Pilot School.
Vdf	The fastest speed an aircraft is test-flown to. A designer will have worked out a theoretical maximum speed known as Vd. The test pilot will then endeavour to test the aircraft to this speed or a lower speed if handling qualities, vibration or other reasons cause him to call an 'end point' before reaching Vd – this then is Vdf.

VFR	Visual Flight Rules. Applicable only when the weather allows the flight to be completed using external visual references – the flight needs to be flown in VMC.
VMC	Visual Meteorological Conditions. Defined visibility and cloud base that permits a pilot to fly visually. Many light aircraft are only permitted to fly within VMC.
Vne	The speed or velocity that must not be exceeded in normal operations. Usually 10 per cent slower than Vdf.
Vs	The aircraft's stall speed in a given configuration.
Wingover	A manoeuvre flown by all types of aircraft whether they have wings or not! Involves a gentle climb from relatively high-speed flight. As the speed reduces the aircraft is rolled into a steep turn of 60-90 degree angle of bank – the aircraft is then dived to its original speed and height. Operationally this is used by helicopters to achieve a rapid reversal of direction but it is also used by all types in air-displays etc.
WRNS	Women's Royal Naval Service – or the Wrens. When I joined the Royal Navy, women were able to join the WRNS but not go to sea in the RN proper.
Yaw	Yaw is the name we give to turning around the centre of the aircraft. A yaw to port would mean the aircraft turning anti-clockwise when viewed from above.
Yaw Pedals	These pedals are operated by a helicopter pilot's feet. Pushing the left pedal, yaws the aircraft left. In a conventional helicopter the yaw pedals effectively change the thrust from the tail rotor, which allows the aircraft to yaw in each direction.

THE STORM WITHIN

CAMERON SMITH

WITH ANDREW WEBSTER

THE STORM WITHIN

THE AUTOBIOGRAPHY OF A LEGEND

FOREWORD BY CRAIG BELLAMY

ALLEN&UNWIN
SYDNEY · MELBOURNE · AUCKLAND · LONDON

First published in 2020

Allen & Unwin
83 Alexander Street
Crows Nest NSW 2065
Australia
Phone: (61 2) 8425 0100
Email: info@allenandunwin.com
Web: www.allenandunwin.com

A catalogue record for this
book is available from the
National Library of Australia

ISBN 978 1 76052 511 8

Statistics by David Middleton, League Information Services
Index by Puddingburn Publishing Services Pty Ltd
Set in 12.75/18.5 pt Adobe Garamond Pro by Midland Typesetters, Australia
Printed in Australia by McPherson's Printing Group

10 9 8 7 6 5 4 3 2 1

The paper in this book is FSC® certified.
FSC® promotes environmentally responsible,
socially beneficial and economically viable
management of the world's forests.

To Barb, Jada, Jasper and Matilda . . .
Thank you.

CONTENTS

FOREWORD

As coach of the Melbourne Storm, I like to think I don't miss much. I've watched Cameron Smith play a lot over the years and thought I pretty much knew all there was to know about him. But, in the lead-up to Cameron's 400th match in 2019, one of our assistant coaches, Marc Brentnall, pointed out something I hadn't noticed before. Whenever one of Cameron's teammates scores a try, Cameron is the first player there to congratulate him.

It sums him up, as a player and person: he enjoys the success of others. That's a real good trait to have when you've done what he's done, when you're the top dog. I've seen other players who are well regarded become envious of another player's success. Cameron wants everyone around him to thrive and to achieve what he's had.

I'd heard a little bit about him as a player before I arrived at the Storm for the 2003 season, but within the first few weeks of preseason I identified that he was training within himself. It wasn't that he was lazy, because he doesn't have that in him, but he was a laidback character with a 'she'll be right' attitude. I wanted him to be the best player that he could possibly be. So I pulled him aside.

'You have to get uncomfortable,' I said. 'All the best players do.'

From the next session onwards, he went full throttle and didn't take his foot off the gas until the last minute of his career.

I've been fortunate to watch his evolution as a player from close range, and it was clear early on that he had a great grounding and education from his father, Wayne, who had been a hooker of note in the Brisbane competition before coaching juniors. When he arrived at the Storm, Cameron also benefited from learning from senior players like Robbie Kearns, Scott Hill and Robbie Ross. In the many years that have followed, he's become the best the game has ever seen.

Before Cameron came along, I considered Steve Walters to be the best dummy half I'd laid eyes on. I'd seen 'Boxhead' up close because I played with him at the Canberra Raiders. Benny Elias from Balmain was also a wonderfully skilful hooker. In recent years, we've seen the likes of Josh Hodgson at Canberra and Damien Cook at Souths. But none come close to Cameron. The quality of his play on both sides of the ball, but especially with the ball, has never wavered. He's also done it for a long period of time. Nobody has done what he's done as well, or as skilfully, or as tough, for eighteen years. Playing for that long in any position is hard. But he's done it in the middle of the ruck, with big blokes lining him up. The tackles he's made, the quality of his defence, has been remarkable.

Cameron adapted as the game changed but always remained old school in his mentality. He comes from a time when work, footy and family were separate. But now, because the game is professional and fulltime, they are intertwined, and that makes things complicated. He doesn't play the games that other people want, especially the media. He's certainly stubborn. People don't realise that. It means he's never veered away from the standards he truly believes in.

Some of the criticism and scrutiny over the last few years of his career was really disappointing. I've always taken the view, whether it's me or the players, that you pay a certain price at this level because it's professional sport. Sometimes you are criticised, sometimes you are praised. But families should never be brought into it. They don't sign up for that. Sometimes the media has overstepped the mark with his family. And that's not right.

To do what he's done in the game, Cameron's had to have some really good support off the field. There have been no bigger supporters than his wife, Barb, who has been with him since they were teenagers, and his three children, Jada, Jasper and Matilda.

I have never made this point publicly before but there were a couple of times after matches early in his career when Cameron could've got himself into a little bit of strife celebrating wins. He never went off the rails, but without Barb's influence things could've gone the other way. She was as important then as she is now. I don't think I've seen a partnership in footy where the other half has made as many sacrifices as Barb has. She's been his anchor and deserves as many accolades as he does.

As coach and captain, we've also been through a lot together. There have been hard times, and none more so than the salary cap scandal in 2010 and the years that followed as we put the club back together. People didn't see how tough Cameron did it during those times—because he hid it from view. He copped a lot of criticism in the papers, which was unfair. It wasn't the players' responsibility to make sure our squad was under the cap—it was the club's. As far as I was concerned, our club made the mistakes, not the players. They were unfairly picked out and picked on.

If there was a silver lining, the club came out of it stronger and more resilient. And so did Cameron. He was better for it, as tough as it had been.

Cameron has enjoyed annoying me over the years, niggling away at times without me even knowing, but our relationship has gone far beyond that of player and coach. He was brought up in the working-class suburb of Logan in Brisbane's south, and I was brought up in the working-class town of Portland in the NSW Central West. We have similar standards and beliefs, and over the years we've become close mates. That's something that will never change, whether or not he is my captain and I'm his coach.

Craig Bellamy
Head Coach, Melbourne Storm, 2003–

PROLOGUE

When I'm on a football field, I feel like I can see into the future. My brain tells me the story of how the game will unfold before it happens.

Rugby league is a series of decisions, made in a split second, under pressure and while fatigued, against the clock or the scoreboard. An average tackle takes 3.8 seconds to complete, and when you're the hooker, when you live at the play-the-ball, you make more decisions than any other player on the field.

I was never the strongest or the fastest player, or the one with the most talent—that's why I had to be the smartest.

I have a checklist in my head to help get it right, ticking the boxes off as my team plays out its set of six tackles.

The first box is how my teammate is carrying the ball. If he's run over the top of a defender, throwing him to one side, that means he'll probably play the ball quickly. If that happens, I know in my mind what I'll do next.

I am running.

The second box is the first marker and how he's standing. If I run, can he get to me? Have I seen anything in the video sessions this week to suggest he won't worry about the dummy half? How long has he been on the field? How many tackles has he made in this set? Is he a prop or a backrower with a good motor? What are his tendencies at marker? Does he like attacking me? Or does he like backing off? Does he want to go back to his position on the right? Or will he turn his left shoulder and open his hips, and come to the open side?

The third box is the defensive line. Who is the 'A defender', the one closest to the ruck? Which foot does he usually start off on? If I run at him, and I show the ball, will he fall for a dummy? Do the defenders have their numbers right? Is the fullback standing in the defensive line or behind it? If he's deep, that leaves them with ten players, so are there five players on one side and five on the other? Or are they six and four? They are—and I know in my mind what I'll do next.

I am passing.

Then there are the times when all it takes is one word, one quick glance, and only three of us know what's going to happen next.

We get a penalty coming out from our own end, I kick for touch and we are now 40 metres or so from our own tryline. We work the ball through our forwards to the middle of the field. One word. One look. It's on.

I look at Cooper Cronk. He is tucked behind the play-the-ball, just to the right. As the ball is being played, Cooper starts his run on a 45-degree angle. That gets the first marker interested. That's his man. He goes after him. As this happens, I move forward with Cooper, and that gets the second marker interested. That was the plan: to split the markers.

In rugby league, you're constantly trying to manipulate the defensive line. If they move up in a line, there's only a small amount of space to get through. You can move a defender forwards or backwards, or laterally, to open up the hole. And the biggest space on the field is behind the markers.

Cooper fires the ball back to me. 'Shit,' the second marker thinks to himself. 'Smith is going to run here.' But I'm not. There's a better runner than me: Billy Slater, our fullback. He'll be the one who's running.

I pass it to him on the inside. With his speed, in a space that big, right in the middle of the ruck, nobody can stop him. Game over.

And if all that fails, I'll just give it to Greg Inglis. Let them try to stop him and his right-hand fend.

There's no secret or magic to it. I don't put a spell on other teams. But the art of rugby league is in deceiving the opposition—and when you've played as many games as I have, when you've watched and analysed every team and player, and when you've played in a position where you touch the ball more than anyone else, with players you've played along-side since you were a teenager, you know how the trick will play out before it happens. You can see into the future.

•

For two decades, in over 427 NRL matches for the Melbourne Storm, 42 State of Origins for Queensland and 56 internationals for Australia, making the right decisions was the easy part about rugby league. These were the things I could control. This was what I loved about the game.

What I never quite understood was the stuff that came outside of those 80 minutes and the hard work preparing for them. When I was a kid playing for Logan Brothers in Brisbane's south, I didn't think this was what rugby league was going to be like. I just wanted to play and be left alone.

On the field, I gave everything I had. Off the field, I often held back, preferring to keep quiet and brush aside the speculation and assumptions.

This is my chance to set the record straight.

1

SCRAPBOOKS

We were walking through the carpark at Wynnum-Manly's home ground, Kougari Oval, when it hit me: I was never going to play in the National Rugby League. No professional football career. No Broncos contract. No contract at all.

I was only seventeen years old, but my dreams had evaporated in just a few short minutes. It was all over before it had even started.

I'd just played in a 'Possibles versus Probables' match, from which the selectors were picking a Queensland under-17s side to play New South Wales. The game would be held at Lang Park as a curtain-raiser before game two of the 2000 State of Origin series.

As soon as I'd heard about that game, I wanted to play in it. Imagine running down the tunnel and out onto Lang Park in a Maroons jumper . . . That was something every Queensland kid dreamed about.

This Queensland kid wanted something more. I knew that playing well in a curtain-raiser before a Lang Park Origin match could help me on the road to a career in the NRL.

I thought I'd played well that afternoon at Kougari Oval. Our team had won. But then my name wasn't read out, and it left me completely shattered. I congratulated the players who had been picked and then quickly left.

When we got to the carpark, I broke down. There was my dream—gone.

'If I can't get picked in an under-17s Queensland side,' I said to my dad, Wayne, 'how am I ever going to play first grade?'

Dad knew how much this meant to me. He also knew more about footy than anyone I knew, so he understood that this setback wasn't the end of the world. He certainly realised it wasn't the end of my career.

'It's okay that you're disappointed,' Dad offered. 'But there's one thing you have to realise: first-grade coaches don't ask for scrapbooks. They don't care about junior rep teams. They only care about what you're doing right now. That's all that matters.'

I've never taken for granted that my earliest football mentor was also my father. I wouldn't have become the player I was, nor would I have achieved everything I did in my career, without him. Without any of my family, for that matter. From the very start, rugby league was part of my DNA—and he was the reason.

People who saw my old man play say I remind them of him when he was a hooker in the Brisbane competition, first with Eastern Suburbs and then with Wynnum-Manly. He had a traditional hooker's build: short and stocky but quick off the mark. In time, I grew taller and became rangier. But we were both left-foot kickers, and some of his former teammates say my playing style reminds them of how he played. That's pretty cool to hear.

Dad played in the 1975 premiership side at Easts when he was just eighteen years old, in his rookie year. Des Morris was the captain-coach, but Dad wasn't getting much game time because the bloke in front of him was Johnny Lang, who also happened to be the Australian hooker. If he was at any other club, he would've got a few more games.

Dad tells a story about Bobby Bax, the legendary coach who won nine Brisbane premierships. 'Come and play for Norths,' Bobby said to him. Then he wrote the contract on the back of a beer coaster—where all good contracts were written in that era.

Dad turned him down because it was going to be too far for him to travel from the south side of Brisbane. In the end, Dad signed with Wynnum-Manly and Bobby signed Greg Conescu, who went on to play for Queensland and Australia. The old man is probably still kicking himself he didn't take up the contract written on the back of the coaster.

Like most players in that era, Dad's rugby league career fitted around his work. He was a bricklayer and worried about getting injured. If he was injured, he couldn't work. And if he couldn't work, he couldn't support his family.

So in 1981, when my mum, Sonia, fell pregnant with my sister, Khirstie, he decided to retire. He was only 24.

Mum and Dad grew up in Brisbane, in a suburb called Carina Heights, but after they married they knew they needed to find an area, build a new home and start their family. Logan City, between Brisbane and the Gold Coast, was starting up. The only problem was there was nothing there.

When my parents bought a home on a quarter-acre block, it was among the first in the housing estate. At the end of their big, sprawling backyard was nothing but bush as far as you could see.

Over the years, it filled with the houses and businesses that now basically join Brisbane to the Gold Coast. There are 350,000 people in the area these days, so it's very different. The community is different, too. Polynesian families started moving in. Future internationals Israel Folau and Josh Papalii also hail from the Logan area.

Logan always remained very working class, and its sport of choice is still rugby league. In the 80s, it was the ideal place for the Smiths to start their family.

First came Khirstie, on 14 December 1981. Then me, on 18 June 1983. Then Matthew, on 2 July 1992.

I was a quiet kid. I was cheeky at home and caused some grief with my older sister—who never got in trouble, of course—but I was always a bit too scared of Mum and Dad to do the wrong thing outside the house. Other people might say something different.

Sport was in our blood. Mum was a good sportswoman, playing netball and softball at a representative level. Our parents never forced rugby league onto us. 'Just because Dad played, you don't have to play it too,' they always told me. We'd have a cricket bat, a basketball, a footy. But, for whatever reason, I was naturally drawn to rugby league.

When I was six years old, Dad planned to take me to join the Browns Plains Bears, but that changed when he bumped into an old Wests player from his era called Billy Whitmore, whose daughter was best friends with Khirstie.

Billy saw me mucking around with a footy. 'Is your young bloke going to play?' he asked Dad.

'I was thinking about taking him to Browns Plains,' Dad replied.

'Why don't you come to St Paul's, where my son plays?'

Brothers' St Paul's Rugby League Club, now known as Logan Brothers, was formed at St Paul's Convent in Woodridge in 1976, after Brisbane Brothers decided a team was needed in the southern suburbs. When Dad and I rolled up for the sign-on day at the home ground, Civic Park, right in the heart of Logan, the first thing he noticed were the steel bars on the clubhouse windows.

'What have you tipped me into here, Bill?' Dad laughed.

But we signed up that day, and from then on I was a proud Brothers player wearing their green-and-gold jumper.

These days, Logan Brothers is a big club. It grew as Logan City grew. It's well financed, with better facilities that are three times bigger than they were when I was starting out. There's a big clubhouse and lots of training fields. They've got an electric scoreboard, which is a far cry from the days when my mates and I would put up tin numbers on the old score board as every point was scored.

Back in the late 1980s, St Paul's was one of those little footy clubs that did its best to punch above its weight—and we did.

We had these ratty old dressing sheds that felt like a bat cave: concrete floor, concrete seats and the lights were really dim. The urinals stunk. But we didn't care. It had the essentials. The canteen had its nutritious fare of Chiko rolls, potato gems and Redskins. There were three footy fields, and as a young kid that's all you really care about: a football and somewhere to play with it.

I've heard Billy Whitmore say that I was never the strongest or the fastest player, but I had great skills. That's nice of him to say, but I think that changed over time. When I was a junior, I did have some speed and some size in comparison to the other kids. That started to change around the under-13s and under-14s, when other boys became stronger and faster and I developed an average teenager's build.

What helped me overcome that was my competitiveness. From a very young age, I *hated* losing. I'd do whatever I could to win. I doubt that will surprise a lot of people!

Nor will the fact that once I started playing, that was all I ever did. Rugby league consumed me. If I wasn't at school, I'd be in the backyard practising my skills, maybe putting in a grubber-kick and then chasing it down. Or throwing a dummy to nobody, before stepping and running. While most kids were having one or two training sessions a week and then playing on the weekend, it was rare for me not to have a footy in my hands.

And when we were at training, Mum had a hard time getting me off the field when it was time to go home. I just loved it so much.

I'd get a new pair of footy boots at the start of each year. I'd take them out of the box and smell the new leather. Then I'd take them to bed. Yes, I loved my new boots so much I would sleep with them. Some might say that's weird, but I see nothing wrong with it.

Then I'd start dreaming of playing for the Brisbane Broncos, the new team coached by Wayne Bennett that had entered the New South Wales Rugby League premiership in 1988. I loved halfback Allan Langer, and of course Wally Lewis in his early days at the club, but the player I followed the most was Michael Hancock, the hard-running winger. We went to a few early matches at Lang Park and I instantly became a Broncos tragic.

It was the same with Queensland. On Origin nights, we'd huddle around the TV in the loungeroom to watch our beloved Maroons take on the Cockroaches from New South Wales. Dad was always very vocal, either about the referee or if Queensland did something wrong. Whatever he said always made sense. He knew the game, and, over time, he passed that knowledge down to me.

In years to come, Dad would become club president and director of coaching at Logan Brothers. But initially he was a coach of the older boys, from under-15s through to under-17s. As soon as I finished my training session, I would run over to the part of Civic Park where he was training his team.

First he'd bring them into those dark, stinky sheds and have a chat about the match they'd just played and the one ahead. They'd be talking about things that were a lot more complex and detailed than what I'd just heard in the under-9s. *When we have the ball, we want to get to this point on the field, then come back this way, because we want to move their defence* . . . I'd sit in the corner and soak it all up like a sponge.

Pretty soon I virtually became a player in Dad's teams. I was constantly into him to let me join in with the various drills and plays. He'd let me warm up but would then drag me out of the way. But I felt a part of his teams as much as my own.

On game day, I'd play in the mornings and then we'd drive over to whichever ground Dad's team was playing at. I'd sit in the rooms with his players beforehand, then I'd watch them warm up, then I'd sit with Dad on the bench and listen to what he said as the game played out. Or else I'd be the ball boy or running the sand, the whole time lapping up whatever knowledge I could.

So from a young age I knew there was so much more to rugby league than running, passing and tackling. I learned those basics of the game back in the under-9s, but in the under-15s I was learning how to play the game. 'Let's take two to this field position, because that will put the defence out of shape,' I'd think to myself. 'Then we want to come back with this sweeping play . . .'

•

In the under-10s I came up against a player who was as obsessed with the game as me. He was a skinny little halfback for Souths Sunnybank, he didn't wear any headgear and he had a lot of talent.

At one point he threw a cut-out pass on the halfway line, one of our boys intercepted it and raced away to score a try. As our team celebrated, I looked back and saw the little halfback in the same spot where he'd thrown the pass – he was down on his haunches, having a cry. Then again, Johnathan Thurston has always been a big sook . . .

I'm kidding, of course. 'JT' was as competitive in his junior years as he was in his senior years. Who would've thought that, years later, we'd play countless matches for Queensland and Australia together?

That JT was so emotional, even in the under-10s, showed how much he cared about his team. It meant that much to him. He felt the same way about his footy as I did.

After that first encounter, we played lots of junior rep footy together. We once had a training session for an under-12s Logan area development squad. JT likes to tell the story of how he was paired up with me for tackling practice. I remember hitting him hard. 'That's the last time I'm pairing up with this bloke,' he insisted.

Defence has always been a big part of my game, even from a young age. I was never overly fazed about playing against bigger kids. I just practised good technique. Back in those days, there was none of this wrapping your arms around your opponent's chest, stopping the offload and keeping them upright. It was about bending your back and going in hard with your shoulder. Unfortunately, that part of the game has all but disappeared.

The defender we all wanted to be was Queensland backrower Trevor Gillmeister, better known as 'The Axe'. But the player I loved the most in Origin was his Maroons teammate Gary Larson, who just got in and made his 50 tackles with little fuss. Gavin Allen was the same. For some reason, I appreciated that sort of player as much as the superstars. They got their job done, every time, and even though they often went unnoticed, I admired them.

As it turned out, JT and I would walk a similar path in rugby league from our young years. We'd get picked in junior rep teams, but struggled to attract interest from the Broncos.

The Broncos' talent scouts were more interested in three players around our age: Dane Campbell, a five-eighth or lock; Daniel Jones, a prop or second-rower who was the size of a man but had ability too; and Mick Daley, a talented young halfback. Mick was touted as the next Alfie Langer. Even though most young halfbacks in Queensland who showed a lot of talent wore that label, he was definitely a smart footballer who had some good ball-playing skills.

In fact, they were all good players—and they all played for Redcliffe.

The Dolphins were one of the most successful clubs in Queensland rugby league at that time, and they're even stronger now. There were a lot of junior clubs on the north side of Brisbane—Deception Bay, Burpengary, Aspley—but many of the talented kids went to Redcliffe, who eventually built a super team.

For the working-class boys from Logan Brothers, Redcliffe were our biggest rivals. We often held our own, and had some great victories, but we struggled to get on top of them in the match that mattered most.

They beat us in the under-13 and under-15 grand finals, and looked like doing the same in our under-16s year, when they dominated the home-and-away rounds. They easily finished as minor premiers, with Logan Brothers finishing second.

In the grand final, they were leading at halftime, but we fought back to score late and send the match into extra time. With only a few minutes remaining, Redcliffe made an error on their own twenty-metre line, right in front of the goalposts.

In my early teens, I usually played five-eighth or lock. I'd played one season at dummy half, in the under-15s, but I never saw myself as a number nine. I was either a six or thirteen.

In this grand final I'd been playing lock, but as the scrum was being set I told my teammates I was going to stand at first receiver. 'Give it to me,' I whispered to the halfback. 'I'm going to kick a field goal.'

My reasoning was that Redcliffe wouldn't be expecting this—I was betting they'd think we would take one tackle first and then set ourselves for the field goal. And I was right. I got myself into position and knocked the field goal over from 25 metres out.

Redcliffe desperately rushed back to kick off, and the siren sounded as the ball was floating in the air. It could've been a lottery and given them one last chance to snatch it, but five of our boys went up, grabbed the ball and sealed the win.

It was the only junior grand final I ever won, but it was a cool moment—and even cooler to finally do it against Redcliffe.

•

It didn't take me too long in life to know what I *didn't* want to be.

In the school holidays, Dad would take me to work with him to help out while he laid bricks. They were long days, getting up at 5 a.m. and leaving there at 5 p.m., and you'd come up with your hands dried out and cracking because you'd been handling cement and picking up bricks all day. It showed me straightaway it was a tough life.

'You see, mate?' Dad told me years later. 'That's why I took you—so you didn't become a brickie.'

I'd already made my mind up anyway: I wanted to be a professional footballer. After winning the under-16s grand final, I could see a pathway to making a career out of it. And I figured the only way to do that was to work hard, play well and get picked in representative teams. Then an NRL club might come knocking. I hoped that club would be the Broncos.

In Queensland, representative footy alternates between schoolboys reps one year and club reps the next. In 2000 I was picked to represent Brisbane under-17s at the Queensland state carnival—but at hooker. Even though I never saw myself as a dummy half, that's where I seemed to get picked in the rep sides.

We won the state title that year without losing a game, and I thought I had played well. I was rewarded with selection to play in the Possibles versus Probables match.

I'd been picked to play for the Queensland Schoolboys under-15s team two years before, but I hadn't been in the starting side. We went down to the national carnival at Seiffert Oval in Queanbeyan, but I shivered on the sidelines and didn't get a start.

Now I had a chance to wear the Maroons jumper at Lang Park before an Origin. How good!

After the match at Kougari Oval, I had a shower, got dressed and waited with the other players and parents in the meeting area as the selectors picked the side.

Time dragged on. We sat there for what seemed like a long, long time, and the longer it went on, the more nervous Dad seemed to get. He was paranoid that the delay was about his young bloke and whether he should be in the side. He had no reason to think it would be about me—he just had a bad feeling. The selectors eventually came out and announced the team. Some of my good mates at Logan Brothers were picked, but I was overlooked.

Dad was right: the long delay had been about me. What I've been told is that two of the three selectors wanted me, but the third one wanted a different player: Jake Walker from Wide Bay. The coach, former Cronulla Sharks forward Dan Stains, apparently also wanted Walker. Neither side would budge, and finally one of the officials went into the room and asked why it was taking so long. He said the coach had the overriding call.

I was lucky to have Dad there. His knowledge of the game has helped me through many rough times. The longer my career went on, the less I had to seek his help—but he's always been there if I needed some frank, simple advice about the game.

Coaches don't ask for scrapbooks. I knew what he was saying: 'You're disappointed, but if you work hard, you will get a shot one day, because coaches are more worried about how you're playing in the present than what you've done in the past.'

So I stopped crying and moved on as best I could, returning to the dark, stinky sheds at Logan Brothers, working harder than ever.

A few weeks later, the phone rang at home. It was the Melbourne Storm.

2

THE LITTLE THREE

There's an old team photo that newspaper editors have regularly dragged out over the years around grand finals or State of Origin matches, showing three happy young footballers with their careers ahead of them. Sitting in the front row, all wearing Norths Devils' sky-blue and gold jumpers, Cooper Cronk, Billy Slater and I have grins from ear to ear.

We all look like boys because we pretty much are: Billy and I were born on exactly the same day in June 1983, while Cooper was born in December that year, so in that photo we are all just seventeen.

Sure, we all had big ambitions, but nothing beyond just doing our best and working hard and hoping that a first-grade start would come along one day. The Devils were the Melbourne Storm's feeder club, and being there meant we had a foot in the door.

The person from the Storm who called my parents' place out of the blue that day was Anthony Griffin, who was coach of the under-19s Colts team at Norths. It was the call that changed everything for me.

'Hook' had seen me play in the under-17s carnival in Rockhampton, and he liked what he saw. He wanted to meet with me and my parents, and he brought along Mark Murray, who was in charge of the senior side that played in the Queensland Cup. Together, they were the Storm's recruitment eyes and ears in Queensland, and they outlined what they thought my future could look like if I signed with Melbourne.

If I'm being honest, I was just chuffed that someone was interested in me. It softened the blow of missing out on the Queensland under-17s. It also softened the blow of never hearing from the Broncos. Other players were getting tracksuits, having training days with the senior squad or even having their schooling paid for.

JT and I weren't even on their radar. And that hurt because I'd grown up as such a massive Broncos fan. If I was ever fortunate enough to play in the NRL, I had always thought, I wanted to play with them because they were my team. Yet they were never interested.

Then, suddenly, they were. When word about the Storm talking to me got out, a call from the Broncos soon followed. 'Mate, come in, we'd love you to meet Wayne Bennett,' an official from the club said. 'He wants to talk to you.'

I was as nervous as they come—I mean, this was Wayne Bennett. Even though Mum and Dad were with me, my mind went blank when I walked into his office. I didn't even know how to introduce myself. I was that scared that I struggled to get the words out of my mouth.

He was typical Wayne with someone he didn't know too well: a wry smile here or there, not a whole lot more. He talked about the Broncos as an organisation, and my place in it.

I didn't say much. Neither did Mum or Dad. It was mostly Wayne talking, short and sharp.

'What do you see as your weaknesses?' Bennett asked me.

'I'm not very fast,' I said.

It was true. When I grew into my body as a teenager, I wasn't an athletic specimen at all. I was not the fastest and not the strongest—but I was trying to be the smartest.

'You aren't quick—but we can make you quick if we have to,' Bennett promised.

Dad and I had long ago discussed my speed around the park, and his feeling was there was no use being something I wasn't. 'You're not fast with your feet—but you're fast between the ears,' he once told me.

Dad always had little sayings like that. It was his way for us kids to understand the message he was giving us. Not dumbing it down, but boiling it down into one sentence.

When he said I was fast between the ears, I knew exactly what he meant. He was saying that if I used my brains, I wouldn't have to rely on leg speed—I could put myself in the right position before others knew I was going to be there. Dad made me realise from an early age that *my* strength was an ability to bend the game the way I wanted it. I had to rely on my knowledge, street smarts and ability to think quickly. That's just as important in a cunning game like rugby league.

When we walked out of Bennett's office, I knew I had a big choice to make. Not one NRL club had shown any interest in me throughout my junior years, and now there were two: the Storm, who had shown interest first, or the Broncos, the team I'd always supported and wanted to play for.

Interestingly, both clubs had the same job in mind for me: they wanted me to be their long-term hooker. That was never where I saw my career going. When I was younger, I'd naturally fallen into a No. 7 or No. 6 jersey. As with most junior sport, you play where your skill base dictates, and for me that was mostly in the halves. There were other guys who were more suited to playing dummy half—plus I was having too much fun one or two off the ruck.

Perhaps the person who really got the ball rolling on my permanent switch to the dummy half role was Brad McLennan, a Queensland Schoolboys' coach, who convinced me to play there in the under-15s because he didn't have much depth in the position. It didn't change the way I played: I was picking up the ball in the ruck but then running to the line, trying to put blokes through holes or set up players outside of me, instead of being a ball distributer or runner. So I didn't come out of the same mould as Issac Luke or Damien Cook. I don't have the speed to dart out of dummy half and race downfield. My first instinct has always been to ball-play and set others up.

Because both clubs saw me as a future hooker, my decision to go to Brisbane or Melbourne really came down to opportunity. At the Broncos, Luke Priddis was the starting No. 9. The next in line was Mick Ryan, another quality dummy half. I figured I'd be third in line. Would I get a start? Possibly. When? Couldn't say. And I certainly didn't see myself as a utility player.

Then I looked at Melbourne. They had one recognised dummy half: Richard Swain. They used Danny Williams as a back-up hooker now and then, but he was really a backrower.

Swainy was a Kiwi international who had played in the Storm's 1999 grand final win against St George Illawarra, and he was also a player who very rarely missed matches. He was very resilient, playing 133 games straight for the club. I knew it was going to be really difficult to jag a start in the NRL at Melbourne, but if I went down there I would be the second-choice hooker behind him—not the third in line like I would be at the Broncos.

The other attractive thing about the Storm was that I didn't have to move away from Brisbane straightaway, because I could learn the game at Norths for a couple of years.

So, in the end, I signed with Melbourne. The contract was done by my manager, Jim Banaghan, for two years. It was worth $30,000.

We informed Brisbane and they understood. They were always stocked with plenty of talent, and they would survive without me.

Mum and Dad were comfortable too. They'd been a big part of the discussion—I was only seventeen, after all. They were really cool. They weren't parents who got starry-eyed, wondering how much their son was going to make from a professional footy career. They had been around sport for a long time, and rugby league in particular. They'd seen bad sporting parents and they were determined to never be like that. And they never were.

•

There was another incentive to stay in Brisbane a little longer.

Barbara Ann Johnson and I had met at Marsden State High School, which was the biggest high school in the Logan area, in 1996, when we were in Year 8. But we didn't really know each other in the junior grades. It wasn't until our last couple of years at school that I became more interested.

Her parents had named her after the Beach Boys' song, but everyone knew her as Barb. I made the first move. My mates had girlfriends who were friends of Barb's, so we often hung out at lunchtime. One day I thought I may as well ask her out. Luckily, she said yes.

You can imagine how excited she was when our first date was a footy game in which I was playing. And they say romance is dead! It was a big game, too: an under-17s semi-final for Logan Brothers against Cannon Hill. 'I need a really big game today,' I thought to myself just before kick-off, knowing who would be watching from the sidelines. We won and I scored two tries. I must have impressed her enough, because I asked her out again after that and we've been together ever since.

Also with me since those days has been my 1971 Holden Kingswood, which I bought with some of the money from my first contract; it's still in my back garage at home to this day. When I got it in 2000, it looked great on the outside, with shiny new wheels and a bottle-green paint job, but it needed some work on the inside.

Four nights a week, Cooper would slide into the front seat and we'd drive to training with the Devils. We both lived on the south side of Brisbane. I was doing an apprenticeship in label printing, working from 7.30 a.m. to 3.30 p.m., and when I knocked off I'd drive to Kingston train station, where Cooper would be after finishing his day. Then we'd drive to Bishop Park, or Nudgee College, on the north side of the city, and train with the Devils.

On those trips together, with the Kingswood sliding this way and that in wet conditions, listening to the local rock'n'roll station because I didn't have a CD player, we got to know each other really quickly. We soon worked out that we'd played against each other in the under-11s, when he was playing for Souths Acacia Ridge. Then he went to St Laurence's College and played rugby union so we hadn't crossed paths again, either at club level or in rep footy.

Coops played in the halves, but he also had some speed so he could play in the centres, too. We played two trials early in 2001 and then, on the Friday night before the third and final preseason trial match, a bloke called Billy Slater arrived. He'd driven eighteen hours in a clapped-out Mitsubishi Magna from Innisfail in North Queensland in search of a start at a Brisbane club. He went to Redcliffe first, but they didn't have a spot. Then he lobbed up at the Devils' training, looking for a run.

I'd never heard of him. He'd played no rep footy in North Queensland, so he was never in those state carnival teams. The first time I laid eyes on Billy was that week leading into the last trial. He was lightning fast, agile, quick off the mark, and good over a long distance. He had it all. He played in the trial match the next day and scored a stack of tries.

At no stage that year did the three of us imagine we'd go on to achieve everything we did. We were content playing under-19s Colts, then watching reserve grade and Queensland Cup matches and having a laugh and enjoying life.

It wasn't long into the 2001 season that things were shaken right up. Down in Melbourne, coach Chris Anderson had fallen out with management and quit after just seven rounds. It was less than two seasons since he'd guided the side to a grand final win over the Dragons. Mark Murray was rushed down as caretaker coach, and Anthony Griffin went as his assistant.

I started the year at hooker, but then found myself playing in the halves or at lock. I liked the freedom of getting the ball one off the ruck and having a run, or using it if I wanted.

But the Storm had signed me with hooker in mind, and midway through that season I got the chance to play some senior football in that position. Terry Matterson had replaced Mark Murray as the Devils' Queensland Cup coach—and he was superb. For starters, 'Box' was a Broncos legend who I'd followed. But he also had a great understanding of the game.

'Listen, you're close to getting a start here,' he said to me. 'If you keep playing well, you might get a run soon.'

That opportunity came when he dropped his starting hooker, Terry Benson, and gave me my senior debut. As soon as he told me I was playing, I scanned the draw: we were playing the Toowoomba Clydesdales—the Broncos' feeder club—who were running first at the time. They had a gun team, including Corey Parker, Brent Tate, Justin Hodges and Kirk Reynoldson.

There wasn't much instruction coming to us from Storm headquarters. Melbourne was only a fledgling club back in those days. It had come into the competition in 1998, after the Super League war, and while it had won the 1999 premiership, the club's finances and resources were still tight.

In the lead-up to the 2002 season, a lot of us in the development group came down to Melbourne for a week for some training. There was no fancy hotel to stay in. Instead, they put us up at a backpackers' hostel at the St Kilda end of Punt Road called The Pint on Punt. It was one of the roughest joints you'd ever find, with communal showers and toilets, and we reckoned there were bedbugs. Something was biting us, anyway. Thankfully, the pub downstairs had the best and biggest parmigianas, which we scoffed down every night after training.

At the end of that preseason, I missed out on Melbourne's 25-man squad, which was okay. I wanted to be there, of course, but I was only eighteen. I had plenty of time to play in the NRL. As it turned out, I wouldn't have to wait long.

I started the 2002 season as the first-choice hooker for Norths in the Queensland Cup. About a month into the season, I was driving the Kingswood home from training when I got a phone call: I had to get down to Melbourne ASAP. I was going to be making my NRL debut—and at halfback.

I was in shock, not just because it had come so quickly, but because of the circumstances. The Storm's halfback, Matt Orford, had been sidelined for a few weeks with a groin and hip injury. Our halfback at Norths, Marty Turner, had been rushed down there to make his NRL debut, but not long after tragedy struck.

Marty and Storm teammate Mick Russo, who had been the 2001 Australian Schoolboys captain, went for a drive down to the coast looking for somewhere to surf. Mick went to do a U-turn on the highway but didn't see a semi-trailer coming along behind him. It rammed straight into their car, and the accident left Marty seriously injured. He was rushed to hospital and placed in a coma for a couple of days with a ruptured spleen, head injuries and broken ribs.

I was rattled when I heard the news. I was happy to be making my first-grade debut, but the circumstances were pretty ordinary. It was through the misfortune of someone else.

Our opponents that week couldn't have been any stronger. The Bulldogs were brimming with talent, with Steve Price, Willie Mason, Mark O'Meley, Luke Patten, Nigel Vagana and Braith Anasta.

Mum, Dad and Barb all came down for the Saturday-afternoon match at Olympic Park in Melbourne. As I sat nervously in the sheds, with the No. 18 jumper on my back, I listened to Mark Murray's clear instructions: 'If you see any opportunities, have a run or kick. Other than that, if Scott Hill wants the ball, give him the ball. And make your tackles.'

I also had some instructions for myself: 'No missed tackles, no dropped balls, no kicks out on the full, don't let anyone down.' Don't make a goose of yourself, basically.

We lost 22–6, with Bulldogs winger Matt Utai scoring two tries, but I was comfortable that I hadn't played too badly. A couple of good kicks, some good darting runs, made some tackles. The following week I was picked at halfback again for the match against St George Illawarra, another Saturday afternoon game at Olympic Park.

We won 12–4, with Mick Russo actually returning to the side and scoring a crucial try. But I was out of the game just before halftime after suffering a leg injury. Someone went to make a tackle, swung their leg around and their studs went straight into my shin. As I was helped from the field, I was convinced something was broken but it turned out I was okay.

Matt Orford returned from injury the following week and I was sent back to Norths, where I played out the season.

As for Marty Turner, unfortunately he never played in the NRL again. He's a lovely bloke, though, and whenever I see him he jokes about how he was responsible for my debut.

•

Midway through the 2002 season, Jim Banaghan phoned to tell me that Canberra coach Matt Elliott was interested in signing me. 'You should go and have a look,' Jimmy advised. So I did.

I went to Canberra for the day and they showed me around the city, took me through their training facilities and gave me their thoughts on what I could do for them. Simon Woolford was their hooker at the time, and I'd be sharing the role with him.

This put me in a tricky situation, because Richard Swain was also coming off contract. Jimmy said that if Richard stayed, I should look at going to Canberra. 'Richard doesn't miss a game,' Jimmy told me. 'He's an 80-minute player.'

I spoke with Swainy. 'I'm not going to make a decision here until you do,' I told him. 'You're a legend of this club so I'm not going to force you into any decision.'

In the end, the decision was made for both of us. Storm chief executive John Ribot had set up the club during the Super League era and wasn't afraid to make some big calls. 'Reebs' told Richard they were going to go with me and that he should look elsewhere. It was a really difficult decision for them, and Reebs had to sell it to the members because Swainy was a fan favourite. Like I said, he was a legend of the club. And now some bloke they barely knew was coming in to replace him.

When I heard the news that the club wasn't re-signing Richard, I took my opportunity with both hands and agreed to a two-year deal worth $110,000.

It wasn't the only big decision Reebs made that year. When the Storm finished in tenth spot, failing to make the finals, Mark Murray was sacked. The question was: who was going to replace him?

In Brisbane, Wayne Bennett's assistant coach had become the hottest property in the game. He'd steered the club's 'Baby Broncos' to victories through the State of Origin period when Bennett and a host of players were away on representative duty.

The Storm went after him and signed him as their coach for the 2003 season.

Sitting at home one day, I received a phone call.

'Yeah, Cameron?' a voice grumbled down the line.

'Yeah, mate,' I said.

'Craig Bellamy.'

Shit. I'd never met the bloke in my life.

'Listen, I just want to tell you when we're starting training,' he said, and he gave me the details. 'You'll be receiving an off-season program from Alex Corvo that we need you to start doing now.'

Alex was the Storm's head of performance—someone we were all about to know a whole lot better.

'Mate,' Craig continued, 'I haven't seen you play but I've spoken to a few people at the club who know a bit about you, and they say you go okay. So all I'll ask is that you train hard in the preseason and I'll give you first crack at hooker.'

'Righto,' I said. 'See you in three weeks.'

Then we hung up.

'Geez,' I thought, 'that bloke was pretty intense.'

3

DOG HEAD

At Craig Bellamy's first training session as coach of the Melbourne Storm, he couldn't have been clearer about his expectations of his new team.

Having just left the Broncos, he shared with us what he thought as an 'outsider' about the Storm's culture. 'Good club, good people, skilful side that can do some wonderful things on the field,' he said. 'But once put under pressure, the side struggles.'

To him, that was a sign of mental weakness.

'That is one thing I won't tolerate around here,' he continued. 'I want tough players who can perform under any conditions. So that's what we're going to do in our training. We're going to become tough, mentally and physically. When the pressure comes, we get better.'

We found out quickly why Craig's nickname was 'Bellyache'. He had his angry head on and, to be honest, there weren't many times over the next few years when it came off. All he had in that period was footy, because his family had stayed in Queensland because of his children's schooling. Every waking minute was dedicated to the Melbourne Storm.

The most notable thing about Craig was that he was up-front, honest and told you how it was. And in all the years I've known him since, nothing has changed.

Bellyache had a simple theory about football: train harder than any situation you would ever find yourself in during a game, so that when it happens out there on the field, you'll find it easy. Well, easier than it might have been, at least. You'll be able to push through. We players had no idea of the torture that was about to come our way.

Every preseason is usually tougher than the last in rugby league. But the training sessions in those early years under Bellyache, driven by Alex Corvo, remain as brutal as any I've ever experienced. They made our club into what it is today. He wanted to build a foundation, not just enjoy instant success, and this was his way of doing it.

Because I was a young fella and didn't have much of that hardened training under my belt, I wasn't used to this type of grind. There was nothing too technical: he just trained the shit out of us. There's no better way to describe it.

The way Bellyache and Alex went about training the shit out of us was making us run. Then run some more. These were the days before each player wore GPS trackers, which record how far you run, your workloads and heart rate, so we were working off rough measurements. But in those early seasons we were running about 50 kilometres per week. That's all we did: run.

And Bellyache loved it, because he would do it all with us.

We'd start the preseason by doing laps of the 'Tan'—the track around the Royal Botanical Gardens in the heart of Melbourne. It's about 3.6 kilometres, and we'd do a time trial around it. Bellyache quickly figured out that one lap wasn't enough. We'd do one lap, have a five-minute break, then do another. That was the opening day of preseason.

I would finish somewhere in the middle of the pack. I was never the fastest runner, but I wasn't too far behind. My best time was about sixteen minutes and 30 seconds, which was respectable. The quickest boys—players like Robbie Ross, Matt Geyer and Billy Slater—were doing roughly fifteen minutes.

And then there was Bellyache himself. He was 43 years old but still running up the front of the pack, trying to set the standard.

Most of the Tan is on the flat, except for one big hill, but as the preseason went on and the weather got warmer, the coaches decided to really challenge us. That meant Studley Park, which had little walking trails in the bush and then a parkland area on the side of a hill. We would do hill sessions out there three times a week.

Any running session in those days had to total roughly seven kilometres per player. We'd start with two long runs. Then each session we'd make our way down to 600s, 400s, through the bush and up that hill.

Most of the blokes were crook in the guts before we ran, feeling so nervous about how hard it was going to be. I always felt like vomiting. Once we had a couple of these sessions, we knew exactly what was coming. Blokes would be nervous, getting goose bumps, worried about the pain that was to come.

'Righto boys,' Alex would say. 'We've got twelve runs to do today. Four 800s, four 600s and then four 400s.'

We suffered through the hell of the hill runs until Christmas, then, when we came back in the New Year, we'd be running on the flat; just doing laps around the training oval. It was a grind but that was the entire purpose of it: braindead training to break us down, mentally and physically.

In the gym it was much the same. Everyone from the full-backs to the front-rowers did the same exercises, just different weights. I couldn't even lift some of the weights given to me—they were too heavy and I didn't have great technique. But that didn't matter: you *had* to lift them.

'Sometimes you just have to get it up, Smithy,' Alex would say. 'Just get it up.'

It makes me laugh now. I'm not bagging Alex, because he's one of the most effective strength and conditioning coaches the game has ever seen, and his influence on the Melbourne Storm can't be underestimated. But I was stronger in the last five years of my career than in those early seasons because I used proper technique, slowly building my strength by lifting the appropriate weights.

But that was the philosophy back then. They'd load up 80 kilograms and I'd struggle to bench-press it. 'Just get it up, Smithy. If you get it up, then you've got it done.'

Attitude was what impressed Bellyache. That's why Billy Slater and Dallas Johnson—who was also playing for Norths, having moved down from the Atherton Tablelands in North Queensland—were the last two players added to the squad of 25 for the 2003 season: their application to training impressed the coach more than anything they did with their feet or hands.

'I've got to have these two,' I recall Bellyache saying.

That's all Bellyache really wanted in those early years. 'I don't care about skill,' he'd say. 'I just want blokes who are going to work hard and get their job done. I'd rather a team of those players than anyone who has great skills but doesn't work hard.'

I considered myself to be one of those players. I worked hard, busted my guts and always gave my best effort. Then, one day after a session at Studley Park, Bellyache pulled me aside.

'Smithy, can I have a quick chat?' he asked.

'No worries,' I said.

'How do you think you're going?'

'I think I'm going alright.'

'Mate, I feel like you're training within yourself,' he told me. 'You look comfortable when you're running and doing your conditioning work.'

'Oh. Okay.'

'The one thing I've learned in my time in the game is that if you want to be a good player, train in your comfort zone and you'll be a good player. But the champions push themselves. They get the best out of themselves. I want to see you push yourself for the remainder of the preseason.'

I went away and thought about what he'd said. I knew that I took most things very literally. If we had to finish a run in three minutes and 40 seconds, I'd get it done in three minutes and 38 seconds. I'd have made my time; what was next?

Bellyache had a point, I realised. He was all about ripping in. If you blow out, you blow out. That was the thing I struggled to get my head around: if I went as hard as I could from the start, I knew I wouldn't make my times at the end. I wanted to make every target, not just the first three. I was cruising along so I could get it all done.

The very next session, I went as hard as I could—and I trained like that all the way up until my final match, whether it was for club, state or country. Every time I hit the training paddock, especially during preseason, that was how I approached my preparation.

If it was a timed routine, then I stopped worrying about what was coming later—I went as hard as I could. And over time, I increased my capacity to train harder for longer. That was what Bellyache was trying to tell me, and it stuck with me for the rest of my career.

For me it was a significant moment. Never again did Craig come over and ask me to train harder. I was always on the red line. Today I wonder: if Bellyache hadn't sat me down and said that to me, would I have played 400 games? Probably not. Would I have played Origin, or for Australia? Maybe—but how many times?

•

The club might've signed me ahead of Richard Swain for the 2003 season, but the only guarantee the coach was giving me was first crack at the No. 9 jumper. That was it.

He mustn't have had great confidence in me, though, because he brought Nathan Friend, who had made his debut the previous season with the Broncos, down from Brisbane with him. Maybe he just needed another dummy half, but the arrival of 'Friendy' kept me on my toes.

Our first three seasons under Bellyache were setting us up for something bigger. We could sense it with each game we played. In 2003 we finished the season in fifth place, setting up a qualifying final in week one of the playoffs against Canberra at Canberra Stadium.

It was an exciting time, but many of us were playing finals for the first time so it was also nerve-racking. I kicked off and the ball sailed dead by about fifteen metres. So my very first touch in finals footy gave away a penalty on halfway. I can only imagine what Bellyache was saying in the box.

We had wanted a strong start because the Raiders had a strong side, including Clinton Schifcofske at fullback and Mark McLinden at halfback. Up front, they had quality forwards like Luke Davico, Ruben Wiki and their captain and hooker, Simon Woolford.

We won 30–18 and I scored a try under the posts to seal the result. It's a funny clip when you watch it. On the last tackle and pressing the Canberra tryline, I take the ball out of dummy half, then come to the right. I dummy to grubber three times, and Woolford gets stuck on his heels, half-trying to block it. I see a gap—between his legs. I dive over and score.

Our celebrations were short-lived, though, as the following week we played the Bulldogs and got hammered 30–0.

It was a similar story for the next two seasons. In 2004, we beat the Broncos 31–14 in front of more than 30,000 people at Suncorp Stadium—but then got flogged again by the Bulldogs, this time 43–18. In 2005 we again beat Brisbane at Suncorp—24–18—but bowed out the following week once more, losing 24–16 to the Cowboys at Aussie Stadium.

It was disappointing, but we knew it was part of a bigger picture. Each year, the preseason work became tougher and tougher. We were becoming stronger, mentally and physically, just as Bellyache had promised.

Nobody ever questioned his methods. Nobody ever stormed off the field saying it was too much. But I do remember two times when players had to be taken to hospital.

We were doing shuttle work one day—twenty metres out, ten metres back—around the field when Semi Tadulala, a young Fijian winger, started dropping off. And we knew that if one player missed the times and targets, the whole squad was handed penalties.

That was a real incentive to bust yourself. I could count on one hand how many times the coaches actually called time early on a session if we reached our goal. The incentive at other clubs was to get your work done so you could finish early. The incentive at the Melbourne Storm was to get it done so you didn't have to do more.

So the boys were into Semi. 'Come on, Semi! You'll cost us!' Alex was also into him. Bellyache was into him. 'Don't be weak! Come on!'

We finished the drill but he was miles behind, so we all had to do penalties, which usually meant extra runs. So now we had to do four 100-metre sprints.

Semi keeled over and didn't move. We all looked around, stunned, and then raced to his aid. He was rushed to hospital and we later found out he had a collapsed lung. The poor bloke was running on one lung but had kept going.

There's a similar story about Cooper, who had been suffering from osteitis pubis and taking a lot of anti-inflammatories so he could keep training. We were doing some conditioning one day and he just fell over and hit the deck.

'Get up!' Bellyache barked, standing over him. 'You're being soft!'

Cooper wasn't being soft. He was seriously ill. He was also rushed to hospital, where it was discovered that the medication had created ulcers in his guts. What happened after, though, was that Cooper looked after his body so well that he became one of the fittest players at the Storm.

After a couple of years, some at the club wondered how much longer the younger blokes could handle this type of brutal training. I lived with Matty Geyer for a few months between the 2004 and 2005 seasons. I was trying to save on rent as Barb and I were looking to buy a house.

'I don't know how much longer you'll last here doing this type of training,' Matt said one day. 'It's too much.'

'Boofa' had played at Penrith, then the Western Reds, then at the Storm under Chris Anderson. They'd trained hard but enjoyed their time off too, getting the afternoon off here or there throughout the week. They'd have a game of golf, then enjoy a couple of quiet beers. That never happened under Bellyache. We'd start at 7 a.m. and end at 5 p.m. Every day.

'You might have to go elsewhere,' Boofa continued.

To be honest, it was in the back of my mind. Could I hack this sort of training for another ten years? Could my body withstand it?

The older blokes in the team, like Boofa, knew a different way. They sometimes said to Alex, 'We're footballers. You're trying to make us weightlifters and marathon runners at the same time.'

The training was hard, but I decided I wasn't going anywhere. I was prepared to tough it out because I believed in Bellyache's philosophy. The relentless preparation didn't hurt my love of footy, or influence my attitude towards the game, because I didn't know any different in the first-grade system.

Also, Barb and I didn't have any commitments at that stage. We didn't have kids. She was working in a pharmacy, then she was working in a secure welfare facility for young girls, so footy wasn't eating into our family time.

I was a fresh young player, and I just thought this was what first-grade was all about. I trusted what Bellyache was building.

•

Often you heard Bellyache before you saw him.

In the club's early years, the Storm used the old greyhound administration offices at Olympic Park as a headquarters. Upstairs was reserved for all the front office staff. There was a kitchen up there, and the stairs fed into the players' room, where we'd have lunch and watch TV. Bellyache's office was down the end, meaning he'd have to walk through us to get there.

In the first few months after he arrived, if anyone heard him chatting and walking towards them, they'd stop talking and drop their eyes to the ground. They didn't want to make eye contact with him. That's how intense and intimidating he was.

'Surely, he's not this sort of bloke 24/7,' I thought. 'Surely not.'

I tried to break him down by playing tricks on him, cracking jokes, doing whatever I could do to get a smile and a laugh. Initially it was just for my own benefit—I wanted to see if he was a normal bloke. But I also wanted to report back to the playing group that this lunatic was okay.

Because, to be truthful, it was sometimes hard to tell. His nickname was 'Bellyache', but we had others for him— including 'Dog Head', 'Dog Face' and 'Dog Features'. Anytime he was riled up, or he was carrying on in the coach's box during a game, he'd start spitting or have saliva building up at the corners of his mouth.

'Look at this bloke!' I'd joke. 'It's like a dog with rabies. He's a rabid dog frothing at the mouth!'

Boofa and I called him 'Dog Head' so often that he began responding to it.

'Hey, Dog Head!' we'd shout at him.

'Yeah?' Craig would calmly reply.

Dog Head was brutally honest when it came to giving an assessment of your performance or form. I've seen him square a few of the boys up, either in video sessions, at halftime or on the training field, and I've been on the end of these assessments myself.

Early on in my career, I wasn't great when passing from left to right. In the NRL, the width of the passes is much greater than what you find in junior footy, or even in reserve grade. Our halfback, Matt Orford, would stand twelve metres away and I'd have to hit him on the chest every time or feel the heat from Dog Head.

In one training drill, I threw some ordinary passes—and the coach let me know.

'If you don't learn how to pass left to right and hit "Ox" like you should, I'll find someone who can,' he shouted during the training session, in front of everyone.

That's the polite version of that story. In those days, it was common for either individuals or groups of players to cop it. He'd often come in at halftime, come straight up to you and provide some feedback about your opening 40 minutes.

Video sessions could also be brutal because there was nowhere to hide. These days, the software is so advanced that you can easily call up every action a player has had in a game: a tackle, a missed tackle, a pass to the left, a pass to the right. Just click on a player's name and there it is.

When we first started at Melbourne, video reviews were done on VHS tape. We would all jam into a little meeting room at

Olympic Park, and Dog Head would show us clips of stuff we'd done wrong. You'd walk in and be saying to yourself, 'Please not me. Please not me. Please not me.' But you knew he wouldn't miss a single thing. If you'd fallen for a dummy, it'd be on there. If you fell off a tackle, it'd be on there. If you threw a bad pass or did something outside the game plan, it'd be on there.

You could tell the players who knew they hadn't done anything wrong at the weekend because they would casually walk into the room. But those who had made errors were just sitting there waiting for the pain to come. Dog Head was so meticulous in his review of matches that he never missed a thing.

I can't recall anyone ever challenging him, although Matt Orford had a strong personality and if he didn't agree with something, he would say so. But there wouldn't have been many times.

Dog Head has an incredible work ethic, but in those early years I think he was trying to make his mark. He knew that if he was going to achieve anything with our group, he had to let us know straightaway what he stood for. And he did. He did a good job of scaring us, while also setting standards that would soon pay off.

Three years after he joined the Storm, he was assistant coach to his former Canberra teammate Ricky Stuart for the Australian team. I'd been picked as hooker for the Tri-Nations series.

The very first day was an eye-opener. It was a totally different Craig Bellamy! He was all smiles, laughing at training, patting blokes on the back. He was even having a beer. I was thinking, 'Who the hell is this bloke?' I'd never seen him so relaxed in his life.

Then the other players came up to me, saying, 'How good is Bellyache? You blokes must love him down there!'

'Boys,' I laughed, 'you've got no idea.'

4

PURPLE REIGN

Shane Webcke is after me. We're deep into the second half of the 2006 grand final between the Storm and the Broncos, and the Queensland and Australian prop is picking me out and running at me every time he's got the ball. It doesn't help that this is his final game of rugby league before he retires, so he's giving it everything.

'Webby' probably senses that I am busted—and I am. I've got a bad cork in my left leg—the one I kick with—and I'm struggling to get around the field. So he keeps charging at me, barrelling me, over and over and over.

The Broncos have come to play, and even though we're favoured to win the match, one look across the halfway line just before kick-off makes you wonder why. It's pretty much an Australian side looking back at us: Justin Hodges, Darius Boyd, Brent Tate, Karmichael Hunt, Darren Lockyer, Petero Civoniceva,

Sam Thaiday, Brad Thorn, Tonie Carroll, Corey Parker and Shane Webcke. Here he comes again.

The Broncos have brought all of their big-game knowledge to the table, like we knew they would, but with ten minutes remaining we are still in the grand final.

I'd been whacked from behind earlier in the half, and now my back and ribs are screaming with pain. The trainers help me from the field, rush me up the tunnel and, while they're injecting me with a painkiller in the dressing-room, I'm watching the TV in the corner as Locky sets himself for a field goal . . .

•

In 2006 it was time for us to cash in on the hard work of the previous three years under Bellyache. The team had come together nicely. We already had an aggressive forward pack with the likes of David Kidwell, Jeremy Smith and Brett White, but it had been boosted by the emergence of Junior Kiwi Adam Blair and the signing of Michael Crocker from the Sydney Roosters.

'Crock' had played for Queensland and Australia and won a competition with the Roosters, but he needed to get out of Sydney. Bellyache took on Crock on certain conditions. 'I'll have you if you behave yourself,' he told him. 'I need you to be a leader for these younger fellas.'

Everyone called him 'Mick' or 'Crock'. Bellyache would call him 'Michael'. That was to help his transition from party boy into a reformed senior player. And it worked: Mick—or Michael, Crock, whatever you want to call him—came to Melbourne and played the house down.

There was another major change that year. Matt Orford had left the club and taken a big contract at Manly, which opened the way for Cooper Cronk to start at halfback along-side Scott Hill.

Until then, Coops had been used all over the place. He'd come down from playing with Norths Devils, coming off the bench to play in the halves, or at dummy half, at centre, even at fullback. He had played all over the field as a schoolboy in rugby and was one of those natural sportsmen who was good at everything. Wherever he was asked to play, he did the job. But he'd arrive, play a game or two, then get sent back to Norths, where he'd continue playing in the Queensland Cup. Now he had a chance to make the Storm's No. 7 jumper his own.

This was also the season when a skinny Indigenous kid from the North Coast of New South Wales became the hottest property in the game. He had a diamond stud in one ear but he was very quiet and reserved, even shy. But he could do it all—run, jump, kick, pass—and he did it with natural athleti-cism and ease.

The big question was whether this young talent could take the next step. He'd played a handful of matches the previous season and got everyone interested—but could he back it up in his second year and build on what he had already shown us?

Of course he could. Greg Inglis scored eighteen tries in nineteen matches for us in 2006, as well as making his State of Origin debut for Queensland. He was incredible for the Storm—and he needed to be, because for much of the year he was there when Billy Slater wasn't.

Billy had a terrible year because of suspension. Early on he was rubbed out for seven matches for kicking Wests Tigers prop John Skandalis in the face. Then, in his first week back, the Roosters' Ryan Cross made a run from dummy half, Billy chased him from marker, got underneath him and tipped him on his head—another two weeks.

When Billy returned, Bellyache decided to send him back to reserve grade because he'd missed so much game time, and when he came back against Wests Tigers he started him off the bench. After halftime Billy kept looking at the coaches' box from the sidelines. His eyes said it all: 'I'm ready to go.' He came on, only to clip the Tigers' fullback, Shannon McDonnell, across the back of the head with a forearm as he was scoring a try—another two weeks.

The frustration just built and built inside Billy. When you're suspended, you don't really train with the NRL team, and at that stage of our careers, when we were young, footy was what we lived for. There wasn't much more in our lives.

But Billy's absence meant GI had to play fullback, and with that time and space to move at the back, he exploded.

We dropped just four matches to claim the minor premiership, and personally I'd never felt better since coming into the NRL. Bellyache had made me one of five captains, in rotation with Kidwell, Hill, Geyer and Crocker, but more critical to my form was Orford's departure in the off-season. Without him there, a lot of our football was focused around our ruck and playing off me.

I reckon that was why, in the first week of the finals, at a black-tie function in Sydney, I was named Dally M Player of the Year.

I went there that night with Barb thinking I had no chance of winning it. Before I knew it, Prime Minister John Howard was trying to get the medal over my woolly hair. It was nice recognition of the season we'd had—but it's never been about that sort of stuff for me. I was more interested in reaching and winning the grand final.

We'd won the minor premiership by a massive eight points, ahead of the Bulldogs, and we got past Parramatta in the qualifying final and then the Dragons in the preliminary final to reach the decider.

The night before we played the Dragons, the Broncos had upset the Bulldogs, who had led 20–6 at halftime and looked certain to win. The significant change to that Brisbane team had been Wayne Bennett's decision to shift Shaun Berrigan from centre to hooker. He scored two tries against the Dogs, including a late 70-metre effort, to turn the match around and set up a grand final between two teams from outside New South Wales for the first time in history.

The Storm had already built up a healthy rivalry with the Broncos, having beaten them in the finals in the past two seasons. There would be greater battles and matches to come, but this was the start of it.

People often asked me what it was about the two of us— why there seemed to be more on the line when the Storm and Broncos met. I felt it was more about Bellyache than anything else.

He'd come to the Storm from the Broncos, leaving Bennett behind. He never wanted his mentor to put one over him, and the feeling was probably mutual. There was no animosity between the two of them, but as a player I just knew there was something different about those games. Bellyache would probably deny that. He'd say he's the same every week—but he wasn't. It's not so much that he wanted to win more than the previous week, but some results just mean more than others. And what could mean more than beating your former club in a grand final?

There had been talk for some years about whether a Melbourne side even deserved a place in the competition, but we didn't feel any pressure to win a premiership to justify our existence. We did feel a little disconnected from the rest of the competition. Our aim was to play well, but also to play a brand of footy that was successful and attractive to the public, to help grow the sport in Victoria.

Our goal every year was to be the best we could. We could feel we were becoming a better footy side, with all the players improving each year. That was Craig's expectation: improvement in our skill, ability and performances. Now, against the Broncos, it was time to make good on all that hard work.

I was given the honour of leading the side out onto Telstra Stadium, out through the big purple banner made by our supporters. We started well, with Scotty Hill—in his final match for the club—getting a round-the-corner pass for winger Steve Turner to score in the corner. The Broncos responded with a try to Justin Hodges.

The turning point for me came early in the second half, when 'Hodgo' whacked me from behind and an all-in brawl erupted. 'I didn't see him coming,' I said at the media conference after the game about Hodgo's stray arm. 'He just got me across the face. They're pretty strict on high tackles. For the last twenty minutes I just couldn't move.'

I took the quick tap from the penalty and sent Matt King over for a try that levelled the scores at 8-all, but I was so battered I couldn't take the conversion. Apart from being whacked, I'd suffered a badly corked leg in the fight that broke out. Boofa took the kick and missed.

As the minutes ticked past we were still in it, but the Broncos, with all their big-match experience, were becoming too difficult to roll back. They knew I was hurting. I hadn't taken any injuries into the match, but they'd got a hold of me that night and roughed me up. They took the lead in the 60th minute with a Brent Tate try in the corner, and soon after set themselves for a field goal that would extend their lead to seven points.

I was in the dressing-room as Locky snapped it from 35 metres out. Could I have made a difference if I was out there? I don't know, but it was tough to take as the match slipped away from us. We'd spent four years getting there. We thought we were a really good chance, but we let a golden opportunity slip.

Plenty was made afterwards about the refereeing of Paul Simpkins in his first and last grand final. Matty King was denied a try in the second half after they ruled Ryan Hoffman had knocked on after the ball had come off Justin Hodges from a Cooper Cronk kick. We were down 14–8 at that stage so it really was a massive call. Another obstruction call also went against us, along with all the fifty-fifties that didn't seem to go our way.

But I don't blame Simpkins for the loss. In the end, we were beaten by a really good side. We came up against a team that knew how to play big games better than we did. A lot of the Broncos had played Origin, they'd played internationals, they'd played big finals matches. They knew what to do when it was needed. In the moments that mattered, they got it done. They noticed I had been taken from the field, and when I came back on, it was pretty clear that the experienced Shane Webcke was directing nearly every hit-up at me. We were young and still had a lot to learn.

Another factor was our preparation. We flew up for the Grand Final Breakfast on the Tuesday, then flew back to Melbourne for the rest of the week. So, during NRL grand final week, we were in Melbourne where there was zero atmosphere. We may have made a mistake by treating the decider like any other game.

That was the worst I ever felt after a game. It was heartbreaking, because you start to wonder: 'Have I just played and lost the only grand final I'll ever be in? Am I ever going to get this chance again?'

●

When we returned for the preseason, I could see a new spirit in everyone's eyes: there was a hunger I hadn't seen before. Belly-ache changed things up here and there, although it didn't alter how wrecked I felt after every session. The big difference in this preseason was that instead of having one freakish talent who could run and jump, now we had two.

At training sessions, he would leap high above his team-mates and latch onto the ball. We understood straightaway that we had a huge advantage on the rest of the competition: all we had to do was get Cooper to toss the ball in the air and this kid couldn't be beaten.

Israel Folau moved into the Logan area just as I was leaving. He went to Marsden State High School, the same school as me. Like Greg Inglis, he was simply a ridiculous talent. But unlike GI, who had many clubs chasing him from the age of fourteen, 'Izzy' had flown under the radar. We had a very smart recruitment manager in Peter O'Sullivan, who snapped up both young stars.

'Sully' wasn't just good at signing talented young players. He also recruited a lot of journeymen based on what the coach wanted. Bellyache was more than happy with the guys in the key positions, but he was happier with the players who worked tirelessly.

That's why the safest bet in footy was the Storm winning our first match of the season. In all my time under Bellyache, he never lost a first-round match. The closest was 2004, when we lost to Newcastle in the second round after having a bye in the first week. The point was we were ready to go from the very start.

We're not a club that builds into the season. We want to knock wins out early, get the runs on the board and then keep going.

And that was what happened in 2007 as we tried to put the disappointment of grand final defeat behind us. We suffered just three losses through the regular season—to Brisbane, Parramatta and Manly—and claimed the minor premiership for a second year running. Our defence was very tight, conceding just eleven points a game on average. But we could also score them, averaging 26 points per match—and many of these came from Izzy, as we had predicted in the preseason. He finished that season with 21 tries, the most from any player in a rookie season, beating Billy's record of nineteen tries in 2003.

So we definitely took an air of confidence into every match that year. Each time we played, I felt strongly that we wouldn't get beaten. I don't mean that in an arrogant way, like we'd just turn up and it would happen. But the way we trained, before and during the season, gave me supreme confidence about our footy side. It's a rare feeling to have in a game as unpredictable as rugby league.

We carried that confidence into the finals series, rarely looking like we'd get beat. At all. We shut out Brisbane 40–0 in the first week of the finals. Under the new McIntyre System, we got the week off before beating Parramatta 26–10 in the preliminary final.

I felt the same confidence heading into the grand final, even though our opponents were Manly, who had finished second to us on the ladder and had been one of the few sides to beat us that year. The Sea Eagles were strong, with Brett and Glenn

56

Stewart, Jamie Lyon, Steve Menzies and, strangely, Matt Orford. I knew it was going to feel weird squaring off against him in a grand final, having started my NRL career with him at the Storm. I loved playing with Ox. He was a competitor, an angry little fella, and they're the type of guys I like playing alongside. Despite the strength of Manly's side, though, I knew a lot would have to go against us if we were to lose that grand final.

It didn't take long for us to score the first points, using a set play we had practised all week. We'd noticed that Manly's right edge would fold back behind the tryline, looking to protect the in-goal area or guard against a crossfield kick on the last tackle, so our plan was this: I would come out from dummy half, shaping to grubber-kick, and then have Billy and Ryan Hoffman run through as decoys. Then I'd get it to GI, who would wrap around those two and get the ball out to winger Anthony Quinn, who would score in the left-hand corner.

When it came off perfectly the first time we tried it, my confidence soared. 'We're going to have a good day, here,' I thought.

And we did. The second try also came from a set play, this time with GI running the ball on our right side. The hole we created for him wasn't as big as we hoped but it didn't matter. This was GI. He brushed aside four defenders and scored anyway. It was something only he could do.

Greg played five-eighth for most of that year, and he was superb. I look back at replays of him from that season, and I reckon I would've preferred to see him keep that leaner physique as his career blossomed. He was doing all our weights and had dietitians involved, but he just didn't seem to put weight on quickly in those early years. That changed later in his career, but in 2007 I felt he was the ideal weight. He was already a big man. He ran over three or four defenders to score tries, and he had that lethal fend that made it nearly impossible to tackle him at times. He also had a lot of skill— sometimes you just had to convince him to use it. Like his right foot.

GI had the biggest boot in the team. He could launch it harder and further into the air than anyone. 'Why don't we utilise it?' Bellyache asked one day. Any time we were down the opposition's end of the field, get GI behind the ruck, throw him the ball and he could put it up—a big spiral bomb or a floater or whatever. Cooper and I usually did all the kicking, but that was something we wanted GI to do more. It was just a matter of convincing the big fella to do it.

Early into the second half of the grand final, GI got the ball and reefed it into the sky. I don't know what type of kick you'd call it, but it went bloody high—and that meant when it came down, it was going to be really difficult to catch.

Waiting underneath it, Brett Stewart was a sitting duck. Crock came charging through and whacked him so hard it took 'Snake' out of the game—and almost took Billy out of it, too, because he had also chased through on GI's kick.

That moment changed the game. It had been 10–4 at halftime, and Snake being helped from the field deflated Manly, no doubt. He was their key man in attack. He'd had a great season for them, scoring nineteen tries. His departure meant Manly had to move Michael Robertson from the wing to fullback, which changed their whole game plan.

A year earlier, Bellyache had taken a chance by signing Crock. Now I wonder: if he wasn't in our team that night, would we have won that grand final? We ran away 34–8 winners, but it could've been a lot more if I'd landed some goals. I kicked three from eight.

At the presentation, I was asked to come on stage to collect the trophy and say a few words. I had been outright captain of the club that year. It was a huge honour. I'd captained every junior side from the under-8s onwards. Even then, I wanted to set a good example for my teammates. I'm not sure if that was a weird thing for a kid to think, but I just didn't want to let anyone down. I'd felt the same obligation as captain of the Melbourne Storm, and I couldn't have been any prouder of what we had achieved.

'Five years of hard work, boys,' I shouted as I lifted the trophy, looking at my teammates, and they responded by roaring their approval.

I wasn't just saying that—it really had been five long, hard years of work. The seeds of our 2007 victory were planted the moment Bellyache joined the club, back in 2003, when he said he wanted to make us physically and mentally tougher players because that's what it took to win premierships.

It took him that long to build us into that sort of team— one that didn't fade away when the pressure was on, as he had observed before joining us. Along the way, we shed a lot of experienced guys. Most of those were foundation players at the Storm and had set the example. Players like Robbie Kearns,

Danny Williams, Rodney Howe and Steve Kearney had been at the club when I started, but others had come in—Billy, Coops, Hoffy, Dallas Johnson, Stevie Turner—and together we helped carry on their hard work.

Bellyache was extremely proud of what we had achieved. I think, too, he was pleased to finally be a premiership-winning coach. He'd worked as hard as any of us. But he didn't dwell on it for too long; he's not that type of guy. After a few weeks of celebrations, his attention would turn to the new crop of rookies about to come into the club.

That night at Telstra Stadium, after completing a slow lap of honour, we took the trophy back into the sheds. It was such a good feeling—we could've sat there forever. Until that point, I don't think people realised just how hard we trained down in Melbourne. Now the way the Storm go about things in preseason is almost legendary.

Five years of hard work. Our success may have snuck up on everyone else—but it didn't sneak up on us.

5

BIG MAL

When people talk about Mal Meninga, they often mention his aura. It sounds like a cliché but it's true: there's a presence about him whenever he walks into the room. It's Mal. A legend of the game.

Everything he's done in rugby league is shrouded in excellence. He's got a strong belief in himself and what he teaches his footy team. When he became coach of Queensland for the 2006 State of Origin series, he wanted to create an environment in which we could have a good time, but also work hard when we needed to.

Mal liked having fun—but when it was time to be serious about the job at hand, he wanted you to focus. So when we were in a team meeting in the days before the third and deciding game of that year's series, and he was fixing those big eyes on us, we listened.

Even though we had taken the game to a decider, to be played at the Telstra Dome in Melbourne, Queensland were under enormous pressure. New South Wales had won the last three series, and there was a lot of talk about the future of the interstate series hingeing on this result. No side had ever won four in a row, and the Blues seemed set to do it.

On top of that, the calls had already started about some members of our team. There was talk that the props Steve Price and Petero Civoniceva were too old and should retire. But most of the criticism was reserved for our captain, Darren Lockyer.

Mal is always very honest—and this team meeting was no different. 'This is what everyone is saying,' Mal said, looking around the room. '*These blokes shouldn't be here. It's time for Lockyer to be punted as captain.* That's what they're saying. The question is what are you blokes going to do about it?'

As one of the players in the leadership group, I felt responsible for ensuring we did whatever we could to take the pressure off these three legends—as well as our team. Queensland were staring at some pretty ordinary history. I didn't want to be a part of it. It was pressure I had never experienced since pulling on the Maroons jersey for the first time three years earlier.

•

In the dressing-room at Canberra Stadium in early July in 2003, Bellyache pulled me aside. 'You're a chance of getting picked for Queensland,' he said. 'Play well today and you'll put yourself in the frame.'

62

The Queensland team for the third match of the series was to be announced the following day. The Maroons had already lost the series, but they needed a hooker for game three at Suncorp Stadium as they went about restoring pride. They'd used PJ Marsh in game one, but he'd hurt his neck. Then they used Mick Crocker and Scott Sattler in tandem in the second. My name had been tossed up as a possible solution for game three, even though I'd only played sixteen NRL matches.

The only problem was I felt crook as a dog before the match against Canberra. It was only the flu, but I was knackered. I hadn't felt great going up there the day before, and now it was worse. Not ideal for a game of footy that could convince the state selectors to pick me for an Origin.

I didn't dare tell Bellyache about how bad I felt. When he first started at Melbourne, one of the first things he said to us was that he didn't tolerate excuses. 'I don't care about the way you feel, how many hours of sleep you had,' he said. 'Just go out and get your job done.'

That was his approach. Definitely no cuddles. And with that attitude deeply ingrained in my mind, I thought, 'No excuses—put that aside and go out and play. You have to find something.'

We won 18–8 and I felt I'd played a reasonably good game, given how poorly I felt. The next day I was sitting in the lounge-room in the Richmond townhouse Barb and I shared with Billy and Hoffy when the phone rang. It was Dad.

'Has anyone from the club spoken to you?' he asked.

'No,' I said, confused.

'I just heard on the radio you've been picked in the Queensland side.'

I got up, walked down the hallway and out the front door. 'Hang on, what did you just say?' I asked in disbelief.

'You're in the Queensland team,' he said. 'You're going to be playing State of Origin.'

I couldn't speak.

'Can you believe that?' Dad went on. 'You're going to be playing State of Origin, mate.'

I walked inside, sat down and took Barb aside. 'Dad just heard that I'm playing State of Origin,' I told her.

Her eyes lit up. I was still in shock.

Billy and Hoffy were quickly onto us. 'What's going on?' they asked.

'Nothing,' I said.

'Tell them!' Barb demanded.

'Um, I think I'm playing State of Origin.'

We all erupted and carried on a bit. Then I spoke to Greg Brentnall, the Storm's football manager at the time, and he confirmed the news for me.

I remember my first Origin camp like it was yesterday. I flew to Brisbane airport and waited for some of the other players to arrive: Matty Bowen and Josh Hannay from North Queensland, and Mick Crocker and Chris Flannery from the Roosters.

I was waiting in the area where you collect your baggage when I spotted Crock and Flanno coming to collect their bags.

'G'day, Crock,' I said, shaking Crocker's hand. 'How are you?'

'Yeah, g'day, mate,' he said—and walked straight on past me. He didn't know who I was—he thought I was a fan! Luckily, Flanno recognised me and stopped.

'That's a good start,' I thought. 'My teammate didn't even recognise me!'

The week that followed was a real eye-opener. We got to the hotel in Brisbane for our medicals, and before I knew it I was shaking hands with legends of the game: Gorden Tallis, Locky, Petero, Pricey, Webby—all these players who I'd been watching as a kid only two years earlier, hoping one day to meet them— or at the very least to one day wear the Maroons jersey like them. Now I was about to play *with* them.

The third Origin match of 2003 was to be Wayne Bennett's last as Queensland coach. I enjoyed being coached by Wayne that week because he didn't complicate the game at all. Origin is different to club footy, where you have a mix of players of skill levels and experience, and Wayne concentrated on our mental attitude towards the game. He really focused us on going out there and not letting each other down. There was very little coaching about the technical side of the game. It was about playing a basic game of footy and doing what we were good at. That suited me.

We had the traditional bonding session on the first night, and I walked home in the early hours of the next morning with Benny Ikin, who is married to Wayne's daughter. 'I can't get in trouble here because I'm with the son-in-law,' I thought.

The next day, we drove south to the Gold Coast and they absolutely smashed us up. I'd never trained while hungover before, but this was Origin so I just did it. I'd heard all the stories about the mateship and enjoying each other's company, and then ripping in at training—and then, at game time, the way the players look after one another. That sense of trust was quickly established.

The week went so fast, and my feeling as kick-off neared was how good it was being an Origin player. We were staying at the Sheraton Mirage on the Gold Coast, eating seafood buffets every night, beers whenever you wanted. 'How good is this?' I thought.

The match was also Gordie's last for Queensland. I'd played against him only once—at ANZ Stadium in Brisbane—and it felt good to be on his side. I knew how passionate he was about wearing the Queensland jersey.

The day before the match, I was walking down the Suncorp Stadium tunnel for our captain's run when I noticed he was walking alongside me. He pulled me aside.

'Mate, the best advice I can give you isn't about the game,' he told me. 'When you walk out this tunnel tomorrow night, take it all in, because you'll remember it for the rest of your life. Playing for Queensland, in Brisbane—there's nothing like it.'

And he was right. I still remember that moment. The roar of a Queensland crowd just goes through you. There might have been Origins I played in after that when it was louder, or when the crowd was bigger, but this was the very first time I experienced that noise, and it hit me between the eyes.

I'd never been more nervous before a game of football. To that point of my career, I'd only played in junior grand finals, and a few Queensland Cup semi-finals. I'd represented Queensland in the juniors, but this was Origin at Suncorp.

As we lined up for the national anthem, I scanned the crowd for my family. I'd organised a tonne of tickets, so they were all there. Dad was beside himself. So were Mum and the rest of the family. Being such a big football family, it was a proud moment for them. At some point in Dad's life, he'd probably had aspirations to play interstate footy but it hadn't happened. Now his son was living that dream.

When I found them sitting in the stands—something I did until I played my final Origin and Test matches—it didn't make me emotional. I'm not that sort of player: I feel the emotion on the inside, but I also have a job to do and I can't let it get the better of me. Some guys use that emotion, they feed off it. But it affects me too much. My emotion comes later.

When the game got underway, I instantly understood what players meant when they said Origin football was the fastest they had ever played. We were also coming up against a gun New South Wales team: Andrew Johns was the captain, Danny Buderus the hooker, props Jason Ryles and Robbie Kearns, a Storm teammate at the time. Out wide they had Matt Gidley and Jamie Lyon, with Anthony Minichiello at fullback. They had the majority of the Australian team.

But we got the jump on them, racing to a 16-nil lead after just seventeen minutes, and the points kept ticking over for the rest of the match. It all seemed to happen so fast.

With about five minutes left, one of our trainers, Gary Belcher—a Maroons legend in his own right—came to me and said they were going to replace me. I was more than okay with that because I was absolutely knackered. My legs were gone. I'd never played footy like this before.

Then we made a break down the right. 'Stay on, back up down the middle!' Belcher screamed at me.

I got going again somehow, my feet feeling like cement blocks, as the play moved towards the right-hand corner of the northern end. Both teams had fed that way, but I stayed out on the left. The ball shifted back towards the posts, and Shaun Berrigan almost scored. Then the ball was shot back to Locky, who zinged it out to me on my own on the wing. I dived over and scored. There you go: my first Origin try, playing hooker, scoring in the corner. The boys got around me and celebrated.

I left the field and collapsed on the bench. 'What just happened?' I thought. Then I saw my family and ran to the fence and hugged them.

Our 36–6 win was, at the time, the largest win Queensland had ever had over New South Wales. I reckon the Blues were complacent because of what had happened in the first two matches. But I've spoken to a few of their players from that game over the years, and they say they came to win. There were no excuses.

It was a great way to start my Origin career but there was a lot of pain to come. In 2004 Brad Fittler returned for New South Wales and they won the series. In 2005 Andrew Johns came back and the Blues won again.

Joey's performance in game two that year is legendary, and for good reason. I've never played in a game of football that one player has dominated so much, from start to finish. That night in Sydney he set up tries, toyed with our defence and kicked goals from everywhere, and his general play kicking was ridiculous. If you took him out of that game, it was a different result.

There was one try that stands out. New South Wales was inside our ten-metre zone. Danny Buderus passed to his right and Joey got the ball. He looked to the right and then came back off his right foot and held the ball just a little bit, then fed a perfect pass in between two of our defenders to 'Bedsy', who scored the try untouched. I was left standing there.

'This sucks,' I thought. 'But it's also unbelievable.'

Joey was someone I admired greatly. I wanted to control footy games like he did. That's your complete footballer: he could tackle, he was a good runner of the footy, he had a good passing game and could kick goals from anywhere. When I think about the complete package, I think of the player Andrew Johns was.

The other player I greatly respected was Bedsy. When I first started, he was the best No. 9 in the game by a mile. Bellyache would often say, 'If you want to be the best in your position, look at who the best is right now.' That was Danny Buderus, the Australian hooker. 'If there's things that work for him, try to build them into your game and see if they work for you as well.'

I watched a lot of vision of him, taking note of the way he positioned himself on the field, and his subtle movements at dummy half when he would show one way and go the other, and when he went to the line. Like me, he'd also played in the halves when he was younger and so there were parts of his game I could relate to.

We always had a healthy respect when we played against each other. I'm not the type of player who comes into a game thinking I want to put one over a rival player. My focus isn't the other No. 9; as I said earlier, I'm more concerned about doing my own job.

Queensland had its moments too, of course, and some great players were unearthed in those years. Billy's chip-and-chase in game two of the 2004 series was one of the greatest tries in Origin history, but they were few and far between. We just lacked the belief that we could beat New South Wales. We were looking at the opposition and seeing a virtual Australian side, with all those gun players.

We needed to become unbeatable players in our own right.

•

In his first few days as Queensland coach, Mal spoke about what he saw as the important values and behaviours our team should hold. At that very first meeting, he stood in front of a whiteboard and asked us to throw words at him about what playing for Queensland meant to us, how we wanted to be perceived by people outside of the team, and what it was going to take for us to be a successful footy side that could beat New South Wales.

Several words kept coming up. Trust. Effort. Aggression.

Mateship. They were the things we spoke about. But we also wanted to be good people, too. Honest. Respectful. Humble.

Mal also introduced some of the history of Queensland rugby league to us: its roots, its former players, the games that had been played. He always wanted past players around us, and we were lucky to have some great ones as part of our staff. When we needed an insight into the history of the Maroons jumper, you got it from the bloke sitting next to you at breakfast: Allan Langer, Trevor Gillmeister, Gavin Allen, Andrew Gee and the great Chris 'Choppy' Close.

Mal opened up about the really tough period Queensland went through before the Origin concept came in, when the likes of Arthur Beetson, Johnny Lang and others represented New South Wales because they were playing for Sydney clubs in the New South Wales Rugby League competition. The Queensland team had been dominated in those times, and it made us understand why winning now was just so important. Queenslanders watching their state during that dark period were embarrassed. We didn't want them to feel that ever again.

In some ways that was still happening in junior footy. In 2002 I captained a Queensland under-19s side that was beaten by New South Wales. When we took the field, I looked up and saw a stack of Queensland-born and bred players wearing sky-blue jumpers.

One of them was Johnathan Thurston. We'd even played together for Queensland under-19s the year before, on the last night of footy at Lang Park before it became Suncorp Stadium. But one year later he was wearing sky-blue, because he'd moved to Sydney to start his NRL career with Canterbury-Bankstown.

'Look at you!' I yelled at him, stirring him up. 'How can you wear that jumper?'

He and Willie Tonga towelled us up in that match, with most of the points coming from players who would go on to wear the Maroons jumper.

Now, in the 2006 series, JT stood proudly alongside me as we tried to stop New South Wales from winning a record fourth consecutive Origin series. The Blues won the first game 17–16 after their halfback, Brett Finch, who was a last-minute call-up, kicked the winning field goal at the death. We won game two in Brisbane easily, 30–6.

In Melbourne, the night before the deciding match, Locky invited just the players into his hotel room. He told us that he could see that the talk about our last performance had really affected us. Then he did what Locky always did: took ownership of it.

'I'm going to go out there and be the best player on the field,' he said. 'I'm going to win you guys this match. And I want every one of you to go in thinking the same way as I am.'

He figured that if we did that, we would win.

We scored the first try, through winger Adam Mogg, who had debuted that series and played well, but that was where our luck seemed to dry up. JT threw a Hail Mary pass to Adam later in the half, only for Blues winger Eric Grothe Jr to intercept it and race away to score.

It was 4-all at halftime, but the Blues took the lead early

into the second half with a try to my Melbourne teammate Matty King.

Then came the moment that broke our hearts.

Blues halfback Craig Gower kicked the ball high, and when it came down it appeared to come off fullback Brett Hodgson's chest, and then arm, before Steve Menzies grabbed it and passed it out for an unmarked Grothe to dive over. It looked like a clear knock-on, but referee Steve Clark still sent it up to the video referee to make a decision.

'Cool,' I thought. 'The video ref will pick it up—surely.' But the longer the video ref took to make a decision, the more I feared his decision.

I was right. They awarded the try, giving New South Wales a 14–4 lead.

'This is not our time,' I thought. 'That went to a video referee and they *still* gave it. It touched him! This is just not going to happen for us tonight.'

Locky had other ideas. He gathered us behind the uprights as the conversion was being lined up. 'Keep your heads,' he said. 'Don't worry about that—it's out of our control. Stay calm.'

With nine minutes left, JT swung around in a tackle on our ten-metre line, saw fresh air ahead of him—and ran. He found Brent Tate, who then ran 65 metres to score under the posts. At 14–10, we were back in the hunt.

What played out next is part of Origin folklore. Hodgson threw a wild pass out of dummy half and Locky was there, in the right place at the right time, as he so often was, to pounce on the loose ball and run just fifteen metres to score the try that levelled the scores.

I ended up playing a lot of games with Darren Lockyer over the years, so I know it was no fluke that he was there to take advantage. He had that football instinct to know where he should put himself at the right moment. He always had time and space on the field, but he also sensed opportunity. Very few players have all those attributes.

In the post-try celebrations, Tonie Carroll hit Locky so hard he nearly broke his rib cage. That's how excited 'Tunsa' was. We all were. Clinton Schifcofske then took about two minutes to slot over the conversion to put us ahead 16–14.

We had to defend two more sets from the Blues, and when the full-time siren sounded it was sheer relief. In that moment, we had a raw feeling of pride in what we'd accomplished for our state. It was bigger than a team—this was for more than 4 million people.

In the dressing-room after the match, Mal was very proud. He thought it was important to enjoy victories and special achievements. And, at the end of the year, boy, did he mean it. Every player got invites late in the season telling us to converge on the Gold Coast to celebrate the series win. We had no idea what was planned, but put it this way: Big Mal never under-delivers. He's the best of the best.

We all flew into town and got a bus to Hope Island. There was a small itinerary without too much information. We caught up at the tavern for lunch and beers, before we were told to get into small groups. Okay, no worries. That was when we heard the commotion outside: three helicopters were landing on the spare block next to the pub.

We climbed in and flew south, to this big property in northern New South Wales, where eskies full of beer, barbecues and a seafood buffet were waiting for us. There was also a golf driving range, a cricket pitch, mini-motorbikes and remote-controlled cars. Did I mention the eskies full of beer?

We were shown a highlights package, and then Mal spoke and congratulated everyone. About four hours later, we were back on the helicopters and returned to Hope Island. Waiting for us was a massive yacht with the same set-up: beers, seafood, beers. The night ended in the nightclubs of Surfers Paradise.

The next thing I remember, I was getting a shuttlebus home, stumbling into my room. Barb was coming to pick me up, but I couldn't find my mobile phone to call her. I called from the phone in the room.

'Oh, what have you been up to?' she asked cheekily. 'What phone are you ringing from?'

'The one in the room,' I said.

'Lose your phone?'

'Um, I can't remember.'

'I know where it is,' she told me.

It turned out that someone walking their dog had found my mobile in the middle of the roundabout outside Hope Island resort. I must have dropped it out of the window of the shuttle-bus when we were coming back to the hotel. I had no idea—all I knew was I'd had a good night.

What none of us knew was what that victory in Melbourne would mean for rugby league in Queensland, and the success it would trigger. The last thing any of us expected was an Origin dynasty.

6

PANIC

There was barely anyone in the stands at Suncorp Stadium an hour before the 2008 semi-final between the Storm and Broncos. But now, as my teammates huddle in the dressing-room with kick-off just minutes away, and as I deliver my last words, it feels like we're about to play an Origin.

When we race out onto the field, the crowd roars. Every seat is taken. As a Queenslander, I'm used to being on their side. So are Billy, Coops, GI, Izzy, Crock. But tonight they hate us.

Many had predicted this game would be the grand final—a repeat of 2006. We'd won the minor premiership for the third year in a row, but then we lost 18–15 to the eighth-placed Warriors at Olympic Park in the first week of the finals, which ruined those plans. Now, if we were to defend our premiership, we'd have to do it the hard way—and playing the Broncos in Brisbane is as hard as it gets.

Things don't start well. We give away a penalty after just three minutes and the Broncos take full advantage, sweeping the ball to the left with a cut-out pass from Karmichael Hunt hitting an unmarked Darius Boyd on the wing for the first try.

In the coaches' box, Wayne Bennett doesn't move. This is potentially his last game as Broncos coach; he's signed with St George Illawarra for the 2009 season. Bellyache is a little more animated in the Storm coaches' box as Corey Parker lands the sideline conversion. Broncos 6, Storm 0.

The game escalates to a ridiculous pace. The Broncos' forwards—Sam Thaiday, Ben Hannant, Joel Clinton—smash through the middle. Then Peter Wallace kicks to our corners, trying to get in behind Billy, and their kick-chase is great.

There have been stories in the media all week about the Storm and our so-called grapple tackling. They're coming from the usual suspects, trying to unsettle us and the referee, and early on it works: referee Shayne Hayne penalises GI for a 'grapple tackle' on Tonie Carroll.

A grapple tackle is when you have your arm around your opponent's neck, and you're choking them. GI is not choking him. Replays show Tunsa has sold it beautifully, with his own arm up and around his neck.

There are subtle moments like that in every game. Minutes after giving away the penalty, GI tries to play the ball, but Corey Parker has hold of his right hand. GI carries the ball in his left hand, so he needs his right hand free to push up from the ground. If he can't use his hand, he can't get up. And we know Corey hasn't just thought of that—it's a tactic he's been taught. Subtleties are everywhere in the game; you just have to know where to look.

Finally we start getting some possession and field position, but we can't turn it into points. Cooper looks to the right, and the Broncos defence expects a crossfield kick to Izzy. Instead, he grubber-kicks behind the line and Billy slides between two defenders to score the try. Well, so we thought. The replay shows him losing possession, and video referees Bill Harrigan and Paul Simpkins rightfully call 'no try'.

As the half rolls on, the Broncos give us cheap possession, but we fail to make the most of it, too often giving possession straight back.

I cop a stray elbow in a tackle, and blood pours out of a gash above my left eye. There's blood all over my jumper but I barely notice as we get the penalty and I kick for touch. We need points. We need to make good on all this possession and field position we've had.

Cooper darts over the tryline but he knows he hasn't got it down, so he races back to the ten-metre line looking for a quick restart. That's not going to happen. The decision is sent up to the video ref, and the delay gives the Broncos valuable minutes to recover—and the trainers a chance to tape up my bleeding head. We get the ball back but then Crock fumbles while running into the defensive line and another chance is blown.

The Broncos have had very little ball and have rarely been out of their own half, but when they do get possession, they make us pay. They move the ball through the hands—seven players in total—from the left touchline over the right, then back towards the middle.

Their winger, Denan Kemp, bursts through the middle and scores, and Broncos hooker Mick Ennis ends up in a fight with Billy in the in-goal. Corey Parker lands the conversion. Broncos 12, Storm 0.

At halftime, we're not panicking. We never do. We're so confident in our own ability. It doesn't matter what the game situation is, or the score. We know that if we keep chipping away, we'll always be in the contest. That's how we've trained. We've got a tough edge from all those hard yards, all those preseasons.

And we're going to need that tough edge, because the second half turns into mayhem.

The Broncos spin it wide from the get-go, and Justin Hodges skips around GI, who has rushed up out of the line. Hodgo passes inside to Locky, but he drops the ball.

It's not a great start for us but, six minutes in, we find our first try. From a penalty in midfield, Cooper runs at the line, then straightens, only slightly, before getting the ball to Billy. That subtle movement from Coops is all that's needed to throw the Broncos' defensive line. Their feet are planted. If Coops keeps running out, they will just shuffle along and adjust their line. When he straightens slightly, they think for a second that he's coming back inside. Then he goes back out, leaving them flat-footed.

That gives Billy the opportunity to come into the backline and create an overlap for Izzy.

We aren't big on overly exquisite plays at the Storm. Coops and Billy are very good at their structures, but we're not known for our trick shots. We keep it simple.

Our target is Izzy: give him space and get him one on one with his opponent, Joel Moon. He gets around Moon, then motors past Darius Boyd, who chases, but Izzy passes inside to Crock, who races away to score under the posts, untouched.

I kick the conversion, and just like that, we're back. Broncos 12, Storm 6.

No sooner have we grabbed the momentum, though, than we give it straight back. Anthony Quinn knocks on from dummy half. Then GI gives the Broncos a tackle restart while on the attack when he knocks on while attempting an intercept. The ball finds Darius on the wing, and he bounces off defender after defender like a pinball and dives over.

'Check grounding first,' Hayne instructs his video referees.

The replay reveals that Boyd's arm carrying the ball bounces just short of the line, with Billy somehow sliding underneath him. To be honest, the vision is inconclusive. It could go either way.

Harrigan and Simpkins send the decision back to Hayne: 'Ref's call.' Hayne says it's held up.

The momentum swings back and forth, until the 53rd minute, when we look like we've scored one of the greatest tries in finals history. On the last tackle, I run to the line and grubber into the in-goal. It looks like it's going dead, but Matty Geyer races through, dives through the air, and with one hand knocks the ball back into the in-goal.

It's still alive but looks like it's about to go into touch in-goal, before Quinny dives and knocks it back towards the tryline, just like Boofa has. That's where GI is standing, with no Broncos player near him. He picks up the ball inches from the ground, and scores a miracle try.

Again Hayne sends it up to the video referee. They take countless looks at whether the ball has gone dead or into touch, but mostly they focus on whether GI is standing in front of me. It looks like he's behind me when I get foot to ball, but it's not clear because of the camera angle. After what feels like an eternity, the try is disallowed, the crowd roars and the greatest try never scored is quickly forgotten.

Now the two forward packs start ripping into each other. The Broncos defence swarm all over Adam Blair. Then Crock clips Kemp slightly high and an all-in brawl starts. When things settle down, Hayne warns our side—and I point out that Ennis had done similar without punishment earlier in the half.

Then, in the 58th minute, something happens that changes the course not just of the game, but of our entire season.

Sam Thaiday is carrying the ball, and Jeremy Smith and I race in to shut him down. I end up around Sam's head, while Jezza is under his arm. Another all-in erupts, with players coming in from everywhere. Crock is prepared to take on the entire Broncos team if necessary.

When things calm down, the touch judges come in. They call out Crock and Brett White. 'This player has held back the player by the neck, there's no need for it, but it's just a caution,' Matt Cecchin says, referring to Whitey, who wasn't even involved in the tackle. Whitey gets cautioned and then waved away. So is Crock for coming into the fight and hitting someone high. 'I want you to tell your team if I see any more around the head or neck area, blokes may sit down,' Hayne says.

'Is that first contact?' I ask.

'And second contact,' Hayne replies. 'Don't touch the head.'

'Sweet, mate.'

At the time, I didn't think much of the incident. Nothing was put on report.

A few tackles later, Locky drops the ball but Ennis is down in back play, rolling around on the ground looking like he's seriously injured. The touch judges come in again, and Jeff Lima is sent to the sinbin for ten minutes for a late shot. As he leaves the field, the replay on the big screen shows he barely touched Ennis.

Against us back in Round 4, Ennis had claimed he was the victim of a chicken wing tackle, earned a penalty and was then caught on camera winking to his teammates. He's done it again. Ennis jumps to his feet and looks fine as Corey Parker lands the penalty goal from in front. Broncos 14, Storm 6.

Even now, down by eight points and with only twelve men on the field, there is no panic in our team. We have some experienced players. Many have played for Australia or their state. If we can hold our nerve, we know the points will come—and in the 63rd minute they do.

We're twenty metres out after Izzy found space on the right. The ball comes to Coops, who kicks high and towards the left upright. Billy soars above four Broncos players, grabs hold of it and scores.

With a player in the sinbin, scoring one try is as good as two at any other time.

Billy asks for that play almost every set. 'Put a grubber through,' he'll say. 'No!' I'll bark back. 'Not now.' He's all about risk. He doesn't mind taking it on because he can see tries. I'm more selective, because where Billy sees tries, I see Bellyache's angry face. So I'm conservative. Cooper's somewhere in between. But that try shows exactly what Billy can do.

I kick the conversion. Broncos 14, Storm 12.

The play goes back and forth, up and down the field. One minute, Karmichael Hunt almost goes over. The next, he's fielding a Cooper kick on his own tryline.

Now Lima is on the sideline, with officials standing next to him with their stopwatches. He's about to come back on. On the fourth tackle, I decide to run from dummy half and get tackled. Instead of me at dummy half for the last tackle, Dallas Johnson finds himself there—and he knocks on. With ten minutes left, it's a critical play.

Still, we survive. Here's a chance on the right again. Izzy is still our go-to guy. We've got an overlap. We take it that way, but he fumbles Billy's pass and another chance goes begging.

On the next set, in the 74th minute Locky doesn't wait until the last to kick. He notices Billy out of position, and places it perfectly into the in-goal. The Broncos pounce on Billy and force a line drop-out. It's a quality play from a champion player. A real professional. In these circumstances, it's as good as points.

I need to do something similar. We need the ball back. If they get possession here, they're a chance of scoring—and if that happens, we're gone. And if they convert, they're up by eight and it's game over.

I get ready for the drop-out. I spot some space on the right. None of the Broncos are set. The short kick is on here . . . Instead, I put it over the sideline, into Row 8. If anything, I hit the ball too well. I was trying to hit it lower and shorter.

In the grandstand, Bellyache puts his head in his hands. I go down on my haunches and shake my head. The boys try to console me but I walk away. I'm shattered. I'm convinced I've cost us the game. The Broncos will surely take two points from the penalty and it's all over.

Unbelievably, the Broncos take the tap. My mind is racing. 'I have to do something here,' I think. 'I've nearly lost us the game. I need to change it.'

As soon as Mick Ennis comes out of dummy half, and takes a couple of steps, I know I'm allowed to attack the ball because he's cleared the ruck. I race up from marker and slap it out of his hands. The ball comes loose. I jump on it. 'You beauty!' I think.

Then, two tackles later, Matty Geyer—in his 22nd finals appearance—loses the ball in the tackle. Now I am panicking.

There's only three minutes left. The Broncos are on their last tackle, metres out from the line. Ennis darts out from dummy half and finds Ben Hannant, who charges over. It looks like he's scored. Suncorp explodes. In the coaches' box, the usually reserved Bennett is on his feet with his arms in the air. Hannant nods to Lockyer, confirming he got it down, but Hayne sends it once more to the video referee.

Here comes the replay . . . Billy Slater is a genius! He's slid underneath the ball again and kept it from touching the ground. We're still alive, but only just.

We're coming off our line, but these are hard metres. The Broncos have been given the chance to set their line and can get up into us. But we do well, working our way downfield to their 30-metre line by the time we're on the last tackle of the set. There's space on the left so we go that way. It finds Billy, who slips through a small gap in the line—but he loses control and knocks on.

Two minutes left. What a game. And we're still not done. We're looking for one last chance—it's all we need.

Kemp runs it up and is tackled. Parker runs it up and gets tackled. Now Ashton Sims charges at the line. Sika Manu and Izzy hit him hard and dislodge the ball. This is it. We've got one minute to score the match-winner.

We work it left, then back towards the middle. Sika has a great run forward, and offloads to Crock, who is tackled right near the uprights.

We're desperate. We put it through the hands. There's space and numbers on the left. I fire a long pass to Cronk. He draws Lockyer and passes to Jeremy Smith. He draws Hodges and passes to Geyer. He draws Kemp and passes to Inglis . . .

Earlier that year, GI had come back from the off-season looking like he'd swallowed a sheep, with his hair and facial hair grown out. Now, he looks lean and fit as he dives over in the corner to score the try that puts us ahead for the first time in 80 minutes.

We hug each other as the Broncos players collapse on the ground. The siren sounds. Bellyache is in the coaches' box with his arms in the air in triumph.

That's the Melbourne Storm for you, in one match. We know we can hold on until the very end. We back ourselves—especially our defence. We're not a side that will let the opposition score twenty while we score 24. Our mindset: 'We'll keep you to ten, and we'll score twelve.' As soon as Craig took over, three-quarters of our training was on defence, and this is the result.

As I line up the sideline conversion, the Broncos fans are hanging over the fence, giving it to me. They do that all the time. I've learned to shut it out. It's all white noise, especially after a victory like that. My kick goes wide but it doesn't matter.

Storm 16, Broncos 14.

7

GUILTY

The 2008 semi-final against Brisbane was the greatest match I played in. For sheer drama and excitement, I can't recall another like it. But it was also the match that I'll long remember as the most controversial.

In the post-match media conference, Channel Nine's Andrew Voss made a real point about the tackle Jeremy Smith and I made on Sam Thaiday. Usually the reporters harp on about an incident with a few questions, then move on. But Vossy made a big deal of it. We'd just played in the best game of footy that season, if not in recent years, but he kept hammering us with questions about that tackle. Clearly, they must have spoken about it a lot in Nine's coverage of the game.

'Geez, he went on about that tackle,' I said to Bellyache as we left the press conference.

By the time we arrived back in Melbourne the next day, the

incident was all over the papers, all through the TV news. And from there it essentially became a circus.

When the charge sheet dropped the next day, Jezza was charged with a grade-one contrary conduct charge of unnecessary contact with the head or neck. I was charged with the same offence—but mine was a whole lot more complicated.

Normally, under the NRL's grading system, an early guilty plea to a grade-one charge will get you off. The problem was that I had 93 carryover points from an incident in Round 1 against the Warriors.

I'd wanted to fight the charge at the time. I'd made a tackle on Brent Tate, my Queensland teammate, and I was over his back and shoulders. My position was just over his head as well. It wasn't a 'grapple'—I didn't have him around the face or neck. He got up and shoved me because I was holding him down, but there wasn't even a penalty. I wasn't put on report at the time, but they charged me for it.

The club had advised me to take the early plea. 'Mate, they'll make an example of you if you fight it,' Bellyache and our new football manager, Frank Ponissi, advised. 'If you fight it, you'll lose and have to miss a game.'

'But I've done nothing wrong,' I argued. 'This happens every third tackle. This is what happens to me when I get tackled.'

Ultimately, I didn't want to miss a game, so I took the early plea. But those 93 carryover points came back to haunt me in a way I never expected. It meant I was now staring down the barrel of a two-match suspension: and those two matches would be the preliminary final and, if we got through, the grand final.

So it was a no-brainer: I had to contest the charge at the judiciary.

Throughout that year, there had been growing commentary about the Storm's wrestling techniques. Terms like the 'grapple', the 'chicken wing', and the 'rolling pin' were tossed around, like we'd come up with some sinister new way to defend and hurt our opposition. We saw the speculation as a ploy to put us off our game, or to get in the minds of the referees or the Match Review Committee, which hands out punishments for on-field incidents.

In the lead-up to my judiciary hearing, things went to another level. As we were in Melbourne, I had no idea about the interest in the story in the northern states. But I heard some of the commentary, with opposition coaches having plenty to say.

We were playing Cronulla in the preliminary final, so their coach, Ricky Stuart, had a lot to offer. There was even a betting market about whether I would be suspended or not. I was at Winx-like odds—$1.10—to be rubbed out.

When I talked to Dad, I told him I felt confident about getting off.

'Expect the worst, hope for the best,' he said.

Then we spoke about the odds being offered.

'I'll just say the bookies rarely get it wrong,' he said. 'They know what's going on.'

That didn't give me a lot of confidence. I felt I had a good case, but when the market had me at such short odds to be suspended, I didn't like my chances.

The other person I spoke to was Sam Thaiday. 'I've been charged over that tackle on you, Sammy,' I said. 'Do you think there was any intention in it? Do you think I meant to hurt you?'

'No, of course not,' Sam said. 'I didn't even know you'd done it to me.'

We were on a collision course with the Sea Eagles. We'd beaten them in the decider the year before, and we were on track to play them again in the grand final—provided each club got through the preliminary finals. There was a market on the outcome of my hearing and opposition coaches had given their opinion in the media.

We flew up to Sydney for the hearing and drove to NRL headquarters at Fox Studios in Moore Park. As we approached the building, we were met by a sea of cameras and reporters. 'Holy hell,' I thought. 'What's this?'

Once we got inside, I became quite nervous. I'd never been to the judiciary before. I'd been suspended, but I'd never fronted a hearing to fight a charge. It felt like I was on trial for murder. The hearing was held in a quiet room. There were three judiciary members—former players Darrell Williams, Royce Ayliffe and Darren Britt—the chairman, the prosecutor, and my legal team, which was headed by Geoffrey Bellew QC.

'Hang on,' I thought. 'We're talking about a tackle here, aren't we? In a game of rugby league?'

When the hearing got underway, five replays in ultra-slow motion were shown to the room, which I felt exaggerated what had happened. It made the tackle look far worse than what it was. The point I wanted to argue was that I'd released Sam's chin as soon as I knew I had hold of it. I'd never put him in a dangerous position. I'd grabbed his chin looking for a lever. When I realised what it was, I let go.

'I thought it was the wrong thing,' I said when it was my turn to speak. 'But my first action is to release Sam. I released almost immediately. The contact with his head area was less than one second. I stepped away from the tackle and the next contact was with his armpit.'

Peter Kite, the NRL prosecutor, grilled me. 'You first of all gave [his head] a pretty good yank to pull him back?' Kite asked during cross-examination.

'That's right,' I replied. 'But if you play the footage back in real time, I don't know how fast you want me to release.'

'You pulled him back by his head, correct?' Kite continued.

'I don't believe there was force made to his head,' I said. 'There's a lot of tackles in our game with contact to the head. At the time, I thought I was not putting Sam in any danger, I was not breaking any rules.'

The thing with the tackle is that he was trying to get to his 'front'. Sam was well known for surrendering in the tackle, so he could get up and make a quick play-the-ball. I didn't have control of the tackle—and I was trying to get control. That was part of what I was trying to argue.

It frustrated me that very few of the replays were shown in real time. They tried to suggest that I had control of Sam's head for an eternity, when actually it was less than a second, and then my hand was off. I didn't have him in an extended hold around the neck, stopping him from breathing, or trying to rip his head off his shoulders.

I felt we were making a good case. Then I looked across the room at the panel members. Several times when I was describing my account of the tackle, I saw only one of the men taking notes. The other two were not, which gave me the impression they'd already made up their minds about my guilt. They were sitting at a desk, facing directly across, but it felt like they weren't listening to what I had to say.

After what seemed like a marathon hearing, both parties gave concluding remarks and left the room so the three panel members could arrive at a verdict. As we left, the judiciary chairman, Paul Conlon, followed us out.

'You've got a great chance to get off here,' he told us. 'I thought that was a great defence.'

When he said that, my mood changed. 'I'm a chance here,' I thought.

Just seventeen minutes later we were called back in. After what Conlon had said, and the short turnaround, we figured the result must be going our way. One of the biggest judiciary hearings of the year, and it had taken them only that long to arrive at a verdict. They had realised the tackle was an accident . . .

Guilty.

I was completely shattered when I heard the word. First, because I didn't feel what I did was worthy of a suspension. Second, I was now going to let down my teammates in the biggest two games of the season. I felt like an arsehole.

'I am very disappointed at the outcome,' I said to the media as I left that evening. 'I still feel that when I play the game, the game I love, I play with the utmost integrity.'

When I got home, I received a lot of support. Barb was great. So were Bellyache and Frank Ponissi. The message from them was: 'You're still part of this squad, and we need you to be up. If you want to play a role in helping us take this out, we need you around.'

There was a triple blow for the preliminary final against Cronulla at Allianz Stadium. Jeremy Smith was missing after making an early plea for his involvement in the Thaiday tackle, but Ryan Hoffman had been ruled out for the rest of the season with an ankle injury that would later require surgery.

That was frustrating too. I was fit and ready to play, but I wasn't allowed to. At least I could still be around the team and train and help out wherever possible.

Around the boys, I remained upbeat. Privately, I was crushed. The times away from training were the hardest because all I thought about was the suspension. I couldn't get the thought out of my mind that the boys would get through and I wouldn't be a part of it.

It was heartbreaking. Having played in the previous two grand finals, I knew how good it was. I just wanted to be there. I was the captain and I wanted to help my footy side. I was letting them down by not being there—it was that simple.

We beat Cronulla 24–0 with Matty Geyer playing hooker. I watched the first half in the coaches' box and then moved to the grandstands with Jezza. I was genuinely happy for our boys. It wasn't an option for me to be jealous that I wasn't out there—that's not what our club is about.

In the dressing-room shortly after fulltime, I could see Belly-ache was unhappy as he made his way out the door, heading for the media conference. With our chief executive, Brian Waldron, sitting next to him, he had a lot to say.

'Cameron Smith, ten minutes after the game last week, was hung out to dry,' he announced. 'The press conference got hijacked by some of you guys in the media that had him hung out to dry straightaway. Then it continued for four or five days. Four or five days you ripped into us, and I know it's not all of you, but there's some sections of the media that seem to have an agenda against Melbourne and certainly on the grapple tackle. To pick out a guy for a grapple tackle at this time of year is certainly unfair . . . You guys, when it's a grapple tackle issue with us it's in the paper for five days, and if it's someone else it might be in there for a day and then it's gone. We're just after a fair go, and I don't think Cameron Smith got a fair go.'

Those remarks caused all sorts of problems down the track, but I really appreciated what he had to say. Bellyache had my back.

We tried to turn our attention to preparing for the grand final. Walking around sulking was only going to be a negative for the team. Russell Aitken was given the job as dummy half for the grand final against Manly, who had beaten the Warriors 32–6 in their preliminary final and were in great touch.

I talked to 'Rusty' a lot that week, and he was great about it. He'd only played a handful of first-grade games at that point, so the situation mustn't have been easy for him. But years later, whenever I ran into him, he'd say, 'That was the worst week of your career—but it was my best!' And I got that. I just had to help him manage the week as best as he could. We had a grand final to win.

Apart from helping our new dummy half, my main job during training that week was to be Matt Orford. In our sessions I trained specifically as Manly's halfback, trying to mimic his game, even to put on some of the set plays he'd do and the structures Manly often played to.

When the game came around, I felt horrible. I was very nervous. Throughout my career, I was terrible at watching my own team play, because I had no control whatsoever over the result.

I took my seat next to Hoffy in the front row of the grandstand, down on the fence at ANZ Stadium. Just before the teams ran out, the cameras flashed to me and my face appeared on the big screen. Of the 82,000 people there, at least 75,000 of them gave it to me. 'That's not good,' I thought. I was determined not to give a reaction and just cop it. So I did.

We trailed 8–0 at halftime but I felt we could still win it. Then Manly scored straight after the break and kept rolling through the points from there. In the end, it got really ugly: 40–0.

The team had been through a lot. We'd lost in the first week of the finals to the Warriors, after finishing minor premiers, so that meant we lost all our home advantage. We travelled to Brisbane and beat the Broncos on the bell. Then I was suspended. Jezza was suspended. We travelled to Sydney and beat the Sharks, but the whole of grand final week was taken up with the drama of what Bellyache had said in the media conference, and what others were saying about our team.

It's easy to say, 'Boys, just worry about the things you can control.' But we're human beings: you hear things, you read things—you can't escape everything. All of that used up a lot of our energy.

After fulltime, I had one thought: to get out onto the field and console my teammates. But when you're suspended, you can't enter the field of play at all—even when it's over.

'Have I served my two matches now?' I asked an NRL official. 'Is my suspension over?'

I didn't wait for a reply and walked out onto the field anyway.

•

When I look back and think about it now, missing the final two matches of the 2008 season makes me feel crook in the guts. Seeing how the game has evolved, how the judiciary and grading system has changed, and also what penalties some players get now for some pretty bad tackles, it makes me sick to think I missed a preliminary and grand final for that minor indiscretion.

What also hurts is that the NRL changed the grading system one year later. Now, for every match played, five carryover points are taken off. Under that system, I would've missed the preliminary final but played in the grand final.

It doesn't matter how many matches I played: these are the big games that I will never get back.

8

GRAPPLED

The events of September 2008 whipped the hysteria about the Melbourne Storm and our so-called wrestling techniques into a frenzy.

There had been growing reports that season about our defensive tactics, although the first story actually dates back to that 2003 semi-final when we played the Raiders in Canberra—my first ever playoffs match. The referee that day, Tim Mander, blew three early penalties against us for holding down in the play-the-ball area, and then warned our captain, Steve Kearney, about contact with the head.

Bellyache had known it was coming because he'd heard a few days earlier that Canberra had spoken to the NRL.

'It's a thing the Raiders were a bit worried about during the week, and they actually spoke to the league about it from what I can gather,' Bellamy said at the media conference. 'It's been happening all year. If they are going to start penalising that, they can penalise in every tackle. I just don't understand why they started on it tonight. Why they want to pick on us because the opposition staff want to complain to the referees or to the league about it, that just astounds me.'

The more success we had as a club, the more rival coaches complained, or the more stories seemed to come out. Every few weeks, a new wrestling technique was invented, and it just happened to come out of a Melbourne Storm game. The grapple tackle. The chicken wing. The rolling pin. The prowler. The crusher. The cannonball. We would read the stories and laugh, because we'd never heard any of these terms.

In 2008 it became ridiculous, though, as rival coaches and officials used the media or complained to the NRL in order to gain an advantage by unsettling either us or the referee. The stories would usually surface ahead of a really big game—or after we'd had a big win.

'The game's rugby league, you tackle people, you don't wrestle,' Wayne Bennett said after the Storm beat the Broncos at Olympic Park in April that year.

Ricky Stuart, who was coach of Australia and the Sharks that season, wrote several columns questioning our tactics. Or he would raise the issue in radio interviews. 'The month or six-week period where the referees are jumping on top of it is over,' he told Sky Sports Radio in the lead-up to the finals in 2008. 'Now they're [Melbourne] back into it again and it's coming into the most important stage of the season. There's a technique on how they attack the head, and they're getting away with it again.'

Was wrestling a Melbourne Storm thing? For as long as I've been involved in the game, every team has had a wrestling coach. When I played State of Origin for Queensland in 2003, we had wrestling coaches there—and Wayne Bennett, one of the greatest so-called opponents of the wrestle, was our coach. The wrestling coach was Chris Haseman, who had been working with the Broncos since 1998.

But it can be traced back further. Frank Ponissi was on the coaching staff at Manly in the mid-1990s, and he has a copy of the club's 1996 annual report that shows a man called Norm Steel was the club's 'wrestling coach' at the time. Des Hasler, the Manly coach in 2008, was still playing for them back then. The Melbourne Storm didn't even exist.

All these coaches deny they use them, but we watched and played a lot of rugby league in 2008 and I can say every team was doing what we were doing. What they probably didn't like was that we just did it better, and more effectively. If anything, the criticism we received was a compliment.

There's a difference between dirty play that hurts an opponent and slowing down the ruck. Craig wanted our defence to evolve so we wouldn't just tackle someone and lay all over them. We were looking at ways to move players onto their back, or other positions, to allow our defence more time to get set. It's groundwork that every team does.

The person charged with doing that for the Storm was John Donahue, a Brazilian jujitsu instructor. John is a very quiet bloke. If you walked past him in the street, you wouldn't know what he did for a living, or that he knew the art of combat sports. You couldn't pick it. In all the years I've known him, he's never raised his voice in an aggressive manner.

When it comes to rugby league tactics, Bellyache is very basic. He's never introduced any sort of set plays; it's always been about getting the basics right. That's why he employed John to work with us: so we could do one of the fundamentals of the game—defence—better than anyone else. The cornerstone of the club wasn't just effort and attitude. It was also repetition. Do it so often that it becomes second nature. No matter what the situation, even under fatigue, we knew what to do.

John never used terms like 'grapple', 'chicken wing' or 'rolling pin'. Those were all terms created by the media. Nor was there ever a time when John said, 'Grab an arm and try to rip it off.' That has never happened. Rather, they were techniques we used when a player running the ball was trying to find his 'front'.

Every ball-carrier is trying to find his front—that is, to position himself square to the opposition's tryline so he can get a quick play-the-ball. We came up with techniques to legally slow him down—to stop them getting to their front in order to gain an advantage.

To learn a technique like that, we needed to train on each other. There was never a time in a defensive session when someone was injured by the things that we'd practised. None of our tackling or wrestling techniques were dangerous to the opposition, because we had to use them on each other over and over to become good at it.

In April 2008, a former Storm player, Brett O'Farrell, came out in the media and said that John Donahue had once put him in a sleeper hold and 'put him to sleep' during the preseason in 2004. He also said that we had tried to 'hide and conceal' that we were being taught by John to do 'grapple tackles'.

I feel comfortable elaborating on the first claim because I was about two metres away from it when it happened. We were doing our weekly session with John at his studio. He wanted to show us a new technique he wanted us to work on, to slow down the play-the-ball. When we worked on new techniques like this, it would be slow and quite mechanical.

On this day he asked Brett to come into the middle to demonstrate. He was talking us through how to position a player on the ground. As he tried to move Brett, Brett resisted and fought against him. John quickly tied him up in a little hold, showing him who was boss. All the boys were laughing. There was some good banter.

John let him go and let Brett walk away, but then Brett came charging at him from behind. I don't know if it was serious or Brett was just trying get a few more laughs out of the boys, but John had enough—he got Brett in a sleeper hold and put him to sleep for two or three seconds. Nobody mucked around when John was trying to introduce a new technique again.

All the boys were really dirty when Brett came out and criticised us like that. He was trying to throw John and our club under the bus. He knew there was never any discussion about how we could inflict injury on a rival player. It was about efficiency in defence.

The simple fact was that we spent more time than other clubs working on our defence, and in particular on how we transitioned from making contact with a ball-carrier to taking him to the ground. We invested a lot of time in getting him to the ground, to make him get up before playing the ball.

When we first started working with John, I listened closely and practised the techniques that helped me. It was beneficial for me because I was giving away a lot of size to the blokes I was playing against.

Before Michael Maguire became a premiership-winning coach at South Sydney, he was an assistant for several years to Craig. He was the one who nicknamed me 'The Accountant' because of my unspectacular physique. I always had natural strength, but because of my size I had to find other ways to bring down and then hold down the big boys in the middle of the field, where I defended.

Later in my career, some people came up with another term for me: 'The Octopus'. I assume they were talking about my ability to get tangled up with the ball-carrier as the tackle is being made. I didn't see myself as an octopus, but I placed a lot of emphasis on my defensive work, especially my groundwork, to slow the play-the-ball. As a dummy half, I knew how important that was.

I'll admit that now more than ever there's a possibility for things to go wrong—especially with the third man coming in. When you have two defenders holding up the ball-carrier, and 'waltzing' him, as they say, as the defence gets back onside, it's dangerous when a third player comes charging in for the 'prowler' or 'cannonball'. The ball-carrier is more vulnerable than ever with that type of tackling technique. That's where the emphasis is on the third defender to be cautious when coming in, to make sure they don't tackle too low, and with too much force.

Another factor that has made these tackling techniques necessary is the change in body shape of the modern-day footballer—the size and strength of players, and their greater ability to offload the football. Coaching, training and the athleticism of the bigger men have all evolved so much.

I look at video from my early years in the NRL and can see it. Forwards would get the ball, pick a defender's shoulder to run at, come off their left or right foot, and that was about it. The big blokes were taught to get the ball and run hard. As a defender, you'd go in with whichever shoulder you wanted, go low and hit him.

That changed as players changed. These days, if someone of my size went low, one on one with someone, the percentage for me to make that tackle would be low. I couldn't tackle the likes of Payne Haas, Sam Burgess and Andrew Fifita in that way. They had a left-foot step, a right-foot step, a fend, an offload. I wouldn't know until they were half a metre away what they were going to do.

Everyone now is taught to make contact high on the ball-carrier's body, wrap up the ball, stop the momentum and then wait for your teammates to help complete the tackle. They hit his legs and together you take him to ground. That's the theory of modern-day defence.

That's how the game has evolved—and defence has had to evolve with it. Teams that don't defend in this way, or don't do it well, struggle. Souths, Roosters, Manly—all the teams that have been successful in the last decade or so have generally been the best defensive sides—and it's because of their ability to control the ruck.

The best at it at the Storm over the years were Brett White and Adam Blair—they were very good at the groundwork. They enjoyed defending and took pride in winning tackles. That's a stat now: whether you've won the tackle or not. At other clubs, North Queensland's Josh McGuire is great at it. There are plenty of players who are good at it. When you played these guys, or watched them, you could tell they had done plenty of work on their technique.

Towards the end of my career, I didn't do as much work on it as I once did. I did contact work, but not as much because I had to preserve my accountant-like body. In the early days, we'd be doing it every Tuesday for an hour in the preseason, plus some of our Saturday session. Again, that's Craig's training philosophy: if you want to be good at something, and consistently good, you have to do a lot of it.

People who complained about my so-called wrestling techniques haven't seen my disciplinary record. After being suspended in 2008, I was charged only four more times during my career—and I missed just one more match through suspension. That's not much across a twenty-year career, in over 500 NRL and representative matches, while playing in the middle of the field and making all those tackles. Only one of those charges since 2008 related to contrary conduct for contact with the head or neck.

The tackle that caused a lot of controversy late in my career didn't even attract a charge. Referee Ben Cummins penalised me after a tackle on Raiders winger Bailey Simonsson in Round 22 of 2019, in a match against Canberra at Canberra Stadium.

'I just wanted some clarification as to what that penalty was for there,' I asked Cummins.

'Rubbish on the face, mate,' Cummins said. 'And it was you.'

'Rubbish on the face?' I laughed. 'Okay, no worries.'

'I can only say it so many times,' he continued. 'I can't tell you any more.'

This was news to me, because nothing had been discussed at all. The allegation that followed in the days to come was that I had tried to squeeze Simonsson's temples in the tackle. I wasn't charged by the Match Review Committee. Instead, I received a 'concerning act notice'.

I remember the tackle clearly. Simonsson took the ball one off the ruck. After the initial contact, I had hold of his jersey and tried to rip him down. From one of the still images taken from the TV coverage, it looks like I've got hold of his ear. But it wasn't his ear—it was his jumper.

When the penalty was given, he just ran back to his position. If someone grabbed hold of my ear like that, I know how I'd react. But he didn't react at all. Let's be realistic: if someone grabbed your ear that hard, where your knuckles are white because you are squeezing them so hard, you're not just getting up and having zero reaction.

I laughed at some of the commentary. 'You can see his ears between his knuckles, and his knuckles are going white.'

Of course they were! I was holding down a bloke who weighed 100 kilograms and he was trying to get up. It's not touch football.

I had a hold of his jersey. He was down on the ground. If you think about it, your body follows your head. I had a grip on his jersey and tried to hold it over his head. If your head is stuck on the ground, you can't get up and play the ball. I don't know why people would say I was trying to push his temples, but I can assure you that was not the case.

Now they had a new dirty tactic from the Melbourne Storm: the 'wingnut'. There was little mention of Canberra's English forward, John Bateman, doing something similar to me in a tackle just before the Simonsson tackle. My head was nearly twisted off my shoulders, but that didn't seem to matter much to the Storm's critics in Sydney.

Wrestling is now part of the game. It's even creeping into junior football. I don't necessarily think that's a good thing. I played junior football because it was fun. Senior football is much more serious. You need to employ tactics to win and get good results. And controlling the ruck is a big part of the game. It always has been. When I watch classic matches from twenty years ago or more, I can see the wrestling techniques used back then. It might not have been coached like it is now, but it was there. And in fact the game was more dangerous then, what with spear tackles, punching, head-high tackles and so on.

With the evolution of the game, new skills have been developed and new tactics employed by all clubs. Slowing down the play-the-ball was just one of them.

9

THE BIG 25

Brett Finch had never liked me. He liked me even less when Mick Crocker asked me to be the MC at his wedding. Finchy thought it should have been him and was filthy he didn't get the gig.

Crock married his long-time partner Sally on the Sunshine Coast on a stinking-hot day in December 2008. The ceremony was on the beach, Clint Newton was his best man and Billy Slater the only other groomsman. Then the reception was held under a marquee near the surf club.

I started off my MC duties with some housekeeping, then I introduced the bride and groom, and then entrees were served. Later, we started the speeches, with some long-time mates of Crock having something to say—including Finchy.

Finchy didn't have a great opinion of me at that time, even though he didn't know me. We'd played against each other, but I think he disliked me because of the success we'd had at the

Storm and Queensland. The teams I was involved in happened to win all the time. Now I'd been given the role of MC at his good mate's wedding. *How does he get a start over me? I've known Crock longer than this bloke . . .*

When he was doing his speech, the microphone kept cutting out. It did it about three or four times, yet he pushed through and got it done. Everyone had a laugh, as you often do whenever you're around Finchy.

When he got back to his table, he was furious. He blamed me for the microphone problems. *It's Smith! He's sabotaged me!*

Neither he nor I could have imagined that less than four months later, he'd be leaving Parramatta after a fallout with coach Daniel Anderson and joining the Storm on a one-year deal.

'I hated you before I met you,' Finchy said to me soon after he arrived at the Storm. 'I never knew you, but you always had this smug look about winning all the time. And you sabotaged the mic at Crock's wedding!'

As the 2009 season played out, with Parramatta paying for him to play at our club after giving him an early release, Finchy and I became really close.

He was an important addition to our squad, because his arrival meant we now had a genuine five-eighth. Greg Inglis moved out to the centres, where he was just as devastating with the ball, given the time and space he now had.

Players like Finchy are what the Melbourne Storm is all about. It has never been about the big-name players, but every player in the squad. That has long been the philosophy of our club. It's something Bellyache fostered.

We were far more than the 'Big Four', a term the media came up with for the quartet of Slater, Inglis, Cronk and me. It seemed a funny term then, and it still feels strange to think of it now. There was never a time when we referred to ourselves as the 'Big Four', or even the 'Big Three' after GI left the club. We were four dominant players who played in key positions, but we never put that sort of label on ourselves. We were four players in a squad of 25—and under Bellyache, no player was more important than any other. So it was just a convenient label the media came up with, but the fans grabbed hold of it and ran with it.

In many ways, our club had been lucky. It was pure chance that Billy, Cooper and I ended up together at Norths Devils. Then they scouted this freak of a talent in GI. The Storm had had their eye on him since he was fourteen, as did a dozen other clubs. We were the ones who got him.

Heading into the 2009 season, we had internationals like Ryan Hoffman, Adam Blair and Dallas Johnson. But we knew that the guys who liked to roll up their sleeves and get to work—like Ryan Hinchcliffe, Aidan Tolman, Jeff Lima, Steve Turner and many others—would be just as crucial if we were to avenge our grand final loss from the season before.

And that was firmly on our minds. That was our motivation: the 40–0 loss to Manly. The mindset was very similar to what we had after losing the 2006 grand final to the Broncos.

For those guys who'd taken part in the 2008 decider, there was something to really play for. They were hungry and had a point to prove. Even though I hadn't played in the grand final, I felt the loss as much as anyone. Maybe more.

The one major departure was Israel Folau, who had left us to join the Broncos on a lucrative contract. I was gutted to lose him. I knew how close he was with his family, who were based in Brisbane, so I understood his reasons for going. But he was such a great talent, and I knew he could have had a long, successful career at our club. I was surprised he left.

I was more surprised when he left rugby league altogether, departing the Broncos at the end of the 2010 season to become a marquee signing for Greater Western Sydney Giants, a new AFL team in 2011. I didn't question the move publicly at the time because he was my mate. It was his decision and I respected it. To be honest, there were six million reasons for him to swap codes—most of them dollars!—but he just didn't seem suited to AFL. He was never the best endurance trainer—terrible, in fact. He was a power athlete, which was why he excelled in rugby league, particularly when leaping into the air. For the AFL he was more of a marketing tool. As a league fan, I was upset that we'd lost a genuine superstar. We never got him back.

Unlike the previous three seasons, when we'd won the minor premiership, the Storm didn't dominate the home-and-away rounds in 2009, finishing fourth. That meant we played the fifth-placed team in the qualifying final, held at Etihad Stadium in the first week of the playoffs.

Who do you reckon finished fifth? You guessed it: Manly. As soon as I realised it was the Sea Eagles first up, I thought, 'Perfect.' The boys thought it was perfect too.

In the last few years, Bellyache has talked about how I had a 'steely look' in my eye when I walked into the dressing-room before that match. 'There was a look in his eye that I've never seen before,' he said. 'And I haven't seen it since.'

I couldn't tell you what my eyes looked like, but I know what was going on in my head. I'd never felt more driven to win a football match in my career.

In the dressing-room before most games, I was quite jovial. Some guys aren't like that, but I enjoyed a chat and a joke. The work had been done during the week. I knew well before game day what would be required. That's why I was relaxed.

But when I came into the rooms at Etihad Stadium that night, I barely spoke a word to anyone. 'I missed out on last year's preliminary and grand final, so I'm going to make this count,' I was thinking. 'You're not going to take this one away from me.'

We couldn't have played any better that night, winning 40–12 with Billy scoring four tries. The other results over the weekend also fell our way, with the third-placed Gold Coast Titans losing to the Broncos, and the minor premiers, St George Illawarra, getting beaten by eighth-placed Parramatta.

The Eels had been struggling mid-season but turned it around with a seven-match winning streak mainly because of one player: their fullback, Jarryd Hayne, who'd just won the Dally M Medal, and then almost single-handedly beat the Dragons, including a brilliant solo try in which he beat six players.

As the finals series went on, as the Eels and Storm kept winning, it became clearer that we'd have to shut Hayne down if we were going to win the 2009 premiership.

•

Parramatta was much more than just one player. They had big Tongan prop Fuifui Moimoi, who could be very hard to handle in his day. They also had Nathan Hindmarsh, one of the most experienced forwards in the NRL and the heart and soul of the famous Parramatta club, who were desperate to win a premiership before he retired.

There were a lot of blokes around Jarryd doing their job, but he was their biggest threat. He just exploded in the second half of the season. He was almost untouchable, scoring freakish tries. Everything he did seemed to come off, and you almost couldn't tackle him.

I'd first met him at the end of 2006, his rookie season, when coach Ricky Stuart picked him in the Kangaroos squad for the Tri-Nations, but Jarryd didn't play in any of the matches.

There was never any doubting his talent, although he did in the early stages of his career struggle under adversity and pressure. But in the final ten weeks of the 2009 season, he caught fire. It was little wonder that most of our preparation in grand final week was around defending Jarryd and trying to minimise his impact on the game.

Bellyache spoke about trying to blunt his influence. Jarryd was most dangerous when he had space and time. He wanted you to stand back and wait for him to do his thing. He wanted to dictate to you, rather than you dictate to him. He'd also bulked up that year and was very strong, fending off defenders almost at will.

We knew all that. We knew he was a very good ball-runner who had pace and power, so our plan was simple: 'If he gets the ball, someone has to go at him.'

Nobody was specifically given the job of doing that in the grand final, because he was popping up everywhere, breaking the line through the ruck, on the edges, chasing kicks and getting onto them and scoring. We just put a huge emphasis on making sure we were aware of where he was when he had the ball—and that anytime he got the ball in his hands, someone went and got him. After that defender went at him, the next one had to follow, and the next one after that, until we smothered him.

In the first half, we suffocated him out of the game just as we planned, driving him backwards and pinning him down whenever he got the ball. Our first try came after just four minutes, with Finchy putting Hoffy through a hole with a beautiful short ball. We then absorbed a lot of Eels pressure, but as soon as we got possession we were in again, this time after Cooper threw a dummy, pushed off Eels prop Tim Mannah and broke through the line to put Adam Blair over.

At 10–0, we felt like we were in control. But it was a grand final, and they had Jarryd Hayne, so we knew it wasn't over until the final siren. Although Eels winger Eric Grothe Jr scored early in the second half, we looked to have control of the match after GI and Billy scored tries to give us a 22–6 lead with 24 minutes left on the clock.

But the Eels refused to give up. Joel Reddy latched onto a high ball in the 70th minute, and when Luke Burt kicked the conversion from out wide, they had a sniff. As we ran back into position, Fuifui was on the sideline, desperate to get back on and give the Eels one last crack at us.

What followed was a frantic final ten minutes of the season. From the restart, Parramatta started to throw the ball around. Then they got the ball to Fui, who went on a twenty-metre arcing run to the tryline, knocking over two of our players and then carrying Billy and Steve Turner over the line to score. Burty's conversion attempt just faded away from the right goalpost, but with seven minutes left to play, the Eels were right back in the match at 22–16.

Things weren't made any easier when Jarryd launched a towering bomb soon after and Billy leapt high and knocked on. Luckily, we kept them out, and as we came off our own line, we got a lucky break that would prove decisive.

Billy took a run from dummy half, then tried to play the ball quite quickly. A Parra player clipped Billy as he tried to play the ball—referee Tony Archer ruled an infringement in the ruck and awarded us a penalty. It was a fifty-fifty decision— and it went our way. We kicked for touch, went down their end and then GI kicked a wobbly field goal, which effectively came off his shin, to add another point.

I was usually on top of this stuff, but in that moment I thought we were leading by four points, not six. So while everyone else was congratulating GI, I didn't even high-five him because I thought we were only five points ahead. I ran straight past him and back to my position for the kick-off, only to realise we were up by seven points.

We tackled out the last couple of minutes and won the grand final. It was the ultimate payback for what had happened the year before, just as we had hoped. Billy won the Clive

Churchill Medal as the best player on the field, but he reckoned it should've gone to Cooper, who had set up two tries and been really dominant.

In truth, it could've gone to anyone. We weren't the Big Four. We were the Big 25. Everyone had played their part.

One of those players who had been critical to our success was Dallas Johnson, who had a year to run on his contract. But late in 2009, when I was in the United Kingdom for the Four Nations tour, he stunned me with a phone call out of the blue.

'I'm not playing next year,' Dallas said. 'I'm going to play for Catalans instead.'

I was shocked. Dallas had played Origins alongside me for Queensland, and a couple of games for Australia. He was as much a part of what the Storm had achieved as any one—we wouldn't have been able to do it without him. He had set the tone for our matches at the start of every game, including that 2009 grand final win.

We had predicted that Parramatta would put Fui on the right side of the field for the kick-off. Because I was a left-foot kicker, most of my kicks went to the right because I could get more purchase on the footy. Coaches can therefore usually predict where you're likely to send the ball from the kick-off.

'Maybe we should kick the other way, to where Nathan Cayless would be standing,' someone suggested in a team meeting in grand final week.

'No, kick it to Fuifui,' Dallas insisted. 'Smithy, kick the ball to him.'

If you watch that first tackle of that grand final, Fui came steaming in off the back fence—and Dallas drove into him. He just put his head down, picked up the big prop and drove him backwards.

Dallas had no thoughts for self-preservation. In one Origin match, he tried something similar on New South Wales prop Brent Kite and knocked himself out from the kick-off. Dallas stumbled around and fell face-first into the turf, but was later allowed back onto the field. That would never happen now because of the strict concussion rules in place.

He suffered many head knocks during his career, and I did become concerned about how it might affect him later in life. Towards the end of his career, he was getting more serious concussions. But his lack of fear was just part of the way he played. That was the way he played as a kid, and it was how he got his start as an NRL player. His strength was being aggressive and inflicting pain on the opposition. He was so mentally strong. His build was only slightly bigger than mine, but he was a tough human being who loved the club and would do anything for us, and the way he put his body on the line in defence was proof of that.

I was happy Dallas could leave the NRL as a winner. I was also really happy for Finchy, who had been pushed out of the Parramatta club earlier in the year. He certainly enjoyed the grand final celebrations—right up until we got to Molly Meldrum's place a few days later.

Molly is an Australian icon, and had been one of the Storm's biggest supporters ever since they entered the competition.

Each year we would have a post-season Christmas party at Molly's house. They have been some really fun and, well, weird times. Molly has some extravagant artworks, sculptures and other bits and pieces around his house. We were told we could do whatever we wanted at his place—but not to touch any of Molly's famous cowboy hats!

The party at Molly's that topped all the others was the one in 2009, which became best known for Finchy's nudie run.

We'd been at Molly's for quite some time, but the evening was getting on and a few people had finished up. All of a sudden Finchy came charging through the house carrying a Storm flag and wearing one of Molly's hats—and nothing else.

Anyone else would have got into a lot of trouble. But Finchy, much like Allan Langer, could get away with anything. If I'd done that, people would have been into me. But because it was Finchy, everyone thought it was hilarious. And it was.

'You know what's even better?' he often said during our celebrations that year. 'Parramatta paid me to beat them in a grand final!'

Winning football games is a lot of fun. You never get tired of it, and you never know when it might end. As we all laughed at Finchy running around Molly Meldrum's place that night wearing nothing but Molly's hat, none of us could have known what was waiting around the corner.

10

GREEN AND GOLD

In October 2006, just days before my international debut for Australia, I received a phone call from Barb. 'Your mum has had a heart attack,' she said.

I could barely speak. It was a mild heart attack, but a heart attack is a heart attack. Typically, Mum had put me first: because I was preparing for such a big game, she had asked everyone not to tell me. 'He needs to concentrate on his footy and I don't want him to know,' she told the rest of the family. 'I don't want him to worry.'

That's just what Mum and Dad are like. They don't want any sympathy, any drama. If things are okay, they just want you to carry on.

But Barb knew me better than anyone. She knew that when I found out post-match what had happened, and realised that nobody had told me, I'd be filthy. She thought the best thing to do would be to tell me.

I'd been named at hooker for the opening match of the Tri-Nations series, to be played against New Zealand at Mount Smart Stadium in Auckland, but this rattled me. Really rattled me. Mum was my first thought, obviously. Was she okay? My family assured me that she was alright, but I was really concerned. I questioned whether playing was the right thing to do. I just wanted to go home and be with her.

Once I spoke to Mum and Dad, and they assured me that the medical advice was she would be fine—she just needed to start taking some medication—I was prepared to take the field. We won 30–18 and I played okay, but Mum was very much in my thoughts.

I was given my start in the green and gold after the incumbent, Danny Buderus, withdrew from the series for personal reasons. He'd announced in August that his fiancée, Kris, was having their first child in November, and naturally he wanted to be there for her.

As I've already explained, Bedsy was a player I hugely admired. Even though I had a great year personally in 2006, and had been awarded the Dally M Medal in September, I was under no illusions about who the Australian hooker would be against the Kiwis and Great Britain. If anything, I felt I was an outside chance of getting picked in the extended 21-man squad. I would've been grateful for that. Maybe I might come off the bench at least.

Then the news broke that Bedsy was standing down for the series, and my chances of making my international debut improved greatly. The fact Queensland had won the year's

Origin series obviously helped too. When I was picked in the squad, though, I still felt fortunate. If Bedsy hadn't made himself unavailable, he would've been picked.

I realised almost straightaway what it meant to wear that jersey. Australia's runaway success over many decades meant there was always an expectation on every national side to win, no matter who they played. The same expectation existed within the team. As soon as you walked into camp, you felt and understood that. We'd all grown up watching the men in the Kangaroos jersey playing to the highest standard. Their legacy was in my mind in every Test match I played. I did not want to be part of the Kangaroos team that lost the honour of being considered the best rugby league team in the world.

Like many my age, when I think about the Kangaroos, I cast my mind back to those early mornings when, as a kid, I'd get up and, still in my pyjamas, watch Australia take on the might of Great Britain. The 1994 Kangaroo tour, which was Mal Meninga's last as a player, stands out for me. Watching them playing in iconic stadiums like Wembley, Old Trafford and Elland Road, with the crowds packed to the rafters, hearing the Poms singing and cheering, was inspiring. 'I'd love to do that one day,' I'd say to my parents.

Playing against Great Britain in those historic stadiums remained my dream, even ahead of playing the Kiwis, although matches against them were always intense. There was something special about representing Australia against England that was embedded deep in my psyche. I guess my other sporting love, cricket, in which the Ashes meant more than any other series, was partly the reason. I just wanted to beat England!

Heading into camp for my first Tri-Nations series was made easier by the fact that there were a group of us making our debuts for Australia: alongside me were Sam Thaiday, Greg Inglis, Anthony Tupou and Jarryd Hayne. It was also Ricky Stuart's first year as Australian coach, after he'd left the Roosters the year before. He'd coached the one-off Anzac Test earlier in the year, but this would be his first series.

'Stick' was one of the game's truly elite players when I was a young fella, so I always had a lot of admiration for him. As halfback for Canberra, he'd played in all the big games, whether it was for the Raiders in grand finals, or for New South Wales (when I hated him!) or for the Kangaroos. I was looking forward to the chance to play under him. His assistant coach was Craig Bellamy—they were former teammates at the Raiders—so that made me a lot more comfortable. Having Craig there would be great for settling my nerves.

Bellyache and Stick showed emotion in different ways. Bellyache was intense at training and extremely passionate about his teams, and on game day he'd have us prepared mentally and physically for the contest, but he was nowhere near as emotional as Stick. He'd reserve that for the coaches' box on game day. Sticky, on the other hand, was emotional from day one, especially about the opposition and what we needed to do to them. We'd talk about the history of the two teams as he built us up emotionally ahead of kick-off.

As I've said, I never played with much emotion. I had a job to do and my emotion came later. But in those representative games, especially in tournaments when we played four or five games at the end of a long NRL season, it was good to have a coach like Stick getting us up for the contest.

The expectation for us to win was running strong during that tournament after Australia, coached by Wayne Bennett, had lost the 2005 Tri-Nations final 24–0 to New Zealand at Elland Road in Leeds. After that loss, a generational change started in the Australian team. In the Anzac Test in April, Johnathan Thurston and Karmichael Hunt made debuts. Seeing those guys getting picked for the mid-season Test gave guys like me something to strive for at the end of the year, and by the time we reached the 2006 Tri-Nations final, again against New Zealand, it was a new-look team in the green and gold jerseys.

Our matches in the lead-up to the decider had been even: we beat the Kiwis in Auckland, then they beat us in Melbourne. The final, played before a great crowd of 30,000 at Allianz Stadium, was similarly close. With eleven minutes to go, and the scores level at 12-all after Kiwi halfback Stacey Jones kicked a penalty goal, it was anyone's game.

The finish was vintage rugby league. In the space of four minutes, Jones missed a field goal attempt, Karmichael threw the ball into touch on our own tryline, and Kiwi fullback Brent Webb missed another field goal attempt that would've won them the tournament.

Suddenly there were only two minutes on the clock. We were deep in our own territory, a long way from field goal range for JT or Locky to snatch victory. I saw that Webb was slightly out of position, so I kicked towards the sideline, aiming for a 40/20. The ball trickled over the sideline, giving us possession, and I figured we'd kick a field goal and that would be it. Instead, JT's attempt was charged down. We had one last chance, in the final minute, with GI looking to have scored a try from a Willie Mason kick. It was disallowed.

Golden point was no less hectic. Locky had another field goal attempt charged down by Webb. Then Jones missed with another attempt. It was going to take something special to break the match apart. It was little wonder that JT was the one to make it happen.

He got the ball inside our half, produced his trademark show-and-go, slipped through the New Zealand defence before passing inside to Locky, who was exactly where he needed to be and scored the match-winning try. Australia 16, New Zealand 12.

It was like Origin all over again—only this time in green and gold. It felt great to be a part of it.

•

Under Sticky, Australia regained its status as the world's best team—and I was determined to hold on to the No. 9 jumper. As soon as Danny Buderus let it go, I backed myself to keep it.

We won the 2007 Anzac Test 30–6 in April. In October that year, I was named captain for the Test against the Kiwis in Wellington; Locky had been ruled out with a knee injury. It was a huge honour to be given the captaincy, even though it felt strange: I captained my country before I captained my state. We won 58–0.

Our form meant we went into the 2008 World Cup, to be held in Australia, as overwhelming favourites. For a rugby league player, this was the pinnacle: winning a World Cup on home soil. And we started accordingly.

We put a score on the Kiwis in the opening match in Sydney, winning 30–6. Then we smashed England in Melbourne, winning 52–4, with Billy scoring four tries. We dusted up Papua New Guinea in Townsville, winning 46–6, to complete our group matches. After beating Fiji 52–0 in the semi-final, we were extremely confident heading into the final against New Zealand.

Perhaps the fact that we'd had a soft run in the lead-up games meant we were underdone, because the Kiwis seemed more battle-hardened than us. We led 10–0 after fifteen minutes but then the match slowly turned away from us.

New Zealand's first try came through Jeremy Smith—my Storm teammate—and it was a worrying sign. We'd spoken about him earlier in the week: how he liked to get the ball ten metres from the tryline and then go on an 'overs' line. 'Don't take any of his shows,' I warned my teammates. He ran the play, showed the ball to a support runner and went through the defensive line to score.

That shifted the momentum. We led 16–12 at halftime but when Kiwi fullback Lance Hohaia scored a converted try in the 47th minute, we were suddenly chasing.

Then came the moment that final will always be remembered for. In the 60th minute, Benji Marshall kicked into our in-goal,

Billy scooped it up and ran down the right touchline. Under pressure from Kiwi winger Manu Vatuvei, he hurled the ball over his shoulder back into the field of play. The only problem was Benji was there waiting for it. He caught it and scored.

That sunk us. The Kiwis went on to win 34–20.

Afterwards, Billy was gutted. We all were. But as much as what happened in that final was a shock, his Storm teammates weren't entirely surprised. All I could do was shrug and say, 'That's Billy!' For all the great things he did for us, there was always the chance of something like that happening.

That's what made Billy so great—he was willing to take on the risky play. High risk but high reward. He's been involved in some ridiculous moments on a footy field. His greatest asset was that he didn't think about negative consequences; he thought about the reward for the team if it came off. And if it didn't, he'd wipe it from his mind straightaway. If he tried to put on a big play and it didn't come off, the next time we had the ball he'd want to try it again. He always backed himself, believing that whatever he did would come off. I was different: I was more conservative.

He was brilliant at letting go of his errors, too. Most players take time to recover from a bad moment like he had in that final. But the great thing about Billy—and it explains a lot about the career he had—is that it didn't haunt him. If he dwelled on the plays that didn't come off, like many players do, he couldn't have kept playing the way he did.

People forget that he was named player of that tournament, which showed what sort of form he'd been in. You couldn't blame him for sneaking up on the blindside and passing infield, given the confidence he was feeling as we went into that final.

After the match we had a few drinks at the team hotel. I recall Ricky being rather upset with some of the decisions by referee Ashley Klein. Nothing in particular stands out in my memory, just that Stick was unhappy with the match officials in general. But the next morning, as we were checking out and about to fly home, we learned there had been an incident in the foyer. Stick had apparently given Klein and referees boss Stuart Cummings a serve, calling them 'cheats' in a heated discussion.

Six days later, Stick apologised and resigned. I understand that it wasn't an ideal situation to have the national coach acting like that towards match officials in a hotel foyer. I'd been coached by him in the national side for three years now, and I was disappointed that he was going. I loved my time under Stick and was sad to see it end the way it did. And we'd lost not only our coach but also our standing as the number one rugby league country in the world.

•

Ricky's departure led to the appointment of Wests Tigers coach Tim Sheens to lead the national side, and I learned straight-away that he was unlike any other coach I'd had.

At senior level, I'd only played under Mark Murray, Craig Bellamy, Wayne Bennett, Mal Meninga, Michael Hagan and Sticky. Apart from Mark Murray and 'Hages', who had coached me in my early years for the Maroons, all those guys had been involved with the Canberra Raiders system. Three of them—Bellyache, Stick and Mal—had been coached by Sheensy.

Tim had a very different approach, in that he was extremely technical. Bellyache hadn't coached me too much in terms of technique or tactics; he was all attitude. Stick was slightly more hands-on because of his knowledge of the game and his playing career as a halfback. Mal was all about man management. So was Bennett. All of them were about training hard, preparing well and then playing with plenty of effort. But Sheensy was very precise about where he wanted certain plays used on the field, where we had to be positioned on certain tackle counts in a set, and where he wanted us to kick the ball.

Our spine at the time was me, JT, Locky and Billy. And our No. 14 was Cooper. When we were doing video sessions, or preparing our game plan, Sheensy wanted to have the most influence on the way we played. That was something that I wasn't used to at this level. It's more common at club level, when your team won't be full of internationals, but whenever I'd played for Queensland or Australia in previous seasons, the coaches generally gave us the freedom to play how we wanted to play.

So Sheensy exerted control over what the team was doing. There wasn't any drama or conflict, but it was a very different environment and approach. We talked to him about certain things that had worked well in the past. He took some convincing, but at times he came around. When it worked in a game, he was happy to go with it.

Tim was also very big on the history of rugby league—he's a walking footy encyclopedia. If you saw him at breakfast, he'd talk about footy straightaway, waxing lyrical about Kangaroos players from the 1940s, 50s and 60s. 'Mate, how do you know this stuff?' I'd think. He loved the history of the national side, and I found that stuff quite interesting. It's important to understand who's worn the jersey before you.

Our first match under Tim was the Anzac Test against New Zealand in Brisbane in May 2009, which we won 38–10. But if we really wanted to reclaim international supremacy, we knew we'd have to do it at the end of the season in the Four Nations tournament.

We played the Kiwis in the first match at the Stoop, which is just across the road from Twickenham Stadium in London. It's a small ground, but the atmosphere, buoyed by a stack of expats from both Australia and New Zealand, was electric. This was my first match in England, and it conjured in my mind the dreams of playing in England I'd had as a boy.

The match finished as a 20-all draw—after I scored a converted try with five minutes remaining. It was funny how that try came about. I turned left and went to pass to Petero Civoniceva, but missed him. Instead the ball was picked up by GI, who then did what GI often did during his career: bumped off a couple of defenders, saw a half-chance, ran to the line and was tackled by two Kiwis. He got his arm free and snuck the pass to me. Adam Blair caught me just before the line, but momentum got me over. JT kicked the goal to tie the scores.

We vowed to be better in the next match, against England at DW Stadium in Wigan, and we were: we won 26–16. The official crowd on the day was 23,122 but it felt like twice as many people. The thing I learned about English crowds that day, and over the years to come, was that even though they were supporting their national side, and wanted us to lose, they also supported the game. They appreciated good rugby league. It was very different from home, where it didn't matter how well you played—if you were at an away venue, they hated you and gave it to you. In the UK, after matches for Australia—or even for the Storm after a World Club Challenge fixture—we'd walk around applauding the crowd and they would all stay behind and applaud and thank us. Some would yell out that we should come to play for their club. When would that ever happen in Australia?

The third stop on our Four Nations tour was Paris, for a match against France that we had to win to secure our place in the final. In the lead-up, Sheensy was confident we could take care of them, so he announced that he was resting me, Billy, Anthony Watmough and Brett White.

As anyone who has played with me will know, this news didn't sit well with me. I was never happy about being rested. If I was fit, why wasn't I playing? It wasn't just because it was a Test match—that was my mentality over my entire career, stretching back to when I was a young fella: if you're fit, you play. I don't even like coming off the field during a game.

I told Tim I wasn't happy about being rested.

'We've got a big game next week, and I don't want to risk injury, so you're being rested,' he said. 'That's the end of it.'

It was the only game I didn't play, when available, during all the years I played for Australia. We won 42–4, meaning we would play the winner of the final group match between England and New Zealand.

In the lead-up to the tournament, we'd spoken a lot about the Kiwis being world champions, and how we wanted to be back at number one again. For a lot of us who'd been involved in the World Cup the year before, that gave us real motivation. Beating New Zealand in the Four Nations final would win back some of the ground we'd lost a year earlier. But England had other ideas, winning 20–12 to book a place against us in the final at Elland Road.

We were coming up against an England team that featured James Graham, Gareth Ellis, Adrian Morley, Kevin Sinfield, Sam Tomkins and a young backrower called Sam Burgess. He'd been playing for Bradford in the Super League but had signed with South Sydney for the 2010 NRL season because he wanted to test himself in Australia. In that final, he certainly showed how much damage he could do, scoring England's first try with an incredible run from 40 metres out. He made a break and even threw a dummy to get around Billy before scoring. When he scored his second try from close range shortly after halftime, England led 16–14.

What followed was one of the most devastating periods of football of any Australian side I've been involved with—with much of it engineered by Billy. He scored from dummy half to hand us back the lead and then scored two more as we tore away with the match. He also delivered one for me after he freakishly leapt over the dead-ball line and slapped the ball back into the in-goal for me to score.

We won 46–16. It was Australia's greatest victory over England in England, and it helped take away some of the pain from the World Cup final the year before.

11

DYNASTY

'See him?' said Justin Hodges, my Queensland teammate, pointing at me. 'He's number one, you're number two.'

He was talking to Danny Buderus, the New South Wales captain, in the first half of the opening match of the 2007 State of Origin series at Suncorp Stadium.

After the miracle of 2006, when we'd won the series in the dying minutes of the deciding match, my Maroons teammates and I were determined to keep the momentum going.

Hodgo's sledge was nothing more than an attempt to put Bedsy off his game. I didn't pay too much attention to it, although I did hear it. Neither side really cared, to be honest. Just another Justin Hodges sledge to get under the skin of one of the opposition's key players. He was always trying to get an edge, especially against a player of Bedsy's calibre. He also never cared what the scoreboard said, because we were down 8–6 when he directed that one at the Blues' captain.

Then things got worse. We went in at halftime down 18–6 after winger Jarryd Hayne scored just before the break. Not ideal in front of your home crowd. But, typical of the Queensland spirit, we clawed our way back. Converted tries to Greg Inglis and Steve Price levelled the scores at 18-all with twenty minutes to go. Then came the moment that swung the result our way.

We were positioned on the right-hand side of the field on the 40-metre line, coming out of our own end. I was thinking about a 40/20 kick, as I could hook the ball off my left foot back towards the right touchline. Because we were on that shorter side, the winger would be up and the fullback positioned towards the long side, waiting for my left-foot kick.

My foot was just over the 40-metre line, but Jarryd must've thought I was behind it, because he played at the ball and batted it back in before it found touch. Guess who was there? Darren Lockyer. He grabbed it and scored. We won 25–18.

In the lead-up to game two, we talked about how we had struggled to win in Sydney over the last decade or so. In particular, how we hadn't won at Telstra Stadium (now called ANZ Stadium) in eleven matches. The closest was an 18-all draw in 2002.

We made a point of talking about that record, and vowed to do something about it. We went to Sydney with the mindset that the New South Wales blokes weren't unbeatable at this ground. Early in our preparation, we accepted that we'd have hardly any fans there. We would be in a hostile environment, and we would be ready for that.

We were also prepared for a low-scoring grind because of the conditions we knew we would face. The dew at the old Olympic Stadium from May through to July would make things greasy and slippery, which was foreign to many of our players. Our side was largely made up of Broncos and Cowboys players who were accustomed to playing on dry, fast tracks in Queensland. So we had to adapt to it, enjoy it, learn how to win when it's cold and damp. The field becomes narrower, the sideline an extra defender to avoid. If you try to go around teams, your wingers and centres will be easily pushed into touch.

We scored the first try after I went down a really narrow short side on the last tackle. I engaged my Storm teammate, winger Matty King, and flicked the ball out towards GI with my left hand. The ball went to ground but GI scooped it up and scored in the corner.

We stayed in the arm wrestle and won 10–6. Afterwards, Locky reckoned it was the 'gutsiest win' he'd been involved in while playing in a Maroons jumper.

Paul Vautin, a Queensland legend, went further, now that we'd secured back-to-back series wins. 'This could be the start of a Queensland dynasty,' he said.

•

The following year, the New South Wales Rugby League did their best to ensure that didn't happen, replacing Blues coach Graham Murray with Craig Bellamy.

For me, it was a no-brainer. This was where Bellyache was headed as a coach. He'd led the Storm to consecutive grand finals and won one. When his name was tossed up after New South Wales lost, it was inevitable that he was going to get an opportunity.

When he accepted the job, I was happy for him. Privately, though, I was also wary because it was bad news for Queensland. I knew better than anyone how well he prepared his teams, and how much homework he did on the opposition. More than that, he also had an intimate knowledge of the way Billy, GI, Cooper and I played. I was worried about his ability to shut down a lot of the stuff we were doing for Queensland. We'd been able to achieve some incredible things together as coach and players. Now we were matched up against each other, and I wasn't ready for him to put one over us.

It became 'us' versus Bellyache.

There was banter. I was probably the worst at dishing it out, but only because of the strong relationship I had with him. But once we got into camp I stopped caring about Bellyache. It didn't matter what he did, his players still had to go out and win the game against an excellent Queensland side.

As it turned out, the acid wouldn't only be on Bellyache in the first match of the 2008 series. It was also on me, because it was my first as Queensland captain as Locky had been ruled out for the season with a serious knee injury. Suddenly, I found myself captain of several players who were much older and more established than me. Guys like Petero Civoniceva,

Michael Crocker, Brent Tate and Carl Webb had played for Queensland and Australia, and now I was their skipper.

I'm the first to admit I didn't handle that week well. I didn't prepare, nor did I play, like I had in every other game I'd played for the Maroons. I felt like I had to be something that I wasn't.

Bellyache had also come up with a simple gameplan. The Blues forwards ran hard at me and Locky's replacement at five-eighth, Karmichael Hunt, all night. He would've told them, 'Listen, we need to get at these blokes and use up their energy to minimise the impact when they have the ball.' So my Storm teammates Brett White and Ben Cross, along with the Roosters' Craig Fitzgibbon (who had been moved into the front row), ran at us all night long.

New South Wales won 18–10 after Anthony Laffranchi scored in the 69th minute. I was filthy on myself, and a little embarrassed because I'd been beaten, as captain, at the first attempt. That week, I'd tried to do too much. I wasn't my usual relaxed self.

In the lead-up to game two, Mal pulled me aside. He knew I was disappointed with the way I'd played. 'Mate, I understand the captaincy is a big deal,' he said. 'It's something you've always wanted. But I don't need you to be something you're not. I just need you to be your normal self. Don't do anything special, just do what you do.'

It put me at ease knowing that he was confident in my ability as a captain. And that I could just do my thing instead of thinking I needed to do more.

There have been a lot of moments, in his time as Queensland and Australian coach, when Mal's had some really influential things to say. But for me that conversation stands out. If he hadn't grabbed me then, I might have done the same thing in game two. And then who knows? If we lost that one in 2008, where would my Origin career have gone after that? Anyway, after that discussion with Mal I felt a lot more comfortable about the captaincy.

We'd been bogged down in game one looking to play the type of grinding footy that suited New South Wales, played through the middle, trying to outmuscle their forwards, which was the wrong way for us to go, because they had a massive pack.

There was a lot of pressure on GI to perform in game two at Suncorp after his opposite, Mark Gasnier, had got the better of him in the first match. We were confident that he had a big game in him.

People used to say about Mal, 'Don't poke the bear.' It was the same with GI. We all knew he had that in him. But it was our responsibility to give him those opportunities, and so far we hadn't given him any quality ball. In game two, our left side of Johnathan Thurston and Ash Harrison did a great job getting it to him. Not only did GI get over the top of Gaz, he also ran over the top of our Storm teammate, New South Wales winger Steve Turner. GI didn't score a try but hand-delivered two to Darius Boyd in our 30–0 victory.

Coming off the ground after that match, I was stunned. 'What an unbelievable performance,' I said to some of the boys about what GI had just delivered. To do that to someone like Mark Gasnier, who was the number one centre in the game at the time, was impressive. GI was rightly named man of the match.

It set up an epic deciding game back in Sydney. The Blues made several changes, but none more significant than the selection of Mitchell Pearce and Braith Anasta in the halves, who played alongside each other at the Roosters. Braith had been around for several years, and won a comp with Canterbury, but Mitchell had only just made his NRL debut the year before.

There was a fiery start to the match with a fight in the opening minute. Another two fights and two knockouts followed, and with thirteen minutes on the clock the score was level at 10-all. In the second match, it had been GI who stepped up. In this game, it was JT.

As he'd done so many times in big matches, it was the trademark show-and-go that allowed him to pierce the line. Locky wasn't there this time to support. Instead, it was Billy who scored the try that edged us ahead. New South Wales threw everything at us in the final minutes to level again, but we held them out. It was a real dogfight for the entire match until that moment when two of our guns once again stood up and created something out of nothing.

It was nice to win, but the overwhelming feeling for me, as captain, was relief. I was glad I hadn't been the captain to end the dynasty before it started. We knew we had a good footy side. If we'd lost, I would've felt like we'd let down the entire state.

•

By the time the 2009 series rolled around, as we attempted to become the first team in the Origin era to win four in a row, going into camp for Queensland felt like going into camp with your club.

That's how tight we were, with so many familiar faces, especially the Storm players who made up a large chunk of the side. It felt like we automatically knew what was required in terms of preparation. We had a clear understanding of who we were and who we were playing for. We didn't have to form any new combinations or friendships. It was a seamless transition from club to state, and heading into the opening match of the series that was invaluable.

I'm led to believe it was the complete opposite for New South Wales, who were under enormous pressure heading into the first match, to be played at Etihad Stadium in Melbourne. They chopped and changed their side, with Terry Campese and Peter Wallace named in the halves.

The constant uncertainty about the Blues' team over the years was great for us. It was always nice, sitting in Queensland on day one of camp, learning who New South Wales had selected and the numerous changes they'd made. It seemed the opposite of what we were: settled and with stability around our team. New South Wales were changing players in key positions, changing centres, changing backrowers, their bench.

We knew how hard it was to put a brand-new side together and gel quickly. It's not like club footy, where you have a sixteen-week preseason and everyone's working within the same system. In Origin you've got ten days. It's easy to say those seventeen blokes are elite players. But you can have the greatest players in the world, and if they don't have the same game plan in mind and are not on the same page, it's just not going to work.

We won game one 28–18, then game two, in Sydney, 24–14, to wrap up the series. Four straight. Who would've thought that could've happened back in 2006? We weren't content with that, though. We wanted the whitewash, especially in front of our home crowd.

On the Sunday night, JT and a few of the other boys had a drink on the Gold Coast. On Monday morning it was obvious that a few quiet drinks had turned into something more, because JT wasn't in a great way. Later that night, when we were having a team meal, I looked across the table and knew he still wasn't right.

The following day we drove up to Brisbane and had our captain's run at Suncorp Stadium. This was our last hit-out before game three, where we would be looking for a rare three-nil result. We wanted that whitewash. I don't know if JT was still crook, but he wasn't in any shape to be training.

I wasn't the only one thinking this. We finished the session and I could see how angry Mal had become. He grabbed some of the senior players to discuss the idea of replacing JT with Cooper Cronk, who was 18th man. In the end, JT kept his spot. But only just.

Game three of the 2009 series is best remembered for a wild all-in brawl late in the second half—and for the up-and-under kick we put up right on fulltime.

Our prop Steve Price was knocked out after Brett White punched him in a one-on-one fight. We didn't take exception to the fight. What incensed us was New South Wales prop Justin Poore grabbing Pricey when he was concussed and throwing him back to the ground. That really got to us. So there was a big scuffle and the game stopped for some time. The refs got it wrong and sinbinned Blues backrower Trent Waterhouse instead of Poore.

We got the penalty and kicked for touch. There were 30 seconds on the clock. What do we want to do? We weren't in the mood to just run the ball back and end the game. So we had a discussion.

'Let's give it back to them,' Locky said.

In hindsight, I reckon he meant to just toss the ball back to them, but I took it as 'Kick it as high as you can and then we come running through'. I tapped the ball, launched it high into the air, and the rest of the boys followed it like a magnet all the way to poor old Kurt Gidley, the New South Wales fullback, who was standing under it at the back.

Now, 'Gids' is one of the nicest blokes you'd ever meet. We'd played for Australia together, as well as in the All Stars match. But it didn't matter: he was wearing a sky-blue jumper and we were going to stand up for our stricken mate no matter what. Gids caught it, we smashed him and another huge brawl erupted.

There have been some big moments at Lang Park over the years when the crowd has gone off and the atmosphere has been electric. But in that moment I felt like the place was going to explode. The only other time I felt something similar was during the Battle of Brookvale. I felt much safer at Suncorp, of course, but once again I maintained my policy of not throwing punches, knowing I'd get beaten if I did. We lost the match 28–16 and I'm still not sure who won the fight!

A few days later, JT phoned. He wanted to apologise. I believe that match represented a line in the sand for him. From that moment on, he realised that letting down the team, and so many people in Queensland, was something he never wanted to do again. He didn't automatically become a stiff, but he knew when it was time to enjoy himself and when it was time to work.

It was a lesson learned the hard way, but one JT never had to learn again.

12

THE DAMAGE DONE

'Where's Bellyache?'

That was the question on all our lips as we trained in the sun at Princes Park on the morning of 22 April 2010, a day I will never forget.

Princes Park was once the home ground of the Carlton Football Club, but they and the rest of the AFL had started playing out of bigger stadiums long ago and now, under the name Visy Park, it had become our training headquarters. It had remained untouched, with old facilities and old grandstands, but it had a lush, green playing surface for us to train on.

Very rarely would Bellyache be missing whenever we had a skills session out in the middle of that field, so it didn't take long for the boys to notice his absence. His assistant coaches, Steve Kearney and Brad Arthur, were running the session instead.

We'd started the season reasonably well. Because construction wasn't quite finished on our new home ground, AAMI Park, we had played our first three rounds on the road. We'd beaten Cronulla, Newcastle and Penrith, before defeating St George Illawarra at Etihad Stadium on Good Friday. But then we'd dropped matches against the Gold Coast and Manly.

As we prepared for our Anzac Day game against the Warriors in Round 7, I reckoned Bellyache must have been hiding in the old grandstands. 'He's up there somewhere to see if we've put the slippers on while he's not around, so he can have a crack at us,' I joked with the boys.

But when the session finished, there was still no sign of the coach. Now, that *was* strange. I started to sense something was wrong.

'Boys, training's over for the day,' we were told. 'Come straight into the meeting room. No showers. Craig will be in there to have a chat to you.'

Straightaway I thought something serious had happened, like someone had passed away or something serious concerning Craig had occurred. My mind was racing. Was there something wrong with him? Had something happened to his family?

Our meeting room was tiny, and to get every player and member of the football staff in there meant we had to jam in. There wasn't much being said because we were all worried about what was happening.

Then Craig walked in. As soon as I saw his face, I knew he was about to deliver some really heavy news—but about what I just didn't know. Even before he started talking, I could tell he was shattered.

In typical Bellyache fashion, he didn't beat around the bush. 'I've just been in a meeting,' he said. 'The club has had some serious salary cap breaches and the NRL has decided to hand out some punishments.'

That left me reeling. Punishments?

He paused, searching for the right words. 'The two premierships we've won in 2007 and 2009—they've been wiped,' he said finally. 'The minor premierships in 2006, '07 and '08, they're gone. The World Club Challenge from earlier this year, that's gone. All the prizemoney too.'

And then the killer blow.

'For the rest of this year, we'll be playing for no points.'

After he said the premierships had been stripped, my first thought was complete devastation. 'Fuck me,' I thought. 'The last six years have been a complete waste of time. All those hill runs, all those laps around the Tan, all those meetings we sat in, getting hammered by Bellyache, chipping each other for not reaching our high standards—it's all been a waste.'

And then I lost it. I broke down. I was wearing a hoodie, and I just pulled my face down into it and cried. My career had been a complete waste. I knew how much all my mates had put into achieving what we had—the hard work and sacrifices we had made in our lives. Even worse, we wouldn't have an opportunity to make up for the loss, because now we weren't playing for points this season.

Bellyache was really upset too. He had to leave the room because he was about to break down. He tapped me on the head a couple of times as he walked out.

Then it was just us, left there in silence. The younger fellas who weren't involved in all those seasons were confused by it all, understandably enough, and not as affected. The room was dead silent, and we all just sat there in disbelief. I was rattled.

'Training's done for the day,' Frank Ponissi said. 'There's likely to be a lot of media outside. When you go to your cars, politely say "no comment". You'll be contacted about what's going to happen in coming days.'

In between the meeting room and our lockers, there was an outside sitting area with some park benches. I walked out of the meeting and sat down on one with Billy. For some minutes neither of us said a word. We were in shock.

'What just happened?' Billy said, finally breaking the silence.

We were devastated about the news of the premierships— all of it, really—but our major concern was not playing for any points for the rest of the season. What would that mean for the club? Was the Melbourne Storm done? Would the club fold? Have we played our last game for it? Are we even playing this weekend? Are they going to break up our squad and send us all over the country to different teams? We sat there for half an hour, just the two of us, and all those questions started coming out.

Finally, I went home. Devastated, I told Barb what had happened. She struggled to get her head around it. She had always been a big part of my footy—she'd been there since day one, and she'd also been a big part of the Storm, and so supportive of the club. It had been such a huge part of our lives.

'How could that happen?' she asked, bewildered. 'How is this happening?'

What added to the confusion was how quickly it had all come about. We knew nothing of any salary cap issue until Craig stood before us and told us the punishment we'd been handed. Usually there'd be a whisper about something, but I'd heard nothing. Not a thing.

Later that afternoon, a media conference was held in Sydney to announce the breaches and the sanctions. NRL chief executive David Gallop sat alongside John Hartigan, the executive chairman of News Limited, which owned the Storm and half-owned the NRL. Our chairman, Dr Rob Moodie, was also present. Gallop announced that we'd breached the salary cap by $1.7 million over five years.

'[The Storm] had a long-term system of effectively two sets of books and the elaborate lengths they have gone through to cover this up has been extraordinary,' he said. 'The rules are the rules, everyone in this competition knows them . . . they knew the risk they were taking. There's no alternative for the NRL in terms of penalties.'

Hartigan said the NRL's salary cap auditor, Ian Schubert, had found that illegal payments had been paid. 'The breakthrough in the investigation was the discovery by the salary cap auditor of a file in a separate room at the Storm, which contained the file with the players' contracts, outlining the payments to the players not disclosed to us,' he said.

Back in Melbourne, I was oblivious to all of this. I had no idea what was being said. I'd turned off my phone and tried to shut it out.

•

The next day, we held a meeting at Steve Kearney's place in Mont Albert, in Melbourne's eastern suburbs. 'Mooks' had been a player of distinction for our club, and had become an important member of the coaching staff. We decided to have the meeting there to avoid the enormous media pack that was now all over the story. The coaching staff, a handful of senior players and our media manager, Dave Donaghy, were the only people in attendance.

We had to work out how we were going to deal with this. We had a game against the Warriors on Anzac Day—in three days' time—which we somehow had to prepare for.

I was unsure of my immediate future, and I'm sure the other players felt the same. We wanted to get some clarity around what was happening. Would we even be playing on the weekend? Would the club be around this year? Next year? And also . . . what just happened?

Craig wasn't in a good way. He was still extremely upset. He was also uncertain if he was going to keep his job following a phone call with John Hartigan the night before. Later that day at Mooks' place, News Limited executive Keith Brodie turned up and assured us our coach wasn't going anywhere. 'Craig Bellamy is the guy to lead you out of this,' Brodie assured us. 'We're going to back him. And we're going to back you.'

Ryan Hoffman became quite vocal at this point, because Craig had told us that he might not be around for much longer. Like all of us, Hoffy was really upset. We loved Craig and we didn't want him wearing any of the blame for this. He had helped us become the players we were, and achieve those special things, so when we heard that Hartigan had gone hard at him, we were pretty upset.

The mood of the playing group—especially those of us who had been around for all those years—quickly changed from shock and disappointment to anger towards News Limited. Our role was to play football, not to know how the salary cap worked or how the business was run.

We decided we had to address the media—and we weren't going to let Bellyache do it alone. I'd seen how much this had affected him, and I was determined, as captain, that he shouldn't have to front this thing on his own. Once I said that, the boys said, 'Fuck it, we'll all go.'

It hurt us to see Craig feeling the way he was. I'd never seen him like that before. He'd been disappointed in our performances at times, or about the result of certain games, but I'd never known anything to get to him like this.

So the next day we gathered with our coach at our new ground, AAMI Park. It was supposed to be a members' day at the new stadium, which was to be opened in May with our match against Brisbane. Now it became something entirely different.

We walked out of the tunnel and made our way towards the media pack on the other side of the field. It was a sign of unity, and a statement that we weren't going to be broken by what had just happened to us.

Flanked by the players, Bellyache read a prepared statement. I was standing right beside him. 'The two things they can never take away are our dignity and our integrity,' he said. 'We know we will be investigated. We welcome that. I love this club. I love these players. These players love our club. This is a great club, a strong club, a very proud club. This is why we stand here today united. We aren't going anywhere. We ain't going to surrender.'

Then we walked away, without taking any questions from the reporters. Our focus became the match against the Warriors.

There was some speculation about that we were going to boycott the game in protest against the NRL sanctions. I can't recall that ever being discussed. In fact, it was the opposite. Our mindset was: 'They've hammered us so hard, and now they want us to throw in the towel? Fuck them! We've got more substance than that. You won't get rid of us that easy.' That's how I was thinking, anyway.

It felt like us versus the world. There had been a lot of jealousy about our club, from a lot of different people. We were out-of-towners, we'd been very successful, and a lot of people didn't like it. Now some people were dancing on our graves.

Part of our discussion at Mooks' place was what we had to play for that year. How were we supposed to get up for the rest of the season when our results didn't matter, when we weren't playing for points? We quickly decided that all we had left was our own pride in our performance. Did we really want to go out and play in a half-hearted way, and drop our high standards? Of course not.

Perhaps strangely, our fan base and our membership actually grew in that period. In those few days between the sanctions being handed down and the Warriors game, we gained 2000 new members. We owed it to all those supporters to play as hard as possible. Some sponsors dropped off, but many stayed. We owed it to them, too.

In the lead-up to the match, Craig told the playing group that he understood if any of us didn't want to take the field. 'If I was in your shoes, I couldn't play,' he said. 'I couldn't.'

To a man, we said we would. And when we lined up for the national anthem at Etihad Stadium, and saw a bumper crowd that had turned up in support, we knew we'd made the right decision.

We had wondered how many would turn up. Would they turn their backs on us because of what had happened? Some angry fans had dumped their jumpers outside our club earlier in the week. But the ones here on this night showed incredible loyalty to the players and coaching staff. As the anthem was played and I looked at that sea of faces, all I was thinking was how proud I was to be part of the Melbourne Storm.

I'm not sure the Warriors knew what was coming that night. It would've been easy for them to assume we wouldn't play well—that we were distracted. Instead, we smashed them, 40–6.

This was one of the few times in my career when I played on emotion. Normally, that's foreign to me. But after I scored the first try, I kicked the ball high into the stands. 'Get that into you!' I thought.

The boys jumped on top of me, and I released some of the anger that had been bubbling inside me. For about a minute.

•

It didn't take long for the blame game to start. First, attention turned to our former chief executive, Brian Waldron, who had left the club six weeks earlier to join a new Super Rugby team, the Melbourne Rebels.

Then it shifted to Matt Hanson, the former chief financial officer who had replaced Waldron but was immediately stood down when the NRL handed down its punishments.

On 24 April, News Limited newspapers published a story about a 'secret dossier'—in a red manila folder—being found at Matt's place. In the dossier were 'letters of offer to three of the Storm's biggest names, with former chief executive Brian Waldron's signature guaranteeing illegal third-party agreements to all three'.

That's when the finger-pointing started being directed at the players, and the three players mentioned in the story. The day after the News Limited story appeared, Channel Nine named the three players: Slater, Inglis and Smith.

Will Chambers, Cooper Cronk, Mick Crocker, Matt Geyer, Ryan Hoffman, Antonio Kaufusi, Dallas Johnson, Anthony Quinn, Steve Turner and Brett White were later brought into it as well.

Day by day things seemed to get worse, and everyone in the organisation started to become increasingly annoyed with News. Apart from the fact that nobody had yet come down to address the entire squad, we were copping a hiding in their newspapers. 'What's happening here?' we would say to each other. 'We're employees of the same company.'

When the sanctions were handed down, at no stage did

I believe I was involved. And at no stage did I believe my team-mates or our coach were knowingly involved either.

The NRL announced it was going to do a thorough investigation. So did News Limited. It would hire accountancy firm Deloitte to do a complete audit of the Storm business. This confused us. Why wouldn't they have done these investigations and audits before handing down the punishments?

Instead, the approach they took—punishing first and asking questions later—created huge amounts of speculation about who had been involved. The big issue in the eyes of the public was whether the players had been aware of it.

News Limited spokesman Greg Baxter said publicly that we could not have known what the letters in the infamous red manila folder meant.

'There is no evidence the players knew they were part of an elaborate scheme,' he said. 'The letters were written in such a way that players reading them could be forgiven for not thinking they were doing anything illegal.'

Yet it didn't seem like anyone listened to Baxter, or believed him. A lot of the commentary had a familiar theme: *surely they knew. Surely the players knew they were over the salary cap.*

In fact, at that stage of my career, I had little idea about how the cap worked at all. As a player, I was aware that we had one, but the club employed people to oversee that part of the operation. How the salary cap worked—and what the salary of every single player in the squad was—was none of my business.

I had even less of a clue about the technicalities around third-party agreements: what could or couldn't be guaranteed by the club, who was allowed to make introductions, and what 'best endeavours' constituted, as is written into NRL contracts frequently these days.

From my end of things, if I was happy with the terms of a deal, and comfortable I could juggle the sponsorship requirements with my footy commitments, that was it.

From a club payment perspective, I knew what I agreed to and how much I was to get paid each month. Beyond those monthly deposits, there were no irregular payments coming in, so I never had any reason to suspect something was wrong. I just got my normal monthly pay, and there were never any random payments that would just turn up out of nowhere. If there had been, I would've asked straightaway where they came from.

I was also audited by the Australian Taxation Office. They didn't just look at 2010, but several years before and after, and they found I had done nothing wrong. I'm not sure about the other players, but that was the case for me.

It was embarrassing to have all these personal financial details being speculated about in the press. It's not something you talk about with your teammates. Do you talk to your colleagues about how much money you're on? I never went into the lunchroom and said, 'Billy, how much did you sign for?' I was raised by a bricklayer and a stay-at-home mum, and we were taught to never talk about how much money you made. You worked hard, made your money and didn't discuss it.

On many occasions throughout my career, the club told me they were under salary cap pressure, and asked me to make small personal sacrifices by deferring payments, which I agreed to. The club always came first.

I assume similar variations happened with my teammates as well, and other players across the game. From my perspective, I knew I had actually *sacrificed* payments, not received extra money, which made me even more confident I'd done nothing wrong, even inadvertently.

And I hadn't. The problem was that it took more than twelve months of investigation by the NRL to clear the players' names. By then, the mud thrown at us had well and truly stuck.

When News Limited handed down the findings from its investigation in July 2010, Hartigan announced that the Deloitte audit found thirteen players had received payments that hadn't been included in the Storm's salary cap. But he also made it abundantly clear that the players weren't to blame.

The NRL didn't hand down its finding until May 2011—more than a year after stripping us of everything. It found that the Storm were $3.78 million over the salary cap over the five-year period from 2006, which was a lot more than the $1.7 million that was initially announced. But they also confirmed that neither the coach nor the players had any knowledge of the illegal payments that had been made.

'Over 136 pages, the report details a sophisticated level of dishonesty on the part of a number of people who were the ones ultimately responsible for plunging the club and the game into disruption,' David Gallop said. 'The fans, the players and those persons at the Storm who were not involved were in fact let down horribly and there can be no doubt from this report that the acts were intentional and pre-meditated.'

We already knew that. But did the public? By then, it was too late. The damage was done. The sanctions had been announced and the players hung out to dry. The picture had already been painted, for the public, the other clubs and the other players.

•

It's been ten years now, but the effects of the salary cap scandal still linger.

I consider myself an optimistic person, but at that time I couldn't see a single positive about the situation we'd found ourselves in. Not one. It felt like the worst thing that had ever happened to us.

Anger, resentment, frustration—you go through the full range of emotions, and they don't go away quickly. I was sure that the doomsayers—and there were plenty—would be overjoyed at a ten-year Melbourne Storm rebuild, if we even managed one at all.

I would lay awake at night, questions swirling relentlessly around in my head. 'Is this stuff true? How could they hand out punishments before completing any investigations? What does the future hold for our team? For our club?'

Time has passed, and it still comes up every now and then, but I have a totally different perspective now. In 2010 our club was the benchmark in the competition and my career was going from strength to strength. Back then, I believed that whatever adversity came my way, I would be able to handle it. But really nothing could have prepared me for that time.

When I came home that afternoon and gave the news to Barb, our eldest child, Jada, was just a toddler, and our second, Jasper, was eight months old. The kids, of course, were too young to be affected, but the situation enveloped Barb and me, along with all the other Storm families, for a long period.

Every day the pressure kept building, and it went well beyond the players, staff and our immediate families. All of a sudden our parents were being peppered with questions about what was going on, as were extended family members and friends. There was a dark cloud over the club and everyone associated with it.

It was Barb and my parents who helped me get through that difficult time. They love the club and were feeling everything that was happening, as we all were, but they always tried to keep things in perspective.

'Cam,' they would say, 'if this is the worst thing that happens in your life, you've lived a good life.'

Simple and straightforward, but they were right.

I look back now and feel sad that I can never get that time back—days, weeks and months when I was not as present as I should have been. I was someone who took football home with me—and when football is good, that's great, but when it's not, it affects everyone around you.

I don't dwell on that period, but it has stayed with me and I've learned from it. From a football perspective, and as a person, I have no doubt it strengthened me. In fact, it might sound strange but I believe that period in the Storm's history has been a big part of the reason I've been able to continue playing for as long as I have.

'Resilience' is a word thrown around footy clubs pretty regularly these days, but what happened in 2010 taught me everything I needed to know about hardship and adversity and what is required to respond to it. After that experience, my footy improved, my leadership improved and my work/life balance improved. I walked away from the episode a better person, comfortable that I could handle whatever was coming at me next.

13

BATTLING BROOKVALE

I was sitting in the dugout at Brookvale Oval, watching our under-20s team, when some of the Manly fans spotted me and started giving it to me. 'Where's your speedboat, Smithy? Taken your new caravan out yet, Smithy? Where's the paper bags, Smithy?'

It had been the same at Parramatta Stadium, where there were banners in the crowd reminding us of the salary cap scandal. I wondered if we'd get out of there alive, such was the bitterness shown towards us.

There were also banners on the hill at Brookvale. It was impossible to ignore them as I sat in the dugout that day. Then a little kid ran up to the wire fence that separates the dugouts and the concourse in front of the main grandstand.

'Hey, Smith!' the kid said.

I turned around and he handed me a wooden spoon.

163

'Thanks, mate,' I laughed. 'No worries.'

It's surprising how young the sledging starts in some families. I got off the team bus at Belmore Sportsground a few years ago and a young kid, about eight years old, was standing there with his dad in the rain. I took my headphones out and was about to go into the sheds when I heard a voice from behind me.

'Hey, Smith!' the kid said—because apparently that's how you address adults these days, by their surname. 'You're a grub!'

My jaw nearly hit the ground. The kid's dad was chuckling as I walked into the dressing-room. It seemed like a snapshot of where society was at that moment. If I took my young bloke to an AFL game and he said, 'Hey, Dusty Martin, you're a grub,' I'd pull him into line straightaway. I know what my old man would've done to me back in the day if I'd called any player a grub.

Whenever you cop a sledge from a fan, no matter how old they are, you have to laugh it off. I definitely had to laugh in 2010—or I would have cried. We copped abuse—proper abuse—at almost every away match that season. It was abuse I never thought was possible at a rugby league game. You always expect banter at the footy, but this was on another level.

By the time we visited Brookvale Oval in Round 22, our emotions were still all over the place. It was bizarre turning up each week to play for pride instead of two competition points. How we felt depended on the day. One day you might bounce into training, and then you'd be down and out the next. Some days, half the squad was in great spirits but the other half wasn't, so we just had to get around each other and get through it together.

Six days after the salary cap sanctions were handed down, News Limited's executive chairman, John Hartigan, came and spoke to us. He talked to us about there being 'rats in the ranks'—he meant the club officials who had been responsible for the pain we were feeling. He also said News was 'backing the club', but he wasn't overly sympathetic.

We felt massively abandoned by News Limited. We felt we were getting hammered from pillar to post, including in the News-owned newspapers. The company seemed to have two massive conflict of interests: they owned us, but they also owned half of the NRL, and its newspapers were smashing us whenever they had a chance. We weren't getting many answers about our future, while the company's business was skyrocketing because people were buying their newspapers so they could read all about the 'darkest day in Australian sport'.

Much of the commentary, whether it was in News Limited papers or not, went along these lines: 'Aha! We knew the Storm were too good to be true. We knew you had to be cheating.' Maybe we were wrong. We didn't know what was happening behind the scenes, but that was the feeling we had: that we had become scapegoats for something bigger. We worried that the NRL, being half-owned by News, had to come down really hard on the News Limited–owned footy club because it couldn't be seen to have a conflict of interest. A light punishment would've been a bad look.

It was really hard for us, as a young group of blokes, to get our heads around it all. We weren't up to speed with the broader politics of the game, mostly because we were based in

Melbourne. As players, we trained hard and then played, and let everyone on that side of the business do their job.

As captain, I felt a real sense of responsibility to absorb the pressure all the players were feeling, but I can't understate the role that Craig and Frank Ponissi played that year. They made sure we maintained our standards, often making the point that it spoke to who we were as a club and the standards we had. They wouldn't allow us to use this as an excuse to slacken off.

Craig's focus and intensity didn't change a lot, although he did come around to the players' wish to be a little more off-the-cuff with our style of play. We'd always been so structured—mechanical, as some described it—and now we wanted to explore new options with our attack. In some ways it was probably a way for us to get through the year. We wanted to experiment a little, but even then Craig wanted some level of control.

'Got any examples?' he asked bluntly when we put it to him one day. Even though he struggled with the idea of us playing ad-lib footy, he often agreed to it. Then we'd try some bullshit play that he would never have allowed in normal circumstances, and he'd lose it. If it got too much, and blokes were chip-kicking or pulling out other silly plays, he'd blow up. 'Fuck that shit off,' he'd grumble. 'No more of that.'

In comparison to Billy I was a conservative player, but even I was prepared to throw caution to the wind that year. In Round 15 we played the Cowboys. It was getting towards the end of the game and we were leading comfortably, so I decided to try something I never normally would. 'I'm chipping it on the first play,' I said to Cooper.

I kicked for touch, about 30 metres out on the right-hand side. I said to one of my teammates, 'I'll drop you off'—in other words, he should drop behind me and run the ball up. I tapped it, showed it to him, but instead of passing I put a chip-kick in over the Cowboys defensive line for Cooper. It was only the first tackle and so Matt Bowen was out of position at fullback. Billy had caught wind of what Cooper and I were up to and raced through to beat Matt to the ball and score the try.

In normal circumstances, that was stuff I would never have dared attempt—and Bellyache wouldn't have allowed it anyway.

Throughout that season, some opposition players and coaches blew up after we'd beaten them. Some players even complained while we were still on the field, frustrated to know, with five minutes to go, that they were about to get beaten by a side that couldn't make the finals. 'You're playing for nothing,' they'd say. 'You shouldn't even be out here. This is a joke.'

It gave our boys a bit of a laugh. I did feel bad for our opponents, though, because I understood where they were coming from: we literally didn't have anything to lose.

'Sorry, boys,' we'd shout back. 'Not our fault. Blame the NRL.'

Finchy, with his unique sense of humour, really boosted our team spirit. After that very first match, against the Warriors, he invited everyone back to his place for a get-together. A few of the boys went pretty hard that night, needing to blow off some steam.

When we played at Canberra Stadium, the boys ran out for the warm-up and spotted a group of Raiders fans waving some pretend banknotes. 'Here's your cash, you fucking cheats,' they said.

Finchy ran over and started grabbing at it. 'I'll take it! I'll take it!' he said. 'I need every cent I can get!'

We were lucky to have a character like him around. His ability to lift the mood of the boys in those dark days was invaluable. Those first couple of matches, in particular, were played on emotion alone. We were still upset about what had happened, and how it had gone down, but then that emotion died off and it became harder to get ourselves up for games.

It says a lot about the character of our club that we didn't put up the white flag. We finished the 2010 season with fourteen wins and ten losses. The year before, when we won the premiership, we had fourteen wins, one draw and nine losses. If we'd been allowed to accrue points, we'd have finished in fifth spot. Our points differential was plus 129—the third-best in the competition. Not bad for a team that supposedly had nothing to play for and was on the verge of collapsing.

We played throughout that year dealing with daily reports about players being moved on so we could fit under the salary cap for the 2011 season. We'd been determined to keep the playing group together, even offering to take pay cuts so we could stay under the salary cap, but the NRL wouldn't allow it.

I felt that was unfair, because we had built that squad into what it was. So many players had been identified and contracted as teenagers. We'd made them into the footballers they now were. And suddenly they had to be moved on.

Hoffy actually put his hand up to leave, and signed with Wigan. He had aspirations of playing in the Super League towards the end of his career, but now he brought it forward to help ease the pressure on the salary cap. It was a really honourable thing for him to do. He knew the club was in strife and that this would help.

But other players were just squeezed out. Brett White went to Canberra, Aidan Tolman went to the Bulldogs, and Jeff Lima followed Hoffy to Wigan. So did Finchy. We lost eleven players in total. While no player was more important than any other, the one departure that hurt us the most was GI.

We were in Adelaide to play the Bulldogs in Round 18 when the phone buzzed in my hotel room.

It was Bellyache. 'I've spoken to GI and he's going to be released,' he told me.

'What's going on?' I thought.

This was GI, a kid we'd had since he was fifteen, and now he was being released to the Broncos. It was heartbreaking. He'd been such a big part of our club, and such a great person to have around. We all loved him. It was nearly impossible to comprehend that he was leaving. Then again, nothing that season seemed real.

•

Another season, another match at Brookvale Oval—and more sledging from the Manly fans. 'You were cheating the cap and we still beat you by 40!' screamed one, making a reference to the result of the 2008 grand final.

The hostility directed at the Storm throughout 2010 continued all the way through 2011. By the time we met Manly at their home ground on a Friday night in Round 25, the hate was running stronger than ever.

We'd done incredibly well that year, defying the loss of all those players to lead the competition by four points heading into the second-last match of the regular season. We'd been on top of the ladder since Round 15, and to be so close to the minor premiership a season after we'd been stripped of everything showed the great resilience and culture of the Melbourne Storm.

Manly was sitting in second place, so it was little wonder the media had described this forthcoming game at Brookie as the biggest of the season.

It had also been an emotional year for the Sea Eagles—and this was going to be an emotional game. It was the first Manly match that David Gallop had attended since he had given a month-long suspension to their fullback, Brett Stewart, after he was charged with sexual assault in 2009—a charge he was later cleared of by the courts. It also happened to be the first time Gallop had attended a Storm match since stripping us of our titles and minor premierships.

We certainly put on a show for him. There had been plenty of fiery matches between Melbourne and Manly over the previous five years, including two grand finals, but nothing like the 'Battle of Brookvale'. This was the night when, for the first and only time in my career, I thought the crowd was going to jump the fence, storm the field and bash us.

We'd started that 2011 season with Craig telling us to move on and forget about what had happened the previous year, as difficult as that might be. 'It's gone,' he said. 'Let's start again and create our own history here.'

But there was no denying that our guys felt a fair bit of motivation. I don't know if we were seeking payback or revenge. But proving people wrong was a huge driving force. We wanted to stick it up those people who thought we were cheats.

Cheats . . . that word sat so uneasily with us. We knew we hadn't bought premierships—we'd worked hard for them. We'd earned those titles. Yes, our club was caught cheating the salary cap, but we believed we had won them off the back of hard work, it didn't just happen.

And we knew that. We were in the grind every day, living and breathing it. The fans see what happens at the end of the week in the space of 80 minutes. They don't see all the hard yards, year on year, that go into those performances. We wanted to prove that we were the benchmark for the rest of the competition for a reason—and it wasn't because of salary cap cheating. We were the benchmark because of the way we went about our day-to-day business. We believed that we worked harder than anyone else. There were standards at the Storm that everyone had to live up to, and if you didn't, you would be found out pretty quickly.

We didn't have a single motto that summed up this attitude, and the phrases we tossed around were all clichés. 'See something, say something' was one. 'The standards you walk past are the standards you accept' was another. But most of it was unspoken. It was deeply ingrained in us.

When Craig first arrived, he said he wanted mentally and physically strong people, and that only came through a really strong work ethic. In time, that philosophy filtered through to every area of the business, from the top to the bottom of our club—from the rookie playing his first season to the most senior player, coach, receptionist, CEO.

Everyone was accountable to each other. Nobody was afraid to have a tough conversation with the bloke standing next to him. That's how you maintain high standards. Better players, better people—that's what the Storm was about.

And if you weren't living by that mantra, you would be found out straightaway. As the captain, if I saw someone showing a lack of effort in a drill or conditioning run, I'd pull him up. 'That's not what we're about here,' I'd say. And I expected every other player to say the same thing to me if they had to.

Everyone played their part during that 2011 season as we climbed back to the top. The emergence of two young rookies from our under-20s team, English five-eighth Gareth Widdop and Junior Kiwi Jesse Bromwich, certainly helped. 'Gaz' had actually made his debut in the Warriors match that came just days after the salary cap sanctions had been announced. Welcome to first grade.

But most of the players who helped keep us winning that year had been plucked from other clubs because they were either unwanted or not getting an opportunity. Players like Adam Woolnough, who came out of retirement to play for us. Beau Champion replaced GI. Jaimon Lowe. Troy Thompson. By the time we arrived at Brookvale Oval for our Round 25 match against Manly, these guys were as full of belief and confidence as the senior players.

We came into the 26 August game having won twelve straight matches—a club record. The most recent of these had been a great win over the Dragons, the defending premiers, before our biggest home crowd of the season at AAMI Park.

Given our grand final history, there was plenty of hostility between Manly and Melbourne—but also plenty of respect. And that was shown early in that match when the Sea Eagles' winger David Williams badly hurt his neck while trying to score in the corner.

The top of Williams' head had gone straight into Billy's guts while going low into the corner. Billy was straight onto what had happened and the seriousness of the situation, and cradled his opponent's head until the trainers and doctors reached them. Eventually they stretchered Williams from the field.

That was in the 22nd minute. The try was disallowed but Manly led 6–0 after Kieran Foran scored soon after kick-off. Only four minutes after play resumed, all hell broke loose.

Ryan Hinchcliffe ran the ball up and was taken to ground, and as he tried to shrug off the defenders he accidentally caught Manly prop Darcy Lussick in the head with his elbow. As Hinchy got up to play the ball, Lussick slapped him across the back of the head. That was the start of it. Hinchy played the ball and then the two of them pushed and shoved before Lussick threw a big right-hand punch. The referee, Shayne Hayne, blew the penalty our way, but his whistle was completely ignored as both teams raced in and started throwing punches.

I was somewhere in the middle, trying to get hold of Lussick, but I didn't throw any punches. I never have—I don't know how to! That's why I try to break up fights, not start them.

Hinchy and Lussick stopped throwing them pretty quickly, but Adam Blair and Manly's lock, Glenn Stewart, were still going at each other, before wrestling around and refusing to let go. They finally came apart, but then 'Blairy' ended up on the ground with Manly's captain, Jamie Lyon.

When things finally settled down, Hayne reversed the penalty. 'The penalty's going against him [Hinchcliffe] for the elbow first,' Hayne explained. 'That's why he [Lussick] retaliated.'

'An elbow?' I asked.

'Even though we've blown the penalty initially for him [Lussick], this is prior foul play,' Hayne said.

Then Hayne called over Blair and Stewart. 'You've come running in,' he said, looking at Stewart. 'You go for ten. Away you go, Glenn.' Then he turned to Blairy. 'You can go too,' Hayne said, raising both hands towards the dressing-room, signalling ten minutes in the sinbin.

But Hayne made a big mistake in not waiting for Stewart to leave the field. As Blairy ran towards the sheds, Stewart slowed down, waiting for him. Blairy tried to get around Stewart but then stopped and they exchanged a few words. Stewart glanced back at Hayne and then started throwing punches. Blairy had no choice but to throw them back in defence, as a pack of Manly players, led by Stewart's brother, Brett, came sprinting in. Brett flew through the air and threw a punch at my teammate's head.

From there, the Battle of Brookvale was on. Some of our interchange players came running out of the dugout, while trainers from both sides got caught up in it too. When things eventually calmed down, Blairy and Stewart ran up the tunnel and into the dressing-room but were soon hauled back out by Hayne. They weren't there for long as the sinbins were upgraded to send-offs. Stewart went first. When Blairy was also sent, I nodded at him to go and not argue the point.

The remaining Storm players stood behind the posts as Jamie Lyon lined up the penalty goal from in front. We could almost feel the crowd on the hill behind us, they were that angry. That was when I worried they were going to jump the fence and charge the field. It was a full house of more than 20,000 people, and the emotion was so intense we felt they were going to lynch us. I'd never felt that at a game of rugby league before, and never did again.

Manly ran out 18–4 winners, but the fallout from the game extended into the following week. Both Blairy and Stewart were referred straight to the judiciary, while another eight players and two trainers were charged for their roles. Each club was also fined $50,000.

Our bench players—Bryan Norrie, Sika Manu, Sisa Waqa and Jaiman Lowe—were all charged for entering the field of play, but they escaped suspension by taking early guilty pleas. Lussick was banned for three matches, while Brett Stewart and Kieran Foran were each sidelined for one match.

Later that week, we lost Adam Blair for the season. He was given three matches for the second fight with Glenn Stewart, but also got an additional two for striking from the initial brawl. Even if we reached the grand final, he would still be suspended. It meant he'd played his last match for the Storm because he'd agreed to join the Wests Tigers in 2012.

The night after Blairy was suspended for five weeks, Glenn Stewart was banned for three. Obviously, we felt we had copped the raw end of the stick there. Stewart had thrown the first punch while Blairy was trying to leave the field, and Blairy had been attacked by three of their players but ended up with the longest suspension. What was he supposed to do when set upon like that?

We felt Brett Stewart was very, very lucky to get away with just a one-week ban. He nearly took Blairy's head off. Out of all of it, he was the one who should've been nailed, but he was playing again the soonest.

Over time, the animosity between the two clubs waned, with players moving on or retiring. But every game between Melbourne and Manly at Brookvale is still known as the 'Battle of Brookvale'.

Losing Blairy was a big loss, but we weren't going to let it derail us. The Roosters beat us 40–6 in the final home-and-away round, but Manly also lost to Brisbane, which meant we held on to win the minor premiership. After the events of the previous season it was a great achievement, and testament to our club's character.

In week one of the finals we beat the Knights 18–8, setting up a home preliminary final against the New Zealand Warriors. Then, with a fairytale appearance in the grand final awaiting us,

Warriors halfback Shaun Johnson tore us to shreds—as he did to most teams that year. He couldn't do anything wrong that night. The Warriors all played well, and everything went their way.

When we walked off the field, having suffered a 20–12 loss, I thought, 'That's as good as any Warriors performance I've ever seen.' I suspected they had played their grand final already, and I was right, as they struggled in the grand final against Manly.

As always, we took the loss hard, even though we had every reason to be proud, given what had happened the year before. We had wanted to send a message to everyone in the comp—and especially to the NRL administrators—that they hadn't got rid of us. We were back, and still a force. To achieve what we did that year was pretty special.

All the Storm players and staff saw that 2011 season as redemption. Being above the salary cap wasn't what had made us a tough team, mentally and physically. Training hard and putting in the long hours is what makes a good footy side and brings you success.

We knew that by winning the minor premiership and reaching the second-last week of the season, we had proven a lot of people wrong. So we left AAMI Park that night feeling proud. But we also knew we had some unfinished business.

Me aged six months in Logan,
Queensland, in 1983.
I grew up in Logan and
in the 1980s it was in the
middle of nowhere, with bush
as far as the eye could see.

Christmas in Logan, 1985.

At home with my sister Khirstie in 1986.

At a family gathering with Khirstie in 1987.

With Grandma Vesley, circa 1989.

At home in Logan, 1990.

My first day of school, 1990.

Under-7's Brothers St Paul's presentation day, 1990. I won most of my awards playing in the halves or at lock. At no stage did I see myself as a hooker of the future, let alone playing more than 400 games in the NRL.

Getting ready to play for the under-8s, 1991.

With Khirstie at the Brothers St Paul's presentation day, 1992.

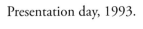
Presentation day, 1993.

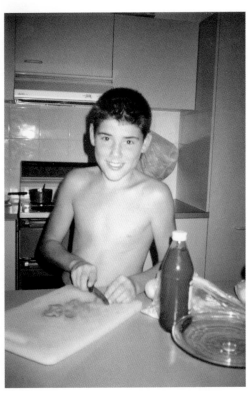

A family holiday on the
Sunshine Coast, 1994.

Holidaying in Cairns following the under-12 state carnival in Townsville.

Under-13 club photo night
at Brothers St Paul's.

Norths Devils RLFC

Colleen Petch/Newspix

Above: Cooper Cronk, Billy Slater and me aged seventeen at Norths Devils. Who could have predicted how much we would achieve together for the Storm, Queensland and Australia over the next two decades?

Left: My NRL debut in 2002 at halfback against Canterbury-Bankstown, who beat us 22–6. The Bulldogs were brimming with talent and couldn't have been any stronger.

Celebrating with Mum after beating Brisbane 24–18 in the quarter-finals in 2005.

Reclaiming the State of Origin shield for Queensland in 2006. This was the start of a record run of eight series wins.

Colleen Petch/Newspix

It was a watershed year for the Storm in 2006. Cooper won Dally M Halfback of the Year, Craig Bellamy won Coach of the Year and I was named Player of the Year.

NRL Imagery

In 2006 I made my debut for Australia and later that year we won the Tri-Nations, beating New Zealand in the final 16–12.

Colleen Petch/Newspix

We put in a mammoth effort to claim the 2007 minor premiership and win the grand final 34–8 against Manly Warringah, but sadly . . .

Colleen Petch/Newspix

. . . it was all just a dream.

Tracey Nearmy/AAP

Entering the NRL judiciary hearing in 2008 for an alleged grapple tackle on Sam Thaiday. We were confident that no offence had taken place, but the outcome was to have significant consequences for me and for the Storm.

NRL Imagery

We beat Parramatta 23–16 in the 2009 grand final, but again, due to salary cap breaches, the title would would be later be stripped from us.

Robert Gray/Getty Images

Training for the Four Nations under new Kangaroos coach Tim Sheens in 2009.

Michael Dodge/Newspix

Training with the Storm at Visy Park on 22 April 2010. We knew something was amiss when Craig didn't join us at training. After the session, the team was taken inside and told the devastating news of the salary cap infringements and resulting penalties.

David Crosling/AAP

24 April 2010. Craig leads us out to address the media in the wake of the salary cap news.

NRL Imagery

The Battle of Brookvale. Manly had been our fiercest opponents for a number of years, and on 26 August 2011 things boiled over.

Cameron Spencer/Getty Images

After the trials of the previous few years, the 2012 grand final win was the sweetest victory of all. We beat Canterbury-Bankstown 14–4.

My younger brother Matt joined the Storm in 2010 and played in the under-20s in 2011 and 2012.

Joined at the hip: training with Matt at Visy Park.

Jasper, me, Barb, Matilda and Jada. Christmas 2012 at Sunshine Beach, Queensland.

14

VINDICATION

No beer tastes better than a beer in the sheds, with your teammates, after a win.

I had a modern approach to football in preparation for a match, but an old-school approach after fulltime. If you've had a good game and a good win, why not celebrate it? A lot of the newer coaches, and particularly those in the high-performance department, didn't agree. They wanted us to have ice baths and protein shakes and massages, and focus solely on recovery.

Not me. I wanted to soak up the moment and the victory. Just let us sit around in a group and talk about this play or that mistake, whatever. Let us have a laugh over half a dozen beers at the end of a hardworking week. And after what happened in 2010, celebrating hard-fought victories with my teammates felt more important than ever before.

It did frustrate the shit out of Bellyache, but that was always something that gave me a good laugh. He was always into me about my punctuality. 'If you're five minutes early, you are five minutes late,' he'd say.

The truth is I was never late. I cut it fine, just to annoy him, but I was never late. Always last, but never late. Last on the bus, last into a meeting, last into the video session—but never late. If we were on an away trip and were boarding the bus, I'd take a couple more sips of my coffee, just to stir him up, then get on with a minute to spare. He hated it because it wasn't the way he did things.

'Fuck, Cameron,' he'd grumble. 'Can't you get here early?'

'It's a 2 p.m. meeting, isn't it?' I'd say. 'If you wanted me earlier . . .'

Bellyache's thing for punctuality went back to when he first started at the Storm, when he wanted us to be disciplined both mentally and physically. It was a product of him being so intense and hard about everything we did.

In 2008, when he was coming off contract, he wondered if his approach might be wearing thin, as Matty Geyer had suggested a few years earlier in relation to the intensity of our training. Bellyache had received a huge offer to return to the Broncos to replace Wayne Bennett, who was heading to the Dragons. He approached the senior players and asked what he should do. 'Should I move on?' he asked me, Billy, Coops, GI and Hoffy. 'Has my time here expired?'

He was questioning whether he could offer the players anything more than he had already, and if his intensity was wearing us down. I'm not sure if he was looking for a reason to go or stay, but we all knew the answer.

'No,' I said. 'We want you to stay.'

If it wasn't for the standards Bellyache set, both before and after the salary cap scandal, we wouldn't have been in the position we were in in 2012, pushing for the premiership we so desperately wanted. While we continued to shed players, we also picked up some good ones with astute recruitment: Jason Ryles from the Roosters and Will Chambers back from the Queensland Reds. And we were given a real lift when Ryan Hoffman returned after one season with Wigan.

We had some quality players across the park. Gareth Widdop, with his footwork and speed, was becoming a quality first-grader. But the heart and soul of this team were those hardworking players who had been discarded by the rest of the game: players who were unwanted by other clubs, had retired to bush footy, or landed in Melbourne in search of an opportunity.

Players like Jaiman Lowe. I'd known him since I was fifteen. We were the same age and played with and against each other in rep sides. There had been such big raps on him as a junior player when he started out, but injuries had cruelled his career and 2012 was going to be his last season before retiring from the game.

Richie Fa'aoso was another. We signed him from Newcastle mid-season because we needed some cover in the forwards after we lost some players because of injury.

Then there was Bryan Norrie. He left the Sharks at the end of 2009 and was headed to England to finish his career, but the deal fell through. He agreed to join Wagga Brothers as captain-coach in Group 9. Then Bellyache called him. 'Wanna come down and have a crack with us?' he asked.

'I can't go back on my word with Brothers,' Nozza said. 'I've committed to them.' That's the sort of bloke he is. But he spoke to the Brothers club and they told him to take his opportunity with the Storm. 'What are you doing?' they said. 'Go for it.'

When he turned up for his first training session in Melbourne, he explained how he could barely run because of his dodgy knees. But our medical staff got him going again. 'You'll have to work hard, though,' they told him.

At a club like ours, that's what was valued above everything else. When they worked hard, those no-nonsense players flourished. Everyone who went through our system came out the other side as better footballers. It all comes back to Craig's coaching. He gives his players simple roles—specific, but simple. These guys don't go out on the field at the weekend unsure what's required of them. They know exactly what they need to do. And if they didn't know, they were expected to ask. That was the same for every player.

Throughout the season, for someone like Nozza, the coaching staff might say something like: 'Mate, we need you to get on these sorts of plays off Smithy. This is what gives you the best carries. And we need quick play-the-balls.'

Craig and his assistants always put that much effort and time into every player. It wasn't just, 'Mate, do your best.' Players would be given detailed tips on the opposition. 'He really struggled last week on that shoulder . . . Use a spin on this bloke—he doesn't like it.'

I'm not sure they go to that level of detail at other clubs. Trent Robinson at the Roosters probably does. And Des Hasler to an extent, because his teams over the years have always been well drilled. You have to play well to beat them. We certainly had to play well in 2012 to beat Des's Bulldogs team.

Des had won the 2011 grand final with Manly, but then stunned the rugby league world a week later when he signed with the Bulldogs. Their form was up and down in the first half of the 2012 season, but then they went on a winning run of twelve matches, including beating us 20–4 in Mackay, and claimed the minor premiership.

The Dogs had some quality players, including England prop James Graham, who arrived from St Helens, but the biggest reason for their success was Ben Barba. He was doing that season for the Bulldogs what Jarryd Hayne had done in 2009 for Parramatta, dominating matches with his speed and footwork, slipping out of tackles almost at will.

While the Bulldogs had started slowly, we started strongly, winning our first nine matches—the club's best start to the season. But we slumped late in the year, losing five straight. That was the most consecutive losses under Bellyache, and the second most in the club's history. It was a frustrating period, but it wasn't for lack of effort. That's never been an issue at our club. We were training as hard as ever. Sometimes there's really no explanation, although it was probably no coincidence that the losing streak came when Billy was sidelined for two months with a knee injury suffered during the Origin series. That upset the balance of our team.

We eventually steadied, finishing second behind the Bull-dogs, and then easily accounted for Souths and then Manly to set up a grand final against Canterbury. Our preparation was much like it had been for Parramatta in 2009: there was one key man we had to shut down. We had to minimise the impact of Ben Barba, just like we had with Jarryd Hayne three years earlier.

So that whole week we trained around defending him: where we were putting our kicks, where we wanted him to return the footy from, and then what we were going to do on his kick return and how to defend him there. He liked to get going off certain plays, usually off Josh Reynolds, or in and around the ruck following big Sam Kasiano around, so we had to be wary of that.

One of our young fellas, Ben Hampton, trained as Ben Barba all week, replicating his speed and agility. That was his role: be Ben Barba. It was invaluable to our preparation, and for most of the grand final we did suffocate Benny out of it, just as we had Jarryd three years earlier.

We took an early lead, with Hoffy running off Gareth Widdop to score after six minutes, but it was clear from the start that our plan was to kick high to Barba, then race through and put him under as much pressure as we could.

When we played the Dogs in Mackay, he had set up the try of the season for Josh Morris. He picked up the ball from a kick just inches from the dead-ball line, then beat five players before drawing our last defender and passing infield for J-Moz to score.

If we couldn't keep the ball away from him, we had decided, let's send it to him and give him no time and space to run. His strength that year was his running. He was busting tackles, making line breaks—it was just impossible to get a hold of him. So we planned to put the ball in the air and rush up on him in one line.

It certainly worked, but the Bulldogs did well to keep us out as we failed to cash in on all the ball and field position we were enjoying. When they finally got their chance down our end, they made the most of it. Their centre, Krisnan Inu, went down the blind side and put in a grubber-kick for winger Sam Perrett, who pounced on it and scored in the corner.

Billy had arrived a second too late to stop the try, and his knees accidentally caught Sam in the back. He was on his knees, and when he went to get up, Inu pushed him to the ground, and that was enough for a wild brawl to break out. Bulldogs forward David Stagg got Bill in a headlock and tossed him towards the fence.

You don't need to invite Billy twice to a fight. He calmly got up and dived straight back in. That's when James Graham grabbed hold of him, and they started wrestling. Just like at the Battle of Brookvale, I was in the middle of it, not throwing punches but trying to break it up, as pockets of fights kept going, sprawling over the sideline and towards the front row of the grandstand.

After Graham was eventually pulled off him, Billy went straight to referee Tony Archer and lodged a pretty heavy complaint. 'He bit me,' Billy told him, pointing to his bloody ear.

When things finally calmed down, the video referee awarded the try and then Inu just missed the sideline conversion. Before play resumed, though, Archer pulled out me and Billy, as well as Bulldogs captain Mick Ennis.

'Are you making an allegation?' he asked Billy.

'Fucken oath,' Billy said, pointing at the bite marks and blood on his ear. 'He bit me on the ear.'

Archer turned to Ben Cummins, the pocket referee. 'You see the incident?' he said. 'You see the blood on the ear? It's on the record—that incident is on report. That's all you can do.'

I wanted Graham sent off. He's a hothead, and his attitude towards footy has made him the player he is, but you can't go around biting people.

'The last person who bit someone got eight weeks,' I said, referring to Bulldogs forward Brad Morrin, who had been suspended for biting Eels centre Timana Tahu on the arm in 2007.

'The incident's on report,' Archer said again. 'It's all you can do.'

To be honest, I was just putting pressure on the referee, trying to seed the idea of a send-off. I was out there to win. If we could play against twelve men, it would make the rest of the match a lot easier.

If Billy was rattled by the incident, it didn't show. He was right there as Cooper double-pumped, sucked Josh Reynolds out of the line and threw a perfect no-look pass for Billy to score our second try. Then, a minute from halftime, Cooper kicked to the corner, and Justin O'Neill climbed over the top of Barba to score our third.

What few could've predicted was that these would be the last points scored in that grand final—the first time it's ever happened in the history of the game.

Despite our 14–4 lead at the break, it's fair to say I kept the Dogs in the grand final because of my left foot. I landed just one from four attempts in the first half.

Early in the second half, Kasiano raised his knee into Justin O'Neill as Justin was playing the ball, and we were given a penalty. I lined up the goal from about 35 metres out—a kick I'd landed countless times before. When I missed it, I chucked the kicking tee away in frustration.

Memories of the 2007 grand final, when I kicked only three from eight, came flooding back. Even though it had been really windy that night, I still blamed myself, just as I had in this grand final five years later. 'You just can't kick at this ground,' I told myself. 'It's got you again . . .'

Goal-kicking can't be underestimated. It can change the game, particularly in the big matches. If I'd converted Justin O'Neill's try in the first half, and also landed the penalty goal attempt, the score would've been 18–4. An advantage like that in a grand final is hard to pull back. At 14–4, though, we weren't unreachable.

Yet I didn't think about handing the kicking duties to someone else—for two reasons.

One day, when I was playing for Norths against Wests Panthers at Purtell Park in the Queensland Cup, we were having a great afternoon, scoring heaps of tries, but I'd only landed a couple of goals. When I missed my sixth attempt, I told one of our trainers to tell Terry Matterson, the coach, that I'd had enough. 'Tell Box I'm not kicking anymore,' I said.

Boxy had been a cool, calm goal-kicker for the Broncos—in the club's 1992 grand final win against St George, he'd landed four goals from five attempts.

'He's a fellow goal-kicker,' I told myself. 'He'll understand.'

The trainer came back out soon after. 'Box said if you want to give the kicking away, you can come off the field as well,' he said. 'You can go sit with him in the coaches' box.'

'Righto. Tell him I'll keep kicking.'

The second reason I wasn't giving away the kicking duties in the 2012 grand final was Michael Maguire, who was our assistant coach at the time. I had the goal-kicking yips, missing them at training and in games, and it was starting to affect the way I was playing, because all I was thinking about was my poor goal-kicking.

'Madge' pulled me aside one day at training. 'Mate, don't worry about your goal-kicking,' he advised. 'If you get it, great. If you miss, whatever. Being captain, being our dummy half, is what matters most.'

So for the rest of the 2012 grand final I put my goal-kicking troubles to one side and concentrated on doing the best I could for our team.

I'd had a plan going into the game to run the ball from dummy half as much as possible, and then when I got tackled

I try to get a super-quick play-the-ball away. I identified an opportunity to do that against their middle forwards. They had some big, powerful blokes like Kasiano and Frank Pritchard, but I felt you could take away their effectiveness by getting them on the back foot.

I didn't usually want to get tackled with the ball that often, but that's what was needed in this game, so I stopped worrying so much about ball playing and focused on running and creating momentum out of dummy half. I had some good runs in the first five minutes, and I could sense that I was going to get more if I stuck at it. In the end, I finished with some ridiculous meterage (for me): 142 metres from sixteen runs, which was only two metres less than Billy.

With twenty minutes to go, Barba finally found space, breaking free down the left touchline. This was his chance to get his side back in the grand final. Josh Morris was looming up on the inside, and he grubber-kicked inside for him. The ball bounced J-Moz's way, he toed it ahead, and then he and Billy jostled to get to the ball first. At the last minute it popped up for J-Moz, and as he tried to grab the ball he fumbled it forward.

Now, if he catches it and scores next to the posts, the Bulldogs are within four points after the straightforward conversion. Instead, Billy got his hand to it first and batted it over the dead-ball line.

Now referee Archer had a crucial call to make, and I was determined to make sure he got it right. 'That's a Bulldogs knock-on!' I screamed. 'That's our feed, that's our ball. Morris touched it first.'

Morris and the rest of the Bulldogs players were adamant it should have been a line drop-out. 'Slater knocked it dead,' they argued. 'We get the feed.'

In the end, Archer got the call right: because Morris had knocked it forward first, it was a Bulldogs mistake.

We thought we had sealed the result minutes later when Bryan Norrie seemed to have scored. He played the ball on the last tackle, and Gareth put in a high kick—again directed at Barba. Billy raced through, went up for the ball and batted it backwards. Nozza was there to grab it and dive over. *Nozza! Grand final try scorer!* We got around him, knowing what he'd gone through to be on the field that night. Then the video ref returned the verdict and said he'd been offside from the kick.

'They'll never take that two minutes off me when I felt like I'd scored a try in a grand final,' Nozza joked later that night.

In the end, we won the 2012 premiership because of our defence. The Bulldogs were coming home with a wet sail, playing right to the 80th minute, like every Des Hasler–coached side. They kept peppering us but they never looked like getting through.

When the match was over, the feeling was sheer relief. I was relieved that we had the chance to go back to a grand final, just two seasons after having everything ripped from us, and that we could win it in a way that nobody could question. Not every Storm player from 2007 or 2009 had the chance to do that.

With the greatest respect to the other clubs, who else could've bounced back a year later and won the minor premiership in one season? And then, the following season, won the whole thing?

When I was asked on stage to accept the premiership trophy, I paid tribute to Bellyache. 'All of your sprays have paid off this year, mate,' I said.

Then I lifted the trophy. How did that feel? Well, I can say that 2007 and 2009 were really nice moments. I will never forget them, no matter what people say about how we won them. But there was no better feeling than doing it in 2012. That was, and remains, my proudest moment in a Storm jumper.

That night, we stayed in the sheds for as long as possible, and Bellyache didn't say a word. Later, we moved out into the middle of ANZ Stadium and huddled on the halfway line.

'I am so proud of this club, I am so proud of this organisation, where we are now after everything that's happened,' I told the group. 'We were told that the Storm were gone, they won't recover from this for a decade . . . Well, have a look at us now.'

I also made special mention of Jaiman Lowe, who had just played his last game of football. Some careers don't turn out how they are supposed to, but it meant a lot for him to go out a winner in his last match. So-called unfashionable players like him and Nozza rarely get mentioned for what they did for us. But if it wasn't for the effort of those sorts of men, where would the Storm be now?

We stayed out on the field for a long time that night, just like we stayed in the freezing cold sheds at Headingly in February 2013, after beating Leeds in the World Club Challenge. They'd beaten us 11–4 at Elland Road in the same match in 2008, before we beat them 18–10 two years later, but that title was stripped from us like everything else. So this was another box for us to tick.

We got over to the United Kingdom about ten days before the game, basing ourselves in Richmond, in south-west London. We did our conditioning work in the freezing-cold weather, then moved up to Leeds for the match.

Jesse Bromwich scored early in the second half, and then we tackled our way to an 18–14 win. Even though it was bloody freezing, we had a good long session in the sheds, enjoying the moment. We went back to the hotel and had an all-nighter there, as you do, staying in the bar area before going back to our rooms until it was time to get an 8 a.m. train back to London.

It was important we got on that train because we were heading to Loftus Road to watch Queens Park Rangers play Manchester United in the English Premier League that afternoon.

'C'mon, Smithy,' Frank Ponissi said as the minutes ticked towards 8 a.m. 'We're cutting it fine.'

Even by my standards, that was true. I only just got on that train—but I still wasn't late. We then started having more beers. The general public sitting near us loved it, singing songs along with us. When we got off at King's Cross Station, it was utter chaos. The place was chock-a-block with people. That's when I saw the pushbike: it wasn't locked up, and it was just begging for me to ride it.

People outside of the footy teams I played in wouldn't understand that I'm a bit of a prankster. 'I'll make the boys laugh here,' I thought. 'This will be funny.'

Our chief executive at the time, Ron Gauci, was with us for this trip. He had come into the club in the wake of the salary cap scandal, but he really enjoyed his time around the boys. Most club bosses might take a dim view of their captain, half-cut, riding through a huge crowd of people at King's Cross Station, but when he saw the top of the trucker hat I was wearing as I swerved in and out of this huge crowd of people, he spun around to the rest of the boys, a big smile on his face, and said, 'How good is *this*?'

Good question. How good was it? After everything we'd been through, it didn't get much better.

•

When people ask me who I'm most angry with for what happened to our club in 2010, they generally think I'll say Brian Waldron, but it's not.

It's true that he made some massive mistakes, but I remember him as a really good chief executive. He understood sport and sporting organisations, having come from AFL club St Kilda. In his five years at the Storm, he brought the football and administration parts of the club together and made us feel like one tight unit. All the admin staff knew the players. He knew all the players' partners by name. He made our working environment an enjoyable place to be. So it's hard for me to be overly critical of him, apart from the really bad decisions he made about our roster and the salary cap.

I've seen him around town a couple of times and had a handful of words with him. Nothing aggressive, and nothing to do with the Storm. It's the same with Matt Hanson. I've run into him a few times too, but 2010 wasn't discussed. Thinking about the way things went down does upset me, because it didn't need to be that way. But apart from decisions concerning the salary cap, I don't feel much anger towards either of them.

My anger is mainly directed at the NRL for the penalties they handed down, and the way the whole matter was handled. And for that I blame David Gallop. He was the one I was most disappointed in because of the way it all unfolded.

By punishing us before undertaking a thorough investigation, Gallop put the players in a position they should never have been in. It allowed the media to give the public the idea that we had knowledge of what had happened. Even though we were cleared of knowing about the cheating that went on, we were hung out to dry by the boss of the game, given no opportunity to defend ourselves and no support during the intense backlash that followed.

There have been three major salary cap breaches since the Storm in 2010—by Manly, Parramatta and Cronulla—and they were all handled far better than ours was. Thorough investigations were conducted for months before any penalties were handed down.

Years later, when Parramatta was sanctioned in 2016 for salary cap breaches, I called the NRL chief executive at the time, Todd Greenberg, and congratulated him on how he'd handled it. Not only were the players cleared of wrongdoing, they were also allowed to play for points that season, even though the twelve competition points they'd won by that time were taken from them.

'I didn't make the decision on Melbourne Storm but I'm making the decision today,' Todd said at the media conference that day. 'The decision we've made gives you an eye to the future and gives some hope to the club, and I hope they take that. When I watched the Melbourne Storm fans and players have to continue to play a season without the ability to accrue points, I thought that was soul-destroying for the players and fans. I have tried hard to find a way forward here that Parramatta Eels can take a step forward today.'

It wasn't like that with us, of course. *Bang! You've cheated. Here's your penalties* ... Then the media went on against us for months, until Deloitte did their independent audit and everyone except a couple of administrators at the top of our club was cleared.

By then, the damage was done. The mud stuck. The whole affair stirred so much speculation about the players, about Craig, about what had happened, about who knew, about who was to blame, about how it had gone down. We lost everything—and then we were told we couldn't play for competition points that year.

People will never know how difficult 2010 was for us. The game was our livelihood. We were there to compete and play for premierships. But what were we playing for? We were told to shut up, go out, put in and fulfil the NRL's broadcast deal, because if we didn't, we wouldn't be fulfilling their contractual obligations.

That was why I called Todd after the Parramatta sanctions were announced after months of investigations and interviews.

'Good on you for taking three or four months to arrive at a decision,' I said to him. 'Because I wouldn't want any player to go through what we went through.'

When Cronulla, on the eve of the 2019 season, were found guilty of serious breaches of the salary cap dating back to 2013, I was asked at the season launch if the NRL should hand back our premierships.

'Absolutely,' I said. 'They have a lot on their plate at the moment, and I don't want to take away from some of the things that have happened over the past six months. But if the NRL can have a look back and go over what happened at the Storm over those years, they may find there is a different outcome.'

Whether we should get back one premiership or both, I'm not too sure. We breached the salary cap by $459,000 in 2007 and lost the title. Cronulla was allowed to keep their premiership from 2016, when they beat us in the grand final, even though there had been systematic cheating over five years for an amount the NRL never revealed publicly. The NRL said they happened to be salary cap compliant during that one year. The Sharks received a $750,000 fine, with $500,000 of it suspended, and lost no competition points. In 2018, Manly were found guilty of breaching the salary cap over five years by $1.5 million. They were fined $750,000 but also didn't lose competition points.

In our case, if the investigations had been done first, rather than after the sanctions had been handed down, there may indeed have been a different result. Not just in terms of the penalties that were given out, but also with regard to the speculation and the finger-pointing directed at members of our team and our staff.

In the end, the Storm players came out of it as stronger people, and our club as a stronger organisation. But I do sometimes wonder: if the whole thing hadn't happened, who knows what we could've achieved in those two seasons—and in the years since?

I haven't seen David Gallop since 2012. If I ran into him in the street, I don't know how I'd react. I'm not sure if I would avoid him or say g'day, let alone bring up the past.

All Storm players get reminded of the salary cap scandal now and then. *Cheats* . . . I do hear that word, but it's mostly faded away with time. I don't think about it too much, and the memories only come back when I start talking about it at length.

I've said I wasn't an emotional player on the field, and that's true. But away from footy, the club and everyone else over those three seasons, there were times when I really struggled. When the initial shock of what had happened faded, I was heartbroken. I'd felt like I'd lost my life's work in one day.

You start playing the game when you're six years old. That grows into a dream to play in the NRL, and that dream becomes a reality. You work tirelessly, year on year, and with luck you may become a premiership player. So when all that was taken away—when the words came out of Craig's mouth that we'd been stripped of everything—that hit me really hard. *What have I been doing for the last twenty years?*

Thankfully, we were able to move on and rebuild our special club. Winning grand finals takes away a lot of the pain.

15

QUEENSLANDER!

The pain and drama of the salary cap scandal was temporarily forgotten whenever I pulled on a Maroons jumper. Those ten days in Origin camp, especially during the 2010 season when we couldn't play for points, brought welcome relief for me and the rest of the Storm players.

It helped that Queensland were carving out a special place in the history of interstate footy, as we broke team and individual records with series win after series win.

We had an air of confidence from the moment we came into camp. We were so comfortable with each other that it felt like being part of your regular club team. We always enjoyed the victories that we had but we never got carried away, which I think allowed us to go on the run that was to come. If you don't have a good handle on the way you go about winning, you can lose control of it pretty quickly.

It helped that we had great continuity in our side. We were settled. The majority of our changes came when a player retired or, more rarely, when a key playmaker was injured. As it turned out, the only match I missed during my fourteen-year Origin career was the first match of the 2010 series.

I dislocated my elbow in the Anzac Test in the first ever rugby league match at AAMI Park, the Storm's new home ground in Melbourne. I found myself in an awkward position while tackling my Storm teammate Adam Blair. When he tried to get to his feet to play the ball, my arm was twisted and out popped my elbow.

I didn't require surgery but the tendon was badly torn, side-lining me for four matches. That didn't just mean I would miss the Storm's first home match at AAMI, against the Broncos, but it also put me in jeopardy for the opening match of the Origin series, to be played at ANZ Stadium in late May.

Despite the uncertainty, the Queensland selectors still named me and I went into camp determined to play. I hate missing games of footy. If I'm not a liability, I'll do whatever I can to take the field. No excuses. I was running fine in the early training sessions. My elbow was heavily strapped, but even I was surprised by how well it had recovered. I took part in some mini games at training. It was still tender, but I could pass and run, and that was half the battle.

My main concern was tackling. I didn't want my elbow to let me down and see me miss a tackle. In Origin, one missed tackle, or one tiny moment when I couldn't reach out and pull someone in, could be all the difference. They're the small plays that determine the result and often the series. 'I'll need to test it,' I told Mal.

I knew that if I wasn't ready to play, we'd need to bring in a replacement. So on the Saturday before the game we went down to the training paddock, and one of our assistants, former Maroons hooker Jason Hetherington, ran at me. 'Let's see how the elbow goes . . .'

There was no problem with contact, but getting a grip was more difficult. The tendon was just too weak—it didn't feel right. Here we were, four days out from an Origin opener in Sydney, and I couldn't grab hold of my opponent. The last thing I wanted to do was let the jersey down—so I was ruled out.

The call went out to Manly hooker Matty Ballin, a quality player and bloke. I was really happy to see him come in. He'd been a consistent player for a long time and this was his reward. We shared a room in the lead-up to the match.

He played well, too, as did the rest of the boys on a terrible wet night at ANZ Stadium. The rain was so heavy there were puddles on the field, but it wasn't enough to stop us from winning 28–24. Sitting in the back of the coach's box, I nearly reinjured my elbow because I was punching the air so hard, hurting it each time we scored.

I was ready to rejoin the side for game two at Suncorp, especially with a series win in front of our home crowd beckoning. We were based at Coolum when the news broke on the Friday before the game about New South Wales winger Timana Tahu leaving their camp.

When it emerged the next day that he walked after Blues assistant coach Andrew Johns had made some derogatory comments about Greg Inglis, it sent shockwaves through our camp. We were stunned by the news. But it didn't affect GI—because he didn't allow it to.

Maybe he wanted to come out and have a good performance because of what happened, but what made Greg Inglis such a special player was that he always delivered on the big stage. There were a handful of matches, in the grind of the season, when he would have a quiet game. But when those headline matches were on, whether they were finals for Melbourne, big State of Origins for Queensland or Test matches for Australia, he always stood up. That's what the great players do: they stand up when it matters most. We won game two 34–6, and therefore our fifth series in a row.

When we headed back to Sydney for game three, our sole intention was the clean sweep. Our Maroons side hadn't achieved it on this run, which had started in 2006. No Queensland side had won three games in a row since Paul Vautin's 1995 team. We challenged ourselves all week to go down to Sydney and get it done—especially with New South Wales stinging about already losing the series. We snuck home 23–18 against a determined Blues side.

People were asking: how much longer could this run go for? We didn't have the answer, but I can tell you we had no intention of stopping.

I did feel sorry for Bellyache, though, who had now lost three series in a row. I knew better than anyone that he was a good coach. I also knew how invested he was in any side he coached. He just came up against a quality Queensland team that was settled and stable, and playing great footy.

It was strange leaving the Queensland camp and coming back to play for Melbourne. The first 24 hours was always weird. But once the next NRL game rolled around, we'd all moved on. That was important for the Storm, given that the whole spine of our club was playing for Queensland.

Nevertheless, I always made sure I reminded Bellyache of the result, just in case he forgot!

•

The following year, Bellyache was replaced as New South Wales coach by Ricky Stuart, his former teammate at Canberra and my first Australian coach.

I knew what Stick was all about. He got his teams up emotionally for the big games. He was very smart in the technical and tactical aspects of the game—particularly when it came to working with his halves, because he'd been such a brilliant playmaker himself. But his greatest asset was his intensity. He'd always have them in an aggressive mindset. I knew he would bring to the Blues what he'd brought to the Kangaroos, so I was wary. Without doubt he'd instil pride and passion in the jersey in his men, and that would override anything they would do tactically. That's what Origin is about.

But we had plenty of incentive too. In March Darren Lockyer had announced that 2011 would be his final season in the NRL. That meant this would be his final Origin series, too. We were determined to send our captain out a winner, just like he deserved.

The series played out accordingly. We won game one in Brisbane 16–12, but New South Wales took it to a decider when they won 18–8 in Sydney after their captain, Paul Gallen, was moved into the front row and played all 80 minutes.

The lead-up to game three back in Brisbane came soon after the devastating Queensland floods that had claimed lives and property. Suncorp Stadium had been flooded, so we were in temporary demountable sheds in the carpark. There was such confidence about our group that week as we prepared for Locky's final game in a Maroons jumper. It didn't matter what people were saying or what the Blues threw at us, we just weren't going to lose that one. As well as it being our captain's last game, we were very aware of the devastation that many Queenslanders had suffered through the terrible floods. We felt this was a great opportunity to bring some joy and positive news back into the community.

I'd learned so much from playing alongside Locky, mostly about being a leader of men. My number one takeaway was making sure my preparation was good—that I was on top of everything around camp and making sure my teammates were doing the same. In that environment, Locky also wanted us to enjoy ourselves in our downtime. We'd worked so hard to get to that point, so we needed to enjoy it.

When it came to game day, Locky was never, ever flustered. It was always about keeping a cool head. If you're lucky enough to have that personality, and those attributes, then regardless of the scoreboard and clock you'll make the right decisions.

That's the greatest lesson I learned from Locky. From 2003 to his final match, there were so many big plays in crucial matches at crucial times, moments that either turned a match or won it for us, because he was there, composed, ready to deliver.

Some people might not have noticed what he did—but I always did. Often it was something like a kick on the third tackle from our own end; a 60-metre drop punt that meant we were tackling the opposition fullback two metres from his own tryline. That would swing the momentum back to us. When you're out there playing alongside him, you're thinking, 'Mate, how are you coming up with that play in such a crucial moment?' He stayed calm in those moments when other players were losing their heads.

I wanted to send him out a winner because he deserved it. It was Bellyache who taught me the importance of playing well in milestone matches for your teammates. If it's important for them, it's important for you. This bloke had been a legend. He was a hero for me when I was a young fella. We had to send him out on a high.

We trained well all week, and it showed when we got onto the park. We led 24–0 after twenty minutes. Out of all my matches for Queensland, those twenty minutes were as good as it ever got for us.

There are a few other things I remember from that game. One was the eight-point try awarded to New South Wales fullback Jarryd Hayne in the second half after I accidentally caught him with my knees as he was scoring a try. Jarryd went across the tryline and wanted to improve his position. I was thinking,

'Mate, if you're coming in closer, you're going to have to earn it.' Because this was Origin.

When I say that, I don't mean I was trying to take his head off. My mindset was: 'I'm wearing a maroon jersey, you're wearing a blue jersey, so if you want to come in and buy some metres then I'm going to make you earn it.' I can't put it any other way. I grew up in an era of Origin where if someone didn't get in a stink or get knocked out, they weren't having a crack.

So it wasn't a late shot in which I dropped my knees into Jarryd. I was half a second late making contact with him after he put the ball down. At the time, I thought the penalty try was harsh.

The other moment concerned JT, who suffered what looked to be a season-ending knee injury. It was a sickening moment in which he hyperextended his knee. When he was going off on the medicab, the painkillers were already kicking in because he gave the thumbs up to his teammates. After the match, which we won 34–24, he emerged from the corner of the stadium in a wheelchair, one hand in the air in celebration, the other holding the green whistle that was numbing his pain.

That night will forever stand out in my career as one to remember. Locky was our hero. To give him an opportunity to win his last game at home, and to win the way we did—there simply was no better feeling.

•

The 2012 series brought back the pressure I felt in 2008 when Locky was out injured. Only this time I was taking over as captain for good. I was hell-bent on making sure I wasn't the man in charge when Queensland's wonderful winning streak ended.

With five minutes remaining in the decider at Suncorp Stadium, with the scores level at 20-all, I was wondering if that was going to happen. We'd won 18–10 at Etihad Stadium in Melbourne in game one, before New South Wales fought back with a 16–12 win in Sydney.

We started well in game three and led 16–8 at halftime. But, like in most Origins, the side that was down found a way to come back. When the Blues' centre Josh Morris scored with ten minutes to go, and five-eighth Todd Carney landed the pressure sideline conversion, it was another Origin going down to the wire.

As the clock wound down, we found ourselves about fifteen metres inside New South Wales' half, working down their left side. When it came to the last tackle, I wasn't thinking field goal. I was thinking we'd work towards a better position on the field and try to get back down there for a cleaner attempt right at the death.

You do a lot of work on field goals in the lead-up to an Origin match because the matches are always so close. I didn't practise them so much—at dummy half you have the markers all over you—but Cooper and JT spent a lot of time on them.

Coops is a right-footed kicker, so we wanted to set up on the left-hand upright so he would be kicking into the middle of the posts. I passed him the ball from way outside the left post, but instead of kicking for field position he went for the long-range field goal right on the 40-metre line.

It was so unexpected. He caught most of us off-guard. He certainly caught the crowd off-guard. I don't think anyone in the commentary box was expecting it either. He just saw an opportunity and went for it.

And he nailed it, with the ball sailing over the dead-ball line. Mitchell Pearce had one last shot, with a long-range attempt in the final minute, but he missed. It was just another game in which we found a way to win.

Through that amazing run of series victories, we found ourselves in a zone in which we could just make things happen without having to think too much about it, without having to construct things. On the rare occasions when we lost, we were completely deflated. We put so much hard work and sacrifice into the result, so when it didn't go our way, or we hadn't performed as well as we could've, it was shattering.

Mal was always positive, though. If we ever lost game one or two, his mindset was, 'We're not out of it. There's another opportunity in a couple of weeks.' He made a point of addressing our mistakes, learning from them and quickly moving on.

That was something he had to do after we lost the first match of the 2013 series, best remembered for an incident involving Paul Gallen and Nate Myles that changed the game of rugby league forever. The Blues won 14–6 in Sydney, but it was the two punches Gal put on Nate's chin that people were talking about for days afterwards.

There was always a dust-up in Origin, and Gal was never far away from it. That's the way he played, and it's what made him such a great player, particularly in the representative arena. He played with his heart on his sleeve. He was out there to win.

After the match, Gal defended punching Nate because he said he was 'over' some of the tactics Nate was employing. Specifically, he was sick of Nate using his big noggin as a weapon when he was tackling. In Nate's defence, he was just a hard man—a player who didn't get the raps he deserved for what he did on the field. He had a lot of respect among his teammates because he played tough. Did he throw his head into a lot of those tackles? Absolutely. Like all players, he did whatever was required to sting the opposition.

As I said before, it's Origin. Unless you've pulled on a jersey, unless you've been out there, it's difficult to understand the hatred the players feel in that moment. Sometimes, if things happen on the field, it can flow over into the rest of the season, and in some cases, for some players, even longer than that. But mostly it's over when the game's done.

After that match, the NRL chief executive at the time, Dave Smith, decided to change the rules. From then on, if a player threw a punch in a game of rugby league, it was an automatic sinbinning. The decree created an outcry, with many people saying the game was going soft.

In reality, the game was moving with the times. It was coming into line with the rest of society. It was harsh to blame Gal. The game had reached a point where it was being watched by more people than ever, and the people who ran the competition were conscious about who was watching: parents, women, children. Did that type of stuff turn people away from our game? In some instances, yes.

The new policy did change rugby league forever, and not entirely for the better. As a result, there's more niggle in the game than ever before. The person who's niggling knows the other player can't punch him, so he feels safe. He might also be prepared to cop a smack in the mouth because it'll put the opposition side one player down. So the plan is to bait the opponent until he throws a silly punch.

That was the negative effect of the new rule. Nowadays, you see open-handed pushes in the face, blokes slapping each other and getting away with it. If you slapped someone before that rule came in, you'd expect a knuckle sandwich in return.

Anyway, as I said, Mal was superb at making sure we moved on from our losses pretty quickly. He made sure we still had fun and enjoyed the camp, as long as we knuckled down when it was time to go to work.

When we came into camp for game two in Brisbane, we headed out for some birthday celebrations for Billy Slater and me. After dinner, we made our way to the Downunder Bar and Grill, which was near the Sofitel, where we often stayed before relocating to the Gold Coast for the remainder of the camp. Its bar was part of a backpacker hostel, and the only thing open that late on a Monday night.

'Righto, if you want a few more drinks we can head to this local bar close to the hotel,' Mal said. 'Once we call last drinks, we'll all walk home together.'

When we got there the bar was pretty busy, and soon the boys were scattered through the place. Mal was after a drink and made his way to the end of the bar. He waited for ages, trying to get the attention of the bar staff without much luck, and in the end, quite innocently, he walked behind the bar to get their attention.

They nabbed him straightaway. 'You've got to go!' the barman said. He must've been from somewhere else, I reckon, because he just rissoled the great Mal Meninga, a Queensland legend.

It was reported in the press that Mal had been pouring himself a drink, but I think that was an embellishment. Nevertheless it was a little embarrassing for Mal. Still, it wasn't the end of the world. He had bigger things to worry about.

So did I. We'd won the 2012 series so that monkey was off my back, but the pressure to keep our series streak alive remained. I didn't want to be the one in charge when our run of wins ended. Then I sat down and thought about it. It was going to happen to someone, I figured, sooner or later. If it was me, so be it. We'd been on a fantastic run.

It wasn't going to be this year, however. There were still victories to come for this Queensland side. We won game two 26–6 to level the series, but the decider back in Sydney was much, much tougher.

Both sides traded tries but, with minutes left we led 12–10 and were looking for the knockout blow. We had momentum. We had field position. Now we were on the Blues' tryline. I made a dart from dummy half and was pulled down metres from the line. I played it back for JT and he spun it to the right, where we had numbers.

For some reason, we also had a dozen or so security guards in fluoro jackets standing in our backline. They were there because there was a large, bald, naked man covered in fake tan running around like a lunatic. The ball found Matt Scott, who scored a try as the security guards wrestled the streaker to the ground and piled on top of him.

Referee Shayne Hayne, standing in the in-goal, didn't know what to do.

'That's a try, eh?' Justin Hodges asked him. 'I'll buy you a beer.'

Hayne sent the decision up to the video referee, who ruled 'no try'. We did get the loosehead and feed from the scrum.

Somehow, both sides composed themselves. The match came down to the last play of the last minute, with Robbie Farah trying for a miracle play with a crossfield kick for winger James McManus, but he knocked the ball into touch.

We'd done it. Again. Eight in a row.

When we sat down with Mal in 2006 and talked about rebuilding the culture of the Maroons, I was optimistic we could turn things around. But I never thought we would reach such a benchmark.

After that 2013 series victory, we set our eyes on a new goal: could we win ten series in a row? If we achieved that, you would think no side would ever come close to matching us. Our place in history would be assured.

16

THE CUP

We are in the dressing-rooms at the famous Wembley Stadium in London, getting strapped and massaged before we head out for our warm-up before the 2013 World Cup semi-final against Fiji.

Our focus should be our opponents. Instead, the members of the Australian side are focused on the small TV screens in the corner of the room as New Zealand and England play out the final minutes of their tense semi-final, the first of a double-header at Wembley in front of 67,000 fans.

You're always told in sport to take it one game at a time. To never think beyond the next 80 minutes, the next opponent, the next tackle. But when I notice that the Poms are winning with a minute to go, it's very hard not to think ahead. If England win and we beat Fiji, we'll be playing them in the final at Old Trafford.

This is the reason we play. The moment takes me back to my childhood, watching from the other side of the world as all these England fans hang from the rafters of their famous sporting cathedrals, singing and cheering on their country.

'How good's this, boys?' I say. 'If we win today, we could be playing England at Old Trafford.'

I've forgotten, though, that rugby league is a funny game. England prop George Burgess hits New Zealand backrower Sonny Bill Williams with a head-high tackle, right on halfway. Now the Kiwis are kicking deep for touch and have a chance to win it at the death.

In the Australian dressing-room, our pre-game preparation has stopped. Everyone's eyes are on the TV screens as the final seconds tick down. We're glued to the monitors like we're fans, instead of getting ready for a World Cup semi.

The ball goes to Shaun Johnson, the Kiwi halfback who has been in great form all tournament. England captain Kevin Sinfield comes flying out of the line to tackle him. He's just broken the number one rule when defending against Shaun Johnson: do not leave your line. Don't let him get you one on one.

Johnson snaps out a left-foot step, beats him, steps again and then scores the try that levels the scores. He's got to land the conversion from about ten metres left of the post to win it. Sure enough, he lines up his kick, slots it, and the Kiwis are through to the final.

In the Australian rooms, it's a strange feeling. Our immediate focus turns to Fiji and our own semi-final. We play well and win 64–0, booking our place in the World Cup Final at Old Trafford the following weekend.

At this stage of the tournament there was a supreme air of confidence among the Australian team. It felt like five years of hard work after losing the 2008 final to New Zealand was about to pay off. We'd gone through generational change, with players retiring or being replaced. We'd seen our captain, Darren Lockyer, retire at the end of 2011, and I'd been given the huge honour of taking on the job.

We had also put to bed any talk about the Australian side being divided along New South Wales and Queensland lines, a story that grew legs because of the hostility between the two states during Origin.

I knew where that perception had come from: the singing of the Queensland victory song after Australia had won a one-off Test in Townsville in 2012. As we were having a team photo with the trophy, JT had kicked off the Queensland team song: '*Aye aye yippee yippee aye . . .*' It's not even really a song; the Maroons don't have a song. It's just something Allan Langer sings, and we all jump on board. It comes from Ipswich, where he started playing with the Walters boys.

There was no malice in it. It was just out of habit that JT started singing it, without even thinking it was the Queensland song. I think some of the New South Wales boys even started singing along until one of their Blues teammates told them to stop.

I can understand why people were upset about what had happened, but the reaction in New South Wales was completely over the top. We were called arrogant Queenslanders, trying to stir up the Blues. Why would we do that? They were our teammates.

It was reported that Paul Gallen, the New South Wales captain and my vice-captain for the national side, was furious. So I got straight on the phone and addressed it with him.

'Mate, the media is carrying on a bit about this,' I said.

'Don't worry about it, Smithy,' Gal replied. 'I know you and the other Queensland boys, and don't think you meant anything by it. You're probably too used to singing that bloody song.'

Still, I wanted to make sure there was no confusion about where we stood. 'If you speak to any more of the New South Wales players, can you please apologise,' I said. 'If they feel like we were taking the piss, we weren't. We're the Australian side. Not Queensland or New South Wales. We're all wearing the same jumper.'

So it wasn't intentional. It was clumsy. It came across poorly and I accept that. But I'm confident that there was never a divide in the national team. There was a period there when there weren't many New South Wales players in the team, simply because Queensland was winning so much at Origin level. But we got on great with all of those New South Wales boys. We'd have beers together on the tours and I was quite close with Greg Bird and Kurt Gidley, as well as several others, and felt we all got on as a big group together.

All the players selected in the national side were united in our goal of making Australia the number one team in the world.

Since losing the 2008 World Cup final, we'd been defeated in just one match: the final of the 2010 Four Nations at Suncorp Stadium, also against the Kiwis.

We'd led that match 12–6 with ten minutes remaining, and felt in control. Then the Kiwis' winger Jason Nightingale scored in the corner and cut the deficit to two points. Right on the bell, Benji Marshall set up hooker Nathan Fien to score the match-winning try.

For the second time in three years, we'd lost a final to New Zealand. And I don't want to take anything away from the Kiwis, because they were a quality team, but I've always felt we lost those finals because we didn't play our best football.

By the time the 2013 World Cup came around, we were determined to make amends.

•

The first match of the tournament was against England at the Millennium Stadium in Cardiff. We beat them 28–20 but it was far from a polished performance.

You'll always take a win at international level, but we knew that type of performance wasn't going to be good enough if we were to win this World Cup. When we returned to our base in Manchester, we had a team meeting to review the match.

At the end, I stood up and told the room I had something to say. 'All the great teams have had success off the back of their defence,' I said. 'Conceding twenty points—that's not good enough. In the big games, the good teams win because they don't give up cheap points. Let's be a team that is almost impossible to score against.'

Everyone was in. And from that game on, we worked tirelessly on our defence at every training session.

We beat Fiji 34–2 in the next match at St Helens. Next up we played Ireland in Limerick, beating them 50–0. That set up a quarter final against the United States at Wrexham, in the north of Wales. The match was to be played at the famous Racecourse Ground, one of the oldest in the United Kingdom. The field is 94 metres long and the in-goals have an incline. If you're running to the south, you just put grubber-kicks in all day because they pull up before the dead-ball line.

The United States team were pumped. They'd reached the quarters of the World Cup and were about to face Australia.

I won the coin toss and said we'd kick off. The whistle goes, I kick off, and what happened next summed up the day for our opponents. The ball hit the right upright near the crossbar and bounced back into the field of play, where Gal dived on it.

'Here we go,' I thought. 'We're going to have a day here.'

We scored within the next 40 seconds. We won 62–0, with Jarryd Hayne and Brett Morris each scoring four tries. You don't see that too often. It was a massacre. I felt sorry for the US boys.

After beating Fiji in the semi-final, we shifted our focus to New Zealand for the final at Old Trafford. Even though I'd wanted to play England in their own backyard, it didn't mean I had less respect for the Kiwis. Shaun Johnson was playing incredible football. So was fullback Roger Tuivasa-Sheck. Up front, they had Jared Waerea-Hargreaves and Jesse Bromwich.

And they also had Sonny Bill. We all knew the type of player he was. He'd shown us that in his return season to the NRL with the Roosters, who had won the premiership earlier in the year.

Even so, as we walked into Old Trafford that day, I had that feeling again: I was just so confident we could not lose. I've said before there were certain matches, whether it was grand finals or Origins, when I just felt we couldn't be beaten. This was one of those times.

The crowd of 74,468 broke the record for a rugby league fixture in the United Kingdom. Leading the side out as captain onto Old Trafford, the ground that Manchester United had made famous, will always be one of the proudest moments of my career. It doesn't get much better than that. I'd dreamed about that as a kid, to be that person, and here I was doing it.

There was carnage early on. Tuivasa-Sheck left the field with an ankle injury. Jarryd Hayne went down with concussion but stayed on the field. The teams traded penalty goals, but when Billy scored off a kick from JT, we were away. Coops scored another just before halftime, and in the second half we tore away with the match. Billy scored in the first set, and by the end we were comfortable 34–2 winners—the biggest margin in a World Cup final.

We'd delivered on what we'd promised after that team meeting in Manchester: we hadn't conceded a single try for the remainder of the tournament. In the final, we didn't even concede a line break, and that really was something when you're facing Sonny Bill Williams playing on an edge.

Our dressing-rooms weren't the same as Manchester United's rooms, unfortunately. We were in the ones beside them, squashed in like sardines. You get accustomed to those sorts of facilities in England. But it didn't matter. It was such an enjoyable moment to have played at a ground with so much history, in so many different sports. To lift the trophy, to be a World Cup–winning captain at this venue was a magnificent feeling. This was the best I ever felt wearing an Australian jumper.

At the end of the tour, Sheensy said we were one of the best sides to have played for the Kangaroos. Comparisons were made with the 1982 Kangaroos, who were known as 'The Invincibles' because they never lost a match on that tour. That in itself was a great honour.

Obviously, I haven't seen as many games as Sheensy. But, having been fortunate to be part of some great Australian sides, I can safely say I was never part of a more complete team.

•

The World Cup victory made up for the disappointing way the Storm had finished its 2013 season. We did quite well throughout the regular season, finishing third behind the Roosters and Souths, but we were quickly bundled out of the finals, losing to the Rabbitohs and then Newcastle.

The World Cup also made me think a lot about my future. Throughout that tournament, and then into the off-season, there was increasing speculation about my long-term future at the Melbourne Storm.

I was coming off contract at the end of 2014. While people on the outside were putting pressure on me to make a call, the real pressure was on my family. Specifically, it was on Barb.

Our young family had really grown. Our younger daughter, Matilda, had just turned two. Our son, Jasper, was four and our elder daughter, Jada, was six. So we had three young kids, living in a foreign city away from family, and because I was playing a lot of football it meant that Barb was doing all of it on her own.

As great as winning the World Cup was, I felt my football career was making life harder for our family. It got to the point where I needed to make a decision that would ease the strain on Barb and take us back to where our family was. And they were all in the south of Brisbane.

During the 2014 season, I pulled Craig aside after a training session. It is still something I remember clearly. We had played the Wests Tigers on a Monday night in Campbelltown, and instead of returning home to Melbourne we based ourselves at Nelson Bay ahead of our Round 22 game against Newcastle on the Saturday. 'I think this is going to be my last year in Melbourne,' I told him.

He was shocked, and I could understand why. The idea that I might leave had seemingly come out of nowhere, without warning.

'Mate, it's the right decision for the family,' I explained to him. 'It's really challenging down in Melbourne at the moment, particularly for Barb, looking after three kids by herself. I don't want her going through that any longer. I want her around her family and friends who can support her when I'm not there. I feel that's the best thing to do.'

I could tell straightaway that Bellyache thought I was making the wrong decision. But then Bellyache did a very Bellyache thing.

'If that's what you and Barb believe is right for you, that's all that matters,' he said.

The Broncos were the obvious choice. They were being coached at the time by Anthony Griffin, although he would later be replaced by Wayne Bennett for the 2015 season. My manager Isaac Moses spoke to the club, and discussions progressed far enough that I knew they were keen to get me up there. There were media reports about them tabling an offer worth more than $1 million a season, but the truth is I never saw an official offer, let alone a contract. It never got that far. Still, in my mind, we were gone.

Then Barb stopped the whole thing in its tracks. As I've said, she knows me better than anyone, and she knew I felt uneasy about moving back home.

So Barb did a very Barb thing.

'Cam, it's going to be challenging down here, but if you want to play for the Storm, which I know you want to do, I'm happy to support you,' she said. 'We will get through it together.'

That uneasiness I felt about leaving Melbourne disappeared straightaway. Several weeks later, I pulled Bellyache aside.

'I've had a change of mind,' I said. 'We're not going anywhere.'

'When I see Barb next,' Bellyache replied, 'I'm going to hug her.'

17

ALEX

I can remember most things that have happened in almost every game of footy I've ever played. Scores, details, how tries came about and how they didn't.

There's only one thing, though, that I recall from the Round 3 match between the Storm and Newcastle at AAMI Park on Monday, 24 March 2014, and that is the incident involving Newcastle Knights forward Alex McKinnon.

This is the hardest chapter of the book for me to write, because of the injury that Alex suffered and the resulting impact it had on his life. It was a tragic accident and a lot of the anger about what happened was directed at the Melbourne Storm and at me. Most of that anger is because of what I said on the field to referee Gerard Sutton, and how things transpired with Alex in the days, weeks and months that followed. This is my chance to clarify what has been said—and reveal what hasn't.

The tackle involving Alex happened in the final minute of the first half. He took the ball up on the 30-metre line, and was tackled by Jordan McLean, Kenny Bromwich and Kenny's brother, Jesse. Jordan had hold of one leg, Kenny was around his shoulders, and Jesse played a minor part as the third man into the tackle. Sutton blew a penalty for a dangerous throw.

I immediately thought it was a rough call. I didn't believe the ball-carrier had gone above the horizontal, which is usually what marks a dangerous throw. I went across to Sutton to ask about the penalty, as I usually would, without really knowing what was happening on the ground with Alex.

'What's the penalty for?' I asked Sutton.

'Lifting,' he said.

'Okay,' I said, nodding.

Then there was some pushing and shoving between the two teams.

'Cameron, just take them back,' Sutton said. 'I'll talk to you in a minute.'

As Sutton was speaking, I looked across to where Alex was on the ground, and I realised the injury was more serious than I'd first thought. Alex was talking and had some movement, but it was clear he was in a bad way.

Having been in the game for such a long time, I'd seen guys in similar positions where there were concerns about an injury around the head or neck, where they were on the ground with the trainer, and sometimes even stretchered off, but they'd all ended up being okay.

So I thought the concern being shown for him was probably precautionary. That's what happens 9.9 times out of ten when a player is injured like that. They leave the field, but they're back the following week. That was my immediate thought.

The longer he was attended to, the greater our concern became for what was happening with Alex. The rest of the Storm players and I stood back, in silence, watching on along with the Knights players. It took eight minutes for Alex to be carefully placed on a stretcher and taken from the field.

It wasn't until the medical staff were carrying him across the sideline that Sutton and I started discussing the penalty, at which point I defended my teammates.

'We've had two lifting tackles against us, where our boys were put in more dangerous positions than that,' I said. 'We can't help when he ducks his head into the ground. It's unfortunate, and I don't want to see that happen at any time in our game, but if he doesn't duck his head, that doesn't happen.'

'I understand what you're saying,' Sutton said.

'How can you penalise that?' I continue.

'But it's lifted . . .'

'So anyone who ducks their head gets a penalty from now on?'

'Cameron, he's put in a dangerous position . . .'

'I understand that . . .'

'It's going on report.'

If you watch the replay, compared to an earlier tackle made against one of our players when they were driven headfirst into the ground and bounced back up, this one looked fairly innocuous. Alex always had one foot on the ground, and at one stage one hand on the ground. He was never lifted into the air and driven, which is why I was asking the question about the penalty.

That dialogue went on for 30 seconds. It was no longer than that, and with no knowledge at all about the seriousness of the situation. Never before and never since in my career have I seen a tackle like that turn into such a life-changing incident.

The play resumed and we won 28–20, but at no stage did I know about the grave concern for Alex in the dressing-room, or that he had been rushed to Royal Melbourne Hospital. That news didn't reach us until the next day, when it emerged that he may have suffered serious spinal injuries.

Everyone at the club, but especially the players who played that night, wanted to make contact with Alex. We actually wanted to go and see him, because we knew he was being treated in Melbourne. Our football manager, Frank Ponissi, was great as always. He was liaising with the Knights about it, but the message kept coming back that Alex needed time; he couldn't have visitors yet. It later came out that he was suffering from pneumonia. All we knew, though, was that he couldn't have visitors because he was in the intensive-care unit.

That's what we were told for days and weeks. Then we were told pretty bluntly: 'No, they don't want you up there at all.' Anthony Quinn, our former winger, was working for the Knights at the time, and was trying to facilitate some of us coming in to visit Alex, but the message that came back was clear: 'You're not welcome.'

I understood that—Alex and his family were going through a terrible situation and wanted space. At the same time, I wanted them to know that I, and we as a club, had genuine concern for Alex and his welfare.

The other person I was worried about was Jordan McLean. From that night on and then for the weeks and months to come, he was in a bad way. He really struggled, and he didn't talk too much about it. Jordan's a country kid and was at the start of his career when that incident occurred. Thinking that he'd contributed to someone being paralysed was a heavy burden to carry for a young player. I checked in with him regularly. He put on a brave face for everyone, but we knew he was hurting deep down.

The truth is what happened to Alex rocked all of us, and from there it didn't take long for the barbs to come out for the Melbourne Storm. Someone had been seriously injured while playing against the Storm, and of course the reason was our 'grubby tactics'. The accusation was that our defensive system was dangerous, and on this occasion the consequences had been devastating.

Some commentators argued that it was a Storm ploy to grab one leg to destabilise them. In fact, if you watch that match, you'll see our players were on the end of some pretty heavy lifting tackles in the first half. Knights backrower Beau Scott was penalised for one on Bryan Norrie in the first minute. Dane Gagai lifted Ryan Hoffman in the eleventh minute in a tackle but wasn't penalised. In the 26th minute, Beau Scott picked up Ben Hampton by one leg and drove him into the ground, a tackle that also didn't attract a penalty.

The other accusation levelled at the club and at me was that we never reached out to Alex to see how he was. As I've said, that's just incorrect. For the two weeks Alex was in hospital in Melbourne, we tried to contact him and even wanted to see him. I don't know if Alex was ever made aware of those approaches, but I was on the front foot every day. 'How is he? Can we go up there? Can we talk to him?'

In early July, Paul Gallen and I launched the 'Rise For Alex Round' to raise funds and honour Alex. In the Round 19 match, I wore No. 16 on my back—the number Alex was playing in on that terrible night back on 24 March.

At the same time, the Storm was still reaching out. It wasn't reported that way, though. There were claims we didn't care. That we had no regard for the injury that he'd suffered.

And that simply wasn't true.

•

In early May 2015, Isaac Moses called to say that Channel Nine's flagship current-affairs show, *60 Minutes*, was doing a story on Alex. 'You may be in it,' he said.

'What does that mean?' I asked, confused.

He explained that the piece might refer to me talking to the referee during the match.

'Oh, okay,' I said. 'No worries.'

At first I didn't think much about potentially featuring in the *60 Minutes* report because I was comfortable with my actions on the night. I don't normally think the worst of people.

'Surely they wouldn't stitch me up,' I figured. As the program got closer, however, and the buzz about the story started to grow, I could sense how this was going to play out.

It soon emerged that the program would air on the Sunday three days before the deciding match of the 2015 State of Origin at Suncorp Stadium.

The timing of the program made me curious. Were they doing this to enhance TV ratings, for the game and the program, or was it a coincidence? But when that Sunday came around, by which time the promos for the program had been aired, it was pretty obvious it was going to be an explosive story.

Barb and the kids came into camp a few days before the Origin match, like all families were allowed under Mal. We refused to watch the program. Why would I put myself through that? Not just because we had a crucial game in a few days' time, but at any time?

Plenty of others did watch it though, and reported back straightaway that it had shown me in a very ordinary light.

I've never seen the program in full. Below is an outline of what apparently occurred, which I am aware of, but I will never watch the episode myself.

What I have been told is that the story, hosted by reporter Liz Hayes, had five parts, and by the end of the third segment the finger was being pointed at me. I was described as 'the one player who has never said sorry'.

After the commercial break, I became the focus of the story. 'Incredibly, Alex feels no anger or resentment towards the Melbourne Storm players who made that tackle,' Hayes says.

'But he's furious about what happened in the minutes after, and the actions of the Australian captain.'

Sitting at Alex's kitchen bench and in front of a laptop, Hayes shows Alex the tackle and my reaction to it. It's a complete misrepresentation of how those eight minutes played out.

'Is he still debating?' Alex says. 'Is he fucking serious?'

'This was the first time that Alex had seen this footage,' Hayes says in her voiceover. 'As Alex lay paralysed, and even eight minutes later when he was carried off the ground, Smith continues to argue that Alex caused his own injury.'

The way it's presented makes out I argued with the referee for the entire time Alex was being attended to on the ground, with no regard for his welfare.

'I don't know what's driving him there,' Hayes says.

'That's the Australian captain there, so well done,' Alex says. 'It's fucking ridiculous.'

'Has Cameron Smith contacted you?' she asks.

'No, I don't know if he's tried or not through Anthony Quinn or the club, but if Jordan McLean could make contact, I haven't heard anything,' he says.

Jordan had texted Alex, but I had kept making approaches to him via our club.

Wayne Bennett, who was Alex's coach at Newcastle at the time of the incident, was also interviewed for the program.

'I know Cameron Smith,' Bennett says. 'I've coached him at different levels, at state level and All Stars, he's a decent person, he's a good person. I have to assume that on the night he got it wrong.'

After the program aired, Isaac called me a few times to see that I was alright. And I was, because I hadn't seen it. Then I went down to the team room at the hotel where we were staying. The players and staff there were on eggshells around me, not knowing if I'd watched the program.

The next morning, when I came down for breakfast, there was concern for me. The story was all over the newspapers— not that I was going to read them. We had the Monday off, so I spent the day with Barb and the kids, then we had a team dinner that night. That was when Mal grabbed me.

'If you need anything, if you don't want to come to dinner, just let me know,' Mal said.

'Mal, I'm all good,' I replied.

'That's great,' he said, 'but I wouldn't mind you letting the guys know at dinner that you're okay, because they're really concerned about you. Being the skipper, it would be good to let them know that you're alright and they can get on with things.'

We got on the team bus to head to dinner, but before we drove off, I stood in the aisle and asked for everyone's attention.

'Boys, I know there's some shit going on at the moment after the *60 Minutes* program,' I said. 'I just want you to know that I haven't watched it. I know some of you have, and it is what it is. I'm fine, my family is fine, I'm just focused on doing what we have to do to beat New South Wales.'

In truth, Barb was very upset. People left me alone—they probably didn't know what to say to me—but she took a lot of calls and text messages. She was rattled by the whole business, and concerned for me like she always is.

The Queensland Rugby League let Nine know how I felt: there was no way I was talking to them before, during or after the match during their telecast on Wednesday night. I said to our team managers that I would do an all-in press conference after the game, but that was it. Anywhere else—at the coin toss, for example—I wouldn't be talking to them. I would be walking away.

It put me in an awkward position because Darren Lockyer—my former captain and a really good mate—was on the Nine panel, and I was going to have to brush him. It had nothing to do with him, but I couldn't have anything to do with him because he was carrying a Nine Network microphone.

My teammates were also unhappy with how I had been portrayed. They carried a lot of that anger into the game.

As I said, this Origin was to be a decider. We'd won the first match, at ANZ Stadium in Sydney, 11–10, thanks to a late Cooper Cronk field goal, but then New South Wales had won the second, at the Melbourne Cricket Ground, 26–18.

It's hard to describe the emotion our team was feeling that night. I don't know if my teammates were convinced the *60 Minutes* program had been a ploy to put us off. We were a very tight team, and someone had come after one of us. My teammates needed to vent that frustration somewhere, and the first opportunity they had was in Origin III.

We ran in three tries in the first half and led 22–2 as we left the field. As we did, the Nine producers on the sideline were looking for players to interview.

That's when Johnathan Thurston stepped in. 'Nobody talks to them,' he barked at our players.

The same thing happened after our record 52–6 victory.

A few weeks after the program aired, I called Alex. He and I had not spoken since the game on 24 March.

I was really pleased to hear directly from Alex that he had improved a lot since the injury occurred. It was also an opportunity to let him know I had attempted to contact him, and visit, but was turned away.

Towards the end of the call we spoke about the *60 Minutes* program and how that played out. The way Alex described it to me, they had that vision on a loop. He said they kept asking him over and over and over until they got the angry reaction out of him that they wanted. He kept apologising to me for that, which I thought was wrong.

'Alex, you don't have to be sorry for anything at all, mate,' I said. 'You're not the one who needs to be apologising. You didn't put the program together.'

I felt bad for him, and wanted to know who was in the room looking after him when *60 Minutes* were filming. Was someone there saying, 'That's enough' when they pushed and pushed him until they got a reaction? Those producers and journalists are trained to get reactions out of people. They knew exactly what they were doing and got exactly what they wanted.

The worst thing about that story was a shifting of the narrative away from Alex and his fiancée, now his wife, Teigan. They had an inspiring story of him overcoming so much adversity, Teigan helping him through it and them getting engaged.

They took that beautiful story away from them by putting me in there and sensationalising things.

•

After the Origin series, my emotions went from shock about what Nine had done, and why they might have done it, to being quite angry that I had been used in this way to get people to watch their show. For ratings.

Within days of the program airing, defamation lawyers reached out to say if I wanted to take on Nine, they'd happily run the case because we would win. At the heart of it was the fact I had never been contacted for my version of events. Instead, they came to me for a right of reply after the program aired. They figured they'd get another show out of it. Unbelievable.

In the end, Barb and I decided that it was best not to pursue any legal action. There were no winners in a situation like that. Mainly, I didn't want to drag Alex through it all again. He'd already suffered a major injury. Me taking on Nine would inevitably have dragged him into it. So we let it go.

What I did say is that I wouldn't be speaking to them on rugby league matters until they apologised. And that's what happened for a long time. I was asked on numerous occasions, but always refused. At the time I was captain of my club, my state and my country, and they regularly wanted to talk to me pre-game, post-game, at halftime. I just said, 'Nope, not doing it.'

Ten months later, on 9 May 2016, things came to a head at a meeting at Crown Casino in Melbourne. On one side of the table were Barb, Isaac and me. On the other were Nine's chief executive, Hugh Marks, Nine Melbourne's managing director, Ian Paterson, and head of sport Tom Malone, who also happened to have been the executive producer of *60 Minutes* the previous year when the program had aired. Sitting in the middle was NRL chief executive Todd Greenberg.

We asked why I hadn't been contacted for comment before the program had aired, and they said they didn't feel like I needed to be in it. That made no sense. Why wouldn't they give me a chance to share my opinion?

But the main point Barb and I made was just how used I felt. We didn't speak solely about the program on Alex—it was about everything.

'When you're making these programs, do you think about the people you line up?' I asked. 'Not just the effect of it on them, but on their families? I've got a mum and dad in Queensland, a brother and sister, and they have children. They have to go to work and out in public. People know I'm their son, their brother . . .

'What about my wife and my children? This is a show that's shown across the entire country, and look at the way you've portrayed me as a person. Is there any responsibility there at all?'

Barb and I got it all off our chests, and I think they were quite taken aback by the emotion from both of us. I didn't get teary, but I did choke up talking about it because of the effect it had on my family.

When Barb spoke, she asked Tom directly how he would feel if he and his family had to walk in our shoes. 'How would you like that said about you?' she asked. 'How would you like your kids to watch that, then take them to school, with all the parents looking at you?'

All we wanted out of that meeting was for them to realise what they had done, and the effect it had had on us as a family. And we wanted an apology. We didn't want money. We didn't want a settlement. But an apology was important. The question was: how were we going to get it?

'*The Footy Show*'s coming up,' Tom said, referring to the long-running Thursday-night league show hosted by Paul 'Fatty' Vautin. 'Why don't you come on and we'll do it there?'

'Why do I have to come on?' I asked. 'Why can't you go on *The Footy Show* and say, "We ran a show on *60 Minutes* and it involved Cameron Smith, we got it wrong, we should've given Cameron an opportunity to be a part of the program, we want to apologise for the way it was handled"?'

'Yep, that sounds fair,' Tom said.

In the end I agreed that I would appear on the show alongside Tom, who would issue an apology. On 25 May, I flew to Sydney. Dave Prentice, who is part of my management group, was there with me, making sure it all went smoothly.

Just before we were about to go on-air, the show's executive producer, Glenn Pallister, came into the green room with a printout of the apology that was going to be read out.

'Mate, this is what we're going to do,' he said. 'The panel will be out there, Fatty will be there, and he will introduce you. You sit down, he asks you a couple of questions, and then just talks to you about the *60 Minutes* program, about what happened, and then he's going to apologise.'

I was stunned. 'What?' I asked. 'Why is Fatty apologising? He's done nothing wrong.'

'He's doing the apology,' Pallister said.

'No, no, no,' I said. 'Where is Tom Malone? He said he would be here doing it, that was the deal.'

'This is the way we're doing it.'

'This is bullshit,' I said.

Dave jumped on the phone to Isaac, because I wasn't going to go on. Five minutes until I was supposed to appear, I was ready to pull the pin.

Fatty was rattled by it too, because he had been lumped with the task just before we went on.

In the end, I just did it. I felt I had to get it over with.

'We know it's been a difficult relationship between Channel Nine and yourself over the past twelve months,' Fatty said. 'With regards to those issues, on behalf of the Nine Network, we want to apologise to you and your family.'

'Yeah, it has been a difficult twelve months, and I want to thank you for that apology on behalf of the network,' I said. 'It's no secret I was pretty disappointed with the *60 Minutes* episode that aired last year, and everything that's happened afterwards too.'

Then we talked about football.

It's been a long time since all that happened. I've moved on. I don't harbour any ill feeling towards Nine now. I've spoken with Tom Malone numerous times since. I've seen him at NRL functions, and it has been fine.

But I walked away that night pissed off about how it had all gone down. After everything that happened, they couldn't even get the apology right.

18

LOSING IT

What happened to Alex that night at AAMI Park had a profound effect on our 2014 season.

In the rare lean times we had at Melbourne, what gave many of our players some respite was Origin football. But for the Queenslanders in our team, this wasn't the case in 2014. There wasn't much fun there, especially for Coops.

We went into the first match hunting down a ninth consecutive series win. We made just one change, and only because of injury: Matt Gillett came into the starting side in place of Sam Thaiday. Aidan Guerra came onto the bench.

New South Wales again made plenty of changes, with Bulldogs halves Trent Hodkinson and Josh Reynolds replacing Mitchell Pearce and James Maloney. Jarryd Hayne also replaced Josh Dugan at fullback. The Blues were also undermanned because of circumstance: Greg Bird was suspended, and Andrew Fifita and Boyd Cordner were ruled out with injury.

Victory in the first game, at Suncorp Stadium, would set us up nicely for the rest of the series. We would also host the third match, but it'd be nice to head to Sydney for game two with one hand on the trophy. Defeat, of course, would mean we'd have to win at ANZ Stadium to keep the series alive.

The game started as we'd hoped, with our winger Darius Boyd scoring after just five minutes. But just minutes later, disaster struck: Cooper left the field with a suspected broken arm. New South Wales scored through Brett Morris and Jarryd Hayne, and then tackled their way to a 12–8 win.

Scans revealed that Cooper would be out for twelve weeks—a devastating blow for Queensland and Melbourne. But as we prepared for the must-win game in Sydney, there were other injury concerns. Greg Inglis, Billy Slater and Coops' replacement at halfback, Manly's Daly Cherry-Evans, were all in doubt. They were ultimately cleared to play but it wasn't an ideal preparation.

The match was a complete grind. The only points in the first half came from two penalty goals off JT's boot. Sammy Thaiday looked to have scored the first try of the match in the 51st minute, but the video referee ruled he'd lost possession while trying to ground the ball.

Then, in the 71st minute, the Blues finally broke our line when Trent Hodkinson threw a dummy and scored. He kicked the pressure conversion of his own try and suddenly, trailing 6–4, our amazing run of Origin series victories was in serious danger of coming to an end.

But we're Queensland. We're never dead. We always find a way.

Then we kicked off and the ball sailed over the dead-ball line. Replays showed that the footy actually brushed Blues prop Aaron Woods, so it should've been a line drop-out. Instead, New South Wales were given a penalty on halfway. As in game one, they then tackled their way to victory.

The Woods moment was very controversial and received plenty of discussion in the days that followed, but we couldn't blame the loss on that one call. In both matches, I felt, we hadn't given ourselves the best opportunity to win. We hadn't played to our capabilities. We'd also fallen into the trap of playing defensive football, which wasn't us.

Losing our first series since 2005 was devastating, mostly because we'd won eight in row. It sounds greedy to say that, doesn't it? But everyone knows we were the type of team that never backed off, that never gave up, that always found something.

I wouldn't say we were complacent, or that we had a lack of respect for New South Wales. They certainly played well. But the most deflating thing for us was that we hadn't given ourselves a chance, starting with our loss at home in the opening match.

It was a very empty feeling in the dressing-room after that defeat, especially because there would be no deciding third match. We still had a game to play, back at Suncorp, but it would be for pride only.

Cooper made a miracle recovery from his broken arm to make his way back into the side for game three, which we won 32–8, but it was little comfort after losing the series.

That series loss was the beginning of speculation about Daly's place in the Queensland team. Rumours started circulating that senior players in the team didn't like him, that he didn't fit in, and that he wasn't welcome. It was rubbish. As far as I was concerned, there was no issue there at all with Daly.

He was a different style of player, no doubt. And very different to Coops. That was the only thing that didn't always work—the footy. It wasn't the relationship or his personality type. I'm not entirely sure why things didn't click on the football front. I wouldn't say it was all because of Daly, either. I played in Australian sides with him over the years and he performed well. So had the team.

As the years went on after that 2014 series loss, the stories and rumours took on a life of their own, as they often do in rugby league. Because it was said so much, it became true in many people's eyes. I never addressed it with Daly personally because I knew it wasn't true and didn't think there was an issue.

Inside the team, we would look at each other and ask, 'Where's this stuff coming from?'

•

The Origin series loss was the start of a really ugly season for me. The Storm won fourteen matches and lost ten to finish sixth on the ladder—the leanest regular season the Storm had had since I became a regular first-grade player. We struggled to string wins together. Just when it looked like we were getting a roll on, we'd suffer back-to-back losses.

A moment that summed things up came in the second-last round, when we played the Roosters at Allianz Stadium. We needed a win to secure a top-four finish, which meant a double bite of the cherry if we lost in the first week of the finals. But I threw a wild pass to our winger Sisa Waqa, which floated out in front of him. He knocked it on—and the Roosters scored. We lost 24–12. I was filthy.

In the final match before the finals, against the Broncos at AAMI Park, I did the syndesmosis ligament in my left ankle. I left the field but later returned as we ran out 22–12 winners, but it wasn't a great sign when I had to hobble into recovery on crutches the next morning.

I couldn't train at all in the lead-up to our match against Canterbury in the first week of the finals. I couldn't even run. A grade-two syndesmosis usually means a six- to eight-week recovery, but I was determined to play. I needed to play. We weren't going well, so I was desperate to take the field.

In reality, I shouldn't have. I didn't get scans on my ankle because I knew how bad it was. I had painkilling injections and put an ankle brace on. So I was in the game but I couldn't feel my foot. The Bulldogs scored in the first set and won 28–4.

It was the end of what had been a season to forget for the Storm. But my year wasn't yet over.

•

Tony Ayoub was the physio for the Storm that year, and also for the Australian team.

'Is this ankle going to be okay for the Four Nations?' I asked him after the loss to the Bulldogs.

'That's five weeks away,' Tony said. 'It should be okay. Just rest up, stay off it and you'll be right to go.'

After three weeks, I figured I had to do *some* training. So I started to run and felt alright. We got into the tournament, but after some high-intensity training and playing, my ankle just didn't feel right. It felt terrible, to be honest.

I shouldn't have played that series but felt obligated to because the Australian squad had already been hit by other players being ruled out with injury. Billy was gone because of a knee complaint. JT and Matt Scott had shoulder injuries.

We went into the tournament with a lot of experience missing, but that didn't mean we had an excuse to not win the series against New Zealand, England and Samoa. We had a great footy team.

Things didn't start well. We lost the opening match 30–12 against New Zealand at Suncorp Stadium. In the second match, my 40th in the green and gold, we only just scraped through 16–12 against England at AAMI Park. We beat Samoa 44–18 at WIN Stadium in Wollongong, setting up the final against the Kiwis in Wellington.

It was the best match we played all tournament—yet we still lost. Shaun Johnson played the house down, as he often did against us, stepping around defenders and kicking goals from the sideline. We had our chances early, and scored the opening try through Michael Jennings, but then the home team got away from us.

They led 22–12 before we mounted a brave fightback. Benny Hunt came off the bench and scored with four minutes left. I converted and we were within touching distance, down by four points with minutes to play.

In the last minute, our eighteen-year-old winger, Newcastle's Sione Mata'utia, looked to have scored in the corner, but English referee Phil Bentham called the last pass forward. A try would've levelled the scores and given me a kick from the sideline to win it. It was a fifty-fifty call, and this time it went against us.

Until that tournament, Australia had suffered just one loss in our previous 36 Tests. Now we'd suffered two in the space of three weeks. That put a lot of pressure on our coach, Tim Sheens, as well as the senior players, and the pressure carried all the way through to the following year's Anzac Test, to be played in Brisbane.

We were meant to play the Kiwis on a Friday night, but Brisbane was smashed by a ridiculous storm and torrential rain, so the match was postponed until the Sunday afternoon. We went back to the hotel, then had to do another captain's run on Saturday and play the following day.

When we finally took the field, we came up against a Kiwi team that was the most confident I ever faced. They seemed to feel unbeatable that day. Their energy, their enthusiasm was immense—it just felt they were faster and stronger than us. I never felt like we were in the game. They just dominated us from start to finish.

It was their first Anzac Test victory in seventeen years, and the first time since 1953 that they'd won three matches in a row against Australia. There had been a turning point in international football. As I've written, there was an expectation on every Australian team to win.

Maybe things would've been different if Sione had been awarded that try in the Four Nations final the year before, and I'd been given a chance to slot the winner from the sideline. But the call didn't go our way. Nothing did that year.

19

GETTING IT BACK

We were in Sydney for a club match in early June 2015 when Billy pulled me aside. We were playing Penrith and he'd been ruled out with a shoulder injury that had been giving him plenty of grief.

'It's busted,' Billy said.

'What do you mean "busted"?' I replied.

'I think I'm done for the year. It's that bad.'

I couldn't believe it. Billy had been playing with this injury all season, as a lot of NRL players do. And Billy was as tough as anyone I'd ever played with, so I knew it was serious if he was accepting he couldn't carry that injury any longer.

Then he did, for one last match. Queensland had won the first game of the Origin series after Cooper once again kicked a field goal to win the match at ANZ Stadium, just like he had in 2012. This time it came in the 72nd minute, securing the win 11–10. Billy made it through that match but was in doubt for the second, at the Melbourne Cricket Ground three weeks later. He played but, as the game went on, he could just tell he wasn't going to be able to be at his best.

We lost 26–18, and soon after it emerged that he needed surgery; if he didn't have it, he risked doing permanent damage. Such was the damage to his rotator cuff that he could barely get his arm above his head. He needed a complete shoulder reconstruction.

The ascendancy, according to the experts, was with New South Wales. Their halfback, Mitchell Pearce, also felt that the tide had turned. Towards the end of the MCG game, Pearcey was a bit chirpy. 'Too old, you blokes,' he told us. 'You need to give it away, you're too old.'

The Blues had played a great game that night. They were quick and skilful, and we had looked a bit slow. Many experts were saying it was time for generational change in our side.

Thankfully, for the decider at Suncorp, the selectors didn't listen. They rarely do.

Late in the game, after we'd reached the 50-point mark, JT spotted Pearcey.

'Go and get a photo with the Wally Lewis statue,' JT said, referring to the sculpture outside the ground. 'That's as close as you'll ever get to the Origin shield.'

After our Origin series win, I returned to Melbourne and set my sights on trying to win the premiership without our number one fullback.

The Storm's 2015 squad was the youngest in our history. We were in a phase when many older players had moved on, but we weren't signing many players from outside our system. We were developing players who had been signed as schoolboys and then played in junior rep sides and the under-20s. Then we started to get some of those younger players into our squad.

That was the path the club thought was the best for our long-term future. And it proved successful straightaway.

Billy's shoulder injury allowed us to blood a kid called Cameron Munster. He was a very talented player who came to us as an outside back, but he had value as a utility as well. He could play in the halves if he had to, although he saw himself as a fullback. That's where he wanted to play. For the rest of the 2015 season, he would play mostly in the No. 1 jumper.

You could tell straightaway that he had something special. Just his ability to come up with plays when you needed it, without even having practised it—that innate ability to make something out of nothing—was impressive. We had a kid who knew the game, knew where he had to be, and was supremely confident.

After everything that had happened in 2014, many experts believed the Storm was finally on the way down the ladder. Instead, we finished the regular season in fourth position, then knocked off the minor premiers, the Roosters, in the first week of the finals.

All of a sudden we had a week off and would be playing the Cowboys in the preliminary final. It set up a showdown with my old mate Johnathan Thurston, as well as the many other Maroons teammates who made up the North Queensland team. Instead of storming into the grand final, though, we were completely outplayed by the Cowboys. They won 32–12, and JT was untouchable.

I left the field with mixed emotions. I was so disappointed with the way we went out but I was really happy for JT, who was getting a chance to finally win a grand final for North Queensland. It had been a decade since the Cowboys had featured in a decider, and there was enormous pressure on him to deliver a premiership for the North Queensland region before he retired.

There were other players in that side like Matt Scott, James Tamou, Ben Hannant, Justin O'Neill and Rory Kostjason who I knew well, having played alongside them for Australia, Queensland or the Storm, but I just wanted the pressure off JT's shoulders. I knew how much he'd put into the Cowboys and the whole North Queensland region. Winning the grand final against the Broncos, who had beaten the Roosters in the other preliminary, would make it even sweeter.

'I hope you win it, mate,' I said to him as we left AAMI Park that night.

I wanted him to win—but that didn't mean I was going to watch. I never do. If I'm not playing in the grand final, I won't watch it. I just can't.

'Did you watch the granny?' my Storm teammates have asked over the years.

'No, I didn't,' I'll say flatly. 'What for? Our season has finished.'

That might sound strange but it's just my mindset. If we're not playing in the grand final, I can't watch. It's too painful.

In fact, the only one I've watched since making my NRL debut was the 2010 decider, and that was because I'd been invited by ANZ Stadium to do some pre-game corporate speaking, so I was at the ground. This was the year of the salary cap scandal, of course, so I'd known since April that I wouldn't be playing.

So as much as I wanted JT to win, I couldn't stomach watching the final match of 2015. That didn't mean I wasn't interested in the result. There were a lot of players in both those sides who I knew, so I was curious about where it was headed.

'Hey, Barb?' I yelled out as I pottered around the backyard that evening. 'Check the score, would you?'

Barb looked it up on her phone.

'Oh my god!' she screamed. 'The Cowboys have just scored on full-time. JT has a kick from the sideline to win it.'

'Turn the TV on!' I shouted, racing into the house.

They were showing a replay of Cowboys winger Kyle Feldt scoring in the corner. JT had his headgear off and was sipping from a water bottle on the sideline, then he lined up the conversion attempt that could win his side the grand final.

'He's taking too long,' I said. 'I know it's a big kick, but he doesn't usually take this long.'

JT looked good with his setup, but I was concerned that the amount of time he was taking would upset his routine. These are the things that go through your head as a goal-kicker.

As he came in to kick the ball, I stood up in the middle of my loungeroom. It looked nice off his boot, but it wasn't curling back for him as much as it usually does. It stayed fairly straight. When the ball hit the upright and the camera showed a close-up of JT, it wasn't hard to read his lips. I was saying the same thing in my loungeroom.

We all know what happened next. It went to golden point and Benny Hunt dropped the ball from the kick-off. As soon as the Cowboys got the scrum feed, I knew that JT would do what he did best and finish it off.

And he did.

•

Missing big matches is hard for most players, but particularly for someone like Billy. When he suffered exactly the same shoulder injury in the opening round of the 2016 season, it was devastating for all of us.

He pulled up sore after the match against the Dragons, but when he was told a couple of days later he'd require another reconstruction and that his season was over, we understood the seriousness of the situation. I grabbed Barb and the kids and we drove down to the Slaters' house to see Bill and his wife, Nicole.

They were just shattered. He'd put in so much work to get back, to get himself ready to go. At the preseason camp he looked fit, he looked lean, he was as fast as I'd ever seen him. Because he hadn't played for most of 2015, he had freshened up and was raring to go.

There was nothing we could say that was going to improve the situation. We were just there to comfort Bill and Nic. Their kids were young at that stage, so they didn't really understand what was going on. But the look on their parents' faces said it all. He'd have to go through the same surgery and same rehab. If he didn't, there was a chance he would have a permanent impingement when moving his arm.

Billy is such a competitor, so I know it was hard for him to sit through that year. Melbourne led the NRL competition, while Queensland was looking to win its first series under new coach Kevin Walters.

Kevie was given the job after Mal had been appointed as the Australian coach following the resignation of Tim Sheens at the end of the 2015 season. I had mixed emotions about Mal giving away the Maroons job. He'd been an outstanding coach and we loved him dearly, but I knew he was exactly what the Kangaroos needed.

Kevie slipped seamlessly into the head coach's role. He'd been a legend as a player and a part of Mal's coaching staff. He was also in charge of a group of players who had been there a long time. He'd toss his ideas in and ask what we thought. 'How do you want to play this game?' We'd give our ideas, tell him how we thought we could win, then we'd go out and train it.

The thing about Kevie, though, was that his passion for the state and the jersey was so intense. It was almost too much at times. 'Mate, are you going too hard here?' I sometimes thought. There were times when he'd be talking to us in meetings and he'd be that revved up that he would get emotional.

'Kevie, you have to compose yourself a little bit,' I'd say afterwards.

The other former player who got that emotional was Allan Langer. In my 42 matches for Queensland, 'Alf' was always part of the coaching staff. I only recall him addressing the team once, and that was the day before the second match of the 2016 series, at Suncorp Stadium.

After winning an incredibly tight opening game 6–4 at ANZ Stadium, we returned to Brisbane to wrap up the series before our home crowd. After the captain's run the day before the game, Kevie asked Alfie to talk about his own career—his memories of Origin and what it meant to him. Alf was the same as Kevie. He could hardly get his words out, and the tears were welling in his eyes.

The match turned out to be another classic Origin with our winger Dane Gagai scoring three tries in our 26–16 win. But that scoreline doesn't reflect how close the Blues had come after their five-eighth, James Maloney, scored a 90-metre intercept try to reduce the margin to four points with ten minutes to go. Once again, though, we found a way to win. When Corey Oates scored, and then JT landed his third sideline conversion of the night, the game and the State of Origin shield were again ours.

That series seemed to ramp up the hype around my relationship with New South Wales captain Paul Gallen, particularly after what happened at the presentation following game three, which we lost 18–14, in Sydney.

After I was handed the shield, I was thanking the New South Wales players when I noticed they were already walking off the field. All of the Queensland players and support staff noticed it. We were annoyed because we always made a point of showing respect to our Origin opponents any time they were talking on stage. You stand together, wait until the speeches are done and then you walk off. That's the done thing in rugby league.

There were media reports that we'd sledged Gal throughout the match, and that was the reason for the snub. I can't recall anything that was said but sledging is just part of the game. Gal has since said he was unaware that I was speaking when they were leaving the field. To be fair, it is different on the ground than being in the stands—it's often hard to hear what's said—but I was standing on the stage and talking into a microphone.

The thing is, I have a lot of respect for Gal. He was a great rival. We brought the best out in each other. And we had a similar attitude towards the game. He always wanted to go out and make a difference, and he was so passionate about the team for which he played. I was no different.

I loved playing alongside him when we wore the Kangaroos jumper. He'd bust his arse every time he pulled that on—or any jersey, for that matter—and did whatever he could to win. That's my kind of player, and I thrived playing alongside blokes like that. Gal would do whatever it takes—and that was the best thing about him. You knew you couldn't break him. You couldn't wear him down; he'd keep coming for the entire time he was out there.

When a player is that strong and determined, he's near impossible to stop—especially when you're trying to tackle him. He brought out the best in me in those Origin matches because I had to tackle him a lot of times, perhaps more than any other player. He made me work for our victories as much as anyone. I respected him for that.

Talking up the personal rivalry between the two Origin captains suited the media. New South Wales snubbing us at the trophy presentation was a good line for the press, and they ran with it for the rest of the season since Melbourne and Cronulla—Gal's team—looked like they were headed for the grand final. When we beat them in the final round to claim the minor premiership, it seemed certain we'd meet them again deep in the finals.

I was really proud of how our team had rebuilt itself over the past two years, and without one of our stars in Billy. We'd won thirteen of fourteen matches, including going five-and-one through the tough Origin period. It was a fair effort.

Munster had been a revelation again. I recall telling some of the senior players as that season progressed that I considered him the best fullback in the NRL that season. We finished that year with very few losses, and as minor premiers, and he was one of the main reasons.

We beat North Queensland and Canberra to reach the grand final, but amid the excitement I felt sorry for Billy. I'd experienced something similar in 2008 when I sat out a preliminary and a grand final because of suspension. But that was just two matches, not a season and a half of rugby league. Typically, Billy never let his disappointment show around our team.

Every grand final has special meaning for whoever plays in it, but the Sharks had a lot to play for. They hadn't won a grand final in 50 years of being in the competition. But we felt comfortable we could handle them. We'd beaten them by twenty points in that match in the final round, so coming into the grand final we knew exactly what we had to do.

Then Cronulla ambushed us. Their game plan was to throw everything they had at us in the first half, and then hold on for dear life.

Their fullback, Ben Barba, scored the first try off a trick play from a scrum, and after that it became a bash-up. The Sharks changed their defensive game plan from earlier in the year, absolutely smothering me when we had the ball, and also getting into Coops, taking away his ball-playing ability and particularly his kicking game.

When they had the ball, it felt like they were running exclusively at me. It took away my energy so I had very little in the tank when we had the ball. I ended up making 73 tackles in that match. They weren't the first team to do this, but it was an effective tactic.

We'd put together a game plan based on what we thought they were going to give us, and in the pressure of a grand final we found it hard to adapt when they surprised us. They seemed to have an answer for everything we threw at them—until the second half.

Soon after the break I played short to Jesse Bromwich, who scored; when I kicked the conversion we were back to 8–6. Then Will Chambers broke through on the right edge, stepped inside, beat a couple of defenders and scored, and all of a sudden we were up 10–8 with seventeen minutes to go. I took as long as possible to kick the goal.

This was the ideal scenario for any Melbourne Storm team. Up by four with fifteen to go—we iced these games, every time.

The only problem was we were completely gassed, because the Sharks' defence had taken so much out of us in the first half. They retook the lead with ten minutes remaining when Andrew Fifita carried three of us over the line and only just managed to ground the ball, straight between the posts.

For the next nine minutes we did everything we could to get the lead back. Our best chance came when Chambers kicked and regathered. All he had to do was pass inside to Cooper, who was trailing him, and we would've scored. Will obviously didn't hear him or see him, and he was tackled.

Even right up to the final siren, it was on. We shifted to their left, they scrambled and shut the door on us. So we went back to the right; then Marika Koribete was tackled and the game was over. We'd come agonisingly close to winning that game. In that last 30 seconds, we felt like we could touch the trophy. If we scored, we win. It was heartbreaking.

Grand final losses are like grand final wins in that they're all different. The first one we lost, in 2006, left us feeling empty. A year of hard work for nothing. But in 2016 it really hurt because I felt like we'd blown a golden opportunity.

How did we lose it? I still don't know. We needed 30 more seconds. That would've done it. They took the game away from us in the first half with their physicality, their aggression and their relentless game plan. We were coming home with a wet sail, but they'd taken so much energy out of us in the first half that we couldn't find that last punch.

One of the oldest sayings in rugby league is that you need to lose a grand final to win one. I've never bought that idea, and in 2016 it made no sense. I'd lost enough grand finals to know what it felt like; I didn't need a reminder.

But there's something to be said for coming so close: it does give you a certain confidence and hunger. I knew we were a good footy side. We just needed to get back to that first weekend in October and do it again.

•

When the Australian coaching position became available following Tim Sheens' departure, I immediately thought Mal would be perfect as his replacement. There had been a late push for Wayne Bennett to get the role, but I believed Mal was the man we needed.

We had to rediscover our identity. In 2006 he'd done that for Queensland, so I knew he could do it for the Australian team too.

We'd been going through a transition in the Australian side, with some older players finishing and some new guys coming in. During that period, I felt that some of those younger guys might not have been aware of, or fully appreciated, the history of the Kangaroos and what it actually meant to wear that jumper. Origin had become so big that some players regarded it as the pinnacle. For the men who came through at the same time as me—Billy, GI, JT, Corey Parker, Gal, Greg Bird—that was playing for Australia, not for your state.

Our first match under Mal was against New Zealand in Newcastle. It was like walking back in time to my first camp for Queensland in 2006. We sat down and brainstormed what it meant to be an Australian player, how we wanted to be seen by our opposition, by the public, by our fans, and what we wanted them to say about us. That process gave the players complete ownership of the side. We concluded the meeting by stating our goal: to become the number one side in rugby league once again.

That journey started in Newcastle, in the Anzac Test of 2016, with a 16–0 win. Then came another win over the Kiwis, this time in Perth in October: 26–6. Then we headed to England for the Four Nations tournament, where we beat Scotland, England and the Kiwis twice, first in the preliminary matches and then the final.

You could say Mal had an immediate influence on the Australian team—for the remainder of my international career we never lost another Test match with him at the helm.

20

THE PERFECT STORM

Just as 2014 was probably the worst year of my career, I'd count 2017 as the best. Everything just fell into place. I never expected that to happen at the age of 34.

'If you want a good season you need a good preseason,' Bellyache told us at the start of every year. I had a limited start to my preparations for the 2017 season because I'd played in the Four Nations, but it didn't take me long to get into the groove. After our grand final loss to Cronulla in 2016, we had fire in our bellies. We were resolute about rebounding in the best possible way.

We decided to adopt a new style of attack that really suited me. It involved plenty of hard and direct play, but we also shifted the ball, which we hadn't done a lot before. We actively tried to move the opposition around.

Our grand final loss to the Sharks had shown us that we needed a change. We couldn't expect to play the same way in

2017 and get a different result. Cronulla had planned really well to counter our game style. They'd nullified us.

We knew we had to play our footy straight up and down through the middle. But after that, we would build in some variations where we moved teams around defensively. We would make their big boys change position on the field—we'd run them off their feet and see if they could stay with us. We always backed our fitness against any other team, particularly at the start of the year, so we were confident it would be difficult for anyone to stay with us.

That game plan suited me, because it meant we were playing through the middle with forwards like Jesse Bromwich, Jordan McLean, Dale Finucane and Nelson Asofa-Solomona. They could all play the ball quickly, particularly Jordan, who finished that season with the fastest play-the-ball in the competition. Not only could I play off the back of that, but I could also switch from dummy half to halfback when we decided to shift from the middle of the field.

And of course we had a backline that could play great attacking football. Billy was back at fullback after his second shoulder reconstruction, so Cameron Munster slotted nicely into the halves.

By now, those young players we had brought through over the past two or three years had 50 games under their belt. They'd played through two finals series, including a grand final, so they knew how to play in the big games. Some had also played some rep footy.

The only new addition to our squad was Josh Addo-Carr— 'The Fox'. We'd signed him from the Wests Tigers, where he'd played a handful of top-grade matches. We'd faced him the year before at Leichhardt and seen his blinding speed. When the Tigers stopped picking him and he was playing in their NSW Cup side, it didn't take long for our recruitment guys to snap him up. So with him on one flank and big Fijian Suli Vunivalu on the other, they were the perfect wingers for the way we wanted to play.

It was all coming together. The perfect storm.

We rolled through the first five rounds of the competition, but in early April received some news few of us were expecting. It concerned Cooper Cronk.

'This will be my last year in Melbourne,' he told us. 'I'm not sure if I'll be playing on or not, but I'm going up to Sydney for family reasons.'

Coops had become engaged to Fox Sports presenter Tara Rushton and would be moving to Sydney to be closer to her. It was a surprise but we got our heads around it, and we wished him the best of course. As the season went on, though, and it started to become a reality that he was leaving, it felt strange knowing this would be the last time Billy, Coops and I would be playing together for the Storm.

We'd been fortunate to achieve a lot of great things as a trio, not just with the Storm but also Queensland and Australia. I'd lived and played so closely with this guy. He'd been such an important part of not only my team's success, but also my personal success.

When we were young fellas and still learning our trade, the three of us worked out how to get the best out of each other.

We talked a lot about what would work on the field and what wouldn't. Billy would come up with plays daily, drawing them on a whiteboard. We'd give it a crack. If it felt good or looked good, we'd try it in a game. If it didn't, we'd park it.

To be doing that as teenagers, and then all the way through our careers into our mid-30s for club, state and country, was amazing. Each of us played over 300 games for the Storm. There hasn't been a combination of a No. 1, 7 and 9 who have played as many games together as we did. If the three of us hadn't had each other, we simply wouldn't have achieved what we did. We needed each other to climb the mountain.

Now we were climbing it one last time.

•

I was never one for a long pre-match speech. I always thought the best person to do that was the coach.

I was cautious about bombarding the team with too many messages. It just wasn't my way. I didn't want to be a contrived captain and say things just for the sake of it. I just wanted to be a captain who people enjoyed being around.

But when I did speak, I wanted the boys to know I meant it. That was never hard when we were preparing for an Origin or a Test match. I was more mindful of what I said at the Storm, though, because I was playing with these guys every week, all year long, and I didn't want to sound like a broken record. And it was challenging to find new things to talk about. My approach to footy was always simple.

So I'd talk in team meetings and at training, but as the game drew closer, I wouldn't say too much. I didn't talk much during the captain's run either. That was the coach's job. It was similar on game day, even during the warm-up. I preferred to leave the boys to themselves.

Only when we had our boots on and mouthguards in, and were about to run onto the field, would I get the boys in nice and tight. I'd remind them what it meant to wear that jersey in that particular game, and who we were representing.

'Let's get out there and get the job done,' I'd say.

So I was always the last to speak before we ran out into battle—and the third match of the 2017 State of Origin series at Suncorp Stadium was certainly going to be that.

'Don't let your mates down,' I demanded of my teammates, grabbing at their maroon jerseys. 'Don't let your state down.'

When I looked into the eyes of the players, I could see real fire. 'We're on here,' I thought.

The match had been built up as the biggest State of Origin match ever played. The storylines were about the significance of the result, where it was going to take New South Wales, and how this was finally their time to go on a run of victories just like Queensland had.

We'd been embarrassed 28–4 in the first match, at Suncorp Stadium, before levelling the series with a gripping 18–16 win at ANZ Stadium—but that victory had come at a huge price. Johnathan Thurston had carried a busted shoulder through most of the match, with his arm dangling by his side, but he bravely continued. When Dane Gagai scored in the 77th minute to level the scores, JT had a sideline conversion attempt to win us the match. Of course, he slotted the goal. It was one of the best plays I'd seen in Origin footy.

Afterwards, there was a lot of criticism of the Blues and their halfback, Mitchell Pearce, for not directing more play towards JT. I understood it—because that's what we would've done. Well, I would've. It sounds harsh, but that's our game: if you're not healthy enough to stay on the field, get off. If you want to stay out there, be prepared to make tackles, even if you're carrying an injury. The game has changed a lot recently, and now there's a lot of protection for playmakers. Sometimes it's warranted, sometimes it's soft. But that's just our game—it's a brutal sport.

JT was unavailable for the decider, back in Brisbane, which opened the door for Cameron Munster to play five-eighth. He was pretty excited to be in his first Origin match. Throughout the week, he was up and about and pretty jovial. He never really let the occasion get to him—at least, he never let on if it did.

His first training session was a shocker, though. He couldn't catch a ball, and every pass he threw went to ground.

Kevie Walters looked concerned.

'Don't worry about it, mate,' I told him. 'That's just him. He's settling in. When he trains badly, he plays well. Trust me.'

The preparation was enjoyable, as it always was in Queensland camp, but I was feeling a lot of pressure personally. At the start of the preparation, we held our open day for the media. I fielded questions from several different journalists about my form in the series so far, and about my thoughts on the first two games and my impact on them.

Believe me, I had a very clear self-assessment of my first two games: I was quiet. New South Wales played well in the first two matches, but I hadn't helped things. I'd looked to promote the football rather than make the play myself. When I reviewed the matches on video, I said to myself, 'You had an opportunity to run there but you tipped on. You put someone else onto the football.'

I'd had a couple of good involvements, but nowhere near enough. Defensively, I was happy. In every Origin game there's a big tackling workload, and I got through my fair share. But in terms of running and kicking, I was almost nonexistent.

The stat that really stood out was that I'd had four runs in Origin I and one run in Origin II. Five runs in two matches? That just wasn't good enough.

Kevie addressed it with me with a few jokes during our training sessions. 'Is the old boy going to have a run this game or what?' he'd laugh.

In any joke there's a little bit of truth. I knew it myself. I wasn't a rookie—I'd played 41 Origin matches. So I knew what I had to do in game three. I had to run the footy.

My mindset that whole week was that I was going to run it early and often. I had to pick my moments, but I also knew I had to get myself into the game early by having a run.

Kevie had once been an assistant coach at the Storm. Back then, he had often told me to be more selfish. In the early years,

I rejected that idea. That wasn't the type of player I was, and it wasn't the type of team the Storm were.

But he wasn't talking about making my stats look good. 'Being selfish will help the team,' Kevie would explain. 'If you run the footy more, good things will happen.'

That week, before game three, he said it again. So after training I practised some dummy half scoots. I wanted it to become a habit, so that when I got out there on Wednesday night, it was already in my mind. Run, run, run.

The look I saw in my teammates' eyes just before we ran into the field wasn't just for show. It was another one of those matches where it just all came together for us.

I made a half break early, tipped onto Billy, who went downfield, went to the right and passed to Cooper, who almost scored under the posts only to be denied by the video referee.

A couple of sets later I came to Boyd Cordner, showed the ball, got on his outside and he just grabbed me by the jersey. I tipped onto Josh Papalii, who nearly scored. It didn't take long for the points to come. Dane Gagai scored—he'd finish with three in total. Cameron Munster had one of the greatest Origin debuts in history.

I was really involved out of dummy half. I kicked early too, putting us on the front foot—and keeping the Blues on the back foot. It all came together perfectly. We couldn't have handled it any better.

I had a bit of a chuckle at some of the commentary afterwards. 'He told them he was going to run the ball. He told them. And what did he do? He ran the ball.'

When it was time for me as captain to be presented with the trophy on stage, I called up JT, his arm in a sling, to hold it up with me, because he was retiring from rep football. I knew how loved he was and wanted him up there alongside me.

Because of his injury, JT hadn't got the proper finale he deserved, but still this was a cool moment. And it was one he deserved. His input into Origin football had been significant. He just knew he was done.

I didn't quite know if I was, too.

•

Throughout my career, I prided myself on playing on the Wednesday night for the Maroons and then backing up for the Storm just days later. I never wanted to let down my teammates. Playing Origin wasn't an excuse for me not to play for my club.

'I'm going to rest you,' Bellyache said after game one that year.

'Good,' was my surprising response.

There had been previous times when I didn't want to back up but I'd made myself play. But not this year. My decision to rest after the three interstate games was critical to me staying fresh as the season went on and we charged towards the minor premiership, which for our club has always been a big deal.

Bellyache puts a lot of significance on the minor premiership—perhaps more than any other coach. He regarded it so highly because it was proof you'd been the best team across

26 weeks, not just in the grand final. Everyone wanted to win the premiership, but the minor premiership showed how good your side had been all year.

Throughout my entire career at the Storm, from day one of the preseason all the way through to my final match, we never had a mindset of just hoping for the best. Our mindset was always: 'Let's train as hard as we can and put ourselves in a position to win it. No excuses.'

Nothing had changed in 2017. We shot to the top of the competition ladder in Round 8 and didn't let go, losing just four matches to finish six points clear of the Roosters and claim the minor premiership. It was the start of a hectic month.

We played Parramatta at AAMI Park in the first week of the finals, but a lot of the talk was around me breaking Darren Lockyer's all-time record of 355 NRL matches. I'll talk about my records later, but the media attention around the milestone that week was a distraction. We trailed 10–4 at halftime but managed to win 18–16.

It was just the wake-up call we needed. In the preliminary final, we beat Brisbane 30–0 to book our place in the grand final against a brave Cowboys side that had been missing JT and Matt Scott through long-term injuries.

Grand final week is always tricky to manage, especially with the Dally M awards being held a few days before the decider. When I won my first, back in 2006, it was held in the first week of the finals. Now, we had to get all dressed up for the awards at Sydney's Star Casino just days before the grand final.

I was blown away when I led throughout the count and eventually won. I claimed 33 votes, to win by eight ahead of Cowboys halfback Michael Morgan. St George Illawarra's Gareth Widdop was third with 24 votes, while Sydney Roosters five-eighth Luke Keary and Cronulla Sharks captain Paul Gallen finished equal fourth with 22.

Making the night even sweeter was that JT was on stage to announce me as the winner.

'This is pretty unique considering I'm at the back end of my career now rather than at the beginning,' I told the room. 'Being 34 and having the opportunity to win another Dally M is pretty special.' Then I paid tribute to my wife.

'She's one of the best, Barb,' I said. 'We were just talking this year when I played my 40th State of Origin game. Each game is ten days in camp, so that's 400 days I've spent away from my family and my beautiful wife. She's been at home that whole time with three children, looking after them, raising them, making sure everything's great at home.'

So 2017 was a year of milestones. I broke the record for most NRL appearances, played my 42nd State of Origin (more than any other player), passed 2000 points and also went past 1000 goals. It didn't surprise me, because I was 34 years old. When you play for as long as I had, you're bound to break a few records. What did surprise me, at that stage of my career, was that I was playing so well, and that my body was in reasonable shape.

Winning the Dally M was the start of an emotional week as the reality sank in that Billy, Coops and I weren't going to play together again. Ahead of the captain's run the night before the match, we were told the jumper presentations would be done in the dressing-room. I knew even before Bellyache had a chance to say it that I would be giving Cooper his jumper.

We had spent so much time together, going back to the days of when we were seventeen, driving to training at Norths in my old Kingswood four times a week. We'd known each other for such a long time, and been through so much. We'd played so much footy alongside one another, most of it in that Storm jumper. Now, I was about to hand that jumper to him for his very last match.

I don't usually get emotional. I can keep it in check. But when it was my turn to speak, I struggled to get the words out.

I spoke about the significance of Coops' role at our club. I spoke about the relationship I'd formed with him, and with Billy as well. He did a good job of holding his emotion in— but I battled. I wasn't a blubbering mess, but it's fair to say the moment got the better of me. The three of us had given so much of our lives to that jersey.

There was talk before the match about the Storm making a lot of grand finals but only having one official title to our name. Of course, two had been taken from us after the salary cap investigation. We'd played in six grand finals, winning three and losing three.

I didn't really feel any pressure to cash in on the amazing year we had. I knew how hard grand finals are to win. It's one match, and any side on their day can play well enough to jag it. But I knew that everyone who had played in that grand final loss to the Sharks the year before was resolved to make amends.

And we did. Again, it was one of those matches when I never felt like we were in danger of losing. I had that rare feeling of confidence that this was going to be our day, and nothing was going to take victory away from us.

When Will Chambers grabbed a loose ball on our line, then beat a couple of defenders before offloading to Josh Addo-Carr, who then sprinted 80 metres for the first try, I knew we were going to have a day out. We led 18–0 at halftime, and scored another three in the second half to win 34–6.

For Billy, Cooper and me, it was the perfect way to end our time together as Melbourne Storm players.

In the aftermath, Billy was awarded the Clive Churchill Medal. I was really happy for him. The comeback that he had was remarkable. There had been a point there when he was advised to stop playing, because of the risk of permanent damage to his shoulder. The way he fought back was just so courageous. So I was over the moon for him.

Some have said this was the greatest Melbourne Storm team ever assembled. Teams of different years are hard to compare, but in terms of performance, definitely.

•

There was only one more thing for me to make 2017 the perfect season: the World Cup, which was being held in Australia for the first time since 2008.

It had been a long season, and Mal did a great job of trying to make the tournament as enjoyable as possible for us.

We'd play a game and then he'd give us three days off to do whatever we wanted before we came back into the camp.

Our first match was in Melbourne, at AAMI Park, against England. After winning 18–4, we were given a few days off. While most of the boys went to watch the Cox Plate at Moonee Valley, I went home. Then we headed to Canberra to take on France, who we beat 52–5. After that I went home again before we played Lebanon in Sydney. Another win: 34–0.

As anyone who knows me will tell you, I love spending time at home around my family. But the desire to get back there was particularly strong during this World Cup. The kids were getting older and I found myself wanting to be at home with them more than ever. A thought started creeping in: was this a sign that I should give up rep footy? It was a question I wasn't ready to answer.

Going back and forth from home helped some of us, but I think it was almost detrimental in the end. We beat Samoa 46–0 in our quarter-final, and then Fiji 54–6 in the semi-final. But by the time we met England in the final, I felt we were a little deconditioned.

We won 6–0 in one of the greatest international arm wrestles I've ever been involved in. Our only points came from Boyd Cordner's try in the 15th minute, and my conversion.

'This was one of the toughest games of my career,' I told the media afterwards. 'We wanted to put ourselves back to number one and we've gone back to back now, and I'm very happy to have the Kangaroos as the best team in the world.'

After the match I embraced Cooper, who'd announced in the lead-up to the final that he was retiring from rep football.

Hanging out with the kids at school pickup, 2013.

My beautiful family. Throughout this incredible ride, everything I've done has been for them.

Barb and me at the Yarra Valley Rodeo, 2017.

A family break on Green Island during a bye round in 2017.

2018: Christmas Day in the Happiest Place on Earth—Disneyland!

Disneyland teacup selfie!

Chowing down on a
Christmas turkey leg
in Disneyland.

Riding the San Francisco cable cars.

Barb and me at a friends' wedding in 2018. I first met Barb in 1996 and I will always be indebted to her for the selfless way she has supported me throughout my career, fought for me and loved me, even when I was a massive pain.

Me and Jasper in our Storm kit in Townsville, 2019.

Me, Rusty and Barb.

Jada's Year 6 graduation.

Family holiday at
Manyana Beach,
New South Wales,
2019.

Gold Coast, 2019. Me, Barb, my sister-in-law Gemma, Matt, Mum, Dad, my
brother-in-law Waylon and Khirstie.

Me and Grandma Vesley.

The 2016 Australian team led by Mal Meninga. Everything 'Big Mal' has done in rugby league has been shrouded in excellence, and it was an honour to be coached by him in the Maroons and the Kangaroos.

Matt King/Getty Images

Just another face in the crowd . . . The Sharks would edge us out in the 2016 grand final, but we wouldn't have to wait long for another tilt.

Shane Myers/NRL Imagery

Cleaning up Mitchell Pearce in 2017 State of Origin game two.

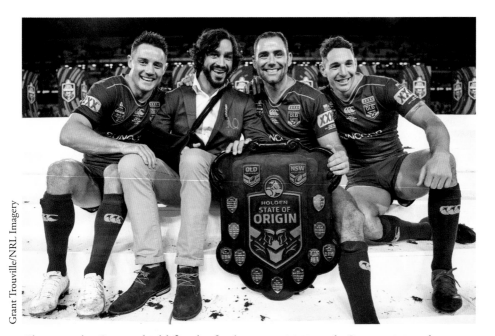

Claiming the Origin shield for the final time in 2017 with Cooper, injured Johnathan Thurston and Billy.

My second Dally M Player of the Year, in 2017.

Taking home the Golden Boot in 2017.

Gregg Porteous/NRL Imagery

Celebrating winning the 2017 grand final with Craig. 'Bellyache' and I worked together for almost twenty years, and it has been an immense privilege to be under the tutelage of possibly the greatest coach the game has known.

Lifting the Provan–Summons trophy with Cooper and Billy after beating North Queensland 34–5 in the 2017 grand final.

Celebrating the 2017 grand final win with Matilda.

I didn't have long to savour our NRL title in 2017—the World Cup began shortly afterwards. We beat England 6–0 in the final. Nothing comes close to your team winning the World Cup for your country.

Part of the captain's job is to discuss decisions with the referee. Some enjoy it more than others!

Breaking the all-time point-scoring record against the Cowboys in Townsville in 2019. Jada and Jasper are watching on from the sidelines.

My 400th NRL game, against Cronulla-Sutherland at AAMI Park in 2019. We beat the Sharks 40–16.

Congratulations from Barb after game 400.

I didn't score very many tries over the course of my career—but I enjoyed them when I did!

Asanka Brendon Ratnayake/NRL Imagery

Returning to training after the 2020 COVID-19 lockdown, complete with iso-beard.

Gregg Porteous/NRL Imagery

It was great to be back playing, but it wasn't the same without the fans.

That meant it was the last time we'd ever play together—although it wouldn't be the last time we met on a footy field, because he'd signed a two-year deal with the Roosters.

To cap off the year, I was awarded the Golden Boot as the best player in the world. It was the second time I won the award, having claimed it in 2007. What a season it had been.

For whatever reason, though, the success I had that year was the tipping point for some people. That's when a whole bunch of lies, rumours and innuendos started about me and my family.

There was media speculation during the World Cup that I had been 'distant' with the rest of the Kangaroos team, which confused me. The only distance came when I went home after matches, as did a number of other players with kids during the tournament, following encouragement from Mal.

I actually really enjoyed being around the younger players in that squad. Manly's Tom Trbojevic came into the team and we'd play golf together every week.

It was hard to get my head around. Why were these lies out there? Was someone trying to chop my legs off because of the year we just had? The way that season unfolded, Origin III, winning the Dally M Medal, winning the premiership, captaining Australia to the World Cup, claiming the Golden Boot . . . It was almost like, 'We better bring this bloke down a few pegs.'

People had been having cracks at me long before that season, so I was accustomed to the criticism. But this was different.

I've got zero evidence about who could've been driving it. It was just coincidental that most of the stuff started coming towards me after such a successful year. There was also speculation about my future.

'Are you going to play on?' I was asked after the grand final.

I threw out a throwaway line in response. 'Not a bad way to finish up—winning a premiership,' I said. 'I'll have to think about it.'

That got tongues wagging, but already I knew I wanted to play on. There was something appealing about finishing with a premiership, but another season—or two, or three—was more appealing.

I wasn't finished just yet.

21

STANDARDS

At the Melbourne Storm, we had no motivational sayings written on the wall in the gym. The standards we had to live up to each day were well known to all of us. They were in the DNA of the club, and they'd been established by Bellyache, his coaching staff and the senior players over a long period of time.

People sometimes ask how we remained competitive for so long. Why we've won so many minor premierships. Why we've made so many preliminary finals and grand finals. How can we be decimated by the salary cap scandal and rebuild so quickly? How can we be down by twenty points but then come back and win in the final minute? How each year we hear people say the Storm will come back to the field, drop out of the top four, won't make the finals, but then defy all of that.

It was all because of the standards we set for ourselves. And they were non-negotiable. We never gave up. We were never dead. People talk about the Melbourne Storm culture. Really it was just about the standards and behaviours we were willing to accept.

When I woke up in Canberra the morning after playing my 50th Test match, against New Zealand in May 2017, it didn't take long for me to find out that one of our players hadn't lived up to the standards of the Storm.

My teammate Jesse Bromwich and former Storm player Kevin Proctor had been caught using illicit drugs after they were offered to them by a person they had met that night. The police had been called but neither Jesse nor Kevin were charged.

Kevin was a former Storm player but had left a few years earlier to sign with the Gold Coast Titans. Jesse was one of our biggest names, and a senior player. I was fuming about what I'd heard.

I wouldn't know what a drug looked like if it was staring me in the face. I've never been offered any drugs during my career, which might surprise you. Each to their own, but I'm as anti-drugs as they come.

To me, taking them just doesn't make sense. Why would a player jeopardise their career by doing drugs? I've seen so many people waste their talent on a range of things—drinking, gambling, abusing drugs. They've been given these football gifts and they've pissed them up against the wall. Blokes make mistakes—I get that. But using drugs is just a no-go for me.

I was worried that other Storm players might have been involved. Jesse's brother, Kenny, also played for the Kiwis that night, but I didn't get a chance to speak to him. Jordan McLean had played for the Kangaroos, and as soon as I spotted him in the hotel foyer that morning I grabbed him.

'Were you out last night with Jesse?' I asked.

'Yeah, but I left fairly early,' Jordan said.

'You weren't involved in this shit, were you?' I asked.

'No, no, no,' Jordan said.

By the time we got to the airport, I was steaming. Because of the milestone, Barb and the kids had come to the game and stayed with me that night. As we made our way through check-in, I was so fired up that I charged ahead, walking five metres in front of them, without even realising.

We went to the Qantas Lounge, where I tried to relax, but when we came down to the gate, which was right at the end of the terminal, Barb realised we were flying on a small QantasLink plane with propellers. She isn't a great flyer at the best of times.

'Oh no,' she said.

'Let's just get on,' I grumbled.

When we boarded the plane, the first head I recognised belonged to Jesse Bromwich. Without acknowledging him or saying hello, I sat down in our row, which was a few ahead of his.

As soon as we landed, I just wanted to get moving. 'Let's go,' I said to Barb.

I knew I would have to talk to him at some stage, but I was too angry to do it now.

As we were walking through the terminal at Melbourne Airport, I heard a voice from behind me. It was Jesse. He was rattled. 'Mate, I just want to talk to you about last night,' he said.

'No worries,' I replied. 'What do you want to say?'

'I just want to apologise for last night. I stuffed up.'

'Is it true?' I asked. 'Did you take drugs or what?'

'Yeah, it's true.'

'Mate, why would you do that? Why would you put your career in jeopardy? Every teammate's name is going to be dragged through the shit, because we're all tarred with the same brush. And your family—you've brought this on them as well. What were you thinking?'

'I don't know.'

'Well, you'll have to live with it now.' I left it at that.

Craig met with him the next day, and Jesse ended up being suspended by the club for four weeks, on top of being dumped from the Kiwis squad for the World Cup later that year. I didn't brush him at training, but I was reserved around him for a while. I wanted him to understand how upset I was.

I get that we are all different, we are all unique personalities, and we make errors of judgement. But this was something I was really disappointed about. As a captain, I care about my teammates. A lot. I want them to be the best they can be, in footy and life, and I knew Jesse was better than that.

Aside from himself and his family, he'd also hurt the club. I'd been a part of the joint since I was seventeen and during that time there had been a lot of people who did everything they could to promote the Storm, and the game, in Melbourne.

It was the legacy that a lot of players had built: Billy, Cooper, Matt Geyer, Steve Kearney, Robbie Kearns, Danny Williams . . . dozens and dozens of people. There was a period there when

Melbourne weren't guaranteed they originally would be in the competition. I'd always appreciated those early players, because if they hadn't built the foundations, where would that have left us younger players? Would we even have got a start in the NRL? Who knows.

The Storm exists in a non-league city and state, so we had made a concerted effort to make sure everything we did only helped to grow the sport in Victoria. We were well aware that any negative press had a detrimental effect on the game's image. We were conscious of not stuffing it up so we could grow the game, and so young people could develop an interest in rugby league and maybe play it.

To his credit, Jesse became a better man and player out of the experience. If you can learn from your mistakes, that's half the battle. And he's done that.

It came back to the standards we'd set for ourselves. Craig had many strong attributes, but his strongest was that he never sugar-coated anything. He just told it how it is. He wouldn't put up with poor decisions or with people carrying on that way in his footy side. It took away from what we were trying to do.

So he had the same conversation with Jesse Bromwich as he had done with Cameron Munster. Cameron's a ratbag, and we loved him for it. He enjoyed a good time away from footy, but at times he went down the wrong path. The thing that was really good about him was that it never affected his footy. If he'd made a poor decision, he was upfront and honest with everyone. If he wasn't aware of his actions, you'd be concerned. He always genuinely cared for the club and his teammates.

Whenever he was around training, he was always doing something to help the team—it was never for his own benefit. For me, that's a really strong behavioural mentality. Team first.

But that didn't mean he never needed to be pulled into line. A few times it was me who did that.

One of those times came early in Cameron's time at the Storm. I grabbed him and told him the expectations I had of him. I understood that he was a young man, and that we all make mistakes. But when you signed on to be a Melbourne Storm player, there were standards you needed to live by. And I didn't mean just when you put the purple jumper on. It was every day of your life.

It didn't matter how young he was, or how many games he'd played. I had the same expectations of him as I did of Billy Slater. That was the point I needed him to understand.

Whenever I spoke to a young player in that way, I explained how poor choices could ruin his career, particularly for a rookie like him who had so much ability. Why would he throw that away? 'You don't want to be one of those guys,' I told Cameron.

The second time I spoke to him was during the 2017 World Cup, when he went off the rails at one point. He had his shenanigans in Darwin when he had an altercation with Benny Hunt. I wasn't there when it happened. I was just told that some of the Emus—the players who trained all week but weren't in the starting team—went for beers and had a disagreement. It was a bit of a push and shove, nothing more, but the incident got out to the papers and turned into an unwelcome story.

'You've worked so hard to be part of the Kangaroos squad,' I told Cameron. 'It's the same as Melbourne: there are standards that you need to adhere to.'

Bellyache was a little more forceful. When he returned to Melbourne after the World Cup, he explained that if those misdemeanours continued, his contract could be torn up. Put simply, we didn't want people like that involved with our organisation. No sugar-coating.

People say Craig has mellowed. It's been a gradual process for him, and becoming a grandfather has softened him a little. I wouldn't say he's mellowed, though—more just that he's evolved, and learned that there are other ways of coaching than being intense. He realised that not everyone responds to a spray.

Whenever I was sprayed, I'd respond strongly to it. Coops, Billy, Will Chambers . . . players like that from those early days also responded well, because we didn't really know any better. But some players in the current generation prefer a cuddle. Bellyache's only just started cuddling blokes to be honest. But at least he's cuddling.

Player misbehaviour in the last few years has become a serious issue for rugby league. I'll be honest: I have no answers about how to improve things. For a period there, it was just one off-season after the other, and I sat there bewildered by how regularly it all seemed to be happening.

I'm certainly not an angel. Nor are my teammates. When a group of Storm players went to Bali at the end of the 2019 season, I knew something would happen because of the location.

Nelson Asofa-Solomona was involved in a streetfight because Suli Vunivalu was about to get hit with a beer bottle. He was banned from playing three Tests for New Zealand, and I thought that was a harsh penalty for sticking up for your mate. That's something that we, as a nation, are all about: looking after your family and your mates.

Most of the players who have come through with me are straight up and down people who haven't caused the code any grief with our behaviour away from the game. It's only a small minority of the 500 or more NRL footballers who make these mistakes. But I've been around long enough to understand that the whole playing group gets tarnished as a result. The clichés come thick and fast: all players are grubs; they're arrogant and entitled; they don't care about the law.

In early 2018, the Australian Rugby League Commission and the NRL's then chief executive, Todd Greenberg, introduced the controversial 'no-fault stand down' policy for serious police charges, especially for incidents involving women. Todd brought that in because he was left with little option. He'd fined and suspended blokes, but things were continuing to happen. The message wasn't getting through. Given the severity of some of the incidents, the pressure from fans, members, the general public and the media, it all became too great for him to not do something.

It was a controversial call, as a footy player who is accused of something is entitled to the presumption of innocence, just like anyone else. But it's different when you're working in a billion-dollar industry like the NRL. So I can understand why the policy came in, even if it divided opinion. I definitely supported it.

I understand life is complicated. And that people make mistakes. Along with those mistakes comes drama and serious consequences. Why would you want that in your life?

22

FINISHING

When I announced on 15 May 2018 that I was retiring from representative football, effective immediately, it shocked a lot of people. The first match of the State of Origin series was only three weeks away.

Until that moment, I had been unsure if I should call time on my career in the Queensland and Kangaroos jerseys. It was extremely difficult to let that part of my life go, no matter how many victories I'd enjoyed while wearing them.

On reflection, the signs were there during the previous season. As I've explained, I was surprised when Bellyache gave me the opportunity to miss a match directly after the 2017 Origin matches—and I gladly took it. The reason I didn't back up was because I just couldn't. I'd return to Melbourne after each match, and spend the next three days in bed or on the lounge. Some days I took the kids to school, but often I couldn't even do that. I was so fatigued, mentally and physically, that I could barely move.

And playing Origin is about more than just the match. You have to be in camp for ten days, and then there are the sponsor and media commitments, and the public appearances—and all of that is fair enough. But it takes a heavy toll in what is already a long season.

So the fact that I couldn't back up for the Storm—and didn't want to—was the first sign I was nearing the end.

Likewise, during the World Cup campaign, I'd taken up coach Mal Meninga's offer to fly home for three days after each match. When I was in camp, I remember thinking, 'This is a lot of footy. I love playing for my country, but I just want to be at home.' I was finding it more difficult to be away from my family. By now Jada was nine, Jasper was eight and Matilda was five. They were getting older and playing junior sports. I felt like I was missing out on their lives.

'I saw a different Cameron in that World Cup,' Mal offered after I'd announced my retirement. 'Not at training or in the games, but that he'd had enough of this.'

He was right—but even then it took me until the last minute to convince myself that this was the right time.

I've never been one to make a rash decision. I like to think things through. But I felt I needed to get close to Origin to sense if I had that buzz, that feeling, again. Which I always had. I always had my eye on the first Origin of the year, knowing that, from two to three matches out, I had to be hitting my straps so I could get into camp and be ready to go. I didn't have that feeling in 2018. I wasn't pumped for Origin. If I'm honest, it was quite the opposite: I felt like I couldn't do it.

Even so, I had to be completely sure that I was making the right decision. I didn't want to walk away and then read about the teams being picked for the opening match and ask myself, 'What have you done?' So I spoke to Barb about it—a lot.

She was typical Barb. 'Cam, it's up to you,' she said. 'It's not up to me. All I care about is your health. I saw you last year and you struggled. I don't want to see you like that.'

There was speculation that she ordered me to give rep footy away, which is simply not true. There were actually a lot of rumours about the reasons why I'd retired from rep footy, and I understand that, it shocked a lot of people.

I wasn't just a guy who'd been in and out of the side, with questions about my selection. I was the current Australian and Queensland captain and, all of a sudden, I decided to stop.

I also talked to Bellyache.

'What are your thoughts on me finishing rep footy?' I asked him.

He sat on the fence a bit. He certainly didn't want to tell me to give it away to benefit the Melbourne Storm.

'Make sure it's the right time,' he said. 'Don't regret giving it away. But it could also be a really good thing to prolong your career. That'll be the upside of it.'

That factored into my decision as well. If I did play on, I knew I'd likely finish my NRL career earlier than I'd like to. If I continued playing Origin through 2018 and even 2019, that would've done me.

I also sought advice from Mum and Dad.

'If you're playing because you have something to prove, that's the wrong reason,' they advised. 'You've got nothing left to prove in that arena.'

In the end, I realised that just asking myself the question was probably a sign—because if you really want to play, there's no question.

The weekend I decided to make the call, the Storm were playing the Dragons at Kogarah. We lost and I knew my head just hadn't been in the game. I played but my mind had been elsewhere. All my thoughts were on giving away Origin.

The last person I needed to speak to was Kevin Walters, the Queensland coach. I'd been talking to him for some weeks about the team—positional changes, what we could do better in our camp—but after the Storm played the Gold Coast at Suncorp Stadium in Brisbane, I decided to tell him. I wanted to do it face to face.

The morning after the match, he caught up with me, Billy, Cameron Munster and Will Chambers for breakfast. When we finished chatting, and it was time for us to get on the bus and get to the airport, I pulled Kevie aside.

'I've been thinking about this for a while,' I told him. 'You're not going to like this, but I've decided to finish up rep footy.'

'This year?'

'Yeah.'

'So this is your last series?'

'No, from right now. I'm done. I won't be available.'

'Ah, okay.'

Kevie wasn't actually surprised. He'd had the same feeling as Mal that my time was up. 'I've been sensing it in our phone calls,' he told me. 'You've been more okay with everything, instead of having your normal input. You seemed to be happy to go with the flow.'

After I finished with Kevie, I boarded the bus. Some of the boys knew something was up.

'Everything sweet?' Will asked.

'All good, mate,' I said.

I planned to make an announcement two days later, but I didn't want a media conference or any fanfare. I never did. I didn't think it was that big a deal, but the Queensland Rugby League decided to fly down Kevie to sit alongside me.

The timing was weird, actually, because that same day the new New South Wales coach, Brad Fittler, and his assistant, Danny Buderus, had come down to watch the Storm train at AAMI Park. They were running an eye over our players who were eligible for the Blues. Suddenly Kevie walked out of the tunnel in a Queensland suit.

'What are you doing here?' they asked him.

He didn't tell them.

I was still on the field training, but the session was coming to an end. I grabbed the Maroons players in our side—Billy, Cameron, Will and Tim Glasby—and told them that I was finishing up with rep footy.

'I'm done,' I said. 'Someone else can have a go.'

One of the first people I'd told was JT, who I'd called the night before.

'Are you serious?' he asked. Then he uncorked a bottle of Grange and our two families FaceTimed and talked about all the good times we'd had representing our state and country. We'd come a long way since playing against each other as teenagers in Brisbane.

I also phoned Mal.

'You sure?' he asked.

'I am,' I said.

'You've done enough. As long as you're happy, I'm happy.'

If arriving at the decision to retire from representative football had been hard, watching it was inconceivably harder. It was horrible. I'm a terrible spectator at the best of times when watching the teams I'm involved in, or have been involved in. But this was torture.

The first match of the 2018 series was played at the Melbourne Cricket Ground. New South Wales had a new-look team, with Freddy picking eleven debutants, as did Queensland.

I told Kevie I wanted to stay away from the team, which was very different to Queensland sides of the past: no Thurston, no Cronk, no Slater, who had been ruled out with injury. When the four of us were playing, we were all very vocal about how the team should be run. I didn't want to go in there now and influence a team I wasn't playing for. I wanted the players to create their own identity and their own footy side. At the captain's run I met with my replacement at hooker, Andrew McCullough from the Broncos, but apart from that I wasn't involved.

So it was a strange week, but I must say I didn't miss it. The only time I felt any emotion about the game was when they ran out and the MCG crowd erupted.

'I'd love to be out there now,' I thought.

Then I started watching some of the hits and I knew I'd made the right decision. I woke up on the Thursday morning and bounced out of bed.

Queensland lost the first match 22–12, then the series with an 18–14 defeat at ANZ Stadium in game two.

I didn't feel any guilt about the result, but I did question myself a few times. If I played, could I have made a difference? But it was silly to think one person would've changed the game. Ultimately, I didn't feel like I'd let anyone down because I knew inside that it wasn't in me anymore.

After the series some comments were made about me leaving the Maroons in the lurch by announcing my retirement three weeks out from the series. Some even labelled it 'selfish'.

I can understand that, but in my mind, that was the right time to make the decision.

As disappointing as it was, the reality was I was done.

To his credit, Kevie was fine about it. No former player has raised it with me, either. On the contrary, some of the boys said, 'Good on you mate, it couldn't have been easy. You deserved to make the decision about when you finished in that arena, and when you know, you know.'

As Kevie said, it had to finish at some stage.

23

STORM VERSUS ROOSTERS

The 2018 NRL season turned out to be one of the closest on record, with the top four teams finishing on 34 points, and the next four finishing on 32. The Roosters won the minor premiership and we came second; it came down to points differential, where we were behind by just eight.

There had been an intense rivalry between the two clubs before Cooper Cronk arrived. In 2017 the Roosters had beaten us by a point in Adelaide, before we got over them by three at AAMI Park later in the season.

Cooper's decision to sign with the Roosters just added to the rivalry, although I wouldn't say the clubs felt the same animosity for each other as the Storm had with Manly a decade earlier. We were just two highly competitive teams that set ourselves high standards, each wanting to be the benchmark of the competition. There was no genuine hatred of each other. There had been with Manly.

Throughout the World Cup in late 2017 there were murmurs that Coops might play on the next year with an NRL club in Sydney, but I thought he would finish after the tournament. Then one day he pulled Billy, Will Chambers and me aside and told us he was joining the Sydney Roosters.

We were happy for him. I was happy for him. 'It's great you're going to keep playing,' I said.

What Coops decided was in the best interests of himself and his family. And after everything he'd given the Storm over so many years, no one could begrudge him that—least of all me, because I understood his reasons and respected them.

Around that same time, he also announced he was retiring from representative football, which gave me the opportunity to present him with his last Test jumper, just as I had with his last Storm jumper.

Fast forward to Round 16 of the 2018 season. Both the Storm and the Roosters were coming into form—sitting fifth and sixth on the ladder, respectively—and with a top four position at stake in the Friday night game, there was everything to play for.

We ran out first, and then the Roosters came on from the other side of the field. As they jogged past us, I saw Coops in the red, white and blue and it struck me: this was the first time I had ever seen him in an opposing team's colours.

So I did what every rugby league player would do: I started heckling him.

'Coopsy!' I shouted at him. 'Here he is!'

He gave me nothing. Donuts.

'Come on, mate,' I joked. 'Don't be like that.'

Nothing again. He had his game face on.

Cooper and I didn't have much contact throughout the match, which we won 9–8 after I landed a field goal in the last minute. It was a classic contest between two strong sides, and we'd been lucky to get away with the win.

After fulltime, the two teams formed two lines and shook hands and hugged, as is the custom at the end of a match. The player before me in our line was backrower Joe Stimson, who might have played ten or twelve matches alongside Cooper. Joe got a big hug. Now it was my turn. I moved in for a hug—but got the cold shoulder. He said nothing and gave me nothing but a quick handshake.

'Wow,' I thought. 'What's up with Cooper?'

I wasn't asked about our encounter in the post-match press conference, but soon enough the vision was given airtime and the story took off. Smith versus Cronk!

At first I didn't pay any attention to it. We'd managed a tough win on the road against a premiership contender. Everything else was just part of the theatre. But the longer the discussion went on, the louder the innuendo got.

The funny thing about it was that there'd never been a time when Coops and I had an argument—or even so much as a disagreement.

'What's going on with you and Cronk?' people started asking.

I wish I could've given them the answer. I had no idea.

•

We snuck through the first week of the finals with a 29–28 win over South Sydney at AAMI Park; we'd led 16–12 at halftime. It was a gritty win, secured with just four minutes remaining when Cameron Munster kicked a 30-metre field goal to regain the lead for us. Things weren't as difficult in the preliminary final against our old sparring partners, Cronulla. We won 22–6 after leading 20–0 at halftime.

The Roosters reached the grand final with a 12–4 win over South Sydney in the other preliminary, in the last ever match at Allianz Stadium.

A grand final between the Roosters and the Storm was big enough as it was, but now Cooper Cronk was going up against his old team. It couldn't have been scripted better. But there was another plot twist to come.

The news soon came through that Cooper was a 'long shot' to play because of a busted shoulder. From there, the week became a media circus surrounding his availability, the seriousness of the injury and what the injury even was.

Externally, the only thing that took the attention away from Cooper's shoulder was Billy having to front the judiciary after he was booked for a shoulder charge on Sharks' winger Sosaia Feki while trying to stop a try. We didn't think he was guilty, but we were concerned about the outcome.

Truth be told, I was very worried. The situation brought back memories of what had happened to me back in 2008, when I was rubbed out of the grand final against Manly. That was the last thing I wanted for Bill. This was to be his final game of footy before retirement, so you can imagine his relief—and ours—when he was cleared to play.

I had no fears about playing the Roosters. I believed we had the players to beat them. When Bill was cleared to play, my confidence grew. We were a much better side when our fullback was taking the field.

An hour before kick-off, Coops was named to play, most likely with the aid of painkillers. That surprised none of us at the Storm.

What shocked us more was the way the Roosters started. They used the same tactics that had worked for the Sharks in the 2016 grand final: they bashed us. The Roosters led 18–0 at halftime and eventually won 21–6.

After the game, some people wanted to look at the Storm negatives, but we just had to give credit to the Roosters. The way they played was as good as anything I'd seen from any team during that era. They were flawless.

Their back three of James Tedesco, Blake Ferguson and Daniel Tupou ran hard and ensured their sets started well. Their forwards were super-aggressive. Then there was five-eighth Luke Keary's kicking game. He launched bombs from halfway, landing them half a metre from our tryline. Cooper did a great job of staying out of harm's way. That's what comes with playing more than 300 games: you know where to position yourself.

That entire first half was played down our end. We had no field position and no ball. The Roosters took the game away from us. They were far better on the night and deserved the premiership—it was as simple as that.

•

Despite all that's been said—mostly by other people—the reality is that Coops and I have never had a bust-up.

It is true we have different personalities, but we've also lived different lives away from the footy field. During our time together at the Storm, I became a father for the first time in 2008 and soon had two more kids, whereas he lived by himself for the most part. As everyone knows, the lifestyles of a young father and a single bloke are like chalk and cheese.

The way the stories around some sort of dramatic falling-out between us gained momentum during 2018 was sad. It became comical when, all of a sudden, I was apparently at odds with Bill as well. Barb was brought into it, again, when stories went around about a spat between her and Billy's wife, Nic, which never happened. They're good friends to this day.

We were stunned. 'Where is this shit coming from?' we asked ourselves.

What was clear enough was that the stories were being fabricated to fit a narrative: Cameron Smith does not get on with his teammates, and vice versa. It couldn't have been any further from the truth, but the more it was written and talked about, the more people seemed to believe it.

Ultimately, Cooper and Bill both know how important they've been in my life over a long period of time. Now that our playing careers are all over, I look forward to having a beer and a laugh with them, just as we have done together for the last twenty years.

24

THE 400

Throughout my whole career, I never cared about accolades or reaching milestones. We all like a pat on the back now and then, when we've done something good. I'm a footy player though. I just wanted to play. I'd rather rip in, play well and work hard for my teammates.

As the years went on though, and the closer I came to the end of my career, there was one record I needed to break. I wouldn't stop until I did . . .

Craig Bellamy's try-scoring record.

'He's broken a whole heap of records, but he still hasn't caught me in the try scoring,' Bellyache said during a series of speeches after the captain's run in the lead-up to my 400th match in July 2019.

That's all I needed to hear. I was sitting on 44 and I wasn't going to stop until I went past Bellyache's record of 46 from his playing days at Canberra.

The revelation came in the theatrette at AAMI Park the day before I became the first NRL player in history to reach the 400 mark. There were different emotions around every record I broke, but 'The 400' was something else. Not so long ago, people thought it was impossible to reach that mark in a brutal sport like ours. Nobody believed a player's body could hold up long enough to play that many games. But because of improvements in training and sports science, players' bodies these days are better preserved. Even someone with an accountant's body like mine could last.

Reaching Darren Lockyer's mark of 355 for most games played was a huge honour, but 400 was significant because it wasn't just a personal achievement. I was proud that a Melbourne Storm player was the first to do it. In their wildest dreams, would anyone ever have thought the first to do it would be representing a rugby league team in Melbourne?

One of the highlights of the week was sharing the limelight with the four players from the VFL/AFL who had also reached that milestone over the years: Kevin Bartlett, Michael Tuck, Dustin Fletcher and Brent Harvey. They came down for a midweek session, watched us train and put on the one-off jersey made for the game. It was nice to share that cross-code connection.

A Richmond legend, 'KB' was the first player to achieve it in either code, and he now spoke about how important that was to him. He felt it was a great accomplishment for himself and also for his sport. It gave other players a goal to strive for, he said. That was how I felt too. But now I'd love to see another rugby league player reach 400 games.

On Bellyache's watch, the Storm enjoyed a strong connection with several AFL clubs in Melbourne. When he first arrived, we did some cross-code training with Richmond and Collingwood. A couple of their players would come in and work with our kickers, fine-tuning our drop-punt technique, helping us get more accuracy and distance out of our kicks.

They also did a of work with our catchers, particularly Billy Slater and Israel Folau. At the time, nobody in the NRL was using the AFL technique of getting up and catching the ball with both hands out in front of your body. In league, you're taught to catch it on your chest, but in Aussie Rules they teach kids to extend their arms and take the ball in their hands.

Izzy had the athletic ability to jump, so they just had to teach him the technique of catching the ball above his body. When he did, he became unstoppable. Billy was so talented he could catch the ball however he wanted. Most of the work he did with the AFL boys was around technique—using defenders' bodies to propel him above the pack towards the ball.

It's no secret that I'm a huge Hawthorn fan. I've been to many games and still have a close relationship with one of their senior players, Shaun Burgoyne. We were introduced to each other as we headed into the 2011 season. Shaun had come to the Hawks the previous year from Port Adelaide, so he was like me: an out-of-towner with a young family, in Melbourne to play footy. Our families have grown close over the years.

I was determined to make sure the build-up to the 400 game was as low-key as possible, after learning hard lessons the year before when I reached Locky's mark. Even when I'd reached 350, when I joined Locky and Canterbury legend Terry Lamb, there had been a big celebration. Six weeks later it was even bigger, with something on every day, including Locky coming down for a luncheon.

It was great to break the record of someone I looked up to so much, but when we got through Parramatta in the first week of the finals I was relieved, mainly because mentally I was completely drained.

In many ways, Locky was like me. He didn't crave the limelight and I am the same. My preference has always been keeping things very simple.

I have never needed attention, or someone patting me on the back so I feel good about myself. I loved playing footy, playing well and competing, but I wasn't driven by what people thought of my performances.

I didn't leave the field hoping for a great write-up in the paper, or gratuitous comments online. Those things never entered my mind coming off a football field, ever.

Perhaps people don't understand that that's just the person I am. I've never felt a need to hear my own voice. If someone has a crack at me, I don't need to reply. Sometimes I was advised that I 'should get on the front foot' about something. What for? I don't need that. I'm happy doing what I'm doing. If people want to think badly of me, good on them. I've only ever wanted to play footy. That's all I was ever about and it's the way I've always wanted it to be.

As long as my family, teammates and coach are proud of my efforts, that's all that matters, and that's why it was special to have them in the room for my jumper presentation after the captain's run. Mum, Dad, Khirstie, Matthew and their families were all there. So were Barb and the kids.

Craig was the first to speak. 'Footy's important to Cameron,' he said. 'It's super-important to him. But his family is more important. He has a genuine love for the game. But that love must have been tested through some periods, especially the suspension from the grand final and salary cap thing. It takes a toll on you. Because he's so balanced, he just moved on. I'm sure he's hated some people in the game, but never the game. He's always got that balance right: his family are first, the game second.'

Bellyache also made mention of a trait that I wasn't aware of.

'It's amazing how many times that after one of our players scores a try, he's the first one there to congratulate him. He would've seen a lot of tries in eighteen years and 400 games. I'm not sure what the message is out of that, but it tells me that he still loves playing the game and he still likes to see other people have success. He's 40 metres away, he'll sprint past guys to congratulate them. Well, probably not sprint. He's about half-pace these days. Let's say he works really hard to get there!'

Then it was Barb's turn to speak. She's an emotional type and doesn't like public speaking. She lasted about three seconds until the tears came, so she got Jada up to read out her words:

'He's the same man now as he was when we met as sixteen-year-old kids. We've never forgotten where we have come from. Most people mumble when they're from a shitty area. You shout it from the rooftops. You've always said it loudly, "I'm from

Logan, mate." This is another quality I love . . . You remind
me every day of how wonderful you are, and you show me and
the kids how to be good people. "Barb, you don't change who
you are. Just keep smiling, that hurts them more." These are
just some of the things he says around our house. He's achieved
a lot in his career, but he's the exact same person he was back
then. He's still a shit-stirrer, he loves his old cars, kids' video
games and singing badly. He's a fantastic husband and the best
dad I could ask for.'

My brother, Matt, presented me with specially designed
golden Nike boots. He's nine years younger than me and played
a handful of under-20s games with the Storm in 2011 and
2012. He was a good little footballer—playing in the No. 9
jersey, of course—but he's built more like our dad than me.
Matt was a handy footballer, but struggled for an opportunity
at Melbourne. He trained hard, which was the main reason he
was down here, and put plenty of effort into his games. Ultimately, he was happy with what he did in those two seasons
before moving home to become an electrician.

Then it was time for the jersey presentation. This was also
a really emotional moment. My best mate, Jared Cumerford,
and his sister, Patricia, came forward.

I've known their family since the age of eight, when Jared
and I went to school together. The Cumerfords were my second
family. If I wasn't at his house, he was at mine. When I first
signed with the Storm, and I had to train with Norths Devils
on the north side of Brisbane, I didn't have a car for the hour-
long drive four times a week. Dad was working. Mum had a car

but usually needed it. And when that was the case, Jared's dad, Mick, would finish his work as a local groundsman early and lend me his car to drive to training.

They were good people, and they didn't deserve the fate that was about to befall them. Just before my 400th game, Patricia was diagnosed with an aggressive cancer, and the prognosis wasn't great. Thankfully, things have since improved but it looked grim there at one stage. She is also like a sister to me. The least I could do was get them both down for that game. Without their support early in my life, would I have played 400 games? Probably not, so it meant a lot to receive my jumper from them.

You don't play a heap of footy games without the support of a lot of people. If Craig hadn't pulled me aside after training at Studley Park that afternoon early in my career and told me I was training within myself—how the difference between being a good player and a great player was busting yourself every session—I would probably have finished my career at 150 games.

Then there was Mum and Dad. We weren't a family that was well off. We got by on the bare minimum. Dad was a brickie for most of our childhood, and he made just enough to cover the mortgage and the bills and put food on the table. When we needed to pay fees to get me to schoolboys' carnivals, or to pay for tracksuits for junior rep teams I'd been picked in, my parents would hold fundraisers and raffles for meat trays to raise the money to send me. There wasn't a spare thousand bucks just sitting there to pay for me to get the team kit and grab a flight to the next carnival. Without their sacrifice, I couldn't have achieved what I did.

Then there were the people who always had my back. My big sister often took on those who attacked me, even jumping on social media to shoot them down. I'd have to call her every now and then. 'Khirst, leave them,' I would tell her. 'It doesn't mean anything.'

The other person who was always an enormous support was Frank Ponissi, our football manager, although that description doesn't seem adequate because of all that he did for our club. Frank had always been very protective of me and my family, particularly as the criticism grew over the years. He had my back, and my family's, and was always quick to call the haters out.

Perhaps the most important people on my way to 400 games were my Storm teammates. Until that moment, I'd played with 157 players across my eighteen seasons.

'Without those 157, without all of you guys, this wouldn't have been possible,' I told the room. 'I really want to thank you boys for what you help me do on the field, but more importantly your friendship away from it. We spend 80 minutes on the field on the weekend but it's so much more to me. That's why I like coming in to training: for a cuddle. I'm a bit of a hugger. I enjoy those good times. That's how I view footy. That's the reason we all started playing: it was never about a pay cheque, being on TV or having anything more than friendships with your mates and enjoying what you did. Every year gets a little bit harder. But Barb is right: I just turned 36 but I feel 26.'

After that, the time for talking was over. I was ready to draw a line under the week and focus on our opponents—Cronulla—at AAMI Park.

'As far as tomorrow is concerned, I'm really excited,' I told the gathering. 'If you can't get up for a game against the Sharkies, I don't know who you can get up for.'

And we did, winning 40–16.

•

The other noticeable milestone in my career was becoming the highest point-scorer in the history of the game, surpassing Bulldogs great Hazem El Masri's mark of 2418.

When I went past him, Hazem posted a funny video on social media, pretending to break a plasma TV in anger, but he also sent me a nice message via social media and an email to the club.

It was a record that just happened along the way from playing so much football, but it's a really cool one because, as a No. 9, you're not expected to score that many points.

As you may have noticed, I didn't score many tries. And when I first started in the NRL, I wasn't a recognised goal-kicker. I had been in junior footy, and at times with Norths Devils, but I was never considered a sharpshooter. That part of my game improved as my career progressed.

Our regular goal-kicker at the Storm when I began was Matty Orford. When he joined Manly in 2006, I was thrown the kicking tee and told, 'Here you go, mate—it's your job.'

At that time my accuracy would have been around 70 to 75 per cent. I was okay without being great. But as my career went on, it became an area of my game I concentrated on. I'd spent so much time on my dummy half craft and defence in my early years, and now I began spending more time on my goal-kicking.

I did some work with former Bulldogs winger Daryl Halligan, one of the greatest goal-kickers the game has seen. He didn't overanalyse my style. I didn't have a big, elaborate, curling kick like Hazem or JT. I was straighter, and 'Chook' gave me tips around my routine, as well as training habits that would help me build consistency. It wasn't about searching for a perfect conversion rate.

A crucial thing was what we call the 'shape' of the kick—the arc from where the ball leaves your boot to where it ends up between the posts. Chook wanted to help me understand the way my shape worked. Then all I had to do was make sure that I had the ball set up correctly on the tee, on the right line, and account for the wind.

As the seasons went by, I paid no attention to how many points I was clocking up—until I came closer to the top of the point-scoring list. The first person I went past was Jason Taylor, who sat on 2107 points. Then Andrew Johns with 2176. Then JT with 2222.

When I was about to edge past Hazem, the Storm was travelling to Townsville for our Round 5 match against the Cowboys. We were very grateful that the NRL allowed Jada and Jasper to be ball kids for the game, something they'd been doing for a few years at Storm home matches.

The moment arrived in the 49th minute. We were awarded a penalty twelve metres out and just to the right of the right-hand upright. It was a straightforward two points that would've levelled the scores at 8-all, but I didn't want to take them just to get the record. Very quickly the message came from the bench to take the two points.

Jada and Jasper came out onto the field and stood behind me. There's a cool pic of them standing there, waiting arm in arm and looking really nervous. They knew what the kick meant for me. Up in the stands, Barb and Tilly were equally nervous.

It was such an easy kick that I could've put it over with my right foot. But the occasion took over. It was a penalty goal, not a conversion, so the game was actually live—so the ball kids shouldn't have been on the field. But they were standing three or four metres behind me. The referee, Gavin Badger, was right behind me and he didn't say anything about it. Everyone stopped thinking. It was only after the match that it dawned on me: 'What would have happened if the ball hit the post and came back in the field of play?' The kids could've been trampled.

Luckily, the kick sailed between the sticks. I gave Jada and Jasper a huge hug and they ran from the field. We won 18–12.

My kids are huge football fans. When we're in the car, I'll ask them footy questions. *Who wears No. 3 for the Raiders? Who's the captain of the Cowboys?* Jada rattles off the answers with ease. She knows what's going on. She's also really athletic and loves playing the game.

The other two, Jasper and Tilly, are my hard nuts. They're maniacs. When they get home from school, they chuck on whatever jersey and shorts they have and play footy with each other for hours. Jasper is two years older, but even though Tilly is a tiny little thing she still rips in.

There's a funny story about Jada's arrival into the world—and it involves Bellyache.

When the Storm won the premiership in 2007, it set up a World Club Challenge match with Super League champions Leeds on 29 February the following year. And that clashed with an important date: Barb was due with our first child.

'There's no way you can go,' Barb told me. 'If I go into labour, you won't be home for three days. It's not like you're playing in Sydney.'

I contemplated missing my first World Club Challenge. 'You'll be right,' I said cautiously.

'Just you getting on the plane will put me into labour,' Barb insisted. 'You can't go.'

I understood. It was my first child. I couldn't miss this.

When I got to training, I knocked on Bellyache's door. 'I can't go to the World Club Challenge,' I told him.

'What do you mean?' he asked.

I explained the situation.

'Oh, mate,' he said. 'First child—they always go past their due date. Always. I'm telling you. Have another chat with Barb about it.'

I walked out knowing I had nothing to think about.

When I got home, I told Barb that I'd spoken to Craig.

'Did he take it okay?' she asked.

'Yeah, not really,' I laughed.

I left it for a couple of days, and then told Bellyache that there was no way I was going. So the boys travelled to London without me. As it happened, hardly any of their bags turned up, and they lost the game. They arrived home—and Jada was born two weeks later.

Bellyache was filthy. 'I told you!' he said when I saw him next. 'I told you so! They always go over!'

Barb wanted to make sure my football wasn't affected when Jasper arrived seventeen months later. He was due in September 2009, in the middle of the finals.

'I'm getting induced so you've got a clear head,' she told me.

It was an incredibly selfless act, so typical of Barb. She understood the disappointment I felt about the previous year when I'd missed the grand final through suspension. She knew how much winning in 2009 meant to me.

We played Newcastle on a Monday night and Barb was booked in on the Tuesday. I caught the first plane out of Newcastle, went straight to the hospital and the big fella was born seven hours after I got there. Our third child, Matilda, came along in 2012.

In a way, I'm glad I played in Melbourne, where AFL is the dominant code. For the most part of their childhood, my kids haven't had a great understanding that I'm in the public eye.

But kids get older. They read stories on the internet. Their friends at school start to talk. We could only shelter them for so long from some of the things being said about their dad.

25

TRUTH

Barb was getting groceries out of the back of her car in front of our house in late July 2018 when someone got out of a nearby car and approached her in the driveway.

'Hi, Barb,' the young man said. 'I'm a reporter from the *Herald Sun*. Can we talk?'

Barb was shocked. Why was a reporter approaching her for comment about anything, especially on our property? How did he even know where we lived?

'About what?' Barb asked.

'About your husband's relationship with his teammates?'

Barb told him to piss off—but even so, the episode rocked her. It didn't help that I was overseas at the time.

I was in Auckland, at the end of our captain's run practising my goal-kicking on a cold, windswept ground ahead of our Round 19 match against the New Zealand Warriors at

Mount Smart Stadium. At one point I noticed Frank Ponissi on the sideline trying to get my attention. That was strange: I knew Frank wouldn't hassle me unless it was about something important. I walked over and he told me about the incident involving Barb and the reporter.

We found out that a request to approach Barb for comment had come to the *Herald Sun* from their News Corp stablemate in Brisbane, the *Courier-Mail*. I have no doubt they knew I was away. If I'd been there, I would've given that bloke a mouthful. He had invaded her privacy—her personal space—and in that space were our three children, all of whom felt upset after seeing their mum get rattled.

At first Barb thought the guy might have been a parent of one of the kids' schoolfriends, or from one of their junior sports teams. He wasn't—and when we later checked our security footage, it showed he'd been snooping around before they got home, looking through the windows and doors.

Things were beginning to get out of hand. Barb and I live a simple life. We're down-to-earth people doing the best we can. It just so happens that my job has a high profile. Away from footy, we just enjoy hanging out at home and being as far from the public eye as possible. This had crossed the line.

•

Unless you were a Storm player, you wouldn't have known.

We were playing the Gold Coast Titans on a Sunday after-noon at AAMI Park in August 2019, and we weren't going that well. We were down by six points, against the team on the bottom of the ladder, and nothing was going right.

Finally we got the ball in a decent position, a few metres out from the tryline. I jumped out of dummy half, went down the short side and played short to Kenny Bromwich. All the big man had to do was break the tackle and score. It was very straightforward. Instead, he busted through and slammed the ball down so hard it went bouncing high into the air. He'd reached back with his left hand and buried it into the turf of the in-goal in pure anger, emotion and frustration.

'Mate, that's exactly how I feel,' I thought, before being the first to embrace him.

We won 24–8 but it was probably the most frustrating match of my career. It was like that back home too, where Barb had been watching with Tilly. She also became frustrated and started gardening before the game was over.

'When will Daddy be home?' Tilly asked Barb.

'You know Dad,' she said. 'Not until later tonight.'

But ten minutes later, I was home. It was well within the hour after fulltime.

'What's wrong with Dad?' Barb asked Jada and Jasper a bit later on.

'Don't know,' they said.

Deep down, Barb knew. So did everyone at the Storm. The campaign to destabilise us had been on in earnest for the past few weeks and it was starting to take its toll. The way Kenny scored that try expressed how the whole side were feeling. We'd had enough.

It had started with a series of strategically placed articles about the Storm's wrestling techniques and so-called illegal tactics. The first of them appeared after we beat South Sydney on the Central Coast, and they didn't really stop until the season was over. This was nothing new, of course. We'd become accustomed to these sorts of stories for many years. But the sheer volume of it, and the timing, showed that there was an orchestrated campaign intended to unsettle us.

The other issue was all this rubbish about me being the 'referee whisperer'. People had joked for a while about how I spoke to referees, and the perception that I got whatever I wanted from them. I can tell you that was never the case. And even if it was, how would that have been my fault? I was just doing what was best for my team. I always figured you got further treating the referees with respect, rather than abusing them like some other players did. You had to be smart about it.

I didn't always get my way with referees. In March 2018 Matt Cecchin sent me from the field for backchatting during a match against Cronulla at Shark Park in which he'd controversially blown 30 penalties during a crackdown. He was making a point that night, and sending me from the field—for the first time in my career—was part of it.

Towards the end of the 2019 season, the myth had been repeated so many times that people were actually believing I had the referees wrapped around my little finger. And because it had been written about and discussed so much, the refs suddenly became dismissive of me. Not just one referee but all of them. Their mindset seemed to be: 'Don't let him converse with you.' Against Gold Coast that afternoon, I was barely given a chance to voice any concerns.

But the story that really got to me and my family was one published in mid-August about a gift the then NRL chief executive Todd Greenberg had given Barb at a special dinner organised a few days before my 400th match.

'I know you guys are very low key, and you don't want to make a fuss,' Todd had said to me at the time. 'But it's a big moment for our game. The first person to play 400 games.'

I told him I wanted everything done early, as far out from the kick-off as possible, because I wanted to avoid the distractions of what had happened in the week in which I broke Locky's games record.

'I want it to be minimal,' I told him.

He assured me it would be. 'But I think it's important to acknowledge Barb's contribution as well,' he said, 'because she's been there for all 400 of them.'

She'd been there longer than that, of course. She'd been there for all of it, all the way back to our first date, when I scored two tries in that under-17s semi-final for Logan Brothers.

'Thanks very much, mate,' I said. 'What do you think would be appropriate? I have no idea.'

'The 300-gamers get rings,' Todd said. 'How about a ring?'

I thought that was a great idea.

At the dinner, Todd got up to say a few words. 'There's a special presentation tonight, but it's not for Cameron,' he said. 'It's for Barb and all the support she's given not just Cameron but the Storm and the game.'

None of the people at the gathering left the restaurant that night thinking it would spark a media story that would take aim at the NRL, and at Barb and me. The gift from the NRL had been a goodwill gesture, at a time when the game was being criticised for how it treats women, and suddenly it became a huge issue. It was claimed this money could've been better spent on grassroots football.

I could not believe this was what our game had become. This had overstepped the mark. And Barb was devastated.

'If it's that much of a problem, I'll give it back,' she said.

What was worse, we got blamed for taking money away from where it should be spent—as if we were stealing money from junior clubs.

'I'll just hand it back,' Barb kept saying. 'I was appreciative that they thought of me, but it's become different from what it was intended to be. If people have a problem with it, I'll hand it back.'

The thing we took most exception to was that the episode painted us as greedy people. It was like the stories around the testimonial match I had with Johnathan Thurston in February 2018. Sections of the media reported that we made huge amounts of money out of the game. We did not. Most of it went to charity, and the whole thing was cleared ahead of time, and afterwards, by the NRL's salary cap auditor.

I'll tell you the type of people we are: ordinary. I loved playing footy, and in other regards I'm just a family man and a normal person.

I felt terrible for Barb. She hadn't signed up for this. We'd been dating before I even started playing NRL, when there was every chance I wouldn't make it to the top grade. Her best memories were the days at Norths Devils, when she would sit on the hill on a Saturday arvo, hanging out with the other punters, watching me play. She has never used the game or the media to gain any benefit for herself. For her it was never about the red carpets or the publicity. She was just there to support me.

The fallout from this story meant we had to have some difficult conversations with our children. Tilly was too young to notice, but Jada and Jasper knew what was going on. We told them not to read the news, and we tried not to turn on the TV. They liked watching the different footy shows, but we stopped putting them on so they wouldn't have to listen to any mistruths about their father.

It was inescapable, though. News is news and everyone reads it, watches it, listens to it. Parents at their school knew what was being said about our family. Other kids knew too. 'Dad's played 400 games and Mum got a gift,' Jada told them. 'I don't know anything else besides that.'

A mother came up to Barb at school one day.

'How are you going?' Barb asked.

'No, how are *you* going?' she asked.

'Why?'

'I've been hearing all this stuff about you and Cam . . .'

Things were getting out of control, and it forced me, at the end of the 2019 season, to ask myself some serious questions. Should I walk away from the game? Or keep playing and continue to put my family through this unwarranted scrutiny?

Football had changed. It was now starting to invade my children's lives. My wife's life. It was sometimes affecting how I played, like in that match against the Titans.

I'd had a good run, and for the most part I'd loved my time in rugby league. Maybe it was time to give it away and go and mow lawns for a living. Nobody would give a rat's about me then, and we'd be left alone.

•

The backdrop to all this stuff was an unfounded rumour about an intimate relationship I was supposedly having with Fox Sports presenter Yvonne Sampson. That one had taken on a life of its own thanks to social media.

In recent years, the rubbish people put about on social media has become a serious issue—and it's getting worse. There's no accountability because they all use pseudonyms. Whether they're intending to cause harm or just gasbagging without thinking, the damage they cause is significant. Lies spread quickly and easily, and the more often people read something, the truer it becomes.

In Melbourne we were usually immune to a lot of this innuendo around rugby league, but this one was inescapable.

The first person to bring it up with me was my manager, Isaac Moses. 'Mate, I need to ask you something,' he said down the phone one day.

'Yeah?'

'No, it's a serious one, mate.'

'Shit,' I thought. 'What's going on here?' I was standing in the backyard and I started expecting the worst.

'Mate, there's a rumour going around that you're having an affair,' Isaac said.

'What?'

'With Yvonne Sampson.'

I started laughing. Honestly, if I was going to have an affair—which is something I never would do—why would I do it with someone with a profile as big as hers? And in my own sport? How could I even hope to get away with that?

Then I got cranky. 'I don't know where this crap has started, or why,' I said. 'But it's laughable.'

I've got the sort of personality that means I can usually brush nonsense stories aside. But when it involves my family, and when it's as personal as this was, that's completely different. I knew the rumour was rubbish, but that didn't mean it wouldn't hurt the ones closest to me.

When I told Barb, she was shattered. It floored her. I want the people who start this garbage—and the ones who spread it—to think about the damage it causes. Barb is married to me, with three children who she takes to school every day. What were the other parents thinking?

Barb's the type of person who wears her heart on her sleeve. She's also the type who stands up for herself and her family. But standing up to it in this case was impossible, because we didn't know which coward had started it and which cowards were spreading it. And because it was on social media, it spread like wildfire.

Our approach was to keep quiet and not give the nonsense any oxygen. When I think back, I wonder whether I should have denied it all publicly straightaway. But the way Barb and I have dealt with things in the past is to let them blow over. No media outlet ever printed it, because they knew it wasn't true— and if they did, they would've been in a lot of legal trouble.

But it all got so silly that one journalist had a photographer follow me every time I came to Sydney, to try to catch me out. The Storm's chief executive, Dave Donaghy, confronted him about it and asked what he found. The answer: nothing! They found that I went to my hotel, went for a swim with my mates, got a coffee, went back to the hotel, went to training, and played the game. Fascinating stuff.

Midway through 2018, I was invited to appear on Fox Sports' *League Life*, which Yvonne hosted with Lara Pitt, Jess Yates and Hannah Hollis. Yvonne wanted to talk about the rumour on air, so we could shut it down once and for all. I wasn't comfortable doing that, but in that moment I saw just how much of an impact this was having on her as well.

'This affects me too, Cameron,' she said.

'I understand that, Vonnie,' I replied. 'But if I comment, it just becomes an even bigger discussion point, and that's not fair on my wife and my children. I'm not doing it to Barb.'

I know how much the rumours hurt Yvonne. It wasn't fair on her, or her partner. It wasn't fair on any of us. I think it says a lot about Barb that she texted Yvonne to see if she was okay. They texted back and forth, each knowing the embarrassment the other was going through. The whole thing was disgusting.

I've copped hurtful criticism and speculation throughout my whole career, so I thought the right thing to do was to leave it. I don't regret that decision, but no one walked away from the whole business in a good place. And there was zero basis to any of it.

•

Despite all the off-field issues, all the nasty rumours and the apparent campaigns to put us off our game, the Storm won the minor premiership in 2019, finishing three wins ahead of the Roosters. Unfortunately, we were bundled out of the finals, with losses to Canberra in the qualifying final and then the Roosters in the preliminary.

That hurt. It really hurt. To finish the regular season three games ahead of the pack was special, but then we lost to the Raiders 12–10 after leading with two minutes remaining. From there it was always going to be difficult to win the premiership.

Bellyache was surprisingly calm about the result. He was proud of what we'd achieved. I felt the same way. In 2018, we lost Cooper Cronk but still made the grand final with a rookie halfback, Brodie Croft. After that, Billy and Ryan Hoffman retired, and suddenly we had a team full of kids—but we still won the minor premiership and made a preliminary final.

That's the thing about the Storm: because we'd been so successful for so long, it was a really empty feeling when we lost.

We let the Roosters out to an 8–0 lead before a try to prop Nelson Asofa-Solomona in the 51st minute put us right back in the game. But their defensive line wouldn't crack. We lost 14–6.

Billy interviewed me on the field for Channel Nine before we entered the dressing-room. 'Are you going to play on next year?' he asked.

'I don't know, mate,' I said. 'Do you need someone to muck out your stables?'

It was just a throwaway line about Billy's horse breeding business. I wasn't trying to plant any seeds or get anyone on edge. But when I plonked down on my seat in the dressing-room soon afterwards, I asked myself a question: 'Do you want to do this again? You've got a decision to make here.'

For the next three or four weeks, I wasn't a good person to be around at home. I didn't have a great outlook on the game. And I was torn about my future.

Bellyache was aware of what I was going through. He'd talked at the Dally M awards about the personal attacks 'wearing Cameron down'. He knew they were a ploy to put me off, to get to me, and said he believed people in the game should respect me more. That was nice of him to say, but that's Bellyache. He's protective of all his players.

The point he was making was that when he was a young fella watching his favourite players, they were shown a lot more respect by the media and the public in general. Something had dramatically changed in recent years, and not for the better. Perhaps it was the race to be first, not right, or the rise of click-bait content online. It's a new world.

Mum and Dad and the rest of my family and close friends had also grown tired of the attacks. They never let on too much, but it chipped away at them when one of their family members was getting hammered all the time. It was hard to cop at times, but I think they understood it was just the Australian way. When someone has success, and particularly sustained success, people look to chop them down.

As for Barb, she thought I should've gone and done something stupid in order to stop the endless stream of stories and comments.

'What do you have to do for them to leave you alone?' she asked me one day. 'Do you have to do something ridiculous to tarnish your reputation, or even break the law? Maybe then they'll say, "Finally we've got something on him—now we can go after someone else".'

I understand that elite sport is of wide interest, and it's reported on in depth. I had no dramas with articles and opinions being written about my performances during my career. But when the media bring my personal life and my family into it, that's crossing the line.

So I had to make a decision. I'd made my NRL debut in 2002, and won premierships, Origins, Test matches. I'd been lucky enough to do all that. Did I really want to go through it all again? My body was fine, but there was every possibility that the personal attacks on my family could happen again. Did I want to put my family through that? Did I want my wife to be in the papers? And all because of what I do for a living?

Rugby league no longer felt like the game that I fell in love with.

Then I looked at it another way. To walk away would have been handing a victory to those critics. I knew I could still play at the top level. And when I thought hard about it, I still wanted to play.

I made a decision: I wasn't going to be driven out of the game. I was going to end my career when the time was right, and on my terms.

26

COVID

This was supposed to be the last chapter of the book. Who'd have thought it would be about a global pandemic that had devastating consequences for the world, including rugby league. COVID-19 changed everything in 2020.

Our club doctor, Jason Chan, had done a great job keeping us informed about what was happening overseas. He gave us a heads-up early on about a virus that had broken out in China, and how it was spreading throughout the world. There was a strong possibility that it would surge in Australia too. Because of Jason's diligence, I felt our club and our playing group were a few steps ahead of the others in understanding what was happening.

Despite the dark shadow of the virus sweeping across the globe, our first match of the season, on Sunday, 15 March against Manly at Brookvale Oval, went ahead in front of a crowd.

That weekend, Prime Minister Scott Morrison had addressed the nation and spoken about major concerns around the coronavirus coming to Australia—but crowds could still go to the footy. The following day, though, no public gatherings of more than 50 people would be allowed.

I couldn't understand it. We were playing at 4 p.m. on a Sunday, but eight hours later it wouldn't be safe to have large crowds?

I don't overthink things. I just think logically. And if the situation in our country was this bad, I didn't believe our game should be pushing ahead. We won 18–4 that afternoon. It was a strange afternoon, with the ball kids washing the balls in buckets of disinfectant on the sidelines after they'd gone over the fence into the crowd.

I was interviewed by Brent Read for Triple M on the field after fulltime.

'If we actually give ourselves an opportunity to step away for a fortnight or even a month, push the season back, then that might give us a chance to take a look at what is happening and the right path on what to do,' I said. 'There's a lot of questions to ask outside of just saying let's pause the comp for four weeks.'

This was clearly much bigger than rugby league; people were losing their lives. I've always thought rugby league should lead the way for the rest of the community. I felt it was the right time to suspend our competition. I wasn't saying we should call it off and not come back, but I thought we needed to suspend it for a short time—until there was a clearer understanding of what was happening. We could come back when it was safe to play and travel again.

And for me, that was the overriding concern: the travel. Our club was on and off planes every second week, going through airports and coming into contact with a lot of different people. The government was telling us these were all things we should be avoiding. But the NRL wanted us to push ahead and keep the competition going. I immediately foresaw that there would be major implications for teams like us, which were flying in and out of cities and then returning to our families.

Some critics didn't like what I had to say, and used the delicate public health issue to have a crack at me. It wouldn't have mattered what I said, of course, as they were always going to launch into me. But I think most people appreciated the point I was making. At this time, other sporting leagues around the world were suspending their competitions—the NBA, the Premier League, the AFL—but we were still pushing ahead.

After we played the Sharks at Jubilee Stadium the following weekend, in front of no crowd, the competition was finally suspended on the advice of the NRL's biosecurity expert. We wouldn't be back for over nine weeks.

To be honest, my first two or three weeks away from the game were great. It was nice to have some time at home with Barb and the kids. That's when we were just social distancing and not in complete lockdown. I was riding bikes with the kids in the morning, and taking them to the park to kick the footy around in the afternoon. But then the country went into lockdown and our activities were far more restricted.

In April and May, things became quite hectic as the game wrestled with how it would survive, and just how long it would be before the players were back on the park. As the general president of the Rugby League Players Association, I was at the front and centre of many discussions with the game's various stakeholders. There were several Zoom calls and phone hook-ups a day with the RLPA, the NRL and the clubs, whose financial viability was under enormous pressure. As players, we were trying to get some clarity around the future of the game and our employment, and what rugby league might look like when we returned.

This was when Australian Rugby League Commission chairman Peter V'landys came to the fore. He'd been appointed in October 2019, but the first time I met him was in the pre-season when he came down to Melbourne to meet the club. He and I spoke only briefly on that occasion, but over the weeks that followed the competition shutdown we started having multiple discussions each day. The thing that came across quickly was that he was a very ambitious leader who was confident in his own ability.

The first discussion between Peter and the players was very positive, and we went away with a lot of confidence about where the game was headed under his direction. After that, though, attentions turned to the financial state of the game.

We had some serious concerns. When we learned that the NRL only had cash reserves of around $120 million, a lot of the boys were really shocked. You didn't have to be a financial guru to understand that when you're bringing in hundreds of millions of dollars a year, through broadcast and other revenue, you should be putting some of it away, whether it's in savings or in assets. What this meant was that if we couldn't play another game in 2020, the NRL wouldn't have the funds to support its players and clubs.

We were also angry when we learned that the players' retirement fund hadn't been paid into for the last two seasons. Our understanding was those funds were deposited at the end of every season. Todd Greenberg's argument was that this wasn't the condition struck under the most recent collective bargaining agreement (CBA). Instead of paying millions of dollars into the fund each year, they only had to pay into it at the end of the five-year cycle of the CBA.

They'd found a loophole, and we felt like we'd been played. Was this the right thing to do, morally, to your players? The whole reason the fund was set up was to help players transition out of footy when their on-field career ended. We were really disappointed when we learned about that, and we aired our grievances.

The 'Project Apollo' committee was formed to work out a way to get the competition started again. The day pencilled in for a restart was 28 May. I had concerns about us rushing back so soon. My number one worry was the safety of our players and their families. I also questioned whether 'bubbles'—where teams would be locked down in a certain place, away from our families, so they could play each other—was the right path to go down.

Many people said we should just deal with our discomfort and go along with that idea. 'Just get on with it,' a few former players said. 'Do what's right for the game.' Well, that was easy for them to say when they weren't the ones doing it. Could they really say whether they would go ahead in that scenario? They'd never been put in a position like this. Ultimately, Peter V'landys canned the bubble concept, and a range of strict biosecurity protocols were put in place instead.

One of the last remaining issues was what the players would be paid when we resumed. Another key difficulty was what this all meant for the New Zealand Warriors, who had found themselves stuck in Australia since March because the New Zealand government had closed its borders. Flying between the two countries meant going into quarantine for fourteen days at either end, so that was never an option.

Days before we were due to return to training, we still didn't know where we stood. Suddenly, stories came out about a 'player revolt', which was apparently being led—surprise, surprise—by Cameron Smith.

It was made out to be a pay dispute, but our main concern was the Warriors. Their players and staff didn't know what sacrifices they were going to have to make, or what conditions they were going to have to live under. We didn't think it was unfair to ask for some clarity around what their pay—and everybody's pay—would look like. Would you leave the country you live in, and leave your family behind, without knowing what you were going to be paid?

We knew we'd be painted as greedy. But as the oldest player in the competition, all I cared about was the safety of my family and the security of my fellow players. I don't apologise for that.

Whether the public looked at me and the players as greedy, I don't care. All we wanted was for the NRL to tell us exactly what we were coming back to. Once we knew that, we could move forward.

At that stage, there was no broadcast deal in place between the NRL and its broadcasters, Channel Nine and Foxtel. There were suggestions that Nine might even walk away from the game. We kept asking questions but could get no answers. The funny thing was, there was no pay dispute because there was no pool of money to be in dispute about.

'Peter, how much money are we getting paid for the rest of the season?' we asked on one Zoom call.

'I don't know,' he said. 'But I'm going to do my very best to get you close to a hundred per cent of your contract. At the very least, I'll guarantee 80 per cent of your wage.'

We went away and talked about it. We were very realistic. They were cutting the season from 25 rounds to twenty. The product was less than what we'd signed up to play, so we considered the 80 per cent offer to be a reasonable one.

Peter also vowed to strip back costs, but promised that would not affect the annual grant the clubs get each year, and the salary cap. The savings would come from stripping back costs from head office. Soon after, Todd Greenberg resigned.

I was disappointed that Todd went. We'd shared a really good relationship through my playing career. I'd never seen a CEO who was more involved with the players than he was. He'd been chief executive of the Bulldogs, so he understood what 'club land' was like.

He also showed the Storm a lot of respect, and that mattered, because in Melbourne we sometimes felt like outcasts from the NRL. Our isolation worked for us in some ways, but no chief executive had visited our club and addressed the players and staff, or come to games as regularly throughout his tenure, as Todd.

Initially, the shutdown was very tough. We weren't allowed out of our houses, we weren't allowed to see anyone, and we couldn't train with a training partner. But we adapted. Towards the end of that period I was in a happy place. I felt fit, fresh, and I'd spent time with the family.

During the nine weeks between the season being suspended and the resumption of training, I didn't have a shave or a haircut. I had nowhere to be, no formal commitments, so I just got lazy. When I returned to training with a full beard, it caused a bit of a stir.

Returning to training and playing presented a whole new challenge. There were 'clean zones', 'dirty zones' and apps we had to fill out every day. I'd arrive at AAMI Park, have my temperature checked, then answer a series of questions. I took my shoes off in the dirty zone, went through a gate and then came into the clean zone. There were all these extra things to remember, so we had to adapt quickly. We knew that if we wanted to play again, this was what we had to do. For me as an older player, it was just one extra challenge I had to get through.

The protocols affected Barb and the kids as well. Barb couldn't have people come over, and all the home responsibilities were pushed onto her. Because I couldn't leave the house, she had to do the shopping and take the kids to and from school, all of it.

I will admit that giving it all away crossed my mind a couple of times. 'Is all this really worth it?' I asked myself. I decided that it was. The beard came off—but I was staying.

•

After our Round 7 match against the Warriors at Jubilee Stadium, Frank Ponissi approached me and asked if I wanted to say a few words to our opponents.

The Warriors had made enormous sacrifices by staying in Australia, with many of them away from their families, in order to keep the NRL going. We owed them a lot. And the strain of being away from home—they were based at Terrigal, on the New South Wales Central Coast—was taking its toll. That week had been particularly difficult for the organisation because the club owner had sacked their coach, Steve Kearney. It had come out of nowhere. The least we could do was thank them, as other clubs had done.

'I do, mate,' I told Frank. 'But I want to do it in the sheds, because I don't want it spread all across the media.'

Other teams had delivered a tribute on the field, but that wasn't my style. I'm not saying there was anything wrong with that, but if you've read this far you'll have realised I don't do things to get pats on the back.

After the match, Bellyache, Ryan Hoffman and I waited outside their sheds, and fifteen minutes later we were invited in.

'Boys, we just want to thank you for doing what you're doing,' I said. 'If you weren't doing this, we wouldn't be having this competition. I know it's tough, but keep your heads up, and look after each other. The one thing I know about the Warriors, you represent your jersey with a lot of pride, so just keep doing that.'

That's all I said.

The next day, we were hammered by some in the media for rubbing their noses in it after winning the game. I didn't expect anything less! The Warriors were shattered after the loss, but they weren't hostile towards us at all. Hoff was actually quite emotional because he'd played for them. Craig spoke about how impressed he was by their ability to get up each week. I'm good mates with Blake Green, Tohu Harris and Adam Blair, so I felt for them in particular.

We didn't go in there out of pity. We were thanking them for what they were doing. If I'd seen the camera in the corner of the dressing-room, I would've covered it up. For starters, it got a great shot of the bald spot on the back of my head. Second, I didn't want the media to see a private moment between us and the Warriors.

Only a few days earlier, we at the Storm were the ones on the move. A spike in the COVID infection rate in Victoria saw us move briefly to Sydney before settling at the Twin Waters Novotel resort on Queensland's Sunshine Coast.

It was nice to be in a place that was warm and sunny, so we got to train and prepare in great conditions. But it wasn't home. Melbourne was wet and cold at that time of the year, but it was where we all lived, and where our families and friends were.

There were fears that Victoria's second wave might reach New South Wales, so Project Apollo moved to ensure the NRL competition didn't stop by sending every player into further lockdowns. That meant we couldn't leave the resort for any reason, even though the rest of Queensland had a very low infection rate.

When a few players and coaches at other clubs were caught breaching the strict protocols, we were angry. We were doing the right thing but others weren't. We had adopted a very simple mindset: 'Don't be the one. Don't be the one who ends the entire competition.'

Most of the Storm players brought their families into the bubble at Twin Waters, but Barb and I decided not to do that. Instead, they relocated to the Gold Coast. It was a tough decision. They could've come in, but then I would have been taking their freedom away from them. By remaining outside our bubble, they could live like every other person in Queensland. They were free to go where they pleased, as long as they obeyed social distancing rules. That was more important for me. I wanted the kids and Barb to live a normal life.

I did have the option to see them, but I'd have to lodge an application with Project Apollo and go through a full screening process: who's in the house? What's their medical history? What medications are they on? Do they have any symptoms?

It was a tough time but I wasn't looking for sympathy. At least I could still play footy. As the season went on though, it forced me to ask myself the question once more: 'Is all this really worth it?'

27

FULL TIME

As we warmed up before a training session at our new home on the Sunshine Coast in late August, Craig approached me and asked for a quiet word. 'If you're playing on next year, why wouldn't it be with us?' he asked.

I was confused. 'Who's been saying that?'

'I've seen a news report.'

Bellyache was referring to several articles that had appeared concerning where I would be playing in 2021 if I didn't retire—something I hadn't decided at that point. At first rumours had me going to the Brisbane Broncos, then it was to the Gold Coast Titans. The weird part about all of it was that I hadn't spoken a single word to anyone from those clubs. Neither had my manager, Isaac Moses. Articles had then appeared saying the Melbourne Storm believed 2020 would be my final season at the club no matter what, because Barb and the kids had relocated to Queensland.

'Was I quoted in the story?' I asked Bellyache.

'No,' he said.

'Well, don't listen to it, mate. It's just speculation.'

For whatever reason, others then painted a completely different picture of how that conversation went. It was claimed the coach had approached me about my future and I'd laughed in his face and walked away.

By this point of my book, I'm sure you have a clear understanding of my relationship with Craig, which has developed over a very long period of time. Our relationship is based on trust and respect for one another. Do you really think I would laugh in his face? Stuff him around? Play mind games with him? I'm not that sort of person—and he's a bloke I respect too much to treat like that anyway.

The strange thing was that the people who were least affected by whether I retired at the end of 2020—the media— seemed to be the ones most obsessed with it. To me it felt like there was a concerted effort being made to force me to make a decision.

Things started to escalate. I was branded a 'liar' and 'dishonest' about discussions I had with the Storm, and in particular with Craig.

The fact is nobody at the club ever asked me to make a call. Our chairman Matt Tripp, coach Craig Bellamy, and football manager Frank Ponissi were all consistent in telling me I'd done enough for the club that I'd earned the right to make the call in my own time. The most important thing, they said, was to focus on the 2020 season.

Never once did Craig ask me straight out, 'Cam, are you going to play next year?' Never once did he even say, 'Cam, we need to know if you're playing on next year.'

I spoke to Frank every day—we were living next door to each other at the Twin Waters Resort—and all he ever wanted me to do was focus on the next game, week by week.

While I did that, he addressed the board in early September about the ongoing speculation. 'The board, given our current situation, wants to know how we're getting on up here, and they asked about the effect of the pressure on Cameron and the uncertainty around the group,' Frank told *The Sydney Morning Herald*. 'I reassured them there are absolutely no problems at all. There's no distraction on the group. This is the closest group I've seen at the Storm in the past 13 years. The way they are playing shows that.'

Matt Tripp checked in with me on a number of occasions, and he was really good about it too. 'There's no pressure on you at all, Smithy,' he told me. 'Just concentrate on what you're doing. If you have a decision, let us know.' We talked again on the phone when it got closer to finals. 'I'm not calling to talk about anything other than football,' he said. 'I just want to see how the team is going and if there's anything you guys need. If there is, let us know.'

As for my teammates, the only time it came up was when they were taking the piss out of me. 'Sign him for another two years!' they would joke after we had a win, just for a laugh. Nobody prodded me about it—and that included Brandon Smith and Harry Grant. Brandon has established himself as the New Zealand No. 9, and Harry played 2020 on a unique swap deal with the Wests Tigers, where he had a standout season.

Let me make it clear that I was always aware it would be beneficial for the Storm to have some notice with regard to my decision so they could juggle their roster ahead of the next season. At the same time, 2020 was an unprecedented year in the way that we had to live and play away from home. But even so, as I've said, the club were really good about it throughout the season. For me, knowing the three most senior people at the Storm had no concerns made things a bit easier.

I was well aware of Brandon's and Harry's situations, and I knew that if I chose to play on in Melbourne, it would be hard for the Storm to retain all three of us, even though the club had said time and time again that it could. I appreciated that Brandon and Harry were building careers of their own. My decision would have a lasting impact, one way or the other.

I discussed it with Craig. 'There's no way I'm re-signing for another twelve months if the club is going to lose either Harry or Brandon,' I said. 'I don't want to see the club struggle in the long term just so I can play one more season.'

Things can be complicated, though. The salary cap is complicated. Juggling rosters is complicated. As I wrote earlier in this book, I was in a similar situation back in 2002 with Richard Swain, a Storm legend. It was different then, however, because neither of us had a contract beyond that season. This time around, Harry had a three-year deal guaranteed, and Brandon had a two-year contract guaranteed.

If anything, the situation showed that the Storm's ability to identify talent was almost too good. They had recruited two great young hookers of the future—for the future. What none of us probably imagined was that I would still be playing when I was 37.

Throughout 2020, I spoke to Harry regularly about how things were going at the Tigers, and I saw Brandon every day. They are both great players and great people. Neither of them raised their future with me at any stage. Some people outside the club have argued that they wouldn't approach a senior player like me about their future, but that was a pretty big assumption to make. I'd like to think that my teammates feel I'm very approachable. If something is bothering them, I don't know why they wouldn't speak to me and ask the question. I'd be upfront and honest with them and tell them the facts, as I had done my entire career at the Storm. I would have told them what I told every other person who asked me: 'I'm not sure what I'm going to be doing.'

That was the truth of it that season: I just didn't know.

I remember talking to Barb on the phone one day when she was still in Melbourne with the kids and I had just relocated to Queensland with the rest of the Storm squad.

'It's not normal, darl,' I said. 'I'm 37 and I feel like I'm playing as well as I've ever played. Nothing is telling me to stop.'

I don't know how to explain it. I just didn't feel the decline at any stage of that 2020 season. If anything, I felt better than I ever had, in all aspects of my footy. I loved waking up and knowing I had to train. I enjoyed getting in there and competing with the younger players. I even enjoyed getting into the gym. Early in my career, the gym was something that I dreaded. The older I got, the more I loved it.

People kept asking me, 'How are you still playing?' The only answer I had was that I continued to train hard. When you look at most footy players, their prime years are from the age of 24 to 30. I felt like I was in better physical shape than I was in my twenties. Why? I honestly cannot say. There must have been some method in the madness of Craig's tough regime. Training as hard as I did over my career must have built some physical and mental resilience. I remember Matt Geyer once wondering how long some of us could last under Bellyache at the Storm. Weirdly, it prolonged our careers. Players like me, Billy, Coops and Hoffy, as well as Adam Blair, all played more than 300 games.

As the year went on, I spoke to a few people whose advice I trusted and valued. I called Billy, who put some things in perspective for me which I had been deliberating on for a while. In the end, he said that if I was making the call based purely on my form, then there was no reason why I shouldn't play on.

My old mate Johnathan Thurston was another I spoke to. I had talked with him regularly during his last season in the NRL, when his body hadn't allowed him to play the football he wanted to. That wasn't the case for me.

Paul Gallen told me that he just knew when it was time. He'd woken up one morning and said, 'I'm done.' I hadn't had that epiphany. I hadn't suffered any chronic injuries through my career, and I still had the hunger to compete. I was conscious that I would likely hit the wall at some point, as Paul had, but it hadn't happened yet. And when it would was an unanswerable question.

And of course I talked a lot about it to Barb and my family, as I had done throughout my career to get a balanced point of view. They never blew any wind up my arse. They were honest and I knew they'd always give me their genuine opinion.

'There's no indication that you're slowing down, but it can happen overnight,' Dad told me. 'I've been watching rugby league for a long time. I've seen it with a lot of athletes in other sports as well.'

As for Barb, she was just typical Barb and left it in my hands—although she agreed with Dad about the danger of going one year too long. 'It's your decision, mate,' she said. 'Whatever you decide, I'll support you. But you've put so much work into your career, and I'd hate to see you go one year too long and struggle through it.'

There was speculation that if I did play on, it would only be with a Queensland club because my family had relocated to south-east Queensland after the Storm was forced to shift north. Of course, with COVID-19 infection rates rising in Melbourne through the winter, we weren't given any choice about that if we wanted to remain in the competition.

Barb had initially wanted to stay in Melbourne, in our family home, but eventually she relocated to be closer to our families in Logan and on the Gold Coast. We enrolled the kids in school there while I was locked in the bubble at Twin Waters. It's possible that's what started the theory that

I wouldn't be playing for Melbourne in 2021, but the truth was I hadn't made any decisions about my playing future.

The other thing swirling around my mind as I considered retirement was the uncertainty that I knew would follow. I've always been a footballer. It's all I've done since I was a little fella. With the end nearing, I was forced to think about how life would look without playing football.

For twenty years or more football was at the centre of my life and my family's life. And it's a job that requires many sacrifices. You can't relax after the working week and go to the pub for a beer and do whatever you want on the weekend. You are always thinking about the next training session, the next game that's coming up. And it's similar for everyone else in your family. The demands of the game dictate so much of your life.

For the most part each week, you're in preparation for a game. You have to knock back social gatherings with family and friends, and if you can go, you're only there for a short time because you have an early training session the next day, or you're playing the next night.

At the same time, the routine of training and playing brings stability. You get handed a schedule, told what you have to do every day, even which clothes to wear and when. What would my life look like when that was no longer there?

A couple of days after Bellyache had approached me, he grabbed me for a second time on the training paddock. 'If you're going to retire, let the club know because we want to put on a celebration for you,' he said.

'What for?' I replied. 'I've had enough celebrations through-out my career, mate. Let's just keep winning. That's all I want to do. When the season's over, let's celebrate then if I'm retiring.'

All I could do, as the weirdest of seasons reached its climax, was concentrate on what I could control—and that was playing good football. The matter could have become a distraction if we allowed it to, but we didn't. We just did what we always do at the Storm: get on with business. Over the past five seasons we had played in five Preliminary Finals—no club had ever played six consecutively. Finals became my focus. My decision would take care of itself.

•

As the 2020 season rolled on, the Storm players and staff shut out the noise and used our isolation to our advantage.

When we'd arrived at the Sunshine Coast in late June, we had a Zoom meeting with NRL chief executive Andrew Abdo and other members from the Project Apollo team. They had prepared a PowerPoint presentation, and told us what had to happen if we were to return to Melbourne. We were all curious and unsure about what the future held and whether we could go home before the season was out.

Late in the presentation, it was pointed out that there had to be 28 consecutive days of single-figure infection rates in metro-politan Melbourne before we could return there. At that stage, the daily numbers of infections, and sadly deaths, were growing significantly. We already suspected that we might be on the

Sunshine Coast for much longer than the NRL were telling us. 'We're not going home this year,' I recall saying to some of the boys.

Once we got our heads around that fact, we spoke about the challenges we would face in living away from home for so long. We spoke about the importance of trying to maintain as much routine as possible, and the risk of the coaches overdoing things, as they had access to us 24/7. Our days off would be days off—there weren't to be any meetings. We wouldn't be asked to do extra sessions. We were trying to live as normally as possible, and that meant our downtime really was downtime.

We also acknowledged that the situation gave us a great opportunity to get to know each other even better than we already did. We had always been a tight-knit group. Almost the entire squad was from outside Victoria, so we didn't have childhood friends and extended family nearby. All we had was ourselves. Being able to spend that extra time together and talk to each other about our experiences outside footy—about where we're from, where we grew up, what our other interests are—would allow us to form an even closer bond.

But I won't lie—I hated being away from home. It didn't take long before I was feeling quite lonely at times, not having Barb and the kids around. We were in a beautiful resort and the weather was amazing, but there was no denying that our lives were constrained, and we were confined to doing the same things and seeing the same people every day.

Barb and the kids were eventually able to come into the 'bubble', but by then I'd spent three long months without them. It was a huge relief.

On the field, too, there were changes we had to keep up with. After the season shut down for nine weeks, it resumed with some new rules in place. The game reverted to one on-field referee, while a new six-again rule came into effect.

Away from the play, there were a few disruptions. The focus on my future shifted when it emerged that the Broncos wanted to sign Craig as their head of football. Bellyache brushed it aside and stated publicly that he would be continuing as head coach of the Storm until the end of 2021. The matter didn't have any effect on our group—other than giving the boys an opportunity to get stuck into Bellyache with some friendly banter. We had the business of winning the premiership to worry about.

Despite these distractions, the quality of the football played by all teams across the competition was incredible. None was better than our Round 8 match in early July against the Roosters at Suncorp Stadium.

We were down 22–12 with ten minutes to go, but as you will know by now, the Storm are never out of it. If any team wants to beat us, they have to play out the full 80 minutes. We scored tries through Jahrome Hughes and Paul Momirovski to take the lead 24–22, before Roosters halfback Kyle Flanagan kicked a difficult penalty. Then Luke Keary bagged a field goal to edge the Roosters ahead by one point.

Then, with 50 seconds left, the impossible happened. We got the ball back from a short kick-off and our fullback, Ryan Papenhuyzen, kicked a field goal with just seconds to go, sending the match into golden point. When Jake Friend was penalised for a ruck infringement, I had an easy penalty kick to win the match.

Another memorable moment came on 19 September, when I crossed the line to beat Craig Bellamy's try-scoring mark of 46. It almost didn't happen, as I suffered a grade-two injury to the AC joint in my shoulder while diving over for a try against the Newcastle Knights seven weeks earlier in Round 12. Really? I couldn't believe it. I'd played 420 NRL games, only scored 46 tries, and I did my AC joint chasing Craig Bellamy's bloody record!

Actually, if Bellyache hadn't alerted me to the record before my 400th match the year before, there's a strong chance I wouldn't have been chasing it at all. He'd brought it up in front of all the boys, though, and from that moment on there was no way I was going to let him have that over me.

In all honesty, the shoulder injury I suffered wasn't career-threatening. It was just painful and annoying because I was out for three matches.

Finally, in the second-last round of the shortened season, I scored the try that edged me ahead of him. After it was awarded, I waved to Bellyache in the coaches' box. He acknowledged that I'd broken his record by giving me the bird. As I said, there's always been a lot of respect between us!

The Storm finished the regular season in second place, behind a young Penrith Panthers side that was flying into the finals. At the Monday-morning captain's call that marked the commencement of the finals, I knew what most of the questions would be.

I was asked if winning a premiership would convince me to retire.

'I think it'd play a part,' I said. 'But that's not a definite for me.'

After all of the challenges, all of the adversity we had faced over the past six months, we couldn't wait to kick off the finals campaign.

•

The game of rugby league is changing in many ways. I don't know how many of the young fellas watch it now. The number of genuine footballers in our game is diminishing, with an increased focus on athletes. It's all about size and power. Catch a ball and run over people, which is a shame.

But there are aspects of the game that will never change, like the camaraderie that comes from being part of a team. Being among a group of mates, working hard for each other, all working towards the same goal of winning a premiership— that's a special thing. After working hard for a long time and achieving special things together, being able to reflect on your accomplishments is wonderful. And it's not something many people get to experience.

Right to the very end, I loved the simple pleasure of going to training. It's all I've ever known since I was a young bloke. That's the environment I grew up in, and the environment I've lived in for most of my life. That's what I will miss the most.

But I am looking forward to the game no longer dictating my life. I get to do things on my terms and spend a lot more time with my family, which has always been the most important thing to me. What does that look like? A few more family holidays will be nice. And I'll be getting out my golf clubs a lot more!

Whether I will stay involved with footy—as a coach, as an administrator or in some role in the media—I simply don't know. After playing the game for so long, and after all the intensity of finals, State of Origins and Test matches, I'm looking forward to a break. Just to hit reset before coming back, in whatever capacity, refreshed and ready to give my very best once again.

It has been some ride, from those early years playing for Logan Brothers, to winning premierships with the Storm, to running out onto Suncorp Stadium in a Maroons jumper for the first time, to captaining my country. I am extremely proud of what I've been able to achieve—not just for myself, but for everyone around me. I'm so proud of the Storm and the club that we've been able to build.

I'm proud of having been able to share this journey with Barb, Mum, Dad, Khirstie and Matthew, and then, in the back half of my career, with Jada, Jasper and Matilda. To have my children so close to the game—and even out on the field when I've been playing, in some of the biggest matches of my career—has been special.

I'm grateful for all the help so many people have given me along the way. If they hadn't been so generous, who knows how it all might have played out?

The one thing that Craig Bellamy always said to me—indeed, always drilled into me—was that the people who work the hardest make their own luck. I'd like to think I've been one of those.

The storm within me allowed me to achieve everything in football I ever dreamed of. Thanks for being a part of it.

INDEX

ACKNOWLEDGEMENTS

Firstly, thank you for getting this far.

Throughout my life I have never been one to overshare, so this whole experience has been a bit out of my comfort zone.

I would like to thank my wife, Barb: you have been the person I've depended on since I was a teenager. I will always be indebted to you for the selfless way you supported me throughout my career, fought for me and loved me, even when I was a pain in the arse. You are one of a kind and I wouldn't have it any other way.

Jada, Jasper and Matilda—what a ride! Although I have been away a lot, everything I have done has always been for you. As your dad I couldn't be prouder and I'm really excited about being right by your side for everything to come moving forward.

Thank you to my parents Sonia and Wayne, and my siblings Khirstie and Matthew, for your unwavering love and support.

As a young fella you instilled the importance of being honest, respecting others and working hard. I am now teaching my own children those same lessons.

Craig, there is so much I could say. You flicked a switch in me and demanded I get the best out of myself. More than that, though, you have been a friend, a confidante and a standout example to others. Apologies if 'Dog Head' starts to gain momentum.

To all of my Melbourne Storm, Queensland and Australian teammates and coaches, I look back with nothing but fondness about all of it—the wins, the losses, the triumphs and tragedies. Even the preseasons and video reviews. Every player in a rugby league team is a sum of their experiences, and none of what transpired throughout my career would have been possible without you.

To my management team at Cove Agency, led by Isaac Moses, thank you for always being there, not just for me but my whole family. We started together over a decade ago and I look forward to many decades to come.

To Andrew Webster, firstly I apologise for being atrocious on the phone! Before jumping into this project I wasn't sure how it would play out, or who would be best to do it with, but I am grateful things came together the way they did. Our sit-downs were cathartic and really enjoyable, which I didn't expect. Thank you for pressing and prodding—as you guys tend to do—but mostly for being respectful and decent. You're a good man.

Publishing companies were completely foreign to me eighteen months ago, but I can't say enough about Kelly Fagan

ACKNOWLEDGEMENTS

and the Allen & Unwin team. You've been professional, supportive and most of all patient, which has helped enormously.

Lastly, thank you to all of the club members and fans of our great game, not just in Melbourne but around Australia and the world. That game, rugby league, is something I dreamed about as a kid and turned into a life I never expected to have.

The greatest game of all.

STATISTICS

Born: 18 June 1983, Brisbane, Queensland

CAREER OVERVIEW

	Games	Tries	Goals	F/Goals	Points
CLUB CAREER *2002–20*					
Melbourne Storm *2002–20*					
Premiership Games *2002–20*	427	47	1279	4	2750
World Club Challenge *2010, 2013, 2018*	3	–	12	–	24
Total	**430**	**47**	**1291**	**4**	**2774**
REPRESENTATIVE CAREER *2003–17*					
QUEENSLAND *2003–17*					
State of Origin *2003–17*	42	5	19	–	58
AUSTRALIA *2006–17*					
Tests and World Cup *2006–17*	56	9	67	–	170
OTHER REPRESENTATIVE *2010–11, 2013, 2016*					
NRL All Stars *2010–11, 2013*	3	–	1	–	2
World All Stars *2016*	1	–	–	–	0
GRAND TOTAL					
All first class matches	**532**	**61**	**1378**	**4**	**3004**

SEASON BY SEASON – Melbourne Storm

Year	Games	Tries	Goals	F/Goals	Points	Won	Lost	Drew	Position
2002	2	–	–	–	0	1	1	–	10th
2003	24	4	8	–	32	15	9	–	Semi-finalists
2004	23	4	43	–	102	12	11	–	Semi-finalists
2005	23	3	30	–	72	13	10	–	Semi-finalists
2006	25	5	79	–	178	21	4	–	Runners-up
2007	24	4	88	–	192	21	3	–	Premiers*
2008	23	4	77	–	170	18	5	–	Runners-up
2009	25	3	65	–	142	16	8	1	Premiers*
2010	20	2	54	–	116	12	8	–	16th (last)
2011	24	2	78	–	164	19	5	–	Prelim finalists
2012	25	2	78	–	164	20	5	–	Premiers
2013	23	2	84	–	176	16	6	1	Semi-finalists
2014	23	2	68	1	145	13	10	–	Quarter finalists
2015	25	1	71	–	146	15	10	–	Prelim finalists
2016	26	2	92	2	194	21	5	–	Runners-up
2017	23	2	92	–	192	21	2	–	Premiers
2018	26	1	98	1	201	18	8	–	Runners-up
2019	27	2	104	–	216	21	6	–	Prelim finalists
2020	16	2	70	–	148	14	2	–	Prelim finalists
Total	**427**	**47**	**1279**	**4**	**2750**	**307**	**118**	**2**	

* Title stripped due to salary cap breaches

RECORD AGAINST OPPOSING NRL CLUBS 2002–20

	Games	Tries	Goals	F/Goals	Points	Won	Lost	Drew
Brisbane	38	4	115	–	246	30	8	–
Canberra	33	2	103	–	214	25	8	–
Canterbury	26	2	57	–	122	14	12	–
Cronulla	29	3	80	–	172	18	11	–
Gold Coast	19	2	81	–	170	15	4	–
Manly	32	4	90	1	197	19	12	1
Newcastle	33	4	110	–	236	25	8	–
North Queensland	31	2	98	1	205	22	9	–
Parramatta	21	3	67	–	146	18	3	–
Penrith	26	5	88	–	196	20	6	–
Souths	29	5	91	1	203	25	4	–
St George Illawarra	27	2	74	–	156	22	5	–
Sydney Roosters	26	3	68	1	149	16	10	–
Warriors	33	3	94	–	200	22	10	1
Wests Tigers	24	3	63	–	138	16	8	–
Grand Total	**427**	**47**	**1279**	**4**	**2750**	**307**	**118**	**2**

Career Summary:

Junior club: Logan Brothers

Premiership Debut: Melbourne v Bulldogs at Olympic Park, 13 April 2002 (Round 5)

Summary of games: played 427, wins 307, losses 118, draws 2. Win%: 71.9

Premierships: 2012, 2017 (titles won by the Storm in 2007 and 2009 were stripped due to the club's salary cap breaches)

Finals series: 2003, 2004, 2005, 2006, 2007, 2008, 2009, 2011, 2012, 2013, 2014, 2015, 2016, 2017, 2018, 2019, 2020

Grand Finals: 2006 (lost), 2007 (won), 2008 (lost), 2009 (won), 2012 (won), 2016 (lost), 2017 (won), 2018 (lost)

World Club Challenge titles: 2013, 2018 (title won in 2010 was subsequently stripped)

Captaincy record (2006–20): Games 324, wins 239, losses 83, draws 2. Win%: 73.8

Goal-kicking: 1279 goals from 1700 attempts (75.2%)

Awards:

Dally M Player of the Year 2006, 2017

Melbourne Storm Player of the Year 2005, 2006, 2007, 2011, 2012, 2013, 2017

Dally M Hooker of the Year 2006, 2008, 2011, 2012, 2013, 2016, 2017, 2019

Dally M Captain of the Year 2011, 2013, 2017, 2018, 2019

RLPA Dream Team 2019

STATISTICS

Records:

Most premiership appearances (427)

Most premiership goals (1279)

Most premiership points (2750)

Most wins in premiership matches (307)

Most appearances as captain (324)

Most wins as captain (239)

Most finals appearances (39)

Most finals goals (100)

Most finals points (212)

STATE OF ORIGIN 2003–17

No.	Date	Venue	Game	Tries	Goals	F/G	Points	Result	Score
1	16/07/03	Suncorp Stadium	3	1	–	–	4	Won	36–6
2	26/05/04	Telstra Stadium	1	–	–	–	0	Lost	8–9
3	16/06/04	Suncorp Stadium	2	–	2	–	4	Won	22–18
4	07/07/04	Telstra Stadium	3	–	3	–	6	Lost	14–36
5	25/05/05	Suncorp Stadium	1	–	5	–	10	Won	24–20
6	22/06/05	Telstra Stadium	2	–	3	–	6	Lost	22–32
7	06/07/05	Suncorp Stadium	3	–	1	–	2	Lost	10–32
8	24/05/06	Telstra Stadium	1	–	–	–	0	Lost	16–17
9	14/06/06	Suncorp Stadium	2	–	–	–	0	Won	30–6
10	05/07/06	Telstra Dome	3	–	–	–	0	Won	16–14
11	23/05/07	Suncorp Stadium	1	–	–	–	0	Won	25–18
12	13/06/07	Telstra Stadium	2	–	–	–	0	Won	10–6
13	04/07/07	Suncorp Stadium	3	–	–	–	0	Lost	4–18
14*	21/05/08	ANZ Stadium	1	–	–	–	0	Lost	10–18
15*	11/06/08	Suncorp Stadium	2	–	–	–	0	Won	30–0
16*	02/07/08	ANZ Stadium	3	–	–	–	0	Won	16–10
17	03/06/09	Etihad Stadium	1	–	–	–	0	Won	28–18
18	24/06/09	ANZ Stadium	2	1	–	–	4	Won	24–14
19	15/07/09	Suncorp Stadium	3	–	–	–	0	Lost	16–28
20	16/06/10	Suncorp Stadium	2	–	–	–	0	Won	34–6

21	07/07/10	ANZ Stadium	3	–	–	0	Won	23–18
22	25/05/11	Suncorp Stadium	1	–	–	0	Won	16–12
23	15/06/11	ANZ Stadium	2	1	–	4	Lost	8–18
24	06/07/11	Suncorp Stadium	3	1	1	6	Won	34–24
25*	23/05/12	Etihad Stadium	1	–	–	0	Won	18–10
26*	13/06/12	ANZ Stadium	2	–	–	0	Lost	12–16
27*	04/07/12	Suncorp Stadium	3	–	–	0	Won	21–20
28*	05/06/13	ANZ Stadium	1	–	1	2	Lost	6–14
29*	26/06/13	Suncorp Stadium	2	–	–	0	Won	26–6
30*	17/07/13	ANZ Stadium	3	–	–	0	Won	12–10
31*	28/05/14	Suncorp Stadium	1	–	–	0	Lost	8–12
32*	18/06/14	ANZ Stadium	2	–	–	0	Lost	4–6
33*	09/07/14	Suncorp Stadium	3	1	–	4	Won	32–8
34*	27/05/15	ANZ Stadium	1	–	–	0	Won	11–10
35*	17/06/15	MCG	2	–	–	0	Lost	18–26
36*	08/07/15	Suncorp Stadium	3	–	–	0	Won	52–6
37*	01/06/16	ANZ Stadium	1	–	–	0	Won	6–4
38*	22/06/16	Suncorp Stadium	2	–	–	0	Won	26–16
39*	13/07/16	ANZ Stadium	3	–	–	0	Lost	14–18
40*	31/05/17	Suncorp Stadium	1	–	–	0	Lost	4–28
41*	21/06/17	ANZ Stadium	2	–	–	0	Won	18–16
42*	12/07/17	Suncorp Stadium	3	–	3	6	Won	22–6

* Indicates captain

Position: starting hooker (all games)

Coaches: Wayne Bennett (2003), Michael Hagan (2004–05), Mal Meninga (2006–15), Kevin Walters (2016–17).

Summary of matches: 42 games, 5 tries, 19 goals, 58 points. Won 26, lost 16. Win%: 61.9

Series victories: 2006, 2007, 2008, 2009, 2010, 2011, 2012, 2013, 2015, 2016, 2017

Captaincy record (2008, 2011–17): games 21, wins 13, losses 8. Win%: 61.9

Goal-kicking: 19 goals from 28 attempts (67.9%)

Man of the Match Awards: Game 2, 2007; Game 1, 2011; Game 3, 2011; Game 2, 2013; Game 1, 2015; Game 2, 2016; Game 3, 2017

Other awards: Dally M Representative Player of the Year 2007, 2011, 2013, 2016; Wally Lewis Medal (State of Origin player of the series) 2007, 2011, 2013, 2016; Dick 'Tosser' Turner Medal (20 Queensland State of Origin appearances) 2013; FOGS Statesman Award (30 Queensland State of Origin appearances) 2013; Ron McAuliffe Medal (Queensland State of Origin player of the series) 2005, 2007, 2013, 2015

Records: Most appearances (42)

TEST CAREER 2006–17

No.	Date	Opponent	Venue	T	G	FG	Pts	Result	Score
1	14/10/06	New Zealand	Mount Smart Stadium	–	–	–	0	Won	30–18
2	21/10/06	New Zealand	Telstra Dome, Melbourne	–	–	–	0	Won	20–15
3	04/11/06	Great Britain	Aussie Stadium, Sydney	–	–	–	0	Lost	12–23
4	18/11/06	Great Britain	Suncorp Stadium	–	–	–	0	Won	33–10
5	25/11/06	New Zealand	Aussie Stadium, Sydney	–	–	–	0	Won	16–12
6	20/04/07	New Zealand	Suncorp Stadium	–	–	–	0	Won	30–6
7*	14/10/07	New Zealand	Wellington	1	6	–	16	Won	58–0
8*	09/05/08	New Zealand	Sydney Cricket Ground	1	–	–	4	Won	28–12
9	26/10/08	New Zealand	Sydney Football Stadium	–	1	–	2	Won	30–6
10	02/11/08	England	Telstra Dome, Melbourne	–	–	–	0	Won	52–4
11*	09/11/08	Papua New Guinea	Townsville	–	–	–	0	Won	46–6
12	16/11/08	Fiji	Sydney Football Stadium	–	–	–	0	Won	52–0
13	22/11/08	New Zealand	Suncorp Stadium (Final)	–	–	–	0	Lost	20–34
14	08/05/09	New Zealand	Suncorp Stadium	–	–	–	0	Won	38–10
15	24/10/09	New Zealand	Twickenham Stoop, London	1	–	–	4	Drew	20–20
16	31/10/09	England	DW Stadium, Wigan	–	–	–	0	Won	26–16
17	14/11/09	England	Elland Road, Leeds	1	–	–	4	Won	46–16
18	07/05/10	New Zealand	AAMI Park	–	–	–	0	Won	12–8

No.	Date	Opponent	Venue	T	G	FG	Pts	Result	Score
19	24/10/10	Papua New Guinea	Parramatta Stadium	1	5	–	14	Won	42–0
20	31/10/10	England	AAMI Park	–	5	–	10	Won	34–14
21*	06/11/10	New Zealand	Eden Park, Auckland	–	3	–	6	Won	34–20
22	13/11/10	New Zealand	Suncorp Stadium	–	2	–	4	Lost	12–16
23	06/05/11	New Zealand	Skilled Park	–	–	–	0	Won	20–10
24	16/10/11	New Zealand	Ausgrid Stadium	–	1	–	2	Won	42–6
25	28/10/11	New Zealand	Warrington	–	–	–	0	Won	26–12
26	05/11/11	England	Wembley Stadium	–	–	–	0	Won	36–20
27*	13/11/11	Wales	Wrexham	1	–	–	4	Won	56–14
28	19/11/11	England	Elland Road, Leeds	–	–	–	0	Won	30–8
29*	20/04/12	New Zealand	Eden Park, Auckland	1	–	–	4	Won	20–12
30*	13/10/12	New Zealand	Dairy Farmers Stadium	1	–	–	4	Won	18–10
31*	19/04/13	New Zealand	Canberra Stadium	–	4	–	8	Won	32–12
32*	26/10/13	England	Millennium Stadium, Cardiff	–	–	–	0	Won	28–20
33*	02/11/13	Fiji	Langtree Park, St Helens	–	–	–	0	Won	34–2
34*	09/11/13	Ireland	Limerick	–	3	–	6	Won	50–0
35*	16/11/13	USA	Wrexham	1	–	–	4	Won	62–0
36*	23/11/13	Fiji	Wembley Stadium	–	–	–	0	Won	64–0
37*	30/11/13	New Zealand	Old Trafford, Manchester (Final)	–	–	–	0	Won	34–2

38*	02/05/14	New Zealand	Allianz Stadium	–	–	–	0	Won	30–18
39*	25/10/14	New Zealand	Suncorp Stadium	–	2	–	4	Lost	12–30
40*	02/11/14	England	AAMI Park	–	2	–	4	Won	16–12
41*	09/11/14	Samoa	WIN Stadium	–	4	–	8	Won	44–18
42*	15/11/14	New Zealand	Westpac Stadium, Wellington	–	3	–	6	Lost	18–22
43*	03/05/15	New Zealand	Suncorp Stadium	–	–	–	0	Lost	12–26
44*	06/05/16	New Zealand	Hunter Stadium, Newcastle	–	1	–	2	Won	16–0
45*	15/10/16	New Zealand	nib Stadium, Perth	–	–	–	0	Won	26–6
46*	28/10/16	Scotland	Lightstream Stadium, Hull	–	–	–	0	Won	54–12
47*	05/11/16	New Zealand	Ricoh Arena, Coventry	–	–	–	0	Won	14–8
48*	13/11/16	England	Olympic Stadium, London	–	–	–	0	Won	36–18
49*	20/11/16	New Zealand	Anfield, Liverpool	–	–	–	0	Won	34–8
50*	05/05/17	New Zealand	GIO Stadium	–	–	–	0	Won	30–12
51*	27/10/17	England	AAMI Park, Melbourne	–	3	–	6	Won	18–4
52*	03/11/17	France	GIO Stadium, Canberra	–	6	–	12	Won	52–6
53*	11/11/17	Lebanon	Allianz Stadium	–	1	–	2	Won	34–0
54*	17/11/17	Samoa	TIO Stadium, Darwin	–	7	–	14	Won	46–0
55*	24/11/17	Fiji	Suncorp Stadium	–	7	–	14	Won	54–6
56*	02/12/17	England	Suncorp Stadium (Final)	–	1	–	2	Won	6–0

* Indicates captain
Bold text indicates World Cup

Position: starting hooker in all Tests except Tri-Nations Test v Great Britain (4/11/06) when he was an interchange player

Coaches: Ricky Stuart 2006–08, Tim Sheens 2009–15, Mal Meninga 2016–17

Summary of matches: 56 Tests, 9 tries, 67 goals, 170 points. Won 49, lost 6, drew 1. Win% 87.5

Series victories: Tri-Nations 2006, Tri-Nations 2009, Four Nations 2011, World Cup 2013 (captain), Four Nations 2016 (captain), World Cup 2017 (captain)

Captaincy record (2007–08, 2010–17): games 33, wins 30, losses 3. Win%: 90.9

Goal-kicking: 67 goals from 94 attempts (71.3%)

Man-of-the-match awards:
Australia v New Zealand, 14 October 2007 (100-year Test)
Australia v New Zealand, 9 May 2008 (Centenary Test)
Australia v Papua New Guinea, 24 October 2010 (Four Nations)
Australia v New Zealand, 19 April 2013 (Trans-Tasman Test)
Australia v England, 2 November 2014 (Four Nations)
Australia v Fiji, 24 November 2017 (World Cup semi-final)

Awards: Rugby League International Federation Player of the Year 2012; Rugby League International Federation Hooker of the Year 2008, 2009, 2011, 2012; Harry Sunderland Medal winner 2014, 2017; Golden Boot award 2007, 2017; Member of the Order of Australia (AM) 2019

Notes on venues
Sydney's Olympic Stadium was commercially known as Telstra Stadium 2002–07 and renamed ANZ Stadium in 2008. Telstra Dome and Etihad Stadium were commercial names for Melbourne's Docklands Stadium. Suncorp Stadium was previously known as Lang Park. MCG refers to Melbourne Cricket Ground.

Statistics to 1 October 2020

Source: David Middleton
League Information Services